Professional SQL Server 7.0 Development Using SQL-DMO, SQL-NS, & DTS

Frank Miller
Rachelle Reese

Wrox Press Ltd. ®

Professional SQL Server 7.0 Development Using SQL-DMO, SQL-NS, & DTS

© 1999 Wrox Press

Published by Wrox Press Ltd, Arden House, 1102 Warwick Road, Acocks Green, Birmingham, B27 6BH, UK
Printed in Canada
ISBN 1-861002-8-07

Trademark Acknowledgements

Wrox has endeavored to provide trademark information about all the companies and products mentioned in this book by the appropriate use of capitals. However, Wrox cannot guarantee the accuracy of this information.

Credits

Author
Frank Miller
Rachelle Reese

Contributing Authors
Steve Danielson
Michael McGrew

Technical Editors
Ian Blackham
Kate Hall

Technical Reviewers
Matt Bortniker
Steve Danielson
Mike Erickson
Tony Greening
Ivor Horton
Ron Landers
Michael McGrew
Todd Robinson
Kenn Scribner

Managing Editor
Joanna Mason

Development Editor
Dominic Lowe

Project Manager
Tony Berry

Design/Layout
Tom Bartlett
Mark Burdett
William Fallon
Jonathan Jones
John McNulty

Proofreader
Christopher Smith

Index
Andrew Criddle

Cover
Chris Morris

About the Authors

Frank Miller

Frank Miller has been working with computers for over 20 years as a user, field engineer, programmer, trainer, and course developer. For the last several years he has specialized in Microsoft operating systems and BackOffice products and is a Microsoft Certified Systems Engineer (MCSE), Microsoft Certified Solution Developer (MCSD), and Microsoft Certified Database Administrator (MCDBA). Lured by chances for greater independence and flexibility, he recently started his own course design and development company.

Frank lives in Desloge, MO, a small town in southeastern Missouri, with his wife Katie, his sons, and an assortment of animals. He runs his business, Cypress Development, Etc. LLC, from his home.

Acknowledgements

First and foremost, I dedicate my portion of this book to my wife, Katie, and my sons, who put up the days, nights, and weekends required to get the book into its final form. Their love and support carried me the through the long hours and frustrations that come with an undertaking like this. An extra thanks goes to Katie for her initial read-throughs and edits. I also have to thank my partner in this endeavor, Rachelle Reese, who was always there when I got lost in my own code.

I'm sure I'll miss some of the folks at Wrox, but I want to make my best attempt. First, a special thank you to Dominic Lowe who offered Rachelle and me this project. Thanks to Tony Berry for keeping things organized throughout the process and staying calm as deadlines loomed. Thanks to Kate Hall and Ian Blackham who helped mold this book into something much better than it would have been without their advice. I also want to thank all of the reviewers and editors for their thoughts, suggestions, and corrections.

Rachelle Reese

Rachelle Reese has been working with computers for over twelve years, although she unabashedly admits that the first computer she *enjoyed* working with was a Macintosh. For several years, she walked the thin line, programming some for the Macintosh and some for the PC. In 1996, she cut the umbilical cord and began programming almost exclusively in Visual Basic. She is currently the Curriculum Manager for Programming and Databases at Wave Technologies International. She holds MCSD, MCSE, and MCDBA certifications.

Rachelle lives in St. Louis, MO with her husband and two dogs, a dachshund named Sassafrass and a basset-mix named Sherlock. When she's not hammering the keyboard, she enjoys reading, counted cross, needlepoint, and brewing.

Special Dedication

In memory of Faltor, my loving cocker spaniel who passed away last summer.

Acknowledgements

I'd like to dedicate my portion of this book to my husband and my dogs, who put up with my late nights and moodiness when things weren't going as smoothly as I wanted. I'd also like to give a special thanks to Frank who helped me through some areas of SQL Server where only well-seasoned database gurus dare to tread. Finally, I'd like to thank my parents for raising me to believe I can accomplish whatever I desire.

I'd also like to say thank you to Dominic Lowe at Wrox for giving us the opportunity to write this book, Tony Berry for making sure we didn't forget any of the pieces along the way, and Kate Hall, Ian Blackham, and the reviewers for giving us great suggestions and helping us ensure that the book addresses the important issues in a clear and accurate manner.

Steve Danielson

Steve has been involved with programming since being introduced to the TRS-80 Model I computer in 1980 during the 6th grade. After his high school years he played lead guitar for different bands and toured up and down the Eastern US Coast and Canada before meeting his wife to be, and returning to his original dream of developing software. He began programming for Microsoft Windows with the release of Visual Basic 3.0, but for the last few years has been working primarily with C++. Steve is currently a consultant for Romac International's Emerging Technologies eServices Practice, where he is developing automated electricity metering software for a client using Microsoft Visual C++. Steve is also a private pilot and flies his Zenair CH-701 kitplane whenever he gets the chance. Steve lives with his family in Wake Forest, NC, and can be reached at stevedanielson@mindspring.com.

Acknowledgements

I would like to thank my wife Donna, and our kids: Stevie Jr, James, Lonnie, and Aundi for supporting me through this effort, and also thank my parents, John and Dianne, for all of the support and guidance I received through my formative years. I would also like to thank Barbara Cheesman, one of my early teachers who introduced me to computers and programming and provided great support throughout my early school years. Thanks also to Wrox Press for all of the great opportunities they have provided over the last few years.

Michael McGrew

Michael McGrew is a software developer who lives in Bremerton, Washington. Michael has been doing software development for almost ten years now and currently works for a Seattle electronic commerce company called VisualCommerce as a Lead Senior Developer in charge of database technology. When not at work, Mike enjoys hiking and fishing with his wife Tonya and his two dogs Penny and Julie in the great northwest.

Acknowledgements

I would like to thank Tonya, my wife, for all of her understanding about all my late nights while helping to put this book together. Without her support I probably wouldn't make it through a single day.

Table of Contents

Chapter 6: Using SQL-NS 217

Chapter 7: Deploying Your Application   259

Chapter 8: Replication Management 295

Chapter 9: Introduction to Data Transformation Services (DTS) 335

Chapter 10: Using DTS Components 375

Chapter 11: Scaling Down with MSDE 399

Introduction

SQL Server 7.0 Distributed Management Framework (SQL-DMF) is a subject that tends to get the same reaction out of a lot of people. Yes, they've heard of it. Yes, it sounds interesting. Yes, they're planning to do something with it eventually, but not right now.

Well for you, the time *is* now. SQL-DMF objects could be the key to the enterprise-wide applications that you want and need. This book focuses on three sets of management objects. SQL Distributed Management Objects (SQL-DMO) encapsulates SQL Server database and replication management. SQL Namespace (SQL-NS) objects give you a way to invoke SQL Server Enterprise Manager user interface components. Data Transformation Services (DTS) objects give you a way to copy or transform data between OLE DB sources and destinations.

The purpose of this book is to lead you through practical examples, and show you how to use SQL-DMF to build applications. Of course, this book is just a jumping off point to get you started. If you take the time to work through the examples we've provided, you'll find yourself well on your way. From there, you'll be ready to go wherever your imagination might take you.

Who Should Read this Book

Be warned. This isn't a book for complete novices. You'll need an intermediate knowledge of both a programming language (in this book we've shown how to use SQL-DMF with C++ and Visual Basic 6.0) and SQL Server 7.0 administration. You need to understand basic object-oriented programming concepts. You also need a working knowledge of Transact-SQL.

We've written this book for programmers who are creating, or planning to create, enterprise applications for SQL Server. Our goal is to give you access to the tools you need to take direct control of SQL Server, using SQL-DMF components to give users access to more robust SQL Server features and functionality.

While obviously not light reading, it doesn't mean that you can't have some fun along the way. If you're interested in getting your hands on SQL Server's real nuts and bolts, hang on tight and get ready to roll.

What's Covered in this Book

The following is a brief roadmap of where this book is going to take us. Throughout, you will see practical examples of how to use SQL-DMF objects. Obviously, it won't be possible to cover every object, property, method, and collection. Instead, we've selected representative samples so you can understand the concepts involved. Where appropriate, we draw parallels between using SQL-DMF, and Enterprise Manager and Transact-SQL statements.

Chapter 1 gets you started. In it, we introduce the SQL-DMF architecture. You'll get a brief look at SQL-DMO, SQL-NS, and DTS. We'll discuss why you would want to use SQL-DMF objects in your applications and some of the benefits you can expect from their use. Finally, we provide you with some guidelines for setting up and configuring a development machine so you can follow along with the examples.

Chapter 2 provides some additional background information, though this time in a slightly different area. Since SQL-DMF applications are most likely to be used in enterprise network solutions, we discuss the Windows DNA architecture and Microsoft Transaction Server (MTS). Don't worry if you're not very familiar with either of these. You don't need to understand them in any great detail, and we'll provide you with what you need to know to follow along. Also, we'll be introducing the business scenario that we'll be using throughout the first part of the book.

With **Chapter 3**, we start getting into the details of working with SQL-DMF, beginning with SQL-DMO. We start with an overview of the SQL-DMO hierarchy, and how to reference and use SQL-DMO objects. The chapter focuses on the `SQLServer` object. We'll see how to manage connections and set configuration values. This chapter wraps up by introducing SQL-DMO errors and provides some guidelines for error handling.

Chapter 4 focuses on the `Database` object and how to create and manage databases with SQL-DMO. We'll also discuss the `Table` object and how we can use it to alter tables in our databases. Finally, we'll look at how SQL-DMO can be used to create indexes.

Chapter 5 continues with SQL-DMO, focusing on administration and management. During this chapter, we will use security objects to manage SQL Server and bring consistency to recurring tasks. We will also discuss how to backup and restore using SQL-DMO objects, the `JobServer` object (through which we can gain access to the tasks performed by the SQL Server Agent), and the objects related to replication.

Moving into **Chapter 6**, we leave SQL-DMO behind and change our focus to SQL-NS objects. As we did with SQL-DMO, we start by introducing the object hierarchy and guidelines for using SQL-NS objects. From there, we move into practical remote management examples using SQL-NS to implement Enterprise Manager functionality.

In **Chapter 7** we pull together all the code segments created in the earlier chapters to create the functional application that we have been building up to. The chapter focuses on issues related to distribution and implementation of your application, including instructions for installing components into MTS and using the Package and Deployment Wizard to deploy the application.

In **Chapter 8**, we discuss how to manage replication using SQL-DMO objects. Specifically, we'll look at how we can use SQL-DMO to allow us to subscribe to a single article in a publication, a feature that is unavailable when managing replication through the Enterprise Manager alone.

In **Chapter 9**, we step away from working with objects briefly to give you an introduction to DTS, which was new to SQL Server 7.0. We start by introducing DTS concepts and components by way of the DTS Designer. During the chapter, we'll create and execute a DTS package to show you how DTS components work together to copy and transform data.

Chapter 10 builds from what you learned in Chapter 9. Once again, we'll be working with DTS. However, instead of using the DTS Designer, we'll be directly implementing DTS objects to create a sample application. You'll see how to use DTS objects to define and execute custom transformations.

With **Chapter 11**, it's back once more to our business scenario as we see how we can use our custom SQL-DMF applications to access the Microsoft Date Engine (MSDE). The MSDE allows developers to distribute exactly the same engine that manages data in SQL Server 7.0 with their own applications.

The final chapter, **Chapter 12**, discusses how to access the SQL-DMF from C++. Three ways in which objects can be accessed will be discussed and an example application will demonstrate the use of each.

How to Get the Most from this Book

You are going to get the most out of this book if you take the time to work through the examples. Chapter 1 gives you some detailed configuration guidelines, but as a short list, you are going to need:

- ❏ SQL Server 7.0 (Standard edition)

- ❏ Visual Basic 6.0 (Professional edition) and/or Visual C++ 6.0 (Professional Edition)

- ❏ Windows NT 4.0 Server (or Windows 2000 Server) is the suggested platform, and will be the required platform for MTS examples. This means that you are going to need the Windows NT Option Pack, which can be ordered (or downloaded free) from Microsoft's web site at
  `http://www.microsoft.com/ntserver/nts/downloads/recommended/NT4Opt Pk/default.asp`.

If you don't have Windows NT 4.0 Server, you can still step through most of the examples in the book. We've identified the examples that require NT Server and MTS to help keep your frustration to a minimum. We have also been careful to point out any significant differences you might encounter using SQL Server 7.0 Desktop edition on Windows NT Workstation or Windows 95/98.

Conventions Used

You are going to encounter different styles as you are reading through this book. This has been done to help you easily identify different types of information and to help you keep from missing any key points. These styles are:

> **Important information, key points, and additional explanations are displayed like this to make them stand out. Be sure to pay attention to these when you find them.**

General notes, background information, and brief asides look like this.

❑ Keys that you press on the keyboard, like *Ctrl* and *Delete*, are displayed in italics

❑ If you see something like, BackupDB, you'll know that it is a filename, object name or function name

❑ The first time you encounter an **important word**, it is displayed in bold text

❑ Words that appear on the screen, such as menu options, are in a similar font to the one used on screen, for example, the File menu

This is how code samples look the first time they are introduced:

```
Private Sub Command_Click
    MsgBox "Don't touch me"
End Sub
```

Whereas code that you've already seen or that doesn't relate directly to the point being made, looks like this:

```
Private Sub Command_Click
    MsgBox "Don't touch me"
End Sub
```

Source Code

Source code for the examples used in this book, as well as the example source database script, can be downloaded from Wrox's web site at:

```
http://www.wrox.com
```

Tell Us What You Think

We want to know what you think about this book. We want to hear your comments, what you liked, what you didn't like, what you think we can do better next time. You can send your comments via the Wrox web site or by e-mail (to feedback@wrox.com). Please be sure to mention the book title in your message.

Introducing SQL-DMF

Many Microsoft SQL Server developers and administrators have been using the **SQL Distributed Management Framework** (**SQL-DMF**) for years (albeit maybe unwittingly). Those that have used it explicitly know the vast development power it offers. Over the course of this book we hope to show how enterprise developers can leverage these technologies to strengthen and enhance their SQL Server applications.

No other SQL Server technology supports the development and management of SQL Server objects like the SQL-DMF. Heck, Microsoft even used this technology to build the new Enterprise Manager for SQL Server 7.0. Why not use this technology to create better applications for your users also?

SQL-DMF allows you to do all the tasks normally associated with Enterprise Manager (such as configuring servers and modifying tables and databases) from within your custom-built applications. There's no longer any need for everyone (no matter what his or her security permissions or level of knowledge) to work with SQL Server via the powerful, but none-the-less complex and somewhat confusing, Enterprise Manager. Now, you can create sophisticated administration and management tools in Visual Basic, C++ or even Delphi, and provide as much functionality and power as is available through the Enterprise Manager.

> With SQL-DMF, you can design a scalable solution that meets your management needs today, but can expand to meet ever-increasing enterprise requirements.

Solutions can be designed to respond directly to the server so that you can minimize the need for user intervention. While you're not likely to ever build a completely self-maintaining database solution, you can take care of selected problem areas.

So in this chapter we're going to cover the following ground:

❑ Overview some features of Microsoft SQL Server 7.0

❑ Introduce the SQL-DMF architecture and its major components

❑ Highlight areas where this technology can be effectively utilized

❑ Describe the system requirements for making full use of this book

Firstly, let's start by talking a little about SQL Server 7.0.

SQL Server 7.0

SQL Server 7.0 represents a major upgrade to Microsoft's SQL Server product. SQL Server is now more powerful, more flexible, and better able to meet the needs of very large databases and enterprise implementations.

Since you're reading this book, you're probably already familiar with SQL Server and have likely been involved in implementing SQL Server business solutions. That's good, because there's a lot about SQL Server, and about relational database systems in general, that we're going to assume that you already know. For example, you should:

❑ Have used Enterprise Manager to create databases and database objects

❑ Be familiar with data organization concepts, including columns, rows, and data types

❑ Understand the how and why of using table indexes

❑ Understand login names, database users, and the purpose of SQL Server roles

❑ Know how to back up and restore databases

❑ Understand basic replication concepts

> **If any of these subjects is unfamiliar to you, it doesn't mean that you won't get your full worth out of this book. It does mean, however, that there may be some areas where you may need to do a little extra review on your own.**

Just in case you're not quite as strong in some of these subjects as you might prefer, we will be providing a few overviews as we go along, especially when we're discussing features that have changed with the release of SQL Server 7.0. Some new features, such as Data Transformation Services, will be covered in quite a bit of detail for you.

Throughout this book, it will help if you think of SQL Server as being a collection of components. These include server and database objects, as well as more abstract components such as server configuration settings. We'll be using SQL-DMF to create components and modify properties of existing server components.

A Few New Features

It's worth our time to take a few moments to look at some of the changes introduced with SQL Server 7.0. This is not meant to be a detailed discussion of all of the changes, but instead a focused look at some significant items that relate to projects we'll discuss in this book. Key areas include:

- ❑ Microsoft Management Console
- ❑ SQL Server Agent
- ❑ Data Transformation Services
- ❑ Windows 95/98 platform support
- ❑ Enhancements to data storage
- ❑ SQL Server security model
- ❑ Replication enhancements

If you've worked with earlier versions of SQL Server, but haven't had much of a chance to become familiar with SQL Server 7.0 yet, these are areas that might throw you off a little initially.

Microsoft Management Console and Enterprise Manager

The **Microsoft Management Console** (**MMC**) is designed to provide a consistent interface for managing Microsoft BackOffice server applications. Management tools can be snapped into the MMC, giving administrators a flexible management environment. It also makes it possible to somewhat customize tools to meet specific management needs.

One of the management tools that runs in this environment is SQL Server's **Enterprise Manager**. Enterprise Manager is designed to meet a full range of management requirements through a single interface. Through Enterprise Manager, you can maintain both local and remote servers with the same relative ease.

Enterprise Manager's strength is also its potential weakness. It may be more power than you want to put into the hands of some database administrators or assistant administrators. This can especially be a problem when supporting remote servers in offices with a high personnel turnover.

SQL Server Agent

SQL Server Agent is the replacement for SQL Executive and is SQL Server's task scheduler. SQL Server Agent is responsible for job scheduling and job execution, creating alerts, notifying operators, replication publishing, and any other items you have set the SQL Server to do on an automated schedule or in response to server events.

Data Transformation Services

Data Transformation Services (**DTS**) gives you a way to move data between any OLE DB, ODBC, or text formats. You can transfer data as simple imports or exports, or include data transformations. Through transformations, you can modify data, calculate new values, and even validate and scrub data. The transformation objects you define through DTS can even be included in other applications.

One of the main uses of DTS is to support data warehousing implementations. DTS allows the transferring and transforming of operational data for import as data warehouse data. Transformations can be scheduled to run on a periodic basis. Data manipulation, scrubbing, and validation can be written into the process, making DTS your gateway between SQL Server 7.0 and SQL Server's OLAP Services.

One point that is sometimes overlooked about DTS is that it doesn't require you to use SQL Server as either your source or destination. That means it can be used to transfer (and transform) data between any two supported data sources.

Windows 95/98 Platform Support

Microsoft SQL Server 7.0 provides support for Windows 95/98, in addition to Windows NT Workstation, Windows NT Server, and Windows NT Server Enterprise Edition. All platforms use common source code to avoid compatibility issues.

Windows 95/98 support gives you a reliable, low-cost alternative for prototyping applications, testing before implementation, and even supporting small database applications. However, there are some potential drawbacks relating directly to the operating system platform. For example, no support is provided for:

❑ Windows NT authentication

❑ Multiple processors

❑ Named pipes

❑ Full-text search

> **It's important to note that the Named Pipes Network Library is not installed when running SQL Server 7.0 on Windows 95/98. The Named Pipes Network Library is installed on Windows 95/98 SQL Server 7.0 clients, and in fact, is the default Network Library.**

One noticeable difference between servers running on Windows NT and those running on Windows 95/98 is that Windows 95/98 servers will not appear in browse lists. For example, if you go to register a server in Enterprise Manager, you won't see it listed. You can, however, type in the server name and still register the server.

Despite these limitations, SQL Server 7.0 on Windows 95/98 is a powerful alternative. For example, it gives you a way of taking SQL Server 7.0 "on the road" as a mobile server. You can even set up replication to receive updates from or pass updates to a central server.

Enhancements to Data Storage

One of the biggest areas of change with the introduction of SQL Server 7.0 is in data storage. Rather than using logical database devices for data storage, SQL Server 7.0 uses operating system files. These system files are defined as part of your CREATE DATABASE statement or when creating the database through Enterprise Manager. You can define automatic growth parameters for database files, letting them expand as your storage requirements increase. Segments are also a thing of the past. SQL Server 7.0 uses file groups (defined sets of files) to let you identify where database objects are created and stored.

The transaction log is no longer implemented as the `syslog` table. It is now a separate operating system data file. You can place the transaction log wherever you wish, and you have the same control over automatic growth as you do with the data files. Should it be necessary, you can even create multiple log files for a database.

Page size has been increased from 2 KB to 8 KB. Row size has increased as well, up to 8060 bytes (as opposed to just over 2000 bytes with SQL Server 6.5). Along with this, the number of columns you can have in a table has increased from 250 to 1024. Pages are still organized as extents, with an extent size of 64 KB. SQL Server supports mixed extents, meaning that one extent can contain multiple tables. This can result in significant reductions in storage space requirements if your database includes a number of small tables.

SQL Server Security Model

There have been a number of changes to the SQL Server security model. It is now more closely integrated with Windows NT security, making it possible to assign database permissions to Windows domain users and groups. You have the option of supporting both Windows NT login authentication (referred to as a trusted connection) and SQL Server login authentication at the same server, or allowing Windows NT authentication only.

For SQL Server authentication, login accounts and passwords are specified on and managed by SQL Server. These login accounts have no relationship to Windows NT domain accounts or, for that matter, any type of network accounts. Each time a user wants to connect with a SQL Server login account, both the user account name and password must be provided.

Windows NT authentication is based around Windows NT users and groups. Users and groups who will be granted login permissions must be identified to SQL Server. Since authentication is based on the Windows NT username and password used to log into the operating system, the user doesn't have to provide either when connecting to SQL Server.

> **Windows NT authentication is not supported at the server side for servers running on Windows 95/98. This means that users must supply a SQL Server user name and password to connect to a Windows 95/98 server. However, this only applies to server-side connections. Windows 95/98 clients that are part of a Windows NT domain will be able to connect through trusted connections to Windows NT-based SQL Servers.**

SQL Server 7.0 also introduces a number of changes to how permissions are managed. Administrators are less likely to encounter situations where it is necessary to manage individual user accounts. Instead, permissions can be managed through roles and Windows NT group accounts.

❑ Roles are somewhat analogous to Windows NT groups. Permissions are assigned to roles, and through the roles, to member users and groups. SQL Server includes a number of predefined server and database roles to meet many of your security needs. For example, the `sysadmin` server role can perform any activity on the SQL Server and the `db_ddladmin` database role can add, modify or drop objects in a database.

❑ Administrators now also have the ability to assign permissions to Windows NT groups, providing even greater flexibility in how security is managed.

Users can be members of multiple roles, making your security administration options even more flexible.

Deserving special mention are application roles. Data permissions can be assigned directly to an application, without having to assign permissions to the user. This gives you a way of keeping even tighter control on access security.

Replication Enhancements

In SQL Server 7.0, Microsoft has made some important changes to replication. One of the most significant is the addition of immediate-updating subscribers. Data is replicated out to the subscribers as normal. Transactions posted at the subscribers are immediately posted back to the distributor, giving you a way to support data modification at multiple sites.

SQL-DMF Introduction

SQL-DMF is the framework of components, objects and services, which manage SQL Server. Enterprise Manager itself is built on SQL-DMF. However, by programming SQL-DMF, instead of staying with Enterprise Manager, you can build a scalable management solution that is adapted entirely to your requirements.

Since SQL-DMF is the framework that underlies SQL Server, you can use it to:

❑   Include wizards and dialog boxes from the Enterprise Manager in your custom applications

❑   Perform database administration and configuration tasks programmatically (at specified times and/or intervals, or when a specified condition occurs)

❑   Programmatically perform data transformation using DTS

The SQL-DMF components give you a way to build custom database management applications. If you are plagued with high turnover and forced to rely on personnel who may not always be up to the task of supporting remote offices, you may find it to your advantage to create some custom management utilities or build automated tools to keep user intervention to a minimum. In addition, with SQL-DMF you have more direct control over database objects. There may be things you want to do that you simply cannot do (or cannot do easily) through SQL Enterprise Manager. SQL-DMF objects open the doors to a more granular level of control.

Better still, because SQL-DMF objects are written to Microsoft's language-independent COM standard, you can program SQL-DMF using any language that supports COM, including Visual Basic, C++ and Delphi.

> **To sum up, SQL-DMF allows you to include any of the functionality of the Enterprise Manager in a custom application (written in the language of your choice), allowing the user to manage a remote SQL Server in a distributed enterprise environment.**

Let's take a look at the SQL-DMF architecture, and how the pieces and parts fit together. Here are the major components:

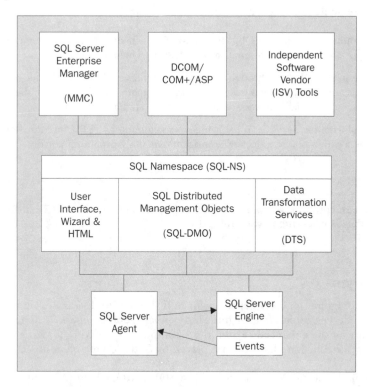

SQL-DMF Applications

At the top of the figure above you can see the three main types of applications that can make use of SQL-DMF. These provide the user interface to the underlying SQL-DMF components:

❑ **SQL Server Enterprise Manager** is the primary administrative tool for SQL Server, running as a snap-in to the MMC. If you've ever used Enterprise Manager, you've been using SQL-DMF objects, even if you didn't realize it.

❑ SQL-DMF objects can be incorporated in **DCOM** or **COM+** applications. They can be implemented as local or remote objects. They can also be used in **Active Server Pages** (**ASP**) for building web-based applications.

❑ **Independent software vendors** (**ISV**) can use the SQL-DMF for server management and configuration. It provides a way of giving targeted support for specific management requirements without confusing the issue by providing more features than are really necessary.

SQL-DMF APIs

SQL-DMF is implemented through three API sets. These are:

❑ **SQL Distributed Management Objects (SQL-DMO)**, which you can use to handle all administrative and configuration tasks programmatically. SQL-DMO includes over 60 management objects.

❑ **SQL Namespace (SQL-NS)**, through which the SQL Server Enterprise Manager user interface components are exposed. What this means to you is that you have many of the Enterprise Manager elements directly available to you, or at least to your applications.

❑ **Data Transformation Services (DTS)**, which lets you import, export, and transform data. The DTS API also lets you import, export, and transform data, only programmatically through the services it exposes.

In some documentation, you may see DTS referred to as Distributed Transformation Services. This is referring to the same API.

SQL-DMF Changes

SQL-DMF has undergone significant changes for SQL Server 7.0. It was introduced with SQL Server 6.0, but with SQL Server 7.0 has been significantly enhanced and expanded. This was done in order to provide support for the enhanced capabilities built into SQL Server 7.0. For example, the SQL Executive objects are gone, and have been replaced by SQL Server Agent objects.

In SQL Server 6.0, the SQL-DMF consisted of just SQL-DMO, which was contained in a library called `Sqlole.dll`. Significant changes were made to the SQL-DMO objects for SQL Server 7.0.

SQL Namespace objects and DTS objects were added with SQL Server 7.0.

SQL-DMF Is Not for Data Access

SQL-DMF should not be used for creating data access applications. Sure, its components can be used for data access, but there are better methods available. You're better off using APIs and object libraries designed specifically for that purpose, like ActiveX Data Objects (ADO) and OLE DB.

Introduction to SQL-DMO

Any server administration functions you can perform through SQL Server Enterprise Manager can be performed with SQL-DMO objects. That's because Enterprise Manager derives its functionality through exactly the same objects. However, with SQL-DMO objects you can automate your management processes and take more detailed control over the server. For example, when you are setting up replication, SQL Server Enterprise Manager will only let you subscribe to publications, but with SQL-DMO, you can subscribe to individual articles.

We can have this level of control because each and every SQL Server object, database object, security object, SQL Server Agent object, and anything else you can think of, is represented by and can be manipulated through SQL-DMO objects. If this sounds like a lot to keep up with, you're right. SQL-DMO includes over 60 different objects and over 1000 different properties and methods (but don't worry there's a comprehensive reference section in the appendices at the end of the book).

The SQL-DMO object model is comprised of objects, collections, and lists. A **collection** is a container object, which means that it is an object that logically contains other objects. Members can be added to and removed from a collection. As an example, SQL-DMO includes a `Databases` collection, which references all of the databases on the server. A **list** is another type of container object. With a list, membership is fixed, that is, a list is a collection of objects that will not change. For example, the fixed server security roles are represented as a list. You can add members to or drop members from fixed server roles, but you cannot add or drop server security roles.

We're going to be looking at these objects in some detail in later chapters, but for now, let's look at a quick example to give you an idea of what we're talking about. A table is a familiar database object, but when you think about it, there's quite a bit of information relating to a table. A database's tables are listed in a `Tables` collection. Each table in the `Tables` collection has collections and objects representing column definitions, check constraints, indexes (with a separate clustered index object), keys (with a separate primary key object), and triggers. Through SQL-DMO, you can create, view and modify properties for, and manage any of these objects.

> **SQL-DMO objects are covered in detail in Chapters 3, 4 and 5.**

Client System Requirements

SQL-DMO clients must have SQL Server ODBC Driver version 3.70 (or later), because SQL-DMO communicates with SQL Server via ODBC. This driver ships with SQL Server 7.0 and installs with the SQL Server management utilities. The driver can also be found in the latest MDAC (Microsoft Data Access Components) installation located at `http://www.microsoft.com/data/`.

SQL-DMO clients must run on one of the following operating systems:

- ❑ Windows 95 (Intel processor computer)
- ❑ Windows 98 (Intel processor computer)
- ❑ Windows NT 4.0 (Intel or Alpha-based)
- ❑ Windows 2000 (Intel or Alpha-based)

In order to communicate with the server, the client must have an appropriate client network library installed and configured.

SQL-DMO Installation

SQL-DMO components install as part of SQL Server or SQL Server client installations. You can select to install C/C++ header and library files, as well as code samples, as part of custom SQL Server setup.

The following is a list of all SQL-DMO files installed during SQL Server setup. The path provided will be on the SQL Server destination drive:

Directory Path	Filename	File Description
\Mssql7\Binn	Sqldmo.dll	All SQL-DMO objects are implemented through this single DLL.
\Mssql7\Binn	Sqldmo.hlp	This is a localized context-sensitive help file for SQL-DMO objects, properties, and methods.
\Mssql7\Binn	Sqldmo.cnt	This is the contents file for SQL-DMO help.
\Mssql7\Binn\Resources*xxxx*	Sqldmo.rll	This is a localized resource file. The *xxxx* directory will be a decimal representation of the SQL Server language identifier.
\Mssql7\Devtools\Include	Sqldmo.h	C/C++ header file – member function prototypes, enumerated data types, and macros.
\Mssql7\Devtools\Include	Sqldmoid.h	C/C++ header file – interface and class identifiers.
\Mssql7\Install	Sqldmo.sql	Only installed on SQL Server. Transact-SQL scripts implement SQL-DMO stored procedures.
\Mssql7\Devtools\Samples \Sqldmo	All files	Sample application files with examples of SQL-DMO use.

The SQL-DMO stored procedures are installed during SQL Server setup. The Sqldmo.sql script file is provided as a means to recreate those stored procedures, should it be necessary.

> **You are unlikely to deal with the SQL-DMO stored procedures under normal circumstances. The stored procedures must be created on the server before SQL-DMO objects or Enterprise Manager can run against the server. They are used internally by SQL Server and are not documented in any of Microsoft's help files. You should only need to recreate the stored procedures if they are deleted or become corrupted in some manner.**

Introduction to SQL-NS

As with SQL-DMO, SQL-NS exposes objects and collections, and their associated properties and methods. Through these, your application can invoke SQL Server Enterprise Manager interface components, such as wizards, dialog boxes, and property sheets.

You should use SQL-NS objects if you want to call SQL Server Enterprise Manager components from within your application. For example, you might create a custom server management utility. If you want to give the user access to the server property sheets as part of this utility without letting the user run SQL Server Enterprise Manager, you can use SQL-NS to display the property sheets from within your application.

Support for SQL-NS objects is installed when you install SQL Server client or server. The operating system requirements are the same as for SQL-DMO; Windows 95/98 (on an Intel-based system) or Windows NT 4.0 or later (on an Intel- or Alpha-based system). The SQL-NS object library is contained in a file named `sqlns.rll` in the directory `\Mssql7\Binn\Resources\xxxx`.

> SQL-NS objects, collections, properties, and methods are discussed in detail in Chapter 6.

Introduction to DTS

Data Transformation Services (DTS) also includes objects, properties, methods, and collections. The purpose of DTS is to move data between OLE DB source and OLE DB destinations. This can be done as a simple copy or can include data transformations.

We will discuss DTS in greater detail later in the book. For now, it might be helpful for you to understand the difference between a copy and a data transformation. A copy is exactly what it sounds like, a one-to-one transfer of data. If you wanted to copy all of the columns from an `Employees` table in one database into an identically structured table in another database (or even in the same database) you would run a data copy. When you run a data transformation, you are manipulating the data in some fashion. If you only wanted to copy selected columns, or if you wanted to combine first and last name columns into a single column containing full names, you would use a data transformation.

Programmers using any language that supports OLE Automation (such as Visual Basic or C++) can create and modify DTS packages through an OLE Automation interface implemented in `Dtspkg.dll`. Through this you can also create custom transformation tasks. Support is provided for ActiveX scripting tasks through the DTSPump, which is implemented in `Dtspump.dll`.

If you are already familiar with the DTS Wizard and DTS Designer, then you'll know that these are powerful, flexible tools. However, this doesn't mean that you won't be able to find reasons for using DTS objects. Keep in mind that DTS doesn't necessarily require SQL Server as a source or destination. You can use DTS objects as part of your application when data copy or data transfer between applications is required.

> DTS and its objects, collections, properties and methods are discussed in detail in Chapters 9 and 10.

DTS Requirements

DTS connects to SQL Server 7.0 using the Microsoft SQL Server OLE DB provider. The Microsoft SQL Server OLE DB provider installs any time you install SQL Server client or server components.

The requirements for DTS are the same as those for SQL-DMO; Windows 95/98 (on an Intel-based system) or Windows NT 4.0 or later (on an Intel- or Alpha-based system). DTS is installed with both SQL Server 7.0 and its client management components.

DTS Files

The following files are installed automatically when you install SQL Server 7.0:

Directory Path	Filename	File Description
\Mssql7\Binn	Axscphst.dll	This is the data pump interface for scripting languages (such as VBScript) used by an ActiveX script transformation.
\Mssql7\Binn	Dtsffile.dll	This is an OLE DB text file provider. The DTS Designer, and the DTS Import and Export Wizards use it.
\Mssql7\Binn	Dtspkg.dll	This is the interface that implements a DTS package.
\Mssql7\Binn	Dtspump.dll	DTS ActiveX script task constants are defined by this interface.
\Mssql7\Binn	Dtsrun.exe	This is a command prompt utility through which a DTS package may be executed.
\Mssql7\Binn	Sqldts.hlp	This is the DTS programming help file.
\Mssql7\Binn	Sqldts.cnt	This is the DTS programming help contents file.
\Mssql7\DevTools\Include	Datapump.h	This is the C/CC++ header file that implements a DTS custom transformation.

Using SQL-DMF

Now you have some idea of what we're talking about with SQL-DMF, but we haven't done much to justify why. After all, SQL-DMF components give you the same functionality as the SQL Server management tools. Why not just use the SQL Server management tools and be done with it?

In most cases, that's what happens. It's a quick solution, but it may not be the best solution. In some cases, it may not even be a safe solution. There are going to be times when you want to be able to make selected administrative functions available, but only those functions. For example, you might want to "hand off" selected management tasks. You have some control by assigning user login names to fixed server roles, but that solution really isn't that flexible. With SQL-DMF you can build management utilities targeted at the exact procedures or processes. You have complete control over what can be done through the utility.

You may encounter situations where you want to automate certain processes rather than having to go through the step-by-step processes using traditional tools. For example, you could have a custom application that has specific requirements for its SQL Server back end. With SQL-DMF, you could make careful, detailed checks and then make changes to the server based on what you find.

Those were some quick examples. Let's take a little closer look at some ideas.

Custom Management Utilities

The traditional view of implementing a database solution involved carefully defined roles and responsibilities. You had the database administrator, responsible for installation, configuration, security, and the like. You had the data architect (or database engineer) who designed and created the database tables, indexes, stored procedures, and other data objects. Finally, you had the programmer writing the client application. While the three roles needed to be in close communication, each knew its place in the overall scheme of things.

Discussions about implementing a database application often still include these roles, but in the real world of modern enterprise networks, the roles often become blurred. There tends to be much more overlap than in the past. Long-term support often means involving people at remote sites (or even at the main database) with limited experience.

Administration is often parceled out, and you don't want to give these limited-responsibility administrators access to too much of the database. You also don't want to spend more time than necessary training (or having them trained) and retraining their replacements.

As an alternative, you can create targeted management tools. You can use SQL-DMF to create management applications that give users and administrators access to only that functionality required to do their jobs. In many cases, you can streamline the interface, making it as intuitive as possible and keeping training to a minimum.

Automated Object Creation

You've come up with the perfect idea for a commercial application. It's going to use SQL Server as the data engine and your custom application as the front end. As part of the installation, you need to have a number of SQL Server objects created and it may be necessary to modify some of the server configuration settings.

The problem is that not every installation is going to be the same. There will be variations in what objects are created, based on user input during the installation program. The solution, though, is right at hand. You can use SQL-DMF as part of your installation process to create custom objects based on user input. The creation process is fully automated, keeping a protective layer between SQL Server and the user.

Commercial Software

One commercial application that leverages the benefits of SQL-DMF is VisualCommerce's Constructor. Constructor is a wizard-based retail software product that assists users in creating e-commerce solutions using Microsoft Site Server Commerce Edition.

One of the many things that Constructor provides to its users is the capability of creating a robust SQL Server e-commerce database for a web storefront. The entire process of enumerating SQL Servers on the network to the creation of a database, its tables, indexes, keys, users, roles and logins, is accomplished using the powerful technology of SQL-DMO.

You can find more information about Constructor and see an animated demo of it in action by visiting the VisualCommerce website at `http://www.visualcommerce.com`:

Redistributable Components

While we're talking about applications, we need to make some mention of redistributable components. We've already mentioned the SQL-DMF components that are installed whenever you set up SQL Server or a SQL Server client. You can also distribute the redistributable components as part of your SQL Server application.

SQL-DMO Components

The redistributable components for SQL-DMO are:

```
Sqldmo.dll          Sqlsvc.dll          Sqlwid.dll
Sqldmo.rll          Sqlsvc.rll          W95scm.dll
Sqlresld.dll        Sqlwoa.dll
```

You will need to use the `regsvr32.exe` utility to register the `sqldmo.dll` file. Place the `sqlwoa.dll` file in the system folder (`\Windows\System` or `\winnt\system32`).

SQL-NS Components

The list of SQL-NS redistributable components is quite extensive:

Sqlns.dll	Semcomn.dll	Semexec.dll
Sqlns.rll	Semcomn.rll	Semexec.rll
Sqlgui.dll	Semcros.dll	Semwiz.dll
Sqlgui.rll	Semcros.rll	Semwiz.rll
Sfc.dll	Semdll.dll	Semrepl.dll
Sfc.rll	Semdll.rll	Semrepl.rll
Semsys.dll	Semmap.dll	Semnt.dll
Semsys.rll	Semmap.rll	Semnt.rll
Semobj.dll	Semwebwiz.dll	Sqllex.dll
Semobj.rll	Semwebwiz.rll	

You will have to use `regsvr32.exe` to register `sqlns.dll` and `sqllex.dll`.

DTS Components

Though not as long as the list for SQL-NS, there are still a number of files included for DTS. The redistributable files are:

Sqlresld.dll	Dtspump.dll	Dtsrun.exe
Dtsffile.dll	Dtspump.rll	Dtsrun.rll
Dtsffile.rll	Axscphst.dll	Sqlwoa.dll
Dtspkg.dll	Axscphst.rll	Sqlwid.dll
Dtspkg.rll		

You will have to register the `dtsffile.dll`, `dtspkg.dll`, `dtspump.dll`, and `axscphst.dll` files. Place the `sqlwoa.dll` and `sqlwid.dll` files in the system folder (`\Windows\System` or `\winnt\system32`).

Getting Ready

As you make your way through this book, you are going to encounter quite a bit of sample code. To help you follow along, the projects discussed in this book are available on the Wrox web site (`www.wrox.com`). To use these, you are going to need to make sure that you have a system available that meets a few simple requirements.

Software

To use the SQL-DMF, you need to use a programming language that is capable of using COM objects, such as Visual Basic, C++, Delphi or Java. In this book, we are going to use Visual Basic 6.0 for the examples (generally, non-VB programmers find it much easier to follow and understand VB code than non-C++ programmers find C++ code). At the back of the book, C++ programmers will find that Chapter 12 is devoted to issues that directly affect them.

Of course, you will also need SQL Server 7.0. Most of the examples were created with Visual Basic 6.0 and SQL Server 7.0 installed on the same Windows NT system.

The SQL Server components you need are installed by running a Typical setup. A Custom setup may be selected, as long as you install (at least) all of the components installed during a Typical setup. In other words, if you select to run Custom setup, you can make additions to the component selections, but don't make any subtractions.

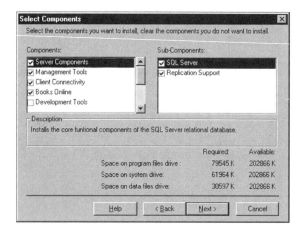

By installing both SQL Server and Visual Basic on the same system, you reduce the number of potential variables should problems arise. You don't have to worry about network communication problems or incompatible network libraries.

Operating System/Hardware Platform

Most of the examples in this book were created on a Windows NT 4.0 Server running on an Intel-based computer. Windows NT (Server or Workstation) is strongly suggested for use as your operating system platform. While most of the examples can be completed on Windows 95 or Windows 98, there will be some features that are not supported due to the limitations of SQL Server running on Windows 95/98.

Summary

In this chapter, we've briefly introduced SQL-DMF. We started with an overview of SQL Server 7.0 and new features significant to the information provided in this book. The chapter has provided a quick look at SQL-DMF components, and an idea of where and why you might want to use SQL-DMF. It also gave some general guidelines for getting ready to follow along with the examples in each of the chapters.

The next chapter also provides some introductory material, this time focusing on the programming environment in which we'll be working. It includes an overview of Windows Distributed interNet Application Architecture (DNA) applications and Microsoft Transaction Server (MTS). It also introduces the application we'll be using as a sample during the book.

Introduction to Windows DNA Applications

Over the last year or so, **Windows Distributed interNet Application** architecture (**Windows DNA**) has become a common buzzword in Microsoft development circles. You can expect to hear the term even more as **Windows 2000** and **Microsoft AppCenter Server** loom closer.

> *Microsoft AppCenter Server was announced in October 1999. Not much has been confirmed as of the date this book went to press, but it is expected to provide advanced features for developing and managing enterprise applications, such as component load balancing and monitoring and management tools.*

What does Windows DNA have to do with applications that use SQL-DMF? As SQL Server is generally used in enterprise environments, applications that access it (including those using SQL-DMF) will usually be enterprise applications. The architecture Microsoft recommends for such applications is Windows DNA.

This chapter will introduce Windows DNA and Microsoft Transaction Server, and describe some potential uses. If you are already familiar with building Windows DNA applications using Microsoft Transaction Server or COM+, you can skip some of this chapter.

> **It is however, important to take a minute to read over the business scenario presented later in the chapter. It describes the application that we will build throughout this book. All of the code for the application (SQL script, VB source and compiled code) is available for download from the Wrox web site at `www.wrox.com`.**

Throughout this book, we're going to employ a twin track approach to looking at the code needed to build our sample application. In this chapter and Chapter 7, we're going to walk you through the coding and deployment of a COM component for use under MTS. In contrast, in Chapters 3, 4, 5 and 6 we're just going to highlight various code snippets that serve to illustrate the aspects of the SQL-DMO and SQL-NS object models we are considering (if you want to see the code in its entirety, you can download it from the Wrox web site).

To summarize, the aims of this chapter are to:

❑ Overview the Windows DNA architecture

❑ Discuss distributed application development using MTS and COM+

❑ Introduce the business scenario we'll use to illustrate the potential of SQL-DMF in the construction of enterprise solutions

Let's start by delving into the concept of Windows DNA.

Windows DNA Applications

Windows DNA is a development strategy for building enterprise applications for the Microsoft Windows platform using Microsoft technologies.

By using Microsoft's Windows DNA architecture, you will be able to build applications that are:

❑ Scalable

❑ Maintainable

❑ Extensible

❑ Available

The strategy involves analyzing the requirements of an application and breaking it down into **components** that provide the services the application requires. By breaking a solution down into a set of components, you can take advantage of the maintainability and reusability offered by COM, as well as the scalability and maintainability features offered by Microsoft Transaction Server.

COM

The **Component Object Model (COM)** specification describes a set of rules for interfaces that can be queried for and bound to either when the component is being compiled or at run-time.

An interface is like a contract with the consumer. To understand how this works, let's look at an example from real life. In building a house, I might decide that I need the services of a contractor to build the foundation. I have the name of the contractor (in COM that's equivalent to the **programmatic identifier** or **ProgID**) I'd like to use, so I look the company up in a directory and look at the list of services the company provides. In COM, this would involve two steps, looking in the registry for the location of the type library and reading the type library. I now know whether the contractor can provide the service I need and I sign a contract with the company to perform this work.

Notice that I have no details about the equipment the contractor uses to build the foundation or the steps that must be taken. I only know that the company can build a foundation. This means that the company is free to change their implementation of the process without notifying me or any other customer, provided the contract (equivalent to a COM interface) does not change. This feature of COM, known as **encapsulation**, provides maintainability by allowing a component to change its implementation without affecting consumers, provided the interface does not change.

Since the fictional contractor provided detailed information about its services in a directory, I was able to get right to the point of negotiating the contract. The COM equivalent of this is **early binding**, which requires the component to have a type library and the consumer to know the identity (the ProgID) of the component. However, suppose the phone directory contained only a phone number. In this case, I would need to call the contractor and ask a series of questions about the services they provide. This process takes more of my time, but the end result is the same. I negotiate a contract with the company to build my foundation. In COM, this process is known as **late binding**.

Microsoft Transaction Server

COM components can run on the same computer as the consumer or on a different computer. One way to allow 32-bit client applications to communicate with 32-bit COM components across a network is through **Distributed COM** (**DCOM**). However, while DCOM is good at handling the underlying packaging of calls to components on different computers, it does not provide efficient tools for managing these components, how they are instantiated, and who can access them.

Microsoft Transaction Server (**MTS**) can be used to fill that gap. It allows you to set attributes that determine whether a component should be launched in its own process or as a library inside MTS. It also lets you control access by configuring security roles that are used to assign access based on Windows NT users and groups. MTS also allows components to be activated and deactivated dynamically. This means that a single instance of a COM component can be shared by multiple users, increasing the scalability of the application.

> **Without MTS, components that run on a different computer are created as out-of-process (EXE) components. A component that runs under MTS must be created as an in-process (DLL) component. This is because it runs within a process that is created by MTS.**

Last but not least, the most important feature of MTS is its ability to perform **transaction processing**. A transaction is just a set of actions that are performed as a whole or not at all. A common, but nevertheless useful, analogy is to think of a transfer of funds between two bank accounts.

When $500 needs to be transferred from Account A to Account B a transaction occurs to ensure that money is not lost "in the system" or that new money is not "created". First, $500 is removed from Account A, and then $500 is added to Account B. If any error occurs, the transaction must roll back to the beginning again.

N-Tier Applications

An n-tier application divides the services the application provides across at least three *logical* tiers, the most common arrangement being:

- ❏ A presentation tier
- ❏ A business tier
- ❏ A data tier

However, n-tier application can consist of any number of logical tiers. A four-tier approach of presentation tier, UI-centric tier, data-centric tier and data tier is also widely used.

Keep in mind that these are logical tiers, not physical tiers. The components of the application may actually reside on a single computer or be spread across many computers.

Windows DNA applications use the n-tier architecture. Let's look at how the n-tier model of Windows DNA applies to the tools and technologies that we will discuss in this chapter:

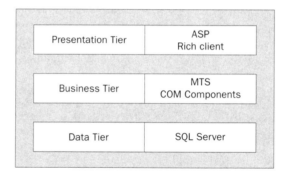

The Presentation Tier

The presentation tier contains services that format and display data and services that accept user input. These services can be implemented as **rich clients**, such as Windows applications written in Visual Basic, C++, or another language or **thin clients**, such as browser-independent HTML generated by an Active Server Page.

> Although sometimes referred to as "fat" clients, Microsoft prefers to use the term "rich" client to refer to a presentation-layer component that executes as an application. A web-based application is known as a thin client.

The Business Tier

The business tier is composed of services that enforce business rules. This tier is generally composed of COM components that run on an application server to validate or manipulate user data before passing it on to a data service, or to perform a business process on stored data before passing it to a user. As you will see a little later in the chapter, MTS can be used to manage COM component activation and deactivation.

The Data Tier

The data tier contains services that handle data integrity, data consistency, data retrieval, and data manipulation. In a Windows DNA application, SQL Server or another relational database management system (RDBMS) like Oracle or Sybase performs these services. However, SQL-DMO is also a data service, as we will see in this chapter.

Logical Tiers Not Physical Tiers

Since these are logical tiers, the Windows DNA architecture does not dictate which machine will run a particular service. In the case of a rich client, the presentation services will need to be run on every client workstation. In the case of a thin browser-based client, the Active Server Pages actually execute on the server and generate the HTML that is displayed by the browser. Business rules that are closely tied to a particular column of data may be best implemented by constraints. Other business rules that involve complex logic or that must process data from a variety of data sources are best implemented as COM components.

Data services will generally provide the best performance when performed by the database management system. However, maintainability and extensibility concerns may require you to abstract data access and data manipulation into a COM component. For example, you might decide to create a data service that can be used with a variety of tables. Alternatively, you may create one that retrieves information about the database schema dynamically so that changes to the schema do not need to propagate down to the business or presentation services.

You may decide to provide business logic that is directly tied to data by writing stored procedures and triggers. By creating a data service component that calls these stored procedures, you shield the rest of your business components, and particularly your client applications, from any changes that are subsequently made in those stored procedures or the database schema itself. SQL-DMO is such an abstraction because it allows you to access your database objects through a consistent object model, even if the system stored procedures or the system tables change.

> Microsoft provides SQL-DMO to abstract developers and their applications from changes that occur in the system tables when a new version of SQL Server is released. If you circumvent the layer of abstraction and write code that accesses system tables directly, it is very likely to break with a subsequent release of SQL Server.

OK, now that we have an idea of what a DNA application is, we should consider where we might find it useful to implement one.

When Does a Distributed Architecture Make Sense?

Applications that required multiple users to interact with a centralized data source were traditionally designed using a client/server architecture. In a client/server architecture, an application runs on the client computer to display the user interface, handle user-input, format data for output, and perform some types of data validation and business processes. The client application calls on the services of the database management system retrieve and manage data.

Choosing a distributed architecture over a traditional client/server architecture is appropriate in situations where maximum scalability is important and/or where maintainability and extensibility requirements make it important to maximize component reuse and minimize redeployment. It is also appropriate when your application requires high availability or access from across the Internet.

Let's take a quick look at how the Windows DNA architecture can allow you to develop solutions that address the issues of:

❑ Scalability

❑ Maintainability

❑ Extensibility

❑ High availability

Scalability

A Windows DNA application can take advantage of MTS to provide increased scalability. The two MTS features most important for scalability are connection pooling and Just in Time object activation.

> *With MTS, component load balancing is a manual process. However, Microsoft AppCenter Server is expected to include dynamic component load balancing for COM+ components. This feature will greatly enhance your ability to scale components across multiple physical machines.*

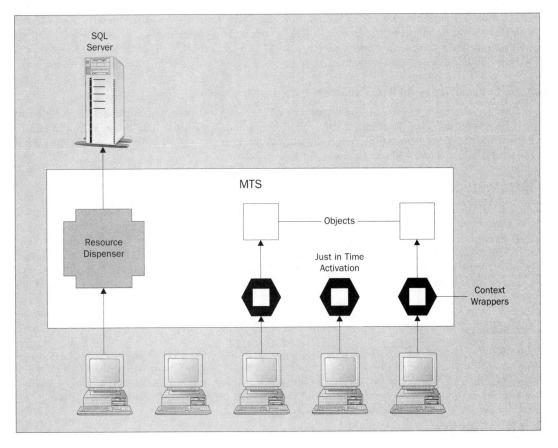

Connection Pooling

Since database connections are time-consuming to open, traditional client/server applications typically opened a connection at the beginning of a session and closed it when the application terminated. As the number of users increases, this architecture becomes very expensive, both in terms of licensing costs and in the amount of processor time and memory spent servicing so many connections. Since a great deal of an application's life is spent waiting for a user to perform some task, it makes sense for database connections that are not being actively used to be pooled and allocated on an as-needed basis so that they can be reused.

MTS provides connection pooling through the **Resource Dispenser**. This enhances scalability because it allows multiple client applications to utilize the same database connection. This gives savings, not only in the time it takes to establish a connection, but also because database licensing is generally based on a particular number of concurrent connections.

Just In Time Activation

MTS provides added scalability through **Just In Time Activation** (**JIT**) (also known as **deferred activation**). When a client application creates a component that is hosted in MTS, the component is not actually activated until the first method of an interface is invoked. Hence, any initialization code that might cause a server's resources to be consumed can be delayed until it is really needed.

MTS also allows the reverse of JIT Activation, called **As Soon As Possible Deactivation**, where an object is deactivated as soon as it is no longer needed. The client application believes that it still holds a reference to the real object, when in fact MTS has released the memory and resources that were being consumed by the object.

Increased Scalability by Adding Machines

Scalability also involves the physical side as well. Making a distributed application scalable often involves being able to spread application processing across multiple machines. MTS can run multiple servers. As demand is placed on an MTS server, additional MTS servers can be added, thus making the overall MTS system scalable.

Maintainability

The Windows DNA architecture allows you to segment your business logic into components that can run on an application server. Since business logic is subject to change as the business grows or as the economic climate and markets shift, an application whose business logic is contained in discrete, server-side components will be much easier to upgrade and maintain than one whose business logic is built into the presentation tier. This is because business logic will only need to be changed on the server as opposed to having to alter the client application and then redistribute it to every workstation.

Extensibility

On a similar note, the Windows DNA architecture encourages developers to create reusable, multipurpose components that can be shared by a variety of applications. By abstracting functionality into more generic interfaces, developers can build applications that can be easily enhanced as the business requirements and the applications needed to meet them evolve.

High Availability

Because the tiers in a Windows DNA application are logical tiers, not physical tiers, you can implement a Windows DNA application that provides high availability for critical system functions by eliminating a single point of failure or by making application services available at several geographic locations.

> *The additional availability enhancements that will become available with Windows 2000 and with the release of Microsoft AppCenter Server will be briefly discussed in Appendix C.*

So now we know what Windows DNA is and what benefits use of that technology can give us, we should really consider how SQL-DMF fits into this architecture.

How SQL-DMF Maps to Windows DNA Tiers

The libraries in the SQL Distributed Management Framework provide services that can be mapped to the tiers of the Windows DNA architecture:

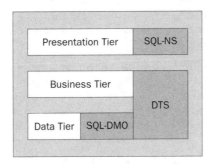

The SQL-NS library provides presentation tier services. As the primary purpose of these services is to display dialogs, wizards, and property pages, they can only be used in rich client applications. Although the library can be used to modify SQL Server and the objects it manages, SQL-NS calls on SQL-DMO to actually perform these services.

Data Transformation Services (DTS) is mostly a data tier component. However, depending on the transformations you configure, it could also be thought of as providing a business tier service. For example, suppose you are using DTS to transfer accounting information from an Excel spreadsheet to a SQL Server database. As part of the transfer, you need to perform a calculation, such as subtracting the sales tax collected from the total of the check, based on the location where the sale occurred. In this case, you are using DTS to perform a business service in addition to performing an actual data transfer.

The role of the SQL-DMO library is to provide an object model for accessing and manipulating SQL Server and the data objects it manages. Therefore, it operates on the logical data tier, even though it may physically be loaded on the client workstation, on a middle-tier server, or on the SQL Server.

To show how SQL-DMO may be used to solve business problems we have set up a scenario involving a fictional company called Surveys Unlimited.

The Surveys Unlimited Business Scenario

Surveys Unlimited is a small market research company that creates and implements web-based surveys for customers, then compiles and analyzes the results. The survey questions and the answers provided by the participants are stored in a SQL Server 7.0 database. Our task is to develop the application that the survey creators will use to create and manage the different databases that are needed to contain the surveys conducted for each customer.

Our solution will be a Windows DNA application with a rich client, created in Visual Basic 6.0. The application is broken down in the following way:

❑ **Presentation Logic**: This is contained in a client application called `SurveyDesigner`. From this application, users will be able to view and establish connections to servers and create and modify the databases needed to contain surveys. It will also include features that allow survey administrators to back up and restore survey databases and manage the security for database objects.

❑ **Business Logic**: The application will have two component libraries on the business tier: `CustomerManager` and `SQLDDL`. The `CustomerManager` component will be a simple component that offers a single service, the ability to log customers and the name of the survey database that belongs to them. The `SQLDDL` component library will provide the functionality required to create and manage databases using SQL-DMO.

❑ **Data Logic**: A small database (`CustomerManagement`) is used to hold information on registered customers, and the location and details of their surveys.

Overall, this can be illustrated as follows:

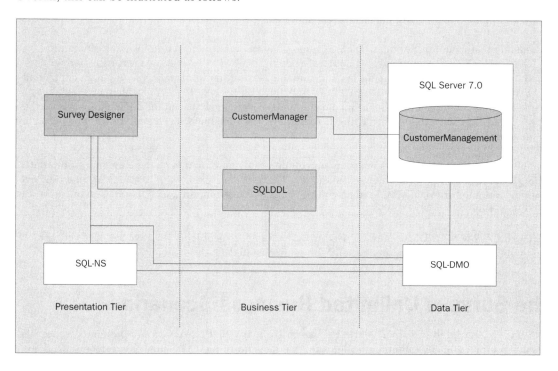

Treatment of the Scenario

The Surveys Unlimited business scenario will form the basis for discussing and highlighting many important points about SQL-DMO. To effectively do this we will follow the dual approach of walking through code development and deployment and examining, in detail, pre-written code.

During the course of this chapter and Chapter 7, we will examine in detail how to code, test and deploy the `CustomerManager` component into MTS. As part of the scenario set up in this chapter we will also provide the information necessary to create the `CustomerManagement` database and to implement a small client application called `SurveyRegTest` (for Survey Registration Test) that will allow us to test our `CustomerManager` component.

In this book, we will walk through most of the coding of the `SQLDDL` component and the `SurveyDesigner` application, making extensive references to the code in each component (during Chapters 3, 4, 5 and 6) to provide examples of the use of SQL-DMO and SQL-NS. However, since there are many forms and class modules, we will not discuss the more fundamental routines that make no use of SQL-DMF.

Since our emphasis in this book is on SQL-DMF, we will not be discussing the design and implementation of the actual application and supporting databases that would implement the web-based survey collection and analysis work of our fictional company.

Let's now have a look at each of these components in more detail.

The Client Application – SurveyDesigner

The client application is a multiple document interface (MDI) application project named `SurveyDesigner`. The parent form is named `frmMDIMain`. It includes a number of child forms for designing databases, viewing server configuration, initiating backup and restore, managing jobs, and creating users. It also has a number of additional forms that are used as dialogs. A quick introduction to the main form is shown below; the child forms and dialogs will be described, and screen shots will be presented, as we discuss the relevant code.

The client application also has a standard module named `modGlobals` that is used to store public variables that are needed by multiple forms in the application. For testing purposes, the client application project and the `SQLDDL` component project are included in a project group.

There are four main menus that can be accessed (screenshots taken after database connection has been established):

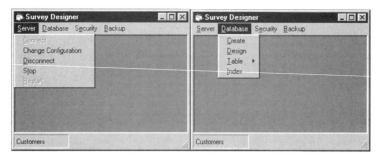

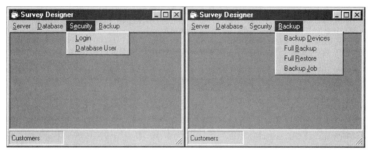

The CustomerManager Component

The CustomerManager component is a very simple component. It has a single class:

Class name	Description
Survey	This component implements a single method, AddSurvey that is used to add a record to the CustomerManagement database.

The SQLDDL Component

The SQLDDL component library has the following components:

Class name	Description
Server	This component implements the methods required to establish a SQL-DMO connection, to stop, start, pause, and resume the MSSQLServer service, and to view and manage server configuration options.
Database	This component implements the methods required to create a database, to add tables to a database, and to add columns to tables.

Class name	Description
Security	This component implements the methods required to allow users to add and delete logins and users.
Management	This component implements the methods required to allow users to create a regularly scheduled job that performs a backup.
BackupDB	This component implements the methods required to configure and run full backups and to restore a database from backup.

In addition, a dependent class module named `Constants.cls` contains enumerations used to identify error numbers and supported column attributes. There is also a standard module named `Strings.bas` that contains constants defining the strings used for error descriptions.

A list of the modules used in each of the projects that form the Surveys Unlimited solution is contained in Appendix A.

Implementing the Surveys Unlimited Solution

Let's now make a start on putting together our application. Within this section, we are going to cover three basic topics:

❑   Creating the `CustomerManagement` database

❑   Initial coding of the `CustomerManager` MTS component and creating the Survey Registration test application

❑   Building an MTS package to test the component

Without further ado, let's get our hands dirty.

Preparing the Database

The component we're going to build is named `CustomerManager.Survey`. Its role is to make an entry in a `CustomerManagement` database that keeps track of customers and the surveys that belong to them. The `CustomerManagement` database has two tables; `Customers` and `Surveys`, which are related as follows:

The columns of the `Customers` table are configured as follows:

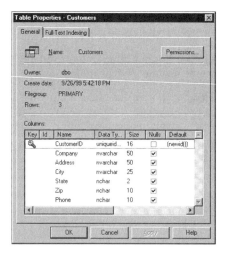

The `CustomerID` column is the primary key with a data type of `uniqueidentifier`. Because the default is specified using the `newid()` function, SQL Server will populate this column with a globally unique identifier (GUID) each time a record is added to the table.

> *A GUID and the* `newid()` *function allow SQL Server to generate values that are to be guaranteed unique, even across servers. This allows you to create unique row identifiers in applications where records are being added to a table on multiple servers, such as when you are using merge replication.*
>
> *Another point to note is that the informational columns use Unicode datatypes. Although these data types are larger than their ASCII equivalents, they allow you to store language-specific characters, a feature that is particularly important if your application needs to be localized.*

The columns of the `Surveys` table are shown below. By specifying a foreign key relationship from the `CustomerID` column of the `Surveys` table to the `CustomerID` column of the `Customers` table, referential integrity is enforced:

The primary key of the Surveys table is composed of two columns: the CustomerID column and a SurveyNum column, which is configured as an Identity column. The Identity column is also populated by SQL Server, using an identity seed for the first record and incrementing each subsequent record by the identity increment value. In this case, both the identity seed and the identity increment are set to 1.

The script for creating the database (also contained in the file CustomerManager.sql) is:

```
CREATE DATABASE CustomerManagement
GO


USE CustomerManagement
CREATE TABLE Customers
    (CustomerID    uniqueidentifier DEFAULT newid(),
    Company        nvarchar(50) NULL,
    Address        nvarchar(50) NULL,
    City           nvarchar(25) NULL,
    State          nchar(2)     NULL,
    Zip            nchar(10)    NULL,
    Phone          nchar(10)    NULL
CONSTRAINT pk_CustomerID PRIMARY KEY(CustomerID))
GO


USE CustomerManagement
CREATE TABLE Surveys
    (CustomerID    uniqueidentifier,
    SurveyName     nvarchar(50) NULL,
    DatabaseName   nvarchar(50) NULL,
    SurveyNum      int          IDENTITY(1, 1)
CONSTRAINT fk_CustomerID FOREIGN KEY(CustomerID)
    REFERENCES Customers (CustomerID),
CONSTRAINT pk_Surveys    PRIMARY KEY (CustomerID, SurveyNum))
GO


USE CustomerManagement
INSERT Customers
    (Company, Address, City, State, Zip, Phone)
VALUES ("Cypress Development, Etc", "Some Street Address", "Anytown",
"MO", "60631", "555-5555")
INSERT Customers
    (Company, Address, City, State, Zip, Phone)
VALUES ("3 Dog Brewery", "Middle of Nowhere", "No Particular Town",
"MO", "60639", "555-1111")
INSERT Customers
    (Company, Address)
VALUES ("Computer Dragon", "Somewhere in Cyberspace")
GO
```

To use the script, launch Query Analyzer and connect to your SQL Server. Run File | Open and locate the script file. Once the script is displayed in your query window run it by pressing *F5*, by clicking on the green arrow, or by running Query | Execute.

As the code we'll write depends on records existing in the Customers table, the above script automatically adds several records. If you wish to add more, launch Query Analyzer and use the INSERT command with the following syntax:

```
USE CustomerManagement
Insert Customers (Company, Address, City, State, Zip, Phone)
   VALUES("company", "address", "city", "state", "zip", "phone")
```

Now we've got a database let's get to grips with the Visual Basic coding required to build our business tier component.

Building the CustomerManager MTS Component with Visual Basic

Building a component that can run under MTS involves the following steps:

- ❏ Creating an ActiveX DLL project
- ❏ Coding the logic of the component
- ❏ Debugging the component inside the Visual Basic IDE
- ❏ Adding a reference to the Microsoft Transaction Server Type Library
- ❏ Adding code to interact with MTS
- ❏ Setting the MTSTransactionMode property of the class module
- ❏ Setting other project options
- ❏ Compiling the ActiveX DLL project

First, we need to create an ActiveX DLL project. MTS components run inside a process created by MTS, so they are always in-process components. If you are starting from scratch, run File | New Project and select ActiveX DLL. Set the Name property of the project to CustomerManager and the Name property of the class module to Survey.

> If you want to convert an existing out-of-process component to run in MTS, you need to open the ActiveX EXE project and display **Project Properties.** Use the **Project Type** drop-down box on the **General** tab to change the project to an ActiveX DLL.

Coding the Logic

In order to make debugging the majority of the code simpler, we're going to build the logic of the component before enabling it for MTS. Since we are going to use **ActiveX Data Objects** (**ADO**) we'll need to set a reference to the Microsoft ActiveX Data Objects 2.1 library:

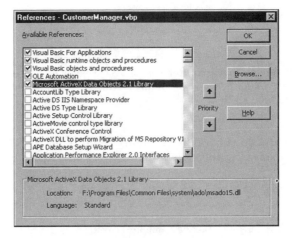

Firstly, we need to declare variables to reference the `Connection` object, the `Command` object, and the `Recordset` object of the ADODB library:

```
Private oConn As ADODB.Connection
Private oCommand As ADODB.Command
Private oRS As ADODB.Recordset
```

In this case, the component is going to implement a single method named `AddSurvey`, which will accept the company name, survey name, and database name from the consumer and make the appropriate entry in the `Surveys` table of the `CustomerManagement` database. We declare the method as follows:

```
Public Sub AddSurvey(sCompanyName As String, sSurveyName As String, _
                sDatabaseName As String)

End Sub
```

Within that method, we need to instantiate the three objects and establish a connection to the `CustomerManagement` database. To keep things simple, we're going to assume that the `CustomerManagement` database is located on the local server and we'll also assume Windows NT authentication:

```
Public Sub AddSurvey(sCompanyName As String, sSurveyName As String, _
                sDatabaseName As String)

    Set oConn = CreateObject("ADODB.Connection")
    Set oCommand = CreateObject("ADODB.Command")
    Set oRS = CreateObject("ADODB.Recordset")
    oConn.Provider = "SQLOLEDB"
    oConn.ConnectionString = _
        "Server=(local);Trusted_Connection=yes;Database=CustomerManagement"
    oConn.CursorLocation = adUseClient
    oConn.Open

End Sub
```

The connection is established using the SQLOLEDB provider (the native OLE DB provider included with SQL Server 7.0).

> **If you're not working on the computer where SQL Server is installed, or if you can't use Windows NT authentication, in order for the code to run the connection string will have to be modified.**

Once the connection is established, we then need to execute a query to retrieve the `CustomerID` based on the company name. The code to perform this action is shown below:

```
Public Sub AddSurvey(sCompanyName As String, sSurveyName As String, _
                     sDatabaseName As String)

    Set oConn = CreateObject("ADODB.Connection")
    Set oCommand = CreateObject("ADODB.Command")
    Set oRS = CreateObject("ADODB.Recordset")
    oConn.Provider = "SQLOLEDB"
    oConn.ConnectionString = _
        "Server=(local);Trusted_Connection=yes;Database=CustomerManagement"
    oConn.CursorLocation = adUseClient
    oConn.Open

    Set oCommand.ActiveConnection = oConn
    sCompanyName = Replace(sCompanyName, "'", "''")
    oCommand.CommandType = adCmdText
    oCommand.CommandText = "SELECT CustomerID FROM Customers WHERE Company = '" _
                          & sCompanyName & "'"
    Set oRS = oCommand.Execute

End Sub
```

Notice that we're setting the `ActiveConnection` property of the `oCommand` object in order to use the connection we just created. Following that, we replace any single apostrophes in the `sCompanyName` string with double apostrophes, using the `Replace` function. The `Replace` function is a new string function, provided through the Microsoft Scripting Runtime library (`scrrun.dll`). You need to set a reference to that library in your `CustomerManager` project:

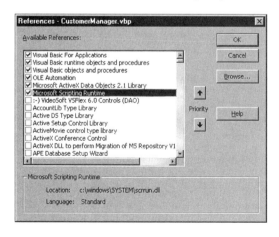

The `Replace` function allows you to specify an expression, a string to find within the expression, and a replacement string. It greatly simplifies the code you need to write to substitute a character in a string.

Next, we set the `CommandType` of `oCommand` to `adCmdText` and the `CommandText` of `oCommand` to a string containing the query we want to execute. We are enclosing the value of `sCompanyName` with single quotes. Finally, the command is executed and the `oRS` object is set to reference the result set.

The next thing we need to do is to insert the appropriate record into the `Surveys` table. However, we only want to do this if the company the consumer passed into the method has an entry in the `Customers` table. We can check this by testing to make sure the `BOF` property of `oRS` is `False`:

```
Public Sub AddSurvey(sCompanyName As String, sSurveyName As String, _
                     sDatabaseName As String)

    Set oConn = CreateObject("ADODB.Connection")
    Set oCommand = CreateObject("ADODB.Command")
    Set oRS = CreateObject("ADODB.Recordset")
    oConn.Provider = "SQLOLEDB"
    oConn.ConnectionString = _
        "Server=(local);Trusted_Connection=yes;Database=CustomerManagement"
    oConn.CursorLocation = adUseClient
    oConn.Open

    Set oCommand.ActiveConnection = oConn
    sCompanyName = Replace(sCompanyName, "'", "''")
    oCommand.CommandType = adCmdText
    oCommand.CommandText = "SELECT CustomerID FROM Customers WHERE Company = '" _
                           & sCompanyName & "'"
    Set oRS = oCommand.Execute

    If oRS.BOF = False Then
        oCommand.CommandText = "INSERT Surveys (CustomerID, SurveyName," & _
            "DatabaseName) VALUES ('" & oRS.Fields(0) & "', '" & sSurveyName & _
            "', '" & sDatabaseName & "')"
        oCommand.Execute
    Else
        Err.Raise vbObjectError + 100, "CustomerManager.Survey", _
                                 "Customer Does Not Exist"
    End If

End Sub
```

If the `RecordCount` exists, the `CommandText` property of `oCommand` is set to a string containing the SQL statement to insert the appropriate record and the command is executed. If it doesn't exist, an error is raised.

In a production application, you would need to either make the Company field a unique index or provide a way for the consumer to specify which customer they would like to add the survey for, when multiple records for the same company exist. However, for simplicity's sake, we're going to assume that the first record in the resulting recordset corresponds to the customer who owns the survey.

Before testing the code, we need to add some error handling:

```
Public Sub AddSurvey(sCompanyName As String, sSurveyName As String, _
                     sDatabaseName As String)

    On Error GoTo abortTran

    Set oConn = CreateObject("ADODB.Connection")
    Set oCommand = CreateObject("ADODB.Command")
    Set oRS = CreateObject("ADODB.Recordset")
    oConn.Provider = "SQLOLEDB"
    oConn.ConnectionString = _
        "Server=(local);Trusted_Connection=yes;Database=CustomerManagement"
    oConn.CursorLocation = adUseClient
    oConn.Open

    Set oCommand.ActiveConnection = oConn
    sCompanyName = Replace(sCompanyName, "'", "''")
    oCommand.CommandType = adCmdText
    oCommand.CommandText = "SELECT CustomerID FROM Customers WHERE Company = '" _
                          & sCompanyName & "'"
    Set oRS = oCommand.Execute

    If oRS.BOF = False Then
        oCommand.CommandText = "INSERT Surveys (CustomerID, SurveyName," & _
            "DatabaseName) VALUES ('" & oRS.Fields(0) & "', '" & sSurveyName & _
            "', '" & sDatabaseName & "')"
        oCommand.Execute
    Else
        Err.Raise vbObjectError + 100, "CustomerManager.Survey", _
                                        "Customer Does Not Exist"
    End If

LeaveIt:
    Exit Sub
abortTran:
    Err.Raise Err.Number, Err.Source, Err.Description
    Resume LeaveIt

End Sub
```

Save the file as `Survey.cls` and the project as `CustomerMgr.vbp`.

Before we add MTS functionality to the component, let's test the code we've just written.

Building the Test Application

Add a simple Standard EXE project (named `SurveyRegTest`) to the project group and set up the single form as shown below.

The three text boxes are named `txtCompany`, `txtSurvey`, and `txtDatabase`, the command button `cmdRegister` and the form `frmTest`:

The next thing we need to do is to set a reference to the `CustomerManager` component (after browsing to the appropriate location):

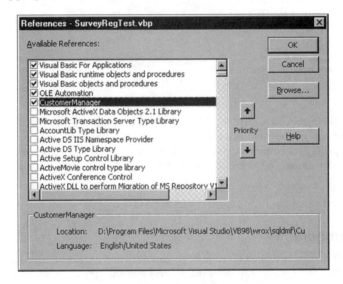

We need to set the test project to be the one that starts when the project is run; to do this right-click on the project's icon in **Project Explorer** and click **Set as Startup**.

We're now ready to add code to test the `CustomerManager` component. First, declare a reference to the component:

```
Private oCMS As New CustomerManager.Survey
```

Now, let's use the `New` keyword to instantiate it in the `Form_Load` event procedure:

```
Private Sub Form_Load()
    Set oCMS = New CustomerManager.Survey
End Sub
```

Next, we code the `Unload` event of the form so that the reference is destroyed when the application closes:

```
Private Sub Form_Unload(Cancel As Integer)
    Set oCMS = Nothing
End Sub
```

Finally, code the `cmdRegister_Click` event so that it calls the `AddSurvey` method of `oCMS`, passing the values in `txtCompany`, `txtSurvey`, and `txtDatabase`. It should display a dialog box to indicate success if no error occurs and failure in the event an error does occur:

```
Private Sub cmdRegister_Click()

    Me.MousePointer = vbHourglass
    On Error GoTo displayErrDialog
    oCMS.AddSurvey txtCompany, txtSurvey, txtDatabase
    MsgBox "Survey record added.", vbOKOnly, "Success!"
ExitHere:
    Me.MousePointer = vbArrow
    Exit Sub
displayErrDialog:
    MsgBox "Error occurred.", vbOKOnly, "Failure!"
    Resume ExitHere

End Sub
```

Now you can run the application and test the code. Verify that the success dialog displays when you specify a company name that exists in the `Customers` table (if you used the given code this will be either "Cypress Development, Etc", "3 Dog Brewery", or "Computer Dragon"). On specifying a company name that does not exist in the `Customers` table an error dialog should appear.

Let's now enable our component for working under MTS.

Adding MTS Functionality

Before we can take advantage of MTS objects in our `CustomerManager` component, we need to set a reference to the Microsoft Transaction Server Type Library (`mtxas.dll`):

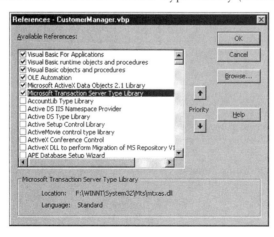

> **If you are building a component to work under Windows 2000 and using Windows 2000 as your development platform, you need to select the COM+ Services Library (`comsvcs.dll`) instead.**

The MTS functionality we'll add to this component is fairly straightforward. First, we set the `MTSTransactionMode` property of the `Survey` class module to 2 – Requires Transaction. This setting causes the component to participate in an existing transaction if one has been started within the object's context or to create a new transaction if one does not exist.

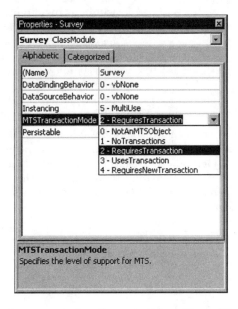

The `MTSTransactionMode` property has five possible settings. They are described in the table below:

Constant	Value	Description
NotAnMTSObject	0	This setting prevents a component from being added to an MTS package. Note that this is the default setting.
NoTransactions	1	This allows a component to be added to an MTS package, but the component cannot be enlisted in a transaction.
RequiresTransaction	2	This setting means a component must be added to an MTS package so that it can run within a transaction. If a transaction has been started when the component is activated, it will be enlisted in that transaction. Otherwise, a new transaction will be started.

Table Continued on Following Page

Constant	Value	Description
UseTransactions	3	This setting allows a component to be added to an MTS package. If a transaction has been started when the component is activated, it will be enlisted in that transaction. Otherwise, the component will be run outside the context of a transaction.
RequiresNewTransaction	4	This setting means that a component will run within its own transaction. When the component is activated, a new transaction will be started, regardless of whether one is already running inside the MTS context. The new transaction will be considered the current transaction and any objects activated inside the package will be added to this new transaction.

Next, we add code to let MTS know that the action was successful if no error occurred or that the action could not be completed if an error occurs. This is accomplished through calling either the `SetComplete` or `SetAbort` method of the `ObjectContext` object returned by `GetObjectContext`. The `SetAbort` method is also called at the beginning of the method to prevent the transaction from committing if an error condition occurs that your component is not aware of, such as a power failure:

```
Public Sub AddSurvey(sCompanyName As String, sSurveyName As String, _
                sDatabaseName As String)

    On Error GoTo abortTran
    GetObjectContext.SetAbort

    Set oConn = CreateObject("ADODB.Connection")
    Set oCommand = CreateObject("ADODB.Command")
    Set oRS = CreateObject("ADODB.Recordset")
    oConn.Provider = "SQLOLEDB"
    oConn.ConnectionString = _
        "Server=(local);Trusted_Connection=yes;Database=CustomerManagement"
    oConn.CursorLocation = adUseClient
    oConn.Open

    Set oCommand.ActiveConnection = oConn
    sCompanyName = Replace(sCompanyName, "'", "''")
    oCommand.CommandType = adCmdText
    oCommand.CommandText = "SELECT CustomerID FROM Customers WHERE Company = '" _
                        & sCompanyName & "'"
    Set oRS = oCommand.Execute

    If oRS.BOF = False Then
        oCommand.CommandText = "INSERT Surveys (CustomerID, SurveyName," & _
            "DatabaseName) VALUES ('" & oRS.Fields(0) & "', '" & sSurveyName & _
            "', '" & sDatabaseName & "')"
        oCommand.Execute
```

```
      GetObjectContext.SetComplete
   Else
      Err.Raise vbObjectError + 100, "CustomerManager.Survey", _
                                     "Customer Does Not Exist"
   End If

LeaveIt:
   Exit Sub
abortTran:
   GetObjectContext.SetAbort
   Err.Raise Err.Number, Err.Source, Err.Description
   Resume LeaveIt

End Sub
```

The final thing we're going to add to the project is code to release the object references our code created when the component is deactivated by MTS. In order for our component to know when MTS activates or deactivates an object, we need to implement the `ObjectControl` interface in our project. To do this add the following statement to the general declarations section:

```
   Implements ObjectControl
```

One of the rules of interface inheritance is that each and every method exposed by the interface must be implemented. The `ObjectControl` interface exposes three methods, which are shown in the table below:

Method	Description
Activate	MTS calls this method when the component is activated. It can be used for initializing object references and private properties.
CanBePooled	This method returns a Boolean. Microsoft may decide to use it someday, but it is currently implemented as a stub. The best way to implement this method is to simply return True.
Deactivate	MTS calls this method right before the component is deactivated. It can be used for destroying object references that were created while the component was active.

In this case, we are only going to place meaningful code in the `Deactivate` method, so we will implement `Activate` and `CanBePooled` as follows:

```
Private Sub ObjectControl_Activate()
   Exit Sub
End Sub
```

```
Private Function ObjectControl_CanBePooled() As Boolean
   ObjectControl_CanBePooled = True
End Function
```

> Note that when creating COM components, it is important that if you implement
> one method of the interface, you implement all of them. Since we don't have any
> initialization code that needs to run, we can implement
> **ObjectControl_Activate** by adding **Exit Sub**.

The Deactivate method will be coded to close the connection if it is open and to destroy the
oConn, oCommand, and oRS objects:

```
Private Sub ObjectControl_Deactivate()
    'Test to make sure the connection is not closed
    If oConn.State <> adStateClosed Then
      oConn.Close
    End If
  Set oConn = Nothing
  Set oCommand = Nothing
  Set oRS = Nothing
End Sub
```

We are now in a position to compile our component.

Compiling Your Component

Before carrying out compilation, display Project Properties and verify that it is set for Unattended
Execution and that the Threading Model is set to Apartment Threaded:

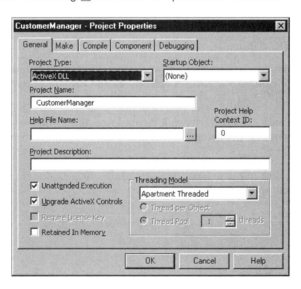

> If we were building this component for use in a production environment, we would
> also want to set versioning properties on the **Make** tab, compile properties
> (especially a unique base address) on the **Compile** tab, and compatibility setting
> on the **Component** tab.

After verifying the properties, run File | Make CustomerMgr.dll to compile a dynamic link library and then compile the SurveyRegTest test application – we'll need it to test the component's behavior inside MTS.

The next stage in the process is to set up an MTS package.

Creating and Adding the Component to an MTS Package

MTS packages are used to group components to run under MTS. Packages are managed through **MTS Explorer**. To launch the MTS Explorer, run Start | Programs | Windows NT 4.0 Option Pack | Microsoft Transaction Server | Transaction Server Explorer.

Like the SQL Server Enterprise Manager, the MTS Explorer is an MMC snap-in:

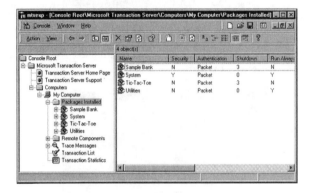

In this section we will:

❑ Create an empty package

❑ Add the component to the package

❑ Test our component

Creating an Empty Package

To add a package, drill down the TreeView control's hierarchy to the Packages Installed icon. Right-click on the icon and run New | Package:

Click on Create an empty package to obtain a dialog prompting for the name of the new package. Name the package SurveyComponents and click on Next:

The next task is to set the package identity – this establishes the Windows NT account under which the components in the package will be run:

> An important thing to keep in mind is that the Interactive user account refers to the user who is physically logged in to the computer running MTS. Since application servers often run when no user is logged in, this setting is only appropriate in a testing environment.

When you click on Finish, an empty package will be created.

Adding the CustomerManager Component to the Package

To add the CustomerManager component to the SurveyComponents package, expand the SurveyComponents package and right-click on Components. Run New | Component.

> You may need to either run New | Window or double-click on the Components icon before you can run New | Component.

Click on Install new component(s); you'll be prompted to add the files containing the component:

Here it might seem that importing a component that is already registered is the right thing to do. However, choosing that option will not read the configuration of the **MTSTransactionMode** property of the component. Therefore, the best way to install a Visual Basic component is to click on Install new component(s) and locate the dynamic link library on the hard drive.

Click on Add files... and browse to locate the CustomerMgr.dll file we compiled earlier. Once a file has been selected, MTS will determine whether the file has a type library, which classes the component implements, and whether their interfaces can be found.

This information will be displayed in the dialog:

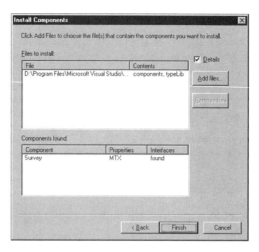

Click on Finish to add the component to the package. The component will be installed into MTS.

Once installation has finished look again at MTS Explorer – our newly installed component is displayed and we can view a number of properties related to it. In the TreeView control, right-click on the Components icon underneath SurveyComponents and select View | Property View. In the Property View, we can see that the component uses apartment threading and a transaction is required. Notice also that two interfaces are listed beneath the Interfaces icon: _Survey, which is the interface that implements the AddSurvey method, and ObjectControl, which is the control interface we implemented in order to clean up object variables when the component is deactivated.

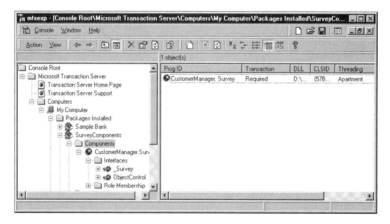

Testing the Component

Now that the component has been successfully installed, we can test its functionality by launching the SurveyRegTest.exe application that was compiled earlier. Firstly, add a survey for a customer that exists in the Customers table. Bring Transaction Server Manager to the foreground, scroll down and click on Transaction Statistics. You should obtain a window looking very similar to:

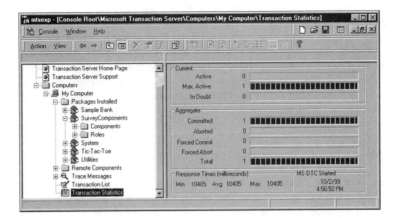

Notice that a single transaction has run and it was committed.

Next repeat the process but try entering a record into the application for a customer that does not exist in the Customers table. On checking Transaction Statistics again, you should see that two transactions have run and one has been aborted:

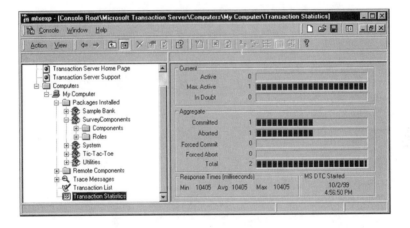

The Transaction Statistics reflect the transactions that have been initiated since the Distributed Transaction Coordinator service was last started. To start gathering new statistics, stop the MS DTC service by right-clicking on the My Computer icon and running Stop MS DTC. Restart the service by right-clicking on the My Computer icon and running Start MS DTC.

Summary

In this chapter, we've introduced you to Windows DNA applications and shown how the SQL-DMF technology fits into this architecture. We then moved on to build an understanding of how to use components in a distributed environment. We rounded off the chapter by introducing the business scenario we'll be using throughout this book to demonstrate how to use SQL-DMO in application development, and building an MTS component as part of that solution.

In the next two chapters, we going to delve into SQL-DMO with a fairly in-depth look at how to use SQL-DMO to connect to and manage the server, and to create databases.

These chapters cover many of the nuts and bolts of SQL-DMO, as well as the concepts behind its object model. By mastering the concepts and techniques introduced in Chapters 3 and 4, you will be able to more easily understand the rest of the objects in SQL-DMO.

3

Introduction to SQL-DMO

The SQL-DMO object library provides objects that allow you to programmatically manage a SQL Server and define your data storage architecture. These objects enable you to create powerful applications and middle-tier components that can automate tasks and make it simple for users to define and modify data structures.

Chapter 1 provided you with an introduction to SQL-DMO and in this chapter we will go into much greater depth by:

- ❑ Providing an overview of the SQL-DMO object hierarchy
- ❑ Discussing the `SQLServer` object in detail including the management of connections and setting of configuration values
- ❑ Introducing error handling for SQL-DMO

In this chapter, we shall be referring to the code in the `SQLDLL.Server` component and `SurveyDesigner` client application constantly, using them to demonstrate how many of the SQL-DMO objects are used. The code examples given in this chapter describe how to use SQL-DMO from Visual Basic. The object model and basic guidelines for using them are the same regardless of the language you are using. Subjects related specifically to using SQL-DMO with C++ are covered in Chapter 12.

> **The Surveys Unlimited project, containing the code samples, can be downloaded from the Wrox web site at www.wrox.com.**

To kick off then, let's begin with an overview of the SQL-DMO object library.

An Overview of the SQL-DMO Hierarchy

The Application object is at the top of the SQL-DMO object library. It exposes the SQLServers collection, which contains references to each instance of the SQLServer object created in the application. The SQLServers collection is automatically maintained by SQL-DMO when objects are created and destroyed.

The SQLServer object is the root object that allows you to access any other object in the tree. It contains objects and collections that allow you to perform a variety of tasks such as establishing a connection, configuring administrative objects such as jobs, operators, and alerts, and creating databases and modifying their schemas. The objects specific to the SQLServer object are shown in this graphic:

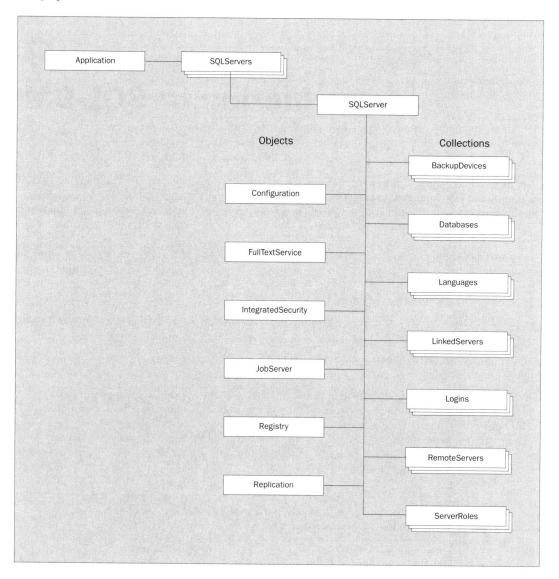

SQLServer Objects

The SQLServer object contains seven objects, six of which are specific to the SQLServer object. The seventh is actually a reference to the Application object, which will be discussed a little later. Let's take a brief look at the purpose of each dependent SQLServer object:

Configuration Object – The Configuration object is used to manage SQL Server configuration options. It contains two collections: ConfigValues and Parameters:

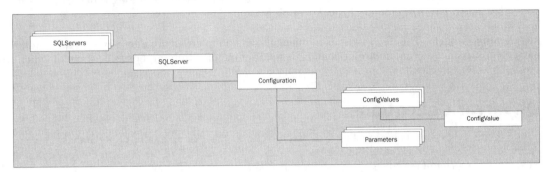

The ConfigValues collection contains ConfigValue objects, which represent the configuration settings for your SQL Server that can be set using sp_configure. These settings include the ability to set a server-wide query governor cost limit to prevent long-running queries and the ability to set a server-wide timeout for remote queries. A specific example of how the ConfigValues collection is used will be covered a little later in the chapter.

The Parameters collection can be used to get information about SQL Server startup options. For example, by default, the Parameters collection contains information about the path to the master database and its log file, and the path to the error log file.

FullTextService Object – The FullTextService object allows you to configure the **Full-Text Search** service on a SQL Server 7.0 Standard or Enterprise installation running on Windows NT Server. Full-Text Search allows you to perform sophisticated queries that locate records containing particular words or phrases in columns that have been indexed for Full-Text Search. With Full-Text Search you can also search on inflected forms of words, such as plurals and various verb tenses. Full-Text Search provides enhanced information retrieval capabilities over what is possible through standard Transact-SQL pattern matching.

The FullTextService object is not covered in this book.

IntegratedSecurity Object – The IntegratedSecurity object allows you to set options that control how the SQL Server handles security. This includes the security mode that should be used and whether auditing should be enabled.

An interesting point to consider is that while SQL Server Enterprise Manager allows you to configure only mixed or Windows NT Authentication, you can use the IntegratedSecurity object to configure your server for SQL Server-only authentication. Another powerful feature of the IntegratedSecurity object is that you can set its ImpersonateClient property to True to allow users to execute operating system commands within their own security context. By default, SQL Server uses the SQL Server Agent account to execute operating system commands.

Using SQL-DMO to manage security will be discussed in Chapter 5.

JobServer Object – The `JobServer` object contains a number of objects and collections that allow you to manage jobs and control the SQL Server Agent.

This object will be discussed in Chapter 5.

Registry Object – The `Registry` object has a number of properties that allow you to retrieve information about the SQL Server that is stored in the registry. Some of these properties are read-only, but others can be modified through this object.

Replication Object – The `Replication` object allows you to configure and manage replication among servers in your enterprise. It contains a number of collections and objects, some of which will be covered in Chapter 8.

SQLServer Collections

SQL-DMO stores objects of the same type in collections. For example, all of the databases on a particular SQL Server are stored in the `Databases` collection. All of the backup devices defined on a server are stored in the `BackupDevices` collection.

The collections under the `SQLServer` object are used to retrieve, add, and remove objects of a particular type. These collections all implement similar functionality, such as the ability to iterate through the collection and the ability to retrieve an object by index or by name. Most of these collections also allow you to modify the objects they contain, add new objects, and remove objects from the collection.

The `Databases` collection will be covered in detail in this chapter, but many of the techniques used on the `Databases` collection can also be used on the other collections. For now, let's take a quick look at the purpose of each collection:

BackupDevices Collection – The `BackupDevices` collection contains references to the backup devices defined on the SQL Server. Although not required when running a backup, these logical devices are used to set properties, such as whether a media header is written. They can also be used to retrieve information about the media headers or the headers for a specific backup.

The `BackupDevices` collection is covered Chapter 5.

Databases Collection – The `Databases` collection contains references to each database on the SQL Server, including system databases, such as `master`, `msdb`, `model`, and `tempdb`.

The `Databases` collection and the `Database` object will be discussed in greater detail in the next chapter.

Languages Collection – Unlike the other collections of the `SQLServer` object, the `Languages` collection can only be used to retrieve information. It contains references to the language records installed during SQL Server setup. These records can be used to respond to different locale ids in your user interface. For example, you can retrieve the name of a month or day of the week in a specific language.

This collection is beyond the scope of this book, but information about using it is available in SQL Server on-line help.

LinkedServers Collection – If your enterprise contains multiple SQL Servers, you may find it necessary to run distributed transactions against them. SQL Server 7.0 allows you to associate servers (through a process called linking) that expose OLE DB interfaces to each other for the purpose of running distributed transactions. The LinkedServers collection allows you to: identify, retrieve information about, set properties for, and run Transact-SQL statements against these servers.

This collection is beyond the scope of this book, but information about using it is available in SQL Server on-line help.

Logins Collection – The Logins collection is used to manage accounts when using SQL Server authentication. You were introduced to SQL Server authentication and the need for login names and passwords in the first chapter.

Chapter 5 provides a more detailed discussion of security concepts and practical examples for account management.

RemoteServers Collection – The RemoteServers collection is similar to the LinkedServers collection, except that it is meant for backward compatibility. It should be used to define servers that do not provide an OLE DB interface, but that need to participate in distributed transactions.

This collection is beyond the scope of this book, but information about using it is available in SQL Server on-line help.

ServerRoles Collection – The ServerRoles collection contains the predefined fixed roles that determine what actions a user is allowed to perform on a SQL Server. Since these are fixed roles (server roles cannot be added to or deleted from a SQL Server), this collection does not have an Add or Remove method. However, you can iterate through the collection and modify the membership of the individual roles.

Using SQL-DMO objects to manage security will be discussed in the Chapter 5.

> SQL Server 7.0 provides a set of fixed server roles and fixed database roles as part of its security system. User-defined roles can also be created, allowing you to customize security. The **ServerRoles** collection deals with fixed server roles only.

A Note on Security

In order to manipulate SQLServer's objects and collections, a user must belong to a role with the appropriate access level. The table below summarizes the minimum role membership required to use the objects and collections that belong to the SQLServer object:

Object or Collection	Role Membership Required	Comments
BackupDevices	sysadmin or diskadmin	Only a sysadmin can remove a device. A diskadmin or sysadmin can add or configure a device.
Configuration	sysadmin	Anyone can view configuration values, but membership in sysadmin is required to change them.
Databases	sysadmin or dbcreator	Restriction applies to adding or removing databases.
FullTextService	sysadmin	The FullTextService object allows you to configure the Microsoft Search Service. Since Microsoft Search runs as a Windows NT service, configuring Microsoft Search through the FullTextService object requires that the user be a member of the Windows NT Administrators group.
IntegratedSecurity	sysadmin	The securityadmin role is able to manage logins for SQL Server authentication, but cannot make changes to Windows NT authentication settings.
JobServer	Depends on activity	Only members of the msdb database public role can add jobs. Only members of the msdb database db_owner role can delete or modify jobs. Only members of sysadmin can add operators.
Languages	No requirements	
LinkedServers	sysadmin or setupadmin	Only members of the sysadmin or setupadmin roles can add or remove linked servers.
Logins	securityadmin or sysadmin	

Object or Collection	Role Membership Required	Comments
Registry	sysadmin	Only sysadmin members may view or modify registry information.
RemoteServers	sysadmin or setupadmin	Only members of the sysadmin or setupadmin roles can add or remove linked servers.
Replication	Depends on activity	Only members of the sysadmin role can enable, modify, or drop Distributors, Publishers, or Subscribers, configure agent profiles, or monitor replication agents. Members of sysadmin or the db_owner database role can create or drop publications or subscriptions, update the publication access list (PAL), and enable snapshots for FTP download.
ServerRoles	Membership in role being modified	The sysadmin role can add and remove members from any role. Any member of a particular role can added members to and delete members from that role. Roles cannot be added to or deleted from the ServerRoles collection.

Using SQL-DMO Objects in Visual Basic

In order to use SQL-DMO objects in Visual Basic, you must first install either SQL Server 7.0 or the SQL Server 7.0 client software on your development computer. Next, we need to set a reference to the Microsoft SQLDMO Object Library by running Project | References from the Visual Basic IDE. In the Surveys Unlimited project, both the SurveyDesigner client application and the SQLDDL component need to have a reference to the Microsoft SQLDMO Object Library:

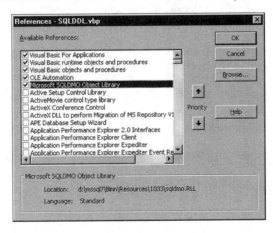

Setting a reference to the library allows you to use early binding, which optimizes performance and simplifies development by providing supported properties and methods to Visual Basic IntelliSense. In addition, setting a reference to the library will ensure that it is listed as a dependency when you package the application using Visual Studio's Package and Deployment Wizard.

> *When early binding is used, Visual Basic is able to detect the object's properties, methods and events before the application is compiled. The alternative, late binding, is the slowest method to invoke the properties and methods of an object, and should be avoided if possible.*

The SurveyDesigner Client Application

In this chapter, we are going to discuss the code behind three forms of the `SurveyDesigner` client application. We will discuss the code behind the Server menu of the `frmMDIMain` form and the `frmConnect` and `frmServerConfig` forms, which are accessible via this menu:

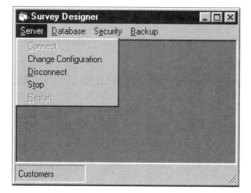

When the application first opens, the Connect menu is enabled. The user can establish a connection by selecting it. The `frmConnect` dialog, which is shown below, will be displayed:

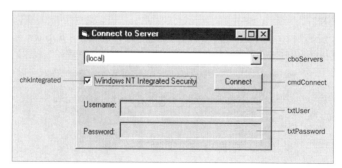

The client application provides the ability to change configuration options through
`frmServerConfig`:

These forms utilize the services of the `SQLDDL.Server` component, which is described in this
chapter.

The Application Object

As we saw in the overview, the `Application` object is the top-level SQL-DMO object and manages
the `SQLServers` collection. It also enables us to retrieve a list of SQL Servers on the network, set
the blocking timeout value for all connections, and retrieve version and installation path information
about the SQL-DMO library. While late-bound declaration is supported, it is best to declare the
variable using the explicit type in order to take advantage of the performance gains provided by early
binding. The following code can be used to declare a variable named `oApp`:

```
Private oApp As SQLDMO.Application
```

As with other COM components, the `SQLDMO.Application` object can be instantiated using either
the `CreateObject` function:

```
Set oApp = CreateObject("SQLDMO.Application")
```

Or the `New` keyword:

```
Set oApp = New SQLDMO.Application
```

You can also declare the object using the `New` keyword. This will cause an instance of the object to be
created the first time it is referenced in the code.

Although it is the top object in the hierarchy, the `Application` object can be referenced directly from any other object. For example, instead of creating a variable to hold the application object's reference, you may decide to instantiate only a `SQLServer` object and reference the `Application` object from there. The code to do this would look like this:

```
Set oServer = New SQLDMO.SQLServer
Set ServerNames = oServer.Application.ListAvailableSQLServers
```

Retrieving Version Information

The properties of the `Application` object shown in the table below allow you to determine SQL-DMO and ODBC Driver Manager version numbers. These properties are read-only:

Property	Description
VersionMajor	Returns the major version number, which is the number to the left of the decimal. For example, for the SQL-DMO object library 7.0, the major version number is 7.
VersionMinor	Returns the minor version number, which is the number to the right of the decimal. For example, for the SQL-DMO object library 7.0, the minor version number is 0.
VersionBuild	Returns the release number of the SQL-DMO object library.
ODBCVersionString	Returns the version string of the ODBC Driver Manager installed on the computer. The version string includes three types of information in the form *major.minor.release*. The major and minor version numbers are two digits. The release number is four digits. All three values are padded with leading zeros if necessary.

Setting the Blocking Timeout

The `BlockingTimeout` property specifies the number of milliseconds that the application will wait to acquire a resource to which it needs an exclusive lock. By default, this value is set to 10,000 milliseconds (10 seconds).

> This property does not govern the length of time the application will wait for a login or a query to succeed. The **LoginTimeout** and **QueryTimeout** properties are set at the level of the **SQLServer** object.

Retrieving a List of Available SQL Servers

Perhaps one of the most important uses for the `Application` object is as a way to retrieve a list of SQL Servers on the network. The `ListAvailableSQLServers` method scans the network to populate the `NameList` object with the name of each SQL Server it finds on the network. If it is executed on a computer that is running the SQL Server service, that server will be listed in the `NameList` as (`local`).

> Using the **NameList** object is similar to using a collection. Like a collection, it has a **Count** property and can be used to iterate through a list of items or reference them by index. Indexing for the **NameList** object begins at 1. However, a **NameList** object contains simple strings instead of objects. Also, it does not implement **Add** or **Remove** methods. The **NameList** object can be thought of as being a 1-based array of strings, except that it implements a **Count** property to allow you to easily determine how many elements it contains.

The following code segments from the Surveys Unlimited solution show how the ListAvailableSQLServers method is used to allow users to choose the server to which they'd like to connect. The first code segment can be found in the SQLDDL.Server component:

```
'ServerNames method of the SQLDDL.Server component
Public Function ServerNames() As SQLDMO.NameList

    'This only works if the component is being run on NT or Windows 2000
    Set ServerNames = oApp.ListAvailableSQLServers

End Function
```

The ServerNames method makes use of an object variable called oApp, which can be found in Strings.bas:

```
Private oApp As New SQLDMO.Application
```

This second code segment can be found in the frmConnect form of the SurveyDesigner project and makes use of the ServerNames method to actually display the available servers to the users:

```
Private Sub Form_Load()

    Dim i As Integer
    Dim oNameList As SQLDMO.NameList

    Set oNameList = conn.ServerNames

    For i = 1 To oNameList.Count
        cboServers.AddItem oNameList(i)
    Next

End Sub
```

The conn variable is declared as type SQLDDL.Server in the standard module modGlobals of the SurveyDesigner client application. Since it is declared using the New keyword, it is instantiated the first time it is used. Notice that the user application iterates through the NameList and adds each string it contains to the cboServers ComboBox control of frmConnect.

> The **ListAvailableSQLServers** method can only be used from a component or
> application that is being run on Windows NT or Windows 2000. In addition, it will
> only locate servers that are running on Windows NT or Windows 2000 with Named
> Pipes selected as the default network library. Servers running on Windows 95/98
> and servers with a default network library other than Named Pipes will not be
> visible. If your servers don't use this protocol, you can set up server aliases that do
> by using the SQL Server Client Network Utility.
>
> Another potential gotcha when using **ListAvailableSQLServers** is that there is
> a delay between the time a SQL Server starts up and the time it can be seen on the
> network. This may cause problems when using the **Shutdown** or **Stop** and
> **Restart** methods from within your application.

Declaring and Instantiating the SQLServer Object

Regardless of the functionality you plan to implement in your application, you will, at the bare
minimum, need to declare and instantiate a SQLServer object. While late-bound declaration is
supported, it is best to declare the variable using the explicit type in order to take advantage of the
performance gains provided by early binding. The following code can be used to declare a variable
named oServer:

```
Private oServer As SQLDMO.SQLServer
```

The SQLServer object raises several events that allow your code to learn the status of various
activities. If you'd like to be able to trap and handle these events, you need to use the WithEvents
keyword in your declaration, as follows:

```
Private WithEvents oServer As SQLDMO.SQLServer
```

This is the method of declaration for the SQLServer object in the SQLDDL.Server component;
you'll find this in the general declarations section.

Again, instantiation of the object can be via either the CreateObject function or the New keyword:

```
Set oServer = CreateObject("SQLDMO.SQLServer")
```

Or:

```
Set oServer = New SQLDMO.SQLServer
```

If you don't need to handle events raised by the SQLServer object, you can declare the object using
the New keyword. This will cause an instance of the object to be created the first time it is referenced
in the code (the downside being that Visual Basic will insert checks into your code to ascertain
whether the object has been created and create it if needed – resulting in inefficient code):

```
Private oServer As New SQLDMO.SQLServer
```

> **If you want to ensure that the object instance is created within the scope of an MTS transaction, you will need to instantiate the object using `CreateInstance`. This problem will not exist with Windows 2000 and COM+.**

As soon as a `SQLServer` object has been instantiated, it is automatically added to the `SQLServers` collection. When you are finished with a `SQLServer` object, you can destroy it in the same manner as you do any other ActiveX component, by setting its reference to `Nothing`:

```
Set oServer = Nothing
```

When all references to a `SQLServer` object have been destroyed, the object will be removed from the `SQLServers` collection.

Establishing a Connection

Once you have created an instance of a `SQLServer` object, you can establish a connection to a particular SQL Server. The `SQLServer` object's `Connect` method allows you to establish connections that are authenticated either through Windows NT Server authentication or through SQL Server authentication. Which you use will depend on how the SQL Server has been configured. The `Connect` method has the following syntax:

```
object.Connect([ServerName], [Login], [Password])
```

The *object* is an instance of the `SQLServer` object. All three arguments are optional. They are defined in the table below:

Argument	Description	Comments
ServerName	This is the name of the `SQLServer`, as returned by the `ListAvailableSQLServers` method of the `Application` object.	If the argument is omitted, a connection to the SQL Server running on the machine where the component is loaded will be attempted.
Login	This is the SQL Server login account name.	If Windows NT Authentication is being used, this argument will be ignored.
Password	This is the SQL Server login account's password.	If Windows NT Authentication is being used, this argument will be ignored.

To use Windows NT Authentication, you need to set the `LoginSecure` property of the `SQLServer` object to `True` before calling the `Connect` method.

The following example shows the implementation of the `ConnectSQLServer` method in the `SQLDDL.Server` component of the sample application:

```
Public Function ConnectSQLServer(ByVal sServername As String, _
                                 Optional ByVal sUser As String, _
                                 Optional ByVal sPassword As String) _
                                 As Long

    Dim oServer As SQLDMO.SQLServer
    Set oServer = CreateObject("SQLDMO.SQLServer")
    If sUser = "" Then
        oServer.LoginSecure = True
        oServer.Connect sServername
    Else
        oServer.Connect sServername, sUser, sPassword
    End If
    ConnectSQLServer = oServer.ConnectionID
    Set oServer = Nothing

End Function
```

The `ConnectSQLServer` method has been implemented in such a way that it can handle both Windows NT authentication and SQL Server authentication. It does this by accepting the `sUser` and `sPassword` arguments as optional arguments. If `sUser` is not passed (for instance, it is an empty string), the `LoginSecure` property will be set to `True` and Windows NT Authentication will be used. Otherwise, the `sUser` and `sPassword` arguments will be passed to the `Connect` method along with the `sServerName` argument. The method returns the `SQLServer` object's `ConnectionID` property. This property will be used by the client application to identify the connection it is referencing when it calls additional methods of the `SQLDDL` component later.

> Once the method has passed the **ConnectionID** property of the **SQLServer** object back to the application, the component's internal reference is destroyed. This technique is important because the **SQLDDL** component is going to be used under MTS (or COM+) in the completed application. It is essential that object references be cleared as soon as they are no longer needed so that they can be reassigned to other clients that may need to use them.

You've already seen how the drop-down list of the `frmConnect` dialog is populated via the `ServerNames` method of `SQLDDL.Server`. The dialog allows the user to choose whether to connect using their Windows NT logon for authentication or by specifying a particular SQL Server account and password. When the user clicks on **Connect**, the `SQLDDL.Server` component's `ConnectSQLServer` method is called with the appropriate parameters. The result of the call is stored in a public variable `lConnID`, which is used throughout the application to identify the connection to the `SQLDDL.Server` and `SQLDDL.Database` components. The server's name and security information are also stored in public variables for later reference. Finally, the event procedure sets the `bConnected` flag to `True`. This flag is used to indicate whether the client application expects the connection to be active:

```
Private Sub cmdConnect_Click()

    If chkIntegrated.Value = vbChecked Then
        lConnID = conn.ConnectSQLServer(cboServers)
        sServer = cboServers
        bIntegrated = True
    Else
        lConnID = conn.ConnectSQLServer(cboServers, txtUser, txtPassword)
        sServer = cboServers
        bIntegrated = False
        sUser = txtUser
        sPassword = txtPassword
    End If
    bConnected = True
    Me.Hide

End Sub
```

The final piece of code we'll add to the frmConnect dialog for now is code that disables the txtUser and txtPassword text boxes and sets their BackColor properties to that of the form when Windows NT security is selected. When NT security is not selected, it enables them and turns their BackColor to white. This code is located in the chkIntegrated_Click event procedure and is shown below:

```
Private Sub chkIntegrated_Click()

    If chkIntegrated.Value = vbChecked Then
        txtUser.Enabled = False
        txtPassword.Enabled = False
        txtUser.BackColor = Me.BackColor
        txtPassword.BackColor = Me.BackColor
    Else
        txtUser.Enabled = True
        txtPassword.Enabled = True
        txtUser.BackColor = vbWhite
        txtPassword.BackColor = vbWhite
    End If

End Sub
```

Disconnecting a SQLServer Object

The connection between a SQLServer object and a SQL Server installation can be closed in one of three ways:

- ❏ The Disconnect method of the SQLServer object will disconnect the object from the SQL Server installation, but keep the object reference in the SQLServers collection.

- ❏ The Close method of the SQLServer object will disconnect the object from the SQL Server installation and remove the object reference from the SQLServers collection.

- ❏ The connection can also be closed by some external factor. By setting the AutoReconnect property of the SQLServer object, you can cause the connection to be re-established when a connection is broken in this manner.

The following method is implemented in the `SQLDDL.Server` component to ensure that the object reference is removed from the `SQLServers` collection when `SurveyDesigner` disconnects the object from the SQL Server. The method accepts a `ConnectionID` from the client application. It then finds the appropriate connection using the `ItemByID` method of the `SQLServers` collection. Finally, it closes the appropriate connection and sets the `oServer` variable to reference `Nothing`:

```
Public Sub DisconnectSQLServer(ByVal lConnid As Long)

    Set oServer = oApp.SQLServers.ItemByID(lConnid)
    oServer.Close
    Set oServer = Nothing

End Sub
```

> The **ConnectionID** property is a long integer. Each connection in the **SQLServers** collection has a unique **ConnectionID** property. We chose to use it here instead of passing an actual object between the client and the component. Since the functionality of the **SQLServer** object is encapsulated in the component, there is no need for the client to receive the **SQLServer** object. By using the **ConnectionID** property to identify the connection, we improve performance by limiting the amount of information that must be marshaled across machine boundaries.

`SurveyDesigner` calls the `DisconnectSQLServer` method in `SQLDDL.Server` when the user chooses **Disconnect** from the **Server** menu of `frmMDIMain`. The `bConnected` flag is also set to `False`:

```
Private Sub mnuDisconnect_Click()

    conn.DisconnectSQLServer lConnID
    bConnected = False

End Sub
```

Configuring the SQL Server

The `Configuration` object allows you to retrieve the values for and modify a variety of SQL Server configuration settings. It contains two collections: `ConfigValues` and `Parameters`. The `ConfigValues` collection contains a variety of other configuration options that allow you to change server-wide values, such as the amount of time to wait on a remote query before timing out. The `Parameters` collection exposes startup parameters. Let's take a look at how you can use these collections to enable users to modify configuration and startup settings programmatically.

ConfigValues Collection

The `ConfigValues` collection contains a `ConfigValue` object for each configuration setting that can be modified using the `sp_configure` stored procedure. The `Configuration` object's `ShowAdvancedOptions` property determines whether advanced configuration settings are included in the collection or only standard options. By default, the `ShowAdvancedOptions` property is set to `True`.

> The SQL-DMO documentation states that the **ShowAdvancedOptions** property is **False** by default. However, it is actually **True** by default.

The `ConfigValue` object exposes a set of properties that allow you to obtain information about the option and set its values. These properties are described in the table below:

Property Name	Data Type	Read-Only or Read/Write	Description
Name	String	Read-only	Contains the string used to identify the property when it is viewed or modified using `sp_configure`.
ID	Long	Read-only	Contains the SQL-DMO constant that identifies this setting. The `SQLDMO_CONFIGVALUE_TYPE` enumeration lists these constants.
Description	String	Read-only	Contains a description of the configuration setting's purpose. This property returns a string.

Table Continued on Following Page

Property Name	Data Type	Read-Only or Read/Write	Description
DynamicReconfigure	Boolean	Read-only	Determines whether the MSSQL Service must be stopped and started before the change can take effect.
MinimumValue	Long	Read-only	Contains the minimum valid setting for the configuration option.
MaximumValue	Long	Read-only	Contains the maximum valid setting for the configuration option.
RunningValue	Long	Read-only	Contains the setting currently being used by the running SQL Server.
CurrentValue	Long	Read/write	This property is used to set a new value for the configuration option. When the ConfigValue is first populated, this property will be equal to RunningValue.

To modify a configuration option, you need to set the ConfigValue object's CurrentValue property to the new value. When properties have been set, you need to call either the Configuration object's ReconfigureCurrentValues method or its ReconfigureWithOverride method. Using the ReconfigureCurrentValues method is a safer choice because it tests the appropriateness of each change before committing it. Since it prohibits values that are not recommended or not valid due to an entry not existing in a system table, it protects the SQL Server from being configured in a way that would result in fatal problems. It is equivalent to executing the sp_configure stored procedure with the RECONFIGURE option.

The ReconfigureWithOverride method does not perform checks to ensure that the value is appropriate and valid. It is equivalent to running the sp_configure stored procedure with the RECONFIGURE WITH OVERRIDE option. Even the ReconfigureWithOverride method will fail if you attempt to set an option to a value that is less than the minimum or greater than the maximum value.

Some of the configuration options require you to stop and restart the Microsoft SQL Server Service. The SQLServer object provides methods that allow you to do this programmatically. These will be discussed a little later in the chapter.

Configuration Settings

The table opposite shows the configuration options that can be set through the ConfigValues collection when the ShowAdvancedOptions property of the Configuration object is set to False:

Option	Minimum	Maximum	Dynamic	Description
allow updates	0	1	True	This option determines whether the system tables can be updated directly (0) or only through system stored procedures (1). It is recommended that this option be set to 0. This option can only be changed with either RECONFIGURE WITH OVERRIDE or ReconfigureWithOverride
default language	0	9999	True	This option determines the language that is used to determine the rules by which dates are displayed and the names for elements of a date. There are 23 languages available. They are listed in the syslanguages table.
language in cache	3	100	False	This option determines how many languages can be kept in the language cache simultaneously.
max text repl size	0	2147483647	True	This option determines the number of bytes that can be added to a replicated text or image column with a single statement.
nested triggers	0	1	True	This option determines whether the server supports cascading triggers. By default, it is set to 1, which allows triggers to be nested up to 16 levels.
remote access	0	1	False	This option determines whether a remote server can access the SQL Server. It is set to 1 (TRUE) by default.
remote login timeout	0	2147483647	True	This option limits the number of seconds the SQL Server will wait for a login to a remote server to succeed. A setting of 0 will cause the server to wait forever for the remote server to respond.

Table Continued on Following Page

Option	Minimum	Maximum	Dynamic	Description
remote proc trans	0	1	True	This option determines whether or not calls initiated on remote servers participate in a transaction coordinated by the Distributed Transaction Coordinator (DTC). A setting of 1 causes sessions with a remote server to be coordinated by DTC.
remote query timeout	0	2147483647	True	This option limits the number of seconds the SQL Server will wait for a query or stored procedure executed on a remote server to succeed. A setting of 0 will cause the server to wait forever.
show advanced options	0	1	True	This option is equivalent to setting the Configuration object's ShowAdvancedOptions property to True.
two digit year cutoff	1753	9999	True	This option sets the time interval assigned to two-digit dates. The interval is always 100 years. The number specified in the two-digit year cutoff option identifies the last year in the interval. For example, the default setting of 2049 will cause two-digit dates to be interpreted as falling between 1950 and 2049.
user options	0	4095	True	This option is a bitmask that identifies defaults that apply to all users.

Using the ConfigValues Collection

To recap from earlier in the chapter, the client application provides the ability to change configuration options through the MDI child form called `frmServerConfig`, part of which is shown below:

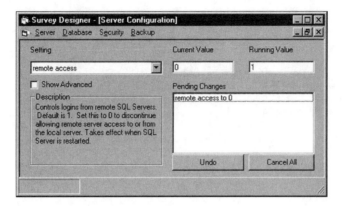

The form's code uses the `SQLDDL.Server` component, which implements a number of methods that allow the client application to retrieve applicable values and modify the setting. Let's look at each of these methods in `SQLDDL.Server` in turn.

GetConfigurationNames Method

The `GetConfigurationNames` method accepts the `ConnectionID` for a `SQLServer` object and a Boolean argument that determines whether the advanced options should be included. It locates the appropriate member of the `SQLServers` collection, based on the `ConnectionID` property. It then sets the `ShowAdvancedOptions` property appropriately, then iterates through the `ConfigValues` collection, adding each configuration setting name to an array of strings. This array is returned to the calling procedure. The code for the `GetConfigurationNames` method is:

```
Public Function GetConfigurationNames(ByVal lConnid As Long, ByVal _
                                bAdvanced As Boolean) As String()

    Dim sConfig() As String
    Dim i As Integer
    Set oServer = oApp.SQLServers.ItemByID(lConnid)
    oServer.Configuration.ShowAdvancedOptions = bAdvanced
    'Dimension the array so that it contains an element for each member of
    'the ConfigValues collection.
    ReDim sConfig(oServer.Configuration.ConfigValues.Count)
    For i = 1 To oServer.Configuration.ConfigValues.Count
        sConfig(i) = oServer.Configuration.ConfigValues(i).Name
    Next
    Set oServer = Nothing
    GetConfigurationNames = sConfig

End Function
```

GetConfig[...]Value Methods

The `SQLDDL.Server` component also implements methods that locate the appropriate `ConfigValue` object, based on its `Name` property and return the value for the `MinimumValue`, `MaximumValue`, `CurrentValue`, `RunningValue`, and `Description` properties. These methods are shown below:

```
Public Function GetConfigCurrentValue(ByVal lConnid As Long, _
                                      ByVal sConfig As String)

    Set oServer = oApp.SQLServers.ItemByID(lConnid)
    GetConfigCurrentValue = _
        oServer.Configuration.ConfigValues(sConfig).CurrentValue
    Set oServer = Nothing

End Function


Public Function GetConfigRunningValue(ByVal lConnid As Long, _
                                      ByVal sConfig As String)

    Set oServer = oApp.SQLServers.ItemByID(lConnid)
    GetConfigRunningValue = _
        oServer.Configuration.ConfigValues(sConfig).RunningValue
    Set oServer = Nothing

End Function


Public Function GetConfigMinValue(ByVal lConnid As Long, _
                                  ByVal sConfig As String)

    Set oServer = oApp.SQLServers.ItemByID(lConnid)
    GetConfigMinValue = _
        oServer.Configuration.ConfigValues(sConfig).MinimumValue
    Set oServer = Nothing

End Function


Public Function GetConfigMaxValue(ByVal lConnid As Long, _
                                  ByVal sConfig As String)

    Set oServer = oApp.SQLServers.ItemByID(lConnid)
    GetConfigMaxValue = _
        oServer.Configuration.ConfigValues(sConfig).MaximumValue
    Set oServer = Nothing

End Function


Public Function GetConfigDescription(ByVal lConnid As Long, _
                                     ByVal sConfig As String)

    Set oServer = oApp.SQLServers.ItemByID(lConnid)
    GetConfigDescription = _
```

```
            oServer.Configuration.ConfigValues(sConfig).Description
        Set oServer = Nothing

    End Function
```

ChangeConfigSetting Method

Finally, the `SQLDDL.Server` component implements a method that accepts the `ConnectionID` for a `SQLServer` object, the name of a configuration option, and its new value, and then attempts to set the option to the new value.

It checks the new value to make sure it is within range before setting the `CurrentValue` property and calling `ReconfigureCurrentValues`. After calling `ReconfigureCurrentValues`, the method checks the `ConfigValue` object's `DynamicReconfigure` property. The `DynamicReconfigure` property will be set to `False` if the configuration change requires that the server be stopped and restarted, and raises an error if the server must be restarted before the change can take effect. The code for this method is as follows:

```
Public Sub ChangeConfigSetting(ByVal lConnid As Long, _
                             ByVal sConfig As String, _
                             ByVal vNewValue As Variant)

    Dim oCfgVal As SQLDMO.ConfigValue
    Set oServer = oApp.SQLServers.ItemByID(lConnid)
    Set oCfgVal = oServer.Configuration.ConfigValues(sConfig)
    If vNewValue >= oCfgVal.MinimumValue Then
        If vNewValue <= oCfgVal.MaximumValue Then
            oCfgVal.CurrentValue = vNewValue
            oServer.Configuration.ReconfigureCurrentValues
            If oCfgVal.DynamicReconfigure = False Then
                Err.Raise sqlddl_ServerRestart, "SQLDDL.Server", _
                          sqlddl_ServerRestartDesc
            End If
        Else
            Err.Raise sqlddl_MaximumExceeded, "SQLDDL.Server", _
                      sqlddl_MaximumExceededDesc
        End If
    Else
        Err.Raise sqlddl_MinimumExceeded, "SQLDDL.Server", _
                  sqlddl_MinimumExceededDesc
    End If
    Set oServer = Nothing
    Set oCfgVal = Nothing

End Sub
```

If the new value is not within range, it raises the appropriate application-defined error. The three errors raised in this method are declared as an enumerated data type in a class in SQLDDL named Constants. The class module's Instancing property is set to PublicNotCreatable. This allows the client application to use the constants in its error handling code:

```
Public Enum ErrorNumbers

    sqlddl_ServerRestart = vbObjectError + 700
    sqlddl_MinimumExceeded = vbObjectError + 701
    sqlddl_MaximumExceeded = vbObjectError + 702

End Enum
```

The SurveyDesigner client application populates most of the controls on frmServerConfig (all but the lstPending ListBox, which shows the pending changes) both when the form is first loaded and when the **Show Advanced** CheckBox is checked. In order to make this code easier to maintain, it is centralized in a sub-procedure in frmServerConfig called LoadOptions as presented below:

```
Private Sub LoadOptions()

    Dim sConfigNames() As String
    Dim i As Integer
    sConfigNames = conn.GetConfigurationNames(lConnID, chkAdvanced.Value)
    cboConfigName.Clear
    For i = 1 To UBound(sConfigNames)
        cboConfigName.AddItem sConfigNames(i)
    Next
    cboConfigName.ListIndex = 0

End Sub
```

Remember that the variable conn contains a reference to the SQLDDL.Server object and lConnID is a public variable that contains the ConnectionID property returned when the connection was established. Notice that the procedure calls the GetConfigurationNames method implemented by this object to retrieve a list of configuration option names. It passes the Value property of the chkAdvanced CheckBox control to determine whether advanced options will be returned. The code then iterates through the array to populate the ComboBox control cboConfigName. Finally, the first item in cboConfigName is selected. This causes the cboConfigName_Click event to fire.

The cboConfigName_Click event procedure passes the selected text to the GetConfigCurrentValue, GetConfigRunningValue, and GetConfigDescription methods to retrieve the data that is used to fill the txtValue, txtRunningValue, and lblDescription controls on the form:

```
Private Sub cboConfigName_Click()

    txtValue = conn.GetConfigCurrentValue(lConnID, cboConfigName)
    txtRunningValue = conn.GetConfigRunningValue(lConnID, cboConfigName)
    lblDescription = conn.GetConfigDescription(lConnID, cboConfigName)

End Sub
```

This form is implemented in such a way that the value of the selected configuration option is modified as soon as the control containing the current value loses focus, if the value in the Current Value field (txtValue) is different from that in the Running Value field (txtRunningValue).

The txtValue_LostFocus event calls the SQLDDL.Server object's ChangeConfigSetting method, and then uses the GetConfigRunningValue method to retrieve the new value of the RunningValue property. Notice that this new value may or may not match the CurrentValue property, depending on whether the update was successful or required a restart. The bulk of this event uses an error handler to display the appropriate error message if either the ChangeConfigSetting method or SQL Server raises an error:

```
Private Sub txtValue_LostFocus()

    On Error GoTo HandleError
    'Prevent server access if value has not changed
    If txtValue.Text <> txtRunningValue.Text Then
        conn.ChangeConfigSetting lConnID, cboConfigName, txtValue
        txtRunningValue = conn.GetConfigRunningValue(lConnID, cboConfigName)
    End If
    Exit Sub
HandleError:
    Select Case Err.Number
        Case sqlddl_ServerRestart
            MsgBox "Value will not change until server is shutdown" _
                & "and restarted"
            lstPending.AddItem cboConfigName & " to " & txtValue
        Case sqlddl_MinimumExceeded
            MsgBox "Value cannot be less than " & _
                conn.GetConfigMinvalue(lConnID, cboConfigName)
        Case sqlddl_MaximumExceeded
            MsgBox "Value cannot be greater than " & _
                conn.GetConfigMaxValue(lConnID, cboConfigName)
        Case Else
            MsgBox Err.Description
    End Select
    Resume Next

End Sub
```

If you're working through the sample application or if you have downloaded the source code from the www.wrox.com, you may want to try setting several configuration options. Try options that succeed without restarting the servers, and those that don't. Try setting options that exceed the maximum or minimum settings. Finally, to see how SQL Server prevents a setting that is not recommended, try setting the 'allows update' option to 1. The application should display an error message generated by SQL Server.

Undoing a Change

If a change to an option requires that the server be stopped and restarted before making the change, or if your code has not yet called either ReconfigureCurrentValues or ReconfigureWithOverride, you can ignore the change by setting the ConfigValue object's CurrentValue property to equal the RunningValue property.

The `SQLDDL.Server` component implements this functionality in the `RevertConfig` method:

```
Public Sub RevertConfig(ByVal lConnid As Long, ByVal sConfig As String)

    Set oServer = oApp.SQLServers.ItemByID(lConnid)
    oServer.Configuration.ConfigValues(sConfig).CurrentValue = _
        oServer.Configuration.ConfigValues(sConfig).RunningValue
    Set oServer = Nothing

End Sub
```

Notice that the appropriate member of the `ConfigValues` collection is being retrieved by name.

The `frmServerConfig` form uses the `RevertConfig` method of `SQLDDL.Server` to implement an Undo feature and a Cancel All feature. The Undo feature reverses the change identified by the selected item in the pending list:

```
Private Sub cmdUndo_Click()

    Dim sPending As String
    sPending = ParsePending(lstPending)
    If sPending <> "No Item Selected" Then
        conn.RevertConfig lConnID, sPending
        lstPending.RemoveItem (lstPending.ListIndex)
        If cboConfigName = sPending Then
            txtValue = conn.GetConfigCurrentValue(lConnID, sPending)
        End If
    End If

End Sub
```

The Cancel All feature reverses all of the pending changes by looping through the pending changes and calling `RevertConfig` for each:

```
Private Sub cmdCancelAll_Click()

    Dim sPending As String
    Do Until lstPending.ListCount = 0
        sPending = ParsePending(lstPending.List(lstPending.ListCount - 1))
        conn.RevertConfig lConnID, sPending
        lstPending.RemoveItem (lstPending.ListCount - 1)
        If cboConfigName = sPending Then
            txtValue = conn.GetConfigCurrentValue(lConnID, sPending)
        End If
    Loop

End Sub
```

Both of these event procedures utilize a function in `frmServerConfig` named `ParsePending` that parses the appropriate item in the `lstPending` control so that it contains the name of an option:

```
Private Function ParsePending(ByVal sPending As String) As String

    Dim iPosition As Integer
    'Parse sPending so that it contains the configuration parameter's name
    iPosition = InStr(1, sPending, " to ", vbTextCompare)
    If iPosition <> 0 Then
        ParsePending = Left(sPending, iPosition - 1)
    Else
        ParsePending = "No Item Selected"
    End If

End Function
```

Parameters Property

The `Configuration` object's `Parameters` property actually exposes a `Names` collection. The `Names` collection is a list of strings that can be iterated through, added, and deleted. In the case of the `Parameters` property, these strings are the startup options used to start SQL Server.

New startup options can be added to the collection using the `Add` method or the `Insert` method:

> `object.Add NewName`

The `Add` method is used to append a string to the end of the collection. The `object` is a reference to the `Parameters` property of the `Configuration` object. The `NewName` argument is the startup option being added. The startup options will be listed a little later in the chapter.

> `object.Insert NewName, InsertBeforeItem`

The `Insert` method inserts the string at a particular position. The `object` and `NewName` placeholders contain the same information as they do for the `Add` method. The `InsertBeforeItem` argument is either a long that indicates the position in the list or a string identifying the name that currently holds that position. The new item will be inserted before the item identified.

> `object.Replace NewName, ExistingName`

Name modification is achieved by using the `Replace` method. The `object` and `NewName` placeholders are the same as those already described. Like the `InsertBeforeItem` argument, the `ExistingName` argument can be either a long that identifies the position of the item to be replaced or the string value of that item.

> `object.Remove index`

The `Remove` method allows you to remove strings from the collection. The `index` argument can be a long that identifies the object's position in the list or the actual string that should be removed.

> `object.FindName(Name) As Long`

The `FindName` method is used to determine whether a string exists in the collection. If the string specified in `Name` does not exist, it will raise the `SQLDMO_E_NAMENOTFOUND` error. If a match is found, it will return the index at which the match occurs.

Startup Options

The table below summarizes the startup options that are available for SQL Server. The first three are enabled by default:

Option	Description
-d*master_file_path*	This option specifies the fully-qualified path to the `master` database. If it is not specified as a startup option, the path identified in the registry will be used.
-e*error_log_path*	This option specifies the fully-qualified path to the error log file. If it is not specified as a startup option, the path identified in the registry will be used.
-l*master_log_path*	This option specifies the fully-qualified path to the `master` database's log file. If it is not specified as a startup option, the path identified in the registry will be used.
-c	This option causes SQL Server to not run as a Windows NT service. This speeds startup time.
-f	This option causes SQL Server to load its minimum configuration and sets the allow updates parameter to 1. This is a helpful startup option if configuration options have been set that prevent SQL Server from starting normally.
-m	This option causes SQL Server to allow only a single user to connect. It also disables `CHECKPOINT` and enables the allow updates configuration option.
-n	This option prevents SQL Server from logging events to the Windows NT application log. It is recommended that you make sure to identify an error log path using the -e option when the -n option is used.
-p*precision_level*	This option allows you to modify the maximum precision allowed for decimal and numeric data types. By default, their precision is limited to 28 decimal places. This value can be set to any number between 1 and 38.
-s*registry_key*	This option allows you to specify a different registry key to load settings from when starting SQL Server. This option cannot be stored as a persistent option.
-T*trace_flag*	This option is used to start SQL Server using non-standard behavior identified by a trace flag. This option should always be specified as a capital `T`.
-x	This option can be used to improve performance by preventing SQL Server from keeping statistics on CPU time and the cache hit ratio.

The **SQLServer** object has an **AddStartupParameter** method that can be used to temporarily add a startup parameter to a **SQLServer** object that is disconnected and that still references a server that is stopped. The parameter will be used when the **SQLServer** object restarts the server. However, parameters added in this manner are not stored in the **Parameters** collection and will not be used on subsequent server restarts. If you want the startup option to be used across multiple server starts, you will need to use either the **Add** or **Insert** method.

Using the Parameters Collection

The Surveys Unlimited application uses the `Parameters` collection to display existing startup options and to allow users to add the `-c`, `-f`, or `-m` startup options. In order to accomplish this, several user interface elements are added to the Server Configuration form as shown in the following graphic:

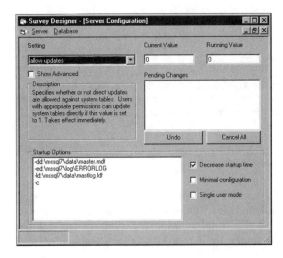

The `SQLDDL.Server` component implements three methods that the client application can use to provide this functionality: `GetStartupOptions`, `AddStartupOption` and `RemoveStartupOption`.

The `GetStartupOptions` method accepts a `ConnectionID` for a `SQLServer` object and returns a `Names` object containing all of that server's startup parameters:

```
Public Function GetStartupOptions(ByVal lConnid As Long) As Names

    Set oServer = oApp.SQLServers.ItemByID(lConnid)
    Set GetStartupOptions = oServer.Configuration.Parameters
    Set oServer = Nothing

End Function
```

The `AddStartupOption` method accepts the `ConnectionID` for a `SQLServer` object and a string. It checks to make sure that the string is a supported startup option, as dictated by the business rules, then uses the `Add` method of the `Names` collection to add the option:

```
Public Sub AddStartupOption(ByVal lConnid As Long, ByVal sOption As String)

    'Business rules for this application support only adding these options
    Set oServer = oApp.SQLServers.ItemByID(lConnid)
    If sOption = "-c" Or sOption = "-f" Or sOption = "-m" Then
        oServer.Configuration.Parameters.Add sOption
    End If

End Sub
```

The `RemoveStartupOption` method accepts the `ConnectionID` and a string. It checks to make sure the option is in the supported list, then calls the `Remove` method of the `Names` collection:

```
Public Sub RemoveStartupOption(ByVal lConnid As Long, _
                               ByVal sOption As String)

    On Error Resume Next
    Set oServer = oApp.SQLServers.ItemByID(lConnid)
    'Business rules support only removing these options
    If sOption = "-c" Or sOption = "-f" Or sOption = "-m" Then
        oServer.Configuration.Parameters.Remove (sOption)
    End If
    Set oServer = Nothing

End Sub
```

The client application displays the current startup options and sets the value of the check boxes when the Server Configuration form loads. It also refreshes the list of startup options when any check box values are changed by a user. To implement this, a module-level flag named `bLoading` is created. It is set to `True` at the beginning of the `Form_Load` event and `False` at the end of the `Form_Load` event:

```
Private Sub Form_Load()

    bLoading = True
    LoadOptions
    RetrieveStartupOptions
    bLoading = False

End Sub
```

The `RetrieveStartupOptions` function of `frmServerConfig` does the work of retrieving the startup options, populating the `lstStartup` ListBox, and setting the CheckBox values if the form is being loaded:

```
Public Function RetrieveStartupOptions()

    Dim oStartupOptions As SQLDMO.Names
```

```
      Dim i As Integer
      lstStartup.Clear
      Set oStartupOptions = conn.GetStartupOptions(lConnID)
      For i = 1 To oStartupOptions.Count
         lstStartup.AddItem oStartupOptions(i)
         'Check these only during Form_Load
         If bLoading = True Then
            Select Case oStartupOptions(i)
               Case "-c"
                  chkQuickStart.Value = vbChecked
               Case "-f"
                  chkMinimal.Value = vbChecked
               Case "-m"
                  chkSingle.Value = vbChecked
            End Select
         End If
      Next

   End Function
```

Notice that `RetrieveStartupOptions` uses the `Count` property of the `Names` collection to iterate through it to retrieve values.

The only other work that needs to be done by the client application is performed in the `Click` event procedure of each of the three check boxes. The `SQLDDL.Server` object's `AddStartupOption` or `RemoveStartupOption` is called, depending on the CheckBox's `Value` property. Then the `RetrieveStartupOptions` function is called to repopulate the ListBox:

```
Private Sub chkMinimal_Click()

   'Avoids duplicate entries due to Click that is fired when
   'the value is set to True on form load.
   If bLoading = False Then
      If chkMinimal.Value = vbChecked Then
         conn.AddStartupOption lConnID, "-f"
      Else
         conn.RemoveStartupOption lConnID, "-f"
      End If
      RetrieveStartupOptions
   End If

End Sub


Private Sub chkQuickStart_Click()

   'Avoids duplicate entries due to Click that is fired when
   'the value is set to True on form load.
   If bLoading = False Then
      If chkQuickStart.Value = vbChecked Then
         conn.AddStartupOption lConnID, "-c"
      Else
         conn.RemoveStartupOption lConnID, "-c"
```

```
        End If
        RetrieveStartupOptions
    End If

End Sub


Private Sub chkSingle_Click()

    'Avoids duplicate entries due to Click that is fired when
    'the value is set to True on form load.
    If bLoading = False Then
        If chkSingle.Value = vbChecked Then
            conn.AddStartupOption lConnID, "-m"
        Else
            conn.RemoveStartupOption lConnID, "-m"
        End If
        RetrieveStartupOptions
    End If

End Sub
```

Retrieving Server Attributes

The `SQLServer` object provides the `EnumServerAttributes` method to allow you to obtain information about the SQL Server's version and the features it supports. This method returns a `QueryResults` object that contains the same information as that returned by the `sp_server_info` stored procedure. The columns returned are shown in the table below:

Column Name	Data type	Description
attribute_id	integer	This column contains the identifier for the attribute.
attribute_name	varchar(122)	This column contains the attribute's name.
attribute_value	varchar(512)	This column contains the attribute's value.

> The number shown in parenthesis next to the varchar data type is the number of bytes required to store that data type as a Unicode character string. It also includes storage for a string terminator character. This means that the actual maximum number of characters the **attribute_name** column can contain is 60 and the maximum number of characters the **attribute_value** column can contain is 255.

Using the QueryResults Object

The `QueryResults` object is designed to make it easy to obtain the information that interests you from the results returned by a variety of SQL-DMO methods, including the `EnumServerAttributes` method. It is a read-only object and does not allow you to add, delete, or modify members of the result set. The columns in the `QueryResults` object will be different depending on the method that returns it. You will see several examples of `QueryResults` objects in this book.

The `QueryResults` object exposes seven properties that allow you to get information about the result set or result sets that the `QueryResults` object represents. These are listed in the table below:

Property	Data Type	Description
ResultSets	Long	This property contains the number of result sets contained in the `QueryResults` object. In the case of `EnumServerAttributes`, this property will be 1. However, some other queries return multiple result sets.
Current ResultSet	Long	This property is used to specify the result set you would like to process. This is the only `QueryResults` object property that is read/write.
Columns	Long	This property contains the number of columns in the current result set.
Rows	Long	This property contains the number of rows in the current result set.
ColumnName	String	This property contains the name of a particular column. To retrieve this property, you must pass the ordinal column number. For example, the following code would retrieve the name of the first column in the `QueryResults` object called oQR: `sColumnName = oQR.ColumnName(1)`
Column MaxLength	String	This property contains the maximum number of bytes you would need to use to store the data in the referenced column. The actual value should be interpreted based on the data type of the data stored in the column. For example, if the column contains data that must be represented as a Unicode string, such as varchar data, the `ColumnMaxLength` returned will be equal to $c * 2 + 2$, where c is the number of characters. Like the `ColumnName` property, you must pass an ordinal column number.
ColumnType	Long	This property contains a number identifying the data type of the referenced column. Like the `ColumnName` property, you must pass an ordinal column number. The values returned are members of the SQL-DMO enumeration, SQLDMO_QUERY_DATATYPE.

The `QueryResults` object provides ten methods for retrieving the contents of a particular cell. These methods, with the exception of `GetRangeString`, accept a row number and column number as arguments and return the data in the cell formatted to a particular data type. For example, the `GetColumnString` method can be used to obtain the data in a particular cell, formatted as a string. Its syntax is:

```
object.GetColumnString(Row, Column) As String
```

If the data in a particular cell cannot be converted to the data type requested, an error will be raised. The table below lists the methods that can be used to return the data in a specific cell, converted to a particular data type:

Method	Description	Data type returned
GetColumnBinary	This method is used to retrieve a pointer to the memory location where a block of binary data resides. In Visual Basic, this method returns an array of integers with the same number of elements as the value returned by GetColumnBinaryLength.	Long
GetColumn BinaryLength	This method is used to retrieve the number of bytes consumed by a binary or variable-length cell.	Long
GetColumnBool	This method returns the value of a cell converted to either True or False.	Boolean
GetColumnDate	This method returns the value of a cell converted to a value of type Date.	Date
GetColumnDouble	This method returns the value of a cell converted to a value of type Double.	Double
GetColumnFloat	This method returns the value of a cell converted to a value of type Single.	Single
GetColumnGUID	This method is used to retrieve a void pointer to the memory location where the storage for a binary data type is being implemented. In Visual Basic, this method returns an array of integers with the same number of elements as the value returned by GetColumnBinaryLength.	Long
GetColumnLong	This method returns the value of a cell converted to a value of type Long.	Long
GetColumnString	This method returns the value of a cell converted to a value of type String.	String

The GetRangeString method can be used to retrieve the text of a block of cells. It has the syntax:

```
object.GetRangeString [Top], [Left], [Bottom], [Right], [RowDelimiter],
[ColDelimiter], [ColWidths] as String
```

The arguments for the GetRangeString method are all optional. They are described in the table below:

Argument	Description	Default if not specified
Top	This argument is the ordinal identifier for the first row you would like included in the string.	The row containing the column names will be used.
Left	This argument is the ordinal identifier for the first column you would like included in the string.	The first column in the result set will be used.
Bottom	This argument is the ordinal identifier for the last row you would like included in the string.	The last row in the result set will be used.
Right	This argument is the ordinal identifier for the last column you would like included in the string.	The last column in the result set will be used.
RowDelimiter	This argument is the string that is used between rows in the returned string.	A carriage return, line feed will be inserted between rows.
ColumnDelimiter	This argument is the string that is used to delimit columns in the returned string.	A tab will be inserted between columns.
ColWidths	This argument is a list of integers, passed as a string. There should be one integer listed for each column included in the return string.	The column width will be the width of the data contained in the column.

Using the EnumServerAttributes Method

The Surveys Unlimited application uses the `EnumServerAttributes` method to provide a listing of the server attributes on the Server Configuration form, as shown below:

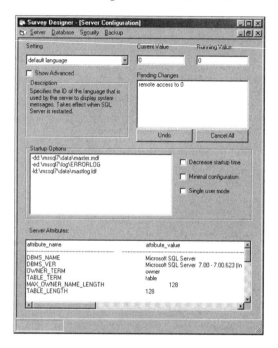

In order to provide this functionality, the `SQLDDL.Server` component provides a `GetServerAttributes` method that accepts a `SQLServer` object and a Boolean argument that indicates whether the names of the columns should be displayed. The method calls `EnumServerAttributes` to populate a `QueryResults` object named `oAttribs`. It then tests the `bShowHeading` argument and sets the `iTopRow` value appropriately. Next, it creates an `sColWidth` string to pass to the `GetRangeString` method of the `QueryResults` object. Finally, it calls the `GetRangeString` method of the `QueryResults` object and returns the formatted string result to the client application:

```
Public Function GetServerAttributes(ByVal lConnid As Long, _
                                    ByVal bShowHeading As Boolean) _
                                    As String

    Dim oAttribs As SQLDMO.QueryResults
    Dim iTopRow As Long
    Dim sColWidth As String
    Set oServer = oApp.SQLServers.ItemByID(lConnid)
    Set oAttribs = oServer.EnumServerAttributes
    If bShowHeading = True Then
        iTopRow = 0
    Else
        iTopRow = 1
    End If
```

```
    sColWidth = UBytesToCharLength(oAttribs.ColumnMaxLength(2)) & ", " _
            & UBytesToCharLength(oAttribs.ColumnMaxLength(3))
    GetServerAttributes = oAttribs.GetRangeString(iTopRow, 2, _
            oAttribs.Rows, oAttribs.Columns, vbCrLf, vbTab, sColWidth)

End Function
```

> **The Bottom (oAttribs.Rows), Right (oAttribs.Columns), RowDelimiter (vbCrLf), and ColumnDelimiter (vbTab) arguments are being passed here for clarity. In reality, the values being passed are the same as those that are used by default.**

Notice that the method makes use of a `UBytesToCharLength` function. `UBytesToCharLength` converts the value returned by the `ColumnMaxLength` property from the number of bytes required for storage of the Unicode string to the actual number of characters the column can hold. This function is a private member of the `SQLDDL.Server` component:

```
Private Function UBytesToCharLength(ByVal uBytes As Long) As Long

    'This function compensates for the fact that ColumnMaxLength returns
    'the number of bytes necessary to store Unicode data, instead of the
    'actual number of characters allowed in the column.
    'Subtract the bytes for the string terminator and divide by two
    UBytesToCharLength = (uBytes - 2) / 2

End Function
```

To implement this functionality in the client application, we call the `GetServerAttributes` method and set its results equal to the `Text` property of `txtAttrib`. That code just needs to be added to the `Form_Load` event procedure of `frmServerConfig`:

```
Private Sub Form_Load()
    bLoading = True
    LoadOptions
    RetrieveStartupOptions
    txtAttrib = conn.GetServerAttributes(lConnID, True)
    bLoading = False
End Sub
```

Stopping and Restarting the MSSQL Service

As we have seen, before certain configuration changes will take effect, the MSSQLServer service needs to be stopped and restarted. This can be achieved programmatically through the `Shutdown` and `Start` methods of the `SQLServer` object:

```
object.Shutdown [Wait]
```

The Shutdown method can be called on any member of the SQLServers collection. The *Wait* argument is an optional argument that determines whether the service will perform an orderly shutdown (when *Wait* is true) or shut down immediately. If no argument is passed, the service will perform an orderly shutdown.

An orderly shutdown is one in which the MSSQLServer service waits to shutdown until all transactions and stored procedures that are in progress have completed executing. It also performs a checkpoint on databases before shutting down. This is the safest way to shut down your MSSQLServer service.

> **The Stop method can also be used to perform an immediate (non-orderly) shutdown. This is not recommended except in circumstances where you need immediate shutdown and are willing to risk aborting the transactions and stored procedures that are in progress.**

It is important to remember that the Shutdown method does not remove the SQLServer from the SQLServers collection. Instead, the object enters a disconnected state. It can still be retrieved through either its ordinal index or the server's name.

You can restart the MSSQLServer service by obtaining a reference to the disconnected SQLServer object and calling the Start method:

```
object.Start StartMode, [Server], [Login], [Password]
```

The *StartMode* argument is a Boolean argument that determines whether SQL-DMO will attempt to connect the object to the server after restart. When set to True, a connection attempt will be made. When set to False, the service will be started, but the object will not be connected to the server. A connection between the object and the server can be established at a later time, using the Connect method.

The *Server* argument is not necessary if you are starting a server that was previously connected and is still a member of the SQLServers collection. If the *Server* argument is not passed, the Name property of the SQLServer object will be used to identify the server. If a *Server* argument is passed that is different from the Name property, the *Server* argument will override the Name property. If a connection is established to the server, the Name property of the SQLServer object will be updated to reflect the new association.

The *Login* and *Password* arguments are used to identify the user if Windows NT Authentication is not used. These arguments are ignored if *StartMode* is set to False.

Note that the SQL-SCM API can also be used to start, pause, and shutdown services.

Shutdown and Start in the Surveys Unlimited Application

The `SQLDDL.Server` component implements a `ShutdownServer` method that accepts a `ConnectionID`, obtains a reference to the `SQLServer` object associated with that connection, and initiates an orderly shutdown for that server:

```
Public Sub ShutdownServer(ByVal lConnid As Long)

    Set oServer = oApp.SQLServers.ItemByID(lConnid)
    oServer.Shutdown True 'Specifying true causes an orderly shutdown
    Set oServer = Nothing

End Sub
```

`SurveyDesigner` implements the **Stop** menu item of `frmMDIMain` by calling the `ShutdownServer` method of the `SQLDDL.Server` object and setting the `bConnected` flag to `False`. A new flag, the `bStopped` flag is set to `True` here. We will see how these flags can be used to control which menus are displayed a little later in the chapter:

```
Private Sub mnuStop_Click()

    conn.ShutdownServer lConnID
    bConnected = False
    bStopped = True

End Sub
```

The `SQLDDL.Server` component implements a `RestartServer` method that accepts a server name, and optionally a username and password. It obtains a reference to the `SQLServer` object associated with that server name and starts the server. The method calls the `Start` method with a *StartMode* of `True`, in order to attempt to reestablish the connection automatically:

```
Public Function RestartServer(ByVal sServer As String, _
                              Optional ByVal sUser As String, _
                              Optional ByVal sPassword As String) As Long

    Set oServer = oApp.SQLServers(sServer)
    If sUser = "" Then
        oServer.LoginSecure = True
        oServer.Start True, sServer
    Else
        oServer.Start True, sServer, sUser, sPassword
    End If
    RestartServer = oServer.ConnectionID
    Set oServer = Nothing

End Function
```

The client application implements a <u>Restart</u> menu item on frmMDIMain by calling the RestartServer method with only the server name if integrated security is being used, or with the stored username and password. Remember, this information was stored in public variables when the connection was first established. The bStopped and bConnected flags are then set appropriately:

```
Private Sub mnuRestart_Click()

    If bIntegrated = True Then
        lConnID = conn.RestartServer(sServer)
    Else
        lConnID = conn.RestartServer(sServer, sUser, sPassword)
    End If
    bConnected = True
    bStopped = False

End Sub
```

Determining Server and Connection Status

So far you have seen how connections can be established and disconnected and how the MSSQLServer service can be stopped and started. However, SQL Server is most commonly used in a multiple user environment. In addition, network problems or other types of system failures can cause connections to be unexpectedly terminated. Luckily, the SQL-DMO SQLServer object provides a VerifyConnection method to allow you to determine whether the connection is still active and a Status property that allows you to find out whether the MSSQLServer service is running, stopped, or in some other state. Let's look at each of these, beginning with the VerifyConnection method.

The VerifyConnection method can be used to verify that a particular SQLServer object is currently connected to a SQL Server installation or to verify that its current connection state is the same as it was the last time a method of the SQLServer object was called. It has the syntax:

```
object.VerifyConnection([ReconnectIfDead]) As Boolean
```

The optional argument determines how you should interpret the value returned by the method. The table below shows the constants that can be passed to this method:

Constant	Value	Returns True	Returns False
SQLDMOConn _LastState	1	The state of the connection is the same as the last time it was used.	The state of the connection has changed since the last time it was used.
SQLDMOConn _CurrentState	2	The SQLServer object is connected to a SQL Server installation.	The SQLServer object is not connected to a SQL Server installation.

Constant	Value	Returns True	Returns False
SQLDMOConn _ReconnectIfDead	6	The SQLServer object is connected to a SQL Server installation.	When this argument is passed, the method does not return false. Instead it raises an error if reconnection fails.

> If no argument is passed, the **VerifyConnection** method uses the **SQLDMOConn_ReconnectIfDead** argument by default. Since the method raises an error when this value is passed and the connection cannot be reestablished, it is essential that you implement the appropriate error handling mechanism in your code when using this option.

VerifyConnection in the Sample Application

We can use the VerifyConnection method to ensure that a connection is valid before attempting to close it. The DisconnectSQLServer method of the SQLDDL.Server component has been modified to implement this functionality. If the SQLServer object is not connected to a SQL Server installation, the method raises an error:

```
Public Sub DisconnectSQLServer(ByVal lConnid As Long)

    Set oServer = oApp.SQLServers.ItemByID(lConnid)
    If oServer.VerifyConnection(SQLDMOConn_CurrentState) Then
        oServer.Close
    Else
        Err.Raise sqlddl_ServerNotConnected, "SQLDDL", _
                sqlddl_ServerNotConnectedMsg
    End If
    Set oServer = Nothing

End Sub
```

The custom error has also been added to the enumeration in Constants.bas:

```
Public Enum ErrorNumbers

    sqlddl_ServerRestart = vbObjectError + 700
    sqlddl_MinimumExceeded = vbObjectError + 701
    sqlddl_MaximumExceeded = vbObjectError + 702
    sqlddl_ServerNotConnected = vbObjectError + 703

End Enum
```

As far as the client application is concerned, the result of this method closing the connection or raising an error that the connection is already closed, is the same. Therefore, the best way to implement error handling for the `mnuDisconnect_Click` event procedure is to use `On Error Resume Next`:

```
Private Sub mnuDisconnect_Click()

    On Error Resume Next
    conn.DisconnectSQLServer lConnID
    bConnected = False

End Sub
```

Determining MSSQLServer Service Status

The status of the MSSQLServer service on a particular computer is contained in the `Status` property of a `SQLServer` object. The `SQLServer` object must have been successfully connected to a SQL Server installation in order for this property to be accessible.

> The **Status** property of a **SQLServer** object can be used to determine whether the MSSQLServer service has successfully completed a shutdown initiated by the **SQLServer** object. However, if the MSSQLServer service is shut down in some other manner, such as through the SQL Server Service Manager, while the object is connected, attempting to access certain properties, including the **Status** property setting will result in the ODBC error shown below.

The MSSQLServer service can have any one of the status settings shown in the table below:

Constant	Value	Description
SQLDMOSvc_Unknown	0	SQL-DMO cannot determine the state of the service.
SQLDMOSvc_Running	1	The MSSQLServer service is running.
SQLDMOSvc_Paused	2	The MSSQLServer service has been paused.
SQLDMOSvc_Stopped	3	The MSSQLServer service is stopped.

Constant	Value	Description
SQLDMOSvc_Starting	4	The MSSQLServer service is in the process of starting after being stopped.
SQLDMOSvc_Stopping	5	The MSSQLServer service is in the process of stopping.
SQLDMOSvc_Continuing	6	The MSSQLServer service is in the process of starting after being paused.
SQLDMOSvc_Pausing	7	The MSSQLServer service is in the process of pausing.

Using the Status Property in the Sample Application

The sample application uses the Status property to ensure that the <u>R</u>estart menu item is not available unless the MSSQLServer service has been fully stopped. To implement this, the SQLDDL.Server component exposes an IsStopped method that accepts the name of a SQLServer object as a string, checks that object's status, and if the status is SQLDMOSvc_Stopped, returns True:

```
Public Function IsStopped(ByVal sServer As String) As Boolean

    Set oServer = oApp.SQLServers(sServer)
    If oServer.Status = SQLDMOSvc_Stopped Then
        IsStopped = True
    Else
        IsStopped = False
    End If

End Function
```

The IsStopped method is used by SurveyDesigner as part of its mnuServer_Click event handling. When the user selects the <u>S</u>erver menu of frmMDIMain, the items enabled in the menu are determined by the value of bConnected, bStopped, and the result of calling the IsStopped method:

```
Private Sub mnuServer_Click()

    'Disable all menus, then enable them according to state
    mnuConnect.Enabled = False
    mnuStop.Enabled = False
    mnuRestart.Enabled = False
    mnuChange.Enabled = False
    mnuDisconnect.Enabled = False
    If bConnected = True Then
        mnuDisconnect.Enabled = True
        mnuChange.Enabled = True
        mnuStop.Enabled = True
    Else
```

```
        If bStopped = True Then
            'If the server is actually stopped
            '(i.e. not still in the process of stopping)
            If conn.IsStopped(sServer) Then
                mnuRestart.Enabled = True
            End If
        Else
            mnuConnect.Enabled = True
        End If
    End If

End Sub
```

Error Handling

Whenever you build an application, you need to take precautions against unexpected occurrences. This is particularly true for distributed applications. A vast number of variables are beyond the control of the component or application developer in a distributed environment. It's always a good idea to code defensively.

An application or component that uses SQL-DMO may receive errors generated from a number of sources. The most common of these are:

❑ SQL-DMO

❑ ODBC Driver Manager

❑ SQL Server

❑ Operating System

SQL Server errors, ODBC Driver Manager errors, and operating system errors are handled the same way you would in any data access application. SQL-DMO errors require a little further discussion.

SQL-DMO Errors

SQL-DMO provides an enumerated list of error constants in SQLDMO_ERROR_TYPES. These constants are listed in SQL Server on-line help at http://msdn.microsoft.com/library/default.htm. Drill down to Building SQL Server Applications | SQL-DMO | SQL-DMO Reference | Constants | E | Error Constants.

Because there are so many possible error conditions, SQL-DMO groups the errors into error types and provides a mask SQLDMO_ECAT_MASK that you can use to determine the category of error you are dealing with. If you need further information about the nature of the error, you can apply a category-specific mask to determine the identity of the error.

Applicable categories will be discussed as applicable errors are encountered throughout the book. For now, let's look at how the SQL-DMO_ECAT_MASK and the specific category mask can be used to identify the error that occurs when you try to restart a server that has not finished shutting down:

```
Public Function RestartServer(ByVal sServer As String, _
                              Optional ByVal sUser As String, _
                              Optional ByVal sPassword As String) As Long


    On Error GoTo handleError
    Set oServer = oApp.SQLServers(sServer)
    If sUser = "" Then
        oServer.LoginSecure = True
        oServer.Start True, sServer
    Else
        oServer.Start True, sServer, sUser, sPassword
    End If
    RestartServer = oServer.ConnectionID
    Set oServer = Nothing

exitFunction:
    Exit Function
handleError:
    If Err.Number And SQLDMO_ECAT_MASK = SQLDMO_ECAT_INVALIDCONTEXT Then
        If Err.Number And SQLDMO_ECAT_INVALIDCONTEXT = SQLDMO_E_ALREADYCONN Then
            'Server has not yet finished shutting down
            Err.Raise sqlddl_ShutdownNotFinished, "SQLDDL", _
                    sqlddl_ServerNotShutdown
        End If
    End If
    Resume exitFunction

End Function
```

Notice how the bitwise And operator is used to determine which bits of Err.Number are the same as those in the mask. Those bits determine the category to which the error belongs. Another And can be performed, using the category mask to determine the actual error.

Timeout Error

While we are discussing error handling for the RestartServer method, it's important to point out that occasionally a timeout error occurs when using the automatic reconnection option of the Start method. The following code shows how that error can be handled by destroying the instance of the oServer variable and raising an error. The code for this is:

```
Public Function RestartServer(ByVal sServer As String, _
                              Optional ByVal sUser As String, _
                              Optional ByVal sPassword As String) As Long

    On Error GoTo handleError
    Set oServer = oApp.SQLServers(sServer)
```

```
        If sUser = "" Then
            oServer.LoginSecure = True
            oServer.Start True, sServer
        Else
            oServer.Start True, sServer, sUser, sPassword
        End If
        RestartServer = oServer.ConnectionID
        Set oServer = Nothing
exitFunction:
    Exit Function
handleError:
    If Err.Number And SQLDMO_ECAT_MASK = SQLDMO_ECAT_INVALIDCONTEXT Then
        If Err.Number And SQLDMO_ECAT_INVALIDCONTEXT = SQLDMO_E_ALREADYCONN Then
            'Server has not yet finished shutting down
            Err.Raise sqlddl_ShutdownNotFinished, "SQLDDL", _
                      sqlddl_ServerNotShutdown
        End If

    ElseIf Err.Number = -2147221504 Then
        'This handles a timeout error that sometimes occurs when trying to
        'automatically reconnect.
        'If reconnection fails, close the object to remove it from SQLServers,
        'set the oServer reference to nothing and raise an error.
        Dim bConnected As Boolean
        Dim iStarted As SQLDMO_SVCSTATUS_TYPE
        bConnected = oServer.VerifyConnection(SQLDMOConn_CurrentState)
        If Not bConnected Then
            oServer.Close
            Set oServer = Nothing
            Err.Raise sqlddl_ConnectionTimeout, "SQLDDL", _
                      sqlddl_ConnTimeoutMsg
        Else
            RestartServer = oServer.ConnectionID
        End If
    End If
    Resume exitFunction

End Function
```

The errors raised within this error handler are declared in the enumeration in the Constants class module:

```
Public Enum ErrorNumbers

    sqlddl_ServerRestart = vbObjectError + 700
    sqlddl_MinimumExceeded = vbObjectError + 701
    sqlddl_MaximumExceeded = vbObjectError + 702
    sqlddl_ServerNotConnected = vbObjectError + 703
    sqlddl_ShutdownNotFinished = vbObjectError + 704
    sqlddl_ConnectionTimeout = vbObjectError + 705
    sqlddl_StillStarting = vbObjectError + 706
    sqlddl_UnableToStartService = vbObjectError + 707

End Enum
```

In addition, an error handler has been added to the `mnuRestart_Click` event procedure in `frmMDIMain`:

```
Private Sub mnuRestart_Click()

    On Error GoTo handleit
    If bIntegrated = True Then
        lConnID = conn.RestartServer(sServer)
    Else
        lConnID = conn.RestartServer(sServer, sUser, sPassword)
    End If
    bConnected = True
DontResetConnected:
    bStopped = False
DontResetAny:
    Exit Sub
handleit:
    Dim iResponse As VbMsgBoxResult
    Select Case Err.Number
        Case sqlddl_ShutdownNotFinished
            'Server has not yet finished shutting down. This should not happen
            'because menu item should not be available until server is stopped.
            MsgBox Err.Description
            Resume DontResetAny
        Case sqlddl_ConnectionTimeout
            'This handles a timeout error that sometimes
            'occurs due to reconnection failing
            iResponse = MsgBox _
                    ("Unable to connect! Would you like to reconnect?", _
                    vbOKCancel, "Server Timeout Error")
            If iResponse = vbOK Then
                frmConnect.Show
            End If
            Resume DontResetConnected
        Case Else
            Resume DontResetAny
    End Select

End Sub
```

Notice that the execution path resumes at a different point, depending on the error that was raised. This keeps the flags we're using to track which menus should be available synchronized with the state of the server and the connection.

SQLServer Events

Before we move on to looking at some of the other objects and collections in the SQL-DMO object model, let's take a quick look at the events fired by the `SQLServer` object. Understanding these events and how they can be used will help you troubleshoot problems when you build your own SQL-DMO applications. They can also be used to build a component that can respond to connection problems and non-fatal SQL Server errors.

Earlier in the chapter, we discussed the syntax required to declare a `SQLServer` object that will allow your application to respond to its events:

```
Private WithEvents oServer As SQLDMO.SQLServer
```

When declared using `WithEvents`, the `SQLServer` can be instantiated using either:

```
Set oServer = CreateObject("SQLDMO.SQLServer")
```

Or:

```
Set oServer = New SQLDMO.SQLServer
```

However, using the `New` keyword as part of the declaration is illegal. For example, you cannot declare the variable as follows:

```
Private WithEvents oServer As New SQLDMO.SQLServer
```

The `SQLServer` object has five events. Let's take a quick look at each of them.

The CommandSent Event

Remember, all SQL Server management ultimately comes down to the execution of SQL statements and stored procedures. Most of the method calls you make to SQL-DMO objects are implemented by calling one or more stored procedures. The `CommandSent` event occurs immediately before a SQL command is sent to the SQL server by SQL-DMO. This command may be a stored procedure, a query, or any other SQL statement.

The `CommandSent` event has the syntax:

```
Private Sub object_CommandSent(SQLCommand As String)
```

This event is particularly useful if you need to understand what is going on behind the scenes when a SQL-DMO method is called. Keep in mind, however, that certain methods, such as `ListAvailableServers` and `Connect` do not send SQL commands to the server. In addition, commands will not be sent unless a valid connection to the server exists.

Using the statement `Debug.Print SQLCommand` inside this event can provide you with valuable insight into the commands being sent to the server while you are debugging:

```
Private Sub oServer_CommandSent(ByVal SQLCommand As String)
    Debug.Print SQLCommand
End Sub
```

The ConnectionBroken Event

The ConnectionBroken event occurs when SQL-DMO discovers that the connection to the server has been broken. This event does not occur in response to the client calling the SQLServer object's Close method. It also does not occur when the SQLServer object's AutoReconnect property is set to True.

The ConnectionBroken event has the syntax:

```
Private Function object_ConnectionBroken(ByVal Message As String) As Boolean
```

The Message argument contains a string, stating that the connection to a particular server has been broken. It does not provide information about the problem that caused the connection to be broken.

The most useful feature of this event is that you can attempt to reconnect to the server by implementing this event to return True. For example, to implement this in the sample project, you would use the code:

```
oServer_ConnectionBroken = True
```

The QueryTimeout Event

The QueryTimeout event is exposed by the SQLServer object, but it is only a stub. In a later release of SQL-DMO, it will be raised when the limit set by the SQLServer object's QueryTimeout property is exceeded when performing a query. At this point, when this limit is exceeded, the ODBC Driver Manager raises a Timeout Exceeded error. This error can be trapped by conventional error trapping methods.

The RemoteLoginFailed Event

The RemoteLoginFailed event is used to notify an application that the SQL Server installation to which the SQLServer object is connected attempted to connect to a remote server and failed. It has the syntax:

```
Private Sub object_RemoteLoginFailed(ByVal Severity As Long, _
                                     ByVal MessageNumber As Long, _
                                     ByVal MessageState As Long, _
                                     ByVal Message As String)
```

The arguments it passes contain information about the SQL Server error that occurred. Most of the information SQL Server uses to populate these arguments is stored in the sysmessages system table. The MessageState is determined by SQL Server, based on the location of the error within SQL Server's code. Although the MessageState value will not be meaningful to most developers, you may be asked for it if you call Microsoft's technical support about a problem.

The ServerMessage Event

The `ServerMessage` event is fired when a call to SQL Server returns success-with-information. It has the syntax:

```
Private Sub object_ServerMessage(ByVal Severity As Long, _
                                 ByVal MessageNumber As Long, _
                                 ByVal MessageState As Long, _
                                 ByVal Message As String)
```

Like `RemoteLoginFailed`, the arguments it passes, with the exception of `MessageState`, correspond to the information in the `sysmessages` table. For example, suppose we add the following code to the `ServerMessage` event of a `SQLServer` object named `oServer` and execute a `Shutdown` (this code is not present in the Surveys Unlimited application):

```
Private Sub oServer_ServerMessage(ByVal Severity As Long, _
                                  ByVal MessageNumber As Long, _
                                  ByVal MessageState As Long, _
                                  ByVal Message As String)

    Debug.Print "Severity=" & Severity
    Debug.Print "MessageNumber=" & MessageNumber
    Debug.Print "MessageState=" & MessageState
    Debug.Print "Message=" & Message

End Sub
```

Results similar to those shown below will be output to the immediate pane:

```
Severity=0
MessageNumber=6001
MessageState=6001
Message=[Microsoft][ODBC SQL Server Driver][SQL Server]SHUTDOWN is waiting for 1
process(es) to complete.
```

> **The documentation for this event states that any messages with a severity of 10 or higher are handled by raising an error, instead of by firing this event. However, in reality, messages of severity 10, like the 5703 message that is passed when a connection with SQL Server is established, are informational messages. They are passed to the application by the `ServerMessage` event and do not result in an error being raised. However, when you check the Severity argument in the `ServerMessage` event, you will notice that it contains 0.**

Summary

In this chapter, we have been introduced to the SQL-DMO hierarchy and in particular to the SQLServer object and the ConfigValues collection. We've seen how to use these objects in code by studying how the management of connections and the setting of configuration values is achieved in the Surveys Unlimited solution. We wrapped up the chapter by discussing how to handle SQL-DMO errors, as well as the events of the SQLServer object.

In the next chapter, we will look at the Databases collection of the SQLServer object in detail and discover how these objects are used in the Surveys Unlimited application.

4

Creating and Managing Databases

In the previous chapter, we had an in-depth look at one of the many objects of the SQL-DMO library, `SQLServer`. In doing so, we familiarized ourselves with several key patterns that will help us to understand how to interact with the other objects in the SQL-DMO library. These key patterns include:

❑ Objects and collections

❑ Methods that enumerate items

❑ Using a `QueryResults` object

❑ Error handling

In our discussion of databases, we'll be using these patterns again, as well as introducing several other patterns of interaction.

In this chapter we're going to:

❑ Inspect the `Databases` collection and `Database` object hierarchy and create a database

❑ Use the `Databases` collection to filter the list of databases we can display

❑ Inspect the `Tables` collection and `Table` object hierarchy and see how to add tables to databases, and columns to tables

❑ Use SQL-DMO to configure the relationships in our databases

❑ Use SQL-DMO to create indexes

> **This chapter concentrates on how to add databases, tables, columns, and indexes. Keep in mind, however, that similar techniques can be used to modify database objects – that topic will be covered in the chapter on SQL-NS, Chapter 6.**

In terms of the business scenario over the next few pages we'll concentrate on the functionality provided through the <u>D</u>atabase menu of frmMDIMain and its associated child forms:

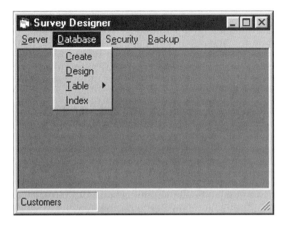

Once again we'll only be highlighting parts of the hierarchy – comprehensive coverage of the objects and collections of the SQL-DMO library is contained in Appendix D.

Databases Collection and Database Object Hierarchy

The Databases collection is a member of the SQLServer object. It contains a Database object for each database managed by the SQLServer, including system databases like master, model, msdb, and tempdb. The Database object is a complex object, with two dependent objects, and eleven dependent collections:

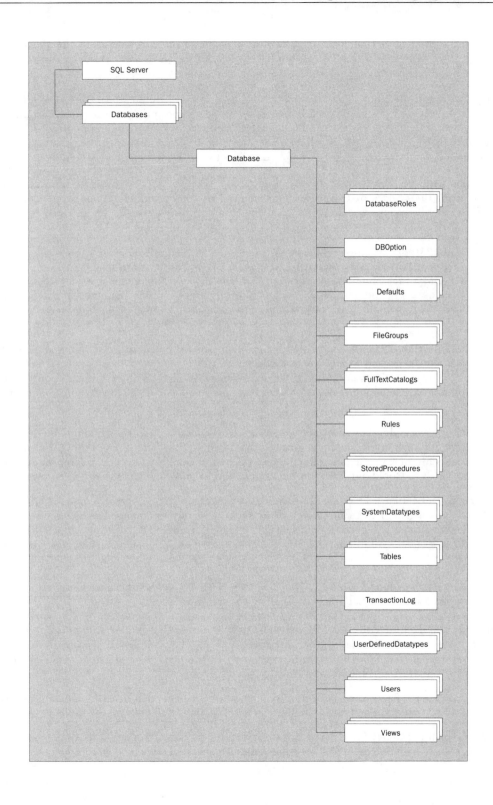

Later in the chapter we'll be looking at how to use some of these objects and collections and drilling down further into some areas, but first let's briefly overview the `Databases` collection and `Database` object hierarchy:

DatabaseRoles Collection – The `DatabaseRoles` collection contains `DatabaseRole` objects. `DatabaseRole` objects are defined in order to grant users permission to perform certain activities on a database. Unlike `ServerRoles`, which are fixed, `DatabaseRoles` are custom-defined. Therefore the `DatabaseRoles` collection supports both `Add` and `Remove` methods. However, all of the members of the role must be removed before the role itself can be removed.

DBOption Object – The `DBOption` object allows us to set the same options for our database as we can set using the `sp_dboption` stored procedure. The `DBOption` object has properties that expose available options and allow us to retrieve the current values and set new values.

> **Manipulating database options is one area in which SQL-DMO gives you more functionality than SQL Enterprise Manager. Several options can be set through SQL-DMO that cannot be set through SQL Enterprise Manager. For example, the "cursor close on commit" and "default to local cursor" options can only be set either through SQL-DMO or by running the `sp_dboption` stored procedure.**

Defaults Collection – The `Defaults` collection contains `Default` objects, which are used to specify default values that should be used when no value is specified for a particular column. Creating `Default` objects provides better maintainability than creating a default constraint on every column – if your requirements change you only need to change the default text in one location.

Consider, for example, that you want to use the text Unavailable as the default value for a number of different columns in the database. By creating a `Default` object, then binding it to the appropriate columns, you avoid redundant work. In addition, if a decision is later made to change the default text to Customer Refused, you only need to make the change in one location.

FileGroups Collection – The `FileGroups` collection contains `FileGroup` objects. Filegroups replaced database devices as an easier and more flexible way to manage the files required to implement a database. When a database is first created, a single `FileGroup` object, named `PRIMARY`, is created. Additional filegroups can be added to the database when tables or indexes are added.

A `FileGroup` object has a `DBFiles` collection. A `DBFile` object stores the properties that determine the name and other attributes of the physical file.

FullTextCatalogs Collection – A `FullTextCatalog` object allows the catalog used to implement **full-text search** on the database to be configured and populated. Full-text search allows flexible searches for fields that contain a specific text string. It supports powerful searches, based on the proximity of words to each other.

Rules Collection – The `Rules` collection contains `Rule` objects that describe a data integrity constraint for the database. Once defined, rules can be bound to columns or to data types.

StoredProcedures Collection – The `StoredProcedures` collection contains all the system stored procedures and the user-defined stored procedures associated with this database.

SystemDatatypes Collection – The `SystemDatatypes` collection contains a `SystemDatatype` object for each base data type supported by SQL Server. Since it only manages the base data types, and they are fixed in number, `SystemDatatypes` does not have an `Add` or `Remove` method.

Tables Collection – The `Tables` collection contains `Table` objects for each of the system tables and user-defined tables in the database.

TransactionLog Object – The `TransactionLog` object allows a transaction log to be configured, truncated, and have information found out about it.

> *The `TransactionLog` object contains a `LogFiles` collection. The `LogFiles` collection has a `LogFile` object for each physical file used to store the transaction log.*

UserDefinedDatatypes Collection – The `UserDefinedDatatypes` collection has a member for each user-defined data type created for the database. Unlike Visual Basic user-defined data types, a SQL Server user-defined data type has a single base data type as its foundation. Additional restrictions are placed on the data type, in terms of length, precision, and nullability.

Users Collection – The `Users` collection holds `User` objects, which are used for authentication when using SQL Server authentication.

Views Collection – The `Views` collection contains `View` objects. Views are used to limit and customize the information made available to particular users. They are also useful for presenting information that is frequently accessed, but that must be compiled using a complex query.

Now that we've familiarized ourselves with the components of the appropriate hierarchy, let's look at what's involved in creating a database through SQL-DMO.

Creating a Database

Firstly, let's overview the steps that must take place in order to create a database on a SQL Server. We have to:

- ❑ Declare and instantiate a `Database` object
- ❑ Declare and instantiate a `DBFile` object
- ❑ Declare and instantiate a `LogFile` object
- ❑ Set properties of the `DBFile` object
- ❑ Add the `DBFile` object to the `DBFiles` collection of the `Database` object's `PRIMARY` filegroup
- ❑ Set properties of the `LogFile` object
- ❑ Add the `LogFile` object to the `LogFiles` collection of the `TransactionLog` object belonging to the `Database` object
- ❑ Add the `Database` object to the `Databases` collection of the `SQLServer` object

To illustrate this we're going to begin by looking at the DBFile and LogFile objects, and then we'll see how they have been used in the SQLDDL component. Since we've already seen how to declare and instantiate SQL-DMO objects, let's start our coverage of this area by moving right into seeing how to handle the DBFile object.

DBFile Object

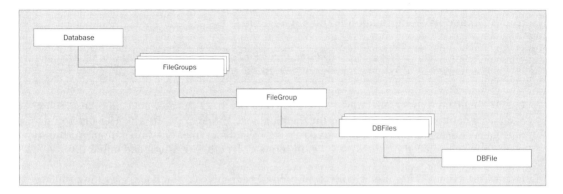

The DBFile object has eleven properties – two of these have to be set before adding the object to the DBFiles collection; the other properties have default values that are used when no specific assignment is made.

The table below shows the DBFile object properties that *should* be set before adding the object to the collection (the complete list of properties is contained in the SQL-DMO reference in Appendix D):

Property	Data type	Description	Default Value
Name	String	This value is the logical name by which the object will be known, both to SQL-DMO and when calling CREATE DATABASE or ALTER DATABASE directly. *This property must be set before adding the object to the collection.*	None
PhysicalName	String	This value contains the Universal Naming Convention (UNC) or path to the location where the file will be stored, plus the file name of the physical file. *This property must be set before adding the object to the collection.*	None

Property	Data type	Description	Default Value
PrimaryFile	Boolean	This value indicates whether the DBFile object is considered primary. There can only be one primary file. By default, the first DBFile that has its Name property set to PRIMARY will automatically have this property set to True.	Depends on name
Size	Long	This value indicates the initial size for the database.	1
FileGrowthType	Enumerated long	This value determines whether the file growth should be based on percentage of the file's total size (SQLDMOGrowth_Percent) or whether the file size should increase by a static number of MB (SQLDMOGrowth_MB).	Percent
FileGrowth	Long	This value determines the number of MB or the percentage by which the file will grow.	10%
MaximumSize	Long	This value determines the maximum size to which the file can grow.	Unlimited

Once the properties of the DBFile object have been set, it is added to the DBFiles collection, using the Add method of the DBFiles collection:

```
object.DBFiles.Add objectToAdd
```

It is recommended that you name the primary physical file with an **.mdf** extension. If you elect to create a database that has multiple data files, additional files should be named with the **.ndf** extension.

LogFile Object

The `TransactionLog` object has a `LogFiles` collection that stores information about the transaction logs associated with the database:

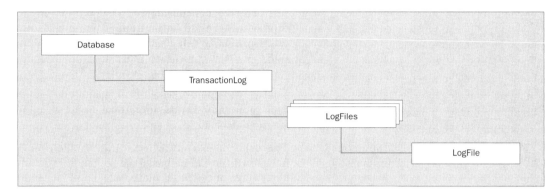

The `LogFile` object exposes the same series of properties that should be set before it is added to the `LogFiles` collection as the `DBFile` object, with the exception of the `PrimaryFile` and `SpaceAvailableInMB` properties (again the full range of properties is in Appendix D). Like `DBFile`, the `Add` method is also used to append the `LogFile` to the appropriate collection.

> **It is recommended that you name the physical file with an `.ldf` extension. As with data files, multiple transaction log files can be associated with a single database. However, all of them should have the `.ldf` extension.**

Database Creation in the Surveys Unlimited Solution

The user of the SurveyDesigner client application can add databases via the `frmCreateDB` form (accessed via Database | Create).

This form creates a database when the Create button is clicked:

```
Private Sub cmdCreate_Click()
    sdbName = db.Create(lConnID, txtSurvey, txtCustomer, bIntegrated, _
                        sUser, sPassword)
    Me.Hide
End Sub
```

The `SQLDDL.Database` component implements this `Create` method with the code shown below:

```
Public Function Create(ByVal lConnID As Long, ByVal sSurveyName As String, _
                       ByVal sCustomerName As String)

    Dim sCustomerID As String
    Dim sDBName As String
    Dim sDFName As String
```

```
        Dim sLFName As String
        Dim sDriveAndPath As String
        Dim oSqlServer As SQLDMO.SQLServer
        Dim oSqldb As SQLDMO.Database
        Dim oSqldf As SQLDMO.DBFile
        Dim oSqllf As SQLDMO.LogFile

        'Object Instantiation
        Set oSqldb = CreateObject("SQLDMO.Database")
        Set oSqldf = CreateObject("SQLDMO.DBFile")
        Set oSqllf = CreateObject("SQLDMO.LogFile")

        'Business Rules to determine names
        sCustomerID = Left(sCustomerName, 6)
        sDBName = sCustomerID & Left(sSurveyName, 5)
        sDFName = Left(sCustomerID, 4) & Left(sSurveyName, 4) & ".mdf"
        sLFName = Left(sCustomerID, 4) & Left(sSurveyName, 4) & ".ldf"

        'Set Database Name property
        oSqldb.Name = sDBName

        'Business Rule to ensure that database is created
        'on the drive with the most space
        Set oSqlServer = oApp.SQLServers.ItemByID(lConnID)
        sDriveAndPath = GetDriveWithMostSpace(lConnID) & "surveydat\"

        'Set DBFile properties
        oSqldf.Name = sDFName
        oSqldf.PhysicalName = sDriveAndPath & sDFName
        oSqldf.Size = 5
        oSqldf.FileGrowthType = SQLDMOGrowth_Percent
        oSqldf.FileGrowth = 20
        oSqldf.MaximumSize = 40

        'Set LogFile properties
        oSqllf.Name = sLFName
        oSqllf.PhysicalName = sDriveAndPath & sLFName
        oSqllf.Size = 2
        oSqllf.FileGrowthType = SQLDMOGrowth_Percent
        oSqllf.FileGrowth = 20
        oSqldf.MaximumSize = 40

        'Add DBFile to the PRIMARY filegroup
        oSqldb.FileGroups("PRIMARY").DBFiles.Add oSqldf

        'Add the LogFile to the LogFiles collection
        oSqldb.TransactionLog.LogFiles.Add oSqllf

        'Add the Database to the Databases collection.
        'At this point, the database is created.
        oSqlServer.Databases.Add oSqldb

        'Return the name of the database
        Create = oSqldb.Name

End Function
```

Notice that the `Create` method implements a business rule that guarantees the database files are stored on the drive that has the most space available:

```
'Business Rule to ensure that database is created
'on the drive with the most space
Set oSqlServer = oApp.SQLServers.ItemByID(lConnID)
sDriveAndPath = GetDriveWithMostSpace(lConnID) & "surveydat\"
```

Let's take a brief detour to see how we implement this functionality.

Enumerating Drives and Determining Free Space

The `EnumAvailableMedia` method of the `SQLServer` object returns a `QueryResults` object that provides you with information about the amount of space available on a specified drive. The type of media included in the results set is determined by the value passed to the method. The valid constants we can pass are:

Value	Constant	Description
1	SQLDMOMedia_Floppy	This option enumerates the floppy drives.
2	SQLDMOMedia_FixedDisk	This option enumerates the fixed hard drives.
4	SQLDMOMedia_Tape	This option enumerates the tape drives.
8	SQLDMOMedia_CDROM	This option enumerates the CD-ROM drives.
15	SQLDMOMedia_All	This option enumerates all of the drives in the system.

The `QueryResults` returned by this method have the following columns:

Column Number	Contents	Description
1	Name	This value is the mapped name of the drive. For example, if the drive is a fixed hard drive, this would be its drive letter.
2	Low free	This column contains the low order value of the amount of available space on the drive.
3	High free	This column contains the high order value of the amount of available space on the drive.
4	Media type	This column contains a constant identifying the media type of the drive.

The `GetDriveWithMostSpace` method of the `SQLDDL.Database` object uses this method to return the name of the drive with the most space available. Its implementation is as follows:

```
Private Function GetDriveWithMostSpace(ByVal lConnID As Long) As String

    Dim oQR As SQLDMO.QueryResults
    Dim i As Integer
    Dim sLargest As String
    Dim lAmountLowFree As Long
    Dim lAmountHighFree As Long
    Dim oSqlServer As SQLDMO.SQLServer

    Set oSqlServer = oApp.SQLServers.ItemByID(lConnID)
    Set oQR = oSqlServer.EnumAvailableMedia(SQLDMOMedia_FixedDisk)
    sLargest = oQR.GetColumnString(1, 1)
    lAmountLowFree = oQR.GetColumnLong(1, 2)
    lAmountHighFree = oQR.GetColumnLong(1, 3)

    For i = 2 To oQR.Rows
        If oQR.GetColumnLong(i, 3) > lAmountHighFree Then
            'Keep track of which has the highest high order value
            sLargest = oQR.GetColumnString(i, 1)
            lAmountHighFree = oQR.GetColumnLong(1, 3)
        ElseIf oQR.GetColumnLong(i, 3) = lAmountHighFree Then
            'If the high order value was the same then determine
            'the low order value
            If oQR.GetColumnLong(i, 2) > lAmountLowFree Then
                sLargest = oQR.GetColumnString(i, 1)
                lAmountLowFree = oQR.GetColumnLong(i, 2)
            End If
        End If
    Next

    GetDriveWithMostSpace = sLargest

End Function
```

Note that the **Create** method that uses this method appends a subdirectory named **surveydat** to the name of the drive. This is done in order to keep the files organized and easy to find. However, when working through this sample code on your own, you will need to create a **surveydat** directory on the drive with the most space available.

Using the Databases Collection

The Databases collection contains Database objects that represent each system and user-defined database on the SQL Server. Like the SQLServers collection, which we looked at in the previous chapter, we can retrieve references to specific databases by passing either their index value or their Name to the Databases collection. This collection also implements the ItemByID method.

Implementation in the SQLDDL.Database Component

The sample application is designed so that each method accepts a string identifying the connection ID and the name of the database. A generic function uses this information to retrieve a reference to the database:

```
Private Function GetDatabase(ByVal lConnID As Long, _
                             ByVal vDatabase As Variant) _
                    As SQLDMO.Database

    Dim oSqlServer As SQLDMO.SQLServer

    Set oSqlServer = oApp.SQLServers.ItemByID(lConnID)
    Set GetDatabase = oSqlServer.Databases(vDatabase)

End Function
```

Returning a List of Non-System Databases

It is likely that you may want to restrict the system databases from being available in an application. This is particularly important if your audience includes users who might be confused by the visibility of databases they don't understand. This functionality can be implemented by iterating through the database and checking the SystemObject property of each Database object before the object is made visible to the user. The SystemObject property is set to True for system databases, like master, and False for user-defined databases.

Implementation in the Surveys Unlimited Solution

The sample application allows users to select the database they would like to modify from a drop-down list. This list is populated by calling the GetDBList method of the SQLDDL.Database object – the method is implemented as shown below:

```
Public Function GetDBList(lConnID As Long)

    Dim nonSystemDBs() As String
    Dim i As Integer
    Dim iDBCount As Integer
    Dim oSqlServer As SQLDMO.SQLServer

    Set oSqlServer = oApp.SQLServers.ItemByID(lConnID)
```

```
      For i = 1 To oSqlServer.Databases.Count
         'Prevent the names of system objects from being returned
         If oSqlServer.Databases(i).SystemObject = False Then
            ReDim Preserve nonSystemDBs(iDBCount)
            nonSystemDBs(iDBCount) = oSqlServer.Databases(i).Name
            iDBCount = iDBCount + 1
         End If
      Next

      'Prevent an undimensioned array from being returned.
      If iDBCount = 0 Then
         ReDim Preserve nonSystemDBs(iDBCount)
      End If

      GetDBList = nonSystemDBs

  End Function
```

Since the name of the database is going to be used to identify it, an array of strings is returned to the client application. The **Database Designer** form (`frmDesign`) of the `SurveyDesigner` client application (accessed through <u>D</u>atabase | <u>D</u>esign) displays these strings in a drop-down list (`cboDBs`) and passes the selected string to retrieve database information when necessary. The code used to populate the drop-down list is:

```
  Private Sub Form_Load()

     Dim i As Integer
     Dim dbList() As String

     dbList = db.GetDBList(lConnID)

     For i = 0 To UBound(dbList)
        cboDBs.AddItem dbList(i)
     Next

     cmdEdit.Enabled = False

  End Sub
```

The `db` variable in the code above references an instance of the `SQLDDL.Database` object.

Now we've looked at how to create databases through the `Database` object hierarchy, let's look into how we can manipulate tables.

Tables Collection and Table Hierarchy

The `Tables` collection contains a `Table` object for each system and user-defined table in the database. Each `Table` object has a set of collections and objects that define its schema and enforce referential and data integrity:

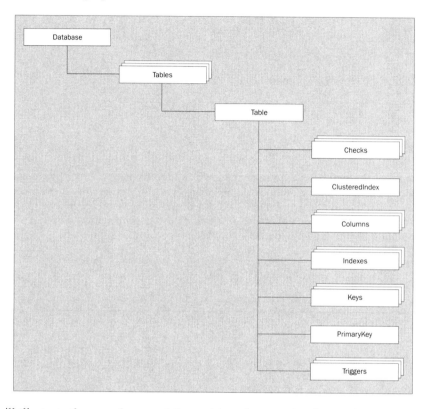

Again, we'll illustrate the use of some of these objects later in the chapter but, as usual, we'll kick off with an overview:

Checks Collection – The `Checks` collection contains rules for ensuring domain integrity. For example, we could define a check to ensure that the value entered in the `HireDate` column is a date earlier than today. Adding `Check` objects is an alternative to defining database-wide rules and binding them to particular columns or data types.

ClusteredIndex Object – The `ClusteredIndex` object defines the columns that are treated as a clustered index. A table can have only one clustered index, since it defines the order in which the data is sorted in physical storage. Clustered indexes should be chosen carefully to optimize performance.

Columns Collection – The `Columns` collection contains a `Column` object for each attribute defined in the table.

Indexes Collection – The `Indexes` collection contains information about the columns involved in clustered and non-clustered indexes.

Keys Collection – The `Keys` collection contains `Key` objects that define the columns that act as primary keys and foreign keys. Keys are used to enforce referential integrity.

PrimaryKey Object – The `PrimaryKey` object contains information about the columns used to define that table's primary key.

Triggers Collection – The `Triggers` collection contains `Trigger` objects. A `Trigger` object is used to cause a Transact-SQL script to run when a particular action occurs on a table. A `Trigger` object has a `Type` property that determines whether it fires when a row is deleted, when a row is inserted, or when a row is updated.

Displaying and Adding Tables

Working with `Tables` is similar to working with `Databases` in several important ways such as:

❑   Retrieving a `Table` object by index, by name, or by ID

❑   Iterating through the `Tables` collection

❑   Determining whether a `Table` object is system or user-defined

❑   Setting properties, then appending the `Table` object to the `Tables` collection

Since we've already seen these concepts in action in the previous section, our discussion of how these interactions are implemented with tables can be kept fairly brief. Let's start by looking at how the sample application allows clients to retrieve a list of the names of each non-system table in a particular database.

Generating a List of Non-System Tables

The `SQLDDL.Database` component exposes a `GetTableList` method that accepts a connection ID and the name of a database and returns an array of strings containing the name of each non-system table in the database. It uses very similar code to the `GetDBList` method that we saw earlier.

In this case however, a `With...End With` statement is used to optimize the code (and save on typing), due to the fact that the `Tables` collection is so far down in the hierarchy:

```
Public Function GetTableList(lConnID As Long, sDatabase As String)

    Dim iT As Integer
    Dim iTCount As Integer
    Dim sNonSystemTables() As String
    Dim oDB As SQLDMO.Database

    Set oDB = GetDatabase(lConnID, sDatabase)
```

```
    'Use With for optimization
    With oDB
       For iT = 1 To .Tables.Count
          'Prevent the names of system tables from being returned.
          If .Tables(iT).SystemObject = False Then
             ReDim Preserve sNonSystemTables(iTCount)
             sNonSystemTables(iTCount) = .Tables(iT).Name
             iTCount = iTCount + 1
          End If
       Next
    End With

    'Prevent an undimensioned array from being returned.
    If iTCount = 0 Then
       ReDim Preserve sNonSystemTables(iTCount)
    End If

    GetTableList = sNonSystemTables

  End Function
```

The SurveyDesigner application uses the GetTableList method to display the list of tables for the database selected on the Database Designer form:

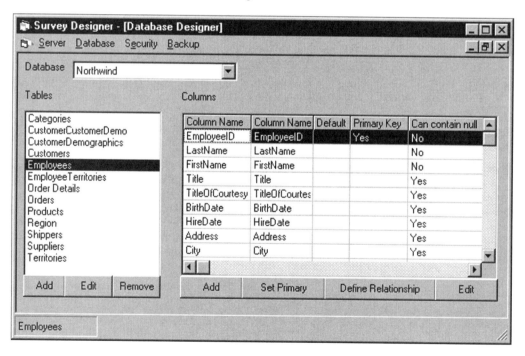

The code for this is shown below – the `cboDBs_Click` event procedure calls the method and uses the returned method to populate the `lstTables` ListBox control:

```
Private Sub cboDBs_Click()

    Dim i As Integer
    Dim sTableList() As String

    lstTables.Clear
    sTableList = db.GetTableList(lConnID, cboDBs)

    For i = 0 To UBound(sTableList)
        lstTables.AddItem sTableList(i)
    Next

    cmdEdit.Enabled = False

End Sub
```

Retrieving a Table by Name in the Surveys Unlimited Solution

As with databases, the interface between the component and the client application is designed in such a way that the client application only needs to pass the connection ID, the database name, and the table name when performing an action on an existing table. To implement this, a general function was created in the `SQLDDL.Database` component:

```
Private Function GetTable(ByVal oDB As SQLDMO.Database, _
                          ByVal vTable As Variant) As SQLDMO.Table
    Set GetTable = oDB.Tables(vTable)
End Function
```

Adding a Table to a Database

Adding a table to a database is fairly similar to adding a database to a `SQLServer` object and involves the following steps:

- ❑ Declaring and instantiating a `Table` object
- ❑ Declaring and instantiating a `Column` object
- ❑ Setting the `Table` object's `Name` property
- ❑ Setting properties of the `Column` object
- ❑ Appending the `Column` object to the `Columns` collection of the `Table`
- ❑ Appending the `Table` object to the `Tables` collection of the `Database`

> **Note: A table cannot be created unless it has at least one column in the `Columns` collection.**

You will need to repeat steps 2 through 5 for each column in the table.

Since SQL Server requires you to define at least one column before adding the table to the `Tables` collection, we'll define an identity column using the name of the table and appending "ID". An identity column is one that allows SQL Server to assign a value based on an identity seed and an identity increment. While this does not ensure uniqueness, especially when multiple servers can modify the table through replication, it does provide a simple way to provide automatic row identifiers. SQL Server automatically assigns a value to the identity column when a row is added, using the identity seed and identity increment you define.

> **Note: A table can only have a single identity column.**

The identity column is established by setting the `Identity` property of the `Column` object to `True` and defining an `IdentitySeed` and an `IdentityIncrement`. The `IdentitySeed` is the starting value and will be the value of the column when the first row is added. `IdentityIncrement` defines the number by which the value should be incremented for each row added.

The code below shows the implementation of the `SQLDDL.Database` object's `AddTable` method:

```
Public Sub AddTable(ByVal lConnID As Long, ByVal sDatabase As String, _
                    ByVal sTable As String)

    Dim oNewTable As SQLDMO.Table
    Dim oIdentity As SQLDMO.Column
    Dim iD As Integer
    Dim oDB As SQLDMO.Database

    'Instantiate table and column
    Set oNewTable = CreateObject("SQLDMO.Table")
    Set oIdentity = CreateObject("SQLDMO.Column")

    'Set Table's Name property
    oNewTable.Name = sTable

    'Requires a column in order for Add to succeed
    oIdentity.Name = sTable & "ID"
    oIdentity.Datatype = "int"

    'Make this column an Identity column
    oIdentity.Identity = True
    oIdentity.IdentitySeed = 0
    oIdentity.IdentityIncrement = 1

    'Append the identity column
    oNewTable.Columns.Add oIdentity

    'Retrieve a reference to the database
    Set oDB = GetDatabase(lConnID, sDatabase)

    'Append the table
    oDB.Tables.Add oNewTable

End Sub
```

SurveyDesigner calls the AddTable method when the **Add** button below the lstTables ListBox is clicked and the cmdAddTable_Click() event is invoked:

```
Private Sub cmdAddTable_Click()

    Dim sTable As String

    sTable = InputBox("Enter the table name:", "Table Name")

    If sTable <> "" Then
        db.AddTable lConnID, cboDBs, sTable
        lstTables.AddItem sTable
    End If

End Sub
```

Displaying and Adding Columns

In the last example, we looked at setting Column properties and adding a Column object to the Columns collection of a table that had not yet been created (see fragments commented as 'Requires a column in order for Add to succeed and 'Append the identity column).

Manipulating columns is pretty much the same as manipulating databases or tables, except that we'll be looking at some different properties. In this part of the chapter we'll:

❑ Look at the properties exposed by the Column object

❑ Investigate the DRIDefault object (exposed by the Column object)

❑ See how to retrieve a list of data types

❑ Walk through the steps required to add a column to a table

❑ Look at how the sample application displays information about columns and provides users with the ability to add new columns

Column Object Properties

The majority of the Column object properties are used to define the data type, defaults, and constraints for the data that will be stored in the column. Most of these properties are fairly straightforward as described below:

Property	Data type	Description
AllowNulls	Boolean	This property determines whether a column can contain null. When set to False, a default for the column must be identified or the column must be an identity column.

Table Continued on Following Page

129

Property	Data type	Description
ANSIPaddingStatus	Boolean	This property determines whether the SQL-92 convention of keeping white space padding around variable length fields is followed (True) or whether these values can be trimmed to conserve space (False). This property is set to False by default.
ComputedText	String	If SQL Server should automatically compute the value of this column, this property will contain the Transact-SQL statement that defines that computation. A computed column is one that is calculated by SQL Server, generally based on some value in another column of another table. For example, you may have an Order table that has a Total column, which SQL Server calculates by adding the Cost of each related item in the Order Details table.
Datatype	String	This property defines the data type of the column. It must be set to a valid base data type or user-defined data type.
Default	String	This property is set to the Name property of a database Default object in order to cause that default to be used when no value is specified.
DefaultOwner	String	This property identifies the database that owns the default bound to this column. This is a read-only property.
FullTextIndex	Boolean	This property determines whether the column will be included in a full-text catalog.
ID	Long	This property is assigned by SQL Server. It is the ID used to retrieve an item using the ItemByID method of the Columns collection.
Identity	Boolean	This property determines whether the column's value will be determined automatically, based on IdentitySeed and IdentityIncrement.
IdentityIncrement	Long	This property defines the amount by which the identity column's value is incremented for each row added.
IdentitySeed	Long	This property defines the starting value for the identity column. It must be a value greater than 0.
InPrimaryKey	Boolean	This property can be used to determine if a column is part of the table's primary key. It is read-only.

Property	Data type	Description
IsComputed	Boolean	This property can be used to determine if the column is a computed column. It is read-only.
IsRowGuidCol	Boolean	This property defines whether a column is part of the globally unique identifier for the table. A GUID column must have a data type of uniqueidentifier.
Length	Long	The number of characters (for text-based data types) or the number of bytes (for numeric data types) that the column can contain.
Name	String	The name by which the column is referenced.
NotForRepl	Boolean	This property determines whether the IDENTITY constraint will be enforced when the table is updated through the replication process. A value of False causes the constraint to be ignored. A value of True causes the constraint to be enforced.
NumericPrecision	Long	This property sets the maximum number of digits that can be stored when the data type is a fixed-precision numeric data type.
NumericScale	Long	This property sets the number of digits to the right of the decimal point that should be stored for a numeric data type.
PhysicalDatatype	String	This property is set automatically, based on the value of the Datatype property. When the Datatype property is set to a user-defined data type, the base data type used as the foundation for that user-defined data type will be stored in PhysicalDatatype. When the Datatype property is set to a base data type, the PhysicalDatatype property will contain the same value. This property is read-only.
Rule	String	This property contains the name of the Rule object used to enforce domain integrity for this column.
RuleOwner	String	This property identifies the database that owns the Rule object bound to this column. It is read-only.

Now we've inspected the Column object, let's move on to see how we can set a default constraint for a column.

The DRIDefault Object

The DRIDefault object is a child of the Column object:

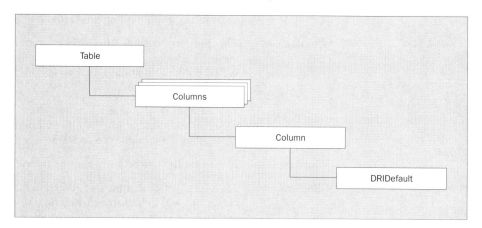

The DRIDefault object allows you to create a default constraint directly on a particular column. To do so, you simply need to set the Text property of the DRIDefault object to the numeric constant or string value you'd like to use as the default. String values must be enclosed in single quotes. For example, to set the default of the column referenced by oTextCol to the value Undefined use the statement:

```
oTextCol.DRIDefault.Text = "'Undefined'"
```

Alternatively, to set the default of the column referenced by oIntCol to the value 100:

```
oIntCol.DRIDefault.Text = 100
```

SQL-DMO then takes this information and uses it to create the actual syntax for the default constraint.

Next, let's briefly digress to see how we can obtain a list of data types.

Handling Data Types

The SystemDatatypes collection and the UserDefinedDatatypes collection of the Database object provide you with the information you need to elegantly handle data types in your code. For example, by iterating through these collections to populate a list of available data types, you can allow user-defined data types to be added at a later time and make them available in your application without the need to recompile.

Another important feature of the objects in these collections is that they allow you to get critical information that you can use to handle the data appropriately. For example, the SystemDatatype object includes an IsNumeric property that lets you determine whether the data type is a numeric data type with a single call. This lets you perform the special handling necessary to correctly define defaults and other data type-specific functionality.

The `UserDefinedDatatype` object allows you to determine the `BaseType`. This `BaseType` value can then be passed to the `SystemDatatypes` collection to retrieve information about what is supported for that base type.

> The **IsNumeric** property returns **False** for **smallmoney** and **money** data types. However, they require a numeric constant for a default. This means that they must be handled as a special case if you are using the **IsNumeric** property to determine the syntax for the default.

We'll see several examples of how these two collections can be used a little later in the chapter when we consider how data type retrieval and column addition is coded in our business solution.

Adding Columns to Existing Tables

Once we've set the necessary properties on a `Column` object, we need to append that object to the `Columns` collection of the `Table` object. If the table already exists in the database, this is performed by calling three methods:

❑ The `Add` method of the `Columns` collection

❑ The `BeginAlter` method of the `Table` object

❑ The `DoAlter` method of the `Table` object

The `BeginAlter` and `DoAlter` methods are similar to `BeginTrans` and `CommitTrans`. The `BeginAlter` method causes all changes to be buffered until the `DoAlter` method is called. To cancel the changes, call `CancelAlter`.

Let's now consolidate the points that we've just covered by having a look at how the business solution makes use of these objects.

Column Manipulation in the Surveys Unlimited Business Solution

Here we're going to look at how the following points are implemented in the case study:

❑ Column display

❑ Data types retrieval

❑ Column addition

Displaying Columns and Selected Attributes

The `SQLDDL.Database` component implements a `GetColumnList` method that allows client applications to pass the connection ID, the database and table names, and a list of constants defining what information it wants returned. The `GetColumnList` method then iterates through the `Columns` collection of the table and returns a two-dimensional array of strings.

This implementation supports only five possible types of information returned. These are defined in the enumeration in the `Constants` module:

```
Public Enum sddlColumnAttributes
    sddl_Name = 0          'Returns the Name property
    sddl_Datatype = 1      'Returns the Datatype property
    sddl_Default = 2        'Returns the Text property of DRIDefault
    SDDL_PRIMARYKEY = 3    'Returns Yes if InPrimaryKey is True
    sddl_nullable = 4      'Returns Yes if AllowNulls is True, No if false
End Enum
```

However, the method could be easily extensible because a `ParamArray` is used to hold the list of constants. The code for the `GetColumnList` method of the `SQLDDL.Database` component is:

```
Public Function GetColumnList(ByVal lConnID As Long, _
                              ByVal sDatabase As String, _
                              ByVal sTable As String, _
                              ParamArray attributeList() As Variant)

    Dim iD As Integer
    Dim iT As Integer
    Dim iRowNum As Integer
    Dim iColNum As Integer
    Dim sAttributeArray() As String
    Dim oDB As SQLDMO.Database
    Dim oTable As SQLDMO.Table

    Set oDB = GetDatabase(lConnID, sDatabase)
    Set oTable = GetTable(oDB, sTable)
    ReDim sAttributeArray(oTable.Columns.Count, UBound(attributeList))

    'Fill the column titles and attributes
    For iRowNum = 0 To oTable.Columns.Count
        For iColNum = 0 To UBound(attributeList)

            Select Case attributeList(iColNum)

                Case sddl_Name
                    If iRowNum = 0 Then
                        sAttributeArray(0, iColNum) = "Column Name"
                    Else
                        sAttributeArray(iRowNum, iColNum) = _
                                oTable.Columns(iRowNum).Name
                    End If

                Case sddl_Datatype
                    If iRowNum = 0 Then
                        sAttributeArray(0, iColNum) = "Datatype"
                    Else
                        sAttributeArray(iRowNum, iColNum) = _
                                oTable.Columns(iRowNum).Datatype
                    End If

                Case sddl_Default
                    If iRowNum = 0 Then
                        sAttributeArray(0, iColNum) = "Default"
```

```
            Else
                sAttributeArray(iRowNum, iColNum) = _
                        oTable.Columns(iRowNum).DRIDefault.Text
            End If

        Case SDDL_PRIMARYKEY
            If iRowNum = 0 Then
                sAttributeArray(0, iColNum) = "Primary Key"
            Else
                If oTable.Columns(iRowNum).InPrimaryKey = True _
                    Then
                    sAttributeArray(iRowNum, iColNum) = "Yes"
                End If
            End If

        Case sddl_nullable
            If iRowNum = 0 Then
                sAttributeArray(0, iColNum) = "Can contain null"
            Else
                If oTable.Columns(iRowNum).AllowNulls = True Then
                    sAttributeArray(iRowNum, iColNum) = "Yes"
                Else
                    sAttributeArray(iRowNum, iColNum) = "No"
                End If
            End If
        End Select

    Next
  Next

  GetColumnList = sAttributeArray

End Function
```

This method is designed for flexibility, extensibility, and its demonstration of retrieving `Column` properties. Dimensioning a two-dimensional array dynamically is not the most efficient option in terms of performance.

Since this method takes some time to execute, `SurveyDesigner` requires either a double-click on the particular table of concern, or an explicit click on the **Edit** button (below the `lstTables` ListBox on the Database Designer form – `frmDesign`) in order to populate the `flxColumns` MSFlexGrid control with column information. The code used to retrieve column information is shown below:

```
Private Sub cmdEdit_Click()

    Dim columnList() As String
    Dim iRow As Integer
    Dim iCol As Integer
```

```
frmMDIMain.sbrStatus.Panels(1).Text = "Retrieving schema"
Me.MousePointer = vbHourglass
columnList = db.GetColumnList(lConnID, cboDBs, lstTables.Text, _
            sqlddl.sddl_Name, sqlddl.sddl_Datatype, sqlddl.sddl_Default, _
            sqlddl.SDDL_PRIMARYKEY, sqlddl.sddl_nullable)
frmMDIMain.sbrStatus.Panels(1).Text = "Filling grid"
flxColumns.Clear


'Loop through the rows in columnList and add the
'appropriate rows to the grid
For iRow = 0 To UBound(columnList)
   If flxColumns.Rows <= iRow Then
      flxColumns.AddItem ""
   End If

   'Loop through the columns in the grid to fill it from columnList
   For iCol = 0 To flxColumns.Cols - 1
      flxColumns.TextMatrix(iRow, iCol) = columnList(iRow, iCol)
   Next
Next


Me.MousePointer = vbDefault
frmMDIMain.sbrStatus.Panels(1).Text = lstTables.Text

End Sub
```

Retrieving a List of Data Types

The SQLDDL.Database component allows client applications to retrieve a list of the names of supported data types for the database by calling the GetDataTypes method. This list includes both base data types and user-defined data types. Its implementation is as follows:

```
Public Function GetDataTypes(ByVal lConnID As Long, _
                          ByVal sDatabase As String)

    Dim sDatatypeNames() As String
    Dim iD As Integer
    Dim iSDT As Integer
    Dim iUDT As Integer
    Dim oDB As SQLDMO.Database

    Set oDB = GetDatabase(lConnID, sDatabase)

    'Dimension the array
    ReDim sDatatypeNames(1 To oDB.SystemDatatypes.Count + _
                    oDB.UserDefinedDatatypes.Count)

    'Fill the array with base data types
    For iSDT = 1 To oDB.SystemDatatypes.Count
        sDatatypeNames(iSDT) = oDB.SystemDatatypes(iSDT).Name
    Next
```

```
      'Add any user-defined data types in the database
      For iUDT = 1 To oDB.UserDefinedDatatypes.Count
          sDatatypeNames(iSDT + iUDT) = oDB.UserDefinedDatatypes(iUDT).Name
      Next

      GetDataTypes = sDatatypeNames

  End Function
```

This method is used by the `SurveyDesigner` client application to populate the `cboDataType` drop-down list on `frmColumns` (click the **Add** button under the **Columns** MSFlexGrid control to bring this form up):

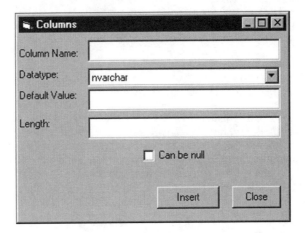

The code that uses this method is the `Form_Load` event procedure of `frmColumns`:

```
  Private Sub Form_Load()

      Dim strDatatypes() As String
      Dim i As Integer

      strDatatypes = db.GetDataTypes(lConnID, frmDesign.cboDBs)

      For i = 1 To UBound(strDatatypes)
          cboDataType.AddItem strDatatypes(i)
      Next

  End Sub
```

Adding a Column

The `SQLDDL.Database` component implements an `AddColumn` method to allow client applications to pass the connection ID, database name, table name, column name, data type, default, length, and whether the column allows nulls. It checks to ensure that either the column will allow nulls or that a default has been defined. It also formats the default as a string or a constant, based on the data type.

The method then sets the appropriate properties of the column and adds it to the table:

```
Public Sub AddColumn(ByVal lConnID As Long, ByVal sDatabase As String, _
                     ByVal sTableName As String, ByVal sColumnName As String, _
                     ByVal sDataType As String, ByVal vDefault As Variant, _
                     ByVal bNullable As Boolean, Optional iLength As Integer)

    Dim oNewcol As SQLDMO.Column
    Dim oDB As SQLDMO.Database
    Dim oTable As SQLDMO.Table
    Dim sBaseDataType As String

    'Test arguments for validity
    If bNullable = False And vDefault = "" Then
        Err.Raise sqlddl_NullableOrDefaultRequired, "SQLDDL.Database", _
                  sqlddl_NullableOrDefaultRequiredMsg
    End If

    'Instantiate Column object
    Set oNewcol = CreateObject("SQLDMO.Column")

    'Retrieve database references
    Set oDB = GetDatabase(lConnID, sDatabase)

    'Determine whether data type is base or user-defined
    If oDB.SystemDatatypes(sDataType) Is Nothing Then
        sBaseDataType = oDB.UserDefinedDatatypes(sDataType).BaseType
    Else
        sBaseDataType = sDataType
    End If

    'Set column properties
    oNewcol.Name = sColumnName
    oNewcol.Datatype = sDataType

    If Not oDB.SystemDatatypes(sBaseDataType).IsNumeric() And _
           sBaseDataType <> "money" And sBaseDataType <> "smallmoney" Then
        oNewcol.DRIDefault.Text = "'" & vDefault & "'"
    Else
        oNewcol.DRIDefault.Text = vDefault
    End If

    oNewcol.AllowNulls = bNullable

    If Not IsMissing(iLength) Then
        oNewcol.Length = iLength
    End If

    'Add the new column to the table
    On Error GoTo CancelTableAdd
    Set oTable = GetTable(oDB, sTableName)
    oTable.BeginAlter
    oTable.Columns.Add oNewcol
    oTable.DoAlter
```

```
exitSub:
   Exit Sub

CancelTableAdd:
   oTable.CancelAlter
   Err.Raise Err.Number, Err.Source, Err.Description
   Resume exitSub


End Sub
```

Notice that the method must determine whether the data type is a user-defined data type or a base data type before determining the format of the default text. If the data type is a user-defined data type, the `BaseType` property is used instead of the actual data type name.

Another thing to note is that an error trap is enabled during the time in which the changes are actually being made. If an error occurs, the `CancelAlter` method is called and the client application is notified of the failure.

The method uses two constants, a string and an enumerated constant to raise an error if a default is not specified and null is not allowed. The string constant can be found in `Strings.bas`:

```
Public Const sqlddl_NullableOrDefaultRequiredMsg = _
   "Columns must either be nullable or have a valid default value."
```

The constant can be found in the `ErrorNumbers` enumeration in `Constants.cls`:

```
Public Enum ErrorNumbers
    sqlddl_ServerRestart = vbObjectError + 700
    sqlddl_MinimumExceeded = vbObjectError + 701
    sqlddl_MaximumExceeded = vbObjectError + 702
    sqlddl_ServerNotConnected = vbObjectError + 703
    sqlddl_ShutdownNotFinished = vbObjectError + 704
    sqlddl_ConnectionTimeout = vbObjectError + 705
    sqlddl_StillStarting = vbObjectError + 706
    sqlddl_UnableToStartService = vbObjectError + 707
    sqlddl_NullableOrDefaultRequired = vbObjectError + 708
End Enum
```

Clicking the **Insert** button on the **Columns** form (`frmColumns`) invokes the following method to create a column:

```
Private Sub cmdInsert_Click()

   On Error GoTo handleit

   If IsNumeric(txtLength) Then
      db.AddColumn lConnID, frmDesign.cboDBs, frmDesign.lstTables, _
                  txtName, cboDataType, txtDefault.Text, chkNullable, txtLength
   Else
      db.AddColumn lConnID, frmDesign.cboDBs, frmDesign.lstTables, _
                  txtName, cboDataType, txtDefault.Text, chkNullable
   End If
```

```
        frmDesign.flxColumns.AddItem txtName

DontAddName:
    Exit Sub

handleit:
    MsgBox "Something went wrong. Table not added.", , "Error!"
    Resume DontAddName

End Sub
```

Establishing Referential Integrity

Referential integrity is established with primary keys and foreign keys. When a foreign key constraint is defined for a column, it ensures that it will always have a valid reference in the table that stores the primary key it references.

SQL-DMO uses the following terminology:

❑   A column with a **foreign key** constraint is termed the **referencing column**

❑   The **primary key** column used to enforce the constraint is termed the **referenced column**

Bear in mind that:

❑   A table can have only one primary key.

❑   A primary key can contain multiple columns. When it does, it is referred to as a composite primary key.

❑   None of the columns in a primary key can allow nulls.

❑   A primary key also enforces entity integrity (each primary will uniquely identify a row).

❑   A primary key cannot be deleted if it is referenced by other tables.

❑   A foreign key constraint can be removed from or added to a table with existing data. However, the ALTER TABLE must be done WITH NO CHECK when adding a foreign key constraint to a table with existing data.

This section looks at the steps that must be taken in order to implement the ability to configure referential integrity with SQL-DMO. In turn we'll address:

❑   Identification of the primary key

❑   How foreign key relationships can be defined using SQL-DMO

In both cases, we'll illustrate the points by referring to our sample application.

Identifying the Primary Key

In order to understand what you need to do to configure a primary key, it is useful to remember the object hierarchy and think about how information about primary keys is mapped to SQL-DMO objects.

The objects involved in setting primary keys are:

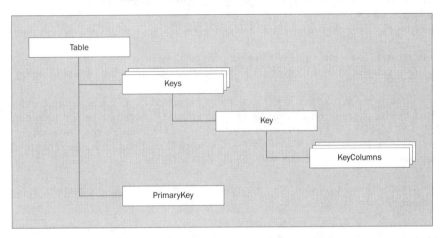

Keys (both primary and foreign) are created by adding a Key object to the Keys collection. However, like other objects we have seen so far, certain Key object properties must be set first (we'll consider those in a moment).

KeyColumn objects – that identify the columns that are included in a particular key – are added to the KeyColumns collection of the Key object. When a key defined as a primary key is added to the Keys collection, the PrimaryKey object is automatically created. The PrimaryKey object can be used to determine whether a table has a primary key and to get information about the columns involved, but is a read-only object and cannot be used directly to configure primary key information.

Setting up a primary key constraint involves several steps. These are:

- ❑ Ensuring the table doesn't already have a primary key
- ❑ Creating and instantiating a Key object
- ❑ Setting the Type property of the Key object to SQLDMOKey_Primary
- ❑ Setting the Name property of the Key object (optional, but recommended)
- ❑ Adding the names of the columns involved to the KeyColumns collection of the Key object
- ❑ Adding the Key object to the table's Keys collection

> If the **Name** property is not set, SQL-DMO will generate one for you. However, this name will not be a human-readable name, so if you plan to expose the names of keys in a user interface or make them easy for programmers to use, you should assign names using a standard naming convention. Primary keys are usually identified by the prefix **PK_**. The name you assign must be unique within the database, so commonly the table name is used to provide the rest of the string. For example, the primary key of the **Employees** table would be named **PK_Employees**.

One way to ensure that a table doesn't have a primary key is to check the PrimaryKey object to see if it holds a valid reference – if it's set to Nothing, a primary key doesn't exist.

If the table already has a primary key, the key can be removed and a new one created, provided the key is not being referenced in a foreign key constraint. The EnumReferencingTables method of the Table object returns a QueryResults object with a row for each foreign key constraint that references that table. If the QueryResults object contains zero rows, the table is not being referenced and its primary key can be deleted.

A primary key is deleted by calling the Remove method of the Keys collection, as shown in the code fragment below:

```
oTable.Keys(oTable.PrimaryKey.Name).Remove
```

The Name property of the PrimaryKey object is used to locate the Key in the collection.

Implementation of Primary Key Definition in the Surveys Unlimited Solution

The SQLDDL.Database component allows client applications to identify a primary key by calling the SetPrimaryKey method:

```
Public Sub SetPrimaryKey(ByVal lConnID As Long, ByVal sDatabase As String, _
                    ByVal sTable As String, ParamArray sColumns() As _
                    Variant)

    Dim oDB As SQLDMO.Database
    Dim oTable As SQLDMO.Table
    Dim oKey As New SQLDMO.Key
    Dim oQR As QueryResults
    Dim i As Integer
    Dim bHasPK As Boolean

    Set oDB = GetDatabase(lConnID, sDatabase)
    Set oTable = GetTable(oDB, sTable)

    'Check to see if the table already has a primary key
    If Not oTable.PrimaryKey Is Nothing Then
        'Check for references to primary key
        Set oQR = oTable.EnumReferencingTables
```

```
            If oQR.Rows = 0 Then
                'Delete primary key
                oTable.Keys(oTable.PrimaryKey.Name).Remove
        Else
                Err.Raise sqlddl_PrimaryKeyReferenced, "SQLDDL.Database", _
                        sqlddl_PrimaryKeyReferencedMsg
        End If
    End If

    'Create new primary key
    oKey.Type = SQLDMOKey_Primary
    oKey.Name = "PK_" & sTable

    For i = 0 To UBound(sColumns)
        oKey.KeyColumns.Add sColumns(i)
    Next

    oTable.Keys.Add oKey

End Sub
```

This method uses two additional constants when raising an error. The
sqlddl_PrimaryKeyReferencedMsg string is defined in `Strings.bas` as shown below:

```
Public Const sqlddl_PrimaryKeyReferencedMsg = _
"Primary key cannot be deleted. It is already referenced in other tables."
```

The sqlddl_PrimaryKeyReferenced constant is held in the `ErrorNumbers` enumeration in
Constants.cls:

```
Public Enum ErrorNumbers
    sqlddl_ServerRestart = vbObjectError + 700
    sqlddl_MinimumExceeded = vbObjectError + 701
    sqlddl_MaximumExceeded = vbObjectError + 702
    sqlddl_ServerNotConnected = vbObjectError + 703
    sqlddl_ShutdownNotFinished = vbObjectError + 704
    sqlddl_ConnectionTimeout = vbObjectError + 705
    sqlddl_StillStarting = vbObjectError + 706
    sqlddl_UnableToStartService = vbObjectError + 707
    sqlddl_NullableOrDefaultRequired = vbObjectError + 708
    sqlddl_PrimaryKeyReferenced = vbObjectError + 709
End Enum
```

The SurveyDesigner client application implements the functionality of setting a primary key through the **Primary Key** dialog (frmKey) accessed via the **Set Primary** button under the Columns MSFlexGrid control:

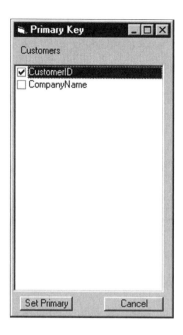

The Form_Load event of the frmKey form populates the lstColumns ListBox by gathering information from the flxColumns MSFlexGrid control on frmDesign. It does not include columns that can contain nulls (those that have the fourth column – **Can contain null** – set to Yes in the flxColumns MSFlexGrid control):

```
Private Sub Form_Load()

    Dim i As Integer

    For i = 1 To frmDesign.flxColumns.Rows - 1
        'Verify that column is not nullable before adding to list
        If frmDesign.flxColumns.TextMatrix(i, 4) = "No" Then
            lstColumns.AddItem frmDesign.flxColumns.TextMatrix(i, 0)
            'Check to see if it is already in the primary key
            'if so, mark it as selected.
            If frmDesign.flxColumns.TextMatrix(i, 3) = "Yes" Then
                lstColumns.Selected(lstColumns.ListCount - 1) = True
            End If
        End If
    Next

    lblTable = frmDesign.lstTables.Text

End Sub
```

When the user clicks the **Set Primary** button on frmKey, information about the items selected in the lstColumns control is passed to the SetPrimaryKey method of the db object. This particular implementation allows only three columns to be included in the primary key although it could be expanded to support more.

The method invoked within the `frmKey` form is:

```
Private Sub cmdSetPK_Click()

    Dim i As Integer
    Dim iSel As Integer
    Dim sColumns() As String

    ReDim sColumns(lstColumns.SelCount)

    For i = 0 To lstColumns.ListCount - 1
        If lstColumns.Selected(i) = True Then
            sColumns(iSel) = lstColumns.List(i)
            iSel = iSel + 1
        End If
    Next

    Select Case UBound(sColumns)
        Case 1
            db.SetPrimaryKey lConnID, frmDesign.cboDBs, lblTable, sColumns(0)
        Case 2
            db.SetPrimaryKey lConnID, frmDesign.cboDBs, lblTable, _
                sColumns(0), sColumns(1)
        Case 3
            db.SetPrimaryKey lConnID, frmDesign.cboDBs, lblTable, _
                sColumns(0), sColumns(1), sColumns(2)
    End Select

    Unload Me

End Sub
```

Creating Foreign Keys

The SQL-DMO objects involved in setting foreign keys are similar to those involved in setting primary keys. However, some additional information must be provided. The hierarchy shown here displays the objects and collections involved in setting up foreign key relationships:

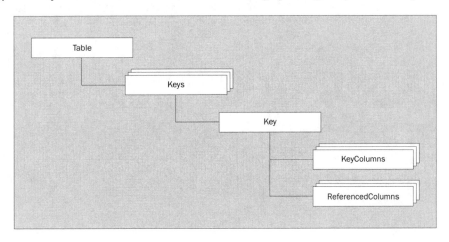

The `ReferencedColumns` collection stores the names of the columns included in the referenced primary key.

The steps we have to take to define a foreign key relationship are:

❑ Ensuring the column does not already have a foreign key constraint

❑ Creating and instantiating a `Key` object

❑ Setting the `Type` property of the `Key` object to `SQLDMOKey_Foreign`

❑ Setting the `Name` property of the `Key` object (optional)

❑ Setting the `ReferencedTable` property of the `Key` object

❑ Adding the names of the columns that define the foreign key to the `KeyColumns` collection of the `Key` object

❑ Adding the names of the columns that define the referenced primary key to the `ReferencedColumns` collection of the `Key` object

❑ Adding the `Key` object to the table's `Keys` collection

> The **`ReferencedKey`** property will be set automatically – it is a read-only property.

Implementation of Foreign Key Creation in the Surveys Unlimited Solution

The `SQLDDL.Database` component implements a `SetForeignKeyConstraint` method that allows client applications to set a foreign key constraint based on a primary key that contains a single column only. While this serves the purposes of the book (showing you how to use SQL-DMO), it would need to be made more flexible for an actual production application:

```
Public Sub SetForeignKeyConstraint(ByVal lConnID As Long, ByVal sDatabase As _
                                   String, ByVal sTable As String, ByVal _
                                   sColumnName As String, ByVal sRefTable As _
                                   String, ByVal sRefKey As String)

    Dim oDB As SQLDMO.Database
    Dim oTable As SQLDMO.Table
    Dim oKeyTable As SQLDMO.Table
    Dim oKey As SQLDMO.Key
    Dim iK As Integer
    Dim iKC As Integer
    Dim bExistingFK As Boolean

    bExistingFK = False

    Set oDB = GetDatabase(lConnID, sDatabase)
    Set oTable = GetTable(oDB, sTable)
```

```
'Check to see if the column already has a foreign key constraint
For iK = 1 To oTable.Keys.Count
   For iKC = 1 To oTable.Keys(iK).KeyColumns.Count
      If oTable.Keys(iK).KeyColumns(iKC) = sColumnName Then
         bExistingFK = True
         oTable.Keys(iK).Remove
      End If
   Next
Next

Set oKey = CreateObject("SQLDMO.key")

Set oKeyTable = oDB.Tables(sRefTable)

oKey.Type = SQLDMOKey_Foreign
oKey.ReferencedTable = sRefTable
oKey.ReferencedColumns.Add oKeyTable.PrimaryKey.KeyColumns(1)
oKey.KeyColumns.Add sColumnName

oTable.BeginAlter
oTable.Keys.Add oKey

If bExistingFK = False Then
   oTable.DoAlter
Else
   oTable.DoAlterWithNoCheck
End If

End Sub
```

SurveyDesigner implements this functionality through the frmRelationship dialog (accessed via the Define Relationship button on the Database Designer form):

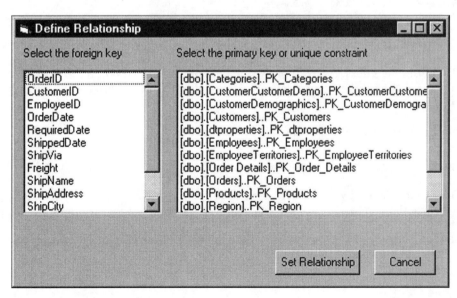

147

The ListBox controls on this form (lstForeign and lstCandidates) are populated during the Form_Load event:

```
Private Sub Form_Load()

    Dim i As Integer

    For i = 1 To frmDesign.flxColumns.Rows - 1
        lstForeign.AddItem frmDesign.flxColumns.TextMatrix(i, 0)
    Next

    Set oQr = db.GetDBPrimaryKeyList(lConnID, frmDesign.cboDBs)

    For i = 1 To oQr.Rows
        lstCandidates.AddItem oQr.GetColumnString(i, 1) & ".." & _
                              oQr.GetColumnString(i, 2)
    Next

End Sub
```

The ListBox on the left (lstForeign) is populated from the flxColumns MSFlexGrid control. The ListBox on the right (lstCandidates) is populated by calling the GetDBPrimaryKeyList method of the SQLDDL.Database object as described below:

```
Public Function GetDBPrimaryKeyList(ByVal lConnID As Long, ByVal sDatabase _
                                    As String) As SQLDMO.QueryResults

    Dim oDB As SQLDMO.Database
    Dim oQR As SQLDMO.QueryResults

    Set oDB = GetDatabase(lConnID, sDatabase)
    Set oQR = oDB.EnumCandidateKeys
    Set GetDBPrimaryKeyList = oQR

End Function
```

Notice that it uses the EnumCandidateKeys method of the SQL-DMO Database object. This method returns a QueryResults object containing a list of all of the primary keys that have been defined in the database.

The frmRelationship form uses the variable declaration:

```
Private oQr As SQLDMO.QueryResults
```

This defines a module-level variable named oQR to store the QueryResults object. It is used not only to populate the lstCandidates ListBox control, but also to pass the appropriate arguments to the SetForeignKeyConstraint method of the SQLDDL.Database component via the cmdSetRelationship_Click event procedure (invoked on clicking the **Set Relationship** button):

```
Private Sub cmdSetRelationship_Click()

    Dim sTableRef As String
    Dim sKeyRef As String

    If lstCandidates.Text <> "" And lstForeign.Text <> "" Then
        sTableRef = oQR.GetColumnString(lstCandidates.ListIndex + 1, 1)
        sKeyRef = oQR.GetColumnString(lstCandidates.ListIndex + 1, 2)
        db.SetForeignKeyConstraint lConnID, frmDesign.cboDBs, _
            frmDesign.lstTables.Text, lstForeign.Text, sTableRef, sKeyRef
        Unload Me
    Else
        MsgBox "You must select a foreign key and a primary key.", , _
                "Error!"
    End If

End Sub
```

Indexes are required to optimize the way that data is accessed via SQL Server, and now is a good time to see how we can use SQL-DMO to set them up.

Creating Indexes

There are several types of indexes, one of which we have already created by creating a primary key. An index is automatically created every time you define a primary key. In general, indexes can be grouped into two categories:

❑ Clustered

❑ Non-clustered

In the remainder of this chapter, we will provide you with a brief overview of how to create indexes on your tables using SQL-DMO. Since the techniques used are very similar to those you have already seen with regards to creating databases, tables, and keys, we will not provide a specific code sample on creating indexes. Instead, we will overview the purpose of indexes and provide a list of properties that should be set, pointing out the differences between indexes and other collections of the Database object where appropriate.

Although we provide an overview of how to create indexes in this chapter, designing an optimal indexing strategy is an important and intricate topic. A detailed discussion of indexing and a variety of other SQL Server issues is covered in Wrox Press's *Professional SQL Server 7.0 Programming*, by Robert Vieira.

Clustered Indexes

A clustered index is one that determines the physical order in which data is stored on the disk. A table is not required to have a clustered index, but at most it can have one. Clustered indexes are the fastest kind of index, particularly when you will be accessing data sequentially or when you will retrieve a range of data based on that index value.

149

Non-Clustered Indexes

A non-clustered index is one that does not influence the physical order in which data is stored on the disk. A table can have up to 249 non-clustered indexes. Non-clustered indexes are slower than clustered indexes, but still provide improved performance over non-indexed columns.

When to Define Indexes

Indexes should be carefully chosen based on the way in which database data will be retrieved and updated. Keep in mind that data that must be updated frequently will also update the index, so choosing the wrong columns can actual have a negative impact on performance. Some basic guidelines for choosing indexes are:

- ❑ Index primary and foreign keys
- ❑ Index columns used in joins required for frequently executed queries
- ❑ Index columns used in ORDER BY clauses
- ❑ Index columns used in GROUP BY clauses
- ❑ Index columns used to retrieve a range of values

> A primary key index is automatically created when you define a primary key. To have this index be the clustered index for the table, set the **Clustered** property of the **Key** object to **True** before adding it to the collection.

Defining Indexes via SQL-DMO

Indexes are created through SQL-DMO by setting the appropriate properties of an Index object and adding it to the Indexes collection of the Table object:

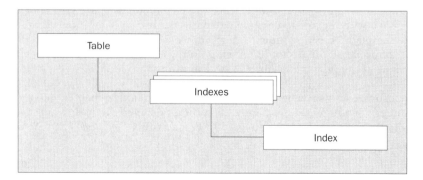

The `Index` object has ten properties but the three we need to set before adding the `Index` object to the collection are shown in the table below:

Property	Data type	Description
Name	String	This property is used to identify the index.
Type	Enumerated long	This property determines the type of index that will be created. For example, whether the index will be clustered (`SQLDMOIndex_Clustered`) or non-clustered and non-unique (`SQLDMOIndex_Default`).
IndexedColumns	SQL-DMO multistring	This property lists the columns that should be included in the index. A SQL-DMO multistring is a list of strings. Each element in the list must be enclosed in square brackets. For example, to include `EmployeeID` and `LastName` in an index, you would set `IndexedColumns = "[EmployeeID],[LastName]"` The `IndexedColumns` property is write-only.

The additional properties, such as `FileGroup` and `FillFactor` can also be set before appending the `Index` object to the table's `Indexes` collection. When adding an index, you should use the `BeginAlter` and `DoAlter` methods to ensure that all properties are set in a single call.

Summary

This chapter has concentrated on using SQL-DMO to define databases, tables, and indexes. In covering this topic we have had a good look at the `Databases` collection and `Database` object hierarchy, the `Tables` collection and `Table` object hierarchy, and the `Column` object.

Furthermore, we have investigated how to use SQL-DMO to set up relationships within our database and indexes to improve the performance of our system. In achieving these aims, we have continued to emphasize and familiarize ourselves with the layout of the SQL-DMO object library.

These working patterns will continue to be important as we move into the next chapter and learn to use SQL-DMO to build applications that perform several common administrative tasks.

SQL Server Administration and Management

Our next port of call on this voyage of discovery through SQL-DMO objects is server management. Once again, we'll be supporting our coverage of the various objects by referring to the Surveys Unlimited business scenario.

This chapter focuses on three general areas:

❑ Security – including a look at selected security objects, specifically logins, database users, and security roles

❑ Backups – backup and restore objects, including backup devices are introduced

❑ Automation of backup procedures – here we'll highlight the use of job server objects

This chapter won't be covering each object and collection in great detail. Instead, the aim is to discuss key points to give a general understanding of how the objects are implemented. Again, we'll observe certain patterns emerging for object usage as we go through the chapter. If you wish to take things further, it should be relatively easy to take the basics contained in this chapter and extend the concepts as far as you need.

As regards the business scenario, in the first part of the chapter we'll be looking at the Security menu and associated child forms that make use of the SQLDDL.Security component. We'll then move onto the Backup menu and child forms that call on the SQLDDL.BackupDB and the SQLDDL.Management components.

OK, let's dive in and look at our first topic – security.

Security

In this section we'll be looking at:

❑ Logins via the `Logins` collection and `Login` object

❑ Database users via the `Users` collection and `User` object

❑ Security roles via the `ServerRole` and `DatabaseRole` hierarchies

However, before trying to look at the various security objects themselves, let's briefly review SQL Server security; if you've worked primarily with earlier SQL Server versions, you'll find that there have been some changes implemented with SQL Server 7.0. The major changes are in:

❑ Login and access

❑ Security roles

Let's begin with logins and access.

Login and Access

Login security deals with connecting to SQL Server. SQL Server 7.0 supports two methods for authenticating logins:

❑ **Windows NT Authentication**

❑ **SQL Server Authentication**

Windows NT Authentication

Windows NT authentication is used to establish a **trusted** connection with the server. To log into a Windows NT workstation we use a Windows NT domain username. If the username, or one of the groups to which the user belongs, is identified as a SQL Server login, we are given access to SQL Server without additional authentication.

In other words, SQL Server "trusts" the authentication made by Windows NT.

One of the advantages of using Windows NT authentication is that you can pass some of the responsibility for login management to Windows NT administrators. Rather than creating logins for individual Windows NT users, you can create logins for groups. A group login gives permission to connect to the server to all members of that Windows NT group. Windows NT administrators can then assign or remove login permissions by adding or removing group members in the Windows NT group.

SQL Server Authentication

With SQL Server authentication, the login is authenticated by SQL Server and we log in using a login name and password that is created on and managed by SQL Server.

> SQL Server running Windows NT can be configured to support SQL Server authentication and Windows NT authentication, or Windows NT authentication only. Obviously, SQL Server running on Windows 95/98 does not support Windows NT authentication.

Logging on only provides you with a connection to SQL Server. It doesn't imply that you have access to any of the databases. This is done through database users. Access is granted to a database by mapping a login name to a database user name. Access permissions are managed primarily through the use of security roles.

Security Roles

Permissions are determined by role membership.

> A role is a collection of access rights that can be assigned to a user en masse simply by assigning a user to that role.

A user (or a Windows NT group) can be assigned membership of multiple roles, making it easier to fine-tune permission assignments. Changing permission assignments, in most cases, is as easy as changing role membership.

SQL Server 7.0 supports three types of user roles:

❏ **Fixed server roles** – predefined security roles with preset server-level permissions

❏ **Fixed database roles** – predefined security roles with preset database-level permissions

❏ **User-defined database roles** – roles for which you define which database permissions they include

You will probably find that you can handle most of your security requirements through the fixed server and database roles. Should it be necessary, you also have the ability to explicitly grant or deny specific permissions to a selected user. This should only be used when you cannot more easily manage security through an **application role**, since it does add to your management overhead.

Application roles give you a means of granting access permissions directly to an application without providing access to the users running the application. Note that you don't assign a user to an application role. A user logs into an application and that application provides the user with its application role for the duration of the user's connection into the application. For this reason, an application role is more like a security alias than a "role".

Fixed Server Roles

Fixed server roles are used for managing server-level security. The fixed server roles are defined by SQL Server. You cannot change the permissions granted by fixed server roles, but you can assign permissions by assigning login accounts' membership to one or more roles.

The fixed server roles are:

- ❏ dbcreator – Members of the database creators role can create and alter databases.
- ❏ diskadmin – Members of the disk administrators role have the ability to manage disk files.
- ❏ processadmin – Assign login accounts to whoever you want to be able to manage SQL Server processes membership in the process administrators role.
- ❏ securityadmin – Security administrators can create and manage SQL Server login accounts as well as manage auditing.
- ❏ serveradmin – Members of the server administrators role can modify server-wide configuration settings.
- ❏ setupadmin – Members of the setup administrators role can install and manage replication.
- ❏ sysadmin – By adding a login account to the system administrators role you give that account the necessary permissions to perform any activity in SQL Server.

Permissions granted to login accounts are additive. If a login account is added as a member to the dbcreator and securityadmin roles, that account will be able to manage databases, logins, and auditing.

Fixed Database Roles

Just like fixed server roles, fixed database roles are defined by SQL Server. Database users and user-defined roles can be added as members of fixed database roles. Members of a role have all of the permissions granted to a role unless otherwise denied. The fixed database roles provided by SQL Server 7.0 are:

- ❏ public – The public role is the only fixed database role to which you can make changes to the permissions assigned. All database users are members of the role and cannot be removed from this role. Any changes made to the public role will impact all users.
- ❏ db_owner – Membership of the database owner role is automatically assigned to the user creating a database. The database owner has access permission equivalent to all of the access permissions granted through fixed database roles.
- ❏ db_accessadmin – Members of the database access administrators role can add and remove database users and user-defined roles.
- ❏ db_ddladmin – Members of the data definition language administrators role can add, modify, and drop database objects.
- ❏ db_securityadmin – Members of the database security administrators role are able to make explicit statement and object permission assignments.
- ❏ db_backupoperator – Make any user who needs to be able to backup or restore a database a member of the database backup operators role.
- ❏ db_datareader – Members of the database data reader role can read data from any table in the database.
- ❏ db_datawriter – Members of the database data write role can add, modify, and delete table data for any table in the database.

❑ `db_denydatareader` – Members of the database deny data reader role cannot read data from any table in the database.

❑ `db_denydatawriter` – Members of the database deny data writer role are prohibited from adding, modifying, or deleting table data.

As with fixed server roles, permissions are additive.

User-Defined Database Roles

User-defined roles are roles that you can create and manage. After creating a user-defined role, you can then grant and deny access permissions to that role. Any users you add as members of the role will automatically be granted and denied the same permissions. User-defined roles can be added as members of fixed database roles and as members of other user-defined roles.

> You have the ability to explicitly deny a permission to a user-defined role or database user. Denying a permission overrides any granting of a permission. For example, if a user is granted SELECT permission to a database through role membership, but denied the SELECT permissions through an explicit assignment to the user, the user will not have the SELECT permission.

Application Roles

Application security roles are a special case. An application security role will not have any members. In fact, you will most commonly use an application security role when you do *not* want to give users direct access permissions to the data.

Application security roles can be used to grant access to client applications or to mid-tier applications, such as business rules running as Microsoft Transaction Server components. They bypass user security and the user's access permissions are ignored when accessing data through the application.

To use application security roles, you will define the security role and assign it appropriate access permissions. The security role is activated when you launch the application by calling the `sp_setapprole` system stored procedure. Once activated, the role remains active until the current connection is released from the server.

Security in the Surveys Unlimited Solution

`Login` objects reference login records for both Windows NT authenticated logins and SQL Server authenticated logins. Our sample application is going to:

❑ List SQL Server logins

❑ Add login records

❑ Remove login records

As we've just seen, logins allow users to connect to a server while database users provide access to server databases. A user's login must be mapped to a database user in order to have access to that database. Logins and database users, then, are very similar in what they do and our application will handle them in a similar way. When working with a database, the application will:

- List database users
- Add database users
- Delete database users

All of these operations are accessed via the Security menu of Survey Designer:

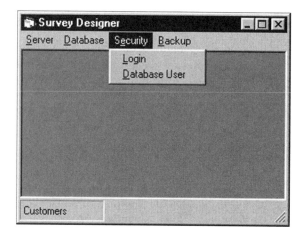

For all the examples throughout this chapter, we've deliberately kept the code as uncomplicated as possible so that, rather than getting bogged down in too much code, we can focus on the main concepts.

Right, enough preamble, let's get to grips with the Login hierarchy:

Logins Collection and Login Object

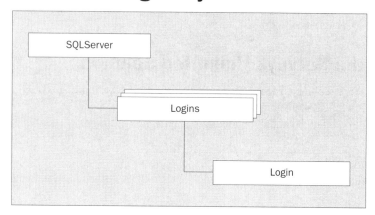

The `Logins` collection is a member of the `SQLServer` object. The hierarchy for SQL Server logins is rather simple, especially when compared to some of the objects in the previous chapter, and contains:

Logins Collection – The `Logins` collection contains references for all login records, Windows NT and SQL Server authenticated. Logins can be created and dropped by adding `Login` objects to or removing them from the `Logins` collection.

Login Object – Each `Login` object represents a login record. The connected user must be a member of the `securityadmin` fixed server role to create or modify login records.

Listing Logins in the Surveys Unlimited Scenario

Running Security | Login in the sample application brings up the `frmLogin` form. Its `Form_Load` event retrieves a list of server logins and displays them in a List Box called `lstLogins`:

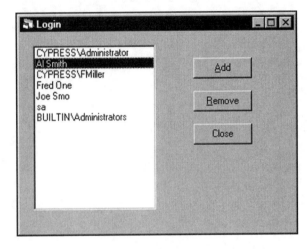

First, let's look at the variables we've declared for this form:

```
Private sLogList() As String
```

We'll be using this array variable to hold the login names we retrieve from SQL Server.

The code for the `Form_Load` event is:

```
Private Sub Form_Load()

    Dim i As Integer

    sLogList = sec.GetLoginList(lConnID)

    For i = 0 To UBound(sLogList)
        lstLogins.AddItem sLogList(i)
    Next

End Sub
```

159

The `GetLoginList` function of the application's `SQLDDL.Security` component generates the login list. The `sec` object variable is declared in the `modGlobals` standard module:

```
Public sec As New SQLDDL.Security
```

The login names are then loaded into the list box so that a list of all logins is displayed.

Implementation of GetLoginList

Generating a list of logins is a straightforward process and is detailed in the code fragment (from the `SQLDDL.Security` component) below.

A reference to the `SQLServer` object is set using the connection ID generated when you connect to the server. It is then a process of just collecting the `Name` property for each of the items in the `Logins` collection by its index value:

```
Public Function GetLoginList(lConnID As Long) As String()

    Dim i As Integer
    Dim iCount As Integer
    Dim oSQLServer As SQLDMO.SQLServer
    Dim sSysLogins() As String

    Set oSQLServer = oApp.SQLServers.ItemByID(lConnID)
    ReDim sSysLogins(0 To oSQLServer.Logins.Count - 1)

    For i = 1 To oSQLServer.Logins.Count
        sSysLogins(iCount) = oSQLServer.Logins(i).Name
        iCount = iCount + 1
    Next

    GetLoginList = sSysLogins

    Set oSQLServer = Nothing

End Function
```

> As with other collections you have seen in this book, members of the `Logins` collection can be referenced by index or by name. You'll see an example of referencing a member by name later in the chapter.

Dropping a Login

The `Logins` collection's `Remove` method is used to drop logins. The syntax for doing this is:

```
object.Remove(index)
```

The `Login` object can be referenced by index or by name.

Removing Logins from the Survey Designer Login List

The DeleteLogin method of the SQLDDL.Security component is used by frmLogin of SurveyDesigner to remove Login objects from the collection, and thereby remove login records from the server. The calling event procedure is:

```
Private Sub cmdDelLogin_Click()

    Dim i As Integer

    sec.DeleteLogin lConnID, lstLogins.Text
    lstLogins.Clear
    sLogList = sec.GetLoginList(lConnID)

    For i = 0 To UBound(sLogList)
        lstLogins.AddItem sLogList(i)
    Next

    cmdDelLogin.Enabled = False

End Sub
```

The lstLogins.Text property is passed as a login name value. In the sample application the cmdDelLogin button starts out as disabled and is enabled by the lstLogin_Click event procedure only if a list member has been selected. The cmdDelLogin_Click event procedure disables the Remove button after refreshing lstLogins.

The DeleteLogin method is implemented as:

```
Public Sub DeleteLogin(ByVal lConnID As Long, ByVal sDelName As String)

    Dim oSQLServer As SQLDMO.SQLServer
    Set oSQLServer = oApp.SQLServers.ItemByID(lConnID)

    On Error Resume Next
    oSQLServer.Logins.Remove (sDelName)

    Set oSQLServer = Nothing

End Sub
```

The connection ID (lConnID) and login name (sDelName) are passed to the method from the client application. The Remove method is being used to remove the Login object, *referencing the object by name.*

Notice that we've told Visual Basic to Resume Next if there is an error. This is because SQL Server will return an error if we try to delete a system login. Therefore, as we are expecting this error to occur occasionally, we just tell Visual Basic to carry on.

Creating a Login

It's relatively easy to create a Login object through SQL-DMO – the steps involved are:

- ❑ Create a Login object
- ❑ Set the Name property
- ❑ Set the Type property
- ❑ Set other properties as applicable
- ❑ Add the Login object to the Logins collection

The Add method is the same as we saw when working with collections in the last chapter.

The Name property must be set for the login. The Type property defaults to SQL Server authentication and the only time it needs to be set is when creating a login for a Windows NT user or group.

The three most commonly used properties of the Login object are:

Property	Data Type	Description
Database	String	The Database property identifies the login's default database.
Name	String	This is the login name. This is how the login is identified to SQL Server or recognized by Windows NT.
Type	Enumeratedlong	The Type property identifies the login as a SQL Server authentication login, a Windows NT user, or Windows NT group.

The Type property will influence how other properties are evaluated – any property values that are supplied, but are inappropriate to the type, are ignored. Please refer to Appendix D for a complete list of properties supported by the Login object.

Adding Logins to the SurveyDesigner Login List

Clicking the **Add** button on frmLogin (cmdAddLogin) brings up the **Add Login** dialog (the frmAddLogin form) where the user will be prompted for a login name, password, and default database:

When you click on C**r**eate the `cmdCreateLogin_Click()` event procedure of `frmAddLogin` is invoked:

```
Private Sub cmdCreateLogin_Click()

    Dim i As Integer

    sLogList = sec.GetLoginList(lConnID)

    If txtLogin.Text = "" Then
        MsgBox "You must enter a login name", vbOKOnly
        Exit Sub
    End If

    For i = 0 To UBound(sLogList)
        If txtLogin.Text = sLogList(i) Then
            MsgBox "Login name already exists", vbOKOnly
            txtLogin.Text = ""
            txtLogin.SetFocus
            Exit Sub
        End If
    Next

    If cboDefDB.Text = "" Then
        MsgBox "You must select a database", vbOKOnly
        Exit Sub
    End If

    sec.AddLogin lConnID, cboDefDB.Text, txtPass.Text, txtLogin.Text
    frmAddLogin.txtLogin.Text = ""
    frmAddLogin.txtPass.Text = ""
    frmLogin.lstLogins.Clear

    sLogList = sec.GetLoginList(lConnID)

    For i = 0 To UBound(sLogList)
        frmLogin.lstLogins.AddItem sLogList(i)
```

```
      Next

      Unload Me

   End Sub
```

This procedure starts by retrieving login names then, before creating the new login, carries out the following verifications:

❑ Verification that a login name has been entered

❑ Verification that the login does not already exist

❑ Verification that a database has been selected

If any of these fails, the procedure exits.

> **We're sure that you're aware of the importance of proper entry data verification as part of your application. This has been provided as an example. The remaining examples in this chapter will include little, if any, verification.**

Next, the procedure calls the `AddLogin` method of the `SQLDDL.Security` component to create the login, passing the server connection ID, default database, password, and login name. After creating the login, the name and password values are cleared:

```
   Public Sub AddLogin(ByVal lConnID As Long, ByVal sDb As String, _
                    ByVal sPass As String, ByVal sName As String)

      Dim oSQLServer As SQLDMO.SQLServer
      Dim oNewLogin As SQLDMO.Login

      Set oSQLServer = oApp.SQLServers.ItemByID(lConnID)
      Set oNewLogin = CreateObject("SQLDMO.Login")

      oNewLogin.Database = sDb
      oNewLogin.Type = SQLDMOLogin_Standard
      oNewLogin.SetPassword "", sPass
      oNewLogin.Name = sName
      oSQLServer.Logins.Add oNewLogin

      Set oSQLServer = Nothing
      Set oNewLogin = Nothing

   End Sub
```

The method declares and instantiates `SQLServer` and `Login` objects. The new `Login` object properties are set using the values passed by the client application and the `Login` object is added to the `Logins` collection.

There is one method being used for defining Login properties, `SetPassword` – it has the syntax:

```
object.SetPassword (oldvalue, newvalue)
```

An empty string is entered as the *oldvalue*, the old password, since the newly created object does not have a default password. A value for the old password must be included, even if it is blank. If you wished to modify this application to let users change login passwords, the same method would be used.

Database Users

We've already seen that there is considerable similarity in the actions of logins and database users. Now that we've seen how we can use and implement features provided by the `Logins` collection and `Login` object, let's move on to the `Users` collection and `User` object.

Users Collection and User Object

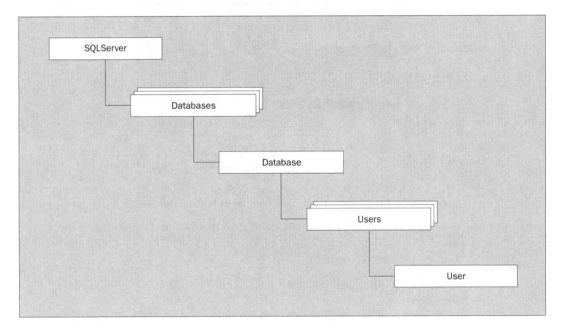

As the hierarchy shows, the `Users` collection is a member of a `Database` object, which in turn is a member of the `SQLServer` object. In more detail we have:

Users Collection – All `User` objects for a particular database are contained in its `Users` collection. Database users are managed separately for each database, including system databases.

User Object – Each User object represents a specific database user. Login names are mapped to database user names to provide access to server databases. If a Login name is removed, database users to which the login name are mapped are *not* removed. This is to avoid leaving orphaned objects in the database.

> **An orphaned object is an object whose owner no longer exists. One way of avoiding orphaned objects is to allow only the database owner to create objects.**

Listing Users by Database in the Surveys Unlimited Scenario

Clicking Security | Database User in SurveyDesigner will bring up the Database Users dialog (the frmDBUser form). As part of its Form_Load event a drop-down list is populated with the server databases:

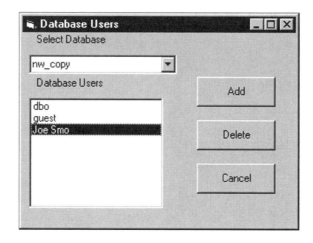

Before we look at Form_Load, here are the module-level variables declared for this form.

```
Private sListDB() As String
Private sListUser() As String
Private sListLogin() As String
```

The sListDB() array is used when generating the list of databases. You will see the others used in later code samples.

The code for Form_Load is very similar to that previously used to display the login list:

```
Private Sub Form_Load()

    Dim i As Integer

    cboDatabases.Clear
    sListDB = sec.GetAllDB(lConnID)
```

```
   For i = 0 To UBound(sListDB)
       cboDatabases.AddItem sListDB(i)
   Next

End Sub
```

The procedure uses the `GetAllDB` function in the `SQLDDL.Security` component to generate the list of database names. This differs from the `GetDBList` method we called from the `SQLDDL.Database` component, in Chapter 4, in that it returns all databases, including system databases:

```
Public Function GetAllDB(lConnID As Long) As String()

   Dim i As Integer
   Dim iCount As Integer
   Dim sAllDBs() As String
   Dim oSQLServer As SQLDMO.SQLServer

   Set oSQLServer = oApp.SQLServers.ItemByID(lConnID)
   ReDim sAllDBs(0 To oSQLServer.Databases.Count - 1)

   For i = 1 To oSQLServer.Databases.Count
       sAllDBs(iCount) = oSQLServer.Databases(i).Name
       iCount = iCount + 1
   Next

   GetAllDB = sAllDBs

   Set oSQLServer = Nothing

End Function
```

Once again, the function is just building an array of names that are then passed back to the client application.

When the application user selects a database from the drop-down list, the `cboDatabases_Click` event of the `frmDBUser` is triggered and this is used to populate the database user name list:

```
Private Sub cboDatabases_Click()

   Dim sDbName As String
   Dim i As Integer

   sDbName = cboDatabases.Text
   lstDBUser.Clear
   sListUser = sec.GetDBUsers(lConnID, sDbName)

   For i = 0 To UBound(sListUser)
       lstDBUser.AddItem sListUser(i)
   Next

End Sub
```

Overall, the general approach is pretty similar to that which we used to list logins – here to generate the user name array we use the GetDBUsers method of the SQLDDL.Security component:

```
Public Function GetDBUsers(ByVal lConnID As Long, ByVal sUDatabase As String)

    Dim i As Integer
    Dim iUCount As Integer
    Dim sDataUsers() As String
    Dim oDB As SQLDMO.Database
    Dim oSQLServer As SQLDMO.SQLServer

    Set oSQLServer = oApp.SQLServers.ItemByID(lConnID)
    Set oDB = oSQLServer.Databases(sUDatabase)
    ReDim sDataUsers(0 To oDB.Users.Count - 1)

    For i = 1 To oDB.Users.Count
        sDataUsers(iUCount) = oDB.Users(i).Name
        iUCount = iUCount + 1
    Next

    GetDBUsers = sDataUsers

    Set oDB = Nothing
    Set oSQLServer = Nothing

End Function
```

Once again, there are no significant differences between generating the user name array and passing it back to the client application, and the GetLoginList method used previously.

> By this time, you should be able to see obvious patterns emerging in some of these procedures. For example, other than the objects and collections involved, there is almost no difference between generating a list of databases, database users, or login names.

Removing a Database User

Once again, the process for deleting a User object is the same as for deleting a Login object – only the objects involved have changed. In this case, it is initiated by the cmdDelete_Click event of frmDBUser:

```
Private Sub cmdDelete_Click()

    Dim i As Integer
    Dim sDbName As String

    sDbName = cboDatabases.Text
```

```
    If lstDBUser.Text = "guest" Or lstDBUser.Text = "dbo" Then
        MsgBox "Cannot delete guest or dbo"
        Exit Sub
    End If

    sec.DeleteUser lConnID, lstDBUser.Text, cboDatabases.Text
    lstDBUser.Clear
    sListUser = sec.GetDBUsers(lConnID, sDbName)

    For i = 0 To UBound(sListUser)
        lstDBUser.AddItem sListUser(i)
    Next

End Sub
```

This time, there is a quick verification check to make sure that the user isn't trying to delete guest or dbo, then the connection ID, user name, and database name are passed to the DeleteUser method of the SQLDDL.Security component:

```
Public Sub DeleteUser(ByVal lConnID As Long, ByVal sDelUser As String, _
                      ByVal sUDatabase As String)

    Dim oSQLServer As SQLDMO.SQLServer
    Dim oDB As SQLDMO.Database

    Set oSQLServer = oApp.SQLServers.ItemByID(lConnID)
    Set oDB = oSQLServer.Databases(sUDatabase)
    oDB.Users.Remove (sDelUser)

    Set oSQLServer = Nothing
    Set oDB = Nothing

End Sub
```

The only real difference between this and what we saw before for deleting a Login object is that DeleteUser must retrieve a reference to the database in which the User object is a member.

> In a production application, we would first use the **User** object's
> **ListOwnedObjects** method to enumerate the database objects owned by the
> user, if any. We would then need to use the **Owner** property for each of those
> objects to change ownership. Ownership is important in determining object
> security. An object's owner has all rights to the object. Often, the proper
> operation of views and stored procedures is dependent on the ownership being
> intact.

Creating a Database User

The process for creating a User object is similar to the process for creating a Login; we need to:

- ❏ Create a User object
- ❏ Set the Login property to the name of an existing login
- ❏ Set other properties as applicable
- ❏ Add the User object to the Users collection

Setting the Login property is mandatory but we have a choice about whether or not to set any of the other properties. The three most commonly referenced User object properties are listed below:

Property	Data Type	Description
Login	String	This property associates a database user with a login record. *You must specify a value for Login.*
Name	String	This is the database user name. If a value is not specified for Name, the associated login's Name property will be entered as the default.
Role	String	This property can only be modified when creating a database user. It specifies the user's initial database security role, defaulting to public.

Note: If only the Login property is set for a User object, its Login and Name property values will be the same.

Refer to Appendix D for additional object properties.

Adding a Database User to the SurveyDesigner Database User List

Clicking on the Add button of the Database Users dialog brings up the Add Database User dialog (frmAddUser form in the SurveyDesigner project):

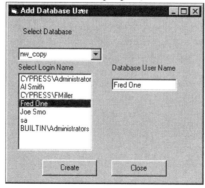

This form uses four module-level variables:

```
Private sListLogin() As String
Private sListUser() As String
Private sListDB() As String
Private sDataName As String
```

The sListDB() and sListLogin() arrays are used when populating the form. Let's look at what happens when this form loads:

```
Private Sub Form_Load()

    Dim i As Integer

    sListDB = sec.GetAllDB(lConnID)

    For i = 0 To UBound(sListDB)
        cboDatabases.AddItem sListDB(i)
    Next

    frmAddUser.cboDatabases.Text = frmDBUser.cboDatabases.Text
    sListLogin = sec.GetLoginList(lConnID)

    For i = 0 To UBound(sListLogin)
        lstLogins.AddItem sListLogin(i)
    Next

End Sub
```

There's nothing here that we haven't already seen in one form or another (with the pun intended) where we've needed to provide lists of logins. The GetAllDB function was used in earlier examples to retrieve a list of databases. We also saw the GetLoginList function, which is used to generate a list of existing login accounts. Two lists are generated, databases and logins, and then added to a drop-down list called cboDatabases (for the databases) and a list box called lstLogins (for the logins). This is to give the application user a way of selecting these two key pieces of information.

When the **Create** button is clicked, we invoke the following:

```
Private Sub cmdAdd_Click()

    Dim sCurrentDB As String
    Dim i As Integer

    sCurrentDB = cboDatabases.Text
    sec.AddUser lConnID, sCurrentDB, txtName.Text, lstLogins.Text
    sListUser = sec.GetDBUsers(lConnID, ByVal sCurrentDB)
    frmDBUser.lstDBUser.Clear

    For i = 0 To UBound(sListUser)
        frmDBUser.lstDBUser.AddItem sListUser(i)
    Next
```

```
      Unload frmAddUser

  End Sub
```

The `cmdAdd_Click` event procedure uses the `AddUser` method of the `SQLDDL.Security` component to create the database user. Afterwards, it refreshes the database user list in the original **Database Users** form and unloads the current form.

> **What's missing here? There is no validation that a login has been selected or that a database user name has been specified. This was left out of the code to keep the examples as simple as possible, allowing us to focus on some key points.**

For each database, you only have **one-to-one mappings** between each login record and a database user. In other words, a login account can only map to one database user name. Each database user name can only have one login account mapping to that database user.

To complete this we need to see what's happening in the `AddUser` method of `SQLDDL.Security`:

```
Public Sub AddUser(ByVal lConnID As Long, ByVal sUDB As String, _
                   ByVal sUName As String, ByVal sULogin As String)

    Dim oSQLServer As SQLDMO.SQLServer
    Dim oDB As SQLDMO.Database
    Dim oNewUser As SQLDMO.User
    Set oSQLServer = oApp.SQLServers.ItemByID(lConnID)
    Set oDB = oSQLServer.Databases(sUDB)
    Set oNewUser = CreateObject("SQLDMO.User")

    oNewUser.Name = sUName
    oNewUser.Login = sULogin
    oDB.Users.Add oNewUser

    Set oSQLServer = Nothing
    Set oDB = Nothing
    Set oNewUser = Nothing

End Sub
```

`AddUser` sets a reference to the connected SQL Server and the selected database. It creates a new `User` object and, since we're passing both the login and user name, sets the `Login` and `Name` properties. The `User` object is then added to the `Users` collection.

Bear in mind that this sample is not a "ready for prime time" application. One of the first things we'd need to do to improve the quality of the application is to use the `EnumDatabaseMappings` method for each `Login` object to generate a list of databases already referencing this login.

The syntax for this is:

```
Query_results = object.EnumDatabaseMappings() as QueryResults
```

This returns a row for each referenced database containing:

❑ The login name

❑ The database to which it is mapped

❑ The database user name

❑ An additional reserved column, not currently used for a value by SQL Server 7.0

When a database is selected from the drop-down list, this information could be used to qualify logins and only display those logins not already referenced by the database.

As we pointed out at the head of the chapter, permissions depend on role membership and we'll now finish off this section on security by looking at the `ServerRole` and `DatabaseRole` hierarchies.

Security Roles

SQL-DMO gives us the ability to manage server roles and database roles, which we discussed at the beginning of this chapter. `ServerRole` objects are fixed; that is, no changes can be made to object properties. Members can, however, be added to and removed from a role. `DatabaseRole` objects include the fixed database roles, but also let us define user-defined database roles.

Many of the procedures for working with `ServerRole` and `DatabaseRole` objects are the same as, or very similar to, those we've already seen for `Login` and `User` objects. Let's take a brief look at them and their use.

ServerRole Hierarchy

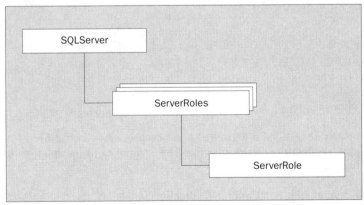

As shown above the `ServerRoles` collection is a member of the `SQLServer` object with the hierarchy containing:

ServerRoles Collection – The `ServerRoles` collection contains all of the fixed server roles. This is a read-only collection so objects can't be added to or removed from it.

ServerRole Object – There is a `ServerRole` object for each fixed server role. Role properties can't be modified, but `Login` objects can be added or removed as members of the role.

ServerRole Object Management

A `ServerRole` object has the following read-only properties:

❑   The `Description` property is a textual description of the role.

❑   The `FullName` property is a "human-friendly" name for the role.

❑   The `Name` property uniquely identifies the role. This can be used to reference the role in the `ServerRoles` collection.

To get a list of logins that are already members of a role, the `EnumServerRoleMember` method is used:

```
Query_results = object.EnumServerRoleMember() as QueryResults
```

The `QueryResults` object returned will contain one column – `mem_col` – containing the role member's `Name` and there will be a row for each role member. We can also use the `Login` object's `ListMembers` method to retrieve `ServerRole` membership information using the syntax:

```
object.ListMembers() as NameList
```

The `NameList` will contain a list of all fixed server roles in which the `Login` object has membership.

> Either **EnumServerRoleMember** or **ListMembers** can be used to verify that a login is not already a member of a specific role before attempting to add the login. They can also be used to verify that the login is a member before attempting to remove it.

The `AddMember` and `DropMember` methods are used to add members to or remove members from a fixed server role with the appropriate syntax being:

```
object.AddMember(user)
object.DropMember(user)
```

The value for `user` must be a valid login name (`Name` property). For either of these methods, the login name used to establish the connection must be a member of the role to which you are attempting to add or drop members.

Let's take a look at an example. Here's a modification to the `AddLogin` method of `SQLDDL.Security` where, after creating the new login account, the login is added to the `sysadmin` (system administrators) security role:

```
Public Sub AddLogin(ByVal lConnID As Long, ByVal sDb As String, _
                    ByVal sPass As String, ByVal sName As String)
```

```
Dim oSQLServer As SQLDMO.SQLServer
Dim oNewLogin As SQLDMO.Login
Dim oServerRole As SQLDMO.ServerRole

Set oSQLServer = oApp.SQLServers.ItemByID(lConnID)
Set oNewLogin = CreateObject("SQLDMO.Login")
Set oServerRole = oSQLServer.ServerRoles("sysadmin")
oNewLogin.Database = sDb
oNewLogin.Type = SQLDMOLogin_Standard
oNewLogin.SetPassword "", sPass
oNewLogin.Name = sName
oSQLServer.Logins.Add oNewLogin
oServerRole.AddMember (sName)

Set oSQLServer = Nothing
Set oNewLogin = Nothing
Set oServerRole = Nothing

End Sub
```

We've added just four lines of code to the earlier example. We declare a ServerRole object variable. We have the variable reference the sysadmin role, and then use its AddMember method to add the login we just created, before finally setting it to Nothing.

DatabaseRole Hierarchy

As the hierarchy shows each DatabaseRoles collection is a member of a specific Database object:

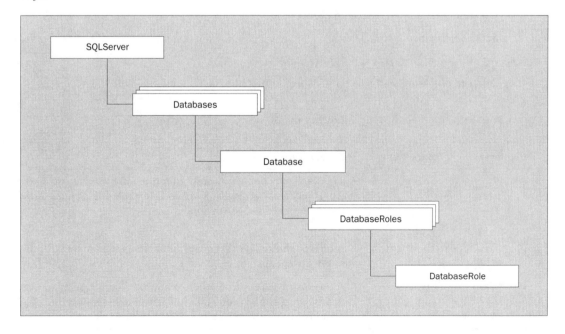

The members of the hierarchy are:

DatabaseRoles Collection – The `DatabaseRoles` collection contains the database's `DatabaseRole` objects. It's slightly different to the `ServerRoles` collection in that it contains both fixed database and user-defined `DatabaseRole` objects. Objects can be added to and removed from the `DatabaseRoles` collection, with the exception of fixed database roles.

DatabaseRole Object – There is a `DatabaseRole` object for each fixed and user-defined database role.

DatabaseRole Management

There are few differences between `DatabaseRole` and `ServerRole` management; the `EnumDatabaseRoleMember` method is used to retrieve a list of role members:

```
Query_results = object.EnumDatabaseRoleMember() as QueryResults
```

As before with the `ServerRoles` collection, the `QueryResults` object will have one column, for database user name, and one row for each member.

`AddMember` and `DropMember` methods are also supported, using exactly the same syntax as for `ServerRoles`.

To round off our coverage of this area we should comment on how to create new `DatabaseRole` objects. The process follows the same pattern as we've previously seen when we've added new objects to a collection in that we need to:

❑   Create a new `DatabaseRole` object

❑   Set the `Name` property

❑   Set additional properties, if applicable

❑   Add the object to the `DatabaseRoles` collection

A `DatabaseRole` object has the following commonly used properties:

Property	Data Type	Description
Name	String	The `Name` property uniquely identifies the user-defined role. An object's name can be used to reference the object in the `DatabaseRoles` collection.
AppRole	Boolean	By default, the `AppRole` property is set to `False`. The property should be given the value `True` when creating an application role.
Password	String	A password is required when the `AppRole` property is `True`. A password is not required (and ignored) when the `AppRole` property is set to `False`.

The `EnumDatabaseRoleMember`, `AddMember`, and `DropMember` methods are all supported for user-defined roles.

What about permissions? Permissions are set after creating the new role and adding it to the `DatabaseRoles` collection. The `Grant`, `Revoke`, and `Deny` methods of the `Database`, `StoredProcedure`, `Table`, and `View` objects are used to manage permission assignments to database roles.

Now let's move on to the second major area addressed in this chapter – backups and restores.

Backup and Restore Overview

Backups are often your first (and possibly only) line of defense when problems occur. One of the keys to proper database management is to run backups on a regular basis and to keep them readily available in case they are needed for recovery. You can manage backups through SQL Server Enterprise Manager or Transact-SQL statements, but you may find situations where it will be more appropriate to use SQL-DMO as at least part of your backup management strategy.

Users who are not that familiar with SQL Server backups and the use of SQL Server Enterprise Manager may find it confusing. Backups are one area where you definitely *do not* want to make any mistakes. You may find it more appropriate to build a simple application, or part of a custom management application, to step users through the backup process with a minimum of interaction. You can provide the user with just those features needed in their specific situation without confusing them with features they won't need. Should a special situation arise requiring those features, SQL Server Enterprise Manager could be used on a case-by-case basis.

So, what does a backup and restore entail?

❑   Firstly, in the backup process we have to define a backup device as a destination, then, to back up the data and store it in the backup device, a `BACKUP` Transact-SQL statement is executed.

❑   If it subsequently becomes necessary to restore the database, the contents of the backup device or devices are used as the source when a `RESTORE` Transact-SQL statement is executed.

SQL Server supports backups to disk, to a locally connected tape drive, and to a named pipe as a way of supporting some available backup devices.

> *A named pipe is required for some third party backup devices. A named pipe is an interprocess communication (IPC) mechanism. Named pipes are commonly used for communications between clients and servers, and provide access to shared network resources. This is an area where you will need to work with the network administrator when setting up for backups if devices of this type are used.*

There are a number of options supported for how backups are run. Over the next few pages we're going to provide a brief overview of those options, however examples in the sample application are going to be limited to full database backups only.

The operations we're looking at now are accessed via the Backup menu of the Survey Designer dialog and will generally involve calling the SQLDDL.BackupDB component:

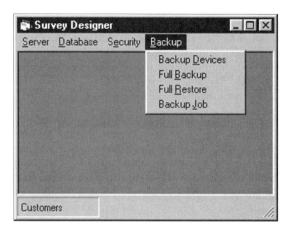

Backup Methods

SQL Server supports four basic backup methods (often, a combination of backup methods is used to optimize backup and restore):

❑ Full backup

❑ Differential backup

❑ File and filegroup backup

❑ Transaction log backup

Let's gain an appreciation of each of these methods in turn:

Full Backup – The entire database is backed up, including any changes in the transaction log occurring after the backup is started.

When we restore, the full database is restored to the point when the backup was run. This can become a very lengthy process as databases expand.

Differential Backup – Only data changes – pages that have changed since the last full backup – are backed up. Since you aren't backing up as much data, the backup doesn't take as long to complete. This is one of the main reasons for using differential backups. A full backup of a large database can take a long time, too long to run backups regularly (more than once a week). By using differential backups, the time to backup is reduced, but will increase with each successive backup. This is because as more changes are made to the database, there are more changes to be backed up.

When restoring, we restore from the most recent full database backup, the most recent differential backup, and then apply transaction log backups, if any. Each differential backup backs up all changes made since the last full backup, so it is only necessary to restore the most recent differential backup.

File and Filegroup Backup – Individual data files and filegroups can be backed up. This gives us an easy method for breaking up the backup process to run over a period of time. When backing up a file or filegroup, we also need to back up the transaction log.

When restoring, restore the file or filegroup and any transaction log backups run since the file or filegroup was backed up.

> *A filegroup is one or more database files, referenced by the filegroup name. You can specify the destination filegroup when adding new database objects. By placing filegroups on different physical hard drives, you can balance the data between the physical drives to give you additional space and to improve database performance.*

Transaction Log Backup – The transaction log is backed up and the inactive portion of the log is truncated. Transaction log backups can also be run just to truncate the log. Transaction log backups give us a quick way of running backups during the day. When restoring, transaction logs must be restored in order.

About Transaction Logs

The **transaction log** is an integral part of SQL Server. Except for a few exceptions (known as **non-logged operations**), any time a statement is executed that modifies a database, the modification is written to the transaction log. This includes the INSERT, UPDATE, and DELETE SQL statements. When a data modification statement is executed, the change is made to data pages stored in memory and is written to the transaction log. Only after the affected data pages are in memory and the log pages are written to disk is the change actually written to the database.

Should a system failure occur, SQL Server will go into an automatic recovery procedure when you restart. SQL Server uses the information stored in the transaction log to return the database to a stable state. Completed transactions in the transaction log will be rolled forward (modifications are written to the database) and uncompleted transactions are rolled back (not written to the database).

Obviously, as you are posting to the database, the transaction log will increase in size. When you backup the transaction log, it will **truncate** (delete) the inactive portion of the transaction log. The transaction log is truncated so that everything occurring before the oldest uncompleted transaction is deleted.

If the Truncate log on checkpoint option of the database is True, transaction log backups can't be used. This is because the information needed to apply changes to the database and retain data consistency is not there. The Truncate log on checkpoint option causes the inactive portion of the transaction log to be truncated each time a **checkpoint** is issued. A checkpoint is a periodic operation, which forces all pages that have changed for the current database to be written to the disk.

Backup Management

To run backups, you need one or more `BackupDevice` objects. You can then use a `Backup` object to define and execute a backup operation. The number of `BackupDevice` objects you need depends on how you are managing the backups and the capacity of each of the objects. You may want each backup in your weekly schedule to be written to a different `BackupDevice` object, or you might organize them by type, one for full backups, one for differential backups, and one for transaction log backups. You may find it necessary to run a full backup to multiple objects because you don't have any single `BackupDevice` object with sufficient capacity.

Backup Device Hierarchy

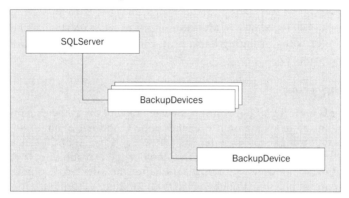

Once again, we have a simple object hierarchy to consider:

BackupDevices Collection – The `BackupDevices` collection contains the `BackupDevice` objects for backup devices on SQL Server. We can add members to or remove members from this collection.

BackupDevice Objects – Each `BackupDevice` object represents a server backup file and gives us access to its properties.

> **The terms "backup device" and "backup file" can be used interchangeably. Both appear at times in Microsoft documentation. Both refer to the physical file used to hold one or more database or transaction log backups.**

Managing Backup Devices in the Surveys Unlimited Solution

Selecting Backup | Backup Devices reveals the **Backup Devices** dialog (frmBackDev in the SurveyDesigner project):

We're on pretty familiar territory when it comes to looking at the code for generating a list of backup devices and the code for removing a backup device. We declare a module-level array to receive the list of existing devices:

```
Private sListBDev() As String
```

The Form_Load event procedure displays the device list in a list box:

```
Private Sub Form_Load()

    Dim i As Integer

    sListBDev = bk.GetDev(lConnID)
    For i = 0 To UBound(sListBDev)
       lstDev.AddItem sListBDev(i)
    Next

End Sub
```

The bk object variable is declared in the modGlobals standard module:

```
Public bk As New SQLDDL.BackupDB
```

The list is generated by the GetDev method of the SQLDDL.BackupDB component:

```
Public Function GetDev(lConnID As Long) As String()

    Dim i As Integer
    Dim iCount As Integer
    Dim oSQLServer As SQLDMO.SQLServer
    Dim sSysDev() As String
```

```
    Set oSQLServer = oApp.SQLServers.ItemByID(lConnID)

    'For the special case where there are no BackupDevices,
    'create an array with a single empty string
    If oSQLServer.BackupDevices.Count = 0 Then
        ReDim sSysDev(0 To 0)
        sSysDev(0) = ""
        GetDev = sSysDev
        Exit Function
    End If

    ReDim sSysDev(0 To oSQLServer.BackupDevices.Count - 1)

    For i = 1 To oSQLServer.BackupDevices.Count
        sSysDev(iCount) = oSQLServer.BackupDevices(i).Name
        iCount = iCount + 1
    Next

    GetDev = sSysDev

    Set oSQLServer = Nothing

End Function
```

Since this is a collection of server devices, it is only necessary to pass the server connection ID to generate the list.

When we remove a backup device, the client application calls the DeleteDev method of the SQLDDL.Backup component as part of the method called on clicking the **Delete** button. After removing the device, the device list is updated:

```
Private Sub cmdDel_Click()

  Dim i As Integer

    bk.DeleteDev lConnID, lstDev.Text
    lstDev.Clear
    sListBDev = bk.GetDev(lConnID)

    For i = 0 To UBound(sListBDev)
        lstDev.AddItem sListBDev(i)
    Next

End Sub
```

The DeleteDev method removes a BackupDevice from the BackupDevices collection using its Remove method:

```
Public Sub DeleteDev(ByVal lConnID As Long, ByVal sDelName As String)

    Dim oSQLServer As SQLDMO.SQLServer
    Set oSQLServer = oApp.SQLServers.ItemByID(lConnID)
    oSQLServer.BackupDevices.Remove (sDelName)
    Set oSQLServer = Nothing

End Sub
```

As was done in previous examples, the `Name` property of the `BackupDevice` is used to reference the device in the `BackupDevices` Collection.

Adding Backup Devices

Once again, the steps for adding backup devices consist of the usual suspects:

- ❏ Create a `BackupDevice` object
- ❏ Set the `Name` property to a unique, recognizable name
- ❏ Set other properties as necessary
- ❏ Add the `BackupDevice` object to the `BackupDevices` collection

The most commonly used `BackupDevice` object properties are:

Property	Data Type	Description
Name	String	This is a unique name identifying the object.
PhysicalLocation	String	The physical location specifies the physical device. For a disk type object, it will be a drive or Universal Naming Convention (UNC) path and filename. For a tape, it will be a local tape drive (local to the server). For a pipe, it will be the pipe name.
SkipTapeLabel	Boolean	This property name can be a little misleading. If True, the backup header describing the backup is ignored when running backup. If False, the default value, headers are read and information such as expiration date is honored.
Type	Enumerated long	This is the device type. A device can be a disk file, floppy disk, tape, or pipe.

Additionally, the object has a `SystemObject` property that is set to `True` for any backup device created during installation. There are also the `DeviceNumber` and `Status` properties, which provide backwards compatibility with older SQL-DMO versions.

Creating a Backup Device in the Surveys Unlimited Scenario

When you attempt to create a backup device the `cmdAdd_Click()` code of the `frmBackDev` is called:

```
Private Sub cmdAdd_Click()

    Dim lGoOn As Long
    lGoOn = MsgBox("This selection creates disk backup devices. Continue?", _
                vbYesNo)

    If lGoOn = vbYes Then
        frmAddDev.Show
    Else
        Exit Sub
    End If

End Sub
```

After receiving, and acknowledging, the warning that this part of the application can only create disk-type backup devices, the user will be taken to the **Add Backup Device** form (`frmAddDev`):

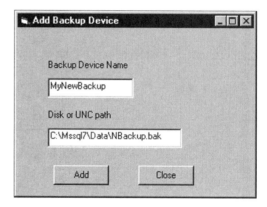

In the `frmAddDev` form, the user enters a name for the device and a disk or UNC path to the device. Notice that the backup device must have an extension of `.bak`.

The `frmAddDev` form has a module-level string array, which holds the list of existing devices:

```
Private sListBDev() As String
```

The backup device name and, since this is creating a disk backup, the destination path must be supplied. The `cmdAdd_Click` event procedure begins by making two quick checks that everything is provided as required:

```
Private Sub cmdAdd_Click()

    Dim i As Integer

    If txtName.Text = "" Then
        MsgBox "Enter Device Name", vbOKOnly
        Exit Sub
    End If
```

```
    If txtPath.Text = "" Then
        MsgBox "Enter Device Path", vbOKOnly
        Exit Sub
    End If

    bk.MakeDev lConnID, txtPath.Text, txtName.Text
    frmBackDev.lstDev.Clear
    sListBDev = bk.GetDev(lConnID)

    For i = 0 To UBound(sListBDev)
        frmBackDev.lstDev.AddItem sListBDev(i)
    Next

    Unload frmAddDev

End Sub
```

The `SQLDDL.BackupDB` component's `MakeDev` method is used to create the device. Afterwards, the device list in `frmBackDev` is updated:

```
Public Sub MakeDev(ByVal lConnID As Long, ByVal sDevLoc As String, _
                   ByVal sDevName As String)

    Dim oSQLServer As SQLDMO.SQLServer
    Dim oNewDev As SQLDMO.BackupDevice

    Set oSQLServer = oApp.SQLServers.ItemByID(lConnID)
    Set oNewDev = CreateObject("SQLDMO.BackupDevice")

    oNewDev.Name = sDevName
    oNewDev.PhysicalLocation = sDevLoc
    oNewDev.Type = SQLDMODevice_DiskDump

    oSQLServer.BackupDevices.Add oNewDev

    Set oSQLServer = Nothing
    Set oNewDev = Nothing

End Sub
```

The `MakeDev` method gets a reference to the connected `SQLServer` object and creates a new `BackupDevice` object. Values are set for the `Name`, `PhysicalLocation`, and `Type` properties. The `BackupDevice` is then added to the `BackupDevices` collection. Since a value was not specified for `SkipTapeHeader`, it will be at its default value.

> This is another example where the sample application is not ready for release to end-users. It would be preferable to display available path information and pre-load a backup filename rather than prompting the user for this information. In addition, SQL Server does not verify the physical device until it is used to run a backup. If you don't provide a list of available directories, you would at least want to verify that a specified path exists.

Now we've seen how to create a backup device let's now see how to use it.

Running Backups

If you've used the Transact-SQL BACKUP statement or run backups through SQL Server Enterprise Manager, you should have no problem working with the Backup object. The difference is that, instead of specifying BACKUP options on the command line, the options are specified through object properties. Even if you haven't run a backup before, the Backup object isn't that difficult to use. For most backups, you only need to provide some basic information – the database you are backing up, the type of backup you are running, and the backup destination device.

The Backup object is a member of the SQL-DMO Application object. Up to now, we've been working with objects that have as a root parent the SQLServer object. Here are the steps to run a backup using the Backup object:

- ❑ Create a new Backup object

- ❑ Set the Database property (for full, differential, and transaction log backups) or DatabaseFiles or DatabaseFileGroups property (for file and filegroup backups)

- ❑ Set the Action property (not required for full or filegroup backups)

- ❑ Identify the destination by setting the appropriate media property

- ❑ Set properties for backup options as desired

- ❑ Call the SQLBackup method to run the backup

There are properties representing all of the BACKUP statement options (22 in all), however we're just going to look at a few that relate to the sample application:

Property	Data Type	Description
Database	String	This is the name of the source database that you want to back up. *A database name must be provided.*
Action	Enumerated long	If a value for Action isn't provided, a full backup is assumed. The Action property lets you specify a full, differential (incremental), file, or transaction log backup.
Devices	SQL-DMO multistring	This is where the destination device or devices is specified.
Initialize	Boolean	If Initialize is False (the default value) the backup is appended to the backups already on the device. If True, existing backup sets are overwritten.

Our sample application is written to run just one type of backup – a full backup to a disk type backup device. The `Action` values for specifying the backup type are:

Constant	Value	Backup Type
SQLDMOBackup_Database	0	This is the default value, specifying that the backup should run as a full backup.
SQLDMOBackup_Differential	1	This value specifies that you want to run a differential backup, backing up only the changes since the last full backup.
SQLDOMBackup_Files	2	Use this option to back up specified files or filegroups.
SQLDMOBackup_Log	3	This value is used to specify a transaction log backup.

Other properties let you specify tape, named pipe, or temporary backup file destinations, as well as set all of the BACKUP statement options, such as the backup expiration date.

The SQLBackup method is called when the backup is to be run:

```
object.SQLBackup (SQLServer)
```

A connection to the SQLServer object used as the backup source must be present.

Running a Backup in the Surveys Unlimited Scenario

Selecting Backup | Full Backup reveals the Full Backup dialog (frmBackup in the SurveyDesigner project):

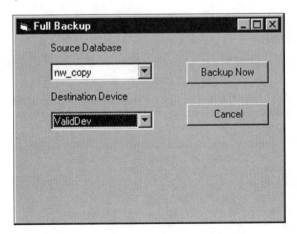

This form has two module-level string arrays:

```
Private sListDB() As String
Private sListDev() As String
```

The `sListDB` array holds the existing databases and `sListDev` holds the existing backup devices.

Since the sample application is running a full backup to an existing backup device, the only things it needs are the database name and the backup device name which are provided to the user through drop-down lists populated by the `Form_Load` event:

```
Private Sub Form_Load()

    Dim i As Integer

    sListDB = sec.GetAllDB(lConnID)
    sListDev = bk.GetDev(lConnID)

    For i = 0 To UBound(sListDB)
        cboDatabase.AddItem sListDB(i)
    Next

    For i = 0 To UBound(sListDev)
        cboBackDev.AddItem sListDev(i)
    Next

End Sub
```

The `GetAllDB` method from the `SQLDDL.Security` component and the `GetDev` method from the `SQLDDL.BackupDB` component have been presented earlier, so let's just look at the code that runs when the user clicks on the **Backup Now** button:

```
Private Sub cmdBack_Click()

    If cboDatabase.Text = "" Or cboBackDev.Text = "" Then
        MsgBox "Select a database and backup device"
        Exit Sub
    End If

    bk.RunBack lConnID, cboDatabase.Text, cboBackDev.Text

End Sub
```

The application verifies that a database and backup device have been selected before calling the `SQLDDL.BackupDB` component's `RunBack` method to back up the database:

```
Public Sub RunBack(ByVal lConnID As Long, ByVal sBDB As String, _
                    ByVal sBDev As String)

    Dim oSQLServer As SQLDMO.SQLServer

    Set oSQLServer = oApp.SQLServers.ItemByID(lConnID)
    Set oBackup = CreateObject("SQLDMO.Backup")

    oBackup.Initialize = True
    oBackup.Database = sBDB
    oBackup.Devices = "[" & sBDev & "]"
```

```
        oBackup.SQLBackup oSQLServer

        Set oBackup = Nothing
        Set oSQLServer = Nothing

    End Sub
```

RunBack creates a backup object, sets its properties, and then calls the SQLBackup method to run the backup. Since a full backup is being run, there is no need to specify a value for the Action property.

> **For the sake of simplicity when demonstrating restore operations, the Initialize property is set to True by the sample application. For a live application, you would probably be running different types of backups to different devices. Thus, you would want to either give the user more access to backup options, or have preset option selections from which the user could choose.**

The oBackup object is not defined as part of the method. Instead, it is part of the general declarations for the BackupDB component. It is declared using the WithEvents keyword:

```
    Private WithEvents oBackup As Backup
```

This lets us, and actually requires us, to set up event procedures for backup events as we discuss below.

Backup Events in the SQLDDL.Backup Component

There are three Backup object events – Complete, NextMedia, and PercentComplete. The Complete event is the only one we're really using for anything in the application:

```
    Private Sub oBackup_Complete(ByVal Message As String)
        MsgBox"Backup Complete"
    End Sub
```

The Complete event occurs when the backup has successfully completed and we generate a message to let the user know this.

A NextMedia event occurs when the media fills up. You would use this event with tape backups if there is a possibility you will need to change the tape before the backup was finished. If the NextMedia event won't occur during your backup, you can omit this procedure (for example, if you are only backing up to a disk file, then the NextMedia event doesn't have any meaning to you):

```
    Private Sub oBackup_NextMedia(ByVal Message As String)
        Exit Sub
    End Sub
```

The `PercentComplete` event occurs each time the percent value is reached, defaulting to ten percent. The percent value at which notification occurs is set through the `PercentCompleteNotification` property. This event could be used to update the user about backup progress on lengthy backups. For the sample application, we're just exiting the procedure:

```
Private Sub oBackup_PercentComplete(ByVal Message As String, _
                                    ByVal Percent As Long)
    Exit Sub
End Sub
```

So we've now learnt how to back our database up, let's now see how to restore it.

Running Restores

The `Restore` object follows the same pattern as the `Backup` object. It is a member of the SQL-DMO `Application` object rather than the `SQLServer` object, and defines how a restore is run. Restore options are set by specifying property values. The steps for running a restore using the `Restore` object are:

- ❑ Create a `Restore` object
- ❑ Set the `Database` property to identify the destination database, or the `DatabaseFiles` or `DatabaseFileGroups` for a destination file or filegroup
- ❑ Set the appropriate media property to identify the source media
- ❑ Set the `Action` property, if necessary, to specify the restore method
- ❑ Set other properties for restore options as necessary
- ❑ Call the `SQLRestore` method

As with `BACKUP`, `RESTORE` options are set through the `Restore` object's property values. We're going to limit ourselves to properties relating to the sample application only:

Property	Data Type	Description
Database	String	This is the name of the target database. *A database name must be provided to run a restore.* If the database name is omitted, SQL Server will verify the backup instead of restoring data.
Action	Enumerated long	Here the options are to restore the database, restore only the indicated files, or restore the database transaction log. The default is to restore the database, which is used to restore full or differential backups.
Devices	String	This is where the destination device or devices is specified.

Our sample application can only run a full restore from a disk type backup containing a single full backup. The values supported by the `Action` property that allow us to specify a different restore type are:

Constant	Value	Backup Type
SQLDMORestore_Database	0	This is the default value and will restore a full database backup or differential backup.
SQLDOMRestore_Files	1	Use this option to restore specified files or filegroups.
SQLDMORestore_Log	2	This value is used to restore from a transaction log backup.

Other properties let us choose a backup from a set, specify different device types, restore to a different location, restore to a point in time, and so on.

After setting the `Restore` properties, the restore is run by calling the `SQLRestore` method:

```
object.SQLRestore (SQLServer)
```

A connection to the SQL Server to which the restoration is being carried out must be present. If the database does not already exist on the server to which the restoration is taking place the `ReplaceDatabase` property must be set to `True` to create a new image of the database. By default, `ReplaceDatabase` is `False`.

Restoring a Database in the Surveys Unlimited Scenario

Clicking <u>B</u>ackup | Full <u>R</u>estore brings up the Full Database Restore dialog (`frmRestore` form):

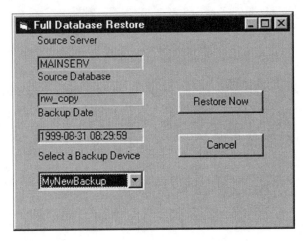

This form has a module-level string array, which holds a list of the existing devices:

```
Private sListDev() As String
```

When you first load this form, the `Form_Load` procedure populates the Select a Backup Device drop-down box with a list of server backup devices:

```
Private Sub Form_Load()

    Dim i As Integer

    sListDev = bk.GetDev(lConnID)

    For i = 0 To UBound(sListDev)
        cboRestDev.AddItem sListDev(i)
    Next

    cmdRestore.Enabled = False

End Sub
```

Note that we're using the `GetDev` method again, the same one that we first encountered when listing backup devices in the Backup Devices dialog.

The user selects a backup source from the `cboRestDev` drop-down list:

```
Private Sub cboRestDev_Click()

    Set oQr = bk.GetHeader(lConnID, cboRestDev.Text)

    If oQr.Rows <> 1 Then
        MsgBox "Wrong device. Select different device."
    End If

    lblServer.Caption = oQr.GetColumnString(1, 9)
    lblDatabase.Caption = oQr.GetColumnString(1, 10)
    lblDate.Caption = oQr.GetColumnString(1, 18)
    cmdRestore.Enabled = True

End Sub
```

We introduced the use of `QueryResults` objects in Chapter 3 and here we make use of one to retrieve backup device header information. This is done by calling the `SQLDDL.BackupDB` component's `GetHeader` method. The backup header describes the backup with information such as the backup name, server and database backed up, and backup date.

Since we are only looking for backup devices containing a single backup, we check the number of rows in the returned object. There is one header row for each backup in the backup set, so if the row count is more than one, we can't use the backup. Once the backup device is verified as having a single backup, the `QueryResults` object's `GetColumnString` method is used to retrieve the source server, database, and backup date. The source database will be used as the target database value for the restore.

The backup will have header information for each backup on the device. If we were preparing to restore from a backup set with multiple backups, we would also want to get position information and display header information in a table.

The `SQLDDL.BackupDB` component's `GetHeader` method is as follows:

```
Public Function GetHeader(ByVal lConnID As Long, ByVal sBkDev As String) _
                    As QueryResults

    Dim oSQLServer As SQLDMO.SQLServer
    Dim oBackDev As SQLDMO.BackupDevice
    Dim oQR As SQLDMO.QueryResults

    Set oSQLServer = oApp.SQLServers.ItemByID(lConnID)
    Set oBackDev = oSQLServer.BackupDevices(sBkDev)
    Set oQR = oBackDev.ReadBackupHeader
    Set GetHeader = oQR

    Set oQR = Nothing
    Set oBackDev = Nothing
    Set oSQLServer = Nothing

End Function
```

`GetHeader` gets a reference to the connected server, then uses the `BackupDevices` collection to get a reference to the specific backup device. The `BackupDevice` object's `ReadBackupHeader` method is called to retrieve the header information.

After making a selection, we can run the `Restore` operation (via the **Restore Now** button):

```
Private Sub cmdRestore_Click()
    bk.RunRest lConnID, lblDatabase.Caption, cboRestDev.Text
End Sub
```

The `cmdRestore_Click` event procedure calls the `BackupDB` component's `RunRest` method and passes the server connection ID, database name, and backup device name:

```
Public Sub RunRest(ByVal lConnID As Long, ByVal sBDB As String, _
                ByVal sBDev As String)

    Dim oSQLServer As SQLDMO.SQLServer

    Set oSQLServer = oApp.SQLServers.ItemByID(lConnID)
    Set oRestore = CreateObject("SQLDMO.Restore")

    oRestore.Database = sBDB
    oRestore.Devices = "[" & sBDev & "]"
    oRestore.SQLRestore oSQLServer

    Set oRestore = Nothing
    Set oSQLServer = Nothing

End Sub
```

The code sample is analogous to the `RunBack` method used for running backups; a `Restore` object is created, the target database and source device identified and the `SQLRestore` method is called to run the restore.

Restore Events

Again, reflecting the coding used for backing up, the `oRestore` object is declared as a general declaration in the `SQLDDL.Backup` component with the `WithEvents` keyword to allow us to use `Restore` events:

```
Private WithEvents oRestore As Restore
```

The same events are supported for `Restore` objects as for `Backup` objects – `Complete`, `NextMedia`, and `PercentComplete`. We are still only using the `Complete` event to accomplish anything (when `PercentComplete` events occur, and should a `NextMedia` event occur, we simply exit the procedure):

```
Private Sub oRestore_Complete(ByVal Message As String)
    MsgBox "Restore Complete"
End Sub

Private Sub oRestore_NextMedia(ByVal Message As String)
    Exit Sub
End Sub

Private Sub oRestore_PercentComplete(ByVal Message As String, _
                                     ByVal Percent As Long)
    Exit Sub
End Sub
```

> An excellent use of the **PercentComplete** event would be to display a progress bar to provide the user with information about how far along the restore process is.

We'll now change our attention to look at how to automate backup procedures, but before we talk about jobs, our real focus in this next section, we need to talk just a little about SQL Server Agent and its associated objects.

SQL Server Agent Overview

The **SQL Server Agent** (prior to SQL Server 7.0 it was called the **SQL Executive**) is responsible for a number of activities, including:

❑   Executing scheduled jobs

❑   Notifying operators of errors or other conditions

❑   Responding to alert conditions

The SQL Server Agent gives you a way of automating SQL Server management activities. Let's begin by defining what a job is.

Jobs

Jobs are used to automate management tasks. A job typically includes:

- ❏   The steps to be performed by the job
- ❏   A schedule defining when the job should execute

Jobs are typically used to define activities that occur on a set schedule. You can also define jobs and use them to respond to alerts. Jobs can be created to execute on the local server or on multiple servers.

A job is comprised of one or more **steps**, which are the actions to be performed by the job. You define the action performed by each job step and the order in which the job steps execute. You can also define **precedence constraints**, which are actions to be taken on completion or failure of a job step. Job steps can include Transact-SQL statements, operating system executable commands, and scripts written in VBScript or JavaScript.

Transact-SQL statement steps let you execute statements, stored procedures, and extended stored procedures. Any required variables or statement parameters must be included with the statement as part of the job step definition. Unless otherwise specified, the job step runs in the job owner's security context.

Operating system commands are executed as **CmdExec job steps**, and can include commands and batches ending with `.com`, `.exe`, `.bat`, or `.cmd` extensions. The full path and filename of the executable (including extension) must be specified. If the job owner is a system administrator or database owner, the command will execute in the job owner's security context. Otherwise, the job will execute in the context of a user named `SQLAgentCmdExec`. This Windows NT user is created automatically during SQL Server 7.0 installation.

You can also have a job step execute a VBScript or JavaScript. You are required to identify the scripting language in which the script is written. You can then either write the script into the job step or open the script file for execution. The script will execute in the job owner's security context.

One common use of jobs is to automate backup procedures. You could define one job to run full backups and schedule it to execute weekly. You could define a second job to run differential backups and schedule that job for daily execution. If you wanted, you could take this a step further and define a job to run transaction log backups based on a schedule you specify.

JobServer and Jobs

We are going to focus on one specific area of automation, creating jobs. To do this, we also need to take a look at the `JobServer` object, which controls scheduled execution.

Only a small portion of the `JobServer` hierarchy is shown below. The full hierarchy (covered in Appendix D) also includes additional job-related collections and objects, as well as collections and objects for managing operators, alerts, and target servers:

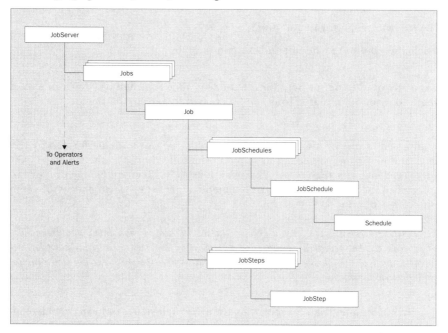

Let's quickly outline what is contained within this part of the hierarchy:

JobServer Object – The `JobServer` object is documented as a member of the SQL-DMO `Application` object. However, it is used as member of the `SQLServer` object. The `JobServer` object lets you start and stop the SQL Server Agent, as well as manage jobs, alerts, and operators.

Jobs Collection – The `Jobs` collection contains all of the `Job` objects, which are references to the jobs that have been defined on the connected server.

Job Object – Each `Job` object represents a specific SQL Server job.

JobSchedules Collection – The `JobSchedules` collection has `JobSchedule` objects as its members.

JobSchedule Object – Each `JobSchedule` object contains the definition for a job execution schedule.

Schedule Object – The `Schedule` object contains the timetable controlling the job execution schedule.

JobSteps Collection – The `JobSteps` collection contains the executable job steps. Multiple steps may be defined, along with the order in which the steps are executed.

JobStep Object – Each executable step in a job is represented by a `JobStep` object. Job steps are executed in a specific order.

Now that we've got a feeling for the objects we're going to be dealing with, let's see how we can use them in our business solution.

Job Creation in the Surveys Unlimited Scenario

The sample application creates a very specific, simple job, which will run a weekly database backup. Much of the information about the job is predefined for the user through text strings in the code.

Before looking at the actual implementation, we need to spend some time talking a little about the process for creating jobs, as well as the properties of the Job, JobSchedule, and JobStep objects.

> *During this discussion, we'll be looking at code snippets from the MakeJob method of the SQLDDL.Management component, and then at the end of the section we'll present the full creation method we've designed.*

Creating a Job

The basic steps for creating a Job object are straightforward:

- ❏ Create a Job object
- ❏ Set the Name property
- ❏ Set other properties as appropriate
- ❏ Add the Job to the Jobs collection

Job objects have over 30 different properties (see Appendix D), most dealing with job status, schedule status, and operator alerts. We're only going to be using the following two properties to create our job:

Property	Data Type	Description
Name	String	Each job must be given a unique name.
Category	String	The Category property is used for grouping jobs into types, such as database management jobs. The JobCategories collection, which is a member of JobServer, contains a list of valid Category objects.

The oJob and oJobServer objects are defined elsewhere in the procedure but the code fragments relevant to Job object creation are:

```
Set oJob = CreateObject("SQLDMO.Job")

oJob.Name = sJobName
oJob.Category = "Database Maintenance"
oJobServer.Jobs.Add oJob
```

After creating oJob and setting the Name and Category properties, it is added to the Jobs collection. At this point, if we were to list all of the Jobs in the collection, we would see our job there. However, the job would never do anything because we haven't defined executable steps, nor have we set an execution schedule.

> It doesn't matter whether you define job steps or the job schedule first after creating a new job. The important thing is that these are added to the job at some point. You can go back, if necessary, and make changes to the steps or schedule at any time.

Creating Job Steps

We can define what a job is going to do by creating a series of job steps; the process for this is:

❑ Create a `JobStep` object

❑ Set the `Name` property to give each step a unique name

❑ Set the `StepID` property to set execution order

❑ Set the `Command` property

❑ Set other properties as appropriate

❑ Add the `JobStep` to the `JobSteps` collection

If you needed to define additional job steps, this process would be repeated for each step. Let's take a look at four of the `JobStep` properties that are particularly appropriate to our application:

Property	Data Type	Description
Name	String	Each job step must be given a unique name.
StepID	Long	Execution order is set by the `StepID` value.
Command	String	This is an executable string to be run when the step is executed, the exact contents of which will depend on the type of job step you are creating. It will contain a Transact-SQL statement, an operating system command, or script, as appropriate.
DatabaseName	String	If the job should execute in a specific database and the database is not identified in the `Command` string, you can specify a database using this property.

Additional properties let you further define the job step, such as including additional parameters for execution, and checking job status. The following code fragments define our `JobStep` object:

```
Set oJobStep = CreateObject("SQLDMO.JobStep")

oJobStep.Name = "Backup Step"
oJobStep.StepID = 1
oJobStep.Command = "BACKUP DATABASE " & sJobDB & _
                   " TO " & sJobDev & " WITH INIT"
oJob.JobSteps.Add oJobStep
oJob.ApplyToTargetServer (oSQLServer.NetName)
```

The sample application is creating a job with a single step, which runs a full database backup. Since only one step is being defined, constant values can be used for the Name and StepID properties.

As we will see later in the full code example, sJobDB is the database we want to backup and sJobDev is the backup device to which the backup will be written. For example, if you were backing up the Northwind database to a backup device named NorthFull, the statement would evaluate as:

```
BACKUP DATABASE Northwind TO NorthFull WITH INIT
```

This could be any executable Transact-SQL statement as long as all of the necessary statement parameters are included.

As the final step in this code fragment, we are calling the ApplyToTargetServer method of the Job object. This identifies the server on which we want the job to execute. We're setting this to the network name of the server for which we've defined a connection. To run the job on the local server, use the local server name or the string "(local)".

Creating a Job Schedule

Multiple schedules can be defined for a job, thereby having it run at different times. To define one schedule, follow these steps:

- ❏ Create a JobSchedule object
- ❏ Set the Name property to identify the JobSchedule
- ❏ Get the Schedule object from the JobSchedule object
- ❏ Set Schedule properties as appropriate
- ❏ Add the JobSchedule object to the JobSchedules collection

We could modify these steps by adding the JobSchedule object to the JobSchedules collection, then using the JobSchedule object's BeginAlter and DoAlter methods to modify Schedule object properties.

> **BeginAlter and DoAlter** can be used at any time to modify a **Schedule** object.

Here we're only going to be concerned with two of JobSchedule properties; the Name property gives the JobSchedule its unique name and the Enabled property (set to True by default) enables the schedule to be used.

The `Schedule` object has fifteen properties; again, we are only concerned with a few of them for scheduling recurring execution within our sample:

Property	Data Type	Description
ActiveStartDate	Long	This is the first effective date for the schedule. The format is *yyyymmdd*: four digits for the year, two for month, and two for day.
ActiveEndDate	Long	This is the last effective date for the schedule. The format is again *yyyymmdd*.
ActiveStartTimeOfDay	Long	This sets when execution should begin. The format for this is a long integer value created as the sum of the hour in 24-hour notation scaled by 10000, the minutes scaled by 100, and the seconds. For 2:10:15 PM, you would have 141015.
ActiveEndTimeOfDay	Long	This sets a time by which the job must run. The format for this is a long integer value created as the sum of the hour in 24-hour notation scaled by 10000, the minutes scaled by 100, and the seconds. For 10:09:03 AM, you would have 100903.
FrequencyType	Enumerated long	The schedule frequency, such as daily, weekly, monthly, and so on, can be specified. Some settings require additional properties to be set. For example, a weekly frequency requires a day of the week to be specified in the `FrequencyInterval` property.
FrequencyInterval	Long	The `FrequencyInterval` property sets additional information for daily, weekly, and monthly schedules, such as setting the day of the week or a date during the month.
FrequencyRecurrenceFactor	Long	This property works with the `FrequencyType` property to help define the recurrence. For example, `FrequencyType` could be set to weekly, and then `FrequencyRecurrenceFactor` could be set to 2 so that the job is scheduled to be executed every other week.

The following values are supported for the FrequencyType property:

Constant	Value	FrequencyInterval Value
SQLDMOFreq_Unknown	0	Either the schedule has no set frequency or the frequency set cannot be applied.
SQLDMOFreq_OneTime	1	The scheduled job occurs once, at the time specified.
SQLDMOFreq_Daily	4	The FrequencyInterval will be set to a long integer value for the number of days. A value of 2 would have the job execute every other day. A value of 4 would have the job run every fourth day. Use a value of 1 to have the job run every day.
SQLDMOFreq_Weekly	8	This will be a bit-packed long integer value describing the days on which the job should execute. The values for use as the FrequencyInterval are listed in the next table.
SQLDMOFreq_Monthly	16	Set the FrequencyInterval to a long integer value representing the day of the month on which you want the job to execute. For example, a value of 15 would have the job execute on the 15th of every month.
SQLDMOFreq_MonthlyRelative	32	Set the FrequencyInterval to a long integer value setting the day of week or indication of a day. Supported values are listed in the second table following.
SQLDMOFreq_Autostart	64	The scheduled job begins when SQL Server Agent starts.
SQLDMOFreq_OnIdle	128	The job will run when the SQL Server Agent is idle.
SQLDMOFreq_Valid	255	Use this to test if the schedule frequency is valid.

If you use the `SQLDMOFreq_Weekly` as your value for `FrequencyType`, you also need to know how to specify days. The values are as follows:

Constant	Value	Days
SQLDMOWeek_EveryDay	127	The job will run every day.
SQLDMOWeek_Sunday	1	Run the job on Sundays.
SQLDMOWeek_Monday	2	Run the job on Mondays.
SQLDMOWeek_Tuesday	4	Run the job on Tuesdays.
SQLDMOWeek_Wednesday	8	Run the job on Wednesdays.
SQLDMOWeek_Thursday	16	Run the job on Thursdays.
SQLDMOWeek_Friday	32	Run the job on Fridays.
SQLDMOWeek_Saturday	64	Run the job on Saturdays.
SQLDMOWeek_WeekDays	62	Run the job on Monday, Tuesday, Wednesday, Thursday, and Friday.
SQLDMOWeek_WeekEnds	65	Run the job on Saturday and Sunday.
SQLDMOWeek_Unknown	0	No day specified.

If you use `SQLDMOFreq_MonthlyRelative` as your value for `FrequencyType`, you can specify the `FrequencyInterval` as:

Constant	Value	Schedule
SQLDMOMonth_Day	8	Execution is scheduled for an occurrence of a day (e.g. the third day of the month).
SQLDMOMonth_Sunday	1	Execution is scheduled for a Sunday.
SQLDMOMonth_Monday	2	Execution is scheduled for a Monday.
SQLDMOMonth_Tuesday	3	Execution is scheduled for a Tuesday.
SQLDMOMonth_Wednesday	4	Execution is scheduled for a Wednesday.
SQLDMOMonth_Thursday	5	Execution is scheduled for a Thursday.
SQLDMOMonth_Friday	6	Execution is scheduled for a Friday.
SQLDMOMonth_Saturday	7	Execution is scheduled for a Saturday.
SQLDMOMonth_WeekDay	9	Execution is scheduled for Monday through Friday.
SQLDMOMonth_WeekEndDay	10	Execution is scheduled for to occur over a weekend.
SQLDMOMonth_MinValid	1	As SQL_DMOMonth_Sunday.
SQLDMOMonth_MaxValid	10	As SQLDMOMonth_WeekEndDay.
SQLDMOMonth_Unknown	0	Invalid value.

When you are using `SQLDMOFreq_MonthlyRelative`, you also have to set the `FrequencyRelativeInterval`, using the values:

Constant	Value	Schedule
SQLDMOFreqRel_First	1	Execution is scheduled for the first occurrence of the value specified in the SQLDMOFreq_MonthlyRelative property.
SQLDMOFreqRel_Second	2	Execution is scheduled for the second occurrence of the value specified in the SQLDMOFreq_MonthlyRelative property.
SQLDMOFreqRel_Third	4	Execution is scheduled for the third occurrence of the value specified in the SQLDMOFreq_MonthlyRelative property.
SQLDMOFreqRel_Fourth	8	Execution is scheduled for the fourth occurrence of the value specified in the SQLDMOFreq_MonthlyRelative property.
SQLDMOFreqRel_Last	16	Execution is scheduled for the last occurrence of the value specified in the SQLDMOFreq_MonthlyRelative property.
SQLDMOFreqRel_Unknown	0	The schedule does not have a relative frequency or relative frequency does not apply.
SQLDMOFreqRel_Valid	31	All valid relative scheduling constants.

This is stored as a bit-packed long integer value. Values can be combined for multiple occurrences.

The following code snippets show how we make use of these properties in the `MakeJob` method:

```
Dim oJobSchedule As SQLDMO.JobSchedule

Dim oSchedule As SQLDMO.Schedule

Set oJobSchedule = CreateObject("SQLDMO.JobSchedule")

oJobSchedule.Name = "Standard Weekly"
oJob.JobSchedules.Add oJobSchedule

Set oSchedule = oJobSchedule.Schedule
oSchedule.BeginAlter
oSchedule.ActiveStartDate = "19990827"
oSchedule.ActiveEndDate = "20200101"
oSchedule.ActiveStartTimeOfDay = "000001"
oSchedule.ActiveEndTimeOfDay = "230000"
oSchedule.FrequencyType = SQLDMOFreq_Weekly
oSchedule.FrequencyInterval = iJobInterval
oSchedule.FrequencyRecurrenceFactor = SQLDMOFreq_Weekly
oSchedule.DoAlter
```

Here we've created the `JobSchedule` and added it to the `JobSchedules` collection, then used the `BeginAlter` and `DoAlter` methods to set the properties of the `Schedule` object. The only property that we are allowing the user to select is the day of the week on which to run backups. Constant values are provided for the remaining properties.

Backup Job Management Sample

Selecting Backup | Backup Job from the Survey Designer form brings up the Backup Job Management dialog (`frmJob`):

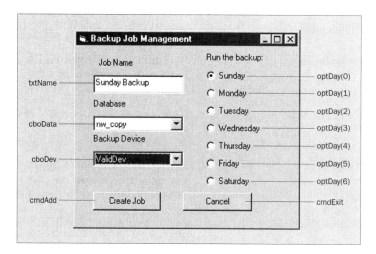

The form presents the user with drop-down lists from which database and backup device choices may be made. The code for this is contained in the `Form_Load` method shown below. Additionally, within the event procedure the `JobServer` object status (SQL Server Agent status) is checked; if the SQL Server Agent isn't running, it is started:

```
Private Sub Form_Load()

    Dim i As Integer

    mgt.CheckJobServer (lConnID)
    sListDev = bk.GetDev(lConnID)
    sListDB = sec.GetAllDB(lConnID)

    For i = 0 To UBound(sListDev)
        cboDev.AddItem sListDev(i)
    Next

    For i = 0 To UBound(sListDB)
        cboData.AddItem sListDB(i)
    Next

    optDay(0).Value = True

End Sub
```

The `mgt` object variable is declared in the `modGlobals` standard module:

```
Public mgt As New SQLDDL.Management
```

The status check is the only variation away from previous list population code segments – it is achieved by calling the `SQLDDL.Management` component's `CheckJobServer` method:

```
Public Sub CheckJobServer(lConnID As Long)

    Dim oJobServer As SQLDMO.JobServer
    Dim oSQLServer As SQLDMO.SQLServer

    Set oSQLServer = oApp.SQLServers.ItemByID(lConnID)
    Set oJobServer = oSQLServer.JobServer

    If oJobServer.Status <> SQLDMOSvc_Running Then
        oJobServer.Start
    End If

    Set oJobServer = Nothing
    Set oSQLServer = Nothing

End Sub
```

`CheckJobServer` gets a reference to the `JobServer` object for the connected server and checks the `Status` property. If `Status` identifies the SQL Server Agent as anything other than running, the `JobServer` object's `Start` method is called to start the SQL Server Agent.

The user must provide a job name, select the source database, and select the target device before creating the job by clicking **Create Job**:

```
Private Sub cmdAdd_Click()

    If cboData.Text = "" Then
        MsgBox "Please select a database"
        Exit Sub
    End If

    If cboDev.Text = "" Then
        MsgBox "Please select a backup device"
        Exit Sub
    End If

    If txtName.Text = "" Then
        MsgBox "Enter a job name"
    End If

    mgt.MakeJob lConnID, txtName.Text, iBkDay, cboData.Text, cboDev.Text

End Sub
```

After running through various code fragments we can now reveal the complete `MakeJob` method of the `SQLDDL.Management` component. The sample application makes only the most minimal of verification checks before calling the `MakeJob` method. The job name, backup day, database, and device are passed when the method is called:

```
Public Sub MakeJob(ByVal lConnID As Long, ByVal sJobName As String, _
                   ByVal iJobInterval As Integer, ByVal sJobDB As String, _
                   ByVal sJobDev As String)

    Dim oJobServer As SQLDMO.JobServer
    Dim oSQLServer As SQLDMO.SQLServer
    Dim oJob As SQLDMO.Job
    Dim oJobSchedule As SQLDMO.JobSchedule
    Dim oJobStep As SQLDMO.JobStep
    Dim oSchedule As SQLDMO.Schedule

    Set oSQLServer = oApp.SQLServers.ItemByID(lConnID)
    Set oJobServer = oSQLServer.JobServer
    Set oJob = CreateObject("SQLDMO.Job")
    Set oJobSchedule = CreateObject("SQLDMO.JobSchedule")
    Set oJobStep = CreateObject("SQLDMO.JobStep")

    oJob.Name = sJobName
    oJob.Category = "Database Maintenance"
    oJobServer.Jobs.Add oJob

    oJobSchedule.Name = "Standard Weekly"
    oJob.JobSchedules.Add oJobSchedule

    Set oSchedule = oJobSchedule.Schedule
    oSchedule.BeginAlter
    oSchedule.ActiveStartDate = "19990827"
    oSchedule.ActiveEndDate = "20200101"
    oSchedule.ActiveStartTimeOfDay = "000001"
    oSchedule.ActiveEndTimeOfDay = "230000"
    oSchedule.FrequencyType = SQLDMOFreq_Weekly
    oSchedule.FrequencyInterval = iJobInterval
    oSchedule.FrequencyRecurrenceFactor = SQLDMOFreq_Weekly
    oSchedule.DoAlter

    oJobStep.Name = "Backup Step"
    oJobStep.StepID = 1
    oJobStep.Command = "BACKUP DATABASE " & sJobDB & _
                       " TO " & sJobDev & " WITH INIT"
    oJob.JobSteps.Add oJobStep
    oJob.ApplyToTargetServer (oSQLServer.NetName)

    MsgBox "Job Created"

    DoEvents

    Set oJobServer = Nothing
    Set oSQLServer = Nothing
    Set oJob = Nothing
```

```
    Set oJobSchedule = Nothing
    oJobStep = Nothing
    oSchedule = Nothing

End Sub
```

The only extra thing that needs to be pointed out here is the call to DoEvents. This is needed so that all the objects will have completed what is required of them before they are set to Nothing.

Now run the Surveys Unlimited application and add a backup job via the Backup Job Management dialog. If you switch to the SQL Server Enterprise Manager and navigate to the SQL Server's Management | SQL Server Agent | Jobs node and you will see the job that we have just created.

Operators

When working with jobs or alerts we are going to encounter references to **operators**. Operators are people we can identify to receive notification when:

❑   A job completes

❑   A job error occurs

❑   A alert event occurs (fires)

You can have an operator notified by e-mail, by pager, or by a Windows NT NET SEND address. When notifying an operator by pager, you can specify the operator's work schedule, limiting the days and times when the operator is notified.

One option you have available when using pager notification is to specify a fail-safe operator. When a notification is generated outside of an operator's work schedule, it is sent to the fail-safe operator instead.

While not a major focus of this chapter, it will be useful to see a quick demonstration of how we can create an operator definition. First, let's take a quick look at the hierarchy.

Operators and OperatorCategories

We are presenting another portion of the JobServer object hierarchy here. This time however, we're only going to discuss those objects relating to operators:

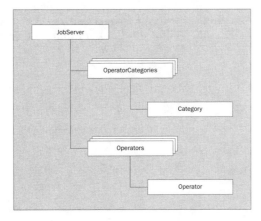

JobServer Object – The `JobServer` object is documented as a member of the SQL-DMO `Application` object. However, it is used as member of the `SQLServer` object. The `JobServer` object lets you start and stop the SQL Server Agent, as well as manage jobs, alerts, and operators.

OperatorCategories Collection – This is a collection of `Category` objects.

Category Object – `Category` objects represent operator, alert, and job categories. These can be used for grouping operators, alerts, and jobs.

Operators Collection – The `Operators` collection contains SQL Server Agent `Operator` objects.

Operator Object – Each `Operator` object represents a SQL Server operator.

Create Operator Sample

This sample application is not part of the Surveys Unlimited application that we've been working with up to this point. Instead, it has been prepared to get you started managing operators through SQL-DMO objects.

You may not find many situations where you would need to use SQL-DMO objects for this purpose. One possibility though, is that you are building a custom management utility for distribution with a SQL Server-based custom application.

To create a SQL Server Agent operator, at a minimum you need to:

❑   Create an `Operator` object

❑   Add the `Operator` object to the `JobServer` object's `Operators` collection

The `Operator` object includes 23 properties, which let you define and manage the operator. We're going to focus on just two of these:

Property	Description
`Name`	This text string sets the operator name. Each operator must have a unique name.
`EmailAddress`	The e-mail address is also entered as a text string.

Other properties let you define items such as the pager address, `NET SEND` address, and pager schedule. Refer to Appendix D at the end of this book for more information about the `Operator` object's properties.

The application has a single form (frmCreate) for entering operator information. The operator name and e-mail address are entered in text boxes called txtName and txtEmail respectively:

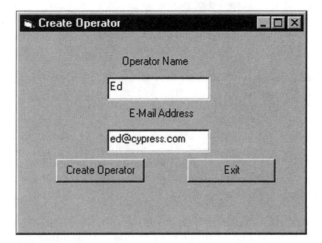

First, let's look at our object variable declarations.

```
Private oServer As SQLDMO.SQLServer
Private oJobServer As SQLDMO.JobServer
Private oOperator As SQLDMO.Operator
```

There is nothing different to what we've seen in the past here.

After entering the operator name and password, the user clicks on the **Create Operator** command button to create the operator. Here's the code that executes:

```
Private Sub cmdCreate_Click()

    Me.Mousepointer = vbHourglass
    Set oServer = CreateObject("SQLDMO.SQLServer")
    oServer.LoginSecure = True
    oServer.Connect
    Set oJobServer = oServer.JobServer
    Set oOperator = CreateObject("SQLDMO.Operator")
    oOperator.Name = txtName.Text
    oOperator.EmailAddress = txtEmail.Text
    oJobServer.Operators.Add oOperator
    Me.Mousepointer = vbDefault

End Sub
```

For the sake of simplicity, we create a SQLServer object and connect to the local server, assuming that the application is running under Windows NT. We set a reference to the connected server's JobServer object, and then create an Operator object. We set the Operator object's Name property equal to the Text property of txtName and its EmailAddress property equal to the Text property of txtEmail. We then add the Operator object to the JobServer object's Operators collection.

The Exit button simply unloads the form and exits the application.

Alerts

The primary use of **alerts** is to respond to potential problem conditions and to SQL Server errors. This is done by defining alerts to respond to user-defined or SQL Server errors. An alert can respond to a specific error number or any errors of a specific severity level. When an alert occurs (fires), you can have the SQL Server Agent notify an operator, execute a job, or both.

Alerts give you a good way of implementing automated monitoring, especially if you are aware of situations that could eventually cause problems. When an error for which you are monitoring occurs, you can either notify someone to respond to the situation or execute a predefined job.

Here's an example of how you might use alerts. You've had to place a database's transaction log on a disk partition that has limited space available. During normal operations, this won't cause a problem, but you run a potential risk of filling the transaction log during end of month activities. Because of the amount of activity going on at that time, you need to have the situation resolved without user intervention if at all possible.

As a solution, you could create an alert to monitor the transaction log. When the transaction log hits a predefined threshold, say 90% full, you could execute a job that you've defined to back up the transaction log. This will truncate the log, giving you additional log space, and give you a backup that can be used should a serious error occur and you need to recover the database from backups.

When defining error alerts, you need to understand that an alert will only fire for errors that are logged in the Windows NT Application log. Even if an error should normally be logged, you can encounter a problem on occasion that operators are not being notified. This will happen when the Windows NT application log fills and is unable to log application events. You will need to clear the application log before any operators will receive notifications.

Alerts and AlertCategories

We are again presenting a portion of the `JobServer` object hierarchy here, but only those objects relating to alerts:

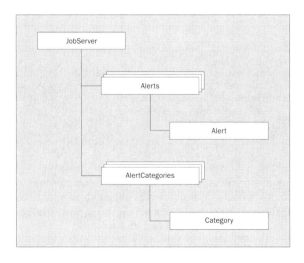

JobServer Object – The `JobServer` object is documented as a member of the SQL-DMO `Application` object. However, it is used as member of the `SQLServer` object. The `JobServer` object lets you start and stop the SQL Server Agent, as well as manage jobs, alerts, and operators.

Alerts Collection – The `Alerts` collection contains SQL Server Agent `Alert` objects.

Alert Object – Each `Alert` object represents a SQL Server alert.

AlertCategories Collection – This is a collection of `Category` objects.

Category Object – `Category` objects represent operator, alert, and job categories. These can be used for grouping operators, alerts, and jobs.

Create Alert Sample

As with the Operators sample application, this is not part of the Surveys Unlimited sample application. It has been provided as a stand-alone example to get you started working with alerts. Both of these sample applications are available for download from the Wrox website.

To create an alert, you will need to, at minimum:

- ❏ Create an `Alert` object
- ❏ Set the `Name` property
- ❏ Set a value defining the severity, message ID, or performance condition for the alert
- ❏ Add the `Alert` object to the `JobServer` object's `Alerts` collection

In our example, we are going to take this one step further by adding an operator notification to the alert. You must add the `Alert` object to the `Alerts` collection before you can add operator notifications.

As we did in the last example, we are keeping the code involved as simple as possible. We are going to create an alert to respond to severity 19 errors at the server. Obviously, this is not a real-world example of how you would use SQL-DMO to manage alerts. Instead, it is designed to let you see what is involved in creating an alert.

> **SQL Server 7.0 automatically creates an alert for severity 19 errors during installation. If you want to run this sample code, you will need to use SQL Server Enterprise Manager to delete the severity 19 alert.**

The sample application will populate a combo box called cboOperators with a list of available operators. After choosing an operator, you will be able to create the alert with the operator to be notified in case of an alert:

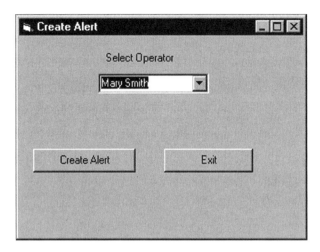

We need to look at a couple of things before we work our way through the sample code. First, the Alert object supports 28 properties. They define the alert and track information about alert occurrences. However, we are only going to be using two properties in our example:

Property	Description
Name	This is a string value for the alert name. Each alert must have a unique name.
Severity	Use the Severity property to set the severity level that will cause this alert to fire.

After creating the alert, we are going to use the AddNotification method to add notification information for the selected operator. When we do this, we will have to provide the operator name and the notification type.

Now we're ready to start looking at the code, starting with our declarations:

```
Private oServer As SQLDMO.SQLServer
Private oJobServer As SQLDMO.JobServer
Private oAlert As SQLDMO.Alert
Private lConnID As Long
```

When the form loads, we establish a connection with the local server and populate cboOperators with a list of available operators:

```
Private Sub Form_Load()

    Dim i As Integer
```

```
     Set oServer = CreateObject("SQLDMO.SQLServer")
     oServer.LoginSecure = True
     oServer.Connect
     lConnID = oServer.ConnectionID
     Set oJobServer = oServer.JobServer

     For i = 1 To oJobServer.Operators.Count
         cboOperators.AddItem (oJobServer.Operators(i).Name)
     Next

     Set oServer = Nothing

 End Sub
```

As you can see, we're not doing anything different here that we haven't done several times before to populate a list or combo box with object names.

The user will select an operator from the combo box and click on **Create Alert** to create the Alert object and add it to the Alerts collection. Let's look at how this is done:

```
 Private Sub cmdAlert_Click()

     If cboOperators.Text = "" Then
         MsgBox "Select an operator", vbOKOnly
         Exit Sub
     End If

     Me.MousePointer = vbHourglass
     Set oServer = oApp.SQLServers.ItemByID(lConnID)
     Set oJobServer = oServer.JobServer
     Set oAlert = CreateObject("SQLDMO.Alert")
     oAlert.Name = "Severity 19 Alert"
     oAlert.Severity = 19
     oJobServer.Alerts.Add oAlert
     oAlert.BeginAlter
     oAlert.AddNotification cboOperators.Text, SQLDMONotify_Email
     oAlert.DoAlter
     Me.MousePointer = vbDefault

 End Sub
```

After verifying that the user has selected an operator we get a reference to the connected server's JobServer object. We then create a new Alert object and set its Name and Severity properties. Once these are set, we add the Alert object to the JobServer object's Alerts collection.

After adding the Alert object to the Alerts collection we can add notification information. We call the Alert object's BeginAlter method. The AddNotification method lets us add the selected operator to the notification list for e-mail notification. Finally, we call the DoAlert method to complete the process.

Summary

Even though they all fell under the general category of SQL-DMO management objects, we've hit on a lot of different areas during this chapter.

We started with security objects and covered the topics of logins, database users, and security roles in this category. The procedures for creating and managing logins and users were introduced, as well as the relationship between these objects. Security roles were introduced and covered as an overview.

Next came backup and restore management. We saw how to manage backup devices, then how to use them to run backups and restores. This led into a short discussion about automating the management process where we looked at how to create a recurring job to run backups. Finally, at the end of the chapter, we discussed how to create operators and alerts using SQL-DMO objects.

After spending some time with SQL-DMO in the next chapter, we're going to move upwards in the Distributed Management Framework and see how we can leverage SQL Namespace (SQL-NS) in application development.

6

Using SQL-NS

The **SQL-Namespace** (**SQL-NS**) object library exposes objects, collections, properties and methods, which can be used to give your application access to many of the user interface elements that are used in SQL Enterprise Manager. By using SQL-NS, your application can include the property pages, wizards and dialog boxes found in the Enterprise Manager. In fact, as we saw in Chapter 1, SQL Enterprise Manager itself uses SQL-NS to provide these elements. Using SQL-NS as part of your application can allow you to provide a powerful user interface to the SQL Server, while writing very little code.

For example, you might want to create an application that could be used by your company's Webmaster to analyze the existing indexes against a workload and create new indexes where appropriate. An easy way to provide this functionality in your application would be to use SQL-NS to launch the wizards on the Webmaster's local computer and connect to the SQL Server.

Since SQL-NS provides user interface elements, it is only appropriate for use in the presentation layer of an application. In addition, it cannot be used as part of an Active Server Pages solution because ASP runs on a server, so cannot display dialogs. While the SQL-NS objects can be used through an Active Scripting language, such as VBScript or JavaScript, you will limit your application's use to browsers that can act as Automation controllers. Essentially, this limits the use of SQL-NS to rich client applications or Web-based applications that run only inside of Internet Explorer or a Netscape browser with an ActiveX plug-in. The most likely use of SQL-NS is in a Windows-based client application like the one we have been building throughout the book.

We've designed this chapter to let you get your feet wet with SQL-NS, but due to the vast number of commands available, we will not be able to cover every possible use of the library. To do so would leave you drowning in a sea of constants. So, in this chapter, we will cover:

❑ The SQL-NS object hierarchy

❑ Walking through the SQL Server namespace and retrieving object references

❑ Displaying the user interface elements SQL-NS provides by executing commands

❑ Error handling when using SQL-NS objects

❑ Integrating SQL-NS into the Surveys Unlimited project

❑ SQL-NS and SQL-DMO integration

❑ Launching wizards from the server level of the SQL-NS

Our strategy for the chapter is to introduce the basic topics (retrieving object references, executing commands, and error handling) by building some code blocks that would facilitate navigation from a root of the `Server` object to the `Table` object named `Customers` in the `Northwind` database. We will then use this knowledge to add functionality to our Survey Designer application, showing how to display SQL Server user interface elements using SQL-NS.

A SQL-NS object reference is contained in Appendix E, but for comprehensive listing of the constants use SQL Server On-Line Help and drill down to **Building SQL Server Applications | SQL-NS**.

So without further ado, let's dip our toes in the water!

The SQL-NS Object Hierarchy

At first glance, the SQL-NS object hierarchy looks very simple. It is composed of a single externally creatable object, called the `SQLNamespace` object, a dependent `SQLNamespaceObject` object, a `SQLNamespaceCommands` collection, and a set of `SQLNamespaceCommand` objects:

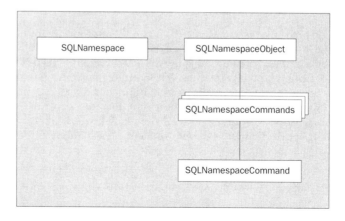

However, the SQL-NS hierarchy is one whose looks are deceiving and there is more to learn regarding the use of these objects than meets the eye. You see, the `SQLNamespaceObject` object is **polymorphic**, meaning that it can represent a variety of SQL Server objects, each with its own user interface elements. A `SQLNamespaceObject` object may represent a `Database` object, a `SQLServer` object, or even a container object.

In case you haven't had a chance to work with polymorphic objects before or perhaps you don't even know what polymorphic means, we're going to take a brief look at the concepts behind polymorphism before moving on to a detailed discussion of how this relates to the `SQLNamespaceObject` object.

Polymorphism

The word polymorphism means having many shapes. Polymorphism means that objects present the same interface to clients, but actually implement that interface in different ways. The best way to understand this is through a real world example:

Consider the domestic dog. All dogs can be counted on to provide certain behaviors. They bark, they run, they eat, and in the case of the well-trained dog, they will even obey certain commands:

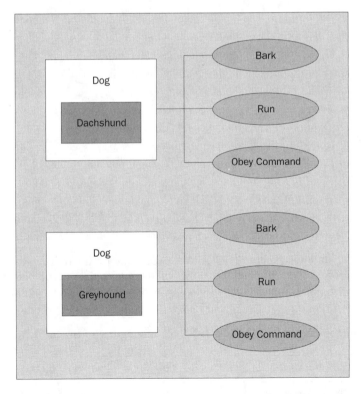

However, each individual dog performs these actions differently. For a graphic image of this, picture a dachshund and a greyhound running across a lawn. The long legs of the greyhound make running a very different activity than it is for the short legs of a dachshund.

Polymorphism in COM is no different. A generic object (the domestic dog) describes the methods and properties available to the client that makes use of that object. Specific objects provide a distinct implementation of those methods and properties.

Polymorphism in the SQLNamespaceObject Object

The `SQLNamespaceObject` object describes an interface that consists of four properties (Commands, Handle, Name, and Type) and two methods (`ExecuteCommandByID` and `ExecuteCommandByName`). Depending on the type of object that the `SQLNamespaceObject` represents, the contents of the `SQLNamespaceCommands` collection returned by the `Commands` property, and therefore the commands that can be executed will be different.

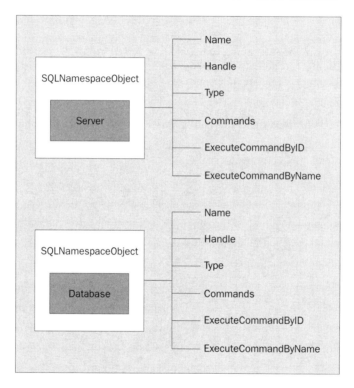

The commands available for execution will differ depending on the object with which you are dealing. For that reason, you will need to be able to know an object's type before you execute a command. There are 103 different types of objects, which are listed in the `SQLNSObjectType` constants enumeration.

We're going to demonstrate how to use SQL-NS by making use of the following five in this chapter:

Constant	Value	SQL Server Object
SQLNSObjectType_Server	3	SQLServer
SQLNSObjectType_Databases	4	Databases collection

Constant	Value	SQL Server Object
SQLNSObjectType_Database	5	Database
SQLNSObjectType_DatabaseTables	24	Tables collection
SQLNSObjectType_DatabaseTable	25	Table

OK, let's return to an overview of the object hierarchy.

The SQL-NS Objects

The objects in the SQL-NS hierarchy are used to navigate through the SQL Server namespace and to display the user interface elements provided by various objects in the namespace. Let's take a brief look at each of them:

SQLNamespace Object – The SQLNamespace object serves as an application's entry point into the SQL Server namespace. It provides a number of methods for navigating through the namespace, obtaining information about objects in the namespace, and providing references to SQLNamespaceObject objects.

SQLNamespaceObject Object – The SQLNamespaceObject object has already been introduced. It represents an object in the SQL Server namespace and, depending on the object it represents, allows the execution of different commands. For example, if the SQLNamespaceObject object represents a database, it allows commands specific to a database to be run; if it represents a table, it allows commands specific to a table to be run.

SQLNamespaceCommands Collection – The SQLNamespaceCommands collection holds and manages the supported commands for a particular SQLNamespaceObject. Access to this collection is exposed through the SQLNamespaceObject object's Commands property. This collection can be used to iterate through the supported commands to locate a particular command or to retrieve a list of commands.

SQLNamespaceCommand Object – The SQLNamespaceCommand object represents a particular command. For example, it may represent a command to display a property page for an object or to launch a wizard.

Now we've looked at the object hierarchy let's see how we can use it, firstly though we have to understand how to negotiate the SQL Server namespace.

Walking through the Namespace

Before we can execute a command, we must locate the object that provides the command. This involves moving through the tree of the namespace until we locate the object we want.

Objects in the tree are located through an understanding of their relationship to an object you have information about, in particular an object for which you have a **handle**. The graphic below illustrates this relationship. The object node represents the object for which you have a handle. The two siblings are at the same level as this object and can be referred to as the next sibling or the previous sibling. The object for which you have a handle is also the parent of two child objects.

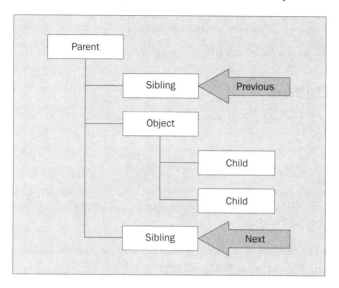

> **A handle identifies the location in memory where a particular object can be found. Visual Basic programmers rarely need to deal with handles directly, however SQL-NS is an exception to this rule. Since memory addresses are stored as Longs, you will declare variables that can store a handle as Long (note that a handle is not really the same thing as a pointer).**
>
> **More information on using handles from Visual Basic can be found in *Visual Basic 6 Win32 API Tutorial, Wrox Press, ISBN 1861002432*.**

You can use this handle with a variety of `SQLNamespace` object methods to retrieve the handles of other objects that have a direct relationship. For example, you can retrieve handles to children, siblings, or the parent object.

The SQLNamespace object provides a number of methods to allow you to walk through the SQL Server namespace which are summarized in the table below:

Method Name	Description
GetRootItem	This method returns the handle to the root object. This will be the starting point for walking the tree.
GetChildrenCount	This method returns the number of children a particular object in the namespace contains.
GetFirstChildItem	This method returns the handle of the first child item that meets particular criteria. If no child item meets the criteria, the method returns 0.
GetParentItem	This method returns the handle to the specified object's parent.
GetNextSiblingItem	This method returns the handle to the next sibling that meets the specified criteria. If no sibling item meets the criteria, the method returns 0.
GetPreviousSiblingItem	This method returns the handle to the previous sibling that meets the specified criteria. If no sibling item meets the criteria, the method returns 0.

We'll be using the GetFirstChildItem method later in the chapter during an example of how to move through a tree.

Now we've covered the ideas underpinning this topic we should now have a look at how to code it. As we mentioned earlier we're going to introduce programming using SQL-NS by generating some relatively general code blocks applicable to the Northwind database. This will build up to using various methods to enable us to display the **Properties** dialog for the Customers table of the Northwind database. We will then see how we can use the coding approaches to enhance the Survey Designer application.

Within this section we'll be covering the following points:

- ❑ Choosing a root
- ❑ Declaring and instantiating the SQLNamespace object
- ❑ Initializing a connection
- ❑ Getting a handle
- ❑ Retrieving an object reference
- ❑ Executing commands

Our starting point is to take a closer look at the root item.

Choosing a Root

The easiest way to understand roots is to look at how they map to the tree displayed in SQL Enterprise Manager:

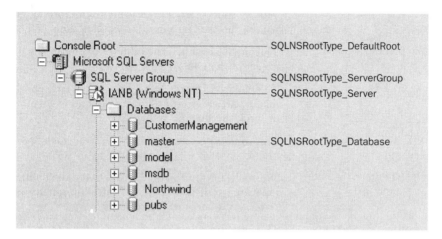

As you can see, the `DefaultRoot` and the `ServerGroup` root are dependent on the configuration of the Microsoft Management Console. Since different users will have different MMC configurations, we recommend that you avoid using either the `DefaultRoot` or the `ServerGroup` as your entry point. Using a specific `Server` or a specific `Database` as your root means that your application will have a consistent entry point, regardless of how a user's MMC is configured.

Another important point to remember when choosing a root is that your application will need to be able to provide the necessary connection information for that entry point. For example, if you are using a server as your root, you will need the server name and login information. If you are using a database as your root, you will also need to know the name of the database.

The four types of roots are defined in the constant enumeration `SQLNSRootType`. Their values are as follows:

Constant	Value
SQLNSRootType_DefaultRoot	0
SQLNSRootType_ServerGroup	1
SQLNSRootType_Server	2
SQLNSRootType_Database	3

Declaring and Instantiating the SQLNamespace Object

The first step in getting to use SQL-NS in your application is to set a reference to the Microsoft SQLNamespace Object Library. As you'll recall from Chapter 1, this library is installed when you install either SQL Server or SQL Server client software and the appropriate file name is `sqlns.rll`:

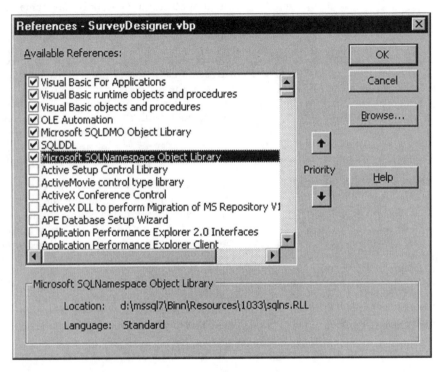

The `SQLNamespace` object is the only externally creatable object in the SQL-NS library. It must be declared and instantiated just as any other object, either by using `New` or by calling `CreateObject`. Its ProgID (programmatic identifier – the fully qualified class name) is `SQLNS.SQLNamespace`.

To declare and instantiate the `SQLNS.SQLNamespace` object the following is used:

```
Public ns As SQLNS.SQLNamespace
Set ns = CreateObject("SQLNS.SQLNamespace")
```

Initializing a Connection

The next step is to establish and initialize your connection to the root. This is achieved by calling the `Initialize` method of the `SQLNamespace` object. Its syntax is as follows:

```
object.Initialize(bstrAppName, [rootType], [pRootInfo], [hWnd])
```

The *object* is the variable that contains an instantiated SQLNamespace object. The other arguments are described in the following table:

Argument	Data Type	Description
bstrAppName	String	This argument contains a string identifying the client application. Generally, the name of the application initializing the connection will be passed. *This is the only required argument.*
rootType	Enumerated, long	This argument identifies the type of object that will serve as the entry point. The root type is a value in the SQLNSRootType constant enumeration. This is an optional argument; if it is not defined, SQLNSRootType_DefaultRoot will be used. We recommend that you define either SQLNSRootType_Server or SQLNSRootType_Database as your entry point.
pRootInfo	Variant pointer	This argument is used to pass the connection string to the method. Although the contents of the variant will be textual, a String argument cannot be passed. This information is not required for a DefaultRoot root type. We'll show some sample connection strings a little later.
hWnd	Window handle	This argument identifies the location in memory where the window requesting initialization is loaded. Visual Basic provides this value through the hWnd property of the Form or MDIForm object.

> **SQL-NS can only be used with SQL Server 7.0. It is important to verify that your server is running the correct version of SQL Server before attempting to initiate a connection. Attempting to initialize a connection to a version other than SQL Server 7.0 will result in Error 1020, SQLNS_E_InvalidServerVersion. We'll show how to check the version of SQL Server using SQL-DMO a little later in the chapter.**

To initialize a connection to the Server root of the SQL Namespace from a form named frmMDIMain the following would be used:

```
ns.Initialize "Survey Designer", SQLNSRootType_Server, sConnect, frmMDIMain.hWnd
```

At the end of this chapter, we'll see how this code can be integrated into the Survey Designer project used in this book.

This code fragment uses a String variable named sConnect to contain the connection string, let's move on to having a look at the syntax for building a connection string for SQL-NS.

Building a Connection String

Either a literal string, or a variable of type Variant, can be passed as the *pRootInfo* argument. This connection string must include all of the information necessary to locate and establish a connection with the root. If you're familiar with building connection strings for use with ODBC, OLE DB, or ADO, you will find building a connection string for use with SQL-NS very familiar.

A connection string is a group of defined parameters, with semi-colons used to separate each parameter and to end the connection string. For example, in order to establish a connection to the local server, using Windows NT authentication, the following connection string would be used:

```
Server=(local);Trusted_Connection=Yes;
```

A few more examples of connection strings are shown below, but firstly let's list the supported parameters for a connection string and when they are used:

Parameter	Description	When Required
Server	This parameter is set to the name of the server or (local) if connecting to the SQL Server running on the local machine.	Use this parameter when the root type is either Server or Database.
SrvGrp	This parameter is set to the name of the SQL Server Group being used as the root type.	Use this parameter when the root type is ServerGroup.
UID	This parameter identifies the login ID for SQL Server authentication.	Use this parameter when the root type is Server or Database and SQL Server authentication is being used.
PWD	This parameter identifies the password for SQL Server authentication.	Use this parameter when the root type is Server or Database and SQL Server authentication is being used.
Trusted_Connection	This parameter determines whether to use SQL Server authentication (No) or Windows NT authentication (Yes).	Use this parameter when the root type is Server or Database.
Database	This parameter identifies the name of the database to be used as the entry point.	Use this parameter when the root type is Database.

So a code fragment that will give two different connection strings, one for a trusted user and one for a SQL Server login, is:

```
sConnect = "Server=" & sServer
If bIntegrated = True Then
    sConnect = sConnect & ";Trusted_Connection=Yes;"
Else
    sConnect = sConnect & ";UID=" & sUser & ";pwd=" & sPassword & ";"
End If
```

In this case, four String variables and one Boolean variable are used. These may be familiar to you, since they are the same variables used in the Survey Designer application (see Chapter 3).

So, if a user named RReese tried to connect to a server named Sherlock, using a password of Sasser, the code would give rise to the following connection string:

```
Server=Sherlock;UID=RReese;pwd=Sasser;
```

Note that this connection string would be used only if you are using SQLNSRootType_Server as the entry point. An entry point of SQLNSRootType_Database would require you to also specify the database you would like to use. For example, to use the Northwind database as your entry point, you might use code similar to:

```
sConnect = " Server=Sherlock;Database=Northwind;UID=RReese;pwd=Sasser;
ns.Initialize "Survey Designer", SQLNSRootType_Database, sConnect, frmMDIMain.hWnd
```

Getting a Handle

Once a connection has been initiated, we can begin moving through the tree. Remember, we do this by retrieving handles of objects and using each handle we retrieve to retrieve yet another handle. This process is loosely analogous to the process used to climb the monkey bars in grade school – once you have a solid grip on one bar, you swing to catch the next, and so on until you reach your destination.

We're going to examine how to climb the SQL-NS monkey bars by looking at the steps required to navigate from a root object of type Server to a Table object. This will require us to understand the syntax for two methods, the GetRootItem method and the GetFirstChildItem method:

The GetRootItem Method

The GetRootItem method is used to obtain the handle of the root object. We'll use this handle as our jumping off point. The GetRootItem method has the syntax:

```
object.GetRootItem()
```

The *object* is the variable that holds the reference to the initialized SQLNamespace object.

The GetFirstChildItem Method

The `GetFirstChildItem` method is used to retrieve the handle of a child object. We can optionally require that the child object be of a certain type and/or have a certain name. The syntax for this method is:

```
object.GetFirstChildItem(ItemIn, [matchType], [matchName])
```

Once again, the `object` is the variable holding the reference to the `SQLNamespace` object. The arguments of this method are described in the table below:

Argument	Data Type	Description
ItemIn	Long	This argument contains the handle of the parent object.
matchType	Enumerated, long	This argument contains a constant identifying the object type. These constants are enumerated in `SQLNSObjectType`. If no match type is specified, the first child object in the hierarchy will be returned, regardless of type.
matchName	String	This argument contains a string identifying the name of the object to be retrieved. If no match name is specified, the first child object in the hierarchy of the appropriate type will be returned.

> If no match is found, the value 0 (null handle) will be returned. As we'll see a little later in the chapter, it's a good idea to check to make sure that a valid (non zero) value is returned before progressing down the namespace tree.

Navigating the Tree

Right, let's see how we can use these methods. Our example is going to involve navigating from a root of the `Server` object to the `Table` object named `Customers` in the `Northwind` database.

This example is not part of the ongoing Surveys Unlimited project, although the project will use somewhat similar code.

In order to make it very clear which objects are referenced by which handle, let's declare some variables:

```
Dim hServer As Long
Dim hDatabases As Long
Dim hDatabase As Long
Dim hTables As Long
Dim hTable As Long
```

Our process can now be divided into five steps:

1. Our first step is to retrieve the handle of the root object. In this case, a variable named ns has been declared as a SQLNamespace object and instantiated, and a connection to a Server object initialized. This latter part of the code should look familiar from a couple of pages ago. To retrieve the handle to that Server object, we need to call the GetRootItem method of the ns object:

```
Dim ns as SQLNS.SQLNamespace
Set ns = CreateObject("SQLNS.SQLNamespace")
sConnect = "Server=" & sServer
If bIntegrated = True Then
    sConnect = sConnect & ";Trusted_Connection=Yes;"
Else
    sConnect = sConnect & ";UID=" & sUser & ";pwd=" & sPassword & ";"
End If
ns.Initialize "My Application", SQLNSRootType_Server, sConnect, frmMDIMain.hWnd
hServer = ns.GetRootItem
```

2. The next step is to retrieve the handle of the Databases collection for that Server object. To do this, we pass the handle of the Server object to GetFirstChildItem, specifying a match type of SQLNSOBJECTTYPE_DATABASES:

```
hDatabases = ns.GetFirstChildItem(hServer, SQLNSOBJECTTYPE_DATABASES)
```

3. Next, we need to retrieve the handle of the Northwind database. This is achieved by passing the handle of the Databases collection, a match type of SQLNSOBJECTTYPE_DATABASE, and a match name of "Northwind":

```
hDatabase = ns.GetFirstChildItem(hDatabases, SQLNSOBJECTTYPE_DATABASE, _
                          "Northwind")
```

4. Our penultimate task is to retrieve the handle of the Northwind database's Tables collection, so we pass the handle of the Northwind database to the GetFirstChildItem method, specifying a match type of SQLNSOBJECTTYPE_DATABASE_TABLES:

```
hTables = ns.GetFirstChildItem(hDatabase, SQLNSOBJECTTYPE_DATABASE_TABLES)
```

5. Finally, we can retrieve the handle for the Customers table by passing the handle of the Tables collection, an item type of SQLNSOBJECTTYPE_DATABASE_TABLE, and a match name of "Customers":

```
hTable = ns.GetFirstChildItem(hTables, SQLNSOBJECTTYPE_DATABASE_TABLE, _
                "Customers")
```

The handles in our application at this point are shown in the screen shot of SQL Server Enterprise Manager below:

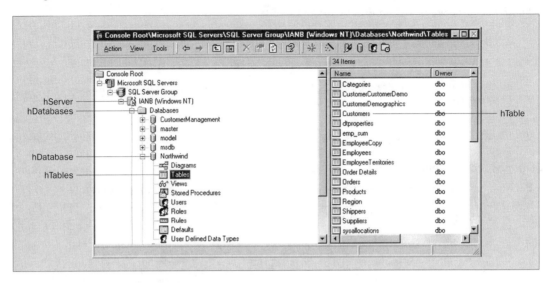

Retrieving an Object Reference

Once we have the handle of the object we need, we can obtain a reference to that object by calling the `GetSQLNamespaceObject` method of the `SQLNamespace` object. This method returns a reference to a `SQLNamespaceObject` object and has the following syntax:

> *object*.GetSQLNamespaceObject(*ItemIn*)

The *ItemIn* argument is the handle of the object to be retrieved. For example, to retrieve an object that references the `Customers` table that we just located we would use the code:

```
Dim ns as SQLNS.SQLNamespace
Set ns = CreateObject("SQLNS.SQLNamespace")
sConnect = "Server=" & sServer
If bIntegrated = True Then
    sConnect = sConnect & ";Trusted_Connection=Yes;"
Else
    sConnect = sConnect & ";UID=" & sUser & ";pwd=" & sPassword & ";"
End If
ns.Initialize "My Application", SQLNSRootType_Server, sConnect, frmMDIMain.hWnd
hServer = ns.GetRootItem
hDatabases = ns.GetFirstChildItem(hServer, SQLNSOBJECTTYPE_DATABASES)
hDatabase = ns.GetFirstChildItem(hDatabases, SQLNSOBJECTTYPE_DATABASE, _
                          "Northwind")
hTables = ns.GetFirstChildItem(hDatabase, SQLNSOBJECTTYPE_DATABASE_TABLES)
hTable = ns.GetFirstChildItem(hTables, SQLNSOBJECTTYPE_DATABASE_TABLE, _
                          "Customers")
Set oSQLNSObj = ns.GetSQLNamespaceObject(hTable)
```

Now we have an object reference to the appropriate `SQLNamespaceObject` object, let's see how we can execute commands.

Executing Commands

There are three ways we can execute a command:

❑ By calling the `ExecuteCommandByID` method

❑ By calling the `ExecuteCommandByName` method

❑ By retrieving a reference to a `SQLNamespaceCommand` object and calling its `Execute` method

We'll look at each of these, but first we'll take a quick look at the `SQLNamespaceCommand` object.

SQLNamespaceCommand Object

Each command that a particular type of `SQLNamespaceObject` can support is stored in that object's `SQLNamespaceCommands` collection. A `SQLNamespaceCommand` object has three properties that allow you to identify a command and an `Execute` method:

Looking at the properties in more detail:

Property	Data Type	Description
CommandID	Enumerated, long	This property identifies the command. The available constants are enumerated in `SQLNSCommandID`.
Name	String	This is the string identifier for the command. This is the string that would be displayed in a menu.
HelpString	String	This property provides a description of what the command does – it's suitable for displaying in a status bar or tool tip.

Executing Commands by CommandID

One way to execute a command is to call the `ExecuteCommandByID` method of the `SQLNamespaceObject` object. This method has the syntax:

```
object.ExecuteCommandByID(SQLCommandID As SQLNSCommandID, _
                          [hWnd] As Long, _
                          [modality] As SQLNSModality)
```

The *object* is a variable containing a `SQLNamespaceObject` reference. The arguments are described below:

SQLCommandID

This argument is the `CommandID` property of an object in the `SQLNamespaceCommands` collection for that object. `CommandID` properties are constants that are defined in the `SQLNSCommandID` enumeration. These enumerations are documented in the SQL-NS documentation of SQL Server 7.0 Help.

The only `CommandID` value we'll use in our sample application is `SQLNS_CmdID_PROPERTIES`, the `CommandID` of the command used to display a **Properties** dialog for an object.

hWnd

This is a Window handle to the window where the command's user interface should be displayed. This is an optional argument and, if it isn't passed, will be set to the window used for initialization.

modality

This optional argument determines whether the dialog should be displayed as modeless or modal. It has the following supported values, enumerated in the `SQLNSModality` constant enumeration:

Constant	Value	Description
SQLNamespace_DontCare	0	The window will be displayed according to the default behavior of the particular user interface element.
SQLNamespace_PreferModal	1	The window will be displayed as a modal dialog. A modal dialog will not allow the user to access any other window in the application until the window is closed. An example of a modal dialog is the **Open** dialog.
SQLNamespace_PreferModeless	2	The window will be displayed as a modeless dialog. A modeless dialog allows the user to access other windows in the application, but the dialog stays on top of the other windows. An example of a modeless dialog is the **Find** dialog.

SQL Namespace may override the specified modality in cases where the user interface element requires a specific modality. For example, the Properties dialog of a Database object is a modal dialog and will display as a modal dialog even if you execute the command using the SQLNamespace_PreferModeless option.

Executing a command by its CommandID property allows code to work regardless of the language settings of the computer running it. This makes it appropriate for applications that require international or multilingual deployment.

For example, to use the ExecuteCommandByID method to display the Properties dialog for the Customers table of the Northwind database we could extend our code as follows:

```
Dim hServer As Long
Dim hDatabases As Long
Dim hDatabase As Long
Dim hTables As Long
Dim hTable As Long
Dim ns as SQLNS.SQLNamespace
Set ns = CreateObject("SQLNS.SQLNamespace")
sConnect = "Server=" & sServer
If bIntegrated = True Then
    sConnect = sConnect & ";Trusted_Connection=Yes;"
Else
    sConnect = sConnect & ";UID=" & sUser & ";pwd=" & sPassword & ";"
End If

ns.Initialize "My Application", SQLNSRootType_Server, sConnect, frmMDIMain.hWnd
hServer = ns.GetRootItem
hDatabases = ns.GetFirstChildItem(hServer, SQLNSOBJECTTYPE_DATABASES)
hDatabase = ns.GetFirstChildItem(hDatabases, SQLNSOBJECTTYPE_DATABASE, _
                        "Northwind")
hTables = ns.GetFirstChildItem(hDatabase, SQLNSOBJECTTYPE_DATABASE_TABLES)
hTable = ns.GetFirstChildItem(hTables, SQLNSOBJECTTYPE_DATABASE_TABLE, _
                        "Customers")
Set oSQLNSObj = ns.GetSQLNamespaceObject(hTable)
oSQLNSObj.ExecuteCommandByID SQLNS_CmdID_Properties, frmMDIMain.hWnd, _
                        SQLNamespace_PreferModal
```

Executing Commands by Name

Using the ExecuteCommandByName method of the SQLNamespaceObject object is very similar to using the ExecuteCommandByID method. The only difference is that instead of passing a CommandID, the Name property of the command is passed. Its syntax is:

```
object.ExecuteCommandByName(bstrCommand As String, _
                        [hWnd] As Long, _
                        [modality] As SQLNSModality)
```

The main drawback to using this method is that it limits an application's use to a computer configured for a specific language.

So, to use the `ExecuteCommandByName` method to the display of the **Properties** dialog for the `Customers` table of the `Northwind` database we would have:

```
Dim hServer As Long
Dim hDatabases As Long
Dim hDatabase As Long
Dim hTables As Long
Dim hTable As Long
Dim ns as SQLNS.SQLNamespace
Set ns = CreateObject("SQLNS.SQLNamespace")
sConnect = "Server=" & sServer
If bIntegrated = True Then
    sConnect = sConnect & ";Trusted_Connection=Yes;"
Else
    sConnect = sConnect & ";UID=" & sUser & ";pwd=" & sPassword & ";"
End If

ns.Initialize "My Application", SQLNSRootType_Server, sConnect, frmMDIMain.hWnd
hServer = ns.GetRootItem
hDatabases = ns.GetFirstChildItem(hServer, SQLNSOBJECTTYPE_DATABASES)
hDatabase = ns.GetFirstChildItem(hDatabases, SQLNSOBJECTTYPE_DATABASE, _
                            "Northwind")
hTables = ns.GetFirstChildItem(hDatabase, SQLNSOBJECTTYPE_DATABASE_TABLES)
hTable = ns.GetFirstChildItem(hTables, SQLNSOBJECTTYPE_DATABASE_TABLE, _
                            "Customers")
Set oSQLNSObj = ns.GetSQLNamespaceObject(hTable)
oSQLNSObj.ExecuteCommandByName "Properties", frmMDIMain.hWnd, _
                        SQLNamespace_PreferModal
```

Using the Command Object

Another way to execute a command is to call the `Execute` method of the `SQLNamespaceCommand` object. The syntax for this method is:

```
object.Execute([hWnd], [modality])
```

This is an appropriate choice in the case that the index of the member of the `SQLNamespaceCommands` collection to be executed is known. For example, we might populate a menu array by iterating through the `SQLNamespaceCommands` and setting the `Caption` of each new menu item to the `Name` property of the appropriate `SQLNamespaceCommand`. Then, when a user selected a menu item, we might execute that command using the index of the menu array to retrieve the appropriate command.

Assuming that a reference to the `SQLNamespaceObject` object has already been obtained and it's been stored in a variable named `oSQLNSObj`, the code to achieve this objective is:

```
Private Sub PopulateMenu()

    Dim i as Integer
    For I = 1 to oSQLNSObj.Commands.Count
        Load mnuCommands(i)
        mnuCommands(i).Caption=oSQLNSObj.Commands(i).Name
    Next

End Sub
```

```
    Private Sub mnuCommands_Click(index As Integer)

        oSQLNSObj.Commands(index).Execute

End Sub
```

An example of this can be seen in the Survey Designer project, with the variation that the menu is a dynamic menu bar menu rather than a popup menu.

Let's complete our run through of the `SQLNamespaceCommand` object by looking at the `HelpString` property.

The HelpString Property

The `HelpString` property contains a short description of what the command does. This description can be used to provide either tool tip help for a graphical toolbar or status bar help. The code below could be used to display the information in the `HelpString` property in the first panel of a status bar control:

```
    Private Sub mnuCommands_Click(index As Integer)

        oSQLNSObj.Commands(index).Execute
        sbrStatus.Panels(1).Text = oSQLNSObj.Commands(Index).HelpString
    End Sub
```

Now we have some ideas on how to use SQL-NS, let's digress to discuss how to handle errors when using this technology.

Error Handling

There are two types of error handling that you need to be concerned with when using SQL-NS:

❑   Trapping errors that are raised by SQL-NS

❑   In the situation when an object is requested using one of the `SQLNamespace` navigational methods and no match is found

The errors that are raised by SQL-NS are enumerated in `SQLNSErrors`. The following code sample shows how this type of error handling can be added to the code fragment shown earlier:

```
    Dim hDatabases As Long
    Dim hDatabase As Long
    Dim hTables As Long
    Dim hTable As Long
    Dim ns as SQLNS.SQLNamespace
    On Error GoTo HandleErr
    Set ns = CreateObject("SQLNS.SQLNamespace")
    sConnect = "Server=" & sServer
```

```
If bIntegrated = True Then
    sConnect = sConnect & ";Trusted_Connection=Yes;"
Else
    sConnect = sConnect & ";UID=" & sUser & ";pwd=" & sPassword & ";"
End If
ns.Initialize "My Application", SQLNSRootType_Server, sConnect, frmMDIMain.hWnd
hServer = ns.GetRootItem
hDatabases = ns.GetFirstChildItem(hServer, SQLNSOBJECTTYPE_DATABASES)
hDatabase = ns.GetFirstChildItem(hDatabases, SQLNSOBJECTTYPE_DATABASE, _
                "Northwind")
hTables = ns.GetFirstChildItem(hDatabase, SQLNSOBJECTTYPE_DATABASE_TABLES)
hTable = ns.GetFirstChildItem(hTables, SQLNSOBJECTTYPE_DATABASE_TABLE, _
                "Customers")
Set oSQLNSObj = ns.GetSQLNamespaceObject(hTable)
oSQLNSObj.ExecuteCommandByName "Properties", frmMDIMain.hWnd, _
SQLNamespace_PreferModal
ExitHere:
    Exit Sub
HandleErr:
    Select Case Err.Number
        Case SQLNS_E_Already_Initialized
            Resume ExitHere
        Case SQLNS_E_InvalidConnectString
            MsgBox "Invalid Connection String. Check server and user information."
            Resume ExitHere
        Case SQLNS_E_InvalidRootInfo
            MsgBox "Could not connect to namespace root"
            Resume ExitHere
        Case SQLNS_E_InvalidServerName
            MsgBox "Check the server name and try again."
            Resume ExitHere
        Case SQLNS_E_DatabaseNotFound
            MsgBox "The Northwind database could not be found."
            Resume ExitHere
        Case SQLNS_E_InvalidLoginInfo
            MsgBox "The login information provided is incorrect."
            Resume ExitHere
        Case SQLNS_E_InvalidObjectHandle
            MsgBox "One of the object handles you tried to use is invalid."
            Resume ExitHere
    End Select
```

The second type of error we mentioned is when an object is requested using one of the SQLNamespace navigational methods and no match is found. It's a good idea to test the handles returned to make sure they are not zero before using them to retrieve another handle or to retrieve an object reference. The following code illustrates how defensive tests can be added to the sample code to prevent the SQLNS_E_InvalidObjectHandle error from occurring:

```
Dim hDatabases As Long
Dim hDatabase As Long
Dim hTables As Long
Dim hTable As Long
Dim ns as SQLNS.SQLNamespace
```

```
On Error GoTo HandleErr
Set ns = CreateObject("SQLNS.SQLNamespace")
sConnect = "Server=" & sServer
If bIntegrated = True Then
    sConnect = sConnect & ";Trusted_Connection=Yes;"
Else
    sConnect = sConnect & ";UID=" & sUser & ";pwd=" & sPassword & ";"
End If
ns.Initialize "My Application", SQLNSRootType_Server, sConnect, frmMDIMain.hWnd
hServer = ns.GetRootItem
If hServer <> 0 Then
    hDatabases = ns.GetFirstChildItem(hServer, SQLNSOBJECTTYPE_DATABASES)
    If hDatabases <> 0 Then
        hDatabase = ns.GetFirstChildItem(hDatabases, SQLNSOBJECTTYPE_DATABASE, _
                                "Northwind")
        If hDatabase <> 0 Then
            hTables = ns.GetFirstChildItem(hDatabase, _
                                    SQLNSOBJECTTYPE_DATABASE_TABLES)
            If hTables <> 0 Then
                hTable = ns.GetFirstChildItem(hTables, _
                                    SQLNSOBJECTTYPE_DATABASE_TABLE, _
                                    "Customers")
                If hTable <> 0 Then
                    Set oSQLNSObj = ns.GetSQLNamespaceObject(hTable)
                    oSQLNSObj.ExecuteCommandByName "Properties", frmMDIMain.hWnd, _
                                    SQLNamespace_PreferModal
                End If
            End If
        End If
    End If
End If
ExitHere:
    Exit Sub
HandleErr:
    Select Case Err.Number
        Case SQLNS_E_Already_Initialized
            Resume ExitHere
        Case SQLNS_E_InvalidConnectString
            MsgBox "Invalid Connection String. Check server and user information."
            Resume ExitHere
        Case SQLNS_E_InvalidRootInfo
            MsgBox "Could not connect to namespace root"
            Resume ExitHere
        Case SQLNS_E_InvalidServerName
            MsgBox "Check the server name and try again."
            Resume ExitHere
        Case SQLNS_E_DatabaseNotFound
            MsgBox "The Northwind database could not be found."
            Resume ExitHere
        Case SQLNS_E_InvalidLoginInfo
            MsgBox "The login information provided is incorrect."
            Resume ExitHere
        Case SQLNS_E_InvalidObjectHandle
            MsgBox "One of the object handles you tried to use is invalid."
            Resume ExitHere
    End Select
```

Now we've had an overview of the area let's see what all this means for our on-going Surveys Unlimited project.

Survey Designer – Displaying Table Properties

We can use SQL-NS to add functionality to the Survey Designer application that allows users to display a table's properties, using the standard SQL Enterprise Manager Properties dialog. So, to illustrate how these enhancements are coded into our application we're going to show how to:

❑ Initialize the namespace

❑ Retrieve the version number

❑ Check if the Table menu item should be enabled

❑ Navigate to the appropriate database and table

❑ Populate the table menu with the names of the commands

❑ Execute the selected commands

So, those are the broad topics we're going to be covering in this section – in detail the code changes we have made to the SurveyDesigner application are:

❑ A Public SQLNamespace object named ns is declared in modGlobals.bas.

❑ A Boolean variable named b7 is declared in modGlobals.bas.

❑ The cmdConnect_Click event of frmConnect has been modified to create an instance of the SQLNamespace object and initialize a connection to the namespace.

❑ A menu named mnuTable and a submenu named mnuCmds have been added to the Database menu of frmMDIMain. The mnuCmds item is a menu array with the Index property set to 0 and the Caption property set to "-".

❑ A set of methods has been added to frmMDIMain to handle populating mnuCmds, showing and hiding the mnuCmds, and destroying the menu commands. These methods are called in response to a table being selected, a database being selected, or frmDesign being unloaded, deactivated, or activated.

❑ The mnuDatabase_Click event has been modified to enable the Table menu only when connected to a valid namespace.

❑ The cboDBs_Click event has been coded to navigate the SQL namespace to the database selected by the user.

❑ The lstTables_Click event has been coded to navigate the SQL namespace to the table selected by the user.

❑ The mnuCmds_Click event has been coded execute the command selected by the user.

❑ A method (called GetVersionNumber) has been added to the SQLDDL.Server object to allow the SurveyDesigner application to retrieve the version number of the connected SQL Server.

OK, let's get to grips with the code itself starting with namespace initialization.

Initializing the Namespace

The `cmdConnect_Click` has been modified to initialize the `SQLNamespace` object after the SQL-DMO connection has been established. This means that there will be two connections open to the same database.

> **A SQL-DMO connection is not required in order to use SQL-NS, but our code depends on it because we use SQL-DMO to check the SQL Server version to make sure SQL-NS can be used.**

First, we make sure that the connection identified by `lConnID` is a connection to a SQL Server 7.0 installation (we'll see the code for doing that in a moment).

If it is a SQL Server 7.0 installation, we build a connection string and store it in `sConnect` (note that `sConnect` is declared as a `Variant`). Once the connection string is built, we can initialize the connection.

In this case, since we do not know the name of the database, we have chosen to use `SQLNSRootType_Server` as our root type. The final argument in the method passes the Window handle of the MDI form:

```
Private Sub cmdConnect_Click()

    Dim sConnect As Variant
    On Error GoTo HandleErr

    If chkIntegrated.Value = vbChecked Then
       lConnID = conn.ConnectSQLServer(cboServers)
       sServer = cboServers
       bIntegrated = True
    Else
       lConnID = conn.ConnectSQLServer(cboServers, txtUser, txtPassword)
       sServer = cboServers
       bIntegrated = False
       sUser = txtUser
       sPassword = txtPassword
    End If
    bConnected = True
    Me.Hide

    'Make sure it's a SQL 7 Server
    If conn.GetVersionNumber(lConnID) = 7 Then

        'Build connection string for SQL-NS
        sConnect = "Server=" & sServer
        If bIntegrated = True Then
           sConnect = sConnect & ";Trusted_Connection=Yes;"
        Else
          sConnect = sConnect & ";UID=" & sUser & ";pwd=" & _
                     sPassword & ";"
```

```
        End If

        'Instantiate the SQLNS.Namespace object
        Set ns = CreateObject("SQLNS.SQLNamespace")
        'Establish SQL-NS Connection
        ns.Initialize "Survey Designer", SQLNSRootType_Server, _
                    sConnect, frmMDIMain.hWnd
        b7 = True
    Else
        b7 = False
    End If

ExitHere:
    Exit Sub

HandleErr:

    Select Case Err.Number
        Case SQLNS_E_Already_Initialized
            Resume ExitHere
        Case SQLNS_E_InvalidConnectString
            MsgBox "Invalid Connection String. Check server and user information."
            Resume ExitHere
        Case SQLNS_E_InvalidRootInfo
            MsgBox "Could not connect to namespace root"
            Resume ExitHere
    End Select

End Sub
```

Retrieving the Version Number

The code below shows the implementation for the SQLDDL.Server component's GetVersionNumber method – note that it returns only the major version number:

```
Public Function GetVersionNumber(lConnID) As Long

    GetVersionNumber = oApp.SQLServers.ItemByID(lConnID).VersionMajor

End Function
```

Enabling the Table Menu Item

Although this code does not relate specifically to implementing SQL-NS in the application, we have shown it here so that you can see how the b7 variable determines whether SQL-NS functionality is available, and hence whether or not the Table submenu of frmMDIMain is available:

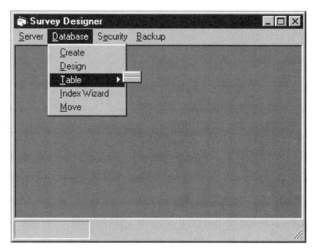

So for this particular submenu the code controlling availability is:

```
Private Sub mnuDatabase_Click()

    If bConnected = True Then
        mnuCreateDB.Enabled = True
        mnuDesign.Enabled = True
        If b7 = True Then
            mnuTable.Enabled = True
        Else
            mnuTable.Enabled = False
        End If
    Else
        mnuCreateDB.Enabled = False
        mnuDesign.Enabled = False
        mnuTable.Enabled = False
    End If

End Sub
```

Declaring Public Variables for the Handles

In order to be able to access objects in the SQL namespace, we need to store the handles to those objects. In this case, we're going to do that by declaring Public variables for each object in the hierarchy in modGlobals.bas. These variables are hServer, hDatabases, hDatabase, hTables, and hTable and since they will store handles, they are declared as Long.

The following code also shows that we have declared ns as the variable to hold the reference to SQLNS.SQLNamespace and b7 as a Boolean variable that keeps track of whether we are connected to a SQL Server 7.0 server. These variables were used when initializing the namespace and checking whether to enable the Table menu. The ns variable will be used in the code samples that follow.

```
Public ns As SQLNS.SQLNamespace
Public sServer As String
Public sUser As String
Public sPassword As String
Public bIntegrated As Boolean
Public bConnected As Boolean
Public bStopped As Boolean
Public b7 As Boolean
Public hServer As Long
Public hDatabases As Long
Public hDatabase As Long
Public hTables As Long
Public hTable As Long
```

Navigating to the Selected Database

The next thing we'll do to the application is to add code to retrieve a handle to the database the user selects in the cboDBs drop-down list on frmDesign. To do this, we'll create a sub procedure in frmDesign named SetNSPositionToDB:

```
Private Sub SetNSPositionToDB()

   If cboDBs.Text <> "" Then

      hServer = ns.GetRootItem

      'Make sure hServer is not 0
      If hServer = 0 Then
         MsgBox "Connection to the server is not initialized!"
         Exit Sub
      End If

      hDatabases = ns.GetFirstChildItem(hServer, SQLNSOBJECTTYPE_DATABASES)

      If hDatabases = 0 Then
         MsgBox "The root does not have a Databases collection."
         Exit Sub
      End If

      hDatabase = ns.GetFirstChildItem(hDatabases, SQLNSOBJECTTYPE_DATABASE, _
                                    frmDesign.cboDBs.Text)

      If hDatabase = 0 Then
         MsgBox "The Database does not exist."
         Exit Sub
      End If

   End If

End Sub
```

This procedure uses the `GetRootItem` method to retrieve a handle to the server, then `GetFirstChildItem` to navigate down to the selected database. This code is very similar to that we showed earlier in the chapter. We'll add code to call this procedure in the `cboDBs_Click` event:

```
Private Sub cboDBs_Click()

    Dim i As Integer
    Dim sTableList() As String

    lstTables.Clear
    sTableList = db.GetTableList(lConnID, cboDBs)

    For i = 0 To UBound(sTableList)
        lstTables.AddItem sTableList(i)
    Next

    cmdEdit.Enabled = False
    SetNSPositionToDB
    hTable = 0
End Sub
```

We also add code to set the `hTable` variable to `0` in case it already references a table in a different database.

Navigating to the Selected Table

We'll follow a similar strategy to retrieve a handle for the selected table. First, we'll create a sub procedure in `frmDesign` named `SetNSPositionToTable`:

```
Public Sub SetNSPositionToTable()

    If frmDesign.lstTables.Text <> "" And hDatabase <> 0 Then
        hTables = ns.GetFirstChildItem(hDatabase, SQLNSOBJECTTYPE_DATABASE_TABLES)

        If hTables = 0 Then
            MsgBox "The database does not have a Tables collection."
            Exit Sub
        End If

        hTable = ns.GetFirstChildItem(hTables, SQLNSOBJECTTYPE_DATABASE_TABLE, _
                                      frmDesign.lstTables.Text)

        If hTable = 0 Then
            MsgBox "The table does not exist."
            Exit Sub
        End If
    End If

End Sub
```

This time the procedure checks to make sure that the `hDatabase` variable does not contain 0 before beginning to crawl down the namespace. We call this procedure from the `lstTables_Click` event:

```
Private Sub lstTables_Click()

    If lstTables.Text <> "" Then
        cmdEdit.Enabled = True
        SetNSPositionToTable
    Else
        cmdEdit.Enabled = False
        hTable = 0
    End If

End Sub
```

If a table name is not selected, we set the `hTable` reference to 0.

Populating the Table Menu

The next step we need to take is to populate the <u>T</u>able submenu with the names of the commands in the `Table` object's `Commands` collection. To do this, we add a method to `frmMDIMain` named `AddTableCommands`:

```
Public Sub AddTableCommands()

    Dim nso As SQLNS.SQLNamespaceObject
    Dim i As Integer

    'Check for null handle
    If hTable <> 0 Then
        'Add table commands
        Set nso = ns.GetSQLNamespaceObject(hTable)
        For i = 1 To nso.Commands.Count
            Load mnuCmds(i)
            mnuCmds(i).Caption = nso.Commands(i).Name
            mnuCmds(i).Visible = True
        Next
    End If

    'Hide the separator bar
    mnuCmds(0).Visible = False

    Set nso = Nothing

End Sub
```

Notice that we are checking to make sure that the `hTable` variable does not contain 0. If it doesn't we get a reference to the `SQLNamespaceObject` object it refers to and iterate through the `Commands` collection, retrieving the name of each command and adding it as a menu item in the `mnuCmds` array.

Finally, we set the Visible property of item number 0 in the mnuCmds array to False, which prevents the separator bar from showing when the mnuCmds contains other items.

> **A menu that has submenus must have at least one visible submenu at all times. For this reason, we cannot set the Visible property of mnuCmds(0) to False until there are other visible items in the menu.**

We call the AddTableCommands method from the lstTables_Click event, provided an item in the list is selected and that the Count property of mnuCmds is equal to 1:

```
Private Sub lstTables_Click()
    If lstTables.Text <> "" Then
        cmdEdit.Enabled = True
        SetNSPositionToTable
        If frmMDIMain.mnuCmds.Count = 1 Then
            'Populate the menu with table commands
            frmMDIMain.AddTableCommands
        End If
    Else
        cmdEdit.Enabled = False
        hTable = 0
    End If
End Sub
```

Executing the Selected Command

The next step is to add code to the mnuCmds_Click event to display the HelpString property of the command the user selects in the StatusBar (called sbrStatus) and execute that command:

```
Private Sub mnuCmds_Click(Index As Integer)

    Dim nso As SQLNS.SQLNamespaceObject

    'Check for null handle
    If hTable <> 0 Then
        Set nso = ns.GetSQLNamespaceObject(hTable)
        sbrStatus.Panels(1).Text = nso.Commands(Index).HelpString
        nso.Commands(Index).Execute
    End If

End Sub
```

Notice that we are using the Index argument to determine which menu item was selected. This is possible because the Commands collection is a 1-based collection and we added items to the mnuCmds array beginning with element 1.

Right, let's see how it all fits together.

The Application in Action

If we want to display the properties dialog for the Employees table of the Northwind database, we take the following steps. Select Database | Design and then select Northwind from the Database drop-down and Employees from the Tables list box:

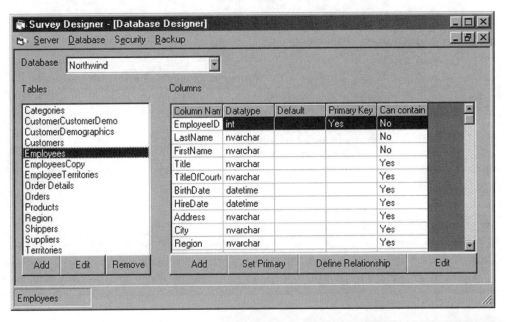

Then select Database | Table | Properties and the properties dialog of the Employees table will appear:

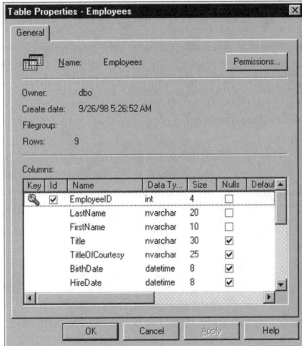

The other menu items that can be chosen are shown in the graphic below. These are all of the commands that belong to the `Commands` collection of the `Table` object:

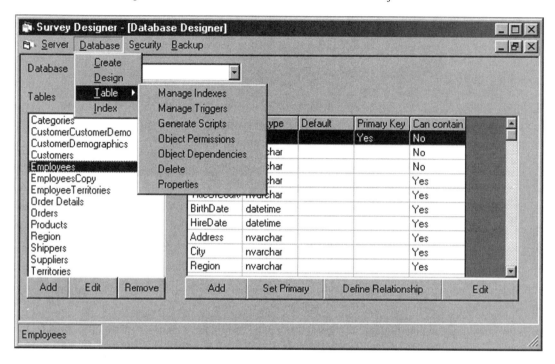

Hiding and Showing the Table Commands

At this point, the <u>T</u>able menu is fully functional. However, once the `Table` commands have been added to the menu, they will still be available even if the `frmDesign` form is deactivated or a table is not selected. To prevent this, we've created three methods in `frmMDIMain`, these are `HideTableCommands`, `ShowTableCommands`, and `RemoveTableCommands`.

The code for these methods is:

```
Public Sub ShowTableCommands()

    Dim i As Integer

    For i = 1 To mnuCmds.Count - 1
        mnuCmds(i).Visible = True
    Next

    'Hide the separator bar
    mnuCmds(0).Visible = False

End Sub
```

```
Public Sub HideTableCommands()

   Dim i As Integer

   'Show the separator bar
   mnuCmds(0).Visible = True

   For i = 1 To mnuCmds.Count - 1
      mnuCmds(i).Visible = False
   Next

End Sub
```

```
Public Sub RemoveTableCommands()

   Dim i As Integer

   'Show the separator bar
   mnuCmds(0).Visible = True

   For i = 1 To mnuCmds.Count - 1
      Unload mnuCmds(i)
   Next

End Sub
```

The ShowTableCommands method and the HideTableCommands method are called from the lstTables_Click event procedure as shown below. ShowTableCommands is used if a table is selected, but the commands have already been added to the mnuCmds array. HideTableCommands is used if a table has not been selected, as would be the case when the control received focus, but it had not been populated with any tables:

```
Private Sub lstTables_Click()
   If lstTables.Text <> "" Then
      cmdEdit.Enabled = True
      SetNSPositionToTable
      If frmMDIMain.mnuCmds.Count = 1 Then
         'Populate the menu with table commands
         frmMDIMain.AddTableCommands
      Else
         frmMDIMain.ShowTableCommands
      End If
   Else
      cmdEdit.Enabled = False
      If frmMDIMain.mnuCmds.Count > 1 Then
         frmMDIMain.HideTableCommands
      End If
      hTable = 0
   End If
End Sub
```

The `Activate` event of `frmDesign` utilizes both the `AddTableCommands` and the `ShowTableCommands` methods using code very similar to that used in the `lstTables_Click` event:

```
Private Sub Form_Activate()

    If lstTables.Text <> "" Then
        If frmMDIMain.mnuCmds.Count = 1 Then
            'Populate the menu with table commands
            frmMDIMain.AddTableCommands
        Else
            frmMDIMain.ShowTableCommands
        End If
    End If

End Sub
```

The `HideTableCommands` method is also called from within `cboDBs_Click` and the `Deactivate` event for `frmDesign`:

```
Private Sub cboDBs_Click()

    Dim i As Integer
    Dim sTableList() As String

    lstTables.Clear
    sTableList = db.GetTableList(lConnID, cboDBs)

    For i = 0 To UBound(sTableList)
        lstTables.AddItem sTableList(i)
    Next
    cmdEdit.Enabled = False
    SetNSPositionToDB
    hTable = 0
    frmMDIMain.HideTableCommands

End Sub


Private Sub Form_Deactivate()
    If frmMDIMain.mnuCmds.Count > 1 Then
        frmMDIMain.HideTableCommands
    End If
End Sub
```

> You can't use the **RemoveTableCommands** method inside the **cboDBs_Click** event procedure because it unloads controls from a control array. This is not legal during a ComboBox **Click** event, **Change** event, or **DropDown** event.

The `RemoveTableCommands` method is called from the `Unload` event of `frmDesign`:

```
Private Sub Form_Unload(Cancel As Integer)
    If frmMDIMain.mnuCmds.Count > 1 Then
        frmMDIMain.RemoveTableCommands
    End If
End Sub
```

Cleaning Up

Finally, we need to add some code to destroy the reference to `ns` if the user severs the SQL-DMO connection or closes the application. The reason we want to free this reference if the user closes the SQL-DMO connection is to prevent the `SQLNS_E_Already_Initialized` error if the user attempts to reconnect to the SQL Server:

```
Private Sub mnuDisconnect_Click()

    On Error Resume Next
    conn.DisconnectSQLServer lConnID
    bConnected = False
    'Release the SQL Namespace connection
    Set ns = Nothing

End Sub


Private Sub MDIForm_Unload(Cancel As Integer)
    Dim frmCurrent As Form
    Set objDB = Nothing
    Set db = Nothing
    If bConnected Then
        conn.DisconnectSQLServer lConnID
        Set conn = Nothing
        Set ns = Nothing
    End If
    For Each frmCurrent In Forms
        Unload frmCurrent
    Next
End Sub
```

SQL-NS Integration with SQL-DMO

SQL-NS is really built on top of SQL-DMO: this means that SQL-NS can allow you to retrieve a reference to the SQL-DMO object associated with a particular namespace handle. The `SQLNamespace` object's `GetSQLDMOObject` method allows you to do just that. It has the syntax:

```
object.GetSQLDMOObject(ItemIn)
```

As with earlier methods, the *ItemIn* argument is the handle of the namespace object.

How do you know the type of object to which you are going to receive a reference? Our recommendation is to use the `GetType` method of the `SQLNamespace` object and check the type before retrieving a reference to the SQL-DMO object. The `GetType` method has the following syntax:

```
object.GetType(ItemIn)
```

It returns a value from the constant enumeration `SQLNSObjectType`. You can use the returned type to ensure that the SQL-DMO object is set to a variable of a particular type to take advantage of early binding.

> **This method can only be used to retrieve references to `Server` and `Database` objects. Attempting to use it on other types of objects will result in an error.**

The code below is *not* part of the sample application, but it does illustrate how to ensure that you only attempt to retrieve a SQL-DMO object when appropriate and that they can use early binding:

```
Dim oServer As SQLDMO.Server
Dim oDatabase As SQLDMO.Database

Select Case ns.GetType(hObject)
   Case SQLNSObjectType_Server
      Set oServer = ns.GetSQLDMOObject(hObject)
   Case SQLNSObjectType_Database
      Set oDatabase = ns.GetSQLDMOObject(hObject)
End Select
```

Invoking Wizards

Before we leave the subject of SQL-NS, let's take a quick look at how we can use SQL-NS to launch the wizards included with SQL Server 7.0. This is one place where SQL-NS can greatly decrease the amount of work we need to do to build a very powerful SQL Server administration tool.

The commands to launch the SQL Server wizards are available through the `Commands` collection of the `SQLNamespaceObject` when that object represents a server. The wizard commands that are available at the server level are listed in the table below:

Name	CommandID Constant	Description
Wizards	SQLNS_CmdID_WIZARDS	This command displays a dialog users can use to select which wizard to run.

Name	CommandID Constant	Description
Create Database Wizard	SQLNS_CmdID_WIZARD_CREATEDB	This command launches a wizard that walks users through creating a database.
Create Index Wizard	SQLNS_CmdID_WIZARD_CREATEINDEX	This command launches a wizard that walks users through creating an index.
Data Import Wizard	SQLNS_CmdID_WIZARD_DTSIMPORT	This command launches a wizard that walks users through configuring a DTS import.
Data Export Wizard	SQLNS_CmdID_WIZARD_DTSEXPORT	This command launches a wizard that walks users through configuring a DTS export.
Create Job Wizard	SQLNS_CmdID_WIZARD_CREATEJOB	This command launches a wizard that walks the user through creating a job.
Security Wizard	SQLNS_CmdID_WIZARD_SECURITY	This command launches a wizard that walks a user through creating a login.
Create Stored Procedure Wizard	SQLNS_CmdID_WIZARD_SP	This command launches a wizard that walks a user through creating a stored procedure.
Create View Wizard	SQLNS_CmdID_WIZARD_VIEW	This command launches a wizard that walks a user through creating a view.
Index Tuning Wizard	SQLNS_CmdID_WIZARD_INDEXTUNING	This command launches the index tuning wizard, which analyzes a sample workload and makes recommendations for the optimal index configuration.
Create Alert Wizard	SQLNS_CmdID_WIZARD_ALERT	This command launches a wizard that walks a user through creating an alert.

Table Continued on Following Page

Name	CommandID Constant	Description
Database Maintenance Plan Wizard	SQLNS_CmdID_WIZARD_MAINTPLAN	This command launches a wizard that walks through creating a plan for routine maintenance, including consistency checks and backups.
Web Assistant Wizard	SQLNS_CmdID_WIZARD_WEBASST	This command launches a wizard that generates HTML based on Transact-SQL queries against a SQL Server 7.0 database.
Backup Wizard	SQLNS_CmdID_WIZARD_BACKUP	This command launches a wizard that walks you through configuring backups.
Create Trace Wizard	SQLNS_CmdID_WIZARD_CREATETRACE	This command launches a wizard that can create traces that can be used when troubleshooting database problems and optimizing performance.

Survey Designer – Launching the Create Index Wizard

The SurveyDesigner client application uses the Create Index wizard to provide users with the ability to create an index via an Index menu item. The menu item is available from the Database menu:

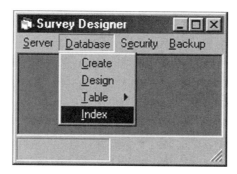

The code for the `mnuIndex_Click` event procedure is actually much simpler than that which we saw in the previous example, because the command is available at the root item identified when the connection is initialized:

```
Private Sub mnuIndex_Click()
    Dim nsObject As SQLNS.SQLNamespaceObject
    hServer = ns.GetRootItem
    If hServer <> 0 Then
        Set nsObject = ns.GetSQLNamespaceObject(hServer)
        nsObject.ExecuteCommandByID (SQLNS_CmdID_WIZARD_CREATEINDEX)
    End If
End Sub
```

Selecting the Index menu item brings up the following screen:

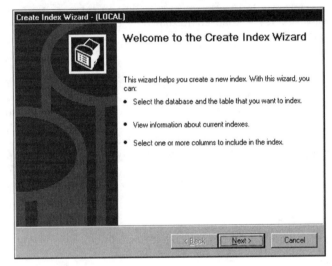

To prevent the Index menu item from being enabled if a connection has not been established, we'll also modify the code of the `mnuDatabase_Click` event:

```
Private Sub mnuDatabase_Click()
    If bConnected = True Then
        mnuCreateDB.Enabled = True
        mnuDesign.Enabled = True
        If b7 = True Then
            mnuTable.Enabled = True
        Else
            mnuTable.Enabled = False
        End If
        mnuIndex.Enabled = True
    Else
        mnuCreateDB.Enabled = False
        mnuDesign.Enabled = False
        mnuTable.Enabled = False
        mnuIndex.Enabled = False
    End If
End Sub
```

Summary

In this chapter we've had a pretty hard look at the SQL-NS object library and, while not giving a comprehensive (and frighteningly exhaustive) treatment of every possible use of the library, we have showed how it allows us to reuse many of the wizards and property dialogs available in SQL Server 7.0 Enterprise Manager.

We started the chapter by looking at the hierarchy of the object model and discussed what the concept of polymorphism means to this model. We then highlighted how to use SQL-NS by building some code blocks that facilitate navigation from a root of the `Server` object to the `Table` object named `Customers` in the `Northwind` database and would allow display the **Properties** dialog for that table.

We then applied this approach to the Surveys Unlimited business scenario and coded some enhancements to the **Database** | **Table** menu selection available in the Survey Designer application. We then finished the chapter by seeing how we could launch the **Create Index Wizard** from within our application.

A further demonstration of the use of SQL-NS is the SQL Namespace Sample Browser that comes with SQL Server 7.0 and can be found in the **\Mssql7\DevTools\Samples\Sqlns\vb\Browse** directory. This sample allows you to view the SQL-NS hierarchy, and view and execute commands.

Our treatment of the Surveys Unlimited business scenario is almost complete – in the next chapter we are going to tidy up a few loose ends and then deploy the application under MTS.

Deploying Your Application

Once our application is finished and tested, we'll need to deploy its parts and pieces to the appropriate users in your organization. This chapter will look at deployment concerns, including:

❑ Installation of libraries on the various machines

❑ Preparing the SQLDDL component for use with MTS

❑ Creating a distribution package for the client application that configures it to work with a remote component

The course this chapter will take is as follows:

❑ An overview of our deployment strategy showing the machines involved and which components will run on each.

❑ Discussion of how to revise previously constructed components to take that architecture into account. We'll need to revise the CustomerManager component to accept the name of a server as an argument, and the SQLDDL component so that it uses CustomerManager and will participate in an MTS transaction.

❑ Deployment of the SQLDDL component into MTS. Here we'll also discuss MTS security and show how roles can be used to limit access to middle-tier components.

❑ Configuration of the client computers and building a Setup program. We have chosen to use the Package and Deployment Wizard to keep things simple.

Deployment Strategy Overview

The n-tier design of our application allows us to be very flexible in how its components are deployed in our environment. Remember, the *n* in n-tier refers to logical tiers only. We could choose to deploy the application all on a single computer, divide the application between client workstations and the SQL Server, or spread the components across multiple computers on the network. For simplicity of design, our example will assume the deployment strategy shown in the graphic below:

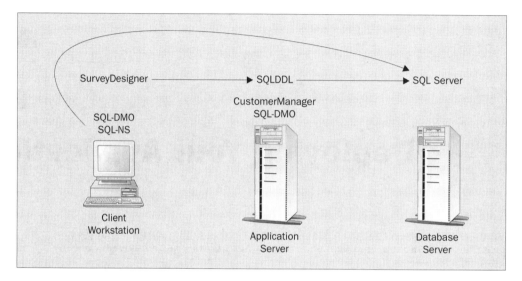

This strategy involves deploying the SQLDDL and CustomerManager components to a middle-tier application server and the SurveyDesigner application to the client workstations.

SQL-DMO and SQL-NS are listed as dependent libraries on the client computer. CustomerManager and SQL-DMO are both dependencies of the SQLDDL component.

> Remember, the ActiveX Data Objects library is also a dependency of the **CustomerManager** library. **CustomerManager** uses ADO to make an entry in the **CustomerManagement** database. The ADO library is not listed in the graphic to keep the drawing straightforward.

Revising and Using the CustomerManager Component

You may recall from Chapter 2 that the design of the CustomerManager component required that it run on the computer where the CustomerManagement database was located. While that was fine for seeing how MTS transactions functioned, it isn't appropriate for our deployment strategy. Therefore, we need to modify the AddSurvey method of the CustomerManager.Survey component so that it accepts a server name and connection information as arguments and dynamically creates the connection string.

> One of the rules of COM is that once an interface is published and used, changes like adding arguments to methods will break compatibility. Going back to our example of a contractor who builds the foundation of a house in Chapter 2, it can be compared to requiring an extra fee after the contract has been signed. That extra fee makes the contract unacceptable to the consumer and effectively breaks the compatibility of the relationship.
>
> The change we're making here will break compatibility with existing consumers and is the type of change that should be stringently avoided in a production environment. However, since our purpose is to learn about building enterprise SQL Server management applications and we know that the component is not yet being used by any consumer other than our test application, we can go ahead and break compatibility without concern.

The code below shows the modified `AddSurvey` method. In addition to dynamically building the connection string, we have also changed all of the arguments to `ByVal`. This will improve performance by minimizing marshaling when the component is called cross-process.

> A component is called cross-process when it is an EXE component or, as in the case of our example, when it is a DLL component running inside MTS on a different computer.
>
> Marshaling is the process by which the arguments are packaged up to be sent across a process or machine boundary, then mapped into memory locations in the process where the component is running.

```
Public Sub AddSurvey(ByVal sCompanyName As String, _
        ByVal sSurveyName As String, ByVal sDatabaseName As String, _
        ByVal sServer As String, ByVal bTrustedConnection As Boolean, _
        Optional sUser As String, Optional sPassword As String)

    On Error GoTo abortTran

    Dim sConnectionString As String
    GetObjectContext.SetAbort

    Set oConn = CreateObject("ADODB.Connection")
    Set oCommand = CreateObject("ADODB.Command")
    Set oRS = CreateObject("ADODB.Recordset")
    oConn.Provider = "SQLOLEDB"

    'Build connection string dynamically
    ' Define the Server parameter by appending the value of sServer
    'after "Server=".
    sConnectionString = "Server=" & sServer & ";"

    'Append the hardcoded database name "CustomerManagement"
    sConnectionString = sConnectionString & "Database=CustomerManagement;"
```

```
      'Check to see if the user is using Windows NT (Trusted) authentication
      'or SQL Server authentication and set the Trusted Connection parameter
      'as appropriate and the UID and Pwd parameters if necessary.
      If bTrustedConnection = True Then
         sConnectionString = sConnectionString & "Trusted_Connection=yes;"
      Else
         sConnectionString = sConnectionString & "Trusted_Connection=no;"
         sConnectionString = sConnectionString & "UID=" & sUser & ";"
         sConnectionString = sConnectionString & "Pwd=" & sPassword & ";"
      End If

      oConn.CursorLocation = adUseClient

      'Set the ConnectionString property of the oConn object equal to the
      'string that was just built.
      oConn.ConnectionString = sConnectionString
      oConn.Open

      Set oCommand.ActiveConnection = oConn
      sCompanyName = Replace(sCompanyName, "'", "''")
      oCommand.CommandType = adCmdText
      oCommand.CommandText = "SELECT CustomerID From Customers Where Company = '" _
                        & sCompanyName & "'"
      Set oRS = oCommand.Execute

      If oRS.BOF = False Then
         oCommand.CommandText = "INSERT Surveys (CustomerID, SurveyName," & _
               "DatabaseName) VALUES ('" & oRS.Fields(0) & "', '" & sSurveyName & _
               "', '" & sDatabaseName & "')"
         oCommand.Execute
         GetObjectContext.SetComplete
      Else
         Err.Raise vbObjectError + 100, "CustomerManager.Survey", _
                              "Customer Does Not Exist"
      End If

   LeaveIt:
      Exit Sub
   abortTran:
      GetObjectContext.SetAbort
      Err.Raise Err.Number, Err.Source, Err.Description
      Resume LeaveIt

   End Sub
```

> We have chosen to use a **ConnectionString** argument to specify the connection
> values in order to remain consistent with the example in Chapter 2. However,
> ADO also allows connection values to be specified by setting individual members
> of the **Connection** object's **Properties** collection.

Once the code modifications have been made, the DLL will need to be re-compiled. However,
since the signature of the interface has been changed, references to the old version of the DLL will
have to be removed before re-compilation.

The old version is referenced both in the test project and in the MTS package; to remove the reference from the test project, open the project in Visual Basic, display the References dialog, and remove the check mark next to CustomerManager. To remove the reference from the MTS package, open the MTS Explorer by running Start | Programs | Windows NT Option Pack | Microsoft Transaction Server | Transaction Server Explorer and delete the component from the SurveyComponents package:

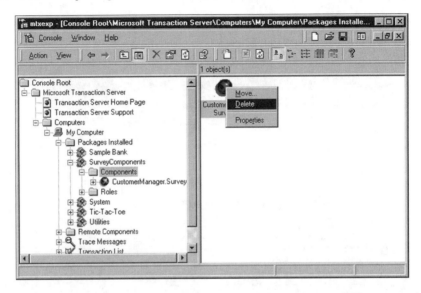

Before compiling CustomerManager again, make its Version Compatibility setting (accessible via the Component tab of the CustomerManager project's Properties dialog) to No Compatibility. This means that when the CustomerManager is recompiled, new GUIDs are created for each class and interface. There is no backwards compatibility with this option and all clients of the project will also have to be recompiled. This is not a problem to us here as we have not yet used CustomerManager with SQLDDL, but be very wary of using this option unless you are prepared to make a clean break between versions.

Let's now move on to address the changes that need to be made to the SQLDDL component.

Integrating MTS Functionality into SQLDDL

The next step in getting ready to deploy our application is to modify the SQLDDL component so that it uses the CustomerManager component to make an entry to the CustomerManagement database's Surveys table when a Survey database is created. This change will involve several steps:

❑ Setting a reference to the necessary libraries

❑ Causing the SQLDDL component to participate in an MTS transaction

❑ Declaring and instantiating the CustomerManager component

❑ Calling the AddSurvey method of the CustomerManager component

Let's look at how this is accomplished.

Setting a Reference to the Necessary Libraries

As with all other components, we'll start by setting references to the libraries we need to use. At this point we need to reference the:

- ❑ `CustomerManager` component's type library
- ❑ Microsoft Transaction Server Type Library
- ❑ Shared Property Manager Type Library

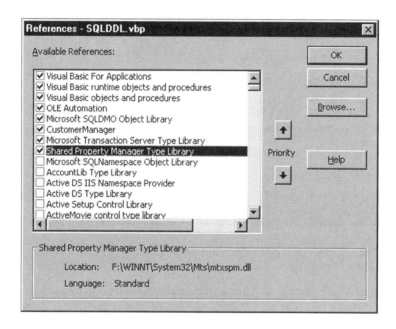

Adding MTS Functionality

In order to allow the `SQLDDL` component to work well with MTS, we need to make it a **stateless component**. A stateless component is one that does not store the values of variables (or read/write properties) between method calls. For example, a "stateful" component might accept a user's account number in one method call, store it in a module-level or global variable, and use it in another. A stateless component would either accept the account number as an argument with each method call or store it in persistent storage or in the **Shared Property Manager** between method calls.

Creating MTS components as stateless components is important because we are going to allow MTS to activate the components when a consumer needs them and deactivate the components when the consumer has finished with them. This will improve your application's scalability by allowing JIT activation, as discussed in Chapter 2. During deactivation, the public variables are all set to `Nothing` and they are re-initialized during reactivation.

The only public variable we are using is the oApp object, which is used to refer to the top-level object of the SQL-DMO hierarchy. The problem is that our component depends on this object, so we can't just delete it; additionally it's also inefficient to have the consumer pass this object back and forth across machine boundaries. We'll solve the problem by using the MTS Shared Property Manager to implement oApp as a property.

The Shared Property Manager allows you to store information that is required by a single component between method calls or by multiple components within the same package. To use it, you add the appropriate reference to your component and create a **Shared Property Group**. The Shared Property Group is given a name that your component and other components can use to access it. You can then add properties to the Shared Property Group and use it to store their values. A **Shared Property** can be of any data type that can be held in a Variant, including object references.

First, delete the Public variable declaration for oApp from the Strings.bas standard module, then add the following code to the Server class:

```
    Private oSPM As MTxSpm.SharedPropertyGroupManager
    Private oSpg As MTxSpm.SharedPropertyGroup
    Private oSProperty As MTxSpm.SharedProperty

  Friend Property Get oApp() As SQLDMO.Application

    Dim bExists As Boolean

    'Create an instance of the SharedPropertyGroupManager or get a reference
    ' to it if it already exists
    Set oSPM = CreateObject("Mtxspm.SharedPropertyGroupManager.1")

    'Create a property group named SharedDMO or retrieve a reference to it if
    'it has already been created.
    Set oSpg = oSPM.CreatePropertyGroup("SharedDMO", 0, 1, bExists)

    'Create a property named oAppReference or retrieve a reference to it if it
    'already has been created.
    Set oSProperty = oSpg.CreateProperty("oAppReference", bExists)

    'If the oAppReference property did not exist previously, create an instance
    'of the SQLDMO.Application object and store its reference in the
    'oAppReference property. Return the reference as oApp. Otherwise, just
    'return the value of the oAppReference property to the consumer.
    If bExists = False Then
        Set oApp = CreateObject("SQLDMO.Application")
        oSProperty.Value = oApp
    Else
        Set oApp = oSProperty.Value
    End If

    Set oSProperty = Nothing
    Set oSpg = Nothing
    Set oSPM = Nothing

  End Property
```

The `oApp Property Get` procedure creates an instance of the
`SharedPropertyGroupManager`. If a `SharedPropertyGroupManager` already exists within
the context of the object, a reference to it will be returned. Next, we use that reference to create a
`SharedPropertyGroup` object named `SharedDMO`. Once again, if the group already exists, a
reference to it is returned to the consumer and the `bExists` variable we pass in is set to `True`.
The `CreatePropertyGroup` method has the following syntax:

```
object.CreatePropertyGroup(name, dwIsoMode, dwrelmode, fExists)
```

The *name* argument is a string that defines the name of the property. The *dwIsoMode* argument
specifies how the properties in the group should be locked. A value of 0 locks an individual
property only while the value is being set or retrieved. A value of 1 locks all of the properties in
the group for the duration of the method the client is executing. The *dwrelmode* argument
determines when the property group will be destroyed. A value of 0 destroys the property group as
soon as all references to it have been set to `Nothing`. A value of 1 causes it to remain in memory
until the process that created it is terminated.

We have set it to 1 here so that the `oApp` property will be persistent as long as the `SQLDDL`
component is running. The final argument is a `ByRef` argument. If the property group existed
before the method was called, this argument will contain `True` when the method returns.

The reference returned to the group is then used to create a property named `oAppReference`. As
with the other methods, if the property already exists, it returns a reference to it and sets the
`bExists` variable we pass in to `True`.

Then we can check the value of `bExists`. If it is `False`, we need to create an instance of
`SQLDMO.Application` and set the `oAppReference` property to reference it. We return the
reference as the value of `oApp`.

If `bExists` is `True`, the property already exists and we simply need to return its value.

Finally, in order to call the `oApp` property procedure, each class module in the project will need to
hold a reference to the `Server` component of `SQLDDL`. To implement this, add the following code
to the General Declarations section of each class module with the exception of `Server` and
`Constants`:

```
Dim oDDLServer As New SQLDDL.Server
```

We will also need to use the fully qualified name with each call to the `oApp` property. The easiest
way to implement this change will be to search on `oApp` and replace it with `oDDLServer.oApp` in
the affected modules (don't forget that this replacement is *not* needed in `Server` itself).

Declaring and Instantiating the CustomerManager Component

Now we must declare and instantiate an instance of the `CustomerManager.Survey` component.
Since the component is only used as part of the `Create` method of the `Database` class, that is
where we'll perform the instantiation. We'll also use a local variable to hold a reference to the
object:

```
Public Function Create(ByVal lConnID As Long, ByVal sSurveyName As String, _
                       ByVal sCustomerName As String)

    Dim sCustomerID As String
    Dim sDBName As String
    Dim sDFName As String
    Dim sLFName As String
    Dim sDriveAndPath As String
    Dim oSqlServer As SQLDMO.SQLServer
    Dim oSqldb As SQLDMO.Database
    Dim oSqldf As SQLDMO.DBFile
    Dim oSqllf As SQLDMO.LogFile
    Dim oCM As CustomerManager.Survey

    'Object Instantiation
    Set oSqldb = CreateObject("SQLDMO.Database")
    Set oSqldf = CreateObject("SQLDMO.DBFile")
    Set oSqllf = CreateObject("SQLDMO.LogFile")
    Set oCM = GetObjectContext.CreateInstance("CustomerManager.Survey")

    'Business Rules to determine names
    sCustomerID = Left(sCustomerName, 6)
    sDBName = sCustomerID & Left(sSurveyName, 5)
    sDFName = Left(sCustomerID, 4) & Left(sSurveyName, 4) & ".mdf"
    sLFName = Left(sCustomerID, 4) & Left(sSurveyName, 4) & ".ldf"

    'Set Database Name property
    oSqldb.Name = sDBName

    'Business Rule to ensure that database is created
    'on the drive with the most space
    Set oSqlServer = oDDLServer.oApp.SQLServers.ItemByID(lConnID)
    sDriveAndPath = GetDriveWithMostSpace(lConnID) & "surveydat\"

    'Set DBFile properties
    oSqldf.Name = sDFName
    oSqldf.PhysicalName = sDriveAndPath & sDFName
    oSqldf.Size = 5
    oSqldf.FileGrowthType = SQLDMOGrowth_Percent
    oSqldf.FileGrowth = 20
    oSqldf.MaximumSize = 40

    'Set LogFile properties
    oSqllf.Name = sLFName
    oSqllf.PhysicalName = sDriveAndPath & sLFName
    oSqllf.Size = 2
    oSqllf.FileGrowthType = SQLDMOGrowth_Percent
    oSqllf.FileGrowth = 20
    oSqldf.MaximumSize = 40

    'Add DBFile to the PRIMARY filegroup
    oSqldb.FileGroups("PRIMARY").DBFiles.Add oSqldf
```

267

```
'Add the LogFile to the LogFiles collection
oSqldb.TransactionLog.LogFiles.Add oSqllf

'Add the Database to the Databases collection.
'At this point, the database is created.
oSqlServer.Databases.Add oSqldb

'Return the name of the database
Create = oSqldb.Name

End Function
```

Note that object instantiation is performed slightly differently for this component. Since we want it to be included in the same transactional context as `SQLDDL.Database`, the `GetObjectContext` function is used to retrieve a reference to the MTS context and call the `CreateInstance` method of the `ObjectContext` to instantiate `CustomerManager.Survey`.

> **Whenever you instantiate one MTS component from another, you want to be sure to do so within the existing transactional context. Otherwise, the component will be created inside a separate context and cannot be enlisted in the current transaction.**

The next step is to call the `AddSurvey` method and to add the `SetComplete` and `SetAbort` calls to allow the `Create` method to let MTS know whether it is satisfied or dissatisfied with the result. In this case, we'll use `SetComplete` if the `Create` method completes without an error. We'll call `SetAbort` to alert MTS that an error occurred and the transaction should not be committed. We'll also call `SetAbort` at the beginning of the method to protect the transaction against a failure our component can't catch. The declaration for the function has also been changed to include the connection parameters the `AddSurvey` method will expect:

```
Public Function Create(ByVal lConnID As Long, ByVal sSurveyName As String, _
                       ByVal sCustomerName As String, _
                       ByVal bIntegrated As Boolean, Optional sUser As String, _
                       Optional sPassword As String)

    Dim sCustomerID As String
    Dim sDBName As String
    Dim sDFName As String
    Dim sLFName As String
    Dim sDriveAndPath As String
    Dim oSqlServer As SQLDMO.SQLServer
    Dim oSqldb As SQLDMO.Database
    Dim oSqldf As SQLDMO.DBFile
    Dim oSqllf As SQLDMO.LogFile
    Dim oCM As CustomerManager.Survey

    GetObjectContext.SetAbort
    On Error GoTo abortTran
```

```
'Object Instantiation
Set oSqldb = CreateObject("SQLDMO.Database")
Set oSqldf = CreateObject("SQLDMO.DBFile")
Set oSqllf = CreateObject("SQLDMO.LogFile")
Set oCM = GetObjectContext.CreateInstance("CustomerManager.Survey")

'Business Rules to determine names
sCustomerID = Left(sCustomerName, 6)
sDBName = sCustomerID & Left(sSurveyName, 5)
sDFName = Left(sCustomerID, 4) & Left(sSurveyName, 4) & ".mdf"
sLFName = Left(sCustomerID, 4) & Left(sSurveyName, 4) & ".ldf"

'Set Database Name property
oSqldb.Name = sDBName

'Business Rule to ensure that database is created
'on the drive with the most space
Set oSqlServer = oDDLServer.oApp.SQLServers.ItemByID(lConnID)
sDriveAndPath = GetDriveWithMostSpace(lConnID) & "surveydat\"

'Register the database
oCM.AddSurvey sCustomerName, sSurveyName, sDBName, oSqlServer.Name, _
              bIntegrated, sUser, sPassword

'Set DBFile properties
oSqldf.Name = sDFName
oSqldf.PhysicalName = sDriveAndPath & sDFName
oSqldf.Size = 5
oSqldf.FileGrowthType = SQLDMOGrowth_Percent
oSqldf.FileGrowth = 20
oSqldf.MaximumSize = 40

'Set LogFile properties
oSqllf.Name = sLFName
oSqllf.PhysicalName = sDriveAndPath & sLFName
oSqllf.Size = 2
oSqllf.FileGrowthType = SQLDMOGrowth_Percent
oSqllf.FileGrowth = 20
oSqldf.MaximumSize = 40

'Add DBFile to the PRIMARY filegroup
oSqldb.FileGroups("PRIMARY").DBFiles.Add oSqldf

'Add the LogFile to the LogFiles collection
oSqldb.TransactionLog.LogFiles.Add oSqllf

'Add the Database to the Databases collection.
'At this point, the database is created.
oSqlServer.Databases.Add oSqldb

'Return the name of the database
Create = oSqldb.Name

GetObjectContext.SetComplete
```

```
exitFunction:
    Exit Function

abortTran:
        GetObjectContext.SetAbort
        Resume exitFunction


End Function
```

Configuring and Exporting the MTS Package

Now we'll need to set project properties and re-compile the SQLDDL component. Set the MTSTransactionMode property of the Database, Management, and Security class modules to 2 – RequiresTransaction. Set the BackupDB and Constants class modules' MTSTransactionMode property to 3 – UsesTransaction. The Server class should have a setting of 1-NoTransactions. Display the Properties dialog and ensure the component has the Threading Model set to be Apartment Threaded and that it is set for Unattended Execution, as was done for the CustomerManager component in Chapter 2, *Compiling Your Component*.

Since it is planned that the consumer will access this component remotely, click on the Component tab and select Remote Server Files. This option will cause a .vbr file to be generated when the component is compiled. The .vbr file will be used by the Setup routine of the client application to configure the client workstation's registry to access the SQLDDL component using Distributed COM (DCOM). The .vbr file will ensure that the appropriate entries are made to the registry, and that the proxy and stub DCOM uses to marshal calls to components will be installed correctly on the client computer.

> **Another way to accomplish this same goal would be to use the MTS Client Export files generated when you export the MTS package. This practice would be particularly useful if you needed to change the location of the component after the client application had been installed. In this case, since we need to install the client application on the workstation, as well as the remote application information, it is easier to create a .vbr file and include it in the client application's Setup program.**

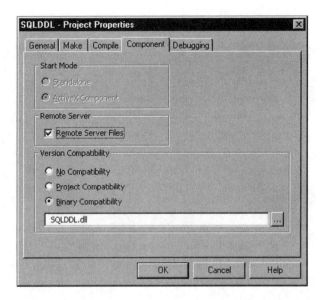

The changes we've made will cause binary compatibility to be broken but since we're not deploying the component for production use, this is fine. However, we still need to modify the client application in order to pass the new arguments for the Create method. Modify the cmdCreate_Click() method of frmCreateDB so that it appears as shown below:

```
Private Sub cmdCreate_Click()
    sdbName = db.Create(lConnID, txtSurvey, txtCustomer, bIntegrated, _
        sUser, sPassword)
    Me.Hide
End Sub
```

Remember, the bIntegrated, sUser, and sPassword variables are public variables stored in the modGlobals module.

Once the SQLDDL component has been compiled, install the latest version of it, as well as the latest CustomerManager component, into the SurveyComponents package under MTS. To do this, follow the process discussed in Chapter 2, *Adding the CustomerManager Component to the Package*.

At this point, we should have:

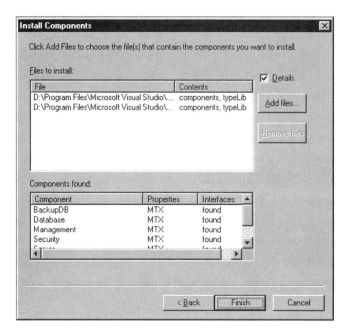

Defining Roles

Security in MTS is managed through roles; MTS roles are similar to user-defined database roles in SQL Server, except that instead of defining access to database objects, they are used to grant access to MTS components.

For this application, we are going to define three roles: SurveyCreators, BackupOperators, and SecurityManagers. To create a role, expand **SurveyComponents**, right-click on the **Roles** folder and run **New** | Role. Type the name of the role and click on OK:

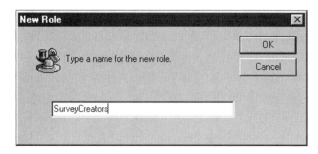

To add users or groups to the role, right-click on the role and run New | User:

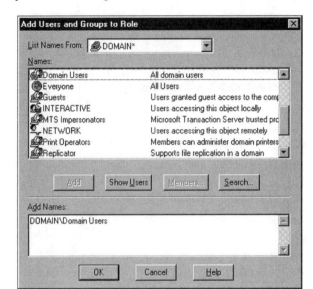

Select the users and groups you would like to associate with the particular role and click on Add and when finished click OK.

Repeat this process for the BackupOperators and SecurityManagers roles. Once defined, these roles can be associated with specific components in the package. Each component has a Role Membership folder and to grant membership to one or more roles, right-click on this folder and run New | Role:

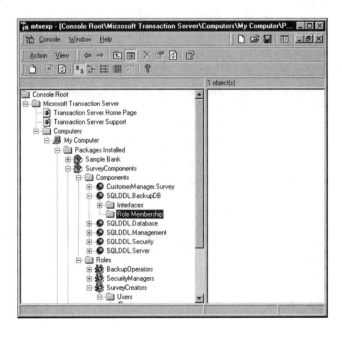

The Select Roles dialog will be displayed. Select one or more roles and click on OK:

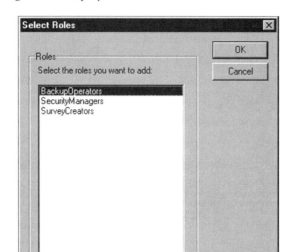

Repeat this process to grant role membership to each component.

One important thing to mention here is that MTS only checks roles when a base client creates an instance of a component. If the component creates an instance of another component in the same package, the user is assumed to be trusted. In the case of the sample project, this means that when the base client creates the SQLDDL.Database component, the user's role membership is checked. However, it is not checked when the SQLDDL.Database component creates an instance of CustomerManager.Survey.

After the task of associating roles with all of the appropriate components has been finished, we're ready to export the package so that it can be installed on the application server. An exported package consists of:

❑ A .pak file that contains the information necessary to register and configure the package on the destination machine. The .pak file is text file (which can be read with Notepad) that contains all the information about the components and roles of the package.

❑ The DLLs and type libraries that the components in the package require.

❑ A clients folder that contains a self-extracting executable that can be used to configure a client computer to access the components over DCOM.

> **It is very important not to run the executable in the clients folder on the MTS computer. Doing so will overwrite the components' registry entries and they will need to be reinstalled.**

To export the package, right-click on it and run Export. A dialog will be displayed to allow selection of the directory in which the .pak file should be created, the name of the file, and whether information about how Windows NT user accounts map to roles should be exported as well:

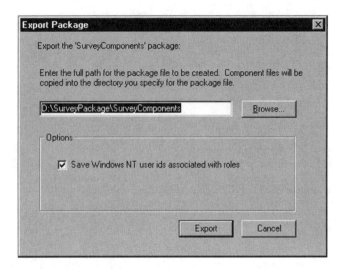

Configuring the Middle-Tier Server

To configure the middle-tier server, the following items need to be installed on it:

- ❑ Windows NT Server
- ❑ Microsoft Transaction Server
- ❑ Windows NT Server Service Pack 4 (or 5)
- ❑ The SQL-DMO libraries
- ❑ The SQL-DDL component into MTS

Of these steps, we'll walk through the last two.

> **The steps shown here would be those used to deploy the application across at least two separate machines (the middle-tier server could be the same computer as the SQL Server). Of course, if you are working through this on a single computer, you installed the SQL-DMO libraries when you installed SQL Server.**

Installing the SQL-DMO Libraries

In order for SQL-DMO to operate, a number of files need to be properly registered and installed to the proper directories:

❏ `sqldmo.dll, sqldmo.dll, sqlrsld.dll, sqlsvc.dll, sqlwid.dll` and `w95scm.dll` should be installed to `\Mssql7\binn`

❏ `sqldmo.rll` and `sqlsvc.rll` should be installed to `\Mssql7\binn\Resources\<language>`

❏ `sqlwoa.dll` should be installed to `%SystemRoot%\system32`

SQL-DMO does not include a dependency file to make it easy to install these files from a `Setup.exe` built with the Package and Deployment Wizard.

SQL-DMO also requires ODBC version 3.5, SQL Server ODBC driver version 3.70, and `Odbcbcp.dll`.

To install SQL-DMO from the SQL Server CD-ROM, click on Install SQL Server 7.0 Components and select Database Server – Standard Edition. You will be prompted to choose either a local installation or a remote installation. If you are logged on interactively at the middle tier server, choose Local Install. Otherwise, choose Remote Install:

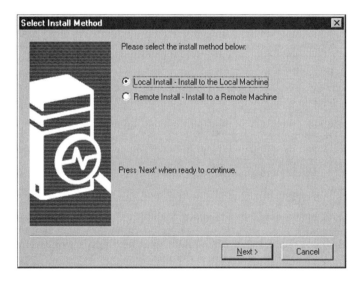

If you choose to install to a remote machine, you will need to provide the name of the computer and a password for an account that belongs to the Domain Admins group or to the Administrators group on the machine to which you are installing:

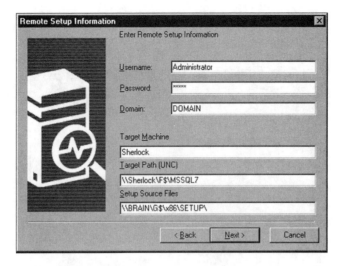

When the name of the Target Machine is entered, the Target Path is automatically filled in. However, the drive (F$ in the graphic) defaults to the drive on which Windows NT is installed on the source computer. The Target Path may need to be adjusted so that SQL-DMO is installed to the appropriate drive on the target computer.

> **Note that this dialog does not include a browse button for either the target path or the setup source files. As you can see in the graphic, these paths are Universal Naming Convention (UNC) paths. The UNC convention is** *servername**sharename**directory*. **In the example, the sharename of the target path is F$. The $ character indicates that it is an administrative or hidden share.**

For the purposes of this demonstration, we'll assume we're installing to the local computer. After acknowledging the welcome screen, accept the license agreement and enter the User information as prompted. At this point, we need to select the type of installation and determine the installation path. Since we only want to install the Client Connectivity tools, select Custom:

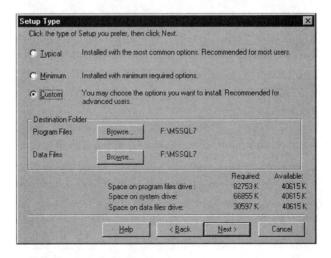

After clicking on Next, a dialog will be displayed to allow installation of specific components. Of the custom installation options offered, the only items we need to install in order for SQL-DMO to work are the Client Connectivity components:

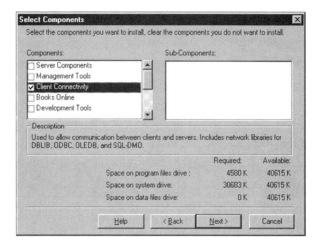

This selection installs the network libraries for DBLIB, ODBC, OLEDB, and SQL-DMO and of these, our middle-tier components require those for SQL-DMO and ODBC. Click on Next twice to continue and install the files. Click on Finish to close the installation program and then Exit to close the SQL Server installation program's auto-menu.

Importing the Package

To import the package into Microsoft Transaction Server on the application server, either share it to the network or copy it to a transfer medium, such as a diskette, CD-ROM, or to the server itself. Launch Transaction Server Explorer. Drill down and right-click on the Packages Installed folder. Run New | Package to display the Package Wizard:

This time, instead of creating an empty package as we did in Chapter 2, we need to install a pre-built package. A dialog will be displayed to allow addition of a package or packages:

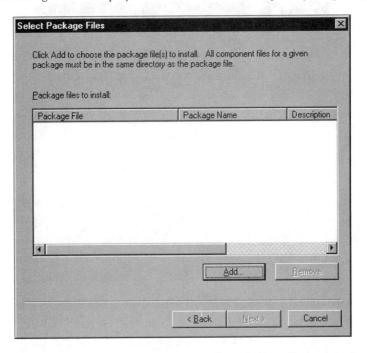

Click on **Add** to locate and select the appropriate package for installation via the browse dialog displayed. Navigate to and select the SurveyComponents.PAK file. Click on **Open**:

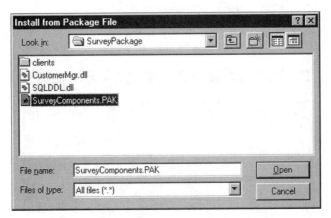

The file will be added to the Select Packages Files dialog:

Click on <u>N</u>ext. At this point, you need to select a user that the package will use as its identity when executing.

Note that the user should not be the interactive user.

The interactive user is the user currently logged on to the computer. Application servers are often left running with no user logged on interactively. If the interactive user is specified here, the component cannot be used when no one is logged on at the computer.

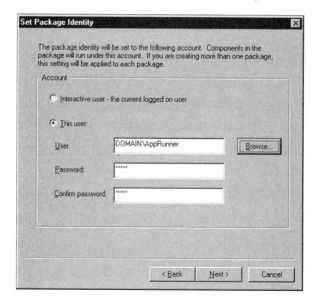

After entering the appropriate user information, click on Next to continue and then select the directory into which the component files should be installed. At this point, you can also choose whether the Windows NT user accounts assigned to roles are added to the package file when it is installed. Click on Finish after completing these options:

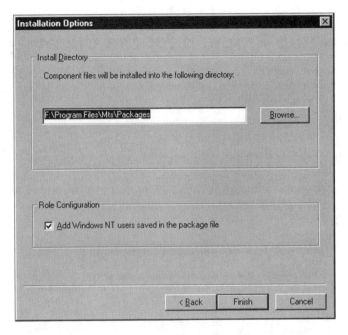

The package will be installed into MTS. Notice in the following graphic that all the components appear in the Components folder and all of the roles previously defined are displayed in the Roles folder:

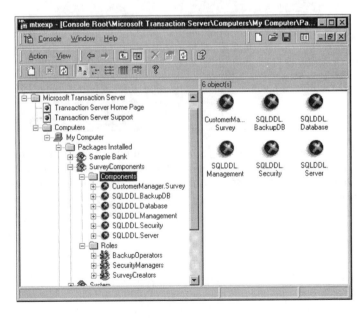

The middle-tier application server is now ready to go and the final step is to build a Setup program to install the client application and configure the client computers. Let's look first at building the client application Setup program. We'll use the Package and Deployment Wizard that comes with Visual Studio 6.0 for this purpose.

Creating a Setup Program for the Client Application

Once we've completed building and testing the Survey Designer, we're ready to package it for deployment. One way to do this is with the Package and Deployment Wizard that comes with Visual Studio 6.0, but you can also create packages for deployment with a variety of third-party tools, such as InstallShield.

To launch the Package and Deployment Wizard, run Start | Programs | Microsoft Visual Studio 6.0 | Microsoft Visual Studio 6.0 Tools | Package and Deployment Wizard.

The first screen of the wizard allows us to select the project for which we'd like to build the installation package. This dialog can also be used for deploying existing packages and managing installation scripts:

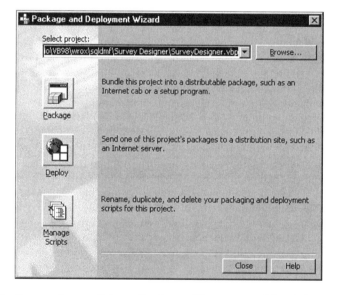

To create a distribution package, click on Package. If an executable of the application already exists and the project files were saved at a later date and time, you'll be asked if you'd like to recompile the project. If there is any chance that the compiled version is not based on the latest project files, choose Yes:

If <u>Yes</u> is selected, the Package and Deployment Wizard will use Visual Basic to recompile the project. If <u>No</u> is clicked, the Package and Deployment Wizard will package the last version of the executable. Selecting Cancel will cause the packaging to be terminated and the main screen of the Package and Deployment Wizard will be displayed.

Next, you'll be prompted to select a script. Scripts are used to save your packaging settings. Since we have not built this package before, we'll set this option to (None):

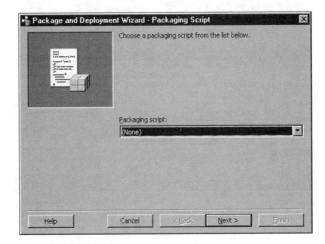

Click on <u>Next</u> to continue. The next screen allows you to choose whether you'd like to build a standard setup package or just a dependency file:

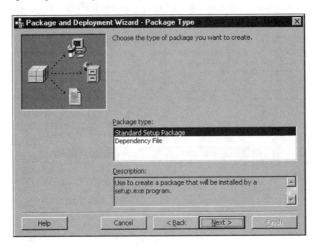

When you select to package a Standard EXE project, you have two choices available. A Standard Setup Package allows you to create a setup program for your application. A Dependency File creates a file that lists the libraries and other files your application depends on.

In this case, since we want to create a setup program for the application, select Standard Setup Package and click on Next.

The next screen allows you to select the destination directory for the package. By default, a Package folder is created inside the project directory but you can specify a different directory if you'd like:

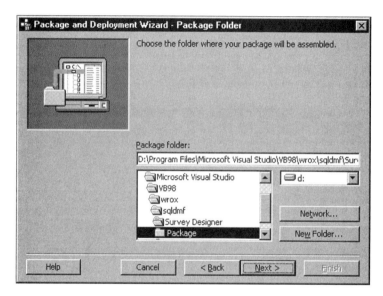

A new folder in which to assemble the package can be created. If you type a folder into the text box and that folder does not exist, you will be prompted to create it.

At this point, the Package and Deployment Wizard will try to determine the dependencies of the application. However, since SQL-DMO and SQL-NS do not have dependency files and we did not build one for the SQLDDL component, you will receive the following warning:

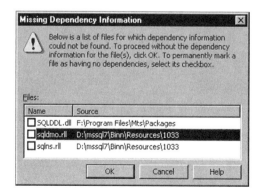

Since we're planning to run the SQLDDL component on a remote server and we already know that we will need to install the SQL-DMO and SQL-NS libraries and dependent files on the client computer, click on OK. We'll look at how to install SQL-NS on the client computer in the next section.

The next screen shows a list of the dependencies the Package and Deployment Wizard could discover. We are going to need to make some changes here:

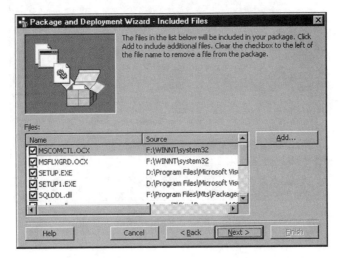

Firstly, remember we're going to run the SLQDDL component remotely. This means that we don't actually want to install the SQLDDL.dll on the client computer. Instead, we want to add the .vbr file, which we created when we compiled the SQLDDL component, to the package in order to have the Setup program configure the client's registry with access information for SQLDDL. Click on Add to add the SQLDDL.vbr file:

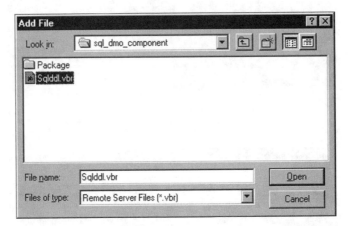

By default the **Files of type** drop-down is set to filter for **.exe** files. You will need to filter for **.vbr** files in order to be able to locate the file.

Once the SQLDDL.vbr file has been located and selected, click on Open. The .vbr file and the .tlb file will be added to the Included Files dialog; the .tlb file is the type library for the component:

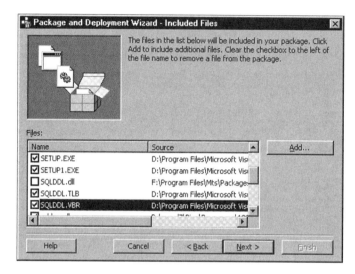

Next, clear the check box next to SQLDDL.dll. Remember, we don't want to actually install this component library to the client.

The final step is to clear the check boxes for the SQLNS.RLL and SQLDMO.RLL files. Remember, we're going to install these libraries in full from the SQL Server 7.0 CD-ROM and we don't want additional copies of the .rll files on the hard drive:

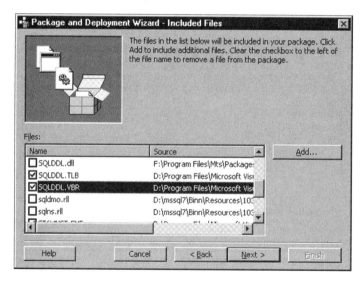

Once you've finished making these changes, click on Next. The next screen prompts you to configure connection information for the remote server component:

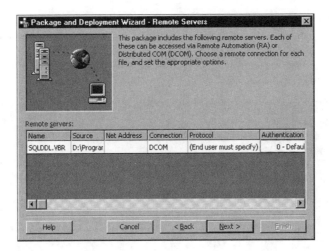

Notice that the default connection is set to DCOM. This is the type of connection that we must use to connect to an MTS component from a Win32 rich client. Remote Automation connections are not supported by MTS.

Since we are connecting via DCOM, the only connection we need to set is the **Net Address**. This is the name of the computer where the remote server will be running. If the **Net Address** is left empty, the user will be prompted for it in during installation.

The next screen allows you to choose whether you want to create a single cab file or multiple cab files.

> **A cab file is a file containing compressed executables for your application and other dependent files, such as the component libraries you set in References.**

Since all Visual Basic applications require files that are larger than can fit on a single diskette, you will need to select multiple cab files if you are planning to install from diskette, otherwise select single cab file:

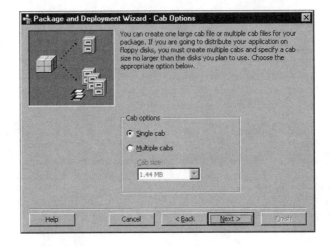

If you select to create multiple cab files, you can determine the size. This allows you to support installing from 1.44 MB diskettes, 2.88 MB diskettes, 720 KB diskettes, and 1.2 MB diskettes. After selecting whether to build a single large cab or multiple cabs of a particular size, click on Next to continue and enter a title for your Setup program. This is the title that will display in the title bar while Setup is running:

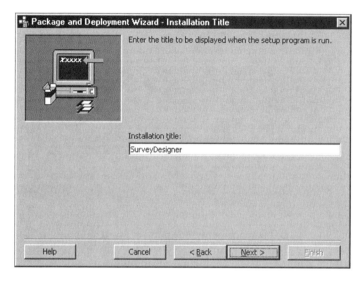

By default, the installation title is the name of the project. Clicking on Next brings up a screen that allows you to determine where the Start menu shortcut should be placed and what it should be called:

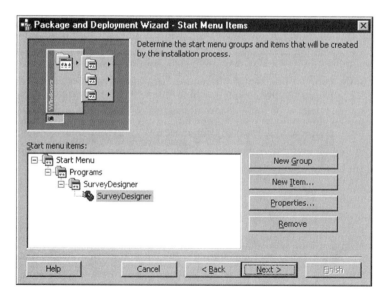

By default, an icon for the application is placed under a menu of the same name. You can change this, add additional options, or remove options. In this case, the only appropriate icon to put in the Start menu is the application icon.

The next screen allows you to configure the installation destinations for the various components you are installing:

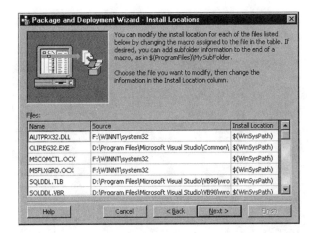

Here you can choose from a list of environmental variables that allow installation of components to the application directory, the `system` directory, the `Program Files` directory, or the `Common` directory. However, you can't type in your own path here, which is one of the main reasons we decided to install the SQL-DMO and SQL-NS libraries through the SQL Server 7.0 installation program. Remember, they must be placed in very specific directories.

> **Other packaging and deployment tools give you more flexibility over the installation destination for specific libraries. For example, you can use the Setup Toolkit that comes with Visual Basic to customize your Setup routine. You could also manually edit the `Setup.1st` file. However, since the crux of this book is not related to deployment, we have decided to limit our discussion to the Package and Deployment Wizard and provide a list of files and their respective installation destinations so that you can build a Setup package using the tool of your choice.**

Once you have verified the installation locations, click on **Next** to continue – the next screen allows components or applications to be marked as shared:

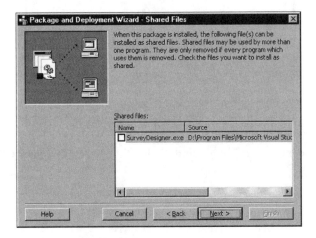

In this case, the only candidate for sharing that is not already configured to be shared automatically is the application itself. Since we do not want to share it, click on <u>N</u>ext to continue.

Finally, you will be prompted to name the script you just created. Give it a name you can easily associate with the project in case you need to rebuild the package at a later date:

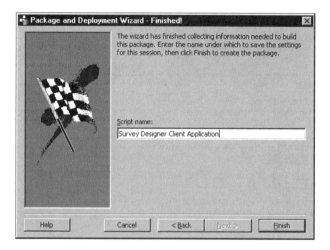

Click on <u>F</u>inish to allow the Package and Deployment Wizard to create the cab files. When it is done, a dialog will be displayed showing the location of the cab files as well as the script that can be used for rebuilding the package at a later date:

Now we are ready to configure the client and deploy the Survey Designer Client Application.

Configuring the Client Computers

SQL-NS also requires a long list of files, which we saw in Chapter 1. These files must be placed in the following locations:

- ❑ `Semcomn.dll`, `Sfc.dll`, `Sqlgui.dll`, `Sqlns.dll`, `Sqlresld.dll`, `Sqlsvc.dll` and `Sqlwid.dll` must be placed in `\Mssql7\Binn`

- ❑ `Semcomn.rll`, `Sfc.rll`, `Sqlgui.rll`, `Sqlns.rll` and `Sqlsvc.rll` must be placed in `\Mssql7\Binn\Resources\<language>`

- ❑ `Sqlwoa.dll` must be placed in `%SystemRoot%\system32`

As with installing SQL-DMO, the easiest way to configure a client computer with these libraries is to install the files from the SQL Server 7.0 CD-ROM.

To do so, follow the same steps as for installation the SQL-DMO libraries. However, on the component selection dialog, select **Management Tools** from the **Components** list and **Enterprise Manager** from the **Sub-Components** list in order to install the SQL-NS files:

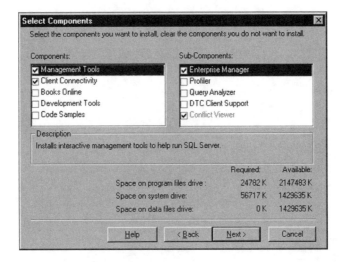

> Notice that **Server Components** is not available. That is because we are installing the libraries on a Windows NT Workstation. When you select to install Standard Edition on either a Windows NT Workstation, Windows 98, or Windows 95 computer, only **Management Tools, Client Connectivity, Books Online, Development Tools,** and **Code Samples** will be available for installation.

Once the SQL-DMO and SQL-NS libraries have been installed, the Survey Designer application can be installed by launching `Setup.exe` from the installation medium. The `Setup.exe` program will install the Survey Designer application and make the appropriate entries to the registry to allow it to access the `SQLDDL` component on the remote computer.

Summary

In this chapter, we've covered some of the issues involved in deploying the SQL-DMO application we've built throughout most of the book. These included:

❑ Configuring the middle-tier components to participate in an MTS transaction

❑ Configuring role-based security in a Windows NT 4.0 environment

❑ Installing the files necessary to use SQL-DMO and SQL-NS

❑ Building a Setup package that can configure a client computer to utilize a remote component

The next chapter takes a brief look at using SQL-DMO to programmatically manage replication, including the ability to subscribe an article inside a publication. SQL Server Enterprise Manager will only allow you to subscribe to publications, so this is one area where programming SQL-DMO objects provides an advantage over using the Enterprise Manager.

Replication Management

8

While we've completed our treatment of the Surveys Unlimited business scenario, there's still more of the SQL-DMO object library to explore. In this chapter we're going to focus on objects used for managing SQL Server replication. To demonstrate the use of these objects we're going to develop a small stand-alone sample application.

The topic of replication is quite complex in the normal run of events and even more so when dealing with it programmatically through SQL-DMO (which includes some 40 objects and collections relating directly to replication and replication management). We will be introducing the subject area before diving into coding, but if you need some further background you could try *Professional SQL Server 7.0 Programming, Robert Vieira, Wrox Press ISBN 1861002319*. As with the earlier chapters, once we get into coding the objects you'll see a number of patterns emerging in the way they can be used.

Our coverage of the subject will be tackled in the following order:

❑   Introduction to replication concepts and terminology

❑   The different types of replication

❑   Setting up replication with SQL Server Enterprise Manager

❑   Overview the replication objects available

❑   Look at a sample application

The reason we're running through a quick discussion of how we can use the SQL Server Enterprise Manager to set up replication is to give us a point of reference for when we move on to discussing the replication objects.

Our sample application will make use of SQL-DMO objects to do something that isn't possible through SQL Server Enterprise Manager – which is to subscribe to an article inside a publication.

As normal, the code for the sample application developed at the end of the chapter can be downloaded from the Wrox website.

First things first; what is replication?

Introduction to Replication

Replication, in its simplest terms, is a way of automatically copying data (for example tables, selected portions of tables, or updated changes) between servers. It can be useful in any situation where you need to have multiple copies of server data. These situations include:

❑ **Remote reference** – In the case of remote servers, especially servers connected through slow links, it can be inefficient to have to connect to the main server to reference relatively stable data. Replication can be used to create copies of the data, such as customer records or inventory files, on the remote servers. Replication can also be used to periodically update the data, based on how often it changes and the available bandwidth for transmitting the data.

❑ **Multi-server applications** – In an especially active application environment, such as an online transaction processing application, one way to optimize performance is to post updates to multiple servers and then have this data consolidated on one central server. Replication allows this to be carried out and gives control over the time delay for making the updates.

❑ **Business support requirements** – It may be found that it is inefficient to try to support both production activity and business analysis on the same server. One server can be used to support the application, updating a second server during periods of reduced activity. The second server can then be used for decision support and business analysis activities.

These are just a few examples that represent some of the most common uses of replication. But this is just a start – organizations are constantly finding new and innovative ways in which replication can support their activities.

Now we know what replication is in general let's get to grips with the concepts and terms prevalent in this area, starting with the different roles servers can play in replication solutions and then moving on to discussing the different replication components.

Server Roles

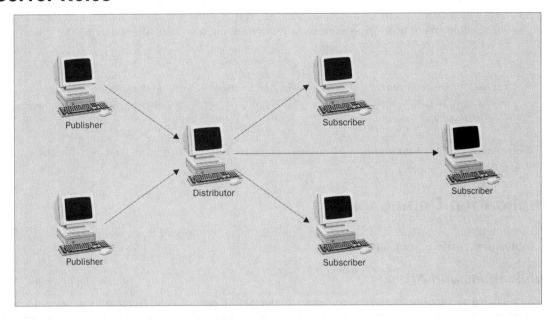

Replication uses a **publishing metaphor** in describing replication components. Servers can be configured to fill three roles: **Publisher**, **Distributor**, and **Subscriber**. Actually, a server can be configured to fill any role or any combination of roles. For example, it is common for a server configured as a Publisher to also act as a Distributor.

> **These are deliberately referred to as** *server roles* **rather than** *SQL Server roles.* **SQL Server replication can be implemented in a heterogeneous server environment. In other words, data servers other than SQL Server (such as Oracle servers) can be included in replication.**

Let's consider each of these roles in turn:

- ❑ **Publisher** – The Publisher is the data source for replication. Databases and tables for replication are located on the Publisher and the Publisher determines what will be sent out as updates. Multiple Publishers can be used to support the data requirements. A Publisher can also be configured as a Distributor, a Subscriber, or both.

- ❑ **Distributor** – The Distributor's responsibility is to move the data from the Publisher out to its Subscribers. One Distributor can support multiple Publishers, but each Publisher will be supported by only one Distributor. Should it become necessary to uninstall a Distributor, this will have serious repercussions for any Publishers it supports. Any **publications** and **subscriptions** supported by the Distributor will be deleted and any Publishers supported by the Distributor will be disabled.

❏ **Subscriber** – The Subscriber is the final consumer or destination of the replicated data. It will receive updates from the Distributor and apply them to a local database. Either the Publisher or Subscriber, depending on the type of subscription, can control the update schedule. We'll be looking at subscription types and how they affect data updates in a moment.

Replication solutions can be configured in a number of ways – any number of Subscribers can receive updates from a Distributor and a single Subscriber can receive updates from multiple Distributors.

We've just glibly used the terms publications and subscriptions, let's now describe what they mean in detail.

Replication Components

The publishing metaphor used to describe replication is built around three components – **publications**, **articles**, and **subscriptions**.

Publications and Articles

Any data to be sent out as updates to Subscribers must be part of a **publication**. A publication will be based on a single database and will include one or more database tables and stored procedures. A database can support multiple publications, letting you fine-tune the data and updates you make available to Subscribers.

You can publish any user database. Additionally, the `Northwind` and `Pubs` databases can also be published since they are just sample user databases. The `master`, `model`, `msdb`, `tempdb`, or `distribution` databases *cannot* be published though.

A publication is made up of one or more **articles**. An article can be a user table, part of a table, or a stored procedure. A publication cannot span databases, so all of the articles must come from the same database.

> **When you set up subscriptions, SQL Server Enterprise Manager will only let you subscribe to a publication. Transact-SQL statements and (as we'll show later) SQL-DMO objects give you the ability to subscribe to individual articles.**

According to Microsoft's SQL Server documentation, the ability to subscribe to articles has been retained to provide backward compatibility with earlier SQL Server versions. Use caution when subscribing to individual articles; in some situations Subscribers will be able to modify replicated data and return the changes to the Publisher. Subscribing to a table, but not to a related table, can lead to data inconsistency.

The information available for replication can be limited by **filtering**:

- ❑ **Vertical filtering** (otherwise termed vertical partitioning in earlier SQL Server versions) – Can be used to limit the columns being replicated to Subscribers.

- ❑ **Horizontal filtering** (otherwise termed horizontal partitioning) – Can be used to limit the rows that are replicated.

Subscriptions

There are two basic **subscription** types supported by SQL Server, **push subscriptions** and **pull subscriptions** (as a variation, SQL Server can also support either subscription type as an **immediate-updating subscription**):

- ❑ **Push subscriptions** – These are set up at and controlled by the Publisher. The Publisher sets the schedule by which updates are sent to the Subscriber. These require more processor overhead at the Distributor than pull subscriptions because the Distributor does the actual *pushing* out to the Subscriber.

- ❑ **Pull subscriptions** – These are set up at and controlled by the Subscriber. The Subscriber sets the schedule by which it receives updates from the Publisher. Pull subscriptions place less of a load on the Distributor, but require more overhead at the Subscriber.

Typically, data sent to the Subscriber is treated as read-only data. There are going to be times when you want to be able to update data at the Subscriber and have the updates applied to the Publisher and one way of doing this is through use of immediate-updating Subscribers.

When a change is posted to an immediate-update Subscriber, the same transactions are applied to the Publisher through a two-phase commit process. This means the change must be made to both systems; if it isn't then neither system will be changed and the change at the Subscriber will be rolled back. This is managed under control of the Microsoft Distributed Transaction Coordinator (MS DTC).

> **Before attempting to implement immediate-updating Subscribers you should carefully review your network configuration. Immediate-updating Subscribers should only be considered if you have a reliable, high-speed connection between the Publisher and Subscriber.**

Replication Types

There are three basic replication types:

- ❑ Snapshot replication
- ❑ Transactional replication
- ❑ Merge replication

Both **Snapshot** and **Transactional** replication can support immediate-updating subscribers, though by default they do not.

Snapshot Replication

Snapshot replication uses a **Snapshot agent** to take a picture of the published data. This includes the table schema and data for publication articles. Since all of the published data is being sent with each update, the amount of data being transferred across the network can be very large. Because of this, there is usually a relatively long **latency** (a term used in replication to refer to the time delay between updates) between changes being applied to the Publisher and those updates being reflected in the Subscriber.

Snapshot replication is typically used with data that changes infrequently. In most implementations, the copy of the data at the Subscriber is treated as read-only. Of course, it doesn't have to be used as read-only; Snapshot replication supports immediate-updating Subscribers, giving you a way of updating the Publisher with changes made at the Subscriber.

One potential use of Snapshot replication is to distribute reference data that changes infrequently to remote servers. For instance you might have a table that contains a list of current reference documents and their document numbers. If the list were updated on a weekly basis, it would be an easy matter to update remote servers over the weekend using Snapshot replication.

Snapshot replication is also a part (in most cases) of **Transactional** and **Merge** replication. Before updates can be replicated to a Subscriber, the Publisher and Subscriber must be synchronized, that is, you must make sure that both contain exactly the same data. This is done by using Snapshot replication to prepare the destination databases. Once that has been done, the Distributor can start sending updates to the Subscriber.

Transactional Replication

Transactional replication works by applying incremental updates to Subscribers. Less data is involved because only transactions that modify data on the Publisher are replicated to the Subscribers. Updates typically occur more frequently than with Snapshot replication, resulting in less latency between changes being made at the Publisher and appearing at the Subscriber. As with Snapshot replication, data is typically treated as read-only at the Subscriber. If you want to be able to make updates at the Subscriber as well, you have the option of using immediate-updating Subscribers.

There are a wide variety of situations where you might want to use Transactional replication. Consider the scenario where three servers are supporting an online transaction processing application. You want to keep the combined sales information on a central server and you need to have the information as up-to-date as possible. You could set up Transactional replication with each of the posting servers configured as a Publisher. The central repository would be configured as a Subscriber, receiving updates from the publishers.

Updates are taken from the Publisher's transaction log. This can potentially lead to a problem as Transactional replication cannot apply changes made to the Publisher through non-logged operations. One way to avoid this and to ensure that the Publisher and Subscriber stay synchronized is to schedule periodic Snapshot replication updates to the Subscriber.

> Transactional replication is not supported for SQL Server running on Windows
> 95 or Windows 98.

Merge Replication

As with Transactional replication, **Merge replication** works by applying incremental updates. There is a significant difference, however, in that changes can be made at the Publisher or Subscriber. Changes made at Subscribers are merged and distributed. Immediate-updating Subscribers are not supported because they are not needed.

Merge replication typically has a longer latency than Transactional replication and, because of this delay, conflicts can occur. When conflicts do occur, they are resolved at the Publisher. Merge replication gives you *eventual* data consistency. Over time, data consistency is assured, but there could be a significant latency involved.

As with Transactional replication, the starting point is to synchronize the Publisher and Subscriber. Merge replication is also similar to Transactional replication in that some changes will not be recognized (non-logged changes to image, text, or ntext type data are not replicated). You may find it appropriate to schedule periodic Snapshot updates to keep the Publisher and Subscriber synchronized.

Now we've put in the foundations let's see how replication can be implemented.

Replication and Enterprise Manager

Before we begin our look at replication objects, we are going to step through setting up replication through SQL Server Enterprise Manager to give an idea of what is involved in managing replication. This isn't a comprehensive treatment of the use of the Create Publication Wizard (depending on your SQL Server 7.0 installation you may see different dialogs at some points) but will give us the background we need to be able to understand the SQL-DMO approach.

Configuring Replication

We're going to work through a relatively simple, straightforward example where we configure our server as a Publisher/Distributor and, in the process, create a transactional publication. This is in fact the default SQL server **replication topology** model (topology models represent the logical and physical connectivity of the servers involved in the replication solution). In this model, one server acts as a Publisher and its own Distributor – it can support any number of Subscribers. The Publisher owns all the replicated data and is the sole data source for replication.

Once we have configured the server we're going to create a push subscription to the publication. In fact for simplicity the same server will be used as a Subscriber but the subscription will be directed to a new database.

Let's get down to work by configuring our Publisher/Distributor.

Publisher/Distributor Configuration

We start by selecting a server from SQL Server Enterprise Manager and running Tools | Replication | Create and Manage Publications..:

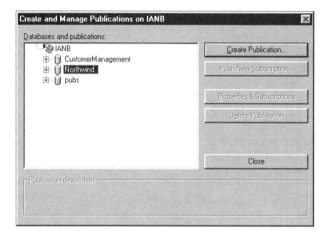

This opens the Create and Manage Publications dialog. From here, select the database to be used as the source for the first publication and click on Create Publication to bring up the Create Publication Wizard.

> *Note: When creating a Distributor through SQL Server Enterprise Manager, you will be prompted to create an initial publication, making it a Publisher/Distributor.*

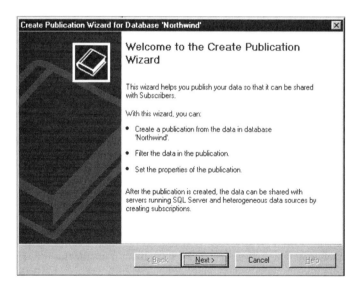

Clicking on Next to continue will bring up a dialog asking the publication type to be specified (unless you have other servers available within the installations SQL Server Group – in this case you will be asked to select the Distributor before choosing the publication type. The default is to configure the Publisher as a Publisher/Distributor).

The default is to create a Snapshot publication but we're going to create a Transactional publication:

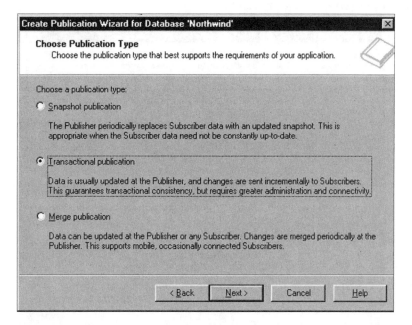

Next we have to decide whether or not we are going to support immediate-updating subscriptions. By default, they are not supported – we're going to accept the default and not provide support:

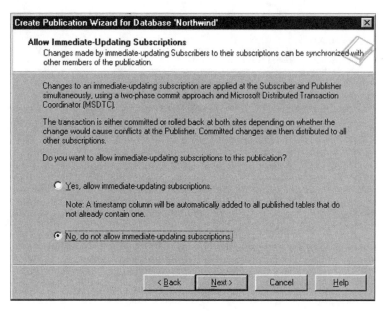

The next screen asks us whether or not all of the Subscribers are running SQL Server. If they are, snapshots can be created using native data format rather than character mode format which helps to optimize snapshot creation and distribution:

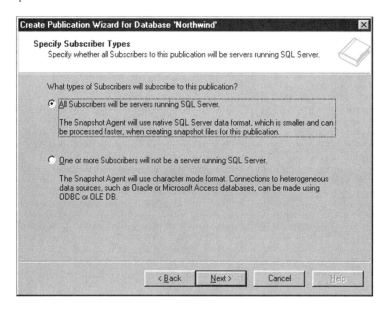

We are next prompted to identify our table articles. As mentioned earlier, an article can be a data table, a portion of a data table, or a stored procedure. By default, only tables are listed initially:

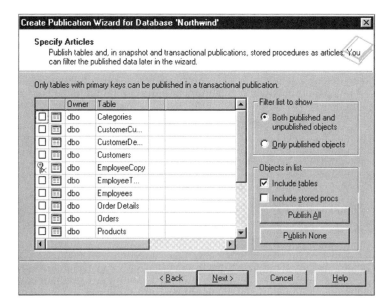

We're going to choose to publish all available tables by clicking on Publish All. This will select all of the tables that can be published as articles:

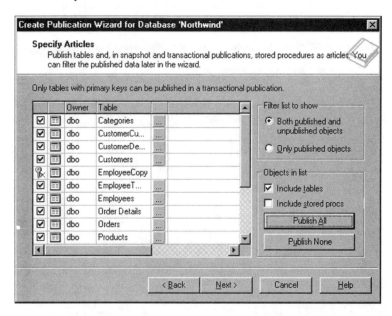

At this point selecting the ...button will bring up the properties for the selected table, allowing a variety of options to be set. Here we are not concerning ourselves with these details and will just move on. The next step is to name the publication; the publication name defaults to the source database name. In our example, we've renamed the publication NorthTran:

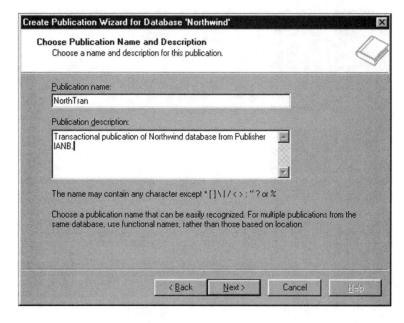

We are next prompted to decide if we want to create the publication using default configuration properties. If we wanted to provide support for anonymous subscribers or add vertical or horizontal filtering, we would have to select to modify the publication properties. Again for simplicity we're going to use the default properties:

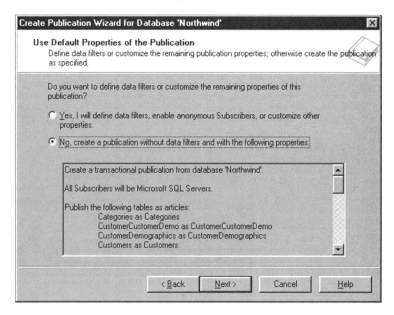

The Create Publication Wizard is now ready to create the publication based on the properties we have defined:

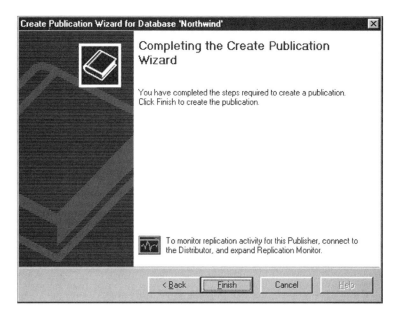

On clicking Finish the Create Publication Wizard will prompt you that it has completed configuring the Publisher/Distributor when it is finished. Additionally, it will inform you that it has added the Replication Monitor to the SQL Server Enterprise Manager console.

The Create and Manage Publications dialog now shows the Northwind database as a published database and lists our new publication:

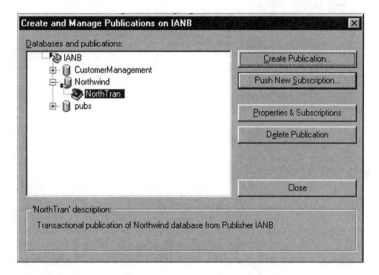

We're now ready to define our Subscribers.

Push Subscriber Configuration

To create a push subscription select the appropriate database in the SQL Server Enterprise Manager, then run either Tools | Replication | Create and Manage Publications...or Tools | Replication | Push Subscriptions to Others...to open the Create and Manage Publications dialog (as shown above).

> As mentioned before, when configuring subscriptions through SQL Server Enterprise Manager, you can only subscribe to the entire publication, not to individual articles.

Select the publication for which you want to create a push subscription (our example will use NorthTran) and click on Push New Subscription.

This will launch the Push Subscription Wizard, the first screen of which is just a welcome:

On clicking on <u>N</u>ext, we are taken to a list of enabled Subscribers. The list of enabled Subscribers will include all of the SQL Server systems that have been registered locally at your system. If you wanted to add an enabled Subscriber to this list, you would exit the Push Subscription Wizard, register the server through SQL Server Enterprise Manager, and then re-launch the Wizard.

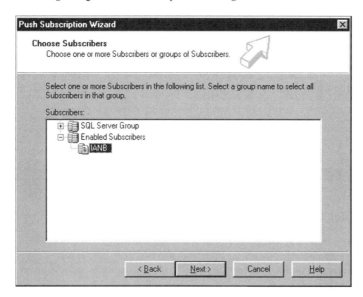

Next, we're prompted to select the destination database, that is the database that will be receiving updates from the Publisher via the Distributor:

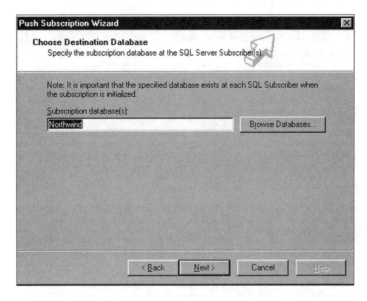

For this example we're going to select B̲rowse Databases...(which will enable us to view a list of databases available on the Subscriber) and then use C̲reate New...to create a new database called PushTest:

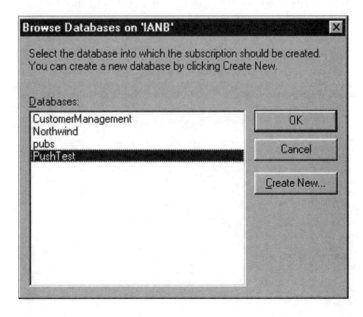

We are now prompted for the distribution schedule. The default schedule for a Transactional publication push subscription is to send updates continuously as they occur, although there is also the option to have updates occur based on a set schedule:

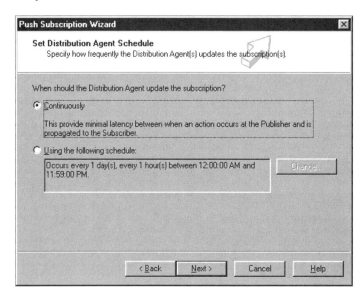

As we previously indicated, a Snapshot publication is used to synchronize the Publisher and Subscriber before updates are applied and that's the next step in our process. In most situations the schema and data at the Subscriber will have to be initialized. The update is made by taking a snapshot of the Publisher and applying it to the Subscriber and if desired the process can be started immediately.

Again we've elected to take the default setting:

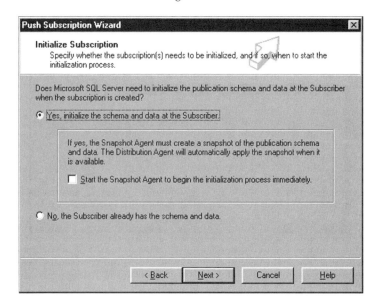

We are now prompted with any services required to support this subscription and the service status:

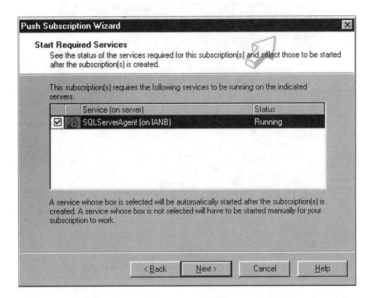

After that, we are prompted to create the subscription from a screen that reviews the options selected:

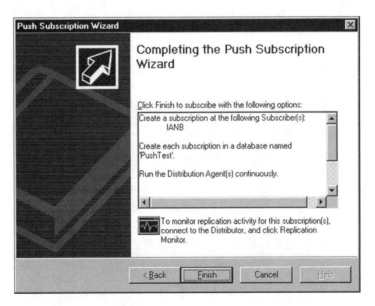

Finally we should receive a dialog telling us that the subscriptions were created:

Although we're not going to go through all of the publication properties in detail, let's see how we can check on the subscriptions defined for a publication.

Quick Check

As with the earlier examples, select the appropriate SQL Server and run Tools | Replication | Create and Manage Publications...Next, drill down to locate the publication, select it and click on Properties & Subscriptions to display the publication's property sheets:

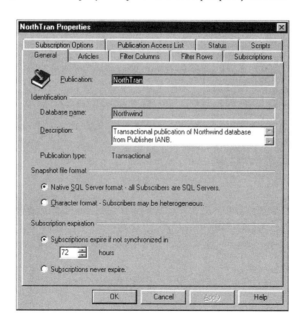

Clicking on the Subscriptions tab enables us to view the subscriptions defined for this publication. Unsurprisingly we have a push subscription that includes all articles:

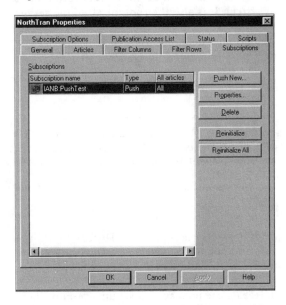

Now that we've seen how to set up replication and define a subscription, let's move back to the main focus of this book, SQL-DMO objects, and more specifically the replication objects.

Replication Objects

Let's take a little while to look at part of the replication hierarchy and some of the replication objects. We'll start with a look at top-level objects, then drill down a little deeper to have a look at the hierarchies revealed by the `Distributor` object and `ReplicationDatabases` collection.

Top-Level Objects

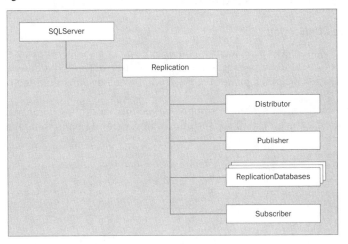

Replication Object

The `Replication` object is the topmost object in the replication hierarchy. It represents the server's entire replication system. It is also the root for all of the server's replication objects.

It's worth our time to highlight one method supported by the `Replication` object, the `Uninstall` method. The syntax for calling this method is:

```
object.Uninstall()
```

> This is mentioned as a caution. Calling the **Uninstall** method will completely remove all replication components from the server. If the server is a Publisher using a remote Distributor, it will attempt to connect to the Distributor and remove all references to itself.

Distributor Object

The `Distributor` object represents the replication Distributor. Obviously, the `Distributor` object can be used to set up and manage a system as a Distributor or the Distributor components of a server set up as a Publisher/Distributor.

What might be less obvious is its use on a system set up as a Publisher only. If a system is configured as a Publisher, it will be attached to a remote Distributor for replication and the `Distributor` object can be used to configure remote distribution.

As with the `Replication` object, the `Distributor` object supports an `Uninstall` method. The same warning applies as for the `Replication` object's `Uninstall` method. Calling the `Uninstall` method for the `Distributor` object will remove all replication components from the server.

Publisher Object

The `Publisher` object represents the replication properties of a Publisher. It could be assumed that it would be the root for all of the server's publications, but it isn't. The only object contained in the `Publisher` object is the `RegisteredSubscribers` collection, which is a collection of servers that can be configured as Subscribers for push subscriptions.

ReplicationDatabases Collection

The `ReplicationDatabases` collection contains `ReplicationDatabase` objects. The `ReplicationDatabase` objects enumerate all of the user-defined databases (including `Northwind` and `Pubs`), whether or not the database has been published for replication.

Each `ReplicationDatabase` object contains collections and objects for managing all of the databases publications, tracking pull subscriptions, and creating and managing push subscriptions.

Subscriber Object

A Subscriber's replication properties are represented by the `Subscriber` object. The `Subscriber` object does not contain any other objects and only has one method, the `Script` method.

> **About one third of the replication objects support a `Script` method (see Appendix D for further details). The `Script` method can be used to generate a Transact-SQL batch file which can be used to recreate the referenced object.**

Now we're going to take some time to follow a few of the branches of this hierarchy, starting with `Distributor` objects. Our discussion is only going to take us a couple of levels deeper in the hierarchy here, but it will help you in understanding how the objects are organized.

Distributor Objects

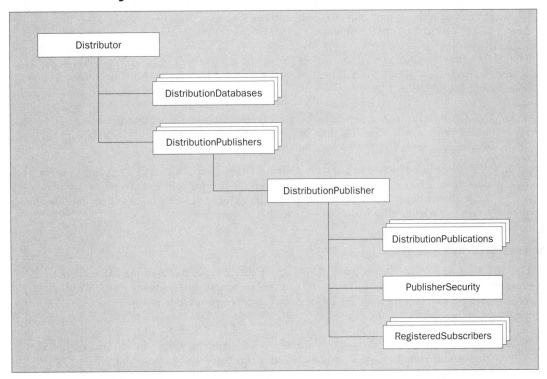

DistributionDatabases Collection

Every `Distributor` will have one or more distribution databases. The `DistributionDatabases` collection contains the Distributor's `DistributionDatabase` objects. Databases can be added to or removed from this collection. `DistributionDatabase` objects represent physical databases on the server that have been identified as distribution databases. Database properties can be viewed or modified through this object.

DistributionPublishers Collection

This contains `DistributionPublisher` objects that, in turn, represent Publishers. Each Publisher that is referenced by the Distributor, that is, each Publisher that is using the Distributor for replication, will be included in the collection.

You can add a Publisher to use this Distributor by adding a `DistributionPublisher` object to its `DistributionPublishers` collection. On doing this the `Name` property must be set to the Publisher's name and the `DistributionDatabase` and `DistributionWorkingDirectory` properties set to identify the database and working directory used to support replication for the Publisher.

Each `DistributionPublisher` is a root for a `DistributionPublications` collection, `PublisherSecurity` property, and `RegisteredSubscribers` collection.

DistributionPublications Collection

This contains `DistributionPublication` objects that represent the Distributor's image of a Snapshot, Transactional, or Merge publication. Each of the Publisher's (`DistributionPublisher` object's) publications will be represented as a `DistributionPublication` object.

The `DistributionPublication` object's properties describe publication attributes and the source database from which the publication was defined. The `DistributionPublication` object contains the following:

❏ A `DistributionArticles` collection that contains `DistributionArticle` objects which reference the articles that define the publication. These can include user tables and stored procedures.

❏ A `DistributionSubscribers` collection that contains `DistributionSubscriber` objects which reference Subscribers defined for this publication. The `DistributionSubscriber` object's `DistributionSchedule` object can also be used to set the schedule by which the Subscriber is updated.

PublisherSecurity Property

The `PublisherSecurity` property (although apparently an object in the MS released hierarchies) returns a `ReplicationSecurity` object that represents the authentication information for connecting with the Publisher. The three properties of the `ReplicationSecurity` object used are:

❏ **SecurityMode** – Sets the security mode used for authenticating the connection; either SQL Server authentication or Windows NT authentication can be selected

❏ **StandardLogin** – On choosing to use SQL Server authentication, this is the login account name that will be used for connecting to the server

❏ **StandardPassword** – On choosing to use SQL Server authentication, this is the login account name password used for connecting to the server

The `StandardLogin` and `StandardPassword` properties are ignored when using Windows NT authentication to establish a trusted connection with the server.

RegisteredSubscribers Collection

We mentioned a `RegisteredSubscribers` collection a little earlier as a child of the `Publisher` object but there is a difference this time. *Previously* the `RegisteredSubscriber` objects in the `RegisteredSubscribers` collection under the `Publisher` object referenced Subscribers registered for the local server. *This time*, the `RegisteredSubscriber` objects reference Subscribers registered for the selected Publisher, which *may or may not* be the Publisher/Distributor to which you are connected.

This might be easier to understand if we attach some SQL Server names to these objects and set up a scenario. Let's consider the situation where you have a Publisher/Distributor named `MAINSERV` on your network and another Distributor named `ADDSERV`.

In the case that you are connected to `MAINSERV` then `MAINSERV` is the local publisher. The subscribers listed under `Replication.Publisher.RegisteredSubscribers` would be registered Subscribers for `MAINSERV`.

Now the point is that the list of registered Subscribers for the two servers may be different. Both `MAINSERV` and `ADDSERV` may be listed under the `Replication.DistributionPublishers` collection. If you selected the `DistributionPublisher` object representing `MAINSERV` from that collection, its `RegisteredSubscribers` collection would be the registered Subscribers for `MAINSERV`. If you selected the `DistributionPublisher` object representing `ADDSERV`, the `RegisteredSubscribers` collection would contain registered Subscribers for `ADDSERV`.

We're going to finish up this investigation of SQL-DMO replication objects by going into some detail in one additional area, the `ReplicationDatabases` collection:

ReplicationDatabases Collection

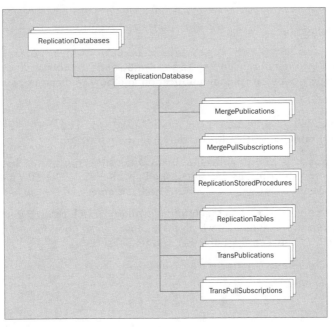

As we wrote earlier, there will be a `ReplicationDatabase` object for each of the user databases on the server to which you are connected. The database is listed whether or not it contains any publications and whether or not it has been enabled for publication.

To get a feel for the object let's have a look at its properties:

- ❑ **AllowMergePublication** – A read-only property, it will return a value of `True` when the referenced database can be published for Merge replication.

- ❑ **DBOwner** – A read-only property that will return a value of `True` if the connected user has database owner rights and permissions. If the connected user is not the database owner or a member of the `db_owner` role, the property will return a value of `False`.

- ❑ **EnableMergePublishing** – Set this property to `True` if you want to enable the database as a source for Merge publications.

- ❑ **EnableTransPublishing** – Set this property to `True` if you want to enable the database as a source for Transactional or Snapshot publications.

- ❑ **Name** – This property allows you view or modify the database name.

> When a database is enabled for Transactional publication, it is also enabled for Snapshot publication. SQL Server does not support enabling a database for Snapshot publication only.

Each database will have one `ReplicationDatabase` object, no matter how many publications have been defined for the database. The `ReplicationDatabase` object is the root for a set of collections that describe its user tables, publications, and pull subscriptions made to those publications.

MergePublications Collection

This collection contains `MergePublication` objects each of which represents a Merge publication defined for the referenced `ReplicationDatabase` object. A `MergePublication` object includes properties describing the publication and how replication conflicts are resolved. It also includes:

- ❑ A `MergeArticles` collection that contains `MergeArticle` objects describing the articles (user tables and stored procedures) in the publication.

- ❑ A `MergeSubscriptions` collection that contains `MergeSubscription` objects that reference push subscriptions defined at the Publisher. You can also define the schedule for a push subscription through its `MergeSchedule` object.

- ❑ A `SnapshotSchedule` object (actually a property which returns a `Schedule` object) which controls the schedule by which the Snapshot is applied for automatic synchronization between the Publisher and its Subscribers.

MergePullSubscriptions Collection

Pull subscriptions are tracked as `MergePullSubscription` objects, which are referenced through the `MergePullSubscriptions` collection (they are Subscriber objects). Merge pull subscriptions are created at and managed by the Subscriber. The `MergePullSubcription` object acts as root for:

- ❑ `DistributorSecurity` (`ReplicationSecurity`) objects that represent the authentication information for connecting with the Distributor

- ❑ `PublisherSecurity` (`ReplicationSecurity`) objects that represent the authentication information for connecting with the Publisher

- ❑ `MergeSchedule` (`Schedule`) objects that represent the schedule for Merge updates

ReplicationStoredProcedures Collection

This collection contains `ReplicationStoredProcedure` objects which reference user-defined stored procedures in a database. Each stored procedure will be represented as a `ReplicationStoredProcedure`, whether or not it is used as an article in a publication. Rather than a collection of published stored procedures, this is a collection of stored procedures that are available to be published.

ReplicationTables Collection

The `ReplicationTables` collection is a collection of `ReplicationTable` objects. Each user table will be represented as a `ReplicationTable` object, whether or not the table has been used as an article in a publication. In other words, you can enumerate the objects in the collection to retrieve a list of tables available for publication.

TransPublications Collection

This collection contains `TransPublication` objects and each `TransPublication` object represents a Transactional or Snapshot publication defined for the referenced database. The `TransPublication` object lets you create, modify, and drop publications.

Each `TransPublication` object includes:

- ❑ A `TransArticles` collection containing `TransArticle` objects that reference the articles making up the publication

- ❑ A `TransSubscriptions` collection containing `TransSubscription` objects that reference the push subscriptions defined for the publication

- ❑ A `SnapshotSchedule` (`Schedule`) object – described above

TransPullSubscriptions Collection

Pull subscriptions are tracked as `TransPullSubscription` objects, which are referenced through the `MergePullSubscriptions` collection. These are Subscriber objects. Merge pull subscriptions are created at and managed by the Subscriber. The `TransPullSubcription` object acts as root for:

❑ `DistributorSecurity` (`ReplicationSecurity`) objects that represent the authentication information for connecting with the Distributor

❑ `PublisherSecurity` (`ReplicationSecurity`) objects that represent the authentication information for connecting with the Publisher

❑ `DistributionSchedule` (`Schedule`) objects that represent the schedule for Merge updates

Using Replication Objects

If you're not familiar with replication and SQL-DMO you may think that Enterprise Manager covers so many bases that replication using these objects looks too much like hard work. But again one can soon envisage a number of uses in an enterprise framework.

For instance, one possible use of this technology could be an application that tracks the replication events and provides statistical analysis on replication events. This would be useful for an end-user who needs the subscription of data aggregated, or for the database administrator who is in charge of the daily publish schedule. Similarly, it may be felt beneficial to build a custom application that facilitates replication of data to another database for data warehousing and aggregation.

> **Of course SQL-DMO objects do have one extra capability in comparison to Enterprise Manager – when working with Subscribers SQL Server Enterprise Manager only supports subscriptions to publications, not to articles. With SQL-DMO objects, you can subscribe to a publication or to individual articles within the publication.**

This facility is of great assistance in the situation where you find yourself distributing an update to a legacy application that has requirements for subscriptions to individual articles.

Replication Sample Application

Now we're ready to take a look at a sample application. This application lets us connect to a server and create a push subscription for a single article of a publication (the unique selling point of SQL-DMO over Enterprise Manager in this area). After connecting to a server, the user running the application selects the:

❑ Destination server

❑ Destination database

❑ Published source database

❑ Source publication

❑ Source article

Our example is straightforward; firstly open a Standard EXE project then set a reference to the SQL-DMO Object Library. We then declare the following variables in a standard module called REPL:

```
Public oApp As SQLDMO.Application
Public oServer As SQLDMO.SQLServer
Public lConnID As Long
Public bConnected As Boolean
```

This is all standard stuff; when you're working with SQL-DMO objects, you can rely on needing to start with an application object, oApp, and a server object, oServer. The variable lConnID will have the connection ID of our connected server as its value.

Next, set up a MDI form as follows:

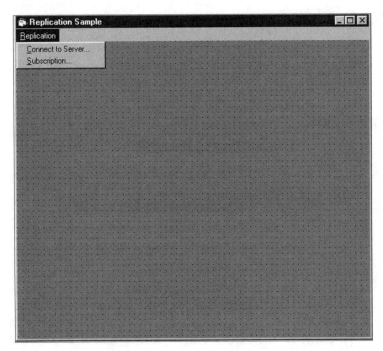

The code for the form is trivial with the menus labeled mnuConnect and mnuSubscriber which will give access to a form enabling connection to the server and, when a connection is made, a form controlling the subscription:

```
Private Sub MDIForm_Load()

'mnuPublisher.Enabled = False
    'mnuSubscriber.Enabled = False
    bConnected = False
End Sub
```

```
Private Sub mnuConnect_Click()
    frmConnect.Show
End Sub


Private Sub mnuReplication_Click()
'Enable the subscriber menu only if the connection has
'been established.
    mnuSubscriber.Enabled = bConnected
'Do not enable the Connect menu if a connection already exists
    mnuConnect.Enabled = Not bConnected
End Sub


Private Sub mnuSubscriber_Click()
    frmSubscribe.Show
End Sub
```

Thus on opening the application the only option available is to make a connection; then, when this is made, the option to subscribe is allowed. Our next task is to set up the server connection form.

Server Connection

The `frmConnect` form should be set up as shown below:

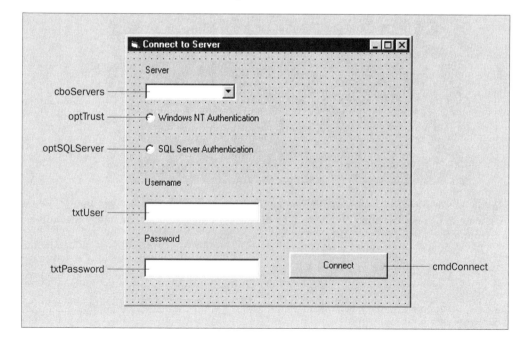

We'll firstly attach some basic screen handling to the form to enable and disable the text boxes as appropriate:

```
Private Sub optSQLServer_Click()
    txtUser.Enabled = True
    txtUser.BackColor = vbWhite
    txtPassword.Enabled = True
    txtPassword.BackColor = vbWhite
End Sub
```

```
Private Sub optTrust_Click()
    txtUser.Enabled = False
    txtUser.BackColor = Me.BackColor
    txtPassword.Enabled = False
    txtPassword.BackColor = Me.BackColor
End Sub
```

Listing the Servers

To make the form usable we need to load the combo box with server names when the form is loaded:

```
Private Sub Form_Load()

    optTrust.Value = True
    Dim i As Integer
    Dim sNameList As SQLDMO.NameList
    Set sNameList = REPL.ServerNames

    For i = 1 To sNameList.Count
        cboServers.AddItem sNameList(i)
    Next

End Sub
```

Within the REPL module we instantiate the Application object and then dimension a SQL-DMO Namelist and call the ServerNames function:

```
Public Function ServerNames() As SQLDMO.NameList
    Set oApp = New SQLDMO.Application
    'This only works if the component is being run on NT or Windows 2000
    Set ServerNames = oApp.ListAvailableSQLServers
End Function
```

This returns a list of SQL Servers running on Windows NT. As mentioned in earlier chapters, only servers running on Windows NT will be listed. A combo box was used to allow the entering of server names that don't appear in the list.

Making the Connection

After selecting the server and entering the connection information, the user will click on the Connect button to make the connection. The `cmdConnect_Click` procedure calls `ConnectServer` in the `REPL` standard module to establish a connection with the selected server. This is the process for establishing a server connection as we saw in the examples provided in earlier chapters:

```
Private Sub cmdConnect_Click()
Dim sServer As String
Dim bIntegrated As Boolean
Dim sUser As String
Dim sPassword As String

    If optTrust.Value = True Then
       Me.MousePointer = vbHourglass
       lConnID = REPL.ConnectServer(cboServers)
       sServer = cboServers
       Me.MousePointer = vbDefault
    End If
    If optSQLServer.Value = True Then
       If txtPassword = "" Then
          MsgBox "Enter a user name", vbOKOnly
          Exit Sub
       End If
       Me.MousePointer = vbHourglass
       lConnID = REPL.ConnectServer(cboServers, txtUser, txtPassword)
       sServer = cboServers
       bIntegrated = False
       sUser = txtUser
       sPassword = txtPassword
       Me.MousePointer = vbDefault
    End If
    bConnected = True
    Me.Hide
End Sub
```

The option buttons let us choose between Windows NT authentication and SQL Server authentication. There is very basic form checking that means if the **SQL Server Authentication** option is selected an error message is given if no user name is entered.

Our next task is to add the `ConnectServer` function to the `REPL` module:

```
Public Function ConnectServer(ByVal sServername As String, _
                    Optional ByVal sUser As String, _
                    Optional ByVal sPassword As String) As Long

    Set oServer = CreateObject("SQLDMO.SQLServer")
    If sUser = "" Then
       oServer.LoginSecure = True
       oServer.Connect sServername
    Else
       oServer.Connect sServername, sUser, sPassword
```

```
    End If
    ConnectServer = oServer.ConnectionID
    Set oServer = Nothing

End Function
```

The server object is created as a new instance of the SQL-DMO object. The application then connects with the Publisher. We only need to supply a login user name (sUser) and password (sPassword) if using SQL Server authentication to connect to the server.

Creating the Subscription

The frmSubscribe form should be set up as shown below:

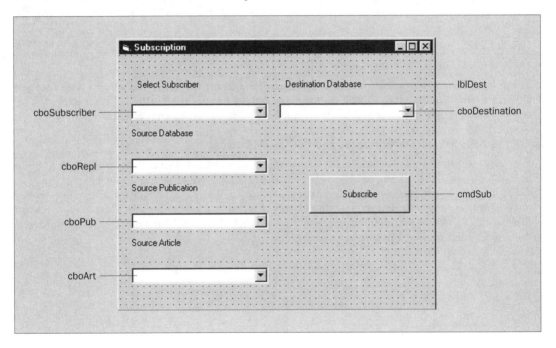

Firstly on the form we dimension three array variables that will be used for receiving enumerated lists:

```
    Private RegSubList() As String
    Private RegDBList() As String
    Private PubsList() As String
```

When the form loads, we retrieve two sets of collection objects, RegisteredSubscribers and ReplicationDatabases:

```
    Private Sub Form_Load()
    Dim i As Integer
```

```
    Me.MousePointer = vbHourglass

    RegSubList = REPL.GetSubList(lConnID)
    For i = 0 To UBound(RegSubList)
        cboSubscriber.AddItem RegSubList(i)
    Next

    PubsList = REPL.GetPubList(lConnID)
    For i = 0 To UBound(PubsList)
        cboRepl.AddItem PubsList(i)
    Next

    cboRepl.Enabled = False
    cboArt.Enabled = False
    cboPub.Enabled = False
    cmdSub.Enabled = False
    Me.MousePointer = vbDefault

End Sub
```

These lists provide our selections for our Subscriber and for the source database. We can't generate a list of destination databases until after the Subscriber has been identified. By the same token, we can't generate a list of source publications until we've selected the source database.

Listing the Subscribers, Destinations, and Source Databases

We call `GetSubList` to retrieve a list of registered subscribers. We call `GetPubList` to get a list of databases available to our publisher (which is the system we connected to earlier in the example). Neither of these should be particularly surprising; we used similar procedures in earlier chapters to retrieve different object lists. In this case, we are retrieving the `Name` property from each of the Subscribers contained in the Publisher's `RegisteredSubscribers` collection and these are added to the `cboSubscriber` combo box.

The `GetSubList` function added to the `REPL` module is as follows:

```
Public Function GetSubList(lConnID As Long) As String()

    Dim SubList() As String
    Dim i As Integer
    Dim dCount As Integer
    Dim oSQLServer As SQLDMO.SQLServer
    Dim oPublisher As SQLDMO.Publisher
    Set oSQLServer = oApp.SQLServers.ItemByID(lConnID)
    Set oPublisher = oSQLServer.Replication.Publisher

    ReDim SubList(0 To oPublisher.RegisteredSubscribers.Count - 1)

    For i = 1 To oPublisher.RegisteredSubscribers.Count
        SubList(dCount) = oPublisher.RegisteredSubscribers(i).Name
        dCount = dCount + 1
    Next
```

```
    If dCount = 0 Then
        ReDim Preserve SubList(dCount)
    End If

    GetSubList = SubList

End Function
```

> We are using combo boxes to simplify our code. We can use the **Text** property of
> the combo boxes to set property values when we create our subscription.

The GetPubList function that we add to the REPL module is very similar. It's used to retrieve a
list of the Publisher's replication databases. When we retrieved databases in the sample used in the
earlier chapters, we had to filter out system databases. That isn't necessary here since the
ReplicationDatabase objects in the ReplicationDatabases collection will only include
user databases, since only user databases can be published. Our GetPubList function is:

```
Public Function GetPubList(lConnID As Long) As String()

    Dim PubList() As String
    Dim i As Integer
    Dim dCount As Integer
    Dim oSQLServer As SQLDMO.SQLServer
    Set oSQLServer = oApp.SQLServers.ItemByID(lConnID)

    ReDim PubList(0 To oSQLServer.Replication.ReplicationDatabases.Count - 1)
    For i = 1 To oSQLServer.Replication.ReplicationDatabases.Count
        PubList(dCount) = oSQLServer.Replication.ReplicationDatabases(i).Name
        dCount = dCount + 1
    Next

    If dCount = 0 Then
        ReDim Preserve PubList(dCount)
    End If
    GetPubList = PubList

End Function
```

When the user clicks on the combo box and makes a selection, the Text property is checked to
verify that a selection has been made (and if so a GetDBList function is called):

```
Private Sub cboSubscriber_Click()
Dim i As Integer
    If cboSubscriber.Text = "" Then
        Exit Sub
    Else
        cboSubscriber.Refresh
        Me.MousePointer = vbHourglass
        cboDestination.Enabled = True
```

```
        lblDest.Enabled = True
        'Clear the ComboBox
        cboDestination.Clear
    End If

    RegDBList() = REPL.GetDBList

    For i = 0 To UBound(RegDBList)
        cboDestination.AddItem RegDBList(i)
    Next

    Me.MousePointer = vbDefault
End Sub
```

Our `GetDBList` function that is placed in the module and used to generate a list of Subscriber databases is:

```
Public Function GetDBList() As String()

    Dim sNonSystemDBs() As String
    Dim sSub As String
    Dim i As Integer
    Dim dCount As Integer
    Dim oSQLServer1 As SQLDMO.SQLServer

    sSub = frmSubscribe.cboSubscriber.Text
    Set oSQLServer1 = CreateObject("SQLDMO.SQLServer")
    oSQLServer1.LoginSecure = True
    oSQLServer1.Connect sSub

    For i = 1 To oSQLServer1.Databases.Count
        'Prevent the names of system objects from being returned
        If oSQLServer1.Databases(i).SystemObject = False Then
            ReDim Preserve sNonSystemDBs(dCount)
            sNonSystemDBs(dCount) = oSQLServer1.Databases(i).Name
            dCount = dCount + 1
        End If
    Next

    'Prevent an undimensioned array from being returned.
    If dCount = 0 Then
        ReDim Preserve sNonSystemDBs(dCount)
    End If

    GetDBList = sNonSystemDBs
    Set oSQLServer1 = Nothing
End Function
```

The user can now select a destination database.

For the purpose of this example, we are assuming that we are establishing a trusted connection to the Subscriber. If you wanted to modify this application to support SQL Server authentication, you would need to let the user select the authentication type and enter a user name and password. Refer to the connection example in this chapter to see how to do this.

After selecting the destination database the user can select a source database from the list retrieved when the form loaded. Our code to handle this in `frmSubscribe` is:

```
Private Sub cboDestination_Click()
    If cboDestination.Text = "" Then
        Exit Sub
    Else
        cboRepl.Enabled = True
    End If
End Sub
```

Listing the Publications and Articles

When the user selects a source database, the application retrieves a list of publications defined for that database. Here we are retrieving the publications and loading them directly into the publications combo box (cboPub). We dimension SQLServer and ReplicationDatabase objects. The cboRepl.Text property is used to select the source database from the ReplicationDatabases collection. We then use the Name property for each of the TransPublication objects in the TransPublications collection to load cboPub as shown below:

```
Private Sub cboRepl_Click()

    Dim oSQLServer As SQLDMO.SQLServer
    Dim oReplicationDatabase As SQLDMO.ReplicationDatabase
    Dim i As Integer

    If cboRepl.Text = "" Then
        Exit Sub
    Else
        cboRepl.Refresh
        Me.MousePointer = vbHourglass
        cboPub.Enabled = True
        'Clear cboPub
        cboPub.Clear
    End If

    Set oSQLServer = oApp.SQLServers.ItemByID(lConnID)
    Set oReplicationDatabase = _
        oSQLServer.Replication.ReplicationDatabases(cboRepl.Text)
    For i = 1 To oReplicationDatabase.TransPublications.Count
        cboPub.AddItem (oReplicationDatabase.TransPublications(i).Name)
    Next
```

```
        Me.MousePointer = vbDefault

End Sub
```

> In our sample application, we are retrieving Transactional publications only. If
> we wanted to create a subscription to a Merge publication, we would have used
> the **MergePublications** collection.

When the user selects a publication, it's then necessary to retrieve all of the articles defining that
publication:

```
Private Sub cboPub_Click()

    Dim oSQLServer As SQLDMO.SQLServer
    Dim oReplicationDatabase As SQLDMO.ReplicationDatabase
    Dim oTransPublication As SQLDMO.TransPublication
    Dim i As Integer

    If cboPub.Text = "" Then
        Exit Sub
    Else
        cboPub.Refresh
        Me.MousePointer = vbHourglass
        cboArt.Enabled = True
        cboArt.Clear
    End If

    Set oSQLServer = oApp.SQLServers.ItemByID(lConnID)
    Set oReplicationDatabase = _
        oSQLServer.Replication.ReplicationDatabases(cboRepl.Text)
    Set oTransPublication = oReplicationDatabase.TransPublications(cboPub.Text)

    For i = 1 To oTransPublication.TransArticles.Count
        cboArt.AddItem (oTransPublication.TransArticles(i).Name)
    Next
    Me.MousePointer = vbDefault
    End Sub
```

The process for loading article names into the cboArt combo box is the same we saw in the last
example. We're dimensioning an additional object variable as a TransPublication object. This
allows us to use the TransArticles collection and the object Name property to retrieve article
names.

When the user makes a selection from cboArt, the cmbSub command button is enabled:

```
Private Sub cboArt_Click()

    If cboArt.Text = "" Then
        Exit Sub
    Else
        cmdSub.Enabled = True
    End If

End Sub
```

Creating the Subscription

We now have all the information we need to create the subscription:

```
Private Sub cmdSub_Click()

    Dim oSQLServer As SQLDMO.SQLServer
    Dim oReplicationDatabase As SQLDMO.ReplicationDatabase
    Dim oTransPublication As SQLDMO.TransPublication
    Dim oTransArticle As SQLDMO.TransArticle
    Dim oTransSubscription As SQLDMO.TransSubscription

    Me.MousePointer = vbHourglass
    Set oTransSubscription = New SQLDMO.TransSubscription
    Set oSQLServer = oApp.SQLServers.ItemByID(lConnID)
    Set oReplicationDatabase = _
        oSQLServer.Replication.ReplicationDatabases(cboRepl.Text)
    Set oTransPublication = oReplicationDatabase.TransPublications(cboPub.Text)
    Set oTransArticle = oTransPublication.TransArticles(cboArt.Text)
    oTransSubscription.Subscriber = cboSubscriber.Text
    oTransSubscription.SubscriptionDB = (cboDestination.Text)
    oTransArticle.TransSubscriptions.Add oTransSubscription

    Me.MousePointer = vbDefault
    MsgBox "Subscription Completed", vbOKOnly


End Sub
```

In this final step we create the TransSubscription object and set its Subscriber and subscription databases properties. We can then use the TransSubscriptions' Add method to add the new TransSubscription object to the collection.

Running the Application

If we wanted to create a subscription to the Customers table in the NorthTran publication, we would make the connection then select Replication | Subscription and fill in the screen as follows:

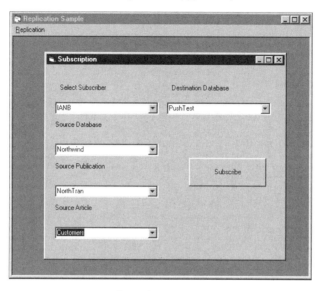

After we click on Subscribe to create the subscription, we can check in SQL Server Enterprise Manager to verify that the subscription was created. Select the Publisher and run Tools | Replication | Create and Manage Publications.

Next, drill down to the publication, right-click select Properties then pick the Subscriptions tab to reveal something like:

This is similar to the subscription example you saw earlier, except that now we are subscribing to some, rather than all, of the articles.

Summary

Over the course of this chapter we've covered a lot of ground very rapidly. Replication is a complicated area and is fully supported with a correspondingly large number of objects in SQL-DMO. Our treatment of the subject has taken us from an overview of the basic concepts through to developing a sample application, via a run through of the appropriate Wizard support given by Enterprise Manager.

While there is a huge amount of material that could still be covered, we hope that this chapter has shown enough material and demonstrated the patterns of implementation that will enable you to apply SQL-DMO to your own replication solutions.

Along the way we've pointed out a few potential reasons for using SQL-DMO in this area (such as tracking replication events, data warehousing) and the fact that through using SQL-DMO to manage replication you can subscribe to an individual article, a facility *not* available through Enterprise Manager.

In the next chapter we move on to a new area – **Data Transformation Services** (**DTS**).

9

Introduction to Data Transformation Services (DTS)

One of the great new features introduced with SQL Server 7.0 was **Data Transformation Services** (**DTS**). The next chapter will introduce working with DTS objects, but first, we're going to give a quick introduction to DTS. Here we're going to use some examples based on the Northwind database. These are going to be simple examples and could be easily modified for use with other databases.

This chapter covers three basic areas:

❑ An overview of DTS basics including an introduction to the DTS Wizard and DTS Designer utilities

❑ Using the DTS Wizard to perform a simple task

❑ Using the DTS Designer to modify existing packages and create new ones

If you're already somewhat familiar with DTS, you may be tempted to skip this chapter; but we suggest you at least scan through the chapter contents – there might be some things you might not have considered before.

> The files built during this chapter (C6Sample1.dts and C6Samp2.dts – for the
> Data Wizard and DTS Designer generated tasks respectively) are available for
> download from the Wrox site at www.wrox.com.

Without further ado let's see what's so good about Data Transformation Services.

DTS Basics

Many people have the same initial reaction to DTS – "Oh no, another option for importing and exporting SQL Server data". Now, while it is an excellent import and export tool, if you limit your use to just those activities, you're going to miss out on other uses that could potentially save you a great deal of time and effort.

For example DTS can be used to carry out tasks such as:

❑ Importing and exporting only selected columns

❑ Transforming and modifying data before transfer

❑ **Scrubbing data** (that is removing bad or inappropriate data) before import

❑ Running periodic transfers based on a schedule defined by the user

❑ Sending notifications when transfers are complete or errors occur

These suggestions are only the tip of the iceberg. Once you start working with DTS, you'll find additional ways it can support your database applications.

> One of the strengths of DTS is that you don't have to specify SQL Server as your
> source or destination. Data can be moved between any supported sources and
> destinations, so enabling data movement between different applications – of
> course, SQL Server client utilities will have to be installed (at minimum) in order
> to have DTS available.

Before we actually start using DTS, via the DTS Wizard and DTS Designer, let's take some time to look over some DTS features and introduce some basic terms.

Source and Destination Support

Before we work with DTS, it might be helpful to know what sources and destinations are supported; these include:

❑ SQL Server installations

❑ Oracle installations

❑ Data files

❑ Other ODBC systems

❑ Microsoft Data Links

When a source is specified, connection information also has to be specified; when defining a data file connection, a file location needs to be provided.

> Data file connections are evaluated in reference to the local machine on which the DTS package is executed. If you're planning to create the package on one machine, but execute the package on a different machine, be very careful how the file location is specified. Either specify the file as a Universal Naming Convention (UNC) path, as *server**shared_path**filename* or as a drive that is mapped the same on both systems. If other words, if it is seen as drive M: on one system, it has to be drive M: on the other.

Source and Destination Options

Let's quickly run through the data connection options:

SQL Server – DTS supports connection using Microsoft OLE DB Provider for SQL Server or Microsoft ODBC Provider for SQL Server. With either, the same information is requested:

❑ Server name, or (local) for a local server

❑ Authentication method – either Windows NT authentication or SQL Server authentication

❑ Default database or database name

Choosing to connect through SQL Server authentication means a username and password for login will also have to be provided.

Oracle – We can connect to Oracle servers through Microsoft OLE DB Provider for Oracle or Microsoft ODBC driver for Oracle. Connection to an Oracle server via either route will trigger a prompt for the following:

❑ Server name

❑ Username

❑ Password

Data File – The information we need to provide when connecting to a data file is somewhat dependent on the file type. File types supported for both source and destination are:

❑ dBase III, dBase IV, and dBase V

❑ Microsoft Access

❑ Microsoft Excel 3.0, 4.0, 5.0, and 8.0

❑ Paradox 3.x, 4.x, and 5.x

❑ Text files

With any of these file types, the full path and filename needs to be provided. With all the file types *except* text files (see below), username and password information can also be provided. Some connection types require additional connection information.

Text Files – Text files are often considered the easiest type of connection to configure and support. In many cases they are, but there can be areas of potential confusion. For instance a text file can take a number of forms and formats and to identify the file correctly, the file format must be understood. Considerations here include finding:

❑ If the file consists of Unicode or ANSI text

❑ If the file has fixed fields or is delimited

❑ If the file has row delimitation

❑ If there are column or field delimiters for delimited files

❑ If there is field alignment for fixed field files

❑ What the text qualifier is

❑ Whether or not the first row contains column names

❑ The rows to skip, if any

This is an area where the intelligence built into DTS can be of assistance. DTS will open the file and attempt, as much as possible, to determine this information automatically and will prompt with its assumptions about how the file is formatted, to let any necessary changes be made prior to execution.

Other ODBC – ODBC connections other than SQL Server or Oracle have their own set of prompts. These include:

❑ User/System DSN or File DSN

❑ Username

❑ Password

The same information is required when connecting to Microsoft Visual FoxPro. Choosing to connect with a User/System DSN through the DTS Wizard gives the option of defining the DSN "on the fly".

Microsoft Data Link Connection – It's possible to connect through the Microsoft Data Link connection and either choose an existing data link file (**Universal Data Link** – **UDL** file), or define a new data link. The data link properties for the connection will need to be specified.

A Microsoft Data Link is a means of connecting to a data source through an OLE DB driver. Connection information is defined through the UDL file describing the link, which includes the:

- ❏ OLE DB provider for the connection

- ❏ Data source name or connection string for connecting to the data source

- ❏ User name and password for connecting to the data source

- ❏ Initial catalog or database

- ❏ Connection timeout

- ❏ Access permissions

One possible reason for using a Microsoft Data Link connection is under the circumstances that one such connection has already been defined to support access to the data by another application (for instance Microsoft Access).

Copy and Transformation Support

DTS lets us run a direct copy between a source and destination, mapping data transfers between source and destination columns, or transform data as part of the copy process. When we transform data, we are formatting the source data to meet our specific needs at the destination. Let's consider each of these in turn.

Data Copy

We have three basic copy options:

- ❏ Copying tables from the source database

- ❏ Using a query to specify the data to be transferred

- ❏ Transferring data and objects between SQL Server 7.0 servers

When copying from a table (or spreadsheet, in the case of Excel) the source columns will copy directly into the destination in the same order, but it's straightforward to map the columns to change the copy order. If only selected columns are needed from the source, a query could be defined as the copy source.

> If it feels easier, you can use a query as your source and do some data manipulation during the transfer. Some things are easy to do through queries – for example combining text columns or generating columns with computed values.

Choosing SQL Server 7.0 servers as both source and destination, gives the option of transferring data and database objects between the servers – all or part of a selected database may be copied.

One potential use of this is in the setting up of a working copy of a database for testing or prototyping. For example, consider the situation where you wanted to make some changes to a database application, but couldn't afford to interrupt activities on the production database. An additional server could be set up and DTS used to copy over the production database. This would enable testing against actual data without operations being affected.

Transformations

Data transformations can be defined as part of the copy process. Transformation scripts can be written in VBScript or JScript. Detailed discussion of such scripts falls outside the scope of this book but they can be used to perform tasks such as:

❑ Data validation

❑ Combination of multiple columns

❑ Breaking of columns into multiple columns

❑ Conversion between types

❑ Reformatting of text data

❑ Calculation of new values

The transformation package can be saved for reuse as required, which gives us a way of automating periodic data transfers where the source data needs to be modified before being written to the destination.

DTS Packages

A DTS package is the complete DTS transformation. It defines the source, the destination, and any manipulation occurring between the two. DTS packages can be defined through the DTS Wizard, DTS Designer, or through use of DTS objects (the first two of these we'll deal with in detail in this chapter, you'll have to wait until Chapter 10 to use the objects). Once you've defined a package, you can:

❑ Run the package immediately

❑ Create a DTS package for replication

❑ Save the package and schedule it for later execution

You can save packages to SQL Server, to the Microsoft Repository, or to an operating system file. It's a good idea to save a package if there's a chance that you're going to need it again later.

OK, let's take a first look at the DTS Wizard and the DTS Designer starting with the DTS Wizard.

DTS Wizard

Within Enterprise Manager highlighting the server group and selecting either Tools | Wizards... or the appropriate icon brings up the following dialog (launching the Wizard by running Start | Programs | SQL Server 7.0 | Import and Export Data will reveal a different screen as detailed later):

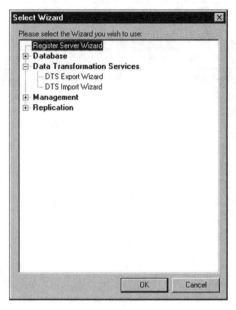

The SQL Server Enterprise Manager Wizard dialog lists two DTS Wizards, Import and Export. In reality, there is one Wizard – data import and export are relative terms, and either choice launches the same Wizard.

> If you prefer working from a command line, you can launch the DTS Wizard from the **Start | Run** prompt or from a command prompt by running `dtswiz.exe`, which will take you into the same Wizard as the other methods.

The DTS Wizard is a powerful utility and will probably meet many (if not most) data transfer requirements. It gives us access to all of the DTS connection types and lets us define connection parameters. We can map data, create transformation scripts, and even transfer data and objects between SQL Server 7.0 servers. It lets us run packages immediately after they've been defined or schedule packages for later execution.

Another use of the DTS Wizard is to build a basic DTS package that can subsequently be opened and modified with the DTS Designer.

In this way it can be a helpful learning tool; different types of package can be created, saved, and then inspected in detail via the DTS Designer enabling a deeper understanding of package structure to be developed and thus facilitating development of more powerful custom packages.

All of which brings us neatly on to our first meeting with the DTS Designer.

DTS Designer

The DTS Designer (we'll see how to access it later so the diagram below is a taster of things to come) gives us options that aren't available through the DTS Wizard.

Here we have more control over package execution – we can execute other tasks, including launching other applications, based on whether a task succeeds or fails, or even based simply on completion.

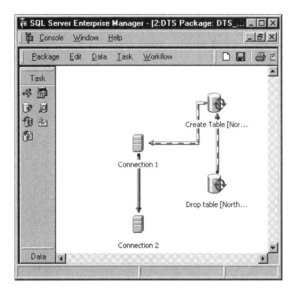

When a package is created through DTS Designer, it will typically include:

❑   One or more connections

❑   Data transformations, moving data between the source and destination

❑   Tasks, which are operations to be performed by the DTS package

❑   Precedence constraints setting the order between tasks

We'll talk about all these features in more detail later, along with an example of using the DTS Designer, but now we've introduced these utilities let's now look in detail at the first – the DTS Wizard.

Using the DTS Wizard to Create a Package

To introduce DTS, let's use the DTS Wizard to create a package to drop and create a table in the Northwind database.

We are going to encounter this example again in the next chapter, but in a different form where we see how to build an application to perform the same tasks, but using DTS objects rather than the DTS Wizard.

Before you start with the DTS Wizard, if you're going to follow the example through, you'll need to create a table named `emp_sum` in the `Northwind` database. The table has four columns. These are:

- ❑ `fname` with data type `nvarchar(10)`
- ❑ `lname` with data type `nvarchar(20)`
- ❑ `hire` with data type `datetime`
- ❑ `phone` with data type `nvarchar(24)`

All of the columns are nullable.

So onto the main event...

Specifying the Source and Destination

The first step is to run Start | Programs | Microsoft SQL Server 7.0 | Import and Export Data and open the DTS Wizard:

Clicking on <u>N</u>ext to continue brings up a dialog that prompts for a data source:

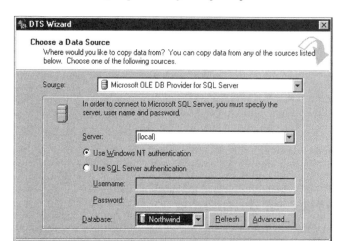

In this case, the local SQL Server is selected, along with the `Northwind` database, as the database connection. You may find that after making a server selection (except for the local server) you will need to click on <u>R</u>efresh to get a list of available databases. The <u>A</u>dvanced...button is used to set advanced OLE DB options, such as timeout information – we won't be using it in our example.

Notice that we're using Windows NT authentication to connect to the server. This will establish a trusted connection with the server. Windows NT authentication can *only* be used if the server is running on Windows NT; if it was running on Windows 95/98, we'd have to use SQL Server authentication and provide a username and password.

The next screen asks us to choose a destination for our data. Since we're copying to a different table in the same database, our destination connection information is the same as for the source connection:

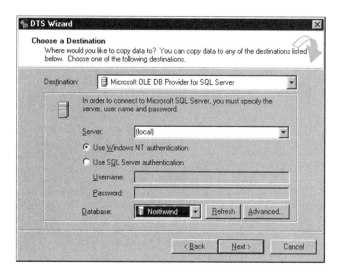

Specifying the Copy Options

We now have the copy options. For this example, we're going to use the default option – copying tables from the source database. We're only going to be copying four columns out of the source table, so we could also select to use a query to define the transfer. This would open an additional dialog so that we could define the query.

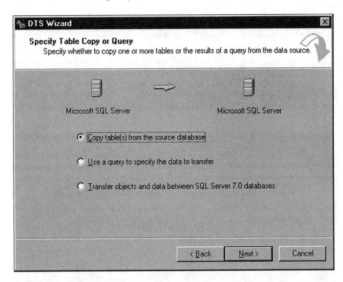

> There are examples in the next chapter of using two different methods for transferring data. In one, a query is used to select the source data. In the other, the individual source and destination columns are selected. This DTS Wizard is following the second example, as you will soon see.

We are now prompted to select the source table (or tables). In this example, we are copying selected columns from the Employees table to the emp_sum table:

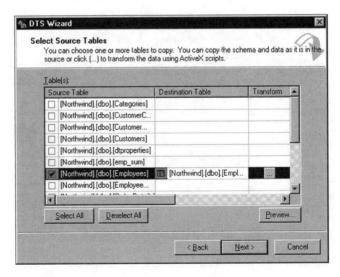

In the figure above, we've expanded that Source Table column to more clearly show the table names and selected the checkbox for the Employees table.

By default, SQL Server assumes that the destination table will have the same name as the source table. If we click in the Destination Table column next to the Employees table, a dropdown arrow will appear. This allows us to select a different destination table. In our example, we're selecting emp_sum as the destination and we now have:

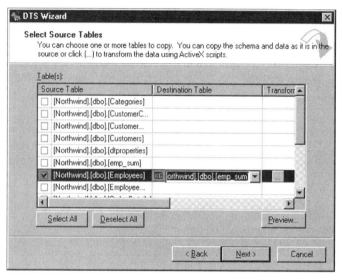

You can see the source and destination tables selected, but before we go further we need to check the source and destination to see if the structures are compatible. Click on the Transform (...) button to bring up the Column Mappings and Transformations dialog.

Here we can see that the source table (Employees) has more columns than the destination table (emp_sum) and that the columns are in different orders, so we are going to use the dialog to facilitate mapping source columns to destination columns and making the necessary transformations:

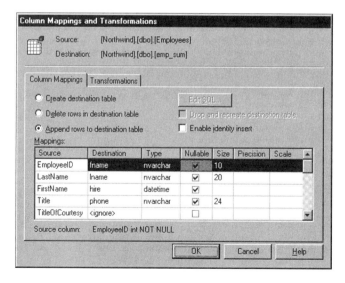

Clicking on any column name under Source, brings up a dropdown arrow allowing the available columns in the source table to be displayed. We are matching `FirstName` to `fname`, `LastName` to `lname`, `HireDate` to `hire`, and `HomePhone` to `phone`. Since there are only four Destination columns available, all of the remaining Source columns will be set automatically to `<ignore>`. After a couple of judicious mouse clicks we should get:

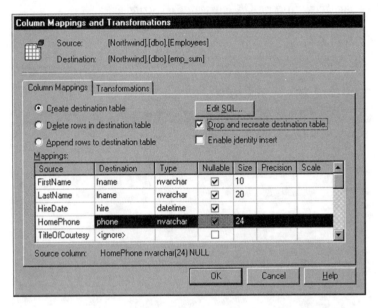

The package will drop and recreate the destination table before copying the data.

To view the transformation script click on the Transformations tab and select Transform information as it is copied to the destination:

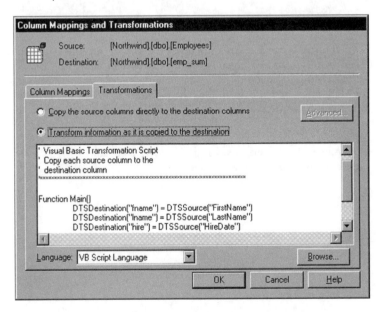

The figure above shows the default transformation script – data transformations can be further defined by modifying this script. DTS supports scripts written in either VBScript or JavaScript.

Incidentally, when you first attempt to display the script in this example, you'll receive a warning that column mappings have changed and will be prompted to generate a default script to reflect those mappings. Click on OK to generate the script.

Clicking on OK from either tab returns to the Source Tables dialog, where clicking on Next to continue brings up a dialog that presents package options:

Saving and Executing the Package

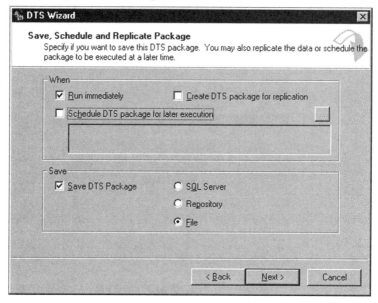

At this point we can choose to run the package immediately, create the package for replication, schedule it for later execution, or any combination of the three. Choosing Schedule DTS package for later execution will bring up a standard SQL Server schedule dialog, letting us set a daily, weekly, or monthly schedule for execution. Selecting Create DTS package for replication will create a package that can be replicated to other servers. This selection will not prompt with any additional screens.

In the example shown, we've selected to save the package as a server file, which means that we'll be prompted for a file location and server name:

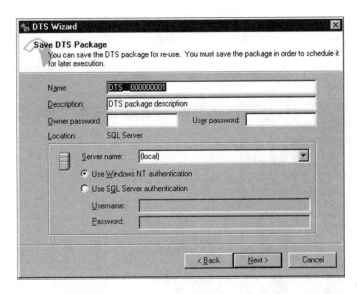

The destination you actually choose for saving the package to will depend on what the future plans are for the package. For instance, if the package is intended to be run on a specific server, it will probably be best to save the package to the server (which also provides version tracking for the package). If the plan is to distribute the package, it will probably be advantageous to save the package to an operating system file. Saving to the Repository is the preferred method in data warehousing applications where data lineage can be used to provide an audit trail.

Here saving as a SQL Server file means that the package should be visible under the LocalPackages icon of the Data Transformation Services folder in Enterprise Manager (though you may need to right-click on the folder and select Refresh to see it).

If the package was to be saved as an operating system file we would be prompted for a file location and filename:

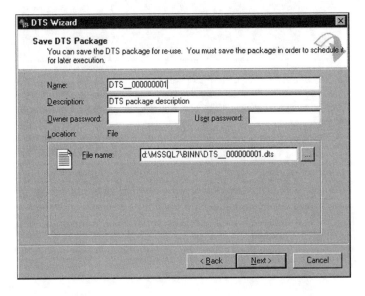

For the purposes of this example, we're going to leave the filename and destination at the default suggestions (although there is the option of changing either, as well as the package description). Click on Next to save the file and continue (remember this file is available for download from the Wrox web site as C6Sample1.dts). The Wizard will review your selections before completing and, if selected, execute the package:

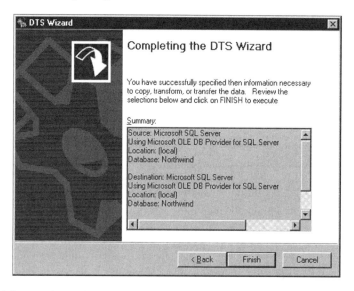

Clicking on Finish completes the Wizard and reveals a dialog showing the progress of the process:

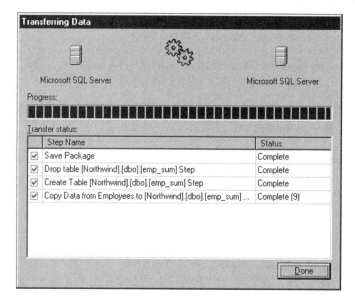

The Wizard will let you know as each step completes. After all is finished click on Done to clear this final dialog and exit the Wizard.

Now let's take a look at the DTS Designer.

The DTS Designer

The basic package operations supported by DTS Designer are:

❑ Creating new packages or opening an existing packages

❑ Editing packages to include connections, tasks, and precedence constraints

❑ Saving packages to SQL Server, Microsoft Repository, or operating system files

❑ Executing packages or scheduling them for execution

When the package is no longer needed, it can be deleted.

The DTS Designer offers additional options for defining packages. To break ourselves into this area gently we're going to look at:

❑ Opening and creating packages

❑ Editing packages

Once we've looked around the utility we'll then use it to recreate the simple package we constructed via the DTS Wizard.

Opening and Creating Packages

The first step is to launch SQL Server Enterprise Manager and expand the server for which the package was created (or is being created):

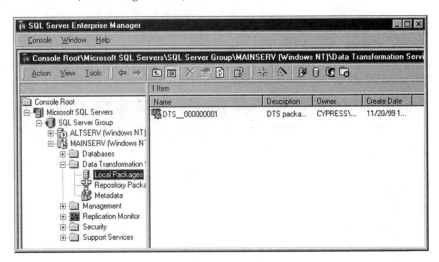

Expanding the Data Transformation Services folder displays three icons. We're going to focus on two of these. The Local Packages icon displays packages stored with SQL Server as their destination (remember you may have to refresh the view to see newly created packages). Packages stored to the Microsoft Repository are listed under the Repository Packages icon. The Microsoft Repository is a common location for information about objects and the relationships between objects. This offers a standard way of describing object-oriented information for use by software tools. With either of these, packages can be opened by double-clicking on the package name or selecting the package and running Action | Design Package.

The Metadata icon (which we won't look into further) gives access to SQL Server metadata. Metadata is data about data, such as data schema information, table lineage data (documenting the source of table data), and version and lineage information about DTS packages.

> *If the package was stored as an operating system file, you will need to select the* Data Transformation Services *folder and run* Action | All Tasks | Open Package.

What about creating a new package? Either select the Data Transformation Services folder, or one of the icons beneath the folder, and run Action | New Package, alternatively right-click on the folder or one of its icons and run New Package from the pop-up menu.

Editing Packages

Once the DTS Designer window is open you can start editing your package. You can add or modify:

❑ Connections

❑ Tasks

❑ Precedence constraints

If we open up our example package created by DTS Wizard to copy from `Employees` to `emp_sum` we'll see that there are two connections, both SQL Server 7.0 connections, and two tasks, both Execute SQL tasks, to drop and then create the `emp_sum` table. Then there is a transformation between the two connections, copying from `Employees` to `emp_sum`. Here the transformation is represented by the solid pipeline between Connection 1 and Connection 2:

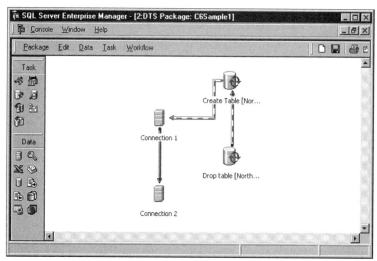

How do we know what is contained in this package? Well in this case it's easy, since it was created by the DTS Wizard example. Otherwise, we'd need to look at properties for each of the package objects to figure out what is happening. In this section we're going to take a quick look at this package first and then recreate the package, with a couple of changes, as a new package.

Now that you can see the package components represented, along with their relationship to one another, let's look at them in a little more detail.

Connections

As with the DTS Wizard, you define a connection through its properties. For example, a SQL Server connection requires you to identify the server, authentication, and database. Connections are selected from the Data menu or Data icons. So selecting Data | 1 Microsoft OLE DB Provider for SQL Server ... would bring up a Connection Properties dialog similar to that shown below.

In the case of a package that already contains connections, right-clicking on a connection and selecting Properties will allow the connection definition to be viewed, so Connection 1 in our example gives:

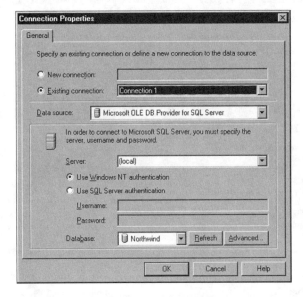

As you can see above, except for giving the connection a name, the information requested for the connection is the same as you saw with the DTS Wizard. This is true for all of the connection types.

You can choose to add a variety of connections (remember to give each one a recognizable name as it is added to the package) either via the Data menu or, as illustrated here, via the icons at the side of the window:

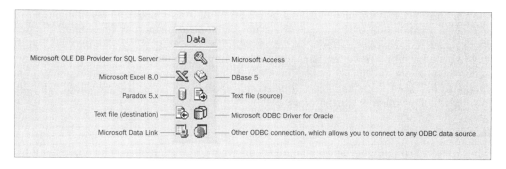

Tasks

Tasks are also defined by task properties. The figure below shows the properties sheet for the Execute SQL Task obtained by right-clicking (and selecting Properties) for the Create Table task in our example:

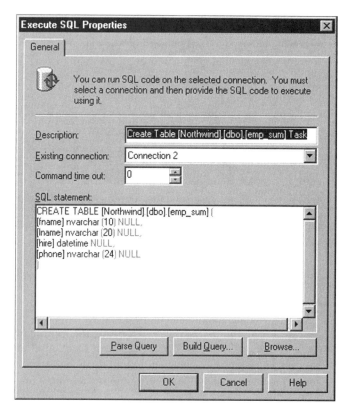

Addition of new tasks can be achieved by selecting the appropriate Task menu item or icon (as illustrated below):

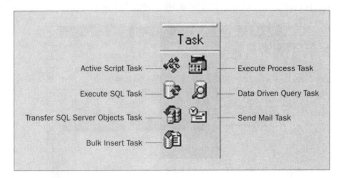

Let's quickly provide a brief description of each of these:

- **Active Script Task** – This can be used to add execution of an active script as part of a package. Script properties, including the scripting language can be defined and script code can be imported or written for the task.

- **Execute Process Task** – This allows an operating system executable (including batch files) to be launched as a package task.

- **Execute SQL Task** – These tasks can be used to write and execute SQL statements. A task can be a single statement, a batch including multiple statements, or a script made up of multiple batches.

- **Data Driven Query Task** – A data driven query task gives the ability to write a query that can perform different operations, selecting the operations to be performed based on the data it finds.

- **Transfer SQL Server Objects Task** – As its name implies, a transfer SQL Server objects task is used to transfer objects (individual objects, all objects in a database, or all objects in all databases) between source and destination servers.

- **Send Mail Task** – Allows the generation of e-mail messages as part of the package.

- **Bulk Insert Task** – Allows the transfer of data as if the bcp utility was being run to import or export data.

You can also register .dll files that define custom tasks.

The same tasks are supported when working with DTS objects. A good way of getting used to DTS task object properties is to work with the tasks first in DTS Designer.

Workflow – Precedence and Transformations

Workflow is controlled through precedence. The precedence between tasks can be:

- **On completion** (blue arrow) – The next task executes when the current task completes, whether or not it is successful

- **On success** (green arrow) – The next task executes when the current task successfully completes execution

- **On failure** (red arrow) – The next task executes if the current task fails

We'll cover how to add and set precedences when we work through using DTS Designer, but for the moment let's satisfy ourselves with looking at the Properties dialog accessed on right-clicking on the blue arrow connecting the Drop Table and Create Table task in our example:

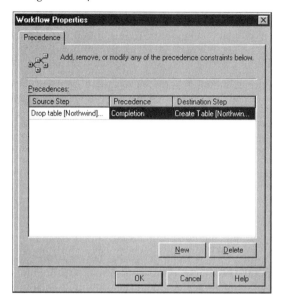

This dialog offers a way of initiating different actions depending on task completion. For example, a task could continue on to the next step if successful, but send a mail notification and stop on failure (this latter option is outlined at the end of this section).

Right-clicking on the arrow linking Connection 1 and Connection 2 gives the choice of Workflow Properties and Properties. Selecting the former brings up a dialog similar to that shown above (with the addition of an Options tab covering transaction attributes).

Let's take a quick look at that Options tab:

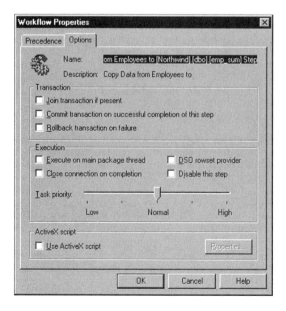

The Options tab allows us to select to join an existing transaction and determine whether to commit the transaction on completion or rollback on failure. The execution options are:

❑ Select Execute on main package thread to have the step execute on the main package thread rather than on a spawned thread.

❑ Select Close connection on completion if the task is associated with a connection and the requirement is to have the connection closed automatically.

❑ Select DSO rowset provider to expose the OLE DB rowset obtained in this step for external query.

❑ Select Disable this step, to disable the step when the package executes.

❑ The Task priority sets the Windows NT thread priority for the step.

To import or write a script to be executed by this step use the ActiveX script option and check the Use ActiveX script box.

Right-clicking on the arrow linking Connection 1 and Connection 2 and selecting Properties brings up:

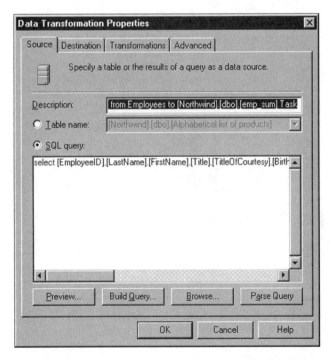

The Data Transformation Properties sheets include tabs for Source, Destination, Transformations, and Advanced. We're going to leave these alone for the moment and look at them in some detail a little later.

Let's move on to creating a package from scratch using the DTS Designer.

Using DTS Designer

Here we're going to duplicate what we did earlier in the DTS Wizard. While perhaps not the most creative example possible, it does give us a chance to compare the two and to focus on the steps for creating a DTS package. As previously when we were working with the DTS Wizard, we are now going to create a package (available from the Wrox web site as C6Samp2.dts) that will drop and recreate the emp_sum table, then copy four columns from Employees to emp_sum.

Now let's see if we can recreate the package. The first step is to highlight the **Data Transformation Services** folder and run **Action | New Package** (or right click on the **Data Transformations** folder and select **New Package**) to create a new package. As you can see, the package starts out empty – don't worry, it won't stay that way for long:

Making Additions to the Package

We'll start by adding our connections. We're going to define two connections and name them Source Database and Destination Database. Both are going to be SQL Server connections, both on the local server, and both using the Northwind database.

To add the connections click on the SQL Server icon in the Data icons or run **Data | 1** Microsoft OLE DB Provider for SQL Server. The setting below would create a connection to attach to the local server and use the Northwind database:

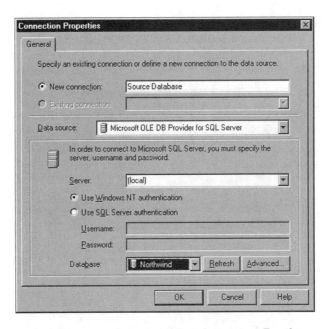

Click on **OK** after entering the connection property information. For this example, we're just going to show the Source Database property sheet. Except for the connection name, the Destination Database properties are identical.

Here's the package so far – the source and destination databases are in place, but nothing else:

Right, let's add some tasks; we're going to be adding two Execute SQL Tasks and here we'll look at the properties for each of them so we can see what's happening inside.

Our first task is to drop the emp_sum table. Bring up the Execute SQL Properties dialog via either clicking the appropriate Task icon or selecting Task | 3 Execute SQL Task...As shown below we'll give the task a descriptive name and type in the SQL statement to be executed. Clicking on Parse Query will check for syntax errors:

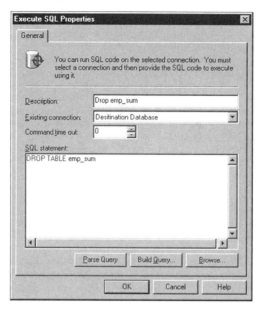

Click on OK after completing the task properties. After we drop the table, we have to recreate it using a CREATE TABLE statement. Add another Execute SQL Task, name it and add the SQL statement as shown below, then click on OK to add the task to the project:

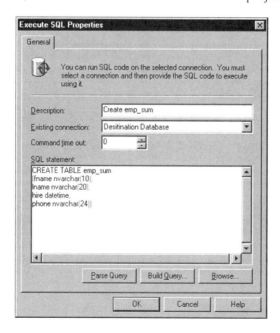

So now we have two connections and two tasks:

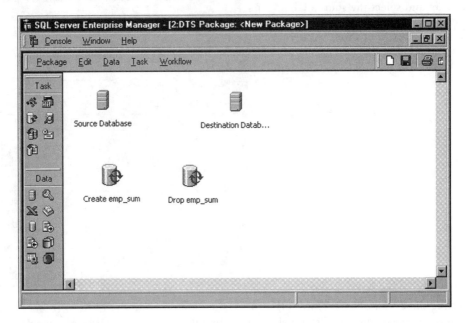

Adding the Transformation

Our next objective is to tell the package the order in which the steps should be executed – the precedence for each step. We're going to start with the data transformation between the source and destination connections. Select **Source Database**, then **Destination Database** (as normal practice hold *Ctrl* down when selecting each icon) and run Workflow | Add Transform (or click on the yellow gear with arrow icon on the taskbar). After that, right-click on the transformation arrow and run Properties from the pop-up menu to set the transformation properties.

We're putting in the transformation first so that we will be able to add our precedents. As it is right now, we can add a precedent between Drop emp_sum and Create emp_sum. The DTS Designer won't let us set a precedent between Create emp_sum and Source Database until the transformation is in place.

On the **Source** tab, we name the transformation and select the source table. If we wanted, we could use a SELECT statement as our source, but we're going to define column mappings as our transformation:

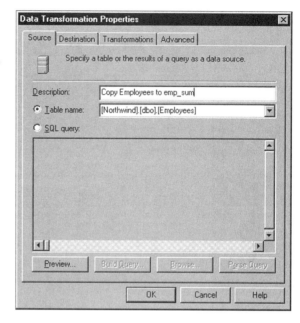

After selecting the **Destination** tab, we select the destination table. If you need to create a table as the destination, you can click on **Create New**...to define the table. In our example, we don't need to create a new table because we're copying to an existing table in the database and we created a new copy of the table as a separate task.

As can be seen, DTS Designer will sometimes provide different options for performing any given operation.

If you're following through this particular example and haven't already done so you'll need to create an emp_sum table in the Northwind database. The figure below has the accurate column information for creating the table:

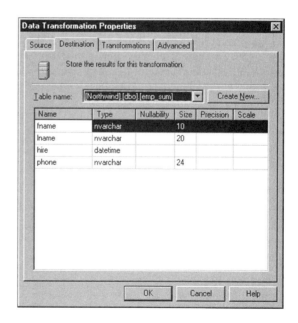

By default, the first four columns in the Employees table are mapped to the emp_sum table. The default mappings before we make any changes are:

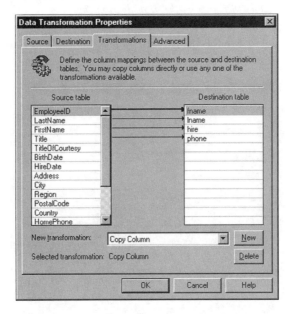

Each mapping that isn't needed can be deleted by clicking on its arrow and pressing *Delete* or clicking on <u>D</u>elete. Click to select source and destination and click on <u>N</u>ew to create new mappings. Double-clicking on any arrow displays a property dialog with dropdown boxes for changing mappings.

Here's how the columns look after re-mapping:

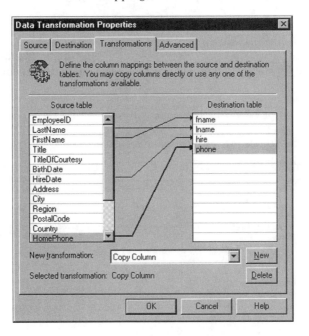

We're running a simple column copy as our transformation. To script the transformation (VBScript and JScript are supported languages) choose one or more source and destination columns, then select ActiveX Script from the drop-down menu.

Additional properties are set through the Advanced tab. The default settings are shown in the figure below:

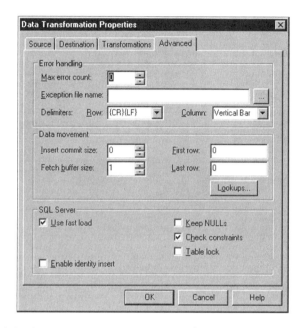

For completeness let's look at the options we have here (although in our example we won't need to alter any).

The Max error count is the maximum number of errors before the task fails and if required an exception file (which is a text file) can be specified in the Exception file name which will record any failing rows. The Row and Column delimiters describe how the exception file will be structured.

The Data movement options describe how data will be copied:

❑ Insert commit size sets the level for commit when copying data; the default is each row.

❑ The Fetch buffer size sets the number of rows to be fetched at a time from the source during the copy.

❑ The First row sets the first row to be copied.

❑ The Last row sets the last row to be copied, with a zero specifying to copy to the end of the table.

The SQL Server options further define the copying process:

- ❑ Use fast load is enabled by default and allows bulk-copy processing.

- ❑ Set Enable identify insert if values need to be inserted into an identity column in the destination.

- ❑ Specify Keep NULLs if empty columns should retain a null value.

- ❑ When Check constraints is enabled, data will be verified by the destination's check constraints.

- ❑ Set Table lock only if table locks are to be acquired during a fast load operation.

Once all of the properties are set, click on OK to save the changes:

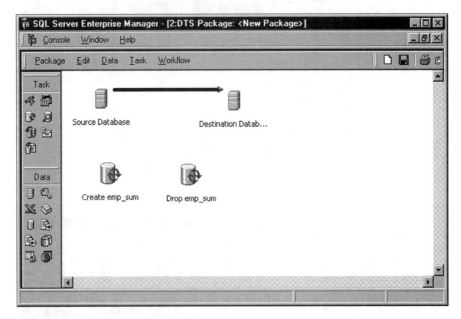

Setting the Precedences

Now we can finish our package by adding the precedences. Select Drop emp_sum, then Create emp_sum, and run <u>W</u>orkflow | On <u>C</u>ompletion. Here we're just concerned that the task completes before going on to the next task. Here's how the properties for the workflow will look (right-click on the blue arrow and select <u>P</u>roperties):

For the next precedence, we select Create emp_sum, then Source Database, then from the menu <u>W</u>orkflow | On <u>S</u>uccess. We're choosing On Success this time because we don't want the copy to run unless the emp_sum table has been created. Here's the property sheet for our On Success workflow:

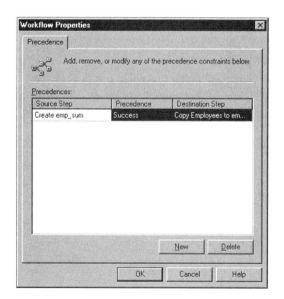

This brings us to our completed package:

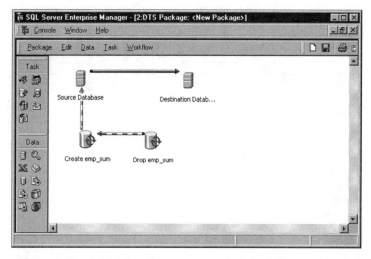

That's it – our package is finished. The objects are in slightly different positions than we saw for the first package, but those can be moved around in the window as needed. The object's screen position doesn't impact the order of execution. That is set by the workflow we've added to the package.

Before we save and execute the package, let's have a quick diversion to look at how we could extend the package functionality to include error handling (which wasn't in the DTS Wizard version).

Variation on a Theme – Adding a Send Mail Task

We've added an On Success constraint on table creation, but what if the table creation failed? Well, we could use a Send Mail task to inform of us of the failure.

To add a Send Mail task, click on the Send Mail icon or run Task | 6 Send Mail either of which will bring up the property sheet for the Send Mail task:

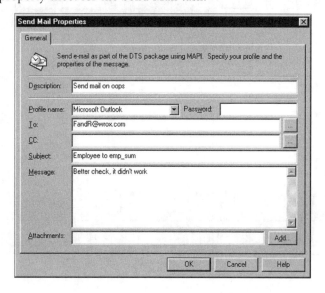

To include a Send Mail task, a mail profile must be defined and the To: and CC: fields need to contain valid e-mail addresses. There is the option of including one or more files as attachments to the message. The Send Mail task is now in place:

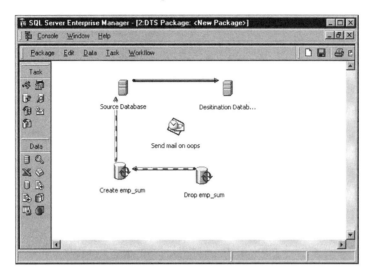

Next, use *Ctrl*-click to select Create emp_sum and Send mail on oops, then run Workflow | On Failure. The property sheet for this is:

Now, let's take a look at our modified package:

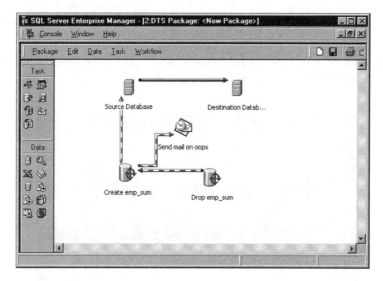

If we wished, we could further expand our package by adding more tasks, or even more connections as necessary.

We now have an improved version of the package we created through the DTS Wizard.

Saving and Executing the Package

Firstly save the package – run Package | Save or Package | Save As depending on your requirements:

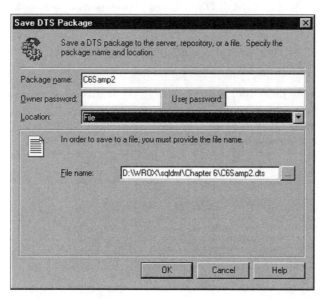

As before, you can save the file to SQL Server, the Microsoft Repository, or as an operating system file (through the Location drop down box). The figure above shows the dialog for saving the package as a file. As mentioned before, this allows you to easily distribute the package. If you want to track versioning information for the package, you'll need to save the package to SQL Server.

The package can be run directly from DTS Designer by running Package | Execute. A dialog similar to that shown below informs us of progress during execution (in the case of a successful execution):

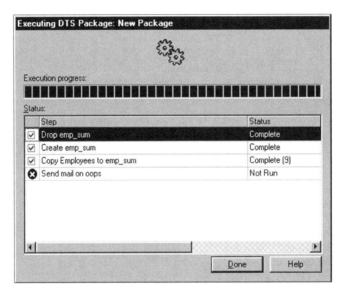

Packages stored as SQL Server or Microsoft Repository packages can be executed or scheduled either through your custom-built SQL-DMO based applications or plain old SQL Server Enterprise Manager.

Using the latter select the package and run Action | Execute Package for immediate execution or Action | Schedule Package to schedule execution for later.

There is also a command line command, DTSRUN.EXE, available for executing DTS Packages. The syntax for this command is:

dtsrun [/? | /[~]S server_name /[~]U username /[~]P password | /E |/[~]F filename /[~]R repository_database /[~]N package_name [/M[~] package_password]|[/[~] package_string] | [/[~]V package_version_string] [/!X] [/!D] [/!Y] [/!C]]

The package will execute immediately unless otherwise specified. The various parameters are described below:

Parameter	Description
/ ?	Use ? to display a list of available option switches.
~	A tilde specifies that the next parameter is a hexadecimal value used to represent the encrypted value of the parameter. This increases security by encrypting server name, user name, and so forth.
/ S *server_name*	This specifies the server to connect to.
/ U *username*	When using SQL Server Authentication, a username which is a valid login account name must be supplied.
/ P *password*	This is the password required for *username* login and validation.
/ E	The / E option specifies a trusted connection. If this is used a login ID isn't required.
/ N *package_name*	This is the name assigned to the package when it was created.
/ M *package_password*	If there is a password associated with the package, use this option to specify the password.
/ G *package_string*	This is a globally unique identifier (GUID) package ID assigned to the package when it was created.
/ V *package_version_string*	This is a GUID version ID that was assigned to the package the first time it was saved or executed.
/ F *filename*	This is the path and filename of the package to be executed. It allows DTS packages stored as COM-structured data files to be executed. If a server_name is also specified, then the contents of the file will be overwritten with the package retrieved from the server.

The path can be specified as a drive ID, directory path, and filename or UNC path and filename. In most cases, it is considered more reliable, especially when using DTSRUN in a batch or stored command string, to use a UNC path and filename. This avoids the potential problem of changes in shared drive IDs. |
| / R *repository_database* | This option can be used to specify the name of the repository database that contains DTS packages. If not specified, the default is assumed. |
| / ! X | With this option, a package can be retrieved from the server and used to overwrite the contents of *filename* without executing the package. |

Table Continued on Following Page

Parameter	Description
/!D	Use this option to delete DTS packages from the Local Packages or Repository Packages folders.
	DTSRUN cannot be used to delete a COM-structured data file. The /F and /S options can however be used to overwrite the file.
/!Y	This is used to display the encrypted command used to execute the package, but without executing the package.
/!C	The DTSRUN command is copied to the Windows clipboard. This option can be used with the /!X and /!Y options.

Summary

OK, so this chapter hasn't made you an expert in Data Transformation Services – but we have put a lot of groundwork in to introduce you to the area.

During this chapter we've seen that DTS accepts data from a variety of sources, enables it to be remapped and then sends it out to a variety of destinations (a discussion of the power of DTS in manipulating data during transformation is beyond the scope of this book).

To show how to use DTS we've developed the same simple package using the DTS Wizard and DTS Designer utilities – we may have only hinted at the power of the latter but, if you hadn't before, at least you've now had an introduction to the tool.

In our package we dropped and created a table in the Northwind database and carefully mapped source columns to destination columns to take account of the different structures of the tables. During our work with DTS Designer we also looked at using automatic generation of e-mails to handle errors.

The next chapter continues our DTS discussion, but shifts the focus back to SQL Server objects. You will be given an introduction to DTS objects and their use. In one of the examples, you'll see how to run the same package created in this chapter, but by using DTS objects.

10

Using DTS Components

Now we're ready to look at our last set of SQL objects, DTS objects. In the last chapter, we introduced Data Transformation Services (DTS) and stepped through the process of creating DTS packages with the DTS Wizard and DTS Designer. In this chapter, we're also going to create DTS packages, but this time the focus will be on creating packages with DTS objects.

As with the previous chapters, the prime objective of this chapter is to introduce you to DTS objects and give you some experience working with the objects. The goal is *not* to try to make you an expert in working with DTS objects or to cover every object, method, and property in detail (indeed that's a book in itself) but again we just want to give you a foundation to build upon.

In this chapter we're going to pick up on the themes and examples we developed in the last chapter. The stand-alone utilities we look at here are designed specifically to run on the local server and to partially replicate the processes we saw in the last chapter. Along the way we'll give a few tips with suggestions on how you might expand these examples to make them even more useful.

More specifically in this chapter we are going to:

- ❑ Introduce the DTS object hierarchy
- ❑ Show how packages can be created in VB using a simple example
- ❑ Develop a DTS package involving mapping, for comparison with that created through the DTS designer in Chapter 9
- ❑ Build on our package example to illustrate the use of precedence constraints

Again the code contained in the chapter is available for download from www.wrox.com.

Incidentally reference material covering the DTS Package Object library and the DTS DataPump Scripting Object library is presented in Appendices F and G respectively.

The DTS Object Hierarchy

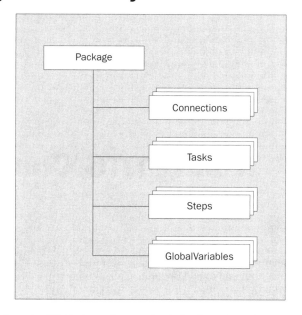

Let's start with a look at the DTS object hierarchy (which is described in detail in Appendix F). For now, we're going to limit the discussion to the `Package` object and its four top-level collections (as shown). As we go through the examples, we'll be looking at some of the collection members in more detail.

Package Object

The first step in creating a DTS package is creating and instantiating the `Package` object. All of the other objects stem from the `Package` object.

Connections Collection

We've already seen that a DTS package will contain one or more connections and this remains true. We will have one or more `Connection` objects as members of the `Connections` collection. The `Connections` collection allows connection pooling and reuse. Tasks reference `Connection` objects by connection ID.

> **Microsoft documentation refers to `Connection` objects as containing information about connections to OLE DB service providers. This is a little misleading. Along with OLE DB providers, ODBC providers are also supported. In fact, the default when defining a `Connection` object is that you will be connecting to an ODBC Data Source Name (DSN).**

Tasks Collection

This is an area where you can get lost if you're not careful. The concept is easy enough – the `Tasks` collection contains `Task` objects and each `Task` object defines an action to be performed when the package executes.

Where this might get confusing is that the `Task` object is polymorphic (we discussed polymorphic objects in Chapter 6, during the discussion about SQL-NS objects). This is necessary to give us a way to create each of the types of tasks we saw in the last chapter. While there are going to be similarities between the `Task` object types, there are also going to be significant differences, due simply to the activities performed by each of the tasks. Here we're going to limit our discussion to a couple of the more commonly used `Task` object types.

Steps Collection

The `Step` objects in the `Steps` collection describe workflow and task execution. Each `Step` object will be associated with a `Task` object. We have the option of creating a `PrecedenceConstraints` collection for each `Step` object and setting precedence constraints as we saw in the previous chapter. You may remember from the last chapter that precedence constraints can be defined as On Success, On Failure, and On Completion. If precedence constraints are not defined, On Completion is assumed as the precedence for each task. As each completes, execution will continue on to the next `Step` and its associated task.

GlobalVariables Collection

The `GlobalVariables` collection contains `GlobalVariable` objects. These objects are used to share data across steps and with ActiveX scripts. The ActiveX scripts are written in a scripting language such as VBScript, JScript, or PerlScript, and are optional programs that can be added to a package. Values can be added to this collection at execution.

So now we've met the family, let's see them in action.

Creating a DTS Package in Visual Basic

The process involved in creating a DTS package in VB is similar to the one we went through when we created packages with the DTS Wizard and DTS Designer. The basic steps include:

- ❑ Creating a `Package` object
- ❑ Creating and adding one or more `Connection` objects to the `Connections` collection
- ❑ Creating and adding one or more `Task` objects to the `Tasks` collection
- ❑ Creating and adding one or more `Step` objects to the `Steps` collection

When this is finished, we are ready to execute the package.

Let's illustrate this by walking through a simple example that will allow us to focus on the use of DTS objects.

Simple Copy Example

This example will copy an existing table in the `Northwind` database on the local server to a new table. If the destination table already exists, it will be dropped and recreated.

To start with, we need to set up a new **Standard EXE** project and set references to the DTS object libraries. As we've seen before, references are set by running <u>P</u>roject | Refere<u>n</u>ces. Set references to the Microsoft DTSDataPump Scripting Object Library and Microsoft DTSPackage Object Library:

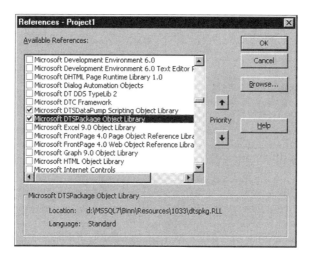

Next, create a form with the following controls as shown below:

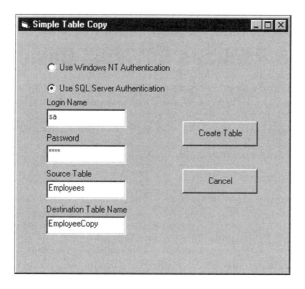

For compatibility with the code that we will discuss in the rest of this chapter, you should set the control names and other properties as shown in this table:

Control	Property	Value
Option Button 1	Name	optWinNT
Option Button 2	Name	optSQL
	TabIndex	0
Label 1	Name	lblUser
Text Box 1	Name	txtUser
Label 2	Name	lblPass
Text Box 2	Name	txtPass
	PasswordChar	*
Label 3	Name	lblSource
Text Box 3	Name	txtSource
Label 4	Name	lblDestination
Text Box 4	Name	txtDestination
Command Button 1	Name	cmdMakeTable
Command Button 1	Name	cmdCancel

We're going to achieve our objective with a single connection (since that's all that is required for running the SQL statements we're using) and two tasks. Let's start by defining the following variables in the General Declarations section of our newly created form:

```
Option Explicit

Private oPackage As DTS.Package
Private oConnection As DTS.Connection
Private oTask As DTS.Task
Private oStep As DTS.Step
Private oExecuteTask As DTS.ExecuteSQLTask
Private strServer As String
Private strDatabase As String
Private strUser As String
Private strPassword As String
Private strSource As String
Private strDestination As String
Private bCheck As Boolean
Private bError As Boolean
```

Here we're declaring object variables for `Package`, `Connection`, `Task`, and `Step` objects with a separate object variable for an `ExecuteSQLTask` object. As you'll see a little later, when we create a `Task` object we have to specify the type of `Task` object we are creating and implement the `CustomTask` object interface, which in our example will be referenced by `oExecuteTask`.

We're also declaring some string and Boolean variables that we'll be using in the application. Even though the server and database name are coded into the application in this version, we're declaring variables for these values to make it easier for future modification of the application to allow the user to select the server name and database name.

We'll instantiate our `Package` object on loading the form:

```
Private Sub Form_Load()
    Set oPackage = New DTS.Package
End Sub
```

General Housekeeping

In addition to the code needed to create and execute the DTS package we can include a few housekeeping routines. First, we're enabling and disabling the login name and password based on the authentication method selected:

```
Private Sub optSQL_Click()
    bCheck = False
    txtUser.Enabled = True
    txtUser.BackColor = vbWindowBackground
    txtPass.Enabled = True
    txtPass.BackColor = vbWindowBackground
    lblUser.Enabled = True
    lblPass.Enabled = True
End Sub
```

```
Private Sub optWinNT_Click()
    bCheck = True
    txtUser.Enabled = False
    txtUser.BackColor = vbButtonFace
    txtPass.Enabled = False
    txtPass.BackColor = vbButtonFace
    lblUser.Enabled = False
    lblPass.Enabled = False
End Sub
```

The heart of the program is in the processes that take place when you click on the Create Table button. Let's declare some local variables that we'll be using in the routine and also load values into our string variables. We've also included some error handling, the code for which is presented later.

```
Private Sub cmdMakeTable_Click()

    On Error GoTo GotError:

    Dim i As Integer

    strServer = "(local)"
    strDatabase = "Northwind"
    strUser = txtUser.Text
    strPassword = txtPass.Text
    strSource = txtSource.Text
    strDestination = txtDestination.Text
```

If you wanted to be able to choose the server and database names, you would need to add code to select the names and load them into the `strServer` and `strDatabase` variables.

Basic Validation

To check that required fields have been given values we need to put in some quick basic validation routines – these don't involve passing values to the SQL Server installation as we're just catching simple errors made during form filling.

Firstly if the user selected SQL Server authentication, we check to make sure that a login name had been entered. We don't check for a password, because the user might have a blank password:

```
'Check for obvious errors
If bCheck = False Then
    If txtUser.Text = "" Then
        MsgBox "Enter user name", vbOKOnly
        Exit Sub
    End If
End If
```

Even though blank passwords are a bad idea, if you give a user the ability to set or change their password, the user can set the password to blank – you can't set a minimum password length for SQL Server authentication passwords as you can for Windows NT passwords.

As you'll see a little later, the password value will be used, whether blank or a string, if we connect using SQL Server authentication. The password will be passed to the server to authenticate the user. In the case that there is no value entered for the password a blank password is passed for authentication.

> **Don't get the idea that this in any way implies that we are in favor of, recommend, or would allow (if it could be helped) blank passwords. A blank password is an open door into a server and will result in problems sooner or later. Unfortunately, as described above, they can occur when using SQL Server authentication.**

Next, there's a quick check made to ensure that the source and destination table names have been entered. Before turning this into a production application, you would probably want to check that a valid table name had been added.

We're not doing anything with the user name, source table, or destination table yet. At this point, we're just checking to make sure that a value has been entered in each of these fields.

```
If txtSource.Text = "" Then
    MsgBox "Please type in source table name", vbOKOnly
    Exit Sub
End If

If txtDestination.Text = "" Then
    MsgBox "Please type in a destination table", vbOKOnly
    Exit Sub
End If
'Turn on wait cursor
Me.MousePointer = vbHourglass
```

As the last step before getting into the DTS package, the cursor is changed to an hourglass. We'll turn it back to the default value after the package executes.

Package and Connections

Just like the DTS Designer example in the last chapter, the first step is to create the package and set up any necessary connections. Actually, we created the `Package` object in our declaration statements, so now we're just naming the object and creating a connection:

```
'Define package and connection
oPackage.Name = "Duplicate Table"
Set oConnection = oPackage.Connections.New("SQLOLEDB")
oConnection.ID = 1
oConnection.DataSource = strServer
oConnection.Catalog = strDatabase

If bCheck = True Then
    oConnection.UseTrustedConnection = True
Else
    oConnection.UserID = strUser
    oConnection.Password = strPassword
End If

oPackage.Connections.Add oConnection
Set oConnection = Nothing
```

We name the `Package` object, and then we use the `Connections` collection's `New` method to create a `Connection` object. If you are creating an OLE DB connection, you must specify the ProgID of the OLE DB provider. In the case of the SQL Server OLE DB provider, that is `SQLOLEDB`.

The `ID` and `DataSource` properties are both required. The `Catalog`, which defines the database context, is optional. If not supplied, the user's default database is assumed, based on the login name used to establish the connection.

> **So, what would happen if we hadn't supplied the OLE DB provider? In that case SQL Server assumes an ODBC connection and we would need to supply a DSN as the `DataSource` property.**

Since we provided two authentication options, an `If` statement is used to support the user's authentication choice. If the user is connecting with Windows NT authentication, the `UseTrustedConnection` property is set to `True`. By default, this property is `False`. For SQL Server authentication, we have to set the `UserID` and `Password` properties.

Finally, we add the `Connection` object to the `Connections` collection, and then set the `oConnection` object reference to `Nothing`.

Tasks and Steps

We also need to add one or more tasks to the DTS package. This package includes two tasks, and firstly we have a task, `Dupe1` that is going to execute a SQL statement to test for the existence of the destination table and drop the destination table if it exists:

```
Set oTask = oPackage.Tasks.New("DTSExecuteSQLTask")
oTask.Name = "Dupe1"
Set oExecuteTask = oTask.CustomTask
oExecuteTask.ConnectionID = 1
oExecuteTask.SQLStatement = "IF EXISTS (SELECT * FROM sysobjects " _
                           & "WHERE name = '" & strDestination _
                           & "' AND TYPE = 'U') DROP TABLE " _
                           & strDestination
oPackage.Tasks.Add oTask
Set oExecuteTask = Nothing
Set oTask = Nothing
Set oStep = oPackage.Steps.New
oStep.Name = "Step1"
oStep.TaskName = "Dupe1"
oPackage.Steps.Add oStep
Set oStep = Nothing
```

We can break this code down into a number of steps:

❑ **Specifying the type of Task object** – When we create a `Task` object, we must specify the type of `Task` object we're creating. In this case, we're creating an Execute SQL Task (`DTSExecuteSQLTask`). The `Name` property is required for any task. Each `Task` object must implement the `CustomTask` object interface, which allows us to define exactly what the task is going to do.

❑ **Defining the Task** – The `ConnectionID` property is set to 1, the only connection defined for this `Package` object and the `SQLStatement` property is set to the string we want executed as a SQL statement. The `Task` object is added to the `Tasks` collection, then the `oExecuteTask` and `oTask` object references are set to `Nothing`. This last operation is done to free up memory – when an object is no longer needed, it is a good practice to set the object variable to `Nothing`.

❑ **Creating a Step object** – When we create a `Task` object, we're also going to need a `Step` object. Each `Step` object must be given a name and be associated with a `Task` object via the `TaskName` property. The `Step` object is then added to the `Steps` collection and the `oStep` variable reference set to `Nothing`.

The second `Task` object, `Dupe2`, is another Execute SQL Task. Except for the names and the SQL statement being executed, everything is set up just like for the first object:

```
Set oTask = oPackage.Tasks.New("DTSExecuteSQLTask")
oTask.Name = "Dupe2"
Set oExecuteTask = oTask.CustomTask
oExecuteTask.ConnectionID = 1
oExecuteTask.SQLStatement = "SELECT * INTO " _
                           & strDestination & " FROM " & strSource
oPackage.Tasks.Add oTask
```

```
Set oExecuteTask = Nothing
Set oTask = Nothing
Set oStep = oPackage.Steps.New
oStep.Name = "Step2"
oStep.TaskName = "Dupe2"
oPackage.Steps.Add oStep
Set oStep = Nothing
```

The package is now complete. All that's left is to execute the package and then set the cursor back to the default. To execute a package we call its `Execute` method. We can check the result of each step by checking its `ExecutionResult` property. After the step executes, the property will be set to either `DTSStepExecResult_Success` or `DTSStepExecResult_Failure`:

```
oPackage.Execute
bError = False
For i = 1 To oPackage.Steps.Count
    If oPackage.Steps(i).ExecutionResult = DTSStepExecResult_Failure Then
        bError = True
        MsgBox "You got an error in step " & i & " of the package.", vbOKOnly
    End If
Next i

If bError = False Then
    MsgBox "Done!", vbOKOnly
End If
txtSource.Text = ""
txtDestination = ""

Me.MousePointer = vbDefault
Exit Sub
```

We also have an error handler included in the code for unexpected errors:

```
GotError:
Dim ErrorMessage As String
ErrorMessage = "You received an unexpected error " & Err.Number
MsgBox ErrorMessage & ": " & Err.Description, vbOKOnly
txtUser.Text = ""
txtPass.Text = ""
txtSource.Text = ""
txtDestination = ""
Me.MousePointer = vbArrow
Exit Sub
End Sub
```

This will report the error number and textual description of the error that occurred. It also clears the user name, password, source table, and destination table text values.

If the user decides to cancel the simple table copy, we unload the form with the following code:

```
Private Sub cmdCancel_Click()
    Unload Me
End Sub
```

Now that you've seen a basic example, let's now look at `Task` objects in a little more detail before we walk through creation of a DTS package. The example will approximately reproduce the first package we created in Chapter 9 (of course we'll tweak things just a little bit just to keep you interested).

A Closer Look at Tasks

As you just saw, each `Task` must have a task type defined and must implement the `CustomTask` object interface. `CustomTask` properties are going to be object type specific. The object types supported are:

- ❑ `ActiveScriptTask` (`DTSActiveScriptTask`)

- ❑ `BulkInsertTask` (`DTSBulkInsertTask`)

- ❑ `CreateProcessTask` (`DTSCreateProcessTask`)

- ❑ `DataDrivenQueryTask` (`DTSDataDrivenQueryTask`)

- ❑ `DataPumpTask` (`DTSDataPumpTask`)

- ❑ `ExecuteSQLTask` (`DTSExecuteSQLTask`)

- ❑ `SendMailTask` (`DTSSendMailTask`)

- ❑ `TransferObjectsTask` (`DTSTransferObjectsTask`)

Assuming you read through Chapter 9, or that you know your way around DTS Designer, you should be somewhat familiar with these task types since they're the same ones that are available through DTS Designer.

You may find it easier to start out working with these task types in the DTS Designer. That will give you a relatively easy to use way to see what each of these task types does and the information that the task needs to be able to do its job.

Let's consider each of these object types in turn:

- ❑ **ActiveScriptTask** – The `ActiveScriptTask` object is used to define a task that will be executing an ActiveX script. The `ActiveScriptTask` object does not have access to the `Connections` collection or DTS source or destination collections. However, information can be passed to an `ActiveScriptTask` object through the `GlobalVariables` collection.

- ❑ **BulkInsertTask** – A `BulkInsertTask` object provides a fast way of copying large amounts of data from a text file into SQL Server. The object is based on the `BULK INSERT` Transact-SQL statement and object properties parallel `BULK INSERT` replaceable parameters. A `BulkInsertTask` object will have a single `ConnectionID`, the destination server. As with the `BULK INSERT` statement, this is a copy operation only. Data transformations are not supported, but a format file can be used to define column mappings.

In case you're not familiar with the term "format file", format files can be used with the bulk copy program, `bcp.exe`, and **BULK INSERT** statement. The format file maps text file fields to data table columns. One of the most common uses of format files is to map text source fields to destination columns when the orders don't match.

❑ **CreateProcessTask** – A `CreateProcessTask` object lets a separate program be run as a task. The program to be run is entered as full path and filename in the `ProcessCommandLine` property, along with any required option switches. A `CreateProcessTask` object does not have access to the `Connections` collection.

❑ **DataDrivenQueryTask** – The `DataDrivenQuery` task specifies the use of queries instead of `INSERT` operations when adding rows to the destination. It requires definition of source and destination connections, as well as description of the source and destination column collections and query statements.

❑ **DataPumpTask** – A `DataPumpTask` object is used for data import and export between data connections. A `DataPumpTask` can include data transformations, and in fact, when a `DataPumpTask` object is used one or more `Transformation` objects have to be created and added to its `Transformations` collection. Here source and destination connections have to be defined. These connections define the source and destination servers, databases, and tables. There is also the option of defining the source and destination table columns. In other words this option allows you to choose the columns you want to copy from and the columns you want to copy to.

❑ **ExecuteSQLTask** – An `ExecuteSQLTask` object allows execution of a SQL statement on the server defined by its connection ID. Use of this object is very straightforward, as we saw in the previous example.

❑ **SendMailTask** – A `SendMailTask` object is often used in conjunction with precedence constraints to send notification on completion of a task or package, or more commonly, when errors occur during execution. To implement this, the Microsoft Messaging API must be installed and a valid user profile must be set up. This gives the ability to set message recipients, message text, and even include file attachments with the message.

❑ **TransferObjectsTask** – A `TransferObjectsTask` object is used to transfer one or more database objects between SQL Server 7.0 servers. A `TransferObjectsTask` object does not use the `Connections` collection. Instead, the source and destination servers and databases must be defined, as well as login authentication information. Here all objects can be transferred or specific types of objects (not individual objects) can be selected for transfer.

So let's see how to duplicate (well almost) the package we created through the DTS Designer in Chapter 9 (it may be useful to refer back to that project as we go along).

DTS Package Example Involving Mapping

As previously, the source and destination servers are set to be the local server, and the source and destination database are set as the Northwind database. As in the DTS Designer example, we're using the Employees table and an additional table created by the package, emp_sum. Source and destination connections are made using Windows NT authentication.

Start a new Standard EXE project, set references to the DTS object libraries and create a form with two command buttons called cmdUpdate and cmdCancel (the database details are all going to be hard-coded into the application):

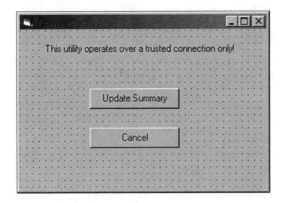

Once again, we'll start by creating the Package object, declare the variables we need and instantiate our Package object on loading the form:

```
Option Explicit

Private oPackage As DTS.Package
Private oConnection As DTS.Connection
Private oTask As DTS.Task
Private oStep As DTS.Step
Private oExecuteTask As DTS.ExecuteSQLTask
Private oDataPumpTask As DTS.DataPumpTask
Private oTransform As DTS.Transformation
Private oColumn As DTS.Column
Private bError As Boolean


Private Sub Form_Load()
    Set oPackage = New DTS.Package
End Sub
```

This time, we're declaring three different object variables. The package uses a DataPumpTask object to transfer data between the source and destination. Along with the DataPumpTask object, we're going to need a Transformation object. The Column object will be used to identify the source and destination columns for mapping between the source and destination.

> We need a **DataPumpTask** this time because we're using the DTS Data Pump to transfer data. This wasn't necessary in the first example because, as far as the DTS package was concerned, we weren't transferring any data. We were just running SQL statements.

Since we're copying data, source and destination connections are required. In this case, the source and destination are the same, both connecting to the local server and using the Northwind database:

```
Private Sub cmdUpdate_Click()

    Dim i As Integer

    Me.MousePointer = vbHourglass
    oPackage.Name = "Update"
    oPackage.Description = "Update Employee Summary"

    'Source connection
    Set oConnection = oPackage.Connections.New("SQLOLEDB")
    oConnection.ID = 1
    oConnection.DataSource = "(local)"
    oConnection.Catalog = "Northwind"
    oConnection.UseTrustedConnection = True
    oPackage.Connections.Add oConnection
    Set oConnection = Nothing


    'Destination connection
    Set oConnection = oPackage.Connections.New("SQLOLEDB")
    oConnection.ID = 2
    oConnection.DataSource = "(local)"
    oConnection.Catalog = "Northwind"
    oConnection.UseTrustedConnection = True
    oPackage.Connections.Add oConnection
    Set oConnection = Nothing
```

The first Task object is an ExecuteSQLTask object, checking for the destination table and dropping it if it exists. This is very similar to the Task object seen in the last example except here the Task object and Step object names have been changed and the SQL statement has the database information coded in:

```
    'Drop summary table if present
    Set oTask = oPackage.Tasks.New("DTSExecuteSQLTask")
    oTask.Name = "Sum01"
    Set oExecuteTask = oTask.CustomTask
    oExecuteTask.ConnectionID = 1
    oExecuteTask.SQLStatement = "IF EXISTS (SELECT * FROM " _
                      & "sysobjects WHERE name = 'emp_sum'" _
                      & "AND TYPE = 'U') DROP TABLE emp_sum"
    oPackage.Tasks.Add oTask
    Set oExecuteTask = Nothing
    Set oTask = Nothing
```

```
    Set oStep = oPackage.Steps.New
    oStep.Name = "Step01"
    oStep.TaskName = "Sum01"
    oPackage.Steps.Add oStep
    Set oStep = Nothing
```

The second `Task` object is another `ExecuteSQLTask` object. This time, the `Task` object is executing a `CREATE TABLE` statement to create the destination table:

```
    'Create summary table
    Set oTask = oPackage.Tasks.New("DTSExecuteSQLTask")
    oTask.Name = "Sum02"
    Set oExecuteTask = oTask.CustomTask
    oExecuteTask.ConnectionID = 1
    oExecuteTask.SQLStatement = "CREATE TABLE emp_sum " _
                & "(fname nvarchar(10), lname nvarchar(20), " _
                & "hire datetime, phone nvarchar(24))"
    oPackage.Tasks.Add oTask
    Set oExecuteTask = Nothing
    Set oTask = Nothing
    Set oStep = oPackage.Steps.New
    oStep.Name = "Step02"
    oStep.TaskName = "Sum02"
    oPackage.Steps.Add oStep
    Set oStep = Nothing
```

> **There is one difference between this example and the DTS Designer package created in the last chapter. We aren't setting any precedence constraints here for simplicity's sake (although we will look at that topic at the end of the chapter). Package execution will continue on to the next `Task` object whether or not the table is created.**

The third `Task` object is a `DataPumpTask` object which moves the data from the source table to the destination table. We have to set the `SourceConnectionID` and `DestinationConnectionID`, as well as the source table (as `SourceObjectName`) and destination table (as `DestinationObjectName`):

```
    'Transfer records
    Set oTask = oPackage.Tasks.New("DTSDataPumpTask")
    oTask.Name = "Sum03"
    Set oDataPumpTask = oTask.CustomTask
    oDataPumpTask.SourceConnectionID = 1
    oDataPumpTask.SourceObjectName = "Employees"
    oDataPumpTask.DestinationConnectionID = 2
    oDataPumpTask.DestinationObjectName = "emp_sum"
```

As mentioned above, since we're using a `DataPumpTask` object, we'll have to create and add at least one `Transformation` object:

```
'Define transformation
Set oTransform = _
    oDataPumpTask.Transformations.New("DTS.DataPumpTransformCopy")
oTransform.Name = "UpCopy"
```

We create the `Transformation` object as a `DataPumpTransformCopy` object. A `Transformation` object can also be defined as a `DataConvert` object (for performing data conversions) or a `DataPumpTransformScript` object (when a transformation script is required).

This tells the package that it's going to be performing a data copy. If we left it at this, a direct source to destination copy would be assumed. That wouldn't work in this case. We already know that the source and destination columns don't match up, so we need to map the columns for copy.

First, we define the source columns. As each column is created, it must be identified both by column name and by ordinal position in the table:

```
'Define source columns
Set oColumn = oTransform.SourceColumns.New("Firstname", 3)
oTransform.SourceColumns.Add oColumn
Set oColumn = Nothing
Set oColumn = oTransform.SourceColumns.New("Lastname", 2)
oTransform.SourceColumns.Add oColumn
Set oColumn = Nothing
Set oColumn = oTransform.SourceColumns.New("Hiredate", 7)
oTransform.SourceColumns.Add oColumn
Set oColumn = Nothing
Set oColumn = oTransform.SourceColumns.New("Homephone", 13)
oTransform.SourceColumns.Add oColumn
Set oColumn = Nothing
```

Since we're adding four columns to the `SourceColumns` collection, we'll need to put four columns in the `DestinationColumns` collection as well. We define destination columns in the same manner, as column name and ordinal position. Both are required parameters when creating a column:

```
'Define destination columns
Set oColumn = oTransform.DestinationColumns.New("fname", 1)
oTransform.DestinationColumns.Add oColumn
Set oColumn = Nothing
Set oColumn = oTransform.DestinationColumns.New("lname", 2)
oTransform.DestinationColumns.Add oColumn
Set oColumn = Nothing
Set oColumn = oTransform.DestinationColumns.New("hire", 3)
oTransform.DestinationColumns.Add oColumn
Set oColumn = Nothing
Set oColumn = oTransform.DestinationColumns.New("phone", 4)
oTransform.DestinationColumns.Add oColumn
Set oColumn = Nothing
```

Now we can add the transformation to the `Task` object and add the `Task` object to the `Package` object's `Tasks` collection. We also have to create a `Step` object, and associate the `Step` object with the `Task` object:

```
oDataPumpTask.Transformations.Add oTransform
oPackage.Tasks.Add oTask
Set oTask = Nothing
Set oStep = oPackage.Steps.New
oStep.Name = "Step3"
oStep.TaskName = "Sum03"
oPackage.Steps.Add oStep
Set oStep = Nothing
```

All that's left is to execute the package and check each `Step` object's `ExecutionResult` property. We've changed this slightly from the last example, to identify which step failed should an error occur:

```
oPackage.Execute
bError = False

For i = 1 To oPackage.Steps.Count
    If oPackage.Steps(i).ExecutionResult = DTSStepExecResult_Failure Then
        bError = True
        MsgBox "Error is in step" & i, vbOKOnly
    End If
Next i

If bError = False Then
    MsgBox "Finished", vbOKOnly
End If

Me.MousePointer = vbDefault

End Sub
```

Again we unload the form if the user decides to cancel the operation:

```
Private Sub cmdCancel_Click()
    Unload Me
End Sub
```

Now let's take a quick look at a variation on this example.

An Alternative Approach

Instead of defining source and destination columns, we can use a query as our copy source. By limiting the query result set to just those columns we want to copy, we can default to copying directly to the destination.

To try this, replace the code for transferring records and defining transformations, source columns, and destination columns by the following:

```
'Transfer records
Set oTask = oPackage.Tasks.New("DTSDataPumpTask")
oTask.Name = "Sum03"
Set oDataPumpTask = oTask.CustomTask
oDataPumpTask.SourceConnectionID = 1
oDataPumpTask.SourceSQLStatement = "SELECT firstname, " _
                 & "lastname, hiredate, homephone FROM employees"
oDataPumpTask.DestinationConnectionID = 2
oDataPumpTask.DestinationObjectName = "emp_sum"

'Define transformation
Set oTransform = _
    oDataPumpTask.Transformations.New("DTS.DataPumpTransformCopy")
oTransform.Name = "UpCopy"
oDataPumpTask.Transformations.Add oTransform
oPackage.Tasks.Add oTask
Set oTask = Nothing
Set oStep = oPackage.Steps.New
oStep.Name = "Step3"
oStep.TaskName = "Sum03"
oPackage.Steps.Add oStep
Set oStep = Nothing
```

As you can see, this simplifies our program code a fair amount. Instead of defining a source object, we use the `SourceSQLStatement` to use a `SELECT` statement as the source. Since the result set matches up with the destination table columns, we can leave the `Transformation` object properties at default and let it copy directly between the source and destination.

> If this is so much simpler, why did we use the `SourceColumns` and `DestinationColumns` collections in the previous example? One reason is that it matches the DTS Designer package example, which is what we set out to do. More importantly, by using the `Columns` collections, you could write a program to let users select source and destination columns, then dynamically fill the collections. This would give you a way to write a program to run custom copies between tables.

OK, let's have one last play with this example to illustrate how we can add precedence constraints to a package.

Precedence Constraints

To show how we can work with precedence constraints via DTS objects we're going extend the above variation and add a SendMail task to the package. As in the previous chapter we'll only send the message if there is a failure when we try to create the table.

Remember that to implement a `SendMailTask` the Microsoft Messaging API (MAPI) needs to be installed with a valid user profile specified on the machine. In this section we're just going to show how to set up the precedence constraints and not concern ourselves with the intricacies of MAPI provider initialization and session management.

In this section we're going to be concerning ourselves (unsurprisingly) with the `SendMailTask` and the `PrecedenceConstraint` objects (remember full coverage of the DTS Package Object library is contained in Appendix F).

Firstly, let's reacquaint ourselves with precedence constraints. As we mentioned in the last chapter the precedence constraints supported are On Completion, On Success, and On Failure. When a precedence constraint is set up we have to define:

❑ The step on which the precedence constraint is based

❑ The step whose execution is controlled by the precedence constraint

❑ The precedence constraint on which execution is based

OK, so that sounds a little confusing. Let's clarify things by setting up a scenario. Let's say your Step2 creates a destination table for data copy and Step3 performs the copy, *but* you only want this step to run if Step2 is successful.

So, Step2 is the step on which the precedence constraint is based and Step3 is the step whose execution is controlled by the precedence constraint. The precedence constraint on which execution is based is On Success.

> **If precedence constraints aren't set, package steps will be executed in step order. There is an assumed precedence constraint of On Completion for each step.**

To carry out our obligations we need to consider the following three properties of the `PrecedenceConstraint` object:

Property	Description
PrecedenceBasis	This determines whether the `Step` object's execution status or execution results are used to specify compliance with the precedence constraint
StepName	The name of the `Step` object being evaluated for the precedence constraint
Value	Sets the value of the `PrecedenceConstraint` object

Within the example we'll be setting the `StepName` property as part of creating the `PrecedenceConstraint` object. The `PrecedenceBasis` and `Value` properties work together to determine the precedence constraint.

Precedence Constraint	PrecedenceBasis	Value
On Completion	`DTSStepPrecedenceBasis_ExecStatus`	`DTSStepExecStat _Completed`
On Success	`DTSStepPrecedenceBasis_ExecResult`	`DTSStepExecResult _Success`
On Failure	`DTSStepPrecedenceBasis_ExecResult`	`DTSStepExecResult _Failure`

Moving on to the `SendMailTask` object here we need to consider the following four properties:

Property	Description
`Name`	Sets the name of the `SendMailTask` object
`ToLine`	The e-mail address to which the mail message will be sent
`Subject`	The text string to be entered in the Subject field of the message
`MessageText`	This is the message text to be sent as the body of the message

We can specify multiple e-mail addresses in the `ToLine` property, but they must be entered as a single text string. Additionally we can also enter CC (carbon copy, to receive a copy of the message) addresses and specify one or more files to be included as attachments to the message.

Much of the code in the example is identical to the code we saw above. Here our declarations are:

```
Private oPackage As DTS.Package
Private oConnection As DTS.Connection
Private oTask As DTS.Task
Private oStep As DTS.Step
Private oExecuteTask As DTS.ExecuteSQLTask
Private oDataPumpTask As DTS.DataPumpTask
Private oTransform As DTS.Transformation
Private oMailTask As DTS.SendMailTask
Private oPrecedence As DTS.PrecedenceConstraint
Private bError As Boolean
```

We're defining precedence constraints for two of the three steps: we're going to copy to the emp_sum table *only* if the table creation step (Step02) is successful. To do this, we'll modify the existing Step03.

```
'Transfer records
Set oTask = oPackage.Tasks.New("DTSDataPumpTask")
oTask.Name = "Sum03"
Set oDataPumpTask = oTask.CustomTask
oDataPumpTask.SourceConnectionID = 1
oDataPumpTask.SourceSQLStatement = "select firstname, lastname, hiredate,
homephone from employees"
```

```
oDataPumpTask.DestinationConnectionID = 2
oDataPumpTask.DestinationObjectName = "emp_sum"

'Define transformations
Set oTransform = oDataPumpTask.Transformations.New("DTS.DataPumpTransformCopy")
oTransform.Name = "UpCopy"
oDataPumpTask.Transformations.Add oTransform
oPackage.Tasks.Add oTask
Set oTask = Nothing
Set oStep = oPackage.Steps.New
oStep.Name = "Step3"
oStep.TaskName = "Sum03"
oPackage.Steps.Add oStep
Set oPrecedence = oStep.PrecedenceConstraints.New("Step02")
oPrecedence.PrecedenceBasis = DTSStepPrecedenceBasis_ExecResult
oPrecedence.Value = DTSStepExecResult_Success
oStep.PrecedenceConstraints.Add oPrecedence
Set oPrecedence = Nothing
Set oStep = Nothing
```

We use the `New` method of the `PrecedenceConstraints` collection to create a `PrecedenceConstraint` object and specify the step to be evaluated for the precedence constraints. This sets the `PrecedenceConstraint` object's `StepName` property.

Since we want the precedence constraint to be On Success, the `PrecedenceBasis` property is set to `DTSStepPrecedenceBasis_ExecResult`. The `Value` property is then set to `DTSStepExecResult_Success`. We then add the `PrecedenceConstraint` object to the `Step` object's `PrecedenceConstraints` collection.

So, what if there is a problem when we try to create the table? To take care of this situation we add another step involving a SendMail task:

```
'Handling table creation problems
Set oTask = oPackage.Tasks.New("DTSSendMailTask")
oTask.Name = "Sum04"
Set oMailTask = oTask.CustomTask
oMailTask.Name = "Mail_on_Error"
oMailTask.Subject = "Error on emp_sum"
oMailTask.MessageText = "Couldn't create emp_sum."
oMailTask.ToLine = "FandR@wrox.com"
oMailTask.InitializeMAPI

oPackage.Tasks.Add oTask
Set oTask = Nothing
Set oStep = oPackage.Steps.New
oStep.Name = "Step4"
oStep.TaskName = "Sum04"
oPackage.Steps.Add oStep
Set oPrecedence = oStep.PrecedenceConstraints.New("Step02")
oPrecedence.PrecedenceBasis = DTSStepPrecedenceBasis_ExecResult
oPrecedence.Value = DTSStepExecResult_Failure
oStep.PrecedenceConstraints.Add oPrecedence
Set oPrecedence = Nothing
Set oStep = Nothing
```

As you can see, the `SendMailTask` object is created in the same manner as the `DTSDataPumpTask` object in the previous step. The `Name`, `Subject`, `MessageText`, and `ToLine` properties of the `SendMailTask` object are set to define our mail message and the `InitializeMAPI` method initializes the MAPI provider.

Since we only want the message sent if there is a failure when we try to create the table, we define an On Failure precedence constraint. Once again, Step02 is being evaluated for the precedence constraint. In fact, the only difference between this `PrecedenceConstraint` object and the one created for the previous example is that the `Value` property is set to `DTSStepExecResult_Failure`.

Lastly, we should slightly modify our error handling routine to ensure that the success of our process (which conversely means that Step04 won't execute) doesn't give us an error message:

```
oPackage.Execute
   bError = False

   For i = 1 To (oPackage.Steps.Count - 1)
If oPackage.Steps(i).ExecutionResult = DTSStepExecResult_Failure Then
         bError = True
         MsgBox "Error is in step" & i, vbOKOnly
      End If
   Next i

   If bError = False Then
      MsgBox "Finished", vbOKOnly
   End If

   Me.MousePointer = vbDefault

End Sub
```

Summary

Between this and the previous chapter, you should now have a good start on working with DTS. In the last chapter we looked at how to create DTS packages through the DTS Wizard and DTS Designer. In this chapter, we repeated the process and created a similar package using DTS objects. Over the course of the chapter we refined the package eventually finishing by adding some precedence constraints. Remember that precedence constraints can only be applied through the DTS Designer or by using DTS objects.

If you don't have prior experience of working with DTS, until you have the concepts firmly established in your mind, you may find it easier to start by working with the DTS Wizard and DTS Designer before moving onto DTS objects.

Whether you're working with DTS Wizard, DTS Designer, or DTS objects, you're working with the same components. They all give you access to connections to data sources and destinations, tasks to be performed, and steps (and precedence constraints) to control execution. These are somewhat hidden when working with the DTS Wizard, and in comparison to what you can do through DTS Designer and using DTS objects, somewhat limited.

Of course, as we said at the head of the chapter, our aim here was just to give you an idea of the potential of DTS objects. Exploration of this area will reveal that there's lots more you can do and just to keep you thinking, let's leave you with another suggestion.

A DTS package can be called (or created etc.) from within another DTS package and in combination with using ActiveX tasks within the packages this can be really helpful. Consider the position where you create a DTS package which imports a text file into a table (easily done through the DTS Wizard). Then you subsequently find out you need to repeat the task for another 100 files, which all have different names but the same data layout. To avoid renaming the text import file name and running the package each time you can automate the task by creating another DTS package with script that loops through all the files in the directory and runs the required package.

11

Scaling Down with MSDE

The **Microsoft Data Engine** (**MSDE**) allows application developers to distribute the same engine that manages data under SQL Server 7.0 with their desktop applications. This not only allows developers to build desktop applications with powerful data access capabilities that can easily scale to SQL Server when necessary, it also allows enterprise applications to implement the ability to work with data and even create databases off-line.

> *Although the use of the MSDE on client machines has not yet become widely used, its usage looks set to increase as more and more developers realize that its 100% compatibility with SQL Server is a major advantage over the JET database engine that Access uses. In fact, many developers believe that MSDE is Microsoft's signal that the life of JET is coming to an end.*

In order to create and design the schema for databases that will be managed by the MSDE inside an application, we will utilize SQL-DMO. In fact, many of the procedures we discussed earlier in this book will be used to interact with MSDE.

In this chapter, you will:

- ❑ Learn what the MSDE is and how it can be obtained
- ❑ Create a local version of the SQLDDL component (we'll revert to the component as it was before adding the MTS functionality and integrating the CustomerTracker)
- ❑ Modify the local version of the SQLDDL component to allow users to move a database created on the local MSDE server to a SQL Server in the enterprise
- ❑ Look at a couple of choices for deploying MSDE with your application

What is MSDE?

To put it simply, the MSDE is really a redistributable version of SQL Server. In fact, it runs as the MSSQLServer service. The main difference between SQL Server and MSDE is that MSDE does not install any user interface components. This means that there is no SQL Server Enterprise Manager, no Query Analyzer, no Service Manager, and so on. So how do you interact with MSDE?

One way would be to install the SQL Server Client tools on the computer running MSDE, another would be to connect to the MSDE server through SQL Server Enterprise Manager, still another, and the one that concerns us most in this book, is to manage the MSDE server through SQL-DMO.

There are a few other differences between MSDE and SQL Server. These are:

❑   Only five concurrent connections are recommended. This is the same limitation as exists with SQL Server Desktop edition.

❑   A single database can be only 2 GB.

❑   An MSDE server cannot act as a publisher for a transactional publication.

❑   An MSDE server does not support full-text search.

❑   An MSDE server cannot participate in a multiple-transaction operation with another computer.

In addition, an MSDE server running on Windows 95 or Windows 98 is subject to the same limitations as SQL Server Desktop edition running on those same platforms. It cannot utilize Windows NT authentication, cannot use certain Net libraries, and does not show up in the browse list in SQL Server Enterprise Manager or when calling `ListAvailableServers` through SQL-DMO.

How to Obtain MSDE

MSDE is included on the Microsoft Office 2000 Developer edition CD-ROMs. Since it was not available when Visual Studio 6.0 shipped, Visual Studio programmers need to obtain it separately. MSDE is available for download from Microsoft's web site at `http://msdn.microsoft.com/vstudio/msde/download.asp` or from the MSDN Subscriber downloads web site at `http://msdn.microsoft.com/subscriptions/resources/subdwnld.asp`. However, it is a 20 MB download, so it will take some time. You can also order the CD-ROM for the cost of shipping and handling. In the United States, shipping and handling costs $7.50. International shipments cost $14.95. One of the advantages of ordering the CD-ROM (particularly if you don't own a copy of SQL Server) is that the CD-ROM includes SQL Server 7.0 Developer Edition. Although this copy of SQL Server is licensed strictly for the developer's use while building the application, it does include all of the GUI tools you need to easily build and test an MSDE application.

Regardless of whether you choose to download MSDE or order it, you must provide proof that you are one of the following:

❑   A registered owner of the Professional or Enterprise edition of Visual Basic 6.0

❑   A registered owner of the Professional or Enterprise edition of Visual C++ 6.0

❑   A registered owner of the Professional or Enterprise edition of Visual Studio 6.0

❑   A registered owner of the Professional edition of Visual FoxPro 6.0

❑   A registered owner of the Professional edition of Visual InterDev 6.0

To prove eligibility, you will need to enter the product ID number of the appropriate product, which can be found in the product's About dialog.

> **If you already have SQL Server, there is no need to obtain MSDE until you are ready to test your application and prepare it for deployment. All development work can be accomplished by using SQL Server and Visual Studio.**

System Requirements for MSDE

The system requirements for installing MSDE are the same as for installing SQL Server Desktop Edition, except that MSDE only requires 40 MB of disk space. Keep in mind, however, that this 40 MB does not include the space you will need for databases and transaction logs. These storage requirements should be estimated, just as you would for SQL Server.

Building SQLDDL_Local

This next section focuses on building a SQLDDL component that can run on the client computer, instead of through MTS. We'll create a SQLDDL_Local component based on the code as it exists at the end of Chapter 6 (before we introduced the MTS code). We'll then modify the SurveyDesigner application to use the SQLDDL_Local component instead of the SQLDDL component.

> **In a production environment, you would probably want to provide users with the flexibility of either working online or offline. However, implementing this in the sample application would have involved more advanced object-oriented techniques and would taken us away from the primary objective of learning to use SQL-DMO. Therefore, for the purposes of this exercise, we'll just modify the client application to work with a different version of the component.**

Since MSDE is 100% compatible with SQL Server, all of the SQL-DMO code in the component should run fine against an MSDE server.

Modifying the Code from SQLDDL

The easiest way to create the SQLDDL_Local component is to begin by copying just the class modules and the standard module (not the SQLDDL.vbp project itself) from the version of SQLDDL created in Chapters 3–6 to a new folder named SQLDDL_local_component. It's safest to keep the modules of the two components distinct.

Once you have copied the .cls and .bas files to the new folder, launch Visual Basic and open the SurveyDesigner.vbp project. Run File | Add Project. Select ActiveX DLL and click on Open.

Change the name of the project to SQLDDL_Local. Remove the Class1 module that was inserted into the project by default. Now we need to add each of the modules in the SQLDDL_local_component folder. To do that, run Project | Add File and select the module you would like to add. You will need to repeat this step for each module in the project.

The final step we must take is to set a reference to the Microsoft SQLDMO Object Library. Now we are ready to begin changing the code.

> In order to avoid getting confused, it is probably best to remove the **SQLDDL** project from your project group before continuing.

Modifying the Client Application

Since we are only modifying the client application to work with this new component, the only modification we need to make is fairly minimal. Remove the reference to SQLDDL and add a reference to SQLDDL_Local:

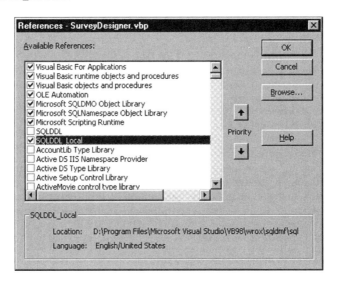

Next, open the `modGlobals` standard module and modify the General Declarations section as follows:

```
Public objSqldmo As SQLDMO.SQLServer 'Comment once all the code
                                     'has been converted
Public lConnID As Long
Public objDB As SQLDMO.Database
Public db As New SQLDDL_Local.Database
Public conn As New SQLDDL_Local.Server
Public sec As New SQLDDL_Local.Security
Public bk As New SQLDDL_Local.BackupDB
Public mgt As New SQLDDL_Local.Management
Public ns As New SQLNS.SQLNamespace
```

Finally, change the code for `cmdEdit` on `frmDesign` as follows:

```
Private Sub cmdEdit_Click()

    Dim columnList() As String
    Dim iRow As Integer
    Dim iCol As Integer

    frmMDIMain.sbrStatus.Panels(1).Text = "Retrieving schema"
    Me.MousePointer = vbHourglass
    columnList = db.GetColumnList(lConnID, cboDBs, lstTables.Text, _
                SQLDDL_Local.sddl_Name, SQLDDL_Local.sddl_Datatype, _
                SQLDDL_Local.sddl_Default, SQLDDL_Local.SDDL_PRIMARYKEY, _
                SQLDDL_Local.sddl_nullable)
    frmMDIMain.sbrStatus.Panels(1).Text = "Filling grid"
    flxColumns.Clear


    'Loop through the rows in columnList and add the
    'appropriate rows to the grid
    For iRow = 0 To UBound(columnList)
        If flxColumns.Rows <= iRow Then
            flxColumns.AddItem ""
        End If

        'Loop through the columns in the grid to fill it from columnList
        For iCol = 0 To flxColumns.Cols - 1
            flxColumns.TextMatrix(iRow, iCol) = columnList(iRow, iCol)
        Next
    Next


    Me.MousePointer = vbDefault
    frmMDIMain.sbrStatus.Panels(1).Text = lstTables.Text

End Sub
```

Moving Databases from MSDE to SQL Server

One of the scenarios you are likely to encounter if you build an application that uses MSDE is that at some point you will need to move a database from the MSDE server to the SQL Server. Moving a database requires:

❏ Detaching the database from the MSDE server

❏ Copying the database file or files from the MSDE server to the SQL Server

❏ Attaching the database to the SQL Server

To accomplish these steps in our sample application, we are adding a Move menu item to `frmMDIMain`. It will display a dialog named `frmMove`. This dialog will allow users to select a database to move and a destination server. Let's start with the user interface, and then look at how we'll accomplish each of the necessary steps in our application.

Designing the User Interface

The user interface for `frmMove` is very similar to the user interface for `frmConnect`. It is shown below:

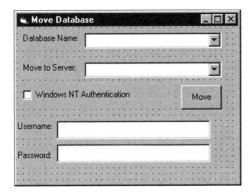

The controls and their names, with the exception of the Label controls, which are not referenced in the code, are shown in the table:

Class	Name
ComboBox	cboDBs
ComboBox	cboServers
CheckBox	chkIntegrated
CommandButton	cmdMove
TextBox	txtPassword
TextBox	txtUser

The `Form_Load` event is coded to populate both of the ComboBox controls by calling the appropriate methods of the `SQLDDL_Local.Server` component and `SQLDDL_Local.Database` component. This code should look familiar. Similar code was used to populate `cboServers` on `frmConnect` and `cboDBs` on `frmDesign`:

```
Private Sub Form_Load()

    Dim i As Integer
    Dim oNameList As SQLDMO.NameList
    Dim SDbList() As String

    Set oNameList = conn.ServerNames

    For i = 1 To oNameList.Count
        cboServers.AddItem oNameList(i)
    Next

    SDbList = db.GetDBList(lConnID)

    For i = 0 To UBound(sDbList)
        cboDBs.AddItem sDbList(i)
    Next

End Sub
```

We have also copied the code of the `chkIntegrated_Click` event procedure from `frmConnect`:

```
Private Sub chkIntegrated_Click()

    If chkIntegrated.Value = vbChecked Then
        txtUser.Enabled = False
        txtPassword.Enabled = False
        txtUser.BackColor = Me.BackColor
        txtPassword.BackColor = Me.BackColor
    Else
        txtUser.Enabled = True
        txtPassword.Enabled = True
        txtUser.BackColor = vbWhite
        txtPassword.BackColor = vbWhite
    End If

End Sub
```

As a reminder, this code disables the `txtUser` and `txtPassword` when Windows NT Authentication is enabled.

Finally, we will add a <u>M</u>ove menu item to the <u>D</u>atabase menu of `frmMDIMain` and code it as follows:

```
Private Sub mnuMoveDB_Click()
    frmMove.Show
End Sub
```

We also add code to the `mnuDatabase_Click` event procedure to enable this menu item only if a connection has been established:

```
Private Sub mnuDatabase_Click()

    Dim i As Integer
    If bConnected = True Then
        mnuCreateDB.Enabled = True
        mnuDesign.Enabled = True
        If b7 = True Then
            mnuTable.Enabled = True
        Else
            mnuTable.Enabled = False
        End If
        mnuIndex.Enabled = True
        mnuMoveDB.Enabled = True
    Else
        mnuCreateDB.Enabled = False
        mnuDesign.Enabled = False
        mnuTable.Enabled = False
        mnuIndex.Enabled = False
        mnuMoveDB.Enabled = False
    End If

End Sub
```

Connecting to the Destination Server

We'll begin coding the `cmdMove` button of `frmMove` with some code that is very similar to that used to connect to the source database in `frmConnect`. It is shown below:

```
Private Sub cmdMove_Click()

    Me.MousePointer = vbHourglass
    If chkIntegrated.Value = vbChecked Then
        lDConnID = conn.ConnectSQLServer(cboServers)
    Else
        lDConnID = conn.ConnectSQLServer(cboServers, txtUser, txtPassword)
    End If
    Me.Hide
    Me.MousePointer = vbDefault

End Sub
```

The only real differences between this code and the code used earlier are that this code does not store persistent information about the connection, user name, and password and it also does not create a SQL-NS connection.

Detaching the Database from the MSDE Server

Now we are ready to start the process of moving the database. First, we'll detach the database from the MSDE server. To implement this functionality, we'll create a DetachDatabase method in the Database class module. The client application will pass it the connection ID for the source database and the name of the database. The DetachDatabase method will retrieve a reference to the SQLDMO.SQLServer object associated with the connection ID, by using the ItemByID method of the SQLServers collection. It will then use the DetachDB method of that SQLServer object to disassociate the database from the MSDE server so that the database file or files can be moved to the SQL Server:

```
Public Sub DetachDatabase(ByVal lSrcConnID As Long, ByVal sDatabase As String)

    Dim oSrcServer As SQLDMO.SQLServer
    Set oSrcServer = oApp.SQLServers.ItemByID(lSrcConnID)
    oSrcServer.DetachDB (sDatabase)

End Sub
```

The syntax for the DetachDB method is as follows:

```
object.DetachDB(DBName As String[, bCheck As Boolean]) as String
```

The DBName argument is the Name property of a database; the bCheck argument specifies whether the query optimization statistics should be updated before detaching the database. A value of True causes them to be updated. If no value is passed for bCheck, a default value of True will be used. The method returns a string to indicate either success or failure.

> The **DetachDB** method calls the **sp_detach_db** system stored procedure.

Next, modify the code of the cmdMove_Click event procedure so that it calls the DetachDatabase method. We also need to add a form to the project and name it frmWaiting. The form contains a Label control, which has its Caption property set to "Local Server Stopping to Release File". This lets the user know what's going on.

The cmdMove_Click event procedure is shown below, modified to detach the database and release the file:

```
Private Sub cmdMove_Click()

    Dim lDConnID As Long

    Me.MousePointer = vbHourglass

    If chkIntegrated.Value = vbChecked Then
        lDConnID = conn.ConnectSQLServer(cboServers)
    Else
        lDConnID = conn.ConnectSQLServer(cboServers, txtUser, txtPassword)
    End If
```

```
        db.DetachDatabase lConnID, cboDBs.Text

        conn.ShutdownServer lConnID
        frmWaiting.Show
        frmWaiting.Refresh

        Do Until conn.IsStopped(sServer) = True
            'Pause until the server has stopped so that the file can be copied.
            DoEvents
        Loop

        frmWaiting.Hide
        conn.RestartServer sServer, sUser, sPassword
        bConnected = False
        Me.Hide
        Me.MousePointer = vbDefault

    End Sub
```

> Note that after calling the **DetachDatabase** method, the code shuts down the
> MSDE server and loops until the server has finished shutting down. Although the
> documentation states that **DetachDB** should allow the files to be copied, I
> received a permissions error when copying the file unless I shutdown and
> restarted the MSDE server. The **bConnected** flag is set to **False** because, after
> the server is restarted, the connection to the MSDE server must be reestablished
> before other activities can be performed.

Copying the Database File to the SQL Server

The next step in moving the database is to move the physical file from the client computer to the
SQL Server. In order to simplify this process, we have hard coded some environmental conditions
into the code. In order for this code to run on your network unmodified, you will need to do the
following:

❑   Create and share a directory named d:\mssql7\data on the SQL Server

❑   Map the share to the drive letter K:\ on the client computer

Determining the Physical File Name

Before you can copy the file, you need to determine its filename and path. This information can be
retrieved by calling the EnumFiles method of the SQLDMO.Database object. The EnumFiles
method returns a QueryResults object with the following columns:

Column Number	Column	Data Type	Description
1	fileid	smallint	This column contains the operating system identifier for the file. This information is generated automatically by the operating system.
2	groupid	smallint	This column contains the identifier for the file group. This information is system generated. If the file is the transaction log (.ldf) file, this field will contain the value 0.
3	size	integer	This column contains the number of pages in the file. Under SQL Server 7.0, a page is 8192 bytes.
4	maxsize	integer	This column contains the maximum size to which the file can grow. A value of –1 indicates that a file's size is limited only by available disk space.
5	growth	integer	This column contains either the percentage by which a file should grow or the number of pages by which a file should grow when the file becomes full.
6	status	integer	This column contains information about the file, such as whether the file grows by percent or by a number of pages and the type of file. The information is retrieved by using a bit mask. The individual flags are listed in SQL Server online help.
7	perf	integer	This column is reserved for later use.
8	name	nchar(129)	This column contains the logical name of the file.
9	filename	nchar(261)	This column contains the physical path and name of the file.

To implement retrieving the physical path and name of the file, we create a `GetPhysicalFileName` method in the `SQLDDL_Local.Database` component. The code is shown below:

```
Public Function GetPhysicalFileName(ByVal lConnID As Long, _
                            ByVal sDatabase As String) As String

    Dim oDB As SQLDMO.Database
    Dim oQRFiles As SQLDMO.QueryResults
    Set oDB = GetDatabase(lConnID, sDatabase)
```

```
      Set oQRFiles = oDB.EnumFiles
      GetPhysicalFileName = oQRFiles.GetColumnString(1, 9)

  End Function
```

The method accepts a connection ID and a database name. It retrieves a reference to the database using that name and calls the `EnumFiles` method on that database. It then returns the value in row 1, column 9 of the `QueryResults` object.

> **Since we have limited the database to only creating databases with a single file, we only need to retrieve the information from row 1, column 9. If you needed to detach multiple files, you would need to build a SQL Server multistring by looping through each record in the `QueryResults` object and concatenating the value in column 9.**

The `GetPhysicalFileName` method is called within the `cmdMove_Click` event. Because it depends on the database being connected to the server, it must be called before we detach the database:

```
Private Sub cmdMove_Click()

   Dim lDConnID As Long
   Dim sFileName As String
   Me.MousePointer = vbHourglass
   If chkIntegrated.Value = vbChecked Then
      lDConnID = conn.ConnectSQLServer(cboServers)
   Else
      lDConnID = conn.ConnectSQLServer(cboServers, txtUser, txtPassword)
   End If
   sFileName = db.GetPhysicalFileName(lConnID, cboDBs.Text)

   db.DetachDatabase lConnID, cboDBs.Text

   conn.ShutdownServer lConnID

   frmWaiting.Show
   frmWaiting.Refresh

   Do Until conn.IsStopped(sServer) = True
      'Pause until the server has stopped so that the file can be copied.
      DoEvents
   Loop

   frmWaiting.Hide

   conn.RestartServer sServer, sUser, sPassword
   bConnected = False
   Me.Hide
   Me.MousePointer = vbDefault

End Sub
```

Using the FileSystemObject Object

The simplest way to copy a file from one location to another is to take advantage of the new `FileSystemObject` object that is included in the Microsoft Scripting Runtime library (`SCRRUN.DLL`) that ships with Visual Basic 6.0. You will need to set a reference to this library:

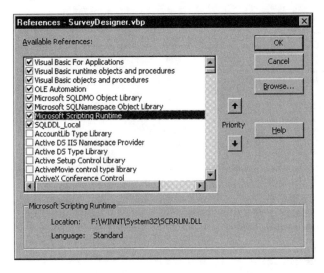

The `FileSystemObject` object allows you to manipulate the file system on a computer. We're going to use two methods of the `FileSystemObject` and the property of its dependent `File` object.

The `CopyFile` method allows you to copy a file from one location to another. Its syntax is shown below:

```
object.CopyFile source, destination [, overwrite]
```

The *source* argument is the full path to the file you wish to copy. The *destination* argument is the full path to the destination. If you do not include the name of the file, you should end this string with a backslash (\). The *overwrite* argument is an optional Boolean argument that determines whether the file should be overwritten if it exists at the location. The value of *overwrite* is `True` by default.

The `GetFile` method returns a reference to the `File` object specified by the *filespec* argument. Its syntax is:

```
object.GetFile(filespec) as File
```

The `File` object has a variety of properties. We will use the `Size` property to determine when the file has finished copying to its destination.

The code below shows how the `FileSystemObject` is used to copy the database file from the client computer to the SQL Server:

```vb
Private Sub cmdMove_Click()

    Dim lDConnID As Long
    Dim fso As New FileSystemObject
    Dim sFileName As String
    Dim sDestPath As String
    Dim sPathParts() As String
    Dim lFileSize As Long
    Dim sPathParts() As String

    Me.MousePointer = vbHourglass

    If chkIntegrated.Value = vbChecked Then
        lDConnID = conn.ConnectSQLServer(cboServers)
    Else
        lDConnID = conn.ConnectSQLServer(cboServers, txtUser, txtPassword)
    End If

    sFileName = db.GetPhysicalFileName(lConnID, cboDBs.Text)
    db.DetachDatabase lConnID, cboDBs.Text
    conn.ShutdownServer lConnID

    frmWaiting.Show
    frmWaiting.Refresh

    Do Until conn.IsStopped(sServer) = True
        'Pause until the server has stopped so that the file can be copied.
        DoEvents
    Loop

    frmWaiting.Hide

    sFileName = Trim(sFileName)
    'Set sDestPath to be the mapped drive letter
    sDestPath = "k:\"
    lFileSize = fso.GetFile(sFileName).Size
    fso.CopyFile sFileName, sDestPath
    sPathParts = Split(sFileName, "\", -1, vbTextCompare)

    Do Until fso.GetFile(sDestPath & sPathParts(UBound(sPathParts))).Size = _
        lFileSize
        MsgBox "Copying file"
        'Wait until the file has finished copying
    Loop

    conn.RestartServer sServer, sUser, sPassword
    bConnected = False
    Me.Hide
    Me.MousePointer = vbDefault
End Sub
```

We have to do some formatting of the `sFileName` string. Let's walk through what the code does to ensure that the right file is copied to the right location and that it finishes copying before anything else is done.

First, we use the `Trim` function to remove the whitespace from around `sFileName`. Next, we set the destination path to be `"k:\"`. Remember, this is a hard coded value of the drive we mapped to the shared directory on the SQL Server. The next step is to retrieve the file size of the source file. We'll use this value to compare against the destination file to be sure it's finished copying before moving on.

The next step involves a string manipulation function introduced with Visual Basic 6.0, the `Split` function (it's actually part of the Visual Basic For Applications library, `msvbvm60.dll`). This is a powerful function for retrieving the parts of strings that are delimited in a consistent way. It returns an array of strings where each element in the array is the part of the string before a known delimiter. It has the following syntax:

```
Split(expression[, delimiter[, count[, compare]]]) as String()
```

The *expression* argument is the string you'd like to parse. The *delimiter* argument is the character that delimits the string. If no delimiter is passed, a space is considered as the delimiter. The *count* argument is the maximum number of elements you'd like the result to contain. If you pass -1, the number of elements in the array will not be limited. The *compare* argument determines whether you'd like to compare the characters in the string based on binary or text. A binary comparison is the default.

Since we know that `sFileName` is delimited with the backslash (\), we can use the `Split` function to easily retrieve the part of the string that is the filename. We use the `UBound` function to indicate the element we are interested in because the filename will always be the last element in a path.

To determine the destination path, we append the name of the file to the `sDestPath` string. We can then retrieve a reference to the new copy of the file and check its size to determine when it has finished copying.

Attaching the Database to the SQL Server

The final step in the process is to attach the database to the SQL Server. For this, we can use either the `AttachDB` method of the `SQLServer` object or the `AttachDBWithSingleFile` method of the `SQLServer` object. The syntax for the `AttachDB` method is shown below:

```
object.AttachDB(DBName, DataFiles) as String
```

The *DBName* argument is the logical name of the database. The *DataFiles* argument is a SQL Server multistring that contains the path to each of the physical files that comprise the database. The method returns a string to indicate success or failure.

> The `AttachDB` method calls the `sp_attach_db` system stored procedure.

The syntax for the `AttachDBWithSingleFile` is meant exclusively for a database that stores all of its data objects in a single file. Its syntax is shown below:

```
object.AttachDBWithSingleFile(DBName, DataFile) as String
```

The only difference between `AttachDB` and `AttachDBWithSingleFile` is that the *DataFile* argument is a string instead of a SQL Server multistring. It must contain the physical path to the primary data file for the database.

> **The `AttachDBWithSingleFile` method calls the `sp_attach_single_file_db` system stored procedure.**

To implement this functionality in the component, we create a `MoveDBtoServer` method:

```
Public Sub MoveDBtoServer(lDestConnID As Long, ByVal sDatabase As String, _
                          ByVal sFileName As String)
    Dim oDestServer As SQLDMO.SQLServer
    Set oDestServer = oApp.SQLServers.ItemByID(lDestConnID)
    oDestServer.AttachDBWithSingleFile sDatabase, sFileName
End Sub
```

It accepts the connection ID for the destination server, the logical name of the database, and the physical path to the file. It then retrieves a reference to the SQL Server and calls that server's `AttachDBWithSingleFile` method. Note that our assumption here is a database composed of a single file. If you are moving a database with multiple files, you will need to use `AttachDB` and pass a SQL Server multistring listing all filenames associated with the database.

The `MoveDBtoServer` method is called within `cmdMove_Click` after the file has finished copying:

```
Private Sub cmdMove_Click()

    Dim lDConnID As Long
    Dim fso As New FileSystemObject
    Dim sFileName As String
    Dim sDestPath As String
    Dim sPathParts() As String
    Dim lFileSize As Long
    Dim sPathParts() As String

    Me.MousePointer = vbHourglass
    If chkIntegrated.Value = vbChecked Then
        lDConnID = conn.ConnectSQLServer(cboServers)
    Else
        lDConnID = conn.ConnectSQLServer(cboServers, txtUser, txtPassword)
    End If
    sFileName = db.GetPhysicalFileName(lConnID, cboDBs.Text)

    db.DetachDatabase lConnID, cboDBs.Text

    conn.ShutdownServer lConnID

    frmWaiting.Show
    frmWaiting.Refresh
```

```
    Do Until conn.IsStopped(sServer) = True
        'Pause until the server has stopped so that the file can be copied.
        DoEvents
    Loop

    frmWaiting.Hide

    sFileName = Trim(sFileName)
    'Set sDestPath to be the mapped drive letter
    sDestPath = "k:\"
    lFileSize = fso.GetFile(sFileName).Size
    fso.CopyFile sFileName, sDestPath

    sPathParts = Split(sFileName, "\", -1, vbTextCompare)

    Do Until fso.GetFile(sDestPath & sPathParts(UBound(sPathParts))).Size =
lFileSize
        MsgBox "Copying file"
        'Wait until the file has finished copying
    Loop

    sFileName = "d:\mssql7\data\" & sPathParts(UBound(sPathParts))
    db.MoveDBtoServer lDConnID, cboDBs.Text, sFileName
    conn.RestartServer sServer, sUser, sPassword
    bConnected = False
    Me.Hide
    Me.MousePointer = vbDefault

End Sub
```

Before we can call the MoveDBtoServer method, however, we need to construct the path to the location on the server where the file exists. Remember, the AttachDBWithSingleFile method will be viewing the file system from the SQL Server's perspective, not from the perspective of the client computer.

This is the basic procedure you will follow when moving a database between an MSDE server and a SQL Server. The process will also work for moving databases between two MSDE servers or two SQL Servers. As you begin to think about the potential uses for MSDE, you will see that knowing SQL-DMO becomes even more useful. Not only can it be used to create and move databases, you can also use it to manage other aspects of MSDE, such as logins and permissions, which is particularly useful as MSDE does not have any user interface components.

Deploying MSDE

MSDE is distributed from Microsoft in a self-extracting executable called `msdex86_pkg.exe` or `msdealpha_pkg.exe`. When the `msdex86_pkg.exe` is extracted, you'll find that it consists of the following files:

Filename	Description
`MSDEx86.exe`	This is a self-extracting executable that installs the files for MSDE in the locations describe in `unattend.iss`.
`license.txt`	This is a license file for MSDE.
`readme.txt`	The Readme file gives instructions on how to run a command-line setup of MSDE.
`unattend.iss`	This `unattend.iss` file is the answer file for an unattended installation of MSDE.

Although you have a number of options for how you'd like to deploy MSDE, we'll just walk through one of them, creating a shortcut for installing MSDE in the Start menu along with your client application's shortcut.

The procedure for doing this involves two additional steps when using the Package and Deployment Wizard to package your application:

❑ Add the four MSDE distribution files on the Included Files screen of the Package and Deployment Wizard

❑ Add a shortcut using the appropriate command line to install MSDE

Adding the MSDE Distribution Files

On the Included Files screen of the Package and Deployment Wizard, click on Add. Browse to locate and select `MSDEx86.exe`, `license.txt`, `readme.txt`, and `unattend.iss`:

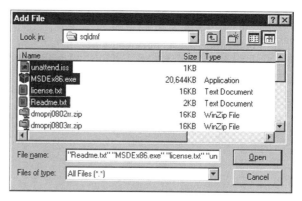

The **Readme.txt** file is not strictly required. However, it is probably useful to have it on the client's computer in case the user deletes the shortcut or selects not to have it created.

Since `MSDEx86.exe` is an executable, you will be prompted that it doesn't have a dependency file. Click on OK.

Defining the Start Menu Shortcut

On the Start Menu Items screen, click on New Item. Define the Start Menu Item as shown in the graphic:

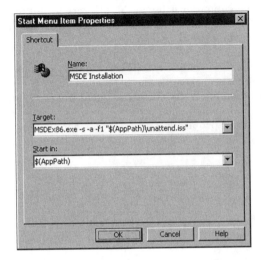

The Name is the text that will appear in the Start menu. In this case, name the shortcut something descriptive like MSDE Installation. The Target should contain the command you will run when the user selects the shortcut. In this case, the shortcut will launch MSDEx86.exe with the following options:

Option	Description
-s	This option switch causes the installation to run in silent mode. This means that the user will not be prompted during installation. Instead, any information that is needed is retrieved from the answer file (in this case unattend.iss).
-a	This option switch causes the remainder of the options to be appended to the internal command.
-f1 "$(AppPath)\unattend.iss"	This option specifies that you should use the file listed immediately following the option switch as the answer file. The $(AppPath) variable is a placeholder for the path where the user selects to install the Survey Designer application.

Make sure to verify your file locations to ensure that both MSDEx86.exe and unattend.iss are copied to the $(AppPath) directory.

Summary

In this chapter, we discussed SQL-DMO in the context of how it can be used with MSDE. We looked at an example of how to scale down the application we have built through most of the book so that it will run on a single computer using an MSDE server. Following that we looked at how to move databases between servers. The chapter wrapped up with a discussion of one strategy for deploying MSDE with your application.

If you are using Visual Basic to develop your SQL-DMF applications then this is the end of the line, as the next chapter discusses accessing the SQL-DMF from C++. This book has provided you with a starting point in programmatically accessing the SQL-DMO, SQL-NS, and SQL-DTS objects. All of the techniques you have learnt over the course of this book can be applied to all the many other objects, collections, properties and methods that we didn't manage to cover. Don't forget that there is an exhaustive reference to all the object libraries in the appendices. Enjoy!

12

Using SQL-DMO with Visual C++

SQL-DMO is a set of COM objects and, as such, can be used from any language that supports the use of COM objects. In this book, Visual Basic has been used to provide working examples of applications using SQL-DMO, but in this last chapter we're going to extend our use of the technology to C++. Again we'll walk you through the code examples, but to get the most from this chapter we assume you are familiar with C++.

We're going to open the chapter by very quickly recapping on the basics of using COM objects and then move on to developing some sample code (the ListServers example) which is adapted from material we have seen earlier in the book. Specifically the example will allow comparison of VB and C++ approaches to enumerating available SQL Servers via the ListAvailableSQLServers method of the SQLDMO.Application object.

Moreover, the focus of this chapter will be on implementation of the example using different methods of accessing COM objects from C++. The three ways we're going to use SQL-DMO COM objects with C++ within this example are:

- ❏ **Raw COM calls**
- ❏ **MFC IDispatch wrappers**
- ❏ **Native compiler COM support**

In this chapter we'll be building our small application with Microsoft Visual C++ and you'll need access to the sqldmo.rll resource file and sqldmo.h and sqldmoid.h header files during the coding (see Chapter 1 for further details).

As previously, the code is available for download from www.wrox.com and, since this chapter moves us away from VB and touches on a number of involved C++ topics, a list of references to sources of more detailed information about the topics discussed is provided at the end of the chapter.

Basics of Working with COM Objects

Just to recap on the three basic steps taken when using COM objects we have:

❑   **Getting a reference to the object** – Getting a reference is the first step to using any COM object. We can get the reference by calling some type of `Create` function, by calling a function that returns a reference to a COM object, or we can be passed a reference to a COM object inside a function that takes a reference as one of its parameters. We're going to be looking at only the first two methods.

❑   **Using the object** – Once the reference is obtained, we can work with the object by calling its methods and properties. In this chapter we'll look at three different ways of working with objects. We'll call the raw COM methods that implement the object, and look at using two different types of wrapper classes that encapsulate the functionality of the object.

❑   **Releasing the reference** – When an object is no longer needed, the reference to the object must be released. We will look at directly calling the `IUnknown` method `Release`, as well as the ways that the wrapper classes we will be using encapsulate the reference counting.

Implementation Specific Information

While the principles are common, different languages will involve some differences in approach. We'll take a practical look at these three steps in the context of our example below, and throughout the remainder of the examples in this chapter. We will also provide more information on these basic steps that are specific to each of the three implementations at the appropriate time.

Setting Up the ListServers Example

The example that we will be using is based on a modified version of an example that was presented in Chapter 3. This example enumerated all of the available SQL Servers using the `SQLDMO.Application` object's `ListAvailableSQLServers` method.

> Remember that the **ListAvailableSQLServers** method is supported only for servers and workstations running Microsoft Windows NT and returns only those SQL Servers using Named Pipes as the default Net-Library protocol. The workaround, if your servers don't use this protocol, is to set up server aliases that do by using the SQL Server Client Network Utility.

Our route through this example is to firstly set up the VB version of the sample, then to set up the bare bones of the C++ example. From that foundation we can then move on to developing the three different methods of getting the list of servers.

The ListServers Example – VB Version

The modified VB version of the sample looks like this:

The code for populating the ListBox with the servers is very similar to the example in Chapter 3, but all of the code to populate the ListBox is contained in a single routine.

To set up this example, create a standard EXE project and add a ListBox (named `lstServers`) and a command button (named `cmdListServers`) to the form as shown above. Add a reference to the Microsoft SQL-DMO Object Library, and then add the code shown below to the `Click` event for the command button:

```vb
Private Sub cmdListServers_Click()

    'Set the mouse pointer
    Me.MousePointer = vbHourglass

    'Empty the list box
    lstServers.Clear

    'Declare the SQL DMO Application object
    Dim oApp As SQLDMO.Application

    'Create the Application object
    Set oApp = New SQLDMO.Application

    'Declare the NameList object
    Dim oNameList As SQLDMO.NameList

    'Get the list of servers
    Set oNameList = oApp.ListAvailableSQLServers

    'Iterate the list and add to the list box
    Dim nCount As Long
    For nCount = 1 To oNameList.Count
        lstServers.AddItem oNameList(nCount)
    Next
```

```
    'Release the references to the
    'NameList and the Application objects
    Set oNameList = Nothing
    Set oApp = Nothing

    'Restore the mouse pointer
    Me.MousePointer = vbDefault

End Sub
```

The first few lines of code set the mouse pointer to the hourglass and clear the ListBox in preparation for being populated with the list of servers:

```
    'Set the mouse pointer
    Me.MousePointer = vbHourglass

    'Empty the list box
    lstServers.Clear
```

The next two lines declare and then instantiate an instance of the SQLDMO.Application object and store a reference to the object in the oApp object variable:

```
    'Declare the SQL DMO Application object
    Dim oApp As SQLDMO.Application

    'Create the Application object
    Set oApp = New SQLDMO.Application
```

The next group of lines declares a SQLDMO.NameList object variable, and then calls the oApp object's ListAvailableSQLServers method. This method returns a reference to a NameList and the Set statement assigns this reference to the oNameList variable:

```
    'Declare the NameList object
    Dim oNameList As SQLDMO.NameList

    'Get the list of servers
    Set oNameList = oApp.ListAvailableSQLServers
```

Now that we have a NameList populated with the list of server names, we iterate this list and add the server names to the ListBox by using the Count property and AddItem method:

```
    'Iterate the list and add to the list box
    Dim nCount As Long
    For nCount = 1 To oNameList.Count
       lstServers.AddItem oNameList(nCount)
    Next
```

Now that we are done using the `NameList` and `Application` objects, we release the references to the two objects:

```
'Release the references to the
'NameList and the Application objects
Set oNameList = Nothing
Set oApp = Nothing
```

Lastly, we finish up by restoring the mouse pointer to the default value:

```
'Restore the mouse pointer
Me.MousePointer = vbDefault
```

These steps represent a typical usage scenario of using any COM objects – get the object, use it, and then release it. In this example we got an object by creating it, and we got another by calling a method that returned an object. Using COM objects in C++ is similar to using them in VB, but the code can look a little different; but it can also look very similar, as we will see in the three examples.

The ListServers Example – Setting up the C++ Version

The C++ example illustrates three ways to use SQL-DMO:

❑ Using raw COM calls

❑ Using the MFC `IDispatch` wrapper classes

❑ Using the native compiler COM support with `#import`

The sample will perform the same function as the VB sample, but in three different ways. The sample uses MFC, but of the actual code that uses SQL-DMO, only the MFC `IDispatch` wrappers code depends on MFC.

The MFC sample will eventually give the following dialog:

The setup for the C++ example is broken down into several smaller steps:

❑ Creating the basic application using AppWizard

❑ Modifying the dialog template

❑ Using ClassWizard to add member variables and message handlers

❑ Adding stubs for the three methods that use SQL-DMO

❑ Adding COM initialization code

❑ Building and running the empty sample shell

We are going to be using a default AppWizard-generated dialog-based application as the foundation for the C++ example, so this is where we start.

Creating the Basic Application via AppWizard

We begin by running Visual C++ and choosing File | New which brings up the New dialog box:

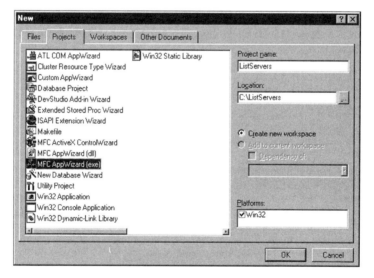

Choose MFC AppWizard (exe) from the Projects tab and give the project the name ListServers. Once these settings are complete, click OK.

From the next screen choose Dialog based:

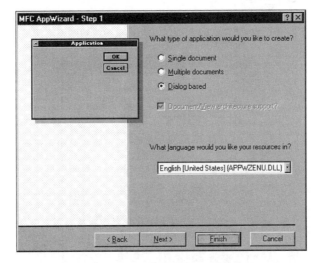

After clicking Finish, a small summary dialog box will display giving information about the new project. Click OK to dismiss this dialog. Visual Studio will then open the new project and present the dialog template for editing:

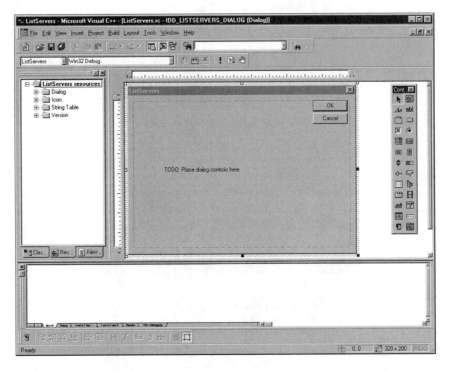

Our next task is to set up the form.

Modifying the Dialog Template

Delete the two buttons and the static control from the dialog template, and then size the template and add controls to resemble the dialog in the following screenshot:

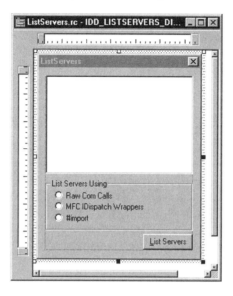

The controls are set up as follows:

❑ Give the ListBox the ID: `IDC_LIST_SERVERS_LIST`, and remove the Sort style

❑ Give the radio buttons the IDs: `IDC_RADIO_RAW_COM`, `IDC_RADIO_DISPATCH_WRAPPERS`, and `IDC_RADIO_IMPORT`

❑ Give the button the ID: `IDC_BUTTON_LIST_SERVERS`

❑ Set the Group style for `IDC_RADIO_RAW_COM`, clear it for the other two radio buttons, and set it for the control next in the tab order, which will be the `IDC_BUTTON_LIST_SERVERS` button

To set these control properties, right-click on the control, and choose Properties from the context menu (to keep the Properties window visible while selecting different controls, push the button with the pin in the upper left corner of the Properties window):

After setting these styles, set the tab order of the controls on the dialog template. Choose the Layout | Tab Order menu item, and click the controls in the desired tab order:

After clicking all of the controls, click outside of the dialog template to return back to the normal dialog template-editing mode.

> **The radio buttons in a radio button group are ordered according to the tab order of the dialog, and grouped by setting the group style of the first radio button and the group style of the first control following the radio button group in the tab order. If the sample doesn't behave as expected the grouping and ordering of the radio button controls may not have been properly set.**

We now move on to the MFC ClassWizard to add the required member variables and message handlers.

Adding Member Variables and Message Handlers

Press *Ctrl+W* to bring up ClassWizard. Add member variables for the ListBox and radio buttons as shown below:

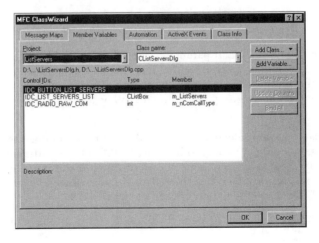

Switch to the **Message Maps** tab and click **Add Function...** (which displays the **Add Member** dialog box) to add a BN_CLICKED handler for IDC_BUTTON_LIST_SERVERS. Click **OK** to accept the default method name and then click **Edit Code** to jump to the implementation of the handler:

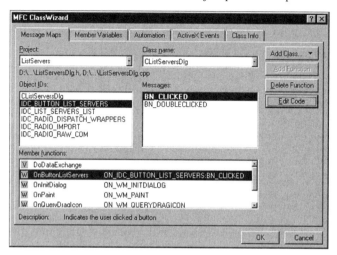

Add the following code to the OnButtonListServers handler:

```
void CListServersDlg::OnButtonListServers()
{
    UpdateData();

    switch(m_nComCallType)
    {
    case 0:
        ListServersRawCom();
        break;
    case 1:
        ListServersMFCDispatch ();
        break;
    case 2:
        ListServersImport();
        break;
    }
}
```

Calling UpdateData with the default parameter, which is TRUE, takes the values from the dialog controls and places them into any variables that have been associated with the controls. For radio button groups, this is a zero-based offset into the button group. In our case, m_nComCallType is associated with the radio button group, and contains either 0, 1, or 2, depending on the radio button the user has selected.

Depending on the radio button selected, we will call routines to populate the ListBox with servers in one of three ways. Since we are going to be using COM in three different ways, we aren't going to use a wizard to add these three functions, but we're going to add them by hand and put the implementations into three different .cpp files. This should reduce any possibility of naming conflicts and simplify the implementation of each method.

At this point we aren't going to add the code for the different methods so stubs are required.

Adding Stubs for the SQL-DMO Methods

Open `ListServersDlg.h` and add the three following method declarations at the top of the `CListServersDlg` class declaration:

```
class CListServersDlg : public CDialog
{
public:
    void ListServersRawCom();
    void ListServersMFCDispatch();
    void ListServersImport();
    ...
```

Create three `.cpp` files, and save them as `ListServersRawCom.cpp`, `ListServersMFCDispatch.cpp`, and `ListServersImport.cpp`. Add the following code to each file, substituting the appropriate method name in each of the three files. Save the changes and then add the files to the project.

```
// ListServersImport.cpp : implementation file
//

#include "stdafx.h"
#include "ListServers.h"
#include "ListServersDlg.h"

#ifdef _DEBUG
#define new DEBUG_NEW
#undef THIS_FILE
static char THIS_FILE[] = __FILE__;
#endif

void CListServersDlg::ListServersImport()
{
}
```

Our penultimate task at this point is to enable our application for COM.

Adding COM Initialization Code

Applications that use COM must initialize the COM libraries before making any other COM calls. Non-MFC applications can use `CoInitialize` and `CoUninitialize` to initialize and uninitialize the COM libraries, or `OleInitialize` and `OleUninitialize` if they use any OLE functionality such as OLE Structured Storage.

MFC applications can call `AfxOleInit` which handles the initialization and uninitialization of the COM libraries.

Open the `ListServers.cpp` file and add the following lines near the top of `CListServersApp::InitInstance`:

```
BOOL CListServersApp::InitInstance()
{
   AfxEnableControlContainer();

   // Standard initialization
   // If you are not using these features and wish to reduce the size
   //  of your final executable, you should remove from the following
   //  the specific initialization routines you do not need.

   AfxOleInit();
```

This will initialize the COM libraries for this application, and cause them to be properly uninitialized when the application terminates.

Building and Running the Sample

Before we can build and run the sample, we need to handle one more detail. In the `CListServersDlg` constructor, we will change the initialization for `m_nComCallType` to select **Raw Com Calls** by default. Change the line of code shown below to initialize `m_nComCallType` to 0 instead of −1:

```
CListServersDlg::CListServersDlg(CWnd* pParent /*=NULL*/)
   CDialog(CListServersDlg::IDD, pParent)
{
   //{{AFX_DATA_INIT(CListServersDlg)
   m_nComCallType = 0; // Raw COM Calls
   //}}AFX_DATA_INIT
   // Note that LoadIcon does not require a subsequent DestroyIcon in Win32
   m_hIcon = AfxGetApp()->LoadIcon(IDR_MAINFRAME);
}
```

The member variable `m_nComCallType` is associated with the radio buttons, and button zero is the first button in the group. This code causes the first radio button in the group to be selected.

It's a good idea to build and run the sample at this point to verify that everything so far works as planned. It won't do much without the code to load the list of servers into the ListBox, but we'll take a look at adding this code in the next section.

Raw COM Calls

The first method that we are going to use to get the list of servers is raw COM calls. To do this we first need to include the header files for the SQL-DMO object interfaces and GUIDs. Add the following include directives at the top of `ListServersRawCom.cpp` after the existing include directives:

```
// ListServersRawCom.cpp : implementation file
//
```

```
#include "stdafx.h"
#include "ListServers.h"
#include "ListServersDlg.h"
```

```
// Include the SQLDMO interfaces and guids
#include <initguid.h>
#include <sqldmo.h>
#include <sqldmoid.h>
```

The first file included, `initguid.h`, must be included once per EXE in order for any GUIDs to be properly defined. We are including this file in this `.cpp` file instead of `sdtafx.h` because we wanted to keep all of the files for each of the different methods of using the SQL-DMO and COM objects specific to each file that used them.

The next two files, `sqldmo.h` and `sqldmoid.h` contain the interface declarations and GUIDs respectively for the SQL-DMO COM objects. These files are in the `MSSQL7\DevTools\Include` directory, and for Visual Studio to find these files this directory must be added to the compiler's include path, by choosing <u>T</u>ools | <u>O</u>ptions, selecting the **Directories** tab, and adding this path as shown below:

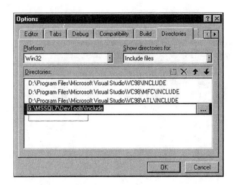

After these include directives, add another include directive for `AtlConv.h`:

```
// Conversion macros
#include <AtlConv.h>
```

`AtlConv.h` declares conversion macros which facilitate conversion between Unicode character strings and ASCII character strings. Since all strings in COM are Unicode strings, we will need to use these macros to convert the returned strings when we retrieve the list of servers. In place of `AtlConv.h` we could have used `AfxConv.h`, which includes `AtlConv.h` and includes a few more conversion macros that we aren't using in this example.

I usually use `AfxConv.h` in an MFC app, but since I said that only the MFC Dispatch Wrappers code would require MFC, we won't use it here. Of course, we are using `CListBox` and `CWaitCursor` in this example, but these are artifacts of the sample application, and the actual code that retrieves the list of servers for this example does not depend on these specific MFC classes or any other MFC code.

The ListServersRawCom Method

The code for the `ListServersRawCom` method is presented below (don't worry, we go through it in detail at the end):

```
void CListServersDlg::ListServersRawCom()
{
    // For conversion macros used below
    USES_CONVERSION;

    // Clear the list box
    m_ListServers.ResetContent();

    m_ListServers.AddString(_T("Raw Com Calls:"));

    // Wait cursor
    CWaitCursor wait;

    // Declare a pointer to an Application
    ISQLDMOApplication* pApplication = NULL;

    HRESULT hr;

    // Create an instance and assign it to the pointer
    hr = CoCreateInstance(CLSID_SQLDMOApplication,
                          NULL,
                          CLSCTX_INPROC_SERVER,
                          IID_IWSQLDMOApplication,
                          reinterpret_cast<void**>(&pApplication));

    // If the creation succeeded
    if(SUCCEEDED(hr))
    {
        // Declare a pointer to a NameList, and pass it to
        // ListAvailableSQLServers
        ISQLDMONameList* pNameList = NULL;
        hr = pApplication->ListAvailableSQLServers(&pNameList);

        // If we got a reference to a NameList
        if(SUCCEEDED(hr))
        {
            // Get the count of servers
            long nCount = 0;
            hr = pNameList->GetCount(&nCount);

            // If getting the count succeeded
            if(SUCCEEDED(hr))
            {
                // Iterate the list
                // Zero based collection here
                for(long i = 0; i < nCount; i++)
                {
                    // Get the server name
                    BSTR bstrServer;
                    hr = pNameList->GetItemByOrd(i, &bstrServer);
```

```
                    // If we got the name
                    if(SUCCEEDED(hr))
                    {
                        // Add it to list
                        LPCTSTR lpszItem = OLE2CT(bstrServer);
                        ASSERT(lpszItem);
                        m_ListServers.AddString(lpszItem);
                        SysFreeString(bstrServer);
                    }
                    else
                    {
                        TRACE1("Failed to get server %d\n", i);
                    }
                }
            }
            else
            {
                TRACE0("Couldn't get NameList count\n");
            }

            // Release our reference to
            // the NameList object
            pNameList->Release();
        }
        else
        {
            TRACE0("Failed to get ISQLDMONameList\n");
        }
    }
    else
    {
        TRACE0("Failed to create ISQLDMOApplication\n");
        return;
    }

    // Release our reference to the
    // Application object
    pApplication->Release();
}
```

Analyzing the ListServersRawCom Method I – Setting Up

The first line of code is used to enable the use of the conversion macros later in the routine:

```
void CListServersDlg::ListServersRawCom()
{
    // For conversion macros used below
    USES_CONVERSION;
```

USES_CONVERSION is declared before any of the conversion macros are used, and expands out to some local variable declarations that the conversion macros use when performing their character string conversions.

The next few lines clear the ListBox and add an item showing the method of server retrieval, and then instantiate a CWaitCursor object. The CWaitCursor object changes the mouse pointer to the hourglass when it is instantiated, and when it goes out of scope, the mouse cursor is restored:

```
// Clear the list box
m_ListServers.ResetContent();

m_ListServers.AddString(_T("Raw Com Calls:"));

// Wait cursor
CWaitCursor wait;
```

Once the setup for the routine is out of the way, the real work begins:

```
// Declare a pointer to an Application
ISQLDMOApplication* pApplication = NULL;

HRESULT hr;

// Create an instance and assign it to the pointer
hr = CoCreateInstance(CLSID_SQLDMOApplication,
                      NULL,
                      CLSCTX_INPROC_SERVER,
                      IID_IWSQLDMOApplication,
                      reinterpret_cast<void**>(&pApplication));
```

ISQLDMOApplication is declared in sqldmo.h, and is the name of the SQL-DMO Application interface. We declare a pointer of this type, and then call CoCreateInstance to create an instance of the object. We have five parameters to consider here:

❑ The first parameter, CLSID_SQLDMOApplication, is the GUID for the Application object. CoCreateInstance uses this GUID to look up the location of the Application object's server, in this case sqldmo.rll.

❑ The next parameter is set to NULL; we don't need to use this and it is beyond the scope of this discussion.

❑ The third parameter tells CoCreateInstance what type of server we want to create, and since SQL-DMO is hosted by an in-process DLL server, we will pass CLSCTX_INPROC_SERVER.

❑ The fourth parameter, IID_IWSQLDMOApplication, is the interface for which we would like a pointer. This is the interface type of which pApplication was declared.

❑ The last parameter is a pointer to the pApplication pointer, cast to be a pointer to a void pointer, which is the type CoCreateInstance expects.

> The interface names and GUIDs used in the sample code for the SQL-DMO
> interfaces were retrieved from **sqldmo.h** and **sqldmoid.h**. If you take a look at
> these files and search for the non-decorated names of the objects you are looking
> for, such as **Application** and **NameList**, you will find these declarations.
> Additionally, you can look at the SQL-DMO reference in Appendix D to see the
> methods and properties that each method supports. In some cases the C++ names
> may be slightly different, for example a **GetCount** method instead of a **Count**
> property in the case of the **NameList** object, but in most cases the intended
> meaning is clear.

CoCreateInstance returns an HRESULT, as do all raw COM methods (except the IUnknown
methods Addref and Release, which return unsigned long). Each COM method returns success
or failure through its HRESULT return value, and the success or failure of the call may be
determined through the use of the SUCCEEDED and FAILED macros:

```
// If the creation succeeded
if(SUCCEEDED(hr))
{
```

Analyzing the ListServersRawCom Method II – Enumerating the Servers

If the call to CoCreateInstance succeeded, then pApplication points to a valid SQL-DMO
Application object. We declare a pointer to the NameList interface, and pass this in to the
ListAvailableSQLServers method. ListAvailableSQLServers returns success or failure
through its HRESULT return value, and if the call was successful we query the NameList for the
count of servers:

```
// Declare a pointer to a NameList, and pass it to
// ListAvailableSQLServers
ISQLDMONameList* pNameList = NULL;
hr = pApplication->ListAvailableSQLServers(&pNameList);

// If we got a reference to a NameList
if(SUCCEEDED(hr))
{
    // Get the count of servers
    long nCount = 0;
    hr = pNameList->GetCount(&nCount);

    // If getting the count succeeded
    if(SUCCEEDED(hr))
    {
```

If the call to GetCount is successful, we enumerate the list of servers and add them to the ListBox.
Note that as we retrieve each server name, we check the HRESULT. If the call to get that particular
server failed, we output a debug message and continue.

```
                // Iterate the list
                // Zero based collection here
                for (long i = 0; i < nCount; i++)
                {
                   // Get the server name
                   BSTR bstrServer;
                   hr = pNameList->GetItemByOrd(i, &bstrServer);

                   // If we got the name
                   if(SUCCEEDED(hr))
                   {
                      // Add it to list
                      LPCTSTR lpszItem = OLE2CT(bstrServer);
                      ASSERT(lpszItem);
                      m_ListServers.AddString(lpszItem);
                      SysFreeString(bstrServer);
                   }
                   else
                   {
                      TRACE1("Failed to get server %d\n", i);
                   }
                }
```

There are a couple of items worth taking a second look at in this code. The first is the odd name of the method to retrieve the server names: `GetItemByOrd`:

```
   hr = pNameList->GetItemByOrd(i, &bstrServer);
```

Sometimes you have to decide which method to call based on a combination of the documentation, the interface declaration in the header files, and the parameters and types used. In this case, we need the `Item` property, which takes a numeric index and returns a string containing the server name. Looking at the `NameList` methods in the `sqldmo.h` header file, we see the following interface declaration:

```
   // Names enumerator object (LPSQLDMONAMELIST).
   #undef INTERFACE
   #define INTERFACE ISQLDMONameList
   DECLARE_INTERFACE_(INTERFACE, ISQLDMOStdObject)
   {
      //*** IUnknown methods
      STDMETHOD(QueryInterface) (THIS_ REFIID riid, LPVOID *ppvObj) PURE;
      STDMETHOD_(ULONG,AddRef) (THIS)  PURE;
      STDMETHOD_(ULONG,Release) (THIS) PURE;

         //*** SQLDMO standard object properties.
      STDMETHOD(GetApplication)(THIS_ LPSQLDMOAPPLICATION *ppApp) PURE;
      STDMETHOD(GetParent)(THIS_ LPSQLDMOSTDOBJECT *ppParent) PURE;
      STDMETHOD(GetTypeOf)(THIS_ SQLDMO_OBJECT_TYPE *pRetVal) PURE;
      STDMETHOD(GetUserData)(THIS_ LPVOID *pRetVal) PURE;
      STDMETHOD(SetUserData)(THIS_ LPVOID lpvNewValue) PURE;
```

```
//*** SQLDMO standard enumeration properties
    STDMETHOD(GetItemByOrd)(THIS_ long lOrdinal, SQLDMO_LPBSTR pRetVal) PURE;
    STDMETHOD(GetCount)(THIS_ LPLONG plCount) PURE;

//*** SQLDMO standard collection methods
    STDMETHOD(Refresh)(THIS) PURE;
    STDMETHOD(FindName)(THIS_ SQLDMO_LPCSTR szName, LPLONG pRetVal) PURE;

};
```

GetItemByOrd fits the bill, and so that's what we used.

Secondly, before we added the server name to the ListBox, we used the conversion macro OLE2CT to convert the BSTR into a null-terminated string of the appropriate data type for either Unicode or non-Unicode builds:

```
LPCTSTR lpszItem = OLE2CT(bstrServer);
```

OLE2CT takes a pointer to an OLE string, and returns a pointer to the string converted to T. T means that under ASCII and MBCS builds, the converted string will be 8 bit ASCII characters, and under Unicode builds, the string will be 16 bit Unicode characters. The C in OLE2CT means that the pointer to the converted string will be a const.

Since OLE characters are Unicode characters, under Unicode builds OLE2CT simply returns back a pointer to the string that was passed in. After this call, lpszItem points to the converted server name, and we can add it to the ListBox.

*For more information about the conversion macros, see the topic **String Conversion Macros** in the MSDN online library.*

Analyzing the ListServersRawCom Method III – Tidying Up

After we do this, we release the BSTR that was allocated inside the GetItemByOrd method:

```
SysFreeString(bstrServer);
```

We need to do this using SysFreeString since the memory for this string may have been allocated by another process.

The conversion macros use _alloca to acquire the memory in which to place the converted character string. This memory is declared on the stack and is not freed until the function in which it is allocated returns, not merely when the stack frame in which it is declared goes out of scope.

If you need to convert large character strings or do multiple conversions inside a single routine, it would be a good idea to put the code using the conversion macros into another function, and call these functions with your own buffer to receive a copy of the converted string.

Note that you must provide a buffer in which to return the string if you use this method. Since the converted string is placed on the stack you cannot return a pointer to the converted string. If your string to be converted is very large, (I use 256K as the limit for my apps) it is a good idea to break this string down into smaller pieces and convert each piece individually by passing it to your helper conversion function. If the conversion macros are called too many times or with strings that are too large, the stack will overflow and crash the application.

The next code closes off a couple of our `if` statements above. If the call to get the count of servers failed, we simply display a diagnostic message to the debug window:

```
    }
    else
    {
        TRACE0("Couldn't get NameList count\n");
    }
```

We then release our reference to the `NameList` object that we received when we called `ListAvailableSQLServers`. If the call to `ListAvailableSQLServers` failed, then we again display a simple diagnostic message:

```
        // Release our reference to
        // the NameList object
        pNameList->Release();
    }
    else
    {
        TRACE0("Failed to get ISQLDMONameList\n");
    }
```

The last code in the routine wraps up our work with the `Application` object:

```
    }
    else
    {
        TRACE0("Failed to create ISQLDMOApplication\n");
        return;
    }

    // Release our reference to the
    // Application object
    pApplication->Release();
}
```

If the call to `CoCreateInstance` failed at the beginning of the routine, we display a message and then exit. If it succeeded, we release our reference to the `Application` object before the routine exits.

Summary of Using Raw COM Calls

Using SQL-DMO with raw COM calls takes more code than the other two methods we are going to take a look at, but it is less dependent on any specific development environment. If you take away the MFC code that is used in this routine to support the sample, all of the code that used SQL-DMO is fairly generic and compiler independent. This code should work with any modern C++ compiler with little modification.

Next we'll look at how to use MFC `IDispatch` wrappers.

MFC IDispatch Wrappers

MFC provides an easy way to use COM objects that expose the `IDispatch` interface. `IDispatch` supports the notion of runtime discovery of methods and properties supported by the client of the object, and was developed to allow scripting of COM objects by interpreted languages, such as VB. SQL-DMO supports `IDispatch`, and MFC provides an easy way to use these objects by generating wrapper classes that have friendly method names and parameters, instead of the more generic `IDispatch` methods.

`IDispatch` has four methods in addition to the three `IUnknown` methods that all COM objects support. These additional methods are:

❑   `GetIDsOfNames`

❑   `GetTypeInfo`

❑   `GetTypeInfoCount`

❑   `Invoke`

`GetIDsOfNames` is used to map method and property names to integer constants known as `DispatchIDs`. A `DispatchID` is passed to the `Invoke` method along with an array of variants wrapped up in a `DISPPARAMS` structure that represents the parameters, to get the return value of the corresponding method, or the value of the corresponding property.

MFC's `COleDispatchDriver` class implements helper functions that use the `IDispatch` interface, and ClassWizard can be used to generate a wrapper class derived from `COleDispatchDriver` that includes the properties and methods of the object that have strongly typed arguments instead of the more generic variant.

Generating the Wrapper Classes

Our example uses the `Application` and the `NameList` objects, so we'll need to generate wrappers for these two classes. Press *Ctrl+W* to bring up ClassWizard, and choose From a type library... from the menu that drops down when the Add Class... button is clicked:

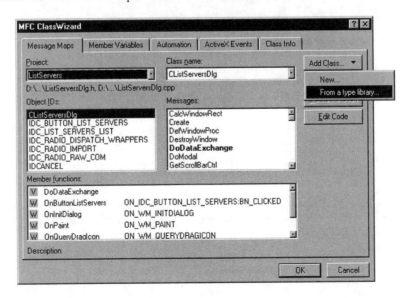

This brings up the Import from Type Library file open dialog:

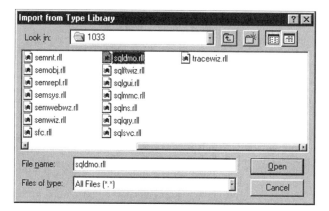

Navigate to `sqldmo.rll` and click **Open**. `Sqldmo.rll` can be found in the `MSSQL7\Binn\Resources\1033\` folder.

Once the file with the type information for the objects is selected, ClassWizard will prompt you to select the classes for which you wish to generate wrapper classes:

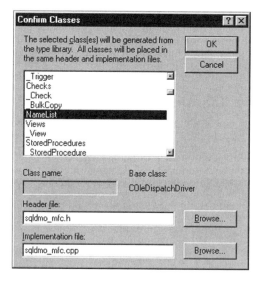

Select Application from the top of the list, and then scroll down and *Ctrl+Click* to additionally select NameList. ClassWizard will suggest filenames of `sqldmo.h` and `sqldmo.cpp` to hold these generated wrapper classes. Change these filenames to include `mfc` before the file extension to help avoid any naming conflicts with the `sqldmo.h` used in the previous section.

Click OK on finishing, and then click OK to dismiss ClassWizard. The files `sqldmo_mfc.h` and `sqldmo_mfc.cpp` will be created in your project directory and added to the project.

Implementing ListServersMFCDispatch

Open `ListServersMFCDispatch.cpp` and include our newly generated header file for the wrapper classes:

```
// ListServersMFCDispatch.cpp : implementation file
//

#include "stdafx.h"
#include "ListServers.h"
#include "ListServersDlg.h"

// Include Class Wizard generated wrappers
#include "sqldmo_mfc.h"
```

The complete code for the routine is:

```
void CListServersDlg::ListServersMFCDispatch()
{
    // Clear the list box
    m_ListServers.ResetContent();

    m_ListServers.AddString(_T("MFC Dispatch Wrappers:"));

    // Wait cursor
    CWaitCursor wait;

    // Declare an instance of the _Application wrapper class
    _Application app;

    // Create an instance and attach to the wrapper
    if(!app.CreateDispatch(_T("SQLDMO.Application")))
    {
        TRACE0("Failed to create application.\n");
        return;
    }

    // Get the IDispatch Interface to the NameList
    LPDISPATCH lpDisp = app.ListAvailableSQLServers();
    if(lpDisp == NULL)
    {
        TRACE0("Couldn't get NameList\n");
        return;
    }

    // Declare an instance of the NameList wrapper
    // and attach it to the returnd IDispatch pointer
    NameList list;
    list.AttachDispatch(lpDisp);

    // Get the count of servers
    long nCount = list.GetCount();
```

```
    // iterate the list and add each server name
    // to the listbox
    for(long i = 1; i <= nCount; i++)
    {
        CString strItem = list.Item(COleVariant(i));
        m_ListServers.AddString(strItem);
    }
}
```

Analyzing the ListServersMFCDispatch Code

The first few lines are straightforward as they clear out the ListBox, and bring up the hourglass cursor as in the previous example.

The next lines create an instance of our _Application wrapper class, and create an instance of a SQL-DMO Application object:

```
    // Declare an instance of the _Application wrapper class
    _Application app;

    // Create an instance and attach to the wrapper
    if(!app.CreateDispatch(_T("SQLDMO.Application")))
    {
        TRACE0("Failed to create application.\n");
        return;
    }
```

CreateDispatch creates an instance of the wrapped object type using the class ID parameter, SQLDMO.Application, queries it for the IDispatch interface, and then stores a pointer to this interface. This interface will be released by default when the wrapper class goes out of scope and is destroyed. If the call fails, the routine exits.

The next code calls ListAvailableSQLServers and is returned a pointer to the IDispatch interface of a NameList object. If the call is successful, we attach the NameList wrapper to the return IDispatch interface:

```
    // Get the IDispatch Interface to the NameList
    LPDISPATCH lpDisp = app.ListAvailableSQLServers();
    if(lpDisp == NULL)
    {
        TRACE0("Couldn't get NameList\n");
        return;
    }

    // Declare an instance of the NameList wrapper
    // and attach it to the returnd IDispatch pointer
    NameList list;
    list.AttachDispatch(lpDisp);
```

AttachDispatch takes a second parameter, BOOL bAutoRelease, which defaults to TRUE. When TRUE, this causes the wrapper class object, in this case NameList, to automatically release its reference to the IDispatch it wraps when the object is destroyed.

Once we have the `NameList` of servers, we can iterate the list and add the servers to the ListBox:

```
        // Get the count of servers
        long nCount = list.GetCount();

        // iterate the list and add each server name
        // to the listbox
        for(long i = 1; i <= nCount; i++)
        {
            CString strItem = list.Item(COleVariant(i));
            m_ListServers.AddString(strItem);
        }
    }
```

To retrieve the count of servers we call `GetCount`. The ClassWizard-generated wrappers implement properties with Get/Set pairs. Since `Count` is a read-only property of `NameList`, there is only a Get implementation for `Count`.

Note that the `Item` method takes a variant and not a long. We can work around this by wrapping our long variable in a `COleVariant`. `COleVariant` is an MFC class that wraps a variant and provides convenience methods such as conversion operators.

After enumerating the servers and adding them to the list, we are done with this method. When the `_Application` and `NameList` wrapper classes are destroyed, they will automatically release the references to the objects they wrap.

Summary of MFC IDispatch Wrappers

Using the MFC `IDispatch` wrappers can result in less application specific code that is simpler to read than the raw COM calls that were covered previously. These wrapper classes were introduced with Visual C++ 4.0, and until the release of Visual C++ 5.0 were the easiest way to quickly wrap and use a COM object in C++.

Visual C++ 5.0 introduced native compiler COM support, and the popularity of the MFC wrapper classes has declined since then in favor of the native support, which we examine in the next section.

Native Compiler COM Support

Native compiler COM support was introduced into Visual C++ with the release of Visual C++ 5.0. This support is implemented primarily by the `#import` directive, and by some smart pointers and `datatype` wrapper classes. Using COM objects via this native support results in code that looks very much like the code used to access objects in VB.

Using #import

The `#import` directive references a type library, or a file that contains a type library such as a DLL, and generates inline wrappers for the objects described by the type library. To add a reference to SQL-DMO from our application, add the following line near the top of the `ListServersImport.cpp` file:

```
// ListServersImport.cpp : implementation file
//

#include "stdafx.h"
#include "ListServers.h"
#include "ListServersDlg.h"

// Import the SQL DMO type library
#import "G:\MSSQL7\Binn\Resources\1033\sqldmo.rll"
```

> **Note, the drive is defined as G: here – if following this example through
> remember to change the download code as appropriate for your installation.**

Once this line is added, we can look in the output directory for our project, and we'll see two new
files:

❑ `sqldmo.tlh` – This file contains declarations of the objects and wrappers for the objects
  in the imported type library

❑ `sqldmo.tli` – This file contains generated inline implementations for the wrapper
  methods

You can open these files and take a look at them, but be sure to close them before editing the line
with the `#import` that generated these files. Visual Studio generates these files as soon as you type
the line with the `#import`, and regenerates them when the `#import` directive changes in any way.
If these files are open in the editor when the editor attempts to regenerate them, you will get a
seemingly endless stream of dialog boxes informing you of this fact.

If you do look in these files, you will see that everything is declared inside the SQL-DMO
namespace. This namespace is named for the library from which the declarations are imported.
This namespace scoping can be turned off by specifying `no_namespace` after the `#import`
directive. We are leaving it in place and will explicitly qualify the objects we reference from this
file with SQL-DMO.

Implementing ListServersImport

Here is the code for `ListServersImport`:

```
void CListServersDlg::ListServersImport()
{
    // Clear the list box
    m_ListServers.ResetContent();

    m_ListServers.AddString(_T("#import:"));

    // Wait cursor
    CWaitCursor wait;
```

```
    try
    {
        // Declare a smart pointer to an _Application
        SQLDMO::_ApplicationPtr spApp;

        // Create an instance of an _Application using __uuidof
        spApp.CreateInstance(__uuidof(SQLDMO::Application));

        // Declare a smart pointer to a NameList
        SQLDMO::NameListPtr spNameList;

        // Get the list of servers and assign to spNameList
        spNameList = spApp->ListAvailableSQLServers();

        // Get the count of servers
        long nCount = spNameList->GetCount();

        // Iterate the list and add to the listbox
        // 1 based
        for(long i = 1; i <= nCount; i++)
        {
            m_ListServers.AddString(
                static_cast<LPCTSTR>(spNameList->Item(_variant_t(i))));
        }
    }
    catch(const _com_error& Err)
    {
        // Disable variable unused warning
        // Not shown in the accompanying text
        #ifndef _DEBUG
            UNUSED_ALWAYS(Err);
        #endif

        TRACE2("Failed to List Servers.\nError: 0x%x\nDescription: %s\n",
               Err.Error(),
               static_cast<LPCTSTR>(Err.Description()));
    }
}
```

Analyzing the ListServersImport Code

The first few lines prepare the ListBox to receive the list of servers, and then the rest of the code is implemented inside a `try` block:

```
try
{
    ...
}
catch(const _com_error& Err)
{
    TRACE2("Failed to List Servers.\nError: 0x%x\nDescription: %s\n",
           Err.Error(),
           static_cast<LPCTSTR>(Err.Description()));
}
```

The wrappers generated by #import throw exceptions to signal error conditions. Taking a look at the wrapper's implementation of ListAvailableSQLServers, shows how this works:

```
inline SQLDMO::NameListPtr SQLDMO::_Application::ListAvailableSQLServers ( ) {
    struct NameList * _result;
    HRESULT _hr = raw_ListAvailableSQLServers(&_result);
    if (FAILED(_hr)) _com_issue_errorex(_hr, this, __uuidof(this));
    return NameListPtr(_result, false);
}
```

The function checks the HRESULT from the call to the raw COM method that this wrapper method implements, and throws an exception if the call fails. Our catch block simply outputs a debug message. The rest of the code in this function may be unfamiliar now but will be covered as we step through the rest of the example.

When using the _com_ptr_t wrappers, all of the raw interface methods are available and have raw_ *prefixed to the method name. Properties are prefixed with* get_ *and* put_. *These methods and properties may be accessed directly as described in the section on using raw COM calls.*

The code inside the try block is where all the action takes place, and that's what we are interested in. The first lines declare and create an instance of the SQL-DMO Application object:

```
// Declare a smart pointer to an _Application
SQLDMO::_ApplicationPtr spApp;

// Create an instance of an _Application using __uuidof
spApp.CreateInstance(__uuidof(SQLDMO::Application));
```

The smart pointers that encapsulate the raw interfaces are named for the interface and have Ptr appended to the name. These are template specializations of the built-in COM smart pointer template class _com_ptr_t. CreateInstance has several overloads, one of which takes a CLSID. The __uuidof operator directly retrieves this from the interface name.

The #import directive has several options, one of which is the named_guids option. If named_guids is appended to the #import declaration in the code, named GUIDs will be generated in the .tlh header. If this option is specified, the above line could be written:

```
// Can do this way when using named_guids
spApp.CreateInstance(SQLDMO::CLSID_Application);
```

The next stage in the process is to declare a smart pointer to a NameList, and then assign it the results of the call to ListAvailableSQLServers:

```
// Declare a smart pointer to a NameList
SQLDMO::NameListPtr spNameList;

// Get the list of servers and assign to spNameList
spNameList = spApp->ListAvailableSQLServers();
```

Once this is done, we can retrieve the count of servers from the NameList, iterate through the list, and add the server names to the ListBox:

```
// Get the count of servers
long nCount = spNameList->GetCount();

// Iterate the list and add to the listbox
// 1 based
for(long i = 1; i <= nCount; i++)
{
   m_ListServers.AddString(
      static_cast<LPCTSTR>(spNameList->Item(_variant_t(i))));
}
```

Properties may be accessed not only via get and set members, but also by directly referencing the property name. The first line of code above could also have been written as:

```
// Property style access
long nCount = spNameList->Count;
```

If we set a breakpoint here and stepped into the code, we would end up in the GetCount wrapper implementation. This is because of the way that the Count data member of the wrapper class was declared.

Inspection of the generated sqldmo.tli file will reveal, in the declaration for the NameList interface, the following apparent data member declaration:

```
__declspec(property(get=GetCount))
long Count;
```

This tells the compiler that any read access to the Count data member should be mapped to a call to GetCount, and since there is no put method specified, the data member is read only. There will be no Count data member added to the class, and any access to Count will be mapped through the designated read and write functions.

The server names are retrieved through the Item method. Item takes a _variant_t, which is a wrapper for the VARIANT type. The _variant_t wrapper has an overloaded constructor for a long, so we wrap our long index with _variant_t and pass it to the method:

```
m_ListServers.AddString(
   static_cast<LPCTSTR>(spNameList->Item(_variant_t(i))));
```

Item returns _bstr_t, which is a wrapper around the BSTR type. This wrapper has assignment operators and other convenience methods, and also handles the memory allocation and de-allocation for the BSTR that it wraps. This wrapper also has operators for returning a NULL-terminated C string pointer to its internal data.

After listing all of the servers, the try block is exited and the smart pointers go out of scope and are destroyed. As they are destroyed, they automatically release the references they hold on the internal objects.

At this point we can build and run the sample and should (fingers crossed) have a fully working application:

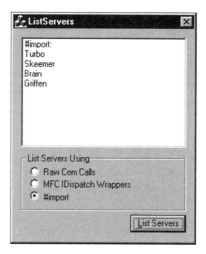

Summary of Compiler COM Support

The compiler COM support provides the ease of use that the MFC `IDispatch` wrapper classes provide without the overhead of calling methods through the `IDispatch` interface and without the dependency on MFC. The direct access to the raw interface is available but its use is not required. All of the `HRESULT` checking and reference counting is implemented by wrapper classes, which reduces the code that has to be written to use COM objects. In turn this can improve readability and reduce the chance for errors to be introduced.

Summary

In this chapter we've developed a simple example application that has enabled us to enumerate available SQL Servers via the `ListAvailableSQLServers` method of the `SQLDMO.Application` object.

We started the chapter by setting up our example in VB to provide a reference point with the code that we've seen in previous chapters. We then moved on to look at three ways to use SQL-DMO with Visual C++. Along the way we have taken a brief look at COM and how to use COM components with Visual C++.

During the course of the chapter we've seen how to work with raw COM calls, we've seen how to use MFC wrappers around COM objects that support the `IDispatch` interface, and we've seen that using the compiler COM support that was introduced with Visual C++ 5.0 combines the best of the previous two approaches. This native support provides us with low overhead wrappers that handle the bookkeeping and provide friendly method and property access through encapsulation of `HRESULTS` and data type wrappers such as `_bstr_t` and `_variant_t`.

Within this chapter we've really moved through the code and in some ways have glossed over a few areas that are well worth exploring in more detail but fell outside the scope of this book. To finish up let's offer a few hints for where to go for further information:

❑ **SQL-DMO** – We've been brief with our coverage of using SQL-DMO in this chapter, but for further information on topics covered in this book the SQL Server Books Online is useful. The VB Object Browser and OLE View can also be used to get more information on the SQL-DMO objects or any COM objects.

❑ **COM Resources** – The Microsoft Developer Network Library has got comprehensive documentation of the COM support available in Visual C++. The `Platform SDK\Component Services\COM` is the location for the MSDN documentation on COM. The `COleDispatchDriver` topic has links to several related topics on OLE Automation as well as documentation on the `COleDispatchDriver` wrapper classes generated by ClassWizard. The `#import` topic and the Compiler COM Support Classes topic has information on using the built-in compiler support for using COM objects.

Of course Wrox Press has a number of books that you might find useful if you want to really delve into some of these topics. Our suggestions are:

❑ *Beginning ATL 3 COM Programming, Richard Grimes et al, ISBN 1-861001-20-7,* has a solid introduction to COM using raw COM calls, and also has good coverage of using COM objects with the native COM compiler support. This book also has a thorough introduction on writing COM components using ATL.

❑ *Beginning MFC COM Programming, Julian Templeman, ISBN 1-874416-87-7,* contains comprehensive coverage of all things COM relating to MFC, including information on `COleDispatchDriver` and ClassWizard generated `IDispatch` wrapper classes.

❑ *Professional MFC with Visual C++ 6, Mike Blaszczak, ISBN 1-861000-15-4,* covers all things MFC, including `COleDispatchDriver`, and using COM components from within MFC applications.

The Surveys Unlimited Application

This appendix lists the modules used in each of the projects that form the Surveys Unlimited solution.

CustomerManager

Module Type	Name	Filename	Description
Class	Survey	Survey.cls	This module implements a method that logs a survey and its owner into the `CustomerManagement` database.

SQLDDL and SQLDDL_Local

Module Type	Name	Filename	Description
Standard	Strings	Strings.bas	This module contains the string constants used when raising errors.

Table Continued on Following Page

Module Type	Name	Filename	Description
Class	BackupDB	BackupDB.cls	This module implements the methods for backup and restore.
Class	Constants	Constants.cls	This module contains the Public enumerations for error numbers and column attributes.
Class	Database	Database.cls	This module implements methods that create, enumerate, and manage databases.
Class	Management	Management.cls	This module implements methods that retrieve information about and create jobs.
Class	Security	Security.cls	This module implements methods for creating and managing logins and users.
Class	Server	Server.cls	This module implements methods for establishing and managing a connection, as well as methods related to enumerating and managing the SQL Server.

SurveyDesigner

Module Type	Name	Filename	Description
Standard	modGlobals	modGlobals.bas	This module contains public variables used throughout the client application.
Form	frmAddDev	frmAddDev.frm	This form is used to gather the information necessary to create a backup device.
Form	frmAddLogin	frmAddLogin.frm	This form is used to gather the information necessary to create a SQL Server login.
Form	frmAddUser	frmAddUser.frm	This form is used to gather the information necessary to create a database user.

Module Type	Name	Filename	Description
Form	frmBackDev	frmBackDev.frm	This form is used to list the backup devices on the server and to add and delete backup devices.
Form	frmBackup	frmBackup.frm	This form is used to initiate a full backup.
Form	frmColumns	frmColumns.frm	This form is used to define a new column.
Form	frmConnect	frmConnect.frm	This form is used to enter the information necessary to establish a SQL-DMO connection to a database.
Form	frmCreateDB	frmCreateDB.frm	This form is used to enter the customer and survey names and to initiate the creation of a new database.
Form	frmDBUser	frmDBUser.frm	This form is used to list the database users in a particular database, and to add and delete users.
Form	frmDesign	frmDesign.frm	This form is used to view information about and design a database schema.
Form	frmJob	frmJob.frm	This form is used to configure and create a job.
Form	frmKey	frmKey.frm	This form is used to list key candidates and select a column to be the primary key.
Form	frmLogin	frmLogin.frm	This form is used to list, add, and delete logins.
MDIForm	frmMDIMain	frmMDIMain.frm	This form is the parent form. It is also the Startup form. All menus are created on frmMDIMain.
Form	frmMove	frmMove.frm	This form is used to move a database from one server to another.

Table Continued on Following Page

Module Type	Name	Filename	Description
Form	frmRelationship	frmRelationship.frm	This form is used to set foreign key relationships.
Form	frmRestore	frmRestore.frm	This form is used to initiate a database restore.
Form	frmServerConfig	frmServerConfig.frm	This form is used to display and modify SQL Server configuration settings and to display server attributes.
Form	frmWaiting	frmWaiting.frm	This form displays a dialog while the SQL Server shuts down to release a database being moved.

Installing and Configuring MTS

Microsoft Transaction Server 2.0 is available in the Windows NT 4.0 Option Pack, which is included with both the Professional and Enterprise editions of Visual Studio 6.0. It is located on CD-ROM #2 inside the `NTOptPk` folder. This folder contains an `x86` folder, which in turn contains three subfolders: `Win.95`, `Winnt.srv`, and `Winnt.wks`. These folders contain the installation files for Windows 95/98, Windows NT Server, and Windows NT Workstation, respectively:

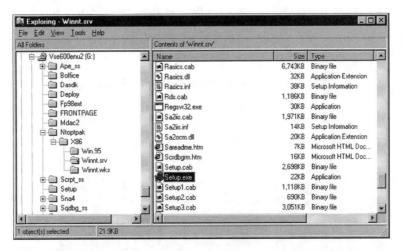

The Windows NT 4.0 Option Pack is also available for download at `http://www.microsoft.com/ntserver/nts/downloads/`. However, be warned: it's a 27 MB download.

To install Microsoft Transaction Server, launch `Setup.exe` from the appropriate subdirectory.

> **If you are running Windows NT Service Pack 4 or later, you will be warned that the Option Pack has not been tested on that service pack. Click on Yes to continue. After installation, you should reinstall the service pack you were running in order to restore versions of DLLs that were replaced by the Windows NT 4.0 Option Pack.**

A welcome screen listing the components that are included in the Windows NT 4.0 Option Pack will be displayed:

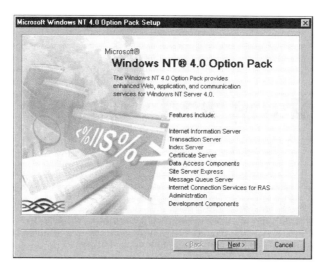

Click on Next to continue. You will be shown a license agreement. After you have read it, click on Accept to agree to its terms and continue with installation. The next screen allows you to choose a minimal, typical or custom installation. Both a minimal and a typical installation install Internet Information Server. Since we are only interested in Transaction Server, click on Custom here:

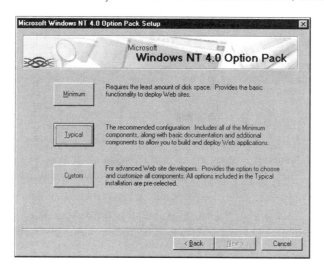

The next screen allows you to choose the parts of the option pack you would like to install. The components that are installed during a typical installation are selected by default:

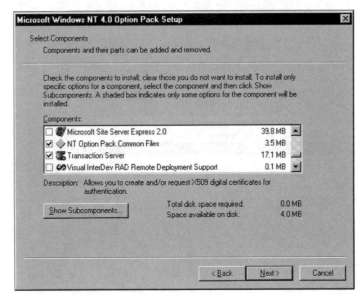

The only components required for running Microsoft Transaction Server are:

❑ Microsoft Data Access Components

❑ Microsoft Management Console

❑ NT Option Pack Common Files

❑ Transaction Server

> **If you are already running Internet Information Server 4.0, some of these components will already be installed on the computer.**

Feel free to clear the check box of any other components you don't wish to install. You will also want to install all of the components of Transaction Server. Either click in the Transaction Server check box twice, or select Transaction Server and click on Show Subcomponents.... By default, the Transaction Server Development components are not selected. Click to select them:

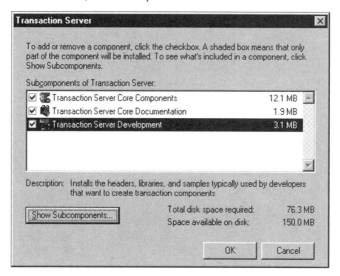

The Transaction Server Development components include the libraries you will need to call from Visual Basic. They also include a Visual Basic add-in you can use to update the MTS package with the latest version of your component as you make changes:

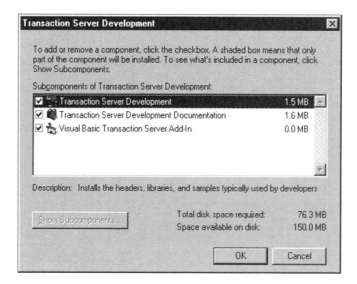

Once you have finished selecting the subcomponents you'd like to install, close all of the subcomponent dialogs by clicking on OK and click on Next to continue the installation. If you are only installing Transaction Server and the components it depends on, you will next be asked to choose a destination for the Transaction Server files:

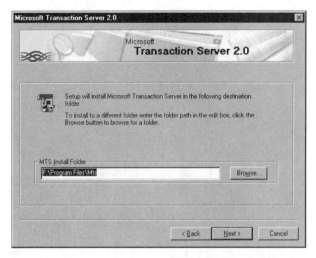

Once you have selected a destination, click on Next to continue. When MTS is installed, it automatically defaults to Local administration where MTS is configured by default to allow administration for the interactive user (the user that is currently logged on to the machine). If you want to enable remote administration, you should select the option button labeled Remote and then enter a login ID and password for an administrator account:

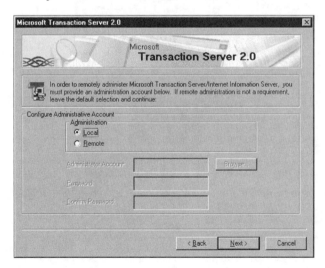

Setup will copy the appropriate files to your computer. You will need to restart after the files have been copied.

Looking Ahead – Windows 2000 as an Application Server

Perhaps your organization already has Windows 2000 servers in the environment or maybe there are plans to deploy them soon. If that's the case, you may already be familiar with the added benefits Windows 2000 offers to application developers, may have already installed an application into the **Component Services Manager** and understand what **COM+** is.

On the other hand, if you haven't yet begun developing applications for Windows 2000 (and are wondering what we're on about), this appendix is provided to whet your appetite. It's not going to be a highly technical section and we won't be providing any actual code. What we *will* attempt to do over the next few pages is to indicate how COM is evolving with the release of Windows 2000.

So in order we're going to:

❑   Outline component services in Windows 2000 and walk through the installation of the MTS package we've already built, into the Component Services Manager

❑   Show how to use the Component Services Manager to export proxy information that clients can use to connect to the server

❑   Describe some aspects of the changes to security handling implemented in Windows 2000

Originally at this point we were going to discuss objects related to managing **IMDB** (**In-Memory Databases**) but in September of 1999, Microsoft announced that IMDB would not form part of Windows 2000.

> The screen shots contained in this appendix were taken using Release Candidate 3.
> There is potential that some of the detail here may change.

Component Services in Windows 2000

In Windows 2000, COM becomes COM+. By the time you've got this far through the book, you'll have gained some awareness of Microsoft Transaction Server so you will find many of the features we'll discuss here familiar. You see, part of the + in COM+ is MTS. COM+ doesn't stop there though, it includes a variety of other features that allow us to more easily create enterprise applications, some of which will be discussed here.

One of the primary goals of COM+ is to provide a better application infrastructure right in the operating system and to allow components and their participation in this infrastructure to be managed from a centralized location.

Our first task is to install the MTS package we created earlier in the book, during the business scenario, onto a Windows 2000 server. But, before we get into the actual procedure, let's clear up some terminology.

MTS Package = COM+ Application

When coming up with the terminology that would be used to describe things under Windows 2000, Microsoft decided that the term **package** was not really a good way to describe a grouping of components, and in my opinion they were right. For one thing, Microsoft had already begun using the term *package* to describe the process used to prepare an application for deployment. For another, the word *package* doesn't have dynamic connotations. It's something that arrives on your doorstep the day before your birthday with your best friend's address inscribed in the upper-left corner. Granted, this is quite pleasing, but it doesn't have much to do with components working together toward a common goal.

Instead, Microsoft decided to use the term **application** to refer to a grouping of components running under **COM+**. At first, their choice of this term may seem equally confusing – after all, the word *application* is nearly a household term in its current meaning of an executable you launch to perform some function. But, if you consider Microsoft's long-term vision of computing, their choice of the term *application* is neither odd nor confusing. Remember under the Windows DNA architecture, an *application* is a set of distributed components, providing services to a consumer.

Microsoft is working hard to position Windows 2000 (and particularly the **AppCenter Server** service – see below – that's expected to be released in 2000) as the preferred platform for running enterprise applications. The particular types of enterprise applications it's designed to run are really groupings of COM+ components that can either run on a single computer or be spread across many computers in the enterprise. These components work together toward a common goal and are therefore not really very different from the monolithic executable we are used to calling an application; they are just designed and built a little differently. So, just as a penthouse apartment is just as much a home to a city-dweller as a two-story house is to a suburban resident, a COM+ application is really just an application built for the 21st century enterprise.

On September 13, 1999, Microsoft announced AppCenter Server, a deployment and management service built on Windows 2000, that includes additional functionality for managing middle-tier components. One feature of AppCenter Server will be Component Load Balancing Services (CLBS). CLBS will provide automatic load balancing and fail-over support for components. Aside from this initial announcement, Microsoft is being tight-lipped (at least as of the date this book went to press) about the features and anticipated ship date of AppCenter Server.

OK, let's see how all this looks in practice.

Launching the *Component Services Manager*

The **Component Services Manager** is a Microsoft Management Console snap-in that allows you to manage COM+ applications, MTS components, and even standard COM components. It is one of the Administrative Tools installed with Windows 2000.

It can be launched either by opening the Administrative Tools icon in Control Panel or from Start | Programs | Administrative Tools | Component Services Manager or it can be launched from the Run dialog by entering `SystemRoot\System32\com\comexp.msc`:

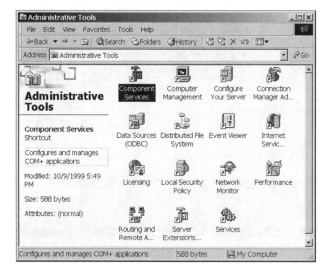

By default, the Component Services Manager can be used to manage components on the local computer. However, other computers can be added to the console, allowing you to manage multiple computers from a single location.

To add a computer to your console, open the Computers folder and either right-click on it or drop-down the Action menu and run New | Computer:

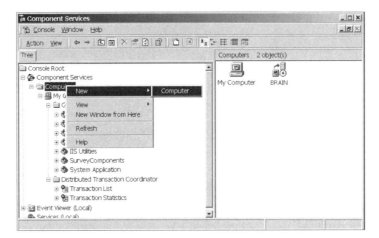

You'll be prompted for the name of the computer you wish to add:

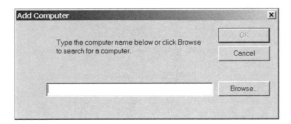

Clicking on Browse...displays a list of computers:

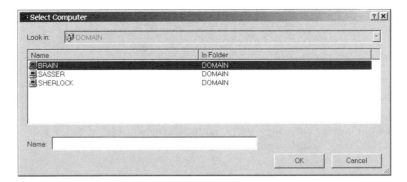

Select the computer you wish to manage and click on OK, then confirm your selection in the subsequent Add Computer dialog.

The new computer should now be visible:

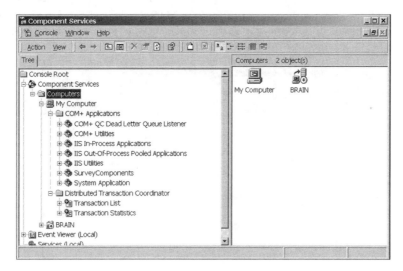

Although you can add Windows NT computers through this dialog to the console, you cannot administer MTS packages on those computers from the Component Services Manager. For example, the graphic shows the server BRAIN added to the console. BRAIN is a Windows NT Server 4.0 computer with MTS installed and packages configured. When you expand BRAIN, you can see a folder for COM+ Applications. However, when you try to open it, you will receive an error that the server catalog version is not supported:

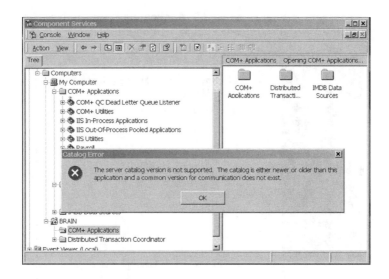

Installing an MTS Package into Component Services Manager

To install an MTS package (here we're installing the MTS package we exported in the deployment chapter, hence the old terminology) as a COM+ application, expand the tree to locate the COM+ Applications folder. Double-click on its icon to open it:

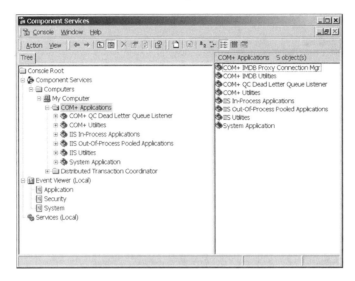

Notice that by default, COM+ Applications contains similar objects to those contained under the MTS Packages icon in Microsoft Transaction Server.

To install the MTS package, right-click on COM+ Applications and run New | Application. The COM Application Install Wizard's Welcome screen will be displayed:

Click on Next to continue. As previously, when we added packages under MTS, we'll get a somewhat familiar prompt asking if we'd like to install a pre-built application or create a new empty application:

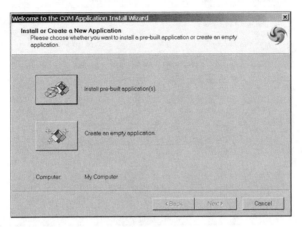

Click on Install pre-built application(s). A dialog will be displayed allowing the application we want to install to be located. By default, the filter is set to show only Windows Installer files (.msi files – discussed later), so change it to display MTS packages (.pak files):

Selecting SurveyComponents.PAK and clicking on Open will list the application:

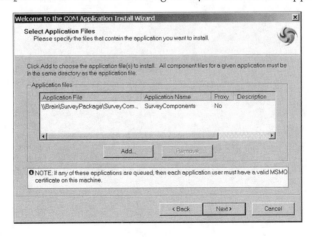

We can add additional applications here if we want to, but in this case we'll continue to the next screen where we are prompted to select an identity for the application:

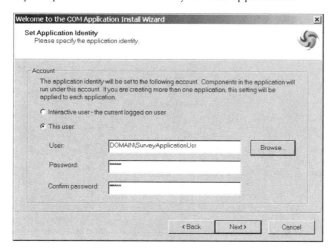

If you're using Windows 2000 in an **Active Directory** environment, there have been some enhancements to what an application running under a particular identity can do – we'll discuss that a little later.

> *Active Directory is the new directory services architecture released with Windows 2000. In order to provide a smooth migration, you have the option of running Windows 2000 using either the traditional domain architecture (to provide backward compatibility while Windows NT 4 computers are still on the network) or in a full Active Directory environment. Some features are only available when all servers on the network are running Windows 2000.*

Once the user is configured, click on Next to continue and select the location to which the application should be installed and whether or not to include the user mappings in the defined roles:

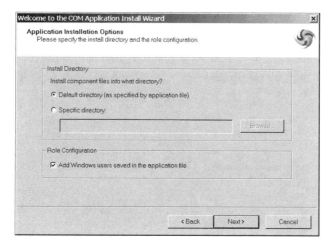

The default location to install components is $d:\Program Files\COM+$
$Applications\CLSID$, where d is the drive where the operating system is installed and $CLSID$ is the GUID associated with the COM+ application. Click on **Next** to continue, then click on **Finish**; the components will be copied to the specified directory and the necessary entries made in the Windows Registry:

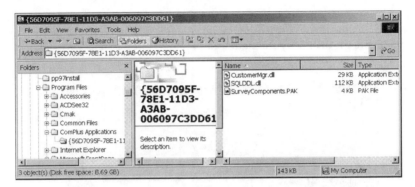

As with MTS, you can export information that allows COM+ applications to be installed on different servers and that provides the proxy information client computers will need to connect to and use the services provided by the COM+ application. This is the next area we'll look at.

Exporting Proxy Information

The major difference between MTS and COM+ in regard to the export of proxy information is that COM+ exports .msi (Windows Installer) files. These files are used by the **Windows Installer** to install files where necessary and to make the required modifications to the registry.

The Component Services Manager allows you to export two types of .msi files:

❑ **Server application** files

❑ **Application proxy** files

Windows Installer is a built-in installation program that will provide a uniform installation interface across multiple applications. Its basic premise is that providing a single interface will make installation easier for users and for network administrators. To allow an application to be installed by the Windows Installer, you must provide an .msi file that describes the features you are making available and the components they require. Users will be presented with a list of features, but will never have to be concerned with the underlying components required to implement them.

> Windows Installer comes bundled as part of Windows 2000. However, if you are running Microsoft Office 2000, you have already installed the Windows Installer, regardless of whether you are running Windows 95, Windows 98, or Windows NT 4.

Exporting the Server application file is similar to exporting an MTS package (again we refer to a package here, as we're referring back to MTS), except that the file is saved in the `.msi` file format used by Windows 2000 and the Windows Installer. The Application Proxy file contains configuration information that allows a client application to be configured to connect to and use the COM+ application.

To export proxy information, right-click on the COM+ Applications icon in Component Services Manager and run Export...from the popup menu. A Welcome screen will be displayed. Click on Next to obtain a prompt to specify the path and filename to be created, as well as the type of export which is about to be performed:

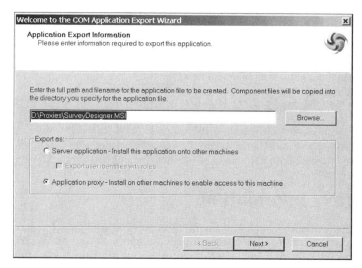

Browse to select where you would like to store the file and name the file. Select the option allowing export of the application proxy information, click on Next to perform the export, and after a minute or so (hopefully) a success screen will be shown indicating the end of the process:

Clicking on Finish closes the COM Application Export Wizard.

Now the client computers can be configured by running the .msi file with the Windows Installer. In an Active Directory environment, the .msi file can be published using **Group Policies**, further simplifying deployment.

Group policies allow system administrators to make applications available to users via a publish and subscribe metaphor. Administrators can choose whether the application is installed immediately or the first time the user launches the shortcut to the application. Configuration of group policies and other Active Directory features are beyond the scope of this book.

Now that we've dealt with component handling, let's have a look at the relevant changes to security handling that come with Windows 2000.

Security Changes Under Windows 2000

The two particularly important changes associated with configuring and running COM+ applications are:

❑   Delegation

❑   Method-level security

Let's take a brief look at each of these.

Delegation

Under Windows NT 4.0, a server component could **impersonate** (act under the security context of) the user running the consumer when accessing resources on the computer where the server component was running, but could not impersonate the consumer when it needed to access a resource across machine boundaries. This was a substantial limitation when it came to spreading components across multiple machines because a user's true identity was lost by the time the second machine boundary was crossed.

To make this a little clearer, consider a situation where there is a user named John who is accessing ComponentA on a middle-tier server named AcctSvcs. ComponentA would know that it was being accessed by a user named John.

Now, if that component called ComponentB on the same computer, ComponentB would also know that John was the user. However, if ComponentA tried to call ComponentC on another middle-tier server (say called ProductSvcs) then ComponentC would know only that it was being accessed by the account used by ComponentA. It would have no knowledge that the originator of the call was John.

Windows 2000 allows a server component to use **delegation** (use the security context of the actual user) to access resources on other machines on behalf of the user. This is illustrated in the following diagram:

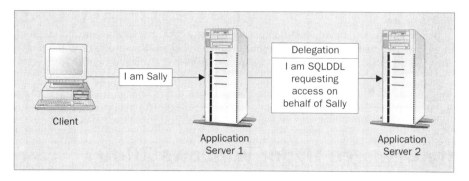

This indicates that a user called Sally can launch the SurveyDesigner application and have her Windows NT logon credentials known to any other computer whose services the SQLDDL component invokes.

For example, if we decided to deploy the CustomerManagement component to a separate computer, either for scalability or geographical convenience, the CustomerManagement component would be able to know of Sally's actual identity.

Method-Level Security

Under Microsoft Transaction Server, we were limited to defining role-based security at a component-level or interface-level granularity. In the context of our sample application this means that we were able to restrict access to the Backup component, for example, but *all* users who had any sort of access to the Server component had access to *all* of its functionality.

Windows 2000 allows us to grant roles permission to specific methods of a component. Let's take a quick look at how it works, using the Server component as an example.

Previously, we defined three roles for our application:

❑   BackupOperators

❑   SecurityManagers

❑   SurveyDesigners

For our discussion, let's assume that we would like to allow the SecurityManagers full access to each method exposed by the SQLDDL.Server component, but we would like to restrict the SurveyDesigners' and BackupOperators' access to ConnectSQLServer, DisconnectSQLServer, GetVersionNumber, IsConnected, IsRunning, IsStopped, and ServerNames.

> Note that while the discussion here may seem to indicate that we can arbitrarily make these decisions and configure a new security model without opening any source code, in reality we would need to carefully consider how we are going to handle the access denied condition in the client application.

To implement this security model, first we'll grant the `SecurityManagers` role permission to the entire `SQLDDL.Server` component. To do this, right-click on **SQLDDL.Server** in Component Services Manager, run **Properties** and click on the **Security** tab:

Make sure the **Enforce component level access checks** option is enabled. Place a check mark in the **SecurityManagers** checkbox. Click on **OK** to close the dialog.

Next, expand the tree until you locate the **ConnectSQLServer** method:

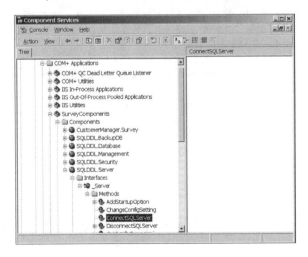

Next, right-click on the ConnectSQLServer method, run Properties and click on the Security tab. Notice that the SecurityManagers role already has permission to this method – the permissions were inherited from the component level:

Place a check mark in the box next to SurveyCreators and BackupOperators. Click on OK to save the changes and then repeat the process for each method you wish SurveyCreators and BackupOperators to have access to.

Summary

In this appendix we've briefly looked at how, in Windows 2000, COM becomes COM+ and have outlined three aspects of Windows 2000 technology that are related to topics we've come across earlier in the book. Specifically in this appendix we've:

❑ Walked through the installation of a previously built MTS package into the Component Services Manager

❑ Showed how to use the Component Services Manager to export proxy information

❑ Looked at the changes to security handling that are made in Windows 2000

D

Microsoft SQL Distributed Management Objects Library Reference

The object model is shown diagrammatically below. The gray boxes represent collection objects and the white boxes represent objects. The main object hierarchy is shown overleaf; other parts of the hierarchy are shown in subsidiary diagrams and are referenced accordingly.

SQL-DMO Object Hierarchy – Main Tree

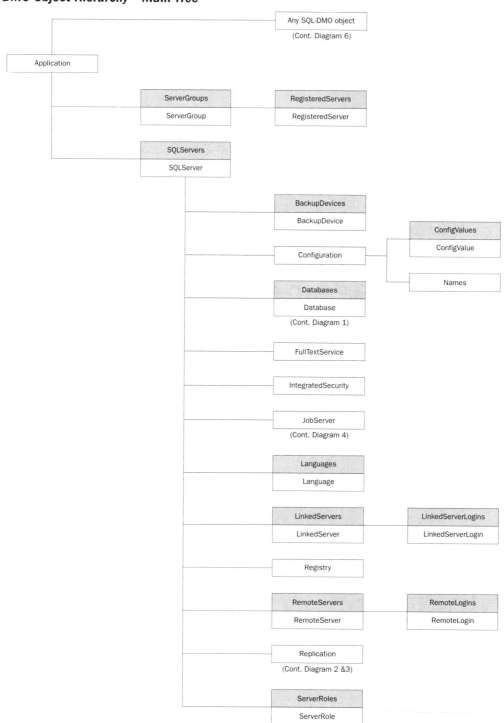

Subsidiary Diagram 1 – Database Objects

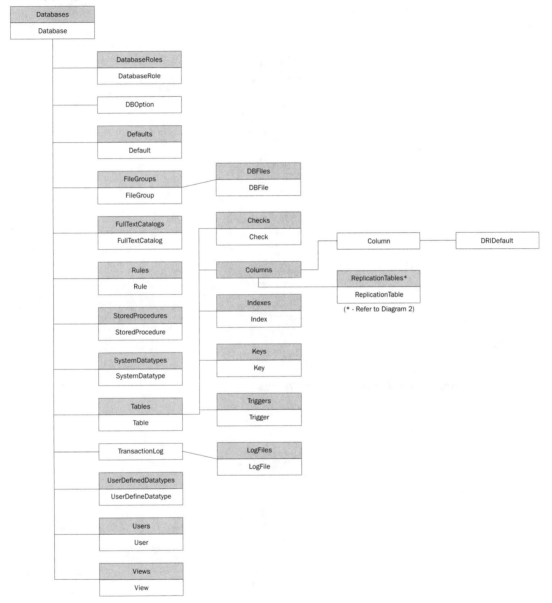

Subsidiary Diagram 2 – Replication and Replication Database Objects

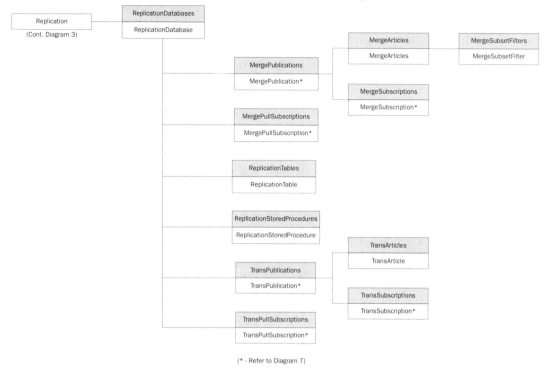

(* - Refer to Diagram 7)

Subsidiary Diagram 3 – Further Replication Objects

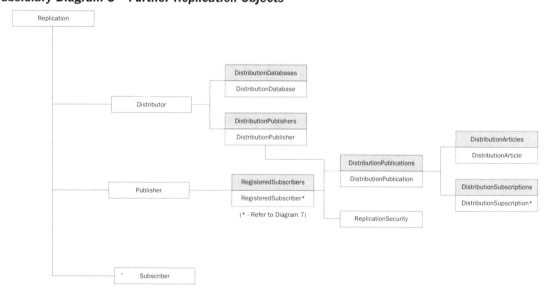

Subsidiary Diagram 4 – JobServer Objects

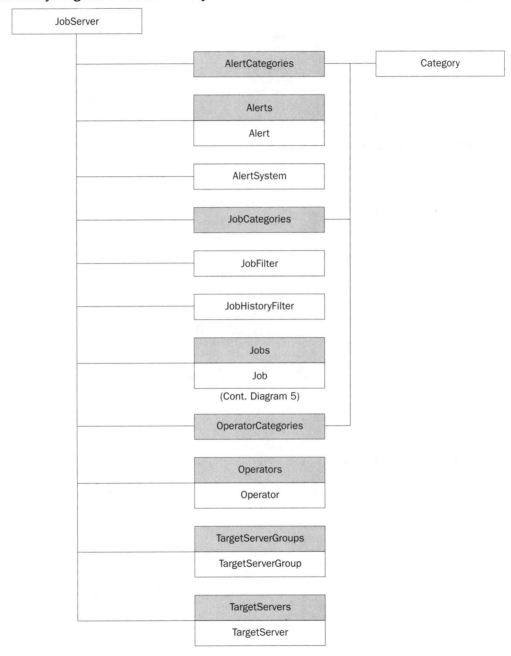

Subsidiary Diagram 5 – Jobs Objects

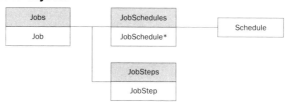

(* - Refer to Diagram 7)

Subsidiary Diagram 6 – Additional Objects

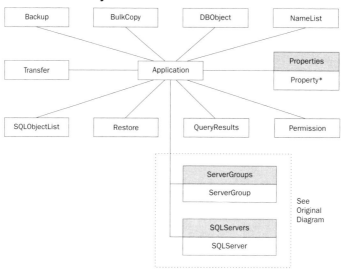

*NB - Not accessible via C/C++

Subsidiary Diagram 7 – Objects Related to the Schedule Object

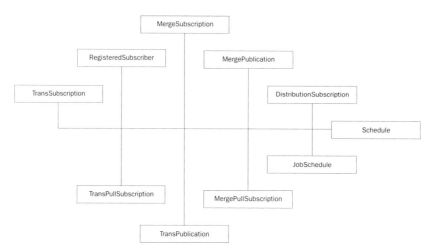

Library File Location

> The source file that contains the Distributed Management Object library is located at `<Drive>:\MSSQL7\Binn\Resources\sqldmo.dll`.

Objects

Name	Description
Alert	Represents a single SQL Server Agent alert.
AlertCategories	A collection containing `Category` objects that reference SQL Server Agent alert categories
Alerts	A collection of SQL Server Agent alerts.
AlertSystem	The properties of the SQL Server Agent alert notification system.
Application	The properties of the SQL-DMO objects and the user application.
Backup	Defines a Microsoft SQL Server database or log backup operation.
BackupDevice	Defines a Microsoft SQL Server database or log backup device.
BackupDevices	A collection of `BackupDevice` objects.
BulkCopy	Used as a parameter to the `ImportData` method of the `Table` object and the `ExportData` method of the `Table` and `View` objects.
Category	Object represents the attributes of a SQL Server Agent alert, job, or operator category.
Check	Represents the attributes of a single Microsoft SQL Server integrity constraint.
Checks	A collection of `Check` objects.
Column	Represents the properties of a single column in a Microsoft SQL Server table.
Columns	A collection of `Column` objects.
Configuration	Represents Microsoft SQL Server engine-configurable parameters and values.
ConfigValue	The attributes of a single Microsoft SQL Server configuration option.

Table Continued on Following Page

Name	Description
ConfigValues	A collection of ConfigValue objects.
Database	Represents the properties of a single database in a Microsoft SQL Server.
DatabaseRole	The properties of a single database role.
DatabaseRoles	A collection of DatabaseRole objects.
Databases	A collection of Database objects.
DBFile	The properties of an operating system file used by SQL Server for table and index data storage.
DBFiles	A collection of DBFile objects.
DBObject	The properties of a Database object (for example, a table, or stored procedure).
DBOption	The settings for SQL Server database options.
Default	The properties of a single SQL Server default.
Defaults	A collection of Default objects.
DistributionArticle	Exposes the attributes of a Distributor's image of replicated articles.
DistributionArticles	A collection of DistributionArticle objects.
DistributionDatabase	A database located at a Distributor that is used to store replication data.
DistributionDatabases	A collection of DistributionDatabase objects.
DistributionPublication	The properties of a Distributor's image of a snapshot, transactional, or merge replication publication.
DistributionPublications	A collection of DistributionPublication objects.
DistributionPublisher	A Publisher that is utilizing the Distributor for replication.
DistributionPublishers	A collection of DistributionPublisher objects.
DistributionSubscription	The properties of a subscription to a publication.
DistributionSubscriptions	A collection of DistributionSubscription objects.
Distributor	The replication Distributor for a server running SQL Server.

Name	Description
DRIDefault	The properties of a SQL Server column default constraint.
FileGroup	The attributes of a SQL Server filegroup.
FileGroups	A collection of SQL Server FileGroup objects.
FullTextCatalog	The properties of a single Microsoft search persistent data store.
FullTextCatalogs	A collection of FullTextCatalog objects.
FullTextService	The attributes of the Microsoft Search full-text indexing service.
Index	The attributes of a single SQL Server index.
Indexes	A collection of Index objects.
IntegratedSecurity	The parameters that affect the logins to SQL Server regardless of the login authentication type.
Job	The attributes of a single SQL Server Agent job.
JobCategories	A collection containing Category objects that expose SQL Server Agent job-organizing methods.
JobFilter	Used to constrain the output of the EnumJobs method of the JobServer object.
JobHistoryFilter	Used to constrain the output of the EnumJobsHistory method of the JobServer object.
Jobs	A collection of SQL Server Agent Job objects.
JobSchedule	The attributes of a single SQL Server Agent executable job schedule.
JobSchedules	A collection of SQL Server Agent JobSchedule objects.
JobServer	The attributes for the SQL Server Agent.
JobStep	The properties for a single SQL Server Agent job execution step.
JobSteps	A collection of SQL Server Agent JobStep objects.
Key	The properties of a single table key.
Keys	A collection of Key objects.
Language	The attributes for the installed SQL Server language record.
Languages	A collection of Language objects.

Table Continued on Following Page

Name	Description
LinkedServer	The properties of an OLE DB data source that allows direct Transact-SQL queries against the data source.
LinkedServerLogin	The properties of an authentication record mapping used to connect to a LinkedServer.
LinkedServerLogins	A collection of LinkedServerLogin objects.
LinkedServers	A collection of LinkedServer objects.
LogFile	The attributes of an operating system file used to maintain transaction log records.
LogFiles	A collection of LogFile objects.
Login	The properties for a single SQL Server login.
Logins	A collection of Login objects.
MergeArticle	A table published as part of a merge publication.
MergeArticles	A collection of MergeArticle objects.
MergePublication	Represents a merge publication.
MergePublications	A collection of MergePublication objects.
MergePullSubscription	A Subscriber-initiated pull or anonymous subscription.
MergePullSubscriptions	A collection of MergePullSubscription objects.
MergeSubscription	A push subscription made from a Publisher.
MergeSubscriptions	A collection of MergeSubscription objects.
MergeSubsetFilter	A filter (or partition) of the data in one article that is based on filtered data in another article.
MergeSubsetFilters	A collection of MergeSubsetFilter objects.
NameList	A string container object returned from a method that enumerates SQL Servers by name.
Names	A string container used to manipulate a list of named objects.
Operator	A single SQL Server operator.
OperatorCategories	A collection that contains Category objects referencing a classification method for SQL Server Agent operators.
Operators	A collection of Operator objects.
Permission	Exposes SQL Server object-access rights.

Name	Description
Properties	A collection of SQL-DMO `Property` objects.
Property	The attributes of a SQL-DMO object property.
Publisher	The replication properties of a SQL Server Publisher.
QueryResults	Represents tabular data returned from various SQL-DMO object methods.
RegisteredServer	The attributes of a single registry-listed server running Microsoft SQL Server.
RegisteredServers	A collection of `RegisteredServer` objects.
RegisteredSubscriber	Shows what a Publisher knows about a Subscriber.
RegisteredSubscribers	A collection of `RegisteredSubscriber` objects.
Registry	Exposes the Registry settings used to maintain a SQL Server installation.
RemoteLogin	Exposes the properties of a single login mapping record for connections to a Microsoft SQL Server installation.
RemoteLogins	A collection of `RemoteLogin` objects.
RemoteServer	The attributes of a remotely connected SQL Server.
RemoteServers	A collection of `RemoteServer` objects.
Replication	Represents the entire replication system on a single SQL Server installation.
ReplicationDatabase	A user database that can participate in replication.
ReplicationDatabases	A collection of `ReplicationDatabase` objects.
ReplicationSecurity	Authentication information used to connect a Distributor or a Publisher.
Replication StoredProcedure	A user stored procedure in a database that can participate in replication.
Replication StoredProcedures	A collection of `ReplicationStoredProcedure` objects.
ReplicationTable	A table that can participate in replication.
ReplicationTables	A collection of `ReplicationTable` objects.
Restore	The behavior of a `RESTORE` statement for a SQL Server database or log.
Rule	The attributes of a single SQL Server data-integrity rule.
Rules	A collection of `Rule` objects.

Table Continued on Following Page

Name	Description
Schedule	The properties for automating SQL Server tasks.
ServerGroup	The properties that organize registered SQL Server installations.
ServerGroups	A collection of ServerGroup objects.
ServerRole	The attributes of a single Microsoft SQL Server security role not constrained to operation within a single database.
ServerRoles	A collection of ServerRole objects.
SQLObjectList	A fixed-membership container for objects enumerated by an object listing method.
SQLServer	The attributes of a server running Microsoft SQL Server.
SQLServers	A collection of SQLServer objects.
StoredProcedure	The properties of a single SQL Server stored procedure.
StoredProcedures	A collection of StoredProcedure objects.
Subscriber	The replication properties of a SQL Server Subscriber.
SystemDatatype	Exposes the attributes of a SQL Server base data type.
SystemDatatypes	A collection of SystemDatatype objects.
Table	Exposes the attributes of a SQL Server table.
Tables	A collection of Table objects.
TargetServer	The SQL Server where a SQL Server Agent job will execute.
TargetServerGroup	The attributes of a multiserver administration target identification shortcut.
TargetServerGroups	A collection of TargetServerGroup objects.
TargetServers	A collection of TargetServer objects.
TransactionLog	The properties of a SQL Server database transaction log.
TransArticle	A table or a stored procedure that is published using a transactional or a snapshot publication.
TransArticles	A collection of TransArticle objects.
Transfer	The Transfer object defines schema and data elements moved from one SQL Server database to another.
TransPublication	A transactional or snapshot publication.

Name	Description
TransPublications	A collection of TransPublication objects.
TransPullSubscription	A Subscriber-originated pull or an anonymous subscription to a transactional or snapshot publication.
TransPullSubscriptions	A collection of TransPullSubcription objects.
TransSubscription	A push subscription (made from the Publisher) to a transactional or snapshot publication.
TransSubscriptions	A collection of TransSubscription objects.
Trigger	The properties of a single SQL Server trigger.
Triggers	A collection of Trigger objects.
User	The properties of a single SQL Server user.
UserDefinedDatatype	The properties of a single SQL Server user-defined data type.
UserDefinedDatatypes	A collection of UserDefinedDatatype objects.
Users	A collection of User objects.
View	The properties of a single SQL Server view.
Views	A collection of View objects.

Alert

Methods

Name	Returns	Description
AddNotification		Operators designated receive notification messages when an event raising the alert occurs.
BeginAlter		Marks the start of a unit of change for the object referenced.
CancelAlter		Marks the end of a unit of change for the object referenced and discards any changes made to object property values.
DoAlter		Method marks the end of a unit of change for the object referenced and submits changes made to property values.

Table Continued on Following Page

Name	Returns	Description
EnumNotifications	QueryResults	Returns a QueryResults object enumerating notifications for a SQL Server Agent operator or alert.
Refresh		Updates the Alert object with current values from the referenced SQL Server installation.
Remove		Drops the referencing object.
RemoveNotification		Drops all SQL Server Agent alert notification assignments for an operator.
ResetOccurrenceCount		Reinitializes history data for a SQL Server Agent alert.
Script	String	Generates a Transact-SQL command batch that can be used to recreate the referenced component.
UpdateNotification		Configures SQL Server Agent operator notification for alerts raised.

Properties

Name	Returns	Description
Application	Application	The top-level Application object for SQL-DMO.
Category	String	The name of a category for SQL Server Agent alerts, jobs, and operators.
CountResetDate	Date	Represents the day and time at which the SQL Server Agent alert occurrence count was reset to 0.
DatabaseName	String	The name of an existing SQL Server database.
DelayBetween Responses	Long	The number of seconds SQL Server Agent waits to generate another response for an alert.
Enabled	Boolean	The state of a SQL Server Agent alert.
EventCategoryID	Long	RESERVED FOR FUTURE USE
EventDescription Keyword	String	Restricts SQL Server Agent alert firing.
EventID	Long	RESERVED FOR FUTURE USE

Name	Returns	Description
EventSource	String	RESERVED FOR FUTURE USE
HasNotification	Long	Returns the number of SQL Server Agent operators assigned to receive notification for an alert.
ID	Long	Used by SQL Server Agent components with defined identifiers.
IncludeEvent Description	SQLDMO_ NOTIFY_TYPE	Indicates response notifications that receive alert error text when SQL Server Agent builds a notification message for an alert.
JobID	String	A string representing the unique identifier of a SQL Server Agent job.
JobName	String	A string representing the name of a SQL Server Agent job.
LastOccurrence Date	Date	The date the most recent occurrence of a SQL Server Agent alert was raised.
LastResponse Date	Date	Identifies the most recent date on which SQL Server Agent generated a notification for a raised alert.
MessageID	Long	Identifies a SQL Server message to a SQL Server Agent alert.
Name	String	The name of a single SQL Server Agent alert.
Notification Message	String	Represents user-supplied text appended to any notification sent when SQL Server Agent responds to an alert.
OccurrenceCount	Long	The number of times an alert has fired after a specific date/time.
Parent	IVSQLDMO StdObject	The hierarchical parent object.
Performance Condition	String	Specifies a Windows NT Performance Monitor counter.
Properties	Properties	A list of properties for the object.
Severity	Long	Identifies a SQL Server error message severity level to a SQL Server Agent alert.
Type	SQLDMO_ ALERT_TYPE	Exposes configured attributes of the referenced SQL Server component.
TypeOf	SQLDMO_ OBJECT_TYPE	The type of SQL DMO object.
UserData	Long	User's private data.

AlertCategories

Methods

Name	Returns	Description
Add		Adds an alert Category object to the collection.
Item	Category	Retrieves an alert Category object.
ItemByID	Category	Retrieves a Category object from the collection by its ID.
Refresh		Updates the collection with current object values.
Remove		Removes a category object from the collection.

Properties

Name	Returns	Description
Application	Application	The top-level Application object for SQL-DMO.
Count	Long	The number of alert Category objects in the collection.
Parent	IVSQLDMOStdObject	The hierarchical parent object.
TypeOf	SQLDMO_OBJECT_TYPE	The type of SQL DMO object.
UserData	Long	User's private data.

Alerts

Methods

Name	Returns	Description
Add		Adds an Alert object to the collection.
Item	Alert	Retrieves an Alert object.
ItemByID	Alert	Retrieves an Alert object from the collection by its ID.
Refresh		Updates the collection with current object values.
Remove		Removes an Alert object from the collection.
Script	String	Generates a Transact-SQL command batch that can be used to recreate the referenced component.

Properties

Name	Returns	Description
Application	Application	The top-level Application object for SQL-DMO.
Parent	IVSQLDMOStdObject	The hierarchical parent object.
TypeOf	SQLDMO_OBJECT_TYPE	The type of SQL DMO object.
UserData	Long	User's private data.

AlertSystem

Methods

Name	Returns	Description
BeginAlter		Marks the start of a unit of change for the object referenced.
CancelAlter		Marks the end of a unit of change for the object referenced and discards any changes made to object property values.
DoAlter		Method marks the end of a unit of change for the object referenced and submits changes made to property values.
Refresh		Updates the object with current values from the referenced SQL Server installation.

Properties

Name	Returns	Description
Application	Application	The top-level Application object for SQL-DMO.
FailSafeOperator	String	Sets an operator to notify when no other operator is defined.
ForwardAlways	Boolean	Controls event forwarding for SQL Server Agent.

Table Continued on Following Page

Name	Returns	Description
ForwardingServer	String	The SQL Server that will receive forwarding events.
ForwardingSeverity	Long	Restricts forwarding events by the severity of the error generated.
NotificationMethod	SQLDMO_ NOTIFY_TYPE	Specifies the method used when notifying a fail-safe operator of a raised alert.
PagerCCTemplate	String	Specifies text used to build the CC: line of an e-mail message implementing pager notification.
PagerSendSubjectOnly	Boolean	Controls message text sent when SQL Server Agent attempts to notify an operator by page.
PagerSubjectTemplate	String	Specifies text used to build the subject line of an e-mail message implementing pager notification.
PagerToTemplate	String	Specifies text used to build the To: address line of an e-mail message implementing pager notification.
Parent	IVSQLDMO StdObject	The hierarchical parent object.
Properties	Properties	A list of properties for the object
TypeOf	SQLDMO_ OBJECT_TYPE	The type of SQL DMO object
UserData	Long	User's private data

Application

Methods

Name	Returns	Description
ListAvailableSQLServers	NameList	Returns a NameList object enumerating network-visible SQL Servers.
Quit		Disconnects all SQLServer objects referenced by an application.

Properties

Name	Returns	Description
Application	Application	The top-level Application object for SQL-DMO.
BlockingTimeout	Long	The timeout interval for resource requests that are blocked due to locks on the SQL Server.
FullName	String	Specifies the path and file name of the DLL implementing SQL-DMO.
GroupRegistration Server	String	RESERVED FOR FUTURE USE
GroupRegistration Version	Long	RESERVED FOR FUTURE USE
Name	String	The name of the Application object.
ODBCVersionString	String	Returns the major and minor build numbers of the installed ODBC driver manager.
Parent	IVSQLDMO StdObject	The hierarchical parent object.
Properties	Properties	A list of properties for the object.
ServerGroups	ServerGroups	A collection of ServerGroup objects.
SQLServers	SQLServers	A collection of SQLServer objects.
TypeOf	SQLDMO_ OBJECT_TYPE	The type of SQL-DMO object.
UseCurrentUser ServerGroups	Boolean	Configures registry entries listing SQL Server installations.
UserData	Long	User's private data.
VersionBuild	Long	The revision number part of the SQL-DMO object library version identifier.
VersionMajor	Long	The major build number part of the SQL-DMO object library version identifier.
VersionMinor	Long	The minor build number part of the SQL-DMO object library version identifier.

Backup

Methods

Name	Returns	Description
Abort		Interrupts a SQL-DMO backup process.
GenerateSQL	String	Returns a string containing a Transact-SQL command batch that can be used to perform the SQL Server database backup.
SQLBackup		Executes the database backup operation.

Events

Name	Returns	Description
Complete		Occurs when a backup operation completes.
NextMedia		Occurs when a backup operation exhausts the media in a device and requests more media.
PercentComplete		Occurs when a backup operation reaches a completion unit.

Properties

Name	Returns	Description
Action	SQLDMO_BACKUP_TYPE	Controls the type of backup performed on the SQL Server.
Application	Application	The top-level Application object for SQL-DMO.
BackupSet Description	String	Descriptive text about the result of the backup operation.
BackupSetName	String	Identifies a unit of backup work.
BlockSize	Long	The formatting size unit for tapes formatted as part of a backup.
Database	String	The database to be backed up.

Name	Returns	Description
Database FileGroups	String	The filegroups that will be backed up.
DatabaseFiles	String	Identifies operating system files storing table or index data as targets of a backup.
Devices	String	Sets one or more backup devices.
ExpirationDate	String	The date that the backup will expire.
Files	String	One or more operating system files used as a database backup target.
FormatMedia	Boolean	Sets whether to format the backup media (tape only) prior to backup operations.
Initialize	Boolean	Controls backup device append/overwrite behavior for a backup.
MediaDescription	String	Descriptive text about the backup media.
MediaName	String	The backup media name.
Parent	IVSQLDMO StdObject	The hierarchical parent object.
PercentComplete Notification	Long	Whether to notify the user of percent completion status during backup operations.
Pipes	String	Specifies one or more named pipes used as a database backup target.
Properties	Properties	A list of properties for the object.
Restart	Boolean	Controls Backup object behavior when the backup or restore operation specified by the object was started and interrupted.
RetainDays	Long	The number of days that must elapse before a backup set can be overwritten.
SkipTapeHeader	Boolean	Sets whether to skip the tape header on backup tape media. Verifies that the correct media was loaded.
Tapes	String	Specifies one or more tape devices used as a database backup target.
TruncateLog	SQLDMO_ BACKUP_LOG_TYPE	Sets whether to truncate the transaction log after backup operations.

Table Continued on Following Page

Name	Returns	Description
TypeOf	SQLDMO_ OBJECT_TYPE	The type of SQL DMO object.
UnloadTapeAfter	Boolean	Specifies whether to unload the backup tape media after backup operations.
UserData	Long	User's private data.

BackupDevice

Methods

Name	Returns	Description
ReadBackupHeader	QueryResults	Enumerates the contents of the media maintained by the backup device.
ReadMediaHeader	QueryResults	Enumerates the values of a backup media header record.
Remove		Removes a reference to a BackupDevice object.
Script	String	Generates a Transact-SQL command batch that can be used to recreate the referenced component.

Properties

Name	Returns	Description
Application	Application	The top-level Application object for SQL-DMO.
DeviceNumber	Long	Maintained for compatibility with earlier SQL-DMO versions.
Name	String	The name of the BackupDevice object.
Parent	IVSQLDMO StdObject	The hierarchical parent object.
PhysicalLocation	String	Specifies an operating system name identifying a backup device.
Properties	Properties	A list of properties for the object.

Name	Returns	Description
SkipTapeLabel	Boolean	Enables or disables, at a device level, backup operation logic that verifies correct media is loaded.
Status	Long	Returns component execution or integrity state information.
SystemObject	Boolean	Returns True for SQL Server database objects whose implementation is owned by Microsoft.
Type	SQLDMO_ DEVICE_TYPE	Exposes configured attributes of a SQL Server backup device.
TypeOf	SQLDMO_ OBJECT_TYPE	The type of SQL DMO object.
UserData	Long	User's private data.

BackupDevices

Methods

Name	Returns	Description
Add		Adds a BackupDevice to the collection.
Item	BackupDevice	Retrieves a BackupDevice object.
Refresh		Updates the collection with current values from the referenced SQL Server installation.
Remove		Removes a BackupDevice from the collection.

Properties

Name	Returns	Description
Application	Application	The top-level Application object for SQL-DMO.
Count	Long	The number of BackupDevice objects in the collection.
Parent	IVSQLDMOStdObject	The hierarchical parent object.
TypeOf	SQLDMO_OBJECT_TYPE	The type of SQL-DMO object.
UserData	Long	User's private data.

BulkCopy

Methods

Name	Returns	Description
Abort		Stops a bulk copy operation.
SetCodePage		Alters the character set used to interpret data during a bulk copy operation.

Events

Name	Returns	Description
BatchImported		Occurs when a bulk copy transaction is committed.
RowsCopied		Occurs when a bulk copy operation completes processing for a system-defined number of rows.

Properties

Name	Returns	Description
Application	Application	The top-level Application object for SQL-DMO
CodePage	Long	Used to interpret data for a bulk-copy operation.
ColumnDelimiter	String	Specifies one or more characters used to delimit a row of data in a bulk copy data file.
DataFilePath	String	The target or source of a SQL Server bulk copy operation.
DataFileType	SQLDMO_ DATAFILE_TYPE	Indicates the format type of the file desired or in use by bulk copy operations.
ErrorFilePath	String	The path where an error file is written if an error occurred during a bulk copy operation.
ExportWideChar	Boolean	Controls character set used in the data file when creating a data file by using the ExportData method of the Table and View object.

Name	Returns	Description
FirstRow	Long	The ordinal value defining the starting point for a bulk data copy.
Format FilePath	String	Exposes the path and file name of a bulk copy format file.
ImportRows PerBatch	Long	The number of rows contained in a bulk copy transaction.
Include IdentityValues	Boolean	Controls the handling of existing values for a column with the SQL Server identity type when data is copied to the SQL Server table.
LastRow	Long	The ordinal value defining the ending point for a bulk data copy.
LogFilePath	String	The path designation for the bulk copy log file.
MaximumErrors BeforeAbort	Long	The maximum number of errors that may occur before a bulk copy operation ends.
Parent	IVSQLDMO StdObject	The hierarchical parent object.
Properties	Properties	A list of properties for the object.
RowDelimiter	String	A character or character sequence that marks the end of a row in a SQL Server bulk copy data file.
ServerBCPData FileType	SQLDMO_ SERVERBCP_ DATAFILE_TYPE	The format for an imported data file.
ServerBCPKeep Identity	Boolean	The handling of existing values for an identity column when importing data into the column.
ServerBCP KeepNulls	Boolean	The handling of missing values for all columns accepting NULL and possessing a default value constraint when importing data.
Suspend Indexing	Boolean	Controls index update when the ImportData method of the Table object is used to copy data.
TruncateLog	Boolean	Controls log file processing for the BulkCopy object.
TypeOf	SQLDMO_ OBJECT_TYPE	The type of SQL-DMO object.
Use6x Compatible	Boolean	Controls interpretation of SQL Server bulk copy native format data files.

Table Continued on Following Page

Name	Returns	Description
UseBulk CopyOption	Boolean	Determines whether the "select into/bulkcopy" option is turned on automatically when the ImportData method of the Table object is executed.
UseExisting Connection	Boolean	Controls bulk copy connection behavior.
UserData	Long	User's private data.
UseServer SideBCP	Boolean	Directs BulkCopy object behavior when implementing a bulk copy import operation.

Category

Methods

Name	Returns	Description
BeginAlter		Marks the start of a unit of change for the object referenced.
CancelAlter		Marks the end of a unit of change for the object referenced and discards any changes made to object property values.
DoAlter		Marks the end of a unit of change for the object referenced and submits changes made to property values.
Refresh		Updates the object with current values from the referenced SQL Server installation.
Remove		Drops the Category object.

Properties

Name	Returns	Description
Application	Application	The top-level Application object for SQL-DMO.
ID	Long	The ID value of the Category object.
Name	String	The name of the Category object.
Parent	IVSQLDMOStdObject	The hierarchical parent object.

Name	Returns	Description
Properties	Properties	A list of properties for the Category object.
Type	SQLDMO_CATEGORYTYPE_TYPE	Exposes attributes of the referenced Category object.
TypeOf	SQLDMO_OBJECT_TYPE	The type of SQL DMO object.
UserData	Long	User's private data.

Check

Methods

Name	Returns	Description
Remove		Drops this Check object from its parent collection.
Script	String	Generates a Transact-SQL command batch that can be used to recreate the Check object.

Properties

Name	Returns	Description
Application	Application	The top-level Application object for SQL-DMO.
Checked	Boolean	Enables/disables integrity or FOREIGN KEY constraint evaluation for an existing integrity or FOREIGN KEY constraint.
Exclude Replication	Boolean	Controls integrity and FOREIGN KEY constraint enforcement when replicated data is inserted.
Name	String	The name of the Check object.
Parent	IVSQLDMOStdObject	The hierarchical parent object.

Table Continued on Following Page

Name	Returns	Description
Properties	Properties	A list of properties for the Check object.
Text	String	Exposes the Transact-SQL or other script that defines the object.
TypeOf	SQLDMO_OBJECT_TYPE	The type of SQL-DMO object.
UserData	Long	User's private data.

Checks

Methods

Name	Returns	Description
Add		Adds a Check object to the collection.
Item	Check	Retrieves a Check object.
Refresh		Updates the collection with current values from the referenced SQL Server installation.
Remove		Removes a Check object from the collection.

Properties

Name	Returns	Description
Application	Application	The top-level Application object for SQL-DMO.
Count	Long	The number of Check objects in the collection.
Parent	IVSQLDMO StdObject	The hierarchical parent object.
TypeOf	SQLDMO_ OBJECT_TYPE	The type of SQL-DMO object.
UserData	Long	User's private data.

Column

Methods

Name	Returns	Description
BindDefault		Implements default binding/unbinding on columns.
BindRule		Implements rule binding/unbinding on columns.
ListKeys	SQLObjectList	Enumerates the primary key and foreign key constraints on a column.
Remove		Drops the Column object.
UpdateStatisticsWith		Forces data distribution statistics update for a referenced index.

Properties

Name	Returns	Description
AllowNulls	Boolean	Exposes the ability of a data type to accept NULL as a value.
AnsiPaddingStatus	Boolean	Returns True if the referenced column is defined to exhibit SQL-92 character padding behavior.
Application	Application	The top-level Application object for SQL-DMO.
ComputedText	String	Contains the Transact-SQL expression used to generate the value of a computed column.
DataType	String	The data type name of the referenced column.
Default	String	Identifies a default bound to a column.
DefaultOwner	String	The name of the database owner for a bound default.
DRIDefault	DRIDefault	A DRIDefault object.
FullTextIndex	Boolean	Identifies if the column participates in a full-text queries.

Table Continued on Following Page

Name	Returns	Description
ID	Long	The ID for the Column object.
Identity	Boolean	Displays whether this is the identity column.
Identity Increment	Long	Displays the increment value for the identity column.
IdentitySeed	Long	Displays the seed value of the identity column.
InPrimaryKey	Boolean	Sets whether the column is part of the primary key.
IsComputed	Boolean	Displays whether the column is computed.
IsRowGuidCol	Boolean	Sets whether the column accepts GUID values for a unique identifier data type.
Length	Long	The maximum number of characters/bytes accepted by the column.
Name	String	The name of the Column object.
NotForRepl	Boolean	Sets whether the column is available for replication.
Numeric Precision	Long	Sets the numeric precision for columns with numeric data types.
NumericScale	Long	Sets the numeric scale for columns with numeric data types.
Parent	IVSQLDMO StdObject	The hierarchical parent object.
Physical Datatype	String	Returns the name of the base data type for the column.
Properties	Properties	A list of properties for the Column object.
Rule	String	Identifies the data integrity constraint bound to the column.
RuleOwner	String	The database user who established the bound integrity constraint on the column.
TypeOf	SQLDMO_ OBJECT_TYPE	The type of SQL-DMO object.
UserData	Long	User's private data.

Columns

Methods

Name	Returns	Description
Add		Adds a `Column` object to the collection.
Count	Long	The number of `Column` objects in the collection.
Item	Column	Retrieves a `Column` object.
ItemByID	Column	Retrieves a `Column` object by the ID value index.
Refresh		Updates the collection with current values from the referenced SQL Server installation.
Remove		Removes a `Column` object from the collection.

Configuration

Methods

Name	Returns	Description
ReconfigureCurrentValues		Applies changes to the configuration options.
ReconfigureWithOverride		Applies changes to the configuration options without appropriate permissions required.

Properties

Name	Returns	Description
Application	Application	The top-level `Application` object for SQL-DMO.
ConfigValues	ConfigValues	A collection of configuration values.
Parameters	Names	Server startup parameters.
Parent	IVSQLDMOStdObject	The hierarchical parent object.

Table Continued on Following Page

Name	Returns	Description
Properties	Properties	A list of properties for the Configuration object.
ShowAdvanced Options	Boolean	Controls ConfigValues collection membership.
TypeOf	SQLDMO_OBJECT_TYPE	The type of SQL-DMO object.
UserData	Long	User's private data.

ConfigValue

Properties

Name	Returns	Description
Application	Application	The top-level Application object for SQL-DMO.
CurrentValue	Long	A configuration parameter value.
Description	String	Information text about the object.
DynamicReconfigure	Boolean	Indicates whether the value maybe modified.
ID	SQLDMO_ CONFIGVALUE_TYPE	The ID value for the ConfigValue object.
MaximumValue	Long	The maximum value for the configuration value.
MinimumValue	Long	The minimum value for the configuration value.
Name	String	The name of the ConfigValue object.
Parent	IVSQLDMOStdObject	The hierarchical parent object.
Properties	Properties	A list of properties for the ConfigValue object.
RunningValue	Long	The current setting value.
TypeOf	SQLDMO_OBJECT_TYPE	The type of SQL-DMO object.
UserData	Long	User's private data.

ConfigValues

Methods

Name	Returns	Description
Item	ConfigValue	Returns a ConfigValue object.
ItemByID	ConfigValue	Retrieves a ConfigValue object by ID value.
Refresh		Updates the collection with current values from the referenced SQL Server installation.

Properties

Name	Returns	Description
Application	Application	The top-level Application object for SQL-DMO.
Count	Long	The number of ConfigValue objects in the collection.
Parent	IVSQLDMOStdObject	The hierarchical parent object.
TypeOf	SQLDMO_OBJECT_TYPE	The type of SQL-DMO object.
UserData	Long	User's private data.

Database

Methods

Name	Returns	Description
CheckAllocations	String	Scans all pages of the referenced SQL Server database, testing pages to ensure integrity.
CheckAllocationsDataOnly	String	Maintained for compatibility with previous versions of SQL-DMO.
CheckCatalog	String	Tests the integrity of the catalog of the referenced database.

Table Continued on Following Page

Name	Returns	Description
Check IdentityValues		Verifies the integrity of all identity columns in tables of the referenced database.
CheckPoint		Forces a write of dirty database pages.
CheckTables	String	Tests the integrity of database pages implementing storage for all tables and indexes defined on the tables of the referenced database.
CheckTables DataOnly	String	Tests the integrity of database pages implementing storage for all tables in the referenced database.
CheckText AllocsFast	String	Executes a DBCC CHECKDB (NOINDEX). (Hidden method)
CheckText AllocsFull	String	Executes a DBCC CHECKDB. (Hidden function)
Deny		Negates a granted database permission.
DisableFull TextCatalogs		Suspends full-text catalog maintenance on the database specified.
EnableFull TextCatalogs		Enables full-text indexing on the referenced database.
Enum CandidateKeys	QueryResults	Enumerates the user tables and constraints on those tables that could define primary keys.
Enum Dependencies	QueryResults	Enumerates database user objects and user object dependency relationships.
Enum FileGroups	QueryResults	Enumerates the filegroups of a SQL Server database.
EnumFiles	QueryResults	Enumerates the OS files to implement database storage.
EnumLocks	QueryResults	Enumerates the locks on a SQL Server database.
EnumLogin Mappings	QueryResults	Enumerates the login mappings for a SQL Server database.
Enum MatchingSPs	QueryResults	Enumerates the stored procedures containing the specified search text.
EnumNTGroups	QueryResults	Enumerates the Windows NT groups for a SQL Server database.
EnumUsers	QueryResults	Enumerates the users for a SQL Server database.

Name	Returns	Description
Execute Immediate		Submits a Transact-SQL command batch on a connection.
Execute WithResults	QueryResults	Executes a Transact-SQL command batch returning batch result sets in a QueryResults object.
ExecuteWith ResultsAnd Messages	QueryResults	Executes a Transact-SQL command batch returning batch result sets in a QueryResults object and capturing messages raised as part of command batch execution.
FullText IndexScript	String	Returns a Transact-SQL command batch enabling full-text indexing on a database.
GenerateSQL	String	Returns a string containing a Transact-SQL command batch that can be used to create the database.
GetDatatype ByName	IVSQLDMO StdObject	Returns an object that references the named system data type.
GetMemoryUsage	String	Retained for compatibility with previous versions of SQL-DMO. Executes DBCC MEMUSAGE system command.
GetObject ByName	DBObject	Returns a DBObject object referencing the specified Database object.
Grant		Assigns a database permission to a user or role.
IsUser	Boolean	Checks if a user is defined for the referenced database.
IsValidKey Datatype	Boolean	Checks to see if the data type is valid for a primary or foreign key.
ListDatabase Permissions	SQL ObjectList	Enumerates database maintenance privilege for security accounts.
ListObject Permissions	SQL ObjectList	Enumerates object access privileges.
ListObjects	SQL ObjectList	Enumerates the list of system and user-defined objects for the database.
Recalc SpaceUsage		Forces the update of data reporting the disk resource usage for the database specified.
Remove		Removes a selected database.

Table Continued on Following Page

Name	Returns	Description
RemoveFull TextCatalogs		Drops all full-text catalogs supporting full-text query on a database.
Revoke		Revokes user privileges on a database.
Script	String	Generates a Transact-SQL command batch that can be used to re-create the database.
ScriptTransfer	String	Generates a Transact-SQL command batch that creates Database objects contained in the Transfer object indicated.
SetOwner		Reassigns ownership for a database.
Shrink		Reduce the size of a referenced operating system file, or attempts to reduce the size of all OS files maintaining the referenced database.
Transfer		Copies database schema and/or data from one database to another.
UpdateIndex Statistics		Forces data distribution statistics update for all indexes on user-defined tables in the database.

Properties

Name	Returns	Description
Application	Application	The top-level Application object for SQL-DMO.
Compatibility Level	SQLDMO_COMP_ LEVEL_TYPE	Sets SQL Server behavior to match either the current or previous versions.
CreateDate	String	The date and time the database was created.
Create ForAttach	Boolean	Controls database file creation when the Database object is added to the Databases collection.
DatabaseRoles	DatabaseRoles	Returns a collection of DatabaseRole objects.
DataSpaceUsage	Single	Indicates the physical disk resource used to maintain the data of a database.
DboLogin	Boolean	Identifies database ownership privilege for the current session
DBOption	DBOption	Returns a DBOption object.

Name	Returns	Description
Defaults	Defaults	Returns the Defaults collection.
FileGroups	FileGroups	Returns the FileGroups collection.
FullText Catalogs	FullText Catalogs	Returns the FullTextCatalogs collection.
Groups	Groups	HIDDEN METHOD
ID	Long	The ID value for the object.
IndexSpace Usage	Single	The database log size in kilobytes.
Isdb_ accessadmin	Boolean	Is the current user a member of db_accessadmin role?
Isdb_ backupoperator	Boolean	Is the current user a member of db_backupoperator role?
Isdb_datareader	Boolean	Is the current user a member of db_datareader role?
Isdb_datawriter	Boolean	Is the current user a member of db_datawriter role?
Isdb_ddladmin	Boolean	Is the current user a member of db_ddladmin role?
Isdb_ denydatareader	Boolean	Is the current user a member of db_denydatareader role?
Isdb_ denydatawriter	Boolean	Is the current user a member of db_denydatawriter role?
Isdb_owner	Boolean	Is the current user a member of db_owner role?
Isdb_ securityadmin	Boolean	Is the current user a member of db_securityadmin role?
IsFull TextEnabled	Boolean	Is the current database full-text enabled?
Name	String	Sets/Gets the name of the Database object.
Owner	String	Gets the owner of the database.
Parent	IVSQLDMO StdObject	The hierarchical parent object.
Permissions	Permission	The permissions of the current user.

Table Continued on Following Page

Name	Returns	Description
Primary FilePath	String	The file path for the primary database file.
Properties	Properties	A list of the properties for this Database object.
Rules	Rules	The Rules collection for the database.
Size	Long	The database size in Megabytes.
SpaceAvailable	Long	The database space available in kilobytes.
Space AvailableInMB	Single	The database space available in Megabytes.
Status	SQLDMO_ DBSTATUS_TYPE	The current status of the database.
Stored Procedures	Stored Procedures	The StoredProcedures collection.
System Datatypes	System Datatypes	The SystemDatatypes collection.
SystemObject	Boolean	Identifies whether the database is a system object.
Tables	Tables	The Tables collection.
TransactionLog	TransactionLog	Returns the transaction log device.
TypeOf	SQLDMO_ OBJECT_TYPE	Returns the SQL Server object type.
UserData	Long	The user's private data.
UserDefined DataTypes	UserDefined Datatypes	The UserDefinedDatatypes collection.
UserName	String	The name of the current database user.
UserProfile	SQLDMO_ DBUSERPROFILE_ TYPE	Is the current user the database owner (dbo) for this database?
Users	Users	The Users collection.
UseServerName	String	Get/Set file prefix for the output files generated through the ScriptTransfer method.
Version	Long	The code version of the database.
Views	Views	The Views collection.

DatabaseRole

Methods

Name	Returns	Description
AddMember		Adds a new user to the current database role.
DropMember		Removes a user from the current database role.
EnumDatabaseRoleMember	QueryResults	Lists the members in the selected database role.
EnumFixed DatabaseRolePermission	QueryResults	Lists the permissions in the selected database role.
IsFixedRole	Boolean	Is the current DatabaseRole a fixed database role?
ListDatabasePermissions	SQLObjectList	Lists database-level (statement) permissions.
ListObjectPermissions	SQLObjectList	List object-level permissions.
Remove		Removes this DatabaseRole object from the parent collection.
Script	String	Generates a SQL Script to recreate this object.

Properties

Name	Returns	Description
Application	Application	The top-level Application object for SQL-DMO.
AppRole	Boolean	Sets the database application role.
Name	String	The name of the DatabaseRole object.
Parent	IVSQLDMO StdObject	The hierarchical parent object.
Password	String	The password for the database application role.
Properties	Properties	A list of properties for the DatabaseRole object.
TypeOf	SQLDMO_ OBJECT_TYPE	The type of SQL-DMO object.
UserData	Long	User's private data.

DatabaseRoles

Methods

Name	Returns	Description
Add		Adds a DatabaseRole object to the collection.
Item	DatabaseRole	Retrieves a DatabaseRole object from the collection.
Refresh		Refreshes data in the collection.
Remove		Removes a DatabaseRole object from the collection.

Properties

Name	Returns	Description
Application	Application	The top-level Application object for SQL-DMO.
Count	Long	The number of DatabaseRole objects in the collection.
Parent	IVSQLDMO StdObject	The hierarchical parent object.
TypeOf	SQLDMO_ OBJECT_TYPE	The type of SQL-DMO object.
UserData	Long	User's private data.

Databases

Methods

Name	Returns	Description
Add		Adds a Database object to the collection.
Item	Database	Retrieves a Database object from the collection.
ItemByID	Database	Retrieves a Database object from the collection by ID.
Refresh		Refreshes data in the collection.
Remove		Removes a Database object from the collection.

Properties

Name	Returns	Description
Application	Application	The top-level Application object for SQL-DMO.
Count	Long	The number of Database objects in the collection.
Parent	IVSQLDMOStdObject	The hierarchical parent object.
TypeOf	SQLDMO_OBJECT_TYPE	The type of SQL-DMO object.
UserData	Long	User's private data.

DBFile

Methods

Name	Returns	Description
Remove		Drops this DBFile object from its collection.
Shrink		Shrink this DBFile to a new size.

Properties

Name	Returns	Description
Application	Application	The top-level Application object for SQL-DMO
FileGrowth	Long	Specifies the size of the increment in MB or as a percentage.
FileGrowthInKB	Single	Specifies the size of the increment in KB.
FileGrowthType	SQLDMO_ GROWTH_TYPE	The type of file growth (in MB or as a percentage).
ID	Long	The DBFile ID.
MaximumSize	Long	The maximum file size restriction for the DBFile growth (in MB).

Name	Returns	Description
Name	String	The name of the DBFile object.
Parent	IVSQLDMO StdObject	The hierarchical parent object.
PhysicalName	String	The physical path and filename for this DBFile.
PrimaryFile	Boolean	Sets whether this is the primary file.
Properties	Properties	A list of properties for the DBFile object.
Size	Long	The current size of the file in Megabytes (MB).
SizeInKB	Single	The current size of the file in kilobytes (KB).
SpaceAvailable InMB	Long	The space available on the DBFile for expansion.
TypeOf	SQLDMO_ OBJECT_TYPE	The type of SQL-DMO object.
UserData	Long	User's private data.

DBFiles

Methods

Name	Returns	Description
Add		Adds a DBFile object to the collection.
Item	DBFile	Retrieves a DBFile object from the collection.
ItemByID	DBFile	Retrieves a DBFile object from the collection by ID.
Refresh		Refreshes data in the collection.
Remove		Removes a DBFile object from the collection.

Properties

Name	Returns	Description
Application	Application	The top-level Application object for SQL-DMO.
Count	Long	The number of DBFile objects in the collection.

Name	Returns	Description
Parent	IVSQLDMO StdObject	The hierarchical parent object.
TypeOf	SQLDMO_ OBJECT_TYPE	The type of SQL-DMO object.
UserData	Long	User's private data.

DBObject

Methods

Name	Returns	Description
EnumDependencies	QueryResults	List of objects which depend on or are depended upon by this object.
ListPermissions	SQLObjectList	List the object permission values on this object.
ListUser Permissions	SQLObjectList	List the user permission values on this object.
Remove		Removes the object from the database.
Script	String	Generate SQL Script to recreate this object.

Properties

Name	Returns	Description
Application	Application	The top-level Application object for SQL-DMO.
CreateDate	String	The DBObject object's creation date.
ID	Long	The ID of the DBObject object.
Name	String	The name of the DBObject object.
Owner	String	The DBObject object's owner.
Parent	IVSQLDMOStdObject	The hierarchical parent object.
Properties	Properties	A list of properties for the DBObject object.

Name	Returns	Description
SystemObject	Boolean	Identifies if this is a system object.
Type	SQLDMO_OBJECT_TYPE	Identifies the object's type.
TypeName	String	Identifies the object type's name.
TypeOf	SQLDMO_OBJECT_TYPE	The type of SQL-DMO object.
UserData	Long	User's private data.

DBOption

Methods

Name	Returns	Description
Refresh		Refreshes the values for the DBOption object.

Properties

Name	Returns	Description
Application	Application	The top-level Application object for SQL-DMO.
AssignmentDiag	Boolean	Gets/Sets the standard assignment diagnostic option.
AutoClose	Boolean	Gets/Sets the auto close option for a database.
AutoCreateStat	Boolean	Gets/Sets the "auto create statistics" option for a database.
AutoShrink	Boolean	Gets/Sets the auto shrink option for a database.
AutoUpdateStat	Boolean	Gets/Sets the "auto update statistics" option for a database.
Columns NullByDefault	Boolean	Gets/Sets the "columns null by default" option for a database.
CompareNull	Boolean	Gets/Sets the "comparison to null yields unknown" option.

Name	Returns	Description
ContactNull	Boolean	Gets/Sets the "contact with null yields null" option.
CursorClose OnCommit	Boolean	Gets/Sets the "cursor close on commit" option.
DBOUseOnly	Boolean	Gets/Sets the "database owner use only" option.
DefaultCursor	Boolean	Gets/Sets whether to default to local cursor option.
Offline	Boolean	Gets/Sets whether the database is offline or not.
Parent	IVSQLDMO StdObject	The hierarchical parent object.
Properties	Properties	A list of properties for the DBOption object.
QuoteDelimiter	Boolean	Gets/Sets whether to delimit identifiers with quotes.
ReadOnly	Boolean	Gets/Sets the read-only option of the database.
Recursive Triggers	Boolean	Gets/Sets whether triggers may be recursive.
SelectInto BulkCopy	Boolean	Gets/Sets the "Select Into/Bulk Copy" option for the database that determines if operations should be logged or not.
SingleUser	Boolean	Gets/Sets the single user option of the database.
TornPageDetection	Boolean	Gets/Sets the "torn page detection" option.
TruncateLog OnCheckpoint	Boolean	Gets/Sets the "automatic log truncation" option.
TypeOf	SQLDMO_ OBJECT_TYPE	The type of SQL-DMO object.
UserData	Long	User's private data.

Default

Methods

Name	Returns	Description
BindToColumn		Binds the Default object to a column.
BindToDatatype		Binds the Default object to a data type.
ListBoundColumns	SQLObjectList	Returns a list of bound columns.
ListBoundDatatypes	SQLObjectList	Returns a list of bound data types.
Remove		Removes the Default object.
Script	String	Creates a SQL script for the Default object.
UnbindFromColumn		Unbinds the Default object from a column.
UnbindFromDatatype		Unbinds the Default object from a data type.

Properties

Name	Returns	Description
Application	Application	The top-level Application object for SQL-DMO.
CreateDate	String	The date the Default object was created.
ID	Long	The ID value of the Default object.
Name	String	The name of the Default object.
Owner	String	The owner of the Default object.
Parent	IVSQLDMOStdObject	The hierarchical parent object.
Properties	Properties	A list of properties for the Default object.
Text	String	The object definition.
TypeOf	SQLDMO_OBJECT_TYPE	The type of SQL-DMO object.
UserData	Long	User's private data.

Defaults

Methods

Name	Returns	Description
Add		Adds a Default object to the collection.
Item	Default	Retrieves a Default object from the collection.
ItemByID	Default	Retrieves a Default object from the collection by its ID.
Refresh		Refreshes data in the Defaults collection.
Remove		Removes a Default object from the collection.

Properties

Name	Returns	Description
Application	Application	The top-level Application object for SQL-DMO.
Count	Long	The number of Default objects in the collection.
Parent	IVSQLDMO StdObject	The hierarchical parent object.
TypeOf	SQLDMO_ OBJECT_TYPE	The type of SQL-DMO object.
UserData	Long	User's private data.

DistributionArticle

Methods

Name	Returns	Description
BeginAlter		Starts a multi–property alteration.
CancelAlter		Cancels a multi–property alteration.
DoAlter		Executes a single alteration sequence.
Remove		Removes the DistributionArticle object.

Properties

Name	Returns	Description
Application	Application	The top-level `Application` object for SQL-DMO.
Description	String	The text description of the object.
ID	Long	The ID value of the object.
Name	String	The name of the object.
Parent	IVSQLDMOStdObject	The hierarchical parent object.
Properties	Properties	A list of properties for the object.
SourceObjectName	String	The name of the source object.
SourceObjectOwner	String	The owner of the source object.
TypeOf	SQLDMO_OBJECT_TYPE	The type of SQL-DMO object.
UserData	Long	User's private data.

DistributionArticles

Methods

Name	Returns	Description
Add		Adds a `DistributionArticle` object to the collection.
Item	Distribution Article	Retrieves a `DistributionArticle` object from the collection.
ItemByID	Distribution Article	Retrieves a `DistributionArticle` object from the collection by ID.
Refresh		Refreshes data in the collection.
Remove		Removes a `DistributionArticle` object from the collection.

Properties

Name	Returns	Description
Application	Application	The top-level Application object for SQL-DMO.
Count	Long	The number of DistributionArticle objects in the collection.
Parent	IVSQLDMO StdObject	The hierarchical parent object.
TypeOf	SQLDMO_ OBJECT_TYPE	The type of SQL-DMO object.
UserData	Long	User's private data.

DistributionDatabase

Methods

Name	Returns	Description
BeginAlter		Begins a multi-property DistributionDatabase alter.
CancelAlter		Cancels a multi-property DistributionDatabase alter.
DoAlter		Executes a DistributionDatabase alter.
Refresh		Refreshes data in the object.
Remove		Drops a DistributionDatabase object from its collection.
Script	String	Generate a SQL script to setup this object.

Properties

Name	Returns	Description
AgentStatus	SQLDMO_TASKS TATUS_TYPE	The status of the cleanup agents associated with the Distributor database.
Application	Application	The top-level Application object for SQL-DMO.

Table Continued on Following Page

Name	Returns	Description
DataFile	String	The name of the data file for the distribution database.
DataFileSize	Long	The size of the data file for the distribution database.
DataFolder	String	The folder of the data file for the distribution database.
Distribution CleanupTaskName	String	The name of the agent that cleans up the transactions in the distribution tables.
HistoryCleanup TaskName	String	The name of the agent that cleans up the history tables in the replication database.
HistoryRetention	Long	The number of hours that the agent history records are retained in the replication database.
LogFile	String	The name of the log file for the distribution database.
LogFileSize	Long	The size of the log file for the distribution database.
LogFolder	String	The folder of the log file for the distribution database.
MaxDistribution Retention	Long	The maximum number of hours that the transactions are retained in the distribution database.
MinDistribution Retention	Long	The minimum number of hours that the transactions are retained in the distribution database.
Name	String	The name of the object.
Parent	IVSQLDMO StdObject	The hierarchical parent object.
Properties	Properties	A list of properties for the object.
SecurityMode	SQLDMO_ SECURITY_TYPE	Security mode used to create distribution database by running script.
StandardLogin	String	Login used to create the distribution database by running a script.
StandardPassword	String	Password used to create the distribution database by running a script.
TypeOf	SQLDMO_ OBJECT_TYPE	The type of SQL-DMO object
UserData	Long	User's private data.

DistributionDatabases

Methods

Name	Returns	Description
Add		Adds a `DistributionDatabase` object to the collection.
Item	Distribution Database	Retrieves a `DistributionDatabase` object from the collection.
Refresh		Refreshes data in the collection.
Remove		Removes a `DistributionDatabase` object from the collection.
Script	String	Generate SQL script to setup this object.

Properties

Name	Returns	Description
Application	Application	The top-level `Application` object for SQL-DMO.
Count	Long	The number of `DistributionDatabase` objects in the collection.
Parent	IVSQLDMO StdObject	The hierarchical parent object.
TypeOf	SQLDMO_ OBJECT_TYPE	The type of SQL-DMO object.
UserData	Long	User's private data.

DistributionPublication

Methods

Name	Returns	Description
BeginAlter		Begins a multi-property alter.
CancelAlter		Cancels a multi-property alter.

Table Continued on Following Page

Name	Returns	Description
DoAlter		Executes an alter.
EnumLog ReaderAgentView	QueryResults	Enumerates the log-reader agent view.
EnumSnapshot AgentView	QueryResults	Enumerates the snapshot agent view.
EnumSubscription Views	QueryResults	Enumerates the subscription agent views.
GetAgentsStatus	SQLDMO_ TASK_TYPE	Status of tasks associated with this publication.
Remove		Drops the object from the parent collection.

Properties

Name	Returns	Description
Application	Application	The top-level Application object for SQL-DMO.
Description	String	The descriptive text about the object.
Distribution Articles	Distribution Articles	A collection of articles for the publication.
Distribution Subscriptions	Distribution Subscriptions	A collection of subscriptions for the publication.
ID	Long	The ID for the object.
LogReaderAgent	String	The name of the log-reader agent associated with the publication.
Name	String	The name of the object.
Parent	IVSQLDMO StdObject	The hierarchical parent object.
Properties	Properties	A list of properties for the object.
Publication Attributes	SQLDMO_ PUBATTRIB_TYPE	The attributes the publication supports.
PublicationDB	String	The name of the publication database.
PublicationType	SQLDMO_ PUBLICATION_ TYPE	The type of the publication.
SnapshotAgent	String	The name of the snapshot agent.

Name	Returns	Description
TypeOf	SQLDMO_OBJECT_TYPE	The type of SQL-DMO object.
UserData	Long	User's private data.
VendorName	String	The object's vendor name.

DistributionPublications

Methods

Name	Returns	Description
Add		Adds a DistributionPublication object to the collection.
Item	Distribution Publication	Retrieves a DistributionPublication object from the collection.
ItemByID	Distribution Publication	Retrieves a DistributionPublication object from the collection by ID.
Refresh		Refreshes data in the collection.
Remove		Removes a DistributionPublication object from the collection.

Properties

Name	Returns	Description
Application	Application	The top-level Application object for SQL-DMO.
Count	Long	The number of DistributionPublication objects in the collection.
Parent	IVSQLDMO StdObject	The hierarchical parent object.
TypeOf	SQLDMO_ OBJECT_TYPE	The type of SQL-DMO object.
UserData	Long	User's private data.

DistributionPublisher

Methods

Name	Returns	Description
BeginAlter		Begin multi-property `DistributionPublisher` alter.
CancelAlter		Cancels multi-property `DistributionPublisher` alter.
DoAlter		Execute `DistributionPublisher` alter.
EnumAgentErrorRecords	QueryResults	Enumerates the error records.
EnumDistribution AgentSessionDetails	QueryResults	Enumerates the distribution agent session details.
EnumDistribution AgentSessions	QueryResults	Enumerates the distribution agent sessions.
EnumLogReader AgentSessionDetails	QueryResults	Enumerates the log-reader agent session details.
EnumLogReader AgentSessions	QueryResults	Enumerates the log-reader agent sessions.
EnumMergeAgent SessionDetails	QueryResults	Enumerates the merge agent session details.
EnumMergeAgent Sessions	QueryResults	Enumerates the merge agent sessions.
EnumSnapshot AgentSessionDetails	QueryResults	Enumerates the snapshot agent session details.
EnumSnapshot AgentSessions	QueryResults	Enumerates the snapshot agent sessions.
GetAgentsStatus		Shows the status of tasks associated with the publications/subscriptions at this publisher.
Refresh		Refreshes the data in the object.
Remove		Drops the object from the collection.
Script	String	Generate SQL script to setup this Distributor.

Properties

Name	Returns	Description
Application	Application	The top-level `Application` object for SQL-DMO.
Distribution Database	String	The name of the associated distributor database.
Distribution Publications	Distribution Publications	A collection of `DistributionPublication` objects.
Distribution WorkingDirectory	String	The name of the distribution working directory.
Enabled	Boolean	Sets whether the publisher is active or not.
Name	String	The name of the object.
Parent	IVSQLDMO StdObject	The hierarchical parent object.
Propeties	Properties	A list of properties for the object.
PublisherSecurity	Replication Security	The security model for the publisher.
Registered Subscribers	Registered Subscribers	A collection of `RegisteredSubscriber` objects.
ThirdParty	Boolean	Is this a third party publisher?
TrustedDistributor Connection	Boolean	Is this a trusted distributor connection from a publisher to a distributor?
TypeOf	SQLDMO_ OBJECT_TYPE	The type of SQL-DMO object.
UserData	Long	User's private data.

DistributionPublishers

Methods

Name	Returns	Description
Add		Adds a `DistributionPublisher` object to the collection.

Table Continued on Following Page

Name	Returns	Description
Item	Distribution Publisher	Retrieves a DistributionPublisher object from the collection.
Refresh		Refreshes data in the collection.
Remove		Removes a DistributionPublisher object from the collection
Script	String	Generate SQL script to setup this object.

Properties

Name	Returns	Description
Application	Application	The top-level Application object for SQL-DMO.
Count	Long	The number of DistributionPublisher objects in the collection.
Parent	IVSQLDMO StdObject	The hierarchical parent object.
TypeOf	SQLDMO_ OBJECT_TYPE	The type of SQL-DMO object.
UserData	Long	User's private data.

DistributionSubscription

Methods

Name	Returns	Description
BeginAlter		Begin multi-property DistributionSubscription alter.
CancelAlter		Cancels multi-property DistributionSubscription alter.
DoAlter		Execute DistributionSubscription alter.
Remove		Drops the object from the collection.

Properties

Name	Returns	Description
Application	Application	The top-level Application object for SQL-DMO.
DistributionAgent	String	The name of the distribution agent.
Distribution Schedule	Schedule	The schedule for the distribution agent.
Name	String	The name of the object.
Parent	IVSQLDMOStdObject	The hierarchical parent object.
Properties	Properties	A list of properties for the object.
Status	SQLDMO_ SUBSTATUS_TYPE	The status of the subscription.
Subscriber	String	The name of the subscriber server.
SubscriptionDB	String	The name of the subscription database.
SubscriptionType	SQLDMO_ SUBSCRIPTION_TYPE	The type of subscription.
SyncType	SQLDMO_ SUBSYNC_TYPE	The synchronization type for the subscriber.
TypeOf	SQLDMO_ OBJECT_TYPE	The type of SQL-DMO object.
UserData	Long	User's private data.

DistributionSubscriptions

Methods

Name	Returns	Description
Add		Adds a DistributionSubscription object to the collection.
Item	Distribution Subscription	Retrieves a DistributionSubscription object from the collection.
Refresh		Refreshes data in the collection.
Remove		Removes a DistributionSubscription object from the collection.

Properties

Name	Returns	Description
Application	Application	The top-level `Application` object for SQL-DMO.
Count	Long	The number of `DistributionSubscription` objects in the collection.
Parent	IVSQLDMOStdObject	The hierarchical parent object.
TypeOf	SQLDMO_OBJECT_TYPE	The type of SQL-DMO object.
UserData	Long	User's private data.

Distributor

Methods

Name	Returns	Description
ChangeAgentParameter		Changes an agent parameter for an agent profile.
ChangeAgentProfile		Modifies an agent profile.
CleanUpDistribution PublisherByName		Clean up the named distribution publisher on this distributor.
CreateAgentProfile	Long	Creates a new agent profile.
DeleteAgentProfile		Deletes an agent profile.
EnumAgentParameters	Query Results	Displays the agent parameters.
EnumAgentProfiles	Query Results	Enumerates the agent profiles.
EnumDistribution AgentViews	Query Results	Displays the distribution agent views.
EnumLogReader AgentViews	Query Results	Displays the log-reader agent views.
EnumMergeAgentViews	Query Results	Displays the merge agent views.
EnumMiscellaneous AgentViews	Query Results	Displays the miscellaneous agent views.

Name	Returns	Description
EnumSnapshotAgent Views	Query Results	Displays the snapshot agent views.
EnumThirdParty Publications	Query Results	Return a result set containing information about third party publications.
GetAgentsStatus		Returns the status of the specified agent.
Install		Installs the distributor.
Refresh		Refreshes the data for the object.
Script	String	Generates SQL script to setup this object.
SetUpDistributor Password		Sets the password for the distributor_admin account.
Uninstall		Uninstalls the distributor.
UpdateAgentProfile		Updates the agent profile for an agent.
UpdateDefault AgentProfile		Updates the default agent profile for the current agent type.

Properties

Name	Returns	Description
AgentCheckupInterval	Long	The agent checkup interval.
Application	Application	The top-level Application object for SQL-DMO.
DistributionDatabase	String	The name of the distributor database.
DistributionDatabases	Distribution Databases	A collection of DistributionDatabases at this distributor.
Distribution Publishers	Distribution Publishers	A collection of DistributionPublishers for this distributor.
DistributionServer	String	The name of the distribution server.
DistributorAvailable	Boolean	Is the distributor is available?
DistributorInstalled	Boolean	Is the distributor is installed?

Table Continued on Following Page

Name	Returns	Description
DistributorLocal	Boolean	Is the distributor local to the current server?
HasRemoteDistribution Publisher	Boolean	Does the local distributor have a remote distribution publisher?
IsDistribution Publisher	Boolean	Is the local distributor also a distribution publisher?
Parent	IVSQLDMOStd Object	The hierarchical parent object.
Properties	Properties	A list of object properties.
TypeOf	SQLDMO_ OBJECT_TYPE	The type of SQL-DMO object.
UserData	Long	User's private data.

DRIDefault

Methods

Name	Returns	Description
Remove		Drops the DRIDefault object.
Script	String	Generates a SQL script for the DRIDefault object.

Properties

Name	Returns	Description
Application	Application	The top-level Application object for SQL-DMO.
Name	String	The name of the DRIDefault object.
Parent	IVSQLDMO StdObject	The hierarchical parent object.
Properties	Properties	A list of object properties.
Text	String	Text of default value.
TypeOf	SQLDMO_ OBJECT_TYPE	The type of SQL-DMO object.
UserData	Long	User's private data.

FileGroup

Methods

Name	Returns	Description
CheckFilegroup	String	Executes DBCC CHECKFILEGROUP.
CheckFilegroup DataOnly	String	Executes DBCC CHECKFILEGROUP (NOINDEX).
EnumFiles	QueryResults	Lists DBFiles in this filegroup.
EnumObjects	QueryResults	Lists objects in this filegroup.
Remove		Drop this object and remove from parent collection.

Properties

Name	Returns	Description
Application	Application	The top-level Application object for SQL-DMO.
DBFiles	DBFiles	A collection of DBFile objects.
Default	Boolean	Set default property to this filegroup.
ID	Long	The ID of the FileGroup object.
Name	String	The name of the FileGroup object.
Parent	IVSQLDMO StdObject	The hierarchical parent object.
Properties	Properties	A list of object properties.
ReadOnly	Boolean	Is the READONLY attribute for this filegroup set?
Size	Long	The size of the file group in MB.
TypeOf	SQLDMO_ OBJECT_TYPE	The type of SQL-DMO object.
UserData	Long	User's private data.

FileGroups

Methods

Name	Returns	Description
Add		Adds a FileGroup object to the collection.
Item	FileGroup	Retrieves a FileGroup object from the collection.
ItemByID	FileGroup	Retrieves a FileGroup object from the collection by ID.
Refresh		Refreshes data in the FileGroups collection.
Remove		Removes a FileGroup object from the collection.

Properties

Name	Returns	Description
Application	Application	The top-level Application object for SQL-DMO.
Count	Long	The number of FileGroup objects in the collection.
Parent	IVSQLDMOStdObject	The hierarchical parent object.
TypeOf	SQLDMO_OBJECT_TYPE	The type of SQL-DMO object.
UserData	Long	User's private data.

FullTextCatalog

Methods

Name	Returns	Description
GenerateSQL	String	Generates a series of Transact-SQL statements that can be used to create the full-text catalog.
Rebuild		Rebuilds this FullTextCatalog without removing it.
Remove		Drops this object and removes it from the collection.

Name	Returns	Description
Script	String	Generates SQL script to create this object.
Start		Start this FullTextCatalog, either full or incremental.
Stop		Stops this FullTextCatalog.

Properties

Name	Returns	Description
Application	Application	The top-level Application object for SQL-DMO.
ErrorLogSize	Long	Returns the full-text error log size.
FullTextCatalogID	Long	Returns the full-text catalog ID.
FullTextIndexSize	Long	Returns the full-text index size.
HasFullText IndexedTables	Boolean	Checks if the full-text catalog contains indexed tables.
ItemCount	Long	Gets the full-text catalog item count.
Name	String	The name of the object.
Parent	IVSQLDMOStdObject	The hierarchical parent object.
Populate CompletionAge	Long	Gets the full-text populate completion age.
Populate CompletionDate	String	Gets the full-text populate completion date.
PopulateStatus	SQLDMO_ FULLTEXTSTATUS_TYPE	Returns the full-text catalog status.
Properties	Properties	A list of properties for the object.
RootPath	String	The full-text catalog root path.
TypeOf	SQLDMO_OBJECT_TYPE	The type of SQL-DMO object.
UniqueKeyCount	Long	Gets the full-text unique key count.
UserData	Long	User's private data.

FullTextCatalogs

Methods

Name	Returns	Description
Add		Adds a `FullTextCatalog` object to the collection.
Item	FullText Catalog	Retrieves a `FullTextCatalog` object from the collection.
Refresh		Refreshes data in the collection.
Remove		Removes a `FullTextCatalog` object from the collection.

Properties

Name	Returns	Description
Application	Application	The top-level `Application` object for SQL-DMO.
Count	Long	The number of `FullTextCatalog` objects in the collection.
Parent	IVSQLDMOStdObject	The hierarchical parent object.
TypeOf	SQLDMO_OBJECT_TYPE	The type of SQL-DMO object.
UserData	Long	User's private data.

FullTextService

Methods

Name	Returns	Description
CleanUp		Directs the Microsoft Search service to locate and remove full-text catalog resources in the file system that do not have corresponding entries in the `sysfulltextcatalogs` system table.
Start		Starts the `FullTextService`.
Stop		Stops the `FullTextService`.

Properties

Name	Returns	Description
Application	Application	The top-level Application object for SQL-DMO.
ConnectTimeout	Long	Gets/Sets the connection timeout.
DefaultPath	String	The default path for the FullTextService.
IsFullText Installed	Boolean	Checks to see if the FullTextService is loaded.
Parent	IVSQLDMOStdObject	The hierarchical parent object.
Properties	Properties	A list of properties for the object.
ResourceUsage	Long	Retrieves the resource usage priority setting.
Status	SQLDMO_ SVCSTATUS_TYPE	The status of the FullTextService.
TypeOf	SQLDMO_OBJECT_TYPE	The type of SQL-DMO object.
UserData	Long	User's private data.

Group

Methods

Name	Returns	Description
ListDatabase Permissions	SQLObjectList	Lists database-level (statement) permissions.
ListObject Permissions	SQLObjectList	Lists object-level permissions.
ListUsers	SQLObjectList	Return a list of all users in this group.
Remove		Drops the object.
Script	String	Generates SQL script to create this object

Properties

Name	Returns	Description
Application	Application	The top-level Application object for SQL-DMO.
ID	Long	The ID value for the object.
Name	String	The name of the object.
Parent	IVSQLDMOStdObject	The hierarchical parent object.
Properties	Properties	A list of properties for the object.
SystemObject	Long	Retrieves the resource usage priority setting.
TypeOf	SQLDMO_OBJECT_TYPE	The type of SQL-DMO object.
UserData	Long	User's private data.

Groups

Methods

Name	Returns	Description
Application	Application	The top-level Application object for SQL-DMO.
Count	Long	The number of Group objects in the collection.
Parent	IVSQLDMOStdObject	The hierarchical parent object.
TypeOf	SQLDMO_OBJECT_TYPE	The type of SQL-DMO object.
UserData	Long	User's private data.

Properties

Name	Returns	Description
Application	Application	The top-level Application object for SQL-DMO.

Name	Returns	Description
Count	Long	The number of Group objects in the collection.
Parent	IVSQLDMOStdObject	The hierarchical parent object.
TypeOf	SQLDMO_OBJECT_TYPE	The type of SQL-DMO object.
UserData	Long	User's private data.

Index

Methods

Name	Returns	Description
CheckIndex	String	DBCC CHECKTABLE on this index.
EnumStatistics	QueryResults	List detailed stats for this index.
GenerateCreationSQL	String	Generate Transact-SQL statement for index creation.
GenerateSQL	String	Generates a series of Transact-SQL statements that can be used to create the index in this table.
ListIndexedColumns	SQLObjectList	Returns a list of columns for this index.
Rebuild		Rebuilds the index.
RecalcSpaceUsage		Recalculate space usage for this index.
Remove		Drops the object and removes it from the collection.
Script	String	Generate SQL script to create this object.
UpdateStatistics		Update index key-value distribution statistics.
UpdateStatisticsWith		Update index key-value distribution statistics with options.

Properties

Name	Returns	Description
Application	Application	The top-level Application object for SQL-DMO.
FileGroup	String	Gets/Sets the index on the selected filegroup.
FillFactor	Long	Percentage to fill index pages on creation.
ID	Long	The ID value of the object.
IndexedColumns	String	Assigns one or more columns to be indexed.
IsFullTextKey	Boolean	Checks to see if this is a full-text key
Name	String	The name of the object.
NoRecompute	Boolean	Specifies that out-of-date index statistics are not automatically recomputed.
Parent	IVSQLDMO StdObject	The hierarchical parent object.
Properties	Properties	A list of properties for the object.
SpaceUsed	Long	Current total space used by this index, in KB.
StatisticsIndex	Boolean	Is this index a statistic_only index?
Type	SQLDMO_ INDEX_TYPE	The type of index.
TypeOf	SQLDMO_ OBJECT_TYPE	The type of SQL-DMO object.
UserData	Long	User's private data.

Indexes

Methods

Name	Returns	Description
Add		Adds an Index object to the collection.
Item	Index	Retrieves an Index object from the collection.
ItemByID	Index	Retrieves an Index object from the collection.
Refresh		Refreshes data in the collection.
Remove		Removes an Index object from the collection.

Properties

Name	Returns	Description
Application	Application	The top-level Application object for SQL-DMO.
Count	Long	The number of Index objects in the collection.
Parent	IVSQLDMO StdObject	The hierarchical parent object.
TypeOf	SQLDMO_ OBJECT_TYPE	The type of SQL-DMO object.
UserData	Long	User's private data.

IntegratedSecurity

Methods

Name	Returns	Description
Refresh		Refreshes data in the collection.

Properties

Name	Returns	Description
Application	Application	The top-level Application object for SQL-DMO.
AuditLevel	SQLDMO_ AUDIT_TYPE	Sets the audit level.
DefaultDomain	String	The default domain name. This property is maintained for compatibility with previous versions.
DefaultLogin	String	The default login identifier. This property is maintained for compatibility with previous versions.
Impersonate Client	Boolean	Impersonate client when executing xp_cmdshell.

Table Continued on Following Page

Name	Returns	Description
MapDollarSign	String	'domain separator', 'space', 'null', character.
MapPoundSign	String	'domain separator', 'space', 'null', character.
MapUnderscore	String	'domain separator', 'space', 'null', character.
Parent	IVSQLDMO StdObject	The hierarchical parent object.
Properties	Properties	A list of properties for the object.
SecurityMode	SQLDMO_ SECURITY_ TYPE	Sets the type of security.
SetHostName	Boolean	Checks if the host name is set.
TypeOf	SQLDMO_ OBJECT_TYPE	The type of SQL-DMO object.
UserData	Long	User's private data.

Job

Methods

Name	Returns	Description
AddStepToJob		Adds the JobStep object to the current job.
ApplyTo TargetServer		Adds the target server name for this job.
ApplyTo TargetServerGroup		Apply to specified TargetServerGroups, up to four groups, comma separated.
BeginAlter		Begins multi-column table alter.
CancelAlter		Cancels multi-column table alter.
DoAlter		Executes a table alter.
EnumAlerts	QueryResults	Enumerate alerts that invoke the job.
EnumHistory	QueryResults	Selectively enumerate server job history
Enum TargetServers	QueryResults	Enumerate TargetServers.

Name	Returns	Description
Invoke		Invokes a job for execution.
PurgeHistory		Purges server job history.
Refresh		Refreshes data in this object.
Remove		Drop this object and remove from parent collection.
RemoveAll JobSchedules		Removes all the job schedules under the current job.
RemoveAll JobSteps		Removes all the job steps under the current job.
RemoveFrom TargetServer		Removes the job from the specified TargetServer.
RemoveFrom TargetServerGroup		Removes the job from the specified TargetServer group.
Script	String	Generate SQL script to create this object.
Start		Starts the job.
Stop		Stops the job.

Properties

Name	Returns	Description
Application	Application	The top-level Application object for SQL-DMO.
Category	String	Gets/Sets the Category name.
CurrentRun RetryAttempt	Long	Retrieves the current number of retry attempts.
Current RunStatus	SQLDMO_ JOBEXECUTION_ STATUS	Returns the current status of the job.
Current RunStep	String	Returns the currently executing job step.
DateCreated	String	The date and time the job was created.
DateLast Modified	String	The date the job was last changed.

Table Continued on Following Page

Name	Returns	Description
DeleteLevel	SQLDMO_ COMPLETION_TYPE	The type of job delete level.
Description	String	A descriptive text about the object.
EmailLevel	SQLDMO_ COMPLETION_TYPE	Completion status that causes sending of e-mail.
Enabled	Boolean	Checks if the job may be executed.
Eventlog Level	SQLDMO_ COMPLETION_TYPE	Completion status that causes log entry.
HasSchedule	Boolean	Checks if job has a schedule.
HasServer	Boolean	Checks if job has a server value.
HasStep	Boolean	Checks if job has a step value.
JobId	String	The ID value for the job object.
JobSchedules	JobSchedules	A collection of JobSchedules for this job.
JobSteps	JobSteps	A collection of job steps for this job.
LastRunDate	Long	The date the job was last executed.
LastRun Outcome	SQLDMO_ JOBOUTCOME_TYPE	The outcome of the last execution of this job.
LastRunTime	Long	The time the job was last executed.
Name	String	The name of the object.
NetSendLevel	SQLDMO_ COMPLETION_TYPE	Get job net send level information.
NextRunDate	Long	The next job run date.
NetRun ScheduleID	Long	The next run job schedule ID.
NextRunTime	Long	The next job run time.
Operator ToEmail	String	The operator's e-mail address.
Operator ToNetSend	String	The operator net send handle.
Operator ToPage	String	Get/Set operator to page.
Originating Server	String	The name of the server that originated the job.

Name	Returns	Description
Owner	String	The owner of the object.
PageLevel	SQLDMO_ COMPLETION_TYPE	The page notification level.
Parent	IVSQLDMO StdObject	The hierarchical parent object.
Properties	Properties	A list of properties for the object.
StartStepID	Long	The starting step ID.
Type	SQLDMO_JOB_TYPE	Returns the job type.
TypeOf	SQLDMO_ OBJECT_TYPE	The type of SQL-DMO object.
UserData	Long	User's private data.
Version Number	Long	The job version number.

JobCategories

Methods

Name	Returns	Description
Add		Adds a Category object to the collection.
Item	Category	Retrieves a Category object from the collection.
ItemByID	Category	Retrieves a Category object from the collection.
Refresh		Refreshes data in the collection.
Remove		Removes a Category object from the collection.

Properties

Name	Returns	Description
Application	Application	The top-level Application object for SQL-DMO.
Count	Long	The number of Category objects in the collection.

Table Continued on Following Page

Name	Returns	Description
Parent	IVSQLDMOStdObject	The hierarchical parent object.
TypeOf	SQLDMO_OBJECT_TYPE	The type of SQL-DMO object.
UserData	Long	User's private data.

JobFilter

Properties

Name	Returns	Description
Application	Application	The top-level Application object for SQL-DMO.
Category	String	Gets/Sets the JobFilter category name.
Current ExecutionStatus	SQLDMO_ JOBEXECUTION_ STATUS	Gets/Sets the current job execution status.
DateFindOperand	SQLDMO_FIND_ OPERAND	Gets/Sets the DateFindOperand.
DateJobCreated	String	Gets the date the job was created.
DateJobLast Modified	String	Gets/Sets the date job last modified.
Enabled	Boolean	Sets whether the JobFilter is available for use.
Owner	String	The name of the owner of the object.
Parent	IVSQLDMO StdObject	The hierarchical parent object.
Properties	Properties	A list of properties for the object.
StepSubsystem	String	Sets/Gets the JobFilter step subsystem.
Type	SQLDMO_JOB_TYPE	Specifies the type of job.
TypeOf	SQLDMO_ OBJECT_TYPE	The type of SQL-DMO object.
UserData	Long	User's private data.

JobHistoryFilter

Properties

Name	Returns	Description
Application	Application	The top-level Application object for SQL-DMO.
EndRunDate	Long	Last date retrieved during execution.
EndRunTime	Long	Last time retrieved during execution.
JobID	String	The job ID value that was retrieved.
JobName	String	The name of the job.
MinimumRetries	Long	The minimum number of retries to display history.
Minimum RunDuration	Long	The minimum run duration.
OldestFirst	Boolean	Sort history by ascending age.
OutcomeTypes	SQLDMO_ JOBOUTCOME_TYPE	Job statuses.
Parent	IVSQLDMO StdObject	The hierarchical parent object.
Properties	Properties	A list of properties for the object.
SQLMessageID	Long	The message ID.
SQLSeverity	Long	The severity level of the SQL execution.
StartRunDate	Long	The starting date to retrieve history data.
StartRunTime	Long	The starting time to retrieve history data.
TypeOf	SQLDMO_ OBJECT_TYPE	The type of SQL-DMO object.
UserData	Long	User's private data

Jobs

Methods

Name	Returns	Description
Add		Adds a Job object to the collection.
Item	Job	Retrieves a Job object from the collection.
Refresh		Refreshes data in the collection.
Remove		Removes a Job object from the collection.
Script	String	Generates a SQL script for creation of the object.

Properties

Name	Returns	Description
Application	Application	The top-level Application object for SQL-DMO.
Count	Long	The number of Job objects in the collection.
Parent	IVSQLDMOStdObject	The hierarchical parent object.
TypeOf	SQLDMO_OBJECT_TYPE	The type of SQL-DMO object.
UserData	Long	User's private data.

JobSchedule

Methods

Name	Returns	Description
BeginAlter		Starts a multi-column table alter.
CancelAlter		Cancels a multi-column table alter.
DoAlter		Executes a table alter.
Refresh		Refreshes data in the collection.
Remove		Drops the object from the collection.

Properties

Name	Returns	Description
Application	Application	The top-level Application object for SQL-DMO.
DateCreated	String	The date and time the job schedule was created.
Enabled	Boolean	Is the job schedule active?
Name	String	The name of the object.
Parent	IVSQLDMOStdObject	The hierarchical parent object.
Properties	Properties	A list of properties for the object.
Schedule	Schedule	A schedule object.
ScheduleID	Long	The job schedule ID.
TypeOf	SQLDMO_OBJECT_TYPE	The type of SQL-DMO object.
UserData	Long	User's private data.

JobSchedules

Methods

Name	Returns	Description
Add		Adds a JobSchedule object to the collection.
Item	JobSchedule	Retrieves a JobSchedule object from the collection.
ItemByID	JobSchedule	Retrieves a JobSchedule object from the collection.
Refresh		Refreshes data in the collection.
Remove		Removes a JobSchedule object from the collection.

Properties

Name	Returns	Description
Application	Application	The top-level `Application` object for SQL-DMO.
Count	Long	The number of `JobSchedule` objects in the collection.
Parent	IVSQLDMOStdObject	The hierarchical parent object.
TypeOf	SQLDMO_OBJECT_TYPE	The type of SQL-DMO object.
UserData	Long	User's private data.

JobServer

Methods

Name	Returns	Description
BeginAlter		Begins a multi-property object alter.
CancelAlter		Cancels a multi-property object alter.
DoAlter		Executes an object alter.
EnumJobHistory	QueryResults	Enumerates server job using job history filter.
EnumJobs	QueryResults	Selectively enumerates server job using `JobFilter`.
EnumSubSystems	QueryResults	Enumerate server scheduling subsystems.
GetJobByID	Job	Retrieves a `Job` object from MSX.
MSXDefect		Ends participation in MSA.
MSXEnlist		Enlist the specified server to MSA.
PurgeJobHistory		Selectively purge server job and alert history.
ReAssignJobsByLogin		Reassign all jobs of a given login to another login.

Name	Returns	Description
Refresh		Refresh the information in this object.
RemoveJobByID		Remove the specified job from MSX.
RemoveJobsByLogin		Drop all jobs of a given login.
RemoveJobsByServer		Drop all jobs from a given server.
Start		Start `JobServer`.
StartMonitor		Start MSX monitor.
Stop		Stop `JobServer`.
StopMonitor		Stop MSX monitor.

Properties

Name	Returns	Description
AlertCategories	AlertCategories	A collection of `AlertCategories` for this `JobServer`.
Alerts	Alerts	A collection of `Alerts` for this `JobServer`.
AlertSystem	AlertSystem	Alert-handling information.
Application	Application	The top-level `Application` object for SQL-DMO.
AutoStart	Boolean	Auto-start `JobServer` on NT boot.
JobCategories	JobCategories	A collection of `JobCategories` for this `JobServer`.
JobFilter	JobFilter	`JobFilter` information.
JobHistoryFilter	JobHistoryFilter	`JobHistoryFilter` information.
Jobs	Jobs	A collection of `Jobs` for the `JobServer`.
MSXServerName	String	Gets MSA server name.
OperatorCategories	OperatorCategories	A collection of `OperatorCategories` for this `JobServer`.
Operators	Operators	A collection of `Operators` for this `JobServer`.
Parent	IVSQLDMO StdObject	The hierarchical parent object.

Table Continued on Following Page

Name	Returns	Description
Properties	Properties	A list of properties for the object.
Startup Account	String	Gets MSA startup account.
Status	SQLDMO_ SVCSTATUS_TYPE	Gets the JobServer's current status.
Target ServerGroups	Target ServerGroups	A collection of TargetServerGroups for this JobServer.
TargetServers	TargetServers	A collection of TargetServers for this JobServer.
Type	SQLDMO_ JOBSERVER_TYPE	The type of job server.
TypeOf	SQLDMO_ OBJECT_TYPE	The type of SQL-DMO object.
UserData	Long	User's private data.

JobStep

Methods

Name	Returns	Description
BeginAlter		Begins a multi-column table alter.
CancelAlter		Cancels a multi-column alter.
DoAlter		Executes a object alter.
Refresh		Refresh the information in this object.
Remove		Drops the object and removes it from the collection.

Properties

Name	Returns	Description
Additional Parameters	String	Get/Set additional parameters for the JobStep.
Application	Application	The top-level Application object for SQL-DMO.
CmdExec SuccessCode	Long	Gets/Sets external command execution returned code.

Name	Returns	Description
Command	String	Gets/Sets JobStep Command.
DatabaseName	String	The database name for the JobStep.
Database UserName	String	The database username for the JobStep.
Flags	Long	Gets/Sets the command flag.
LastRunDate	Long	Retrieves the last execution date.
LastRun Duration	Long	Retrieves the last execution duration.
LastRunOutcome	SQLDMO_ JOBOUTCOME_TYPE	Retrieves the last execution result.
LastRunRetries	Long	Retrieves the last execution retry count.
LastRunTime	Long	Retrieves the last execution time.
Name	String	The name of the object.
OnFailAction	SQLDMO_ JOBSTEPACTION_TYPE	Action performed when JobStep fails.
OnFailStep	Long	Gets/Sets JobStep that failed.
OnSuccess Action	SQLDMO_ JOBSTEPACTION_TYPE	Get/Set action to perform when JobStep succeeds.
OnSuccessStep	Long	Get/Set JobStep succeed.
OSRunPriority	SQLDMO_ RUNPRIORITY_TYPE	Get/Set OS processing priority for the JobStep.
OutputFileName	String	The output file name.
Parent	IVSQLDMOStdObject	The hierarchical parent object.
Properties	Properties	A list of properties for the object.
RetryAttempts	Long	Get/Set retry attempts for the JobStep.
RetryInterval	Long	Get/Set retry interval for the JobStep.
Server	String	Get/Set JobStep server name.
StepID	Long	Get/Set JobStep ID.
SubSystem	String	Get/Set JobStep subsystem.
TypeOf	SQLDMO_OBJECT_TYPE	The type of SQL-DMO object.
UserData	Long	User's private data.

JobSteps

Methods

Name	Returns	Description
Add		Adds a JobStep object to the collection.
Item	JobStep	Retrieves a JobStep object from the collection.
ItemByID	JobStep	Retrieves a JobStep object from the collection.
Refresh		Refreshes data in the collection.
Remove		Removes a JobStep object from the collection.

Properties

Name	Returns	Description
Application	Application	The top-level Application object for SQL-DMO.
Count	Long	The number of JobStep objects in the collection.
Parent	IVSQLDMOStdObject	The hierarchical parent object.
TypeOf	SQLDMO_OBJECT_TYPE	The type of SQL-DMO object.
UserData	Long	User's private data.

Key

Methods

Name	Returns	Description
RebuildIndex		Rebuild the index enforcing this constraint (primary and unique keys only).
Remove		Drops the object and removes it from the collection.
Script	String	Generates a SQL script for the object.

Properties

Name	Returns	Description
Application	Application	The top-level Application object for SQL-DMO.
Checked	Boolean	CHECK or NOCHECK of this key if a foreign key.
Clustered	Boolean	Is this (primary or unique) key clustered?
Exclude Replication	Boolean	Should constraint be ignored for data inserted under replication?
FileGroup	String	Get/Set FileGroup of this key if a primary key/unique key.
FillFactor	Long	Percentage to fill (primary or unique) key's index pages on creation.
KeyColumns	Names	Columns involved in key.
Name	String	The name of the object.
Parent	IVSQLDMO StdObject	The hierarchical parent object.
Properties	Properties	A list of properties for the object.
Referenced Columns	Names	The columns in ReferencedTable's key.
ReferencedKey	String	Name of key in ReferencedTable.
ReferencedTable	String	Get/Set ReferencedTable name.
Type	SQLDMO_ KEY_TYPE	The DRI key type.
TypeOf	SQLDMO_ OBJECT_TYPE	The type of SQL-DMO object.
UserData	Long	User's private data.

Keys

Methods

Name	Returns	Description
Add		Adds a Key object to the collection.
Item	Key	Retrieves a Key object from the collection.
Refresh		Refreshes data in the collection.
Remove		Removes a Key object from the collection.

Properties

Name	Returns	Description
Application	Application	The top-level Application object for SQL-DMO.
Count	Long	The number of Key objects in the collection.
Parent	IVSQLDMOStdObject	The hierarchical parent object.
TypeOf	SQLDMO_OBJECT_TYPE	The type of SQL-DMO object.
UserData	Long	User's private data.

Language

Properties

Name	Returns	Description
Alias	String	Gets/Sets the language alias.
Application	Application	The top-level Application object for SQL-DMO.
Day	String	Get language full names for specified numerical day.
Days	String	Get language day names.

Name	Returns	Description
FirstDayOfWeek	Long	Get the first day of the week.
ID	Long	The ID value for the object.
LangDateFormat	String	The language date-component sequence.
Month	String	Get language's full name for specified numerical month.
Months	String	Get language's full month names.
Name	String	The name of the object.
Parent	IVSQLDMOStdObject	The hierarchical parent object.
Properties	Properties	A list of properties for the object.
ShortMonth	String	Get language's abbreviated name for specified numerical month.
ShortMonths	String	Get language's abbreviated month names.
TypeOf	SQLDMO_OBJECT_TYPE	The type of SQL-DMO object.
Upgrade	Long	SQL Server version of last language upgrade.
UserData	Long	User's private data.

Languages

Methods

Name	Returns	Description
Item	Language	Retrieves a Language object from the collection.
ItemByID	Language	Retrieves a Language object from the collection
Refresh		Refreshes data in the collection.

Properties

Name	Returns	Description
Application	Application	The top-level Application object for SQL-DMO.
Count	Long	The number of Language objects in the collection.
Parent	IVSQLDMOStdObject	The hierarchical parent object.
TypeOf	SQLDMO_OBJECT_TYPE	The type of SQL-DMO object.
UserData	Long	User's private data.

LinkedServer

Methods

Name	Returns	Description
EnumColumns	QueryResults	Returns available columns for the selected table.
Enumtables	QueryResults	Returns the available tables on the selected database.
ExecuteImmediate		Executes a remote stored procedure via pass-through, with no results.
ExecuteWithResults	QueryResults	Executes a remote stored procedure via pass-through and returns a QueryResults object.
ExecuteWith ResultsAndMessages	QueryResults	Executes a command via pass-through and return a QueryResults object and any generated messages.
Remove		Drops the object and removes it from the collection.
SetOptions		Sets one or more options true/false.

Properties

Name	Returns	Description
Application	Application	The top-level Application object for SQL-DMO.
Catalog	String	Gets/Sets a linked server's catalog.
DataSource	String	Gets/Sets a linked server's data source.
DropLogins	Boolean	Get/Set the option to remove all the associated linked server logins when removing the LinkedServer.
LinkedServerLogins	Linked ServerLogins	A collection of LinkedServerLogins.
Location	String	Gets/Sets the location of the linked server.
Name	String	The name of the object.
Options	SQLDMO_ SRVOPTION_TYPE	The linked server's option type.
Parent	IVSQLDMO StdObject	The hierarchical parent object.
ProductName	String	Get or set linked server's product name.
Properties	Properties	A list of properties for the object.
ProviderName	String	The name of the linked server's provider name.
ProviderString	String	Gets/Sets the linked server's provider string.
TypeOf	SQLDMO_ OBJECT_TYPE	The type of SQL-DMO object.
UserData	Long	User's private data.

LinkedServerLogin

Methods

Name	Returns	Description
Remove		Drops the object and removes it from the collection.

Properties

Name	Returns	Description
Application	Application	The top-level Application object for SQL-DMO.
Impersonate	Boolean	Gets/Sets whether the login should impersonate another user.
LocalLogin	String	Gets/Sets the LinkedServerLogin's local login name.
Parent	IVSQLDMOStdObject	The hierarchical parent object.
Properties	Properties	A list of properties for the object.
RemotePassword	String	Gets/Sets the LinkedServerLogin's remote login password.
RemoteUser	String	Gets/Sets the LinkedServerLogin's remote login name.
TypeOf	SQLDMO_OBJECT_TYPE	The type of SQL-DMO object.
UserData	Long	User's private data.

LinkedServerLogins

Methods

Name	Returns	Description
Add		Adds a LinkedServerLogin object to the collection.

Name	Returns	Description
Item	LinkedServer Login	Retrieves a LinkedServerLogin object from the collection.
Refresh		Refreshes data in the collection
Remove		Removes a LinkedServerLogin object from the collection.

Properties

Name	Returns	Description
Application	Application	The top-level Application object for SQL-DMO.
Count	Long	The number of LinkedServerLogin objects in the collection.
Parent	IVSQLDMOStdObject	The hierarchical parent object.
TypeOf	SQLDMO_OBJECT_TYPE	The type of SQL-DMO object.
UserData	Long	User's private data.

LinkedServers

Methods

Name	Returns	Description
Add		Adds a LinkedServer object to the collection.
Item	LinkedServer	Retrieves a LinkedServer object from the collection.
Refresh		Refreshes data in the collection.
Remove		Removes a LinkedServer object from the collection.

Properties

Name	Returns	Description
Application	Application	The top-level `Application` object for SQL-DMO.
Count	Long	The number of `LinkedServer` objects in the collection.
Parent	IVSQLDMOStdObject	The hierarchical parent object.
TypeOf	SQLDMO_OBJECT_TYPE	The type of SQL-DMO object.
UserData	Long	User's private data.

LogFile

Methods

Name	Returns	Description
Shrink		Shrinks the log file to a new size.

Properties

Name	Returns	Description
Application	Application	The top-level `Application` object for SQL-DMO.
FileGrowth	Long	Specifies the size of the increment in KB or as a percentage.
FileGrowthInKB	Single	Specifies the size of the increment in KB.
FileGrowthType	SQLDMO_GROWTH_TYPE	The type of file growth in MB or as a percentage.
ID	Long	The ID value for the object.
MaximumSize	Long	Specifies the maximum size of the log file in MB.
Name	String	The name of the object.
Parent	IVSQLDMOStdObject	The hierarchical parent object.

Name	Returns	Description
PhysicalName	String	The physical name for this log file.
Properties	Properties	A list of properties for the object.
Size	Long	The size of the log file in MB.
SizeInKB	Single	The size of the log file in KB.
TypeOf	SQLDMO_OBJECT_TYPE	The type of SQL-DMO object.
UserData	Long	User's private data.

LogFiles

Methods

Name	Returns	Description
Add		Adds a LogFile object to the collection.
Item	LogFile	Retrieves a LogFile object from the collection.
ItemByID	LogFile	Retrieves a LogFile object from the collection by ID.
Refresh		Refreshes data in the collection.

Properties

Name	Returns	Description
Application	Application	The top-level Application object for SQL-DMO.
Count	Long	The number of LogFile objects in the collection.
Parent	IVSQLDMOStdObject	The hierarchical parent object.
TypeOf	SQLDMO_OBJECT_TYPE	The type of SQL-DMO object.
UserData	Long	User's private data.

Login

Methods

Name	Returns	Description
EnumDatabaseMappings	QueryResults	Enumerates databases in which this login is a user, or aliased to one.
GetAliasName	String	Get this login's alias name in specified database.
GetUserName	String	Get this login's user name in specified database.
IsMember	Boolean	Checks if the login is a member of selected server role.
ListMembers	NameList	Lists the server roles the login belongs to.
Remove		Drops the object and removes it from the collection.
Script	String	Generates a SQL script for the object.
SetPassword		Sets login password.

Properties

Name	Returns	Description
Application	Application	The top-level Application object for SQL-DMO.
Database	String	Gets/Sets the login's default database.
DenyNTLogin	Boolean	Sets the current NT login as a granted or denied login.
Language	String	Gets/Sets the login's language.
LanguageAlias	String	Gets the language alias name for this login.
Name	String	The name of the object.

Name	Returns	Description
NTLoginAccessType	SQLDMO_ NTACCESS_TYPE	Retrieves the access type for the NT user.
Parent	IVSQLDMOStdObject	The hierarchical parent object.
Properties	Properties	A list of properties for the object.
SystemObject	Boolean	Checks to see if the object is a system object.
Type	SQLDMO_LOGIN_TYPE	Get/Set the new login type: NT user, NT group, or standard login.
TypeOf	SQLDMO_OBJECT_TYPE	The type of SQL-DMO object.
UserData	Long	User's private data.

Logins

Methods

Name	Returns	Description
Add		Adds a Login object to the collection.
Item	Login	Retrieves a Login object from the collection.
Refresh		Refreshes data in the collection.
Remove		Removes a Login object from the collection.

Properties

Name	Returns	Description
Application	Application	The top-level Application object for SQL-DMO.
Count	Long	The number of Login objects in the collection.
Parent	IVSQLDMOStdObject	The hierarchical parent object.
TypeOf	SQLDMO_OBJECT_TYPE	The type of SQL-DMO object.
UserData	Long	User's private data.

MergeArticle

Methods

Name	Returns	Description
BeginAlter		Begins a multi-property object alter.
CancelAlter		Cancels a multi-property object alter.
DoAlter		Executes an object alter.
Remove		Drops the object and removes it from the collection.
Script	String	Generates a SQL script for the object.
ScriptDestinationObject	String	Generates a SQL script to create the schema for this object.

Properties

Name	Returns	Description
Application	Application	The top-level Application object for SQL-DMO.
Article Resolver	String	The name of the module that reconciles changes to this article.
ArticleType	SQLDMO_ ARTICLE_TYPE	The type of article.
ColumnTracking	Boolean	Checks if the article has column-level tracking turned on.
ConflictTable	String	The fully-qualified name of the conflict table generated on the article.
Creation ScriptOptions	SQLDMO_ CREATIONSCRIPT_ TYPE	The creation script options.
Creation ScriptPath	String	The path to the snapshot creation script.
Description	String	A descriptive text about the object.
ID	Long	The ID value for the object.

Name	Returns	Description
Merge SubsetFilters	Merge SubsetFilters	A collection of subset filters for this merge article.
Name	String	The name of the object.
Parent	IVSQLDMO StdObject	The hierarchical parent object.
PreCreation Method	SQLDMO_ PREARTICLE_TYPE	The article precreation command.
Properties	Properties	The properties of the object.
ResolverInfo	String	Information needed by the custom conflict resolver.
Snapshot ObjectName	String	The none-qualified name of table or view to use as template for initial sync.
Snapshot ObjectOwner	String	The owner name of table or view to use as template for initial sync.
Source ObjectName	String	The none-qualified name of the source object being replicated.
Source ObjectOwner	String	The owner name of the source object being replicated.
Status	SQLDMO_ ARTSTATUS_TYPE	The status of the merge article.
Subset FilterClause	String	The filter clause to define the subset publication.
TypeOf	SQLDMO_ OBJECT_TYPE	The type of SQL-DMO object.
UserData	Long	User's private data.

MergeArticles

Methods

Name	Returns	Description
Add		Adds a MergeArticle object to the collection.
Item	MergeArticle	Retrieves a MergeArticle object from the collection.

Table Continued on Following Page

Name	Returns	Description
ItemByID	MergeArticle	Retrieves a `MergeArticle` object from the collection by ID.
Refresh		Refreshes data in the collection.
Remove		Removes a `MergeArticle` object from the collection.

Properties

Name	Returns	Description
Application	Application	The top-level `Application` object for SQL-DMO.
Count	Long	The number of `MergeArticle` objects in the collection.
Parent	IVSQLDMOStdObject	The hierarchical parent object.
TypeOf	SQLDMO_OBJECT_TYPE	The type of SQL-DMO object.
UserData	Long	User's private data.

MergePublication

Methods

Name	Returns	Description
BeginAlter		Begins a multi-property object alter.
CancelAlter		Cancels a multi-property object alter.
DoAlter		Executes an object alter.
EnumAll SubsetFilters	QueryResults	Enumerate all subset-filters of all articles for this publication.
EnumGenerated SubSetFilters	QueryResults	Enumerate the generated subset-filters for an article.
EnumPublication Accesses	QueryResults	Enumerate the logins in the access list of this publication.
EnumPublication References	QueryResults	Returns a result set of the tables that are references to existing tables in the publication.

Name	Returns	Description
Enum Subscriptions	QueryResults	Enumerate the subscriptions.
GenerateFilters		Generate filters for this publication.
GrantPublication Access		Adds a login to the access list of this publication.
RefreshChildren		Refreshes the object and its child collections.
ReInitializeAll Subscriptions		Re-synchronize subscriptions on all subscribers.
Remove		Drops the object and removes it from the collection.
RevokePublication Access		Remove a login to the access list of this publication.
Script	String	Generates a SQL script for this object.

Properties

Name	Returns	Description
Application	Application	The top-level Application object for SQL-DMO.
Centralized Conflicts	Boolean	The publication has centralized conflict reporting.
Description	String	A description of the object.
DynamicFilters	Boolean	Checks if the publication is filtered on a dynamic clause.
Enabled	Boolean	Is the publication available for use?
HasSubscription	Boolean	Checks whether the publication has any subscription unsynchronized anonymous subscriptions.
ID	Long	The ID value for the object.
MergeArticles	MergeArticles	A collection of merge articles for this merge publication.
Merge Subscriptions	Merge Subscriptions	A collection of merge subscriptions for this merge publication.

Table Continued on Following Page

Name	Returns	Description
Name	String	The name of the object.
Parent	IVSQLDMO StdObject	The hierarchical parent object.
Priority	Single	The priority of the replica available at this publisher.
Properties	Properties	The properties of the object.
Publication Attributes	SQLDMO_ PUBATTRIB_TYPE	The attributes the publication supports.
RetentionPeriod	Long	The retention period of the publication.
Snapshot Available	Boolean	Is this merge publication's snapshot available?
SnapshotJobID	String	The job ID of the snapshot.
SnapshotMethod	SQLDMO_ INITIALSYNC_ TYPE	The initial synchronization method.
SnapshotSchedule	Schedule	The schedule for the snapshot agent associated with this publication.
TypeOf	SQLDMO_ OBJECT_TYPE	The type of SQL-DMO object.
UserData	Long	User's private data.

MergePublications

Methods

Name	Returns	Description
Add		Adds a MergePublication object to the collection.
Item	MergePublication	Retrieves a MergePublication object from the collection.
ItemByID	MergePublication	Retrieves a MergePublication object from the collection by ID.
Refresh		Refreshes data in the collection.
Remove		Removes a MergePublication object from the collection.
Script	String	Generates a SQL script for the object.

Properties

Name	Returns	Description
Application	Application	The top-level `Application` object for SQL-DMO.
Count	Long	The number of `MergePublication` objects in the collection.
Parent	IVSQLDMOStdObject	The hierarchical parent object.
TypeOf	SQLDMO_OBJECT_TYPE	The type of SQL-DMO object.
UserData	Long	User's private data.

MergePullSubscription

Methods

Name	Returns	Description
BeginAlter		Begins a multi-property object alter.
CancelAlter		Cancels a multi-property object alter.
DoAlter		Executes an object alter.
EnumJobInfo	QueryResults	Enumerates the job info for this subscription.
ReInitialize		Re-initializes this subscription.
Remove		Drops the object and removes it from the collection.
Script	String	Generates a SQL script for the object.

Properties

Name	Returns	Description
Application	Application	The top-level `Application` object for SQL-DMO.
Description	String	A descriptive text about the object.
Distributor	String	The name of the distribution server.

Table Continued on Following Page

Name	Returns	Description
Distributor Security	Replication Security	Replication security attributes for the distributor.
EnabledFor SyncMgr	Boolean	Checks if the subscription is registered with SynchMgr.
FTPAddress	String	The address of the FTP server.
FTPLogin	String	The username used to log on to the FTP server.
FTPPassword	String	The password used to log on to the FTP server.
FTPPort	Variant long	The IP port for the FTP server.
MergeJobID	String	The merge job ID.
MergeSchedule	Schedule	The schedule for the merge agent associated with this merge subscriber subscription.
Name	String	The name of the object.
Parent	IVSQLDMO StdObject	The hierarchical parent object.
Priority	Single	The priority for this subscriber.
Properties	Properties	The properties for the object.
Publication	String	The name of the subscription source for the article.
PublicationDB	String	The name of the publication database.
Publisher	String	The name of the publisher server.
Publisher Security	Replication Security	The replication security attributes for the publisher.
Subscriber Login	String	The login record used by the merge agent to logon subscribing server.
Subscriber Password	String	The password used by the merge agent to logon subscribing server
Subscriber SecurityMode	SQLDMO_ SECURITY_TYPE	Security mode used by the merge agent to logon subscribing server.
SubscriberType	SQLDMO_ MERGESUBSCRIBER_ TYPE	The type of subscriber.

Name	Returns	Description
Subscription Type	SQLDMO_ SUBSCRIPTION_TYPE	The type of subscription.
SyncType	SQLDMO_ SUBSYNC_TYPE	The synchronization type for this subscriber.
TypeOf	SQLDMO_OBJECT_TYPE	The type of SQL-DMO object.
UserData	Long	User's private data.

MergePullSubscriptions

Methods

Name	Returns	Description
Add		Adds a MergePullSubscription object to the collection.
Item	MergePullSubscription	Retrieves a MergePullSubscription object from the collection.
ItemByID	MergePullSubscription	Retrieves a MergePullSubscription object from the collection by ID.
Refresh		Refreshes data in the collection.
Remove		Removes a MergePullSubscription object from the collection.
Script	String	Generates a SQL script for the object.

Properties

Name	Returns	Description
Application	Application	The top-level Application object for SQL-DMO.
Count	Long	The number of MergePullSubscription objects in the collection.
Parent	IVSQLDMOStdObject	The hierarchical parent object.
TypeOf	SQLDMO_OBJECT_TYPE	The type of SQL-DMO object.
UserData	Long	User's private data.

MergeSubscription

Methods

Name	Returns	Description
BeginAlter		Begins multi-property object alter.
CancelAlter		Cancels multi-property object alter.
DoAlter		Executes an object alter.
ReInitialize		Re-initializes this subscription.
Remove		Drops the object and removes it from the collection.
Script	String	Generates a SQL script for the object.

Properties

Name	Returns	Description
Application	Application	The top-level Application object for SQL-DMO.
Description	String	A descriptive text about the object.
EnabledForSyncMgr	Boolean	Register this subscription with SyncMgr?
MergeJobID	String	The merge job ID.
MergeSchedule	Schedule	The merge schedule.
Name	String	The name of the object.
Parent	IVSQLDMOStdObject	The hierarchical parent object.
Priority	Single	The priority for this subscription.
Properties	Properties	The properties for this object.
Status	SQLDMO_SUBSTATUS_TYPE	The status for the subscription.
Subscriber	String	The name of the subscriber server.
SubscriberType	SQLDMO_MERGESUBSCRIBER_TYPE	The type of subscriber.
SubscriptionDB	String	The name of the subscription database.

Name	Returns	Description
SubscriptionType	SQLDMO_ SUBSCRIPTION_TYPE	The type of subscription.
SyncType	SQLDMO_ SUBSYNC_TYPE	The synchronization type for this subscriber.
TypeOf	SQLDMO_ OBJECT_TYPE	The type of SQL-DMO object.
UserData	Long	User's private data.

MergeSubscriptions

Methods

Name	Returns	Description
Add		Adds a MergeSubscription object to the collection.
Item	Merge Subscription	Retrieves a MergeSubscription object from the collection.
Refresh		Refreshes data in the collection.
Remove		Removes a MergeSubscription object from the collection.
Script	String	Generates a SQL script for the object.

Properties

Name	Returns	Description
Application	Application	The top-level Application object for SQL-DMO.
Count	Long	The number of MergeSubscription objects in the collection.
Parent	IVSQLDMOStdObject	The hierarchical parent object.
TypeOf	SQLDMO_OBJECT_TYPE	The type of SQL-DMO object.
UserData	Long	User's private data.

MergeSubsetFilter

Methods

Name	Returns	Description
BeginAlter		Begins multi-property object alter.
CancelAlter		Cancels multi-property object alter.
DoAlter		Executes an object alter.
Remove		Drops the object and removes it from the collection.

Properties

Name	Returns	Description
Application	Application	The top-level Application object for SQL-DMO.
ID	Long	The ID value for the object.
JoinArticleName	String	The name of the join article.
JoinFilterClause	String	The filter clause to qualify the join filter.
JoinUniqueKey	Boolean	Does the join have a unique key?
Name	String	The name of the object.
Parent	IVSQLDMOStdObject	The hierarchical parent object.
Properties	Properties	A list of properties for the object.
TypeOf	SQLDMO_OBJECT_TYPE	The type of SQL-DMO object.
UserData	Long	User's private data.

MergeSubsetFilters

Methods

Name	Returns	Description
Add		Adds a `MergeSubsetFilter` object to the collection.
Item	Merge SubsetFilter	Retrieves a `MergeSubsetFilter` object from the collection.
ItemByID	Merge SubsetFilter	Retrieves a `MergeSubsetFilter` object from the collection by ID.
Refresh		Refreshes data in the collection.
Remove		Removes a `MergeSubsetFilter` object from the collection.

Properties

Name	Returns	Description
Application	Application	The top-level `Application` object for SQL-DMO.
Count	Long	The number of `MergeSubsetFilter` objects in the collection.
Parent	IVSQLDMOStdObject	The hierarchical parent object.
TypeOf	SQLDMO_OBJECT_TYPE	The type of SQL-DMO object.
UserData	Long	User's private data.

NameList

Methods

Name	Returns	Description
FindName	Long	Finds the ordinal position of, or name in the collection.
Item	String	Retrieves a name.
Refresh		Refreshes data in the object.

Properties

Name	Returns	Description
Application	Application	The top-level Application object for SQL-DMO.
Count	Long	The number of items.
Parent	IVSQLDMOStdObject	The hierarchical parent object.
TypeOf	SQLDMO_OBJECT_TYPE	The type of SQL-DMO object.
UserData	Long	User's private data.

Names

Methods

Name	Returns	Description
Add		Adds a name to the collection.
FindName	Long	Retrieves the ordinal value or name from the collection.
Insert		Insert a name into the collection before the name or a specified ordinal.
Item	String	Retrieve a name from the collection.
Refresh		Refreshes data in collection.
Remove		Removes a name from the collection.
Replace		Replace a name (preserving position) or ordinal in the collection.

Properties

Name	Returns	Description
Application	Application	The top-level Application object for SQL-DMO.
Count	Long	The number of items.
Parent	IVSQLDMOStdObject	The hierarchical parent object.
TypeOf	SQLDMO_OBJECT_TYPE	The type of SQL-DMO object.
UserData	Long	User's private data.

Operator

Methods

Name	Returns	Description
AddNotification		Adds an alert notification for this operator.
BeginAlter		Begins multi-column table alter.
CancelAlter		Cancels multi-column table alter.
DoAlter		Executes a table alter.
EnumJobNotifications	QueryResults	Enumerates the job notifications this operator receives.
EnumNotifications	QueryResults	Enumerate this operator's notifications.
Refresh		Refreshes the data for this object.
Remove		Drops the object and removes it from the collection.
RemoveNotification		Removes an alert notification for this operator.
Script	String	Generates a SQL script for the object.
UpdateNotifcation		Updates this operator's notification methods for an alert.

Properties

Name	Returns	Description
Application	Application	The top-level Application object for SQL-DMO.
Category	String	Gets/Sets the Category name.
EmailAddress	String	The e-mail address of the operator.
Enabled	Boolean	Is the operator available?
ID	Long	The ID value for the object.

Table Continued on Following Page

Name	Returns	Description
LastEmailDate	Date	The date/time the operator last received an e-mail notification.
LastNetSendDate	Long	The last date the operator received a net send.
LastNetSendTime	Long	The last time the operator received a net send.
LastPageDate	Date	The date/time the operator last received an pager notification.
Name	String	The name of the object.
NetSendAddress	String	Get/Set net sent address for the operator.
PagerAddress	String	The page address for the operator.
PagerDays	SQLDMO_WEEKDAY_TYPE	A bitmask of days this operator can be paged.
Parent	IVSQLDMOStdObject	The hierarchical parent object.
Properties	Properties	A list of properties for the object.
Saturday PagerEndTime	Date	Latest Saturday time to send pages to this operator.
Saturday PagerStartTime	Date	Earliest Saturday time to send pages to this operator.
Sunday PagerEndTime	Date	Latest Sunday time to send pages to this operator.
Sunday PagerStartTime	Date	Earliest Sunday time to send pages to this operator.
TypeOf	SQLDMO_OBJECT_TYPE	The type of SQL-DMO object.
UserData	Long	User's private data.
Weekday PagerEndTime	Date	Latest weekday time to send pages to this operator.
Weekday PagerStartTime	Date	Earliest weekday time to send pages to this operator.

OperatorCategories

Methods

Name	Returns	Description
Add		Adds a Category object to the collection.
Item	Category	Retrieves a Category object from the collection.
ItemByID	Category	Retrieves a Category object from the collection by ID.
Refresh		Refreshes data in the collection.
Remove		Removes a Category object from the collection.

Properties

Name	Returns	Description
Application	Application	The top level Application object for SQL-DMO.
Count	Long	The number of items.
Parent	IVSQLDMOStdObject	The hierarchical parent object.
TypeOf	SQLDMO_OBJECT_TYPE	The type of SQL-DMO object.
UserData	Long	User's private data.

Operators

Methods

Name	Returns	Description
Add		Adds an Operator object to the collection.
Item	Operator	Retrieves an Operator object from the collection.
ItemByID	Operator	Retrieves an Operator object from the collection by ID.
Refresh		Refreshes data in the collection.
Remove		Removes an Operator object from the collection.
Script	String	Generates a SQL script for the object.

Properties

Name	Returns	Description
Application	Application	The top-level Application object for SQL-DMO.
Count	Long	The number of items.
Parent	IVSQLDMOStdObject	The hierarchical parent object.
TypeOf	SQLDMO_OBJECT_TYPE	The type of SQL-DMO object.
UserData	Long	User's private data.

Permission

Methods

Name	Returns	Description
ListPrivilegeColumns	SQLObjectList	Returns a list of columns.

Properties

Name	Returns	Description
Application	Application	The top-level Application object for SQL-DMO.
Granted	Boolean	True = granted, False = deny
Grantee	String	User or group granted this privilege.
ObjectID	Long	The object's database ID.
ObjectName	String	The name of the object.
ObjectOwner	String	The object owner's name.
ObjectType	SQLDMO_OBJECT_TYPE	The object's type.
ObjectTypeName	String	The object type's name.
Parent	IVSQLDMO StdObject	The hierarchical parent object.

Name	Returns	Description
PrivilegeType	SQLDMO_ PRIVILEGE_TYPE	A bitmask of privilege types.
PrivilegeTypeName	String	The privilege type's name.
Properties	Properties	A list of properties for the object.
TypeOf	SQLDMO_OBJECT_TYPE	The type of SQL-DMO object.
UserData	Long	User's private data.

Properties

Methods

Name	Returns	Description
Item	Property	Retrieves a Property object from the collection.

Properties

Name	Returns	Description
Application	Application	The top-level Application object for SQL-DMO.
Count	Long	The number of items.
Parent	IVSQLDMOStdObject	The hierarchical parent object.
TypeOf	SQLDMO_OBJECT_TYPE	The type of SQL-DMO object.
UserData	Long	User's private data.

Property

Properties

Name	Returns	Description
Application	Application	The top-level Application object for SQL-DMO.
Get	Boolean	Retrieves whether the value can be read.
Name	String	The name of the object.
Parent	IVSQLDMO StdObject	The hierarchical parent object.
Properties	Properties	A list of properties for the object.
Set	Boolean	Retrieves whether the value can be written to.
Type	Long	Returns the type value.
TypeOf	SQLDMO_OBJE CT_TYPE	The type of SQL-DMO object.
UserData	Long	User's private data.
Value	Variant	The value for the Property object.

Publisher

Methods

Name	Returns	Description
Enum Publications	QueryResults	Enumerate publications on databases on this server, which have been enabled for replication.
Script	String	Generate SQL script to setup this object.
Uninstall		Disables publishing.

Properties

Name	Returns	Description
Application	Application	The top-level Application object for SQL-DMO.
Parent	IVSQLDMO StdObject	The hierarchical parent object.
Properties	Properties	A list of properties for the object.
Registered Subscribers	Registered Subscribers	A collection of RegisteredSubscriber objects.
TypeOf	SQLDMO_ OBJECT_TYPE	The type of SQL-DMO object.
UserData	Long	User's private data.

QueryResults

Methods

Name	Returns	Description
GetColumnBinary	Integer	Gets a binary column as an array of bytes.
GetColumn BinaryLength	Long	Get the binary length of the cell.
GetColumnBool	Boolean	Converts a cell to a Boolean; returning 1 if nonzero, else 0.
GetColumnDate	Date	Converts a cell to a string data type date and returns its value.
GetColumnDouble	Double	Converts a cell to double-precision float and returns its values
GetColumnFloat	Single	Converts a cell to a single-precision float and return its value.
GetColumnGUID	Integer	Get a GUID column as an array of bytes.
GetColumnLong	Long	Converts a cell to a long and returns its value.
GetColumnString	String	Converts a cell to a string and return its value.
GetRangeString	String	Converts a range of cells into a delimited, width-padded string.
Refresh		Refreshes cached values.

Properties

Name	Returns	Description
Application	Application	The top-level Application object for SQL-DMO.
ColumnMaxLength	String	The maximum length of a column in current result set.
ColumnName	String	The name of a column in current result set.
Columns	Long	The number of columns in current result set.
ColumnType	SQLDMO_QUERY_DATATYPE	The data type of a column is the current result set.
CurrentResultSet	Long	The current result set.
Parent	IVSQLDMOStdObject	The hierarchical parent object.
Properties	Properties	A list of properties for the object.
ResultSets	Long	The number of result sets.
Rows	Long	The number of rows in the current result set.
TypeOf	SQLDMO_OBJECT_TYPE	The type of SQL-DMO object.
UserData	Long	User's private data.

RegisteredServer

Methods

Name	Returns	Description
Remove		Drops the object and removes it from the collection.

Properties

Name	Returns	Description
Application	Application	The top-level Application object for SQL-DMO.

Name	Returns	Description
Login	String	The registered server login ID.
Name	String	The name of the object.
Parent	IVSQLDMOStdObject	The hierarchical parent object.
Password	String	The registered server login's password.
PersistFlags	Long	The persistent flags stored with this registered server.
Properties	Properties	A list of properties for the object.
SaLogin	Boolean	Checks if the registered server's login ID is the server admin.
TypeOf	SQLDMO_OBJECT_TYPE	The type of SQL-DMO object.
UserData	Long	User's private data.
UseTrusted Connection	Long	Login via SQL authentication, NT authentication, or SQL authentication prompt for password.
VersionMajor	Long	The RegisteredServer version major number.
VersionMinor	Long	The RegisteredServer version minor number.

RegisteredServers

Methods

Name	Returns	Description
Add		Adds a RegisteredServer object to the collection.
Item	RegisteredServer	Retrieves a RegisteredServer object from the collection.
Refresh		Refreshes data in the collection.
Remove		Removes a RegisteredServer object from the collection.

Properties

Name	Returns	Description
Application	Application	The top-level `Application` object for SQL-DMO.
Count	Long	The number of items.
Parent	IVSQLDMOStdObject	The hierarchical parent object.
TypeOf	SQLDMO_OBJECT_TYPE	The type of SQL-DMO object.
UserData	Long	User's private data.

RegisteredSubscriber

Methods

Name	Returns	Description
BeginAlter		Begins a multi-property `RegisteredSubscriber` alter.
CancelAlter		Cancels a multi-property `RegisteredSubscriber` alter.
DoAlter		Executes a `RegisteredSubscriber` alter.
Refresh		Refreshes data in the object.
Remove		Drops the object and removes it from the collection.
Script	String	Generates a SQL script for the object.

Properties

Name	Returns	Description
Application	Application	The top-level `Application` object for SQL-DMO.
Default Distribution Schedule	Schedule	The default distribution schedule for this subscription server.
Default MergeSchedule	Schedule	The default merge schedule for this subscriber.
Description	String	A descriptive text about the object.

Name	Returns	Description
Name	String	The name of the object.
Parent	IVSQLDMO StdObject	The hierarchical parent object.
Properties	Properties	A list of properties for the object.
Replication Security	Replication Security	The replication security attributes for this subscription server.
Type	SQLDMO_ SUBSCRIBER_TYPE	The subscriber type.
TypeOf	SQLDMO_ OBJECT_TYPE	The type of SQL-DMO object.
UserData	Long	User's private data.

RegisteredSubscribers

Methods

Name	Returns	Description
Add		Adds a RegisteredSubscriber object to the collection.
Item	Registered Subscriber	Retrieves a RegisteredSubscriber object from the collection.
Refresh		Refreshes data in the collection.
Remove		Removes a RegisteredSubscriber object from the collection.
Script	String	Generates a SQL script for this object.

Properties

Name	Returns	Description
Application	Application	The top-level Application object for SQL-DMO.
Count	Long	The number of items.

Table Continued on Following Page

Name	Returns	Description
Parent	IVSQLDMOStdObject	The hierarchical parent object.
TypeOf	SQLDMO_OBJECT_TYPE	The type of SQL-DMO object.
UserData	Long	User's private data.

Registry

Properties

Name	Returns	Description
Application	Application	The top-level Application object for SQL-DMO.
AutostartDTC	Boolean	Starts DTC when Windows NT starts.
AutostartLicensing	Boolean	Start license logging when server starts.
AutostartMail	Boolean	Start mail when SQL Server starts.
AutostartServer	Boolean	Start SQL Server when OS starts.
CaseSensitive	Boolean	Is server case sensitive?
CharacterSet	String	The character set loaded on the SQL Server.
ErrorLogPath	String	The error log path.
MailAccountName	String	The SQL mail account name.
MailPassword	String	The SQL mail account password.
MasterDBPath	String	The master database path.
NTEventLogging	Boolean	Does the SQL Server record events in the NT event log?
NumberOfProcessors	Long	The number of processors on the server machine.
Parent	IVSQLDMO StdObject	The hierarchical parent object.
PerfMonMode	SQLDMO_ PERFMON_ TYPE	The performance monitor mode.
PhysicalMemory	Long	The MB of physical RAM on the server machine.

Name	Returns	Description
Properties	Properties	A list of properties for the object.
Registered Organization	String	The registered organization that is set at install time.
RegisteredOwner	String	The registered owner that is set at install time.
Replication Installed	Boolean	Are replication files installed by setup?
SortOrder	String	The sort order installed on the SQL Server.
SQLDataRoot	String	The SQL Server data root path.
SQLRootPath	String	The SQL Server root path.
TapeLoadWaitTime	Long	The wait time for the tape to load.
TypeOf	SQLDMO_ OBJECT_TYPE	The type of SQL-DMO object.
UserData	Long	User's private data.

RemoteLogin

Methods

Name	Returns	Description
Remove		Drops the object and removes the object from the collection.

Properties

Name	Returns	Description
Application	Application	The top-level Application object for SQL-DMO.
LocalName	String	Get/Set RemoteLogin's name on local server.
Parent	IVSQLDMO StdObject	The hierarchical parent object.
Properties	Properties	The properties for the object.
RemoteName	String	Get or set RemoteLogin's name on remote server.
Trusted	Boolean	Is this RemoteLogin's password checking skipped?
TypeOf	SQLDMO_ OBJECT_TYPE	The type of SQL-DMO object.
UserData	Long	User's private data.

RemoteLogins

Methods

Name	Returns	Description
Add		Adds a RemoteLogin object to the collection.
Item	RemoteLogin	Retrieves a RemoteLogin object from the collection.
Refresh		Refreshes data in the collection.
Remove		Removes a RemoteLogin object from the collection.

Properties

Name	Returns	Description
Application	Application	The top-level Application object for SQL-DMO.
Count	Long	The number of items.
Parent	IVSQLDMOStdObject	The hierarchical parent object.
TypeOf	SQLDMO_OBJECT_TYPE	The type of SQL-DMO object.
UserData	Long	User's private data.

RemoteServer

Methods

Name	Returns	Description
ExecuteImmediate		Execute a remote stored procedure via pass-through, with no results.
ExecuteWithResults	QueryResults	Execute a remote stored procedure via pass-through and return a QueryResults object.
ExecuteWith ResultsAndMessages	QueryResults	Execute a command via pass-through and return a QueryResults object and any generated messages.

Name	Returns	Description
Remove		Drops the object and removes it from the collection.
SetOptions		Sets one or more options true/false.
SetTopologyXY		Set topology coordinates.

Properties

Name	Returns	Description
Application	Application	The top-level `Application` object for SQL-DMO.
ID	Long	The ID value for the object.
Name	String	The name of the object.
NetName	String	Gets/Sets the server network name.
Options	SQLDMO_SRVOPTION_TYPE	The remote server options.
Parent	IVSQLDMOStdObject	The hierarchical parent object.
Properties	Properties	A list of properties for the object.
RemoteLogins	RemoteLogins	The remote logins collection.
TopologyX	Long	Gets topology X coordinate.
TopologyY	Long	Gets topology Y coordinate.
TypeOf	SQLDMO_OBJECT_TYPE	The type of SQL-DMO object.
UserData	Long	User's private data.

RemoteServers

Methods

Name	Returns	Description
Add		Adds a `RemoteServer` object to the collection.
Item	RemoteServer	Retrieves a `RemoteServer` object from the collection.

Table Continued on Following Page

Name	Returns	Description
ItemByID	RemoteServer	Retrieves a RemoteServer object from the collection by ID.
Refresh		Refreshes data in the collection.
Remove		Removes a RemoteServer object from the collection.

Properties

Name	Returns	Description
Application	Application	The top-level Application object for SQL-DMO.
Count	Long	The number of items.
Parent	IVSQLDMOStdObject	The hierarchical parent object.
TypeOf	SQLDMO_OBJECT_TYPE	The type of SQL-DMO object.
UserData	Long	User's private data.

Replication

Events

Name	Returns	Description
PercentComplete		Percentage completed in the current stage of replication.
StatusMessage		The status message during the replication process.

Methods

Name	Returns	Description
EnumCustom Resolvers	QueryResults	Enumerate the custom resolvers registered at the given distributor.
EnumData SourceNames	QueryResults	Enumerate the DSNs registered at the distributor.

Name	Returns	Description
Script	String	Generates a SQL script for the object.
Uninstall		Uninstalls the replication setup of the server.
Validate DataSource		Validates that the ODBC data source is a valid SQL subscriber by attempting to connect to the designated source.

Properties

Name	Returns	Description
Application	Application	The top-level Application object for SQL-DMO.
Distributor	Distributor	The replication distributor object.
Parent	IVSQLDMO StdObject	The hierarchical parent object.
Properties	Properties	A list of properties for the object.
Publisher	Publisher	The replication publisher object.
Replication Databases	Replication Databases	The collection of replication databases for this server.
Subscriber	Subscriber	The replication subscriber object.
TypeOf	SQLDMO_ OBJECT_TYPE	The type of SQL-DMO object.
UserData	Long	User's private data.

ReplicationDatabase

Methods

Name	Returns	Description
DisableMerge Subscription		Removes a merge subscription from this database's publication.
DisableTrans Subscription		Removes a transacted subscription from this database's publication.

Table Continued on Following Page

Name	Returns	Description
EnableMerge Subscription		Adds a merge subscription to this database's publication.
EnableTrans Subscription		Adds a transacted subscription to this database's publication.
EnumConflictTables	QueryResults	Returns a result set containing information about conflict tables.
EnumInitial Accesses	QueryResults	Returns a result set containing information about initial login access list.
RefreshChildren		Refreshes the object and its child collections.
Script	String	Generates a SQL script for the object.

Properties

Name	Returns	Description
AllowMerge Publication	Boolean	Retrieves whether a merge publication is allowed in this database.
Application	Application	The top-level Application object for SQL-DMO.
DBOwner	Boolean	Whether the current user is owner of the database.
EnableMerge Publishing	Boolean	Enable this database for merge publishing.
EnableTrans Publishing	Boolean	Enable this database for transactional publishing.
Merge Publications	Merge Publications	Collection of merge publications for this database.
MergePull Subscriptions	MergePull Subscriptions	Collection of merge pull subscriptions in this database.
Name	String	The name of the object.
Parent	IVSQLDMO StdObject	The hierarchical parent object.
Properties	Properties	A list of properties for the object.
Replication StoredProcedures	Replication StoredProcedures	The collection of stored procedures that can be replicated.

Name	Returns	Description
Replication Tables	Replication Tables	The collection of user tables that can be replicated.
Trans Publications	Trans Publications	Collection of transaction publications for this database.
TransPull Subscriptions	TransPull Subscriptions	Collection of transactional pull subscriptions in this database.
TypeOf	SQLDMO_ OBJECT_TYPE	The type of SQL-DMO object.
UserData	Long	User's private data.

ReplicationDatabases

Methods

Name	Returns	Description
Item	ReplicationDatabase	Retrieves a ReplicationDatabase object from the collection.
ItemByID	ReplicationDatabase	Retrieves a ReplicationDatabase object from the collection by ID.
Refresh		Refreshes data in the collection.
Script	String	Generates a SQL script for the object.

Properties

Name	Returns	Description
Application	Application	The top-level Application object for SQL-DMO.
Count	Long	The number of items.
Parent	IVSQLDMOStdObject	The hierarchical parent object.
TypeOf	SQLDMO_OBJECT_TYPE	The type of SQL-DMO object.
UserData	Long	User's private data.

ReplicationSecurity

Properties

Name	Returns	Description
Application	Application	The top-level Application object for SQL-DMO.
Parent	IVSQLDMOStdObject	The hierarchical parent object.
Properties	Properties	A list of properties for this object.
SecurtiyMode	SQLDMO_ REPLSECURITY_TYPE	Integrated or standard security mode for the replication server.
StandardLogin	String	The login name to this server in standard security mode.
StandardPassword	String	The password to this server in standard security mode.
TypeOf	SQLDMO_OBJECT_TYPE	The type of SQL-DMO object.
UserData	Long	User's private data.

ReplicationStoredProcedure

Methods

Name	Returns	Description
EnumDependencies	QueryResults	Lists SQL Server database user objects and user object dependency relationships.
Enum PublicationArticles	QueryResults	Enumerate the articles in publications that this object is part of.

Properties

Name	Returns	Description
Application	Application	The top-level Application object for SQL-DMO.

Name	Returns	Description
Name	String	The name of the object.
Owner	String	The owner of the object.
Parent	IVSQLDMOStdObject	The hierarchical parent object.
Properties	Properties	A list of properties for this object.
SystemObject	Boolean	Is the object a system stored procedure?
TypeOf	SQLDMO_OBJECT_TYPE	The type of SQL-DMO object.
UserData	Long	User's private data.

ReplicationStoredProcedures

Methods

Name	Returns	Description
Item	Replication StoredProcedure	Retrieves a ReplicationStoredProcedure object from the collection.
Refresh		Refreshes data in the collection.

Properties

Name	Returns	Description
Application	Application	The top-level application object for SQL-DMO.
Count	Long	The number of items.
Parent	IVSQLDMOStdObject	The hierarchical parent object.
TypeOf	SQLDMO_OBJECT_TYPE	The type of SQL-DMO object.
UserData	Long	User's private data.

ReplicationTable

Methods

Name	Returns	Description
Enum Publication Articles	QueryResults	Enumerate the articles in publications that replicate the table.

Properties

Name	Returns	Description
Application	Application	The top-level application object for SQL-DMO.
Columns	Columns	A column collection.
HasGuidColumn	Boolean	Does this object have a globally unique identifier column?
HasPrimaryKey	Boolean	Does the object have a primary key?
HasTimeStampColumn	Boolean	Does the object have a timestamp column?
Name	String	The name of the object.
Owner	String	The owner of the object.
Parent	IVSQLDMO StdObject	The hierarchical parent object.
Properties	Properties	A list of object properties.
TypeOf	SQLDMO_ OBJECT_TYPE	The type of SQL-DMO object.
UserData	Long	User's private data.

ReplicationTables

Methods

Name	Returns	Description
Item	ReplicationTable	Retrieves an object from the collection.
Refresh		Refreshes data in the collection.

Properties

Name	Returns	Description
Application	Application	The top-level application object for SQL-DMO.
Count	Long	The number of items.
Parent	IVSQLDMOStdObject	The hierarchical parent object.
TypeOf	SQLDMO_OBJECT_TYPE	The type of SQL-DMO object.
UserData	Long	User's private data.

Restore

Events

Name	Returns	Description
Complete		Executes when restore has completed.
NextMedia		Request for next volume in restore.
PercentComplete		Percent completion message during restore process.

Methods

Name	Returns	Description
Abort		Aborts a restore process
GenerateSQL	String	Generates a series of T-SQL statements that can be used to restore the database.
ReadBackupHeader	QueryResults	Retrieves the backup header information for all backups on a particular backup file.
ReadFileList	QueryResults	Retrieves the list of the database and log files contained in the backup set.
ReadMediaHeader	QueryResults	Retrieves the media header information from the backup media.
SQLRestore		Restores the database or transaction log.
SQLVerify		Verifies the integrity of the backup.

Properties

Name	Returns	Description
Action	SQLDMO_RESTORE_TYPE	Flag to indicate the type of action to perform.
Application	Application	The top-level application object for SQL-DMO.
BackupSetName	String	The name of the backup set.
Database	String	The name of the database to restore.
DatabaseFileGroups	String	The filegroup(s) that are to be restored.
DatabaseFiles	String	The file(s) that are to be restored.
Devices	String	The backup device names.
FileNumber	Long	The set of file(s) to restore.
Files	String	Temporary restore files.
LastRestore	Boolean	Checks if this is the last restore operation to perform.
LoadHistory	Boolean	TRUE if the history information on the backup media will be loaded into the tables in MSDB.
MediaName	String	The media name for the entire backup media set.
Parent	IVSQLDMO StdObject	The hierarchical parent object.
PercentComplete Notification	Long	Percentage completion to send notification.
Pipes	String	The Pipe Device Names.
Properties	Properties	A list of properties for the object.
RelocateFiles	String	A list of logical files that are to be restored to a different location.
ReplaceDatabase	Boolean	Create the database when True.
Restart	Boolean	The operation should attempt to restart when True.
StandbyFiles	String	Standby file(s) that are to be used for RECOVERY.

Name	Returns	Description
Tapes	String	The Tape Device Names.
ToPointInTime	String	Date and time to stop restore restoration at.
TypeOf	SQLDMO_ OBJECT_TYPE	The type of SQL-DMO object.
UnloadTapeAfter	Boolean	Unload any tapes used, when restore is complete.
UserData	Long	User's private data.

Rule

Methods

Name	Returns	Description
BindToColumn		Binds to a column.
BindToDatatype		Binds to a datatype.
ListBoundColumns	SQL ObjectList	Returns a list of all bound columns.
ListBoundDatatypes	SQL ObjectList	Returns a list of all bound datatypes.
Remove		Drops the object and removes it from the collection.
Script	String	Generates a SQL Script for the object.
UnbindFromColumn		Unbinds from a column.
UnbindFromDatatype		Unbinds from a datatype.

Properties

Name	Returns	Description
Application	Application	The top-level application object for SQL-DMO.
CreateDate	String	The date of creation of the object.
ID	Long	The ID value for the object.

Table Continued on Following Page

Name	Returns	Description
Name	String	The name of the object.
Owner	String	The owner of the object.
Parent	IVSQLDMOStdObject	The hierarchical parent object.
Properties	Properties	A list of properties for the object.
Text	String	The text of object definition.
TypeOf	SQLDMO_OBJECT_TYPE	The type of SQL-DMO object.
UserData	Long	User's private data.

Rules

Methods

Name	Returns	Description
Add		Adds a Rule object to the collection.
Item	Rule	Retrieves a Rule object from the collection.
ItemByID	Rule	Retrieves a Rule object from the collection by ID.
Refresh		Refreshes data in the collection.
Remove		Removes a Rule object from the collection.

Properties

Name	Returns	Description
Application	Application	The top-level application object for SQL-DMO.
Count	Long	The number of items.
Parent	IVSQLDMO StdObject	The hierarchical parent object.
TypeOf	SQLDMO_ OBJECT_TYPE	The type of SQL-DMO object.
UserData	Long	User's private data.

Schedule

Methods

Name	Returns	Description
BeginAlter		Begins a multi-property schedule alter.
CancelAlter		Cancels a multi-property schedule alter.
DoAlter		Executes a schedule alter.
Refresh		Drops the object.

Properties

Name	Returns	Description
ActiveEndDate	Long	Gets/Sets the ending date for the active Job.
ActiveEnd TimeOfDay	Long	Gets/Sets the active job ending time of day.
ActiveStartDate	Long	Gets/Sets the active job starting date.
ActiveStart TimeOfDay	Long	Gets/Sets the active job starting time of day.
Application	Application	The top-level application object for SQL-DMO.
FrequencyInterval	Long	Get/Set job frequency interval.
Frequency RecurrenceFactor	Long	Get/Set job frequency recurrence factor.
Frequency RelativeInterval	SQLDMO_ FREQRELATIVE_ TYPE	Get/Set job frequency relative interval.
FrequencySubDay	SQLDMO_ FREQSUB_TYPE	Get/Set job frequency submit day.
Frequency SubDayInterval	Long	Get/Set job frequency submit interval.
FrequencyType	SQLDMO_ FREQUENCY_ TYPE	Get/Set job frequency type.

Table Continued on Following Page

Name	Returns	Description
Parent	IVSQLDMOStdObject	The hierarchical parent object.
Propeties	Properties	A list of object properties.
TypeOf	SQLDMO_OBJECT_TYPE	The type of SQL-DMO object.
UserData	Long	User's private data.

ServerGroup

Methods

Name	Returns	Description
Remove		Drops the object and removes it from the collection.

Properties

Name	Returns	Description
Application	Application	The top-level application object for SQL-DMO.
Name	String	The name of the object.
Parent	IVSQLDMO StdObject	The hierarchical parent object.
Properties	Properties	A list of object properties.
RegisteredServers	Registered Servers	A collection of RegisteredServers for this ServerGroup.
ServerGroups	ServerGroups	A Servergroup collection.
TypeOf	SQLDMO_ OBJECT_TYPE	The type of SQL-DMO object.
UserData	Long	User's private data.

ServerGroups

Methods

Name	Returns	Description
Add		Adds a ServerGroup object to the collection.
Item	ServerGroup	Retrieves a ServerGroup object from the collection.
Refresh		Refreshes data in the collection.
Remove		Removes a ServerGroup object from the collection.

Properties

Name	Returns	Description
Application	Application	The top-level application object for SQL-DMO.
Count	Long	The number of items.
Parent	IVSQLDMO StdObject	The hierarchical parent object.
TypeOf	SQLDMO_ OBJECT_TYPE	The type of SQL-DMO object.
UserData	Long	User's private data.

ServerRole

Methods

Name	Returns	Description
AddMember		Add a new login to the current server role.
DropMember		Drops a login from the current server role.
EnumServer RoleMember	QueryResults	Lists members in this server role.
EnumServer RolePermission	QueryResults	Lists permissions in this server role.

Properties

Name	Returns	Description
Application	Application	The top-level application object for SQL-DMO.
Description	String	A descriptive text about the object.
FullName	String	The server role user friendly name.
Name	String	The name of the object.
Parent	IVSQLDMO StdObject	The hierarchical parent object.
Properties	Properties	A list of properties for the object.
TypeOf	SQLDMO_ OBJECT_TYPE	The type of SQL-DMO object.
UserData	Long	User's private data.

ServerRoles

Methods

Name	Returns	Description
Item	ServerRole	Retrieves a ServerRole object from the collection.
Refresh		Refreshes data in the collection.

Properties

Name	Returns	Description
Application	Application	The top-level application object for SQL-DMO.
Count	Long	The number of items.
Parent	IVSQLDMO StdObject	The hierarchical parent object.
TypeOf	SQLDMO_ OBJECT_TYPE	The type of SQL-DMO object.
UserData	Long	User's private data.

SQLObjectList

Methods

Name	Returns	Description
Item		Retrieves a fixed membership container for objects enumerated by an object.
Refresh		Refreshes data in the object.

Properties

Name	Returns	Description
Application	Application	The top-level application object for SQL-DMO.
Count	Long	The number of items.
Parent	IVSQLDMO StdObject	The hierarchical parent object.
TypeOf	SQLDMO_ OBJECT_TYPE	The type of SQL-DMO object.
UserData	Long	User's private data.

SQLServer

Events

Name	Returns	Description
CommandSent		The SQL command sent to the server.
ConnectionBroken		The SQLServer connection has been broken; return TRUE to reconnect.
QueryTimeout		A Query Timeout has occurred; return TRUE to continue.
RemoteLoginFailed		A remote login failed during operation.
ServerMessage		A server informational message is returned.

Methods

Name	Returns	Description
Abort		Abort the query in progress.
AddStartParameter		Adds a startup parameter.
AttachDB	String	Attaches a database with multiple files to the SQL Server.
AttachDBWith SingleFile	String	Attaches a database with a single file to the SQL Server.
BeginTransaction		Begins a transaction.
Close		Disconnects from the SQL Server and removes the object.
CommandShell Immediate		Executes an external command-shell command.
CommandShell WithResults	QueryResults	Executes an external command-shell command and return results.
Commit Transaction		Commits current transaction.
Connect		Connects to a server.
Continue		Continues a server after pause.
DetachDB	String	Detach a database from the server.
DisConnect		Suspends connection to server but don't close the object.
EnumAccountInfo	QueryResults	Returns account info or members of an account.
EnumAvailable Media	QueryResults	Returns the available media.
EnumDirectories	QueryResults	Returns the directories of pathname.
EnumErrorLogs	QueryResults	Returns the ErrorLog entries.
EnumLocks	QueryResults	Return all current locks on server.
EnumLogin Mappings	QueryResults	Enumerate each login name and whether it is mapped to a user or alias in one or more databases.
EnumNT DomainGroups	QueryResults	Return NT groups within a domain.

Name	Returns	Description
EnumProcesses	QueryResults	Returns the active processes on this server.
EnumServer Attributes	QueryResults	Return the server attributes.
EnumVersionInfo	QueryResults	Returns the version information.
ExecuteImmediate		Execute a command via pass-through, with no results.
Execute WithResults	QueryResults	Execute a command via pass-through and return a QueryResults object.
ExecuteWith Results AndMessages	QueryResults	Execute a command via pass-through and return a QueryResults object and any generated messages.
IsLogin	Boolean	TRUE if login name exists already, FALSE otherwise.
IsNtGroupMember	Boolean	Is the specified NT user a member of the specified NT group?
IsOS	Boolean	What kind of OS we are running on?
IsPackage	SQLDMO_ PACKAGE_TYPE	What kind of SQLServer Package type we are running on?
KillDatabase		Executes DBCC DBREPAIR(DROPDB), which drops the database from the SQL Server.
KillProcess		Kills an active process.
ListMembers	NameList	The current login is a member of these roles.
ListStartup Procedures	SQLObject List	Lists the procedures executed on server startup.
Pause		Pause a server.
PingSQLServer Version	SQLDMO_ SQL_VER	Pings for the SQLServer version.
ReadBackupHeader	QueryResults	Return header info for all server backups on devices specified in LoadSpec.
ReadErrorLog	QueryResults	Return ErrorLog entries.
ReConnect		Reconnect to a disconnected server.
Rollback Transaction		Rollback transaction.

Table Continued on Following Page

Name	Returns	Description
SaveTransaction		Specify a transaction savepoint.
Shutdown		Shutdown this SQL Server through SHUTDOWN command.
Start		Start this SQL Server.
Stop		Stop server through SCM.
UnloadODSDLL		Unload specified DLL from server's process.
VerifyConnection	Boolean	Verify the state of a connected SQL Server object's connection to its server.

Properties

Name	Returns	Description
AnsiNulls	Boolean	Sets ANSI NULL property.
Application	Application	The top-level application object for SQL-DMO.
ApplicationName	String	The connecting application's name.
AutoReConnect	Boolean	Sets whether SQL-DMO will automatically reconnect a dead server at start of operations.
BackupDevices	BackupDevices	A BackupDevices collection.
BlockingTimeOut	Long	Sets the period in milliseconds for which a call will block trying to acquire this server object's lock.
CodePage	Long	Gets the SQL Server codepage.
CodePageOverride	Long	Overrides the codepage value.
CommandTerminator	String	The command terminator for scripting, ExecuteImmediate, etc.
Configuration	Configuration	The Configuration object.
ConnectionID	Long	The connection ID of this Server object.
Databases	Databases	A collection of databases for this server.

Name	Returns	Description
EnableBcp	Boolean	Set whether SQL-DMO will enable bcp option for the particular connection.
FullTextService	FullText Service	The FullTextService object.
HostName	String	The connection host (workstation) name.
Integrated Security	Integrated Security	The IntegratedSecurity object.
Isdbcreator	Boolean	Is current login a member of dbcreator role?
Isdiskadmin	Boolean	Is current login a member of diskadmin role?
Isprocessadmin	Boolean	Is current login a member of processadmin role?
Issecurityadmin	Boolean	Is current login a member of securityadmin role?
Iserveradmin	Boolean	Is current login a member of serveradmin role?
Issetupadmin	Boolean	Is current login a member of setupadmin role?
Issysadmin	Boolean	Is current login a member of sysadmin role?
JobServer	JobServer	The JobServer object.
Language	String	The server language.
Languages	Languages	The Languages collection.
LinkedServers	LinkedServers	The LinkedServers collection.
Login	String	The current login ID.
Logins	Logins	The Logins collection.
LoginSecure	Boolean	Login via integrated security.
LoginTimeout	Long	Login timeout in seconds for this server.
MaxNumeric Precision	Long	Maximum numeric/decimal precision.
Name	String	The name of the SQL Server.

Table Continued on Following Page

Name	Returns	Description
NetName	String	Server network (machine) name.
NetPacketSize	Long	Network packet size for this server.
NextDeviceNumber	Long	The next available device number.
ODBCPrefix	Boolean	Gets/Sets the ODBC message prefix.
Parent	IVSQLDMO StdObject	The hierarchical parent object.
Password	String	Password for current login.
ProcessID	Long	The ID of the current process.
Process InputBuffer	String	Gets a process input command buffer contents.
Process OutputBuffer	String	Get a process' output command-buffer contents.
Properties	Properties	A list of properties for the object.
QueryTimeout	Long	Query timeout in seconds for this server.
QuotedIdentfier	Boolean	Sets QUOTED IDENTIFIERS on or off.
RegionalSetting	Boolean	Sets regional setting ON or OFF
Registry	Registry	The Registry object.
RemoteServers	RemoteServers	The RemoteServers collection.
Replication	Replication	The Replication object.
SaLogin	Boolean	Is the current login the system administrator?
ServerRoles	ServerRoles	The ServerRoles collection
ServerTime	String	Gets the SQL Server current datetime.
Status	SQLDMO_ SVCSTATUS_TYPE	The status of the server.
StatusInfo RefetchInterval	Long	Number of seconds past which cached status info will be re-fetched.
TranslaateChar	Boolean	Perform translation for character data?
TrueLogin	String	Current login ID on the server.

Name	Returns	Description
TrueName	String	The true server name (@@servername).
TypeOf	SQLDMO_OBJECT_TYPE	The type of SQL-DMO object.
UserData	Long	User's private data.
UserProfile	SQLDMO_SRVUSERPROFILE_TYPE	Gets current login user's profile bits.
VersionMajor	Long	SQL Server version major number.
VersionMinor	Long	SQL Server version minor number.
VersionString	String	The version string.This is the same as @@Version.

SQLServers

Methods

Name	Returns	Description
Item	SQLServer	Retrieves a SQLServer object from the collection.
ItemID	SQLServer	Retrieves a SQLServer object from the collection by ID.

Properties

Name	Returns	Description
Application	Application	The top-level application object for SQL-DMO.
Count	Long	The number of items.
Parent	IVSQLDMO StdObject	The hierarchical parent object.
TypeOf	SQLDMO_OBJECT_TYPE	The type of SQL-DMO object.
UserData	Long	User's private data.

StoredProcedure

Methods

Name	Returns	Description
Alter		Alter text for this existing stored procedure.
Deny		Deny privileges.
EnumDependencies	QueryResults	List objects which depend on, or are depended on by, this object.
EnumParameters	QueryResults	Return a list of all parameters.
Grant		Grant privileges.
ListPermissions	SQLObjectList	List users with permissions on this object.
ListUserPermissions	SQLObjectList	List specified user's permissions on this object.
Remove		Drops the object and removes it from the collection.
Revoke		Removes privileges for this stored procedure.
Script	String	Generates a SQL script for this object.

Properties

Name	Returns	Description
AnsiNullsStatus	Boolean	Checks if ANSI NULLS was ON when the object was created.
Application	Application	The top-level application object for SQL-DMO.
CreateDate	String	The date the object was created.
ID	Long	The ID value for the object.
Name	String	The name of the object.
Owner	String	The owner of the stored procedure.

Name	Returns	Description
Parent	IVSQLDMO StdObject	The hierarchical parent object
Properties	Properties	A list of properties for the object.
Quoted IdentiferStatus	Boolean	Checks if quoted_identifier was ON when this object was created.
Startup	Boolean	Is procedure executed automatically on server startup?
SystemObject	Boolean	Is the object a system object?
Text	String	The text value of the object.
Type	SQLDMO_ PROCEDURE_TYPE	The stored procedure type.
TypeOf	SQLDMO_ OBJECT_TYPE	The type of SQL-DMO object.
UserData	Long	User's private data.

StoredProcedures

Methods

Name	Returns	Description
Add		Adds a StoredProcedure object to the collection.
Item	StoredProcedure	Retrieves a StoredProcedure object from the collection.
ItemByID	StoredProcedure	Retrieves a StoredProcedure object from the collection by ID.
Refresh		Refreshes data in the collection.
Remove		Removes a StoredProcedure object from the collection.

Properties

Name	Returns	Description
Application	Application	The top-level application object for SQL-DMO.
Count	Long	The number of items.
Parent	IVSQLDMOStdObject	The hierarchical parent object.
TypeOf	SQLDMO_OBJECT_TYPE	The type of SQL-DMO object.
UserData	Long	User's private data.

Subscriber

Methods

Name	Returns	Description
Script	String	Generates a SQL script for the object.

Properties

Name	Returns	Description
Application	Application	The top-level application object for SQL-DMO.
Parent	IVSQLDMO StdObject	The hierarchical parent object.
Properties	Properties	A list of properties for the object.
TypeOf	SQLDMO_ OBJECT_TYPE	The type of SQL-DMO object.
UserData	Long	User's private data.

SystemDatatype

Properties

Name	Returns	Description
AllowIdentity	Boolean	Can columns of this type (with 0 scale, if IsNumeric) allow identity?
AllowLength	Boolean	Does this datatype require a length?
AllowNulls	Boolean	Does datatype allow Nulls?
Application	Application	The top-level application object for SQL-DMO.
IsNumeric	Boolean	Is this datatype a numeric or decimal base type?
IsVariableLength	Boolean	Is this datatype a variable length datatype?
MaximumChar	Long	Maximum number of characters allowed for this datatype.
MaximumLength	Long	Maximum number of bytes used to store this datatype.
Name	String	The name of the object.
Parent	IVSQLDMOStdObject	The hierarchical parent object.
Properties	Properties	A list of properties for the object.
TypeOf	SQLDMO_OBJECT_TYPE	The type of SQL-DMO object.
UserData	Long	User's private data.

SystemDatatypes

Methods

Name	Returns	Description
Item	System Datatype	Retrieves a SystemDatatype object from the collection.

Properties

Name	Returns	Description
Application	Application	The top-level application object for SQL-DMO.
Count	Long	The number of items.
Parent	IVSQLDMO StdObject	The hierarchical parent object.
TypeOf	SQLDMO_ OBJECT_TYPE	The type of SQL-DMO object.
UserData	Long	User's private data.

Table

Methods

Name	Returns	Description
BeginAlter		Begins a multi-column table alter.
CancelAlter		Cancels a multi-column table alter.
Check IdentityValue		Checks the identity value integrity for this table's identity column.
CheckTable	String	Executes DBCC CHECKTABLE.
Check TableDataOnly	String	Executes DBCC CHECKTABLE with NOINDEX.
Check TextAllocsFast	String	Checks the tables integrity by executing DBCC CHECKTABLE (NOINDEX).
Check TextAllocsFull	String	Checks the tables integrity by executing DBCC CHECKTABLE.
Deny		Deny privileges.
DoAlter		Execute table alter.
DoAlter WithNoCheck		Execute table alter without checking constraint validation.
EnumDependencies	QueryResults	List objects which depend on, or are depended on by, this object.

Name	Returns	Description
EnumLast Statistics Updates	QueryResults	Lists the last update for all statistics (optionally, only one) in this table.
Enum ReferencedKeys	QueryResults	Lists DRI keys from other tables (optionally, for a single table) which are referenced by this table.
Enum ReferencedTables	QueryResults	Lists names of tables which are referenced by this table's DRI keys.
Enum ReferencingKeys	QueryResults	Lists DRI keys from other tables.
Enum Referencing Tables	QueryResults	Lists names of tables which reference this table's DRI keys.
ExportData	Long	Exports data to a file.
FullText IndexScript	String	Generate SQL script to create full-text index on the table.
GenerateSQL	String	Generates a series of T-SQL statements that can be used to create the table in this database.
Grant		Grants privilege.
ImportData	Long	Import data from file.
InsertColumn		Inserts a new column into the table.
ListAvailable UniqueIndexes ForFullText	NameList	List the available unique index candidates.
ListPermissions	SQLObjectList	List users with permissions on this object.
ListUserPermissi ons	SQLObjectList	List specified user's permissions on this object.
RebuildIndexes		Rebuilds all indexes on this table (optionally specifying sorted data optimization and new fillfactor).
RecalcSpaceUsage		Recalculate space usage for this table.
Recompile References		Cause recompilation of all access plans referencing this table.
Refresh		Refreshes table and child collections.
Remove		Drop this object and remove from parent collection.

Table Continued on Following Page

Name	Returns	Description
Revoke		Removes privileges.
Script	String	Generates a SQL string for the object.
TruncateData		Non-logged deletion of all rows in table.
UpdateStatistics		Updates all table index distribution statistics.
Update StatisticsWith		Updates table index distribution statistics with options.

Properties

Name	Returns	Description
Application	Application	The top-level application object for SQL-DMO.
Attributes	SQLDMO_ TABLEATT_TYPE	The table attributes.
Checks	Checks	A collection of DRI checks for this table.
ClusteredIndex	Index	Direct retrieval of DRI primary key for this table.
Columns	Columns	A columns collection for this table.
CreateDate	String	The creation date of the table.
DataSpaceUsed	Long	Current total space used by rows in table, in KB.
FakeSystem Table	Boolean	Is this object a fake system table?
FileGroup	String	Get/Set table on the specified FileGroup.
FullText CatalogName	String	The full-text catalog name for the table.
FullTextIndex	Boolean	Create or drop full-text index on table.
FullText IndexActive	Boolean	Activate or deactivate full-text index on table.
FullText KeyColumn	Long	Get full-text key column ID on this table.
HasClustered Index	Boolean	Does this table contain a clustered index?
HasIndex	Boolean	Does this table contain at least one index?

Name	Returns	Description
ID	Long	The ID value for the table.
InAlter	Boolean	Is table currently between `BeginAlter` and `Do/CancelAlter`?
Indexes	Indexes	A collection of indexes for the table.
IndexSpaceUsed	Long	Current total space used by indexes on table, in KB.
Keys	Keys	Collection of DRI keys for this table.
Name	String	The name of the object.
Owner	String	The owner of the object.
Parent	IVSQLDMO StdObject	The hierarchical parent object.
PrimaryKey	Key	Direct retrieval of DRI primary key for this table.
Properties	Properties	A list of properties for the object.
Rows	Long	The current row count in the table.
SystemObject	Boolean	Is this a system object?
TextFileGroup	String	Get/Set the text image filegroup for the selected table.
Triggers	Triggers	A collection of triggers for the table.
TypeOf	SQLDMO_ OBJECT_TYPE	The type of SQL-DMO object.
UniqueIndex ForFullText	String	Get/Set unique full-text index for the table.
UserData	Long	User's private data.

Tables

Methods

Name	Returns	Description
Add		Adds a `Table` object to the collection.
Item	Table	Retrieves a `Table` object from the collection.

Table Continued on Following Page

Name	Returns	Description
ItemByID	Table	Retrieves a `Table` object from the collection by ID.
Refresh		Refreshes data in the collection.
Remove		Removes a `Table` object from the collection.

Properties

Name	Returns	Description
Application	Application	The top-level application object for SQL-DMO.
Count	Long	The number of items.
Parent	IVSQLDMO StdObject	The hierarchical parent object.
TypeOf	SQLDMO_ OBJECT_TYPE	The type of SQL-DMO object.
UserData	Long	User's private data.

TargetServer

Methods

Name	Returns	Description
Refresh		Refresh data in this object.

Properties

Name	Returns	Description
Application	Application	The top-level application object for SQL-DMO.
EnlistDate	String	Get target server enlist date.
LastPollDate	String	Get last target server poll date.
LocalTime	String	Get local time.
Location	String	Get/Set target server location.

Name	Returns	Description
Parent	IVSQLDMO StdObject	The hierarchical parent object.
Pending Instructions	Long	Get pending instructions.
Polling Interval	Long	Get the frequency with which the target server polls to MSA.
Properties	Properties	A list of properties for the object.
ServerID	Long	The target server ID.
ServerName	String	The target server name.
Status	Long	Retrieves the current status.
TimeZone Adjustment	Long	Get target server time zone adjustment.
TypeOf	SQLDMO_ OBJECT_TYPE	The type of SQL-DMO object.
UserData	Long	User's private data.

TargetServerGroup

Methods

Name	Returns	Description
AddMemberServer		Adds a member to the TargetServerGroup.
BeginAlter		Begins a multi-column table alter.
CancelAlter		Cancels a multi-column table alter.
DoAlter		Executes a table alter.
ListMember Servers	NameList	Lists the member servers in the TargetServerGroup.
Refresh		Refresh data in this object.
Remove		Drop this object and remove from parent collection.
Remove MemberServer		Removes a member from the TargetServerGroup.

Properties

Name	Returns	Description
Application	Application	The top-level application object for SQL-DMO.
GroupID	Long	The `TargetServerGroup` ID value.
Name	String	The name of the object.
Parent	IVSQLDMOStdObject	The hierarchical parent object.
Properties	Properties	A list of properties for the object.
TypeOf	SQLDMO_OBJECT_TYPE	The type of SQL-DMO object.
UserData	Long	User's private data.

TargetServerGroups

Methods

Name	Returns	Description
Add		Adds a `TargetServerGroup` object to the collection.
Item	TargetServerGroup	Retrieves a `TargetServerGroup` object from the collection.
ItemByID	TargetServerGroup	Retrieves a `TargetServerGroup` object from the collection by ID.
Refresh		Refreshes data in the collection.
Remove		Removes a `TargetServerGroup` object from the collection.

Properties

Name	Returns	Description
Application	Application	The top-level application object for SQL-DMO.
Count	Long	The number of items.

Name	Returns	Description
Parent	IVSQLDMOStdObject	The hierarchical parent object.
TypeOf	SQLDMO_OBJECT_TYPE	The type of SQL-DMO object.
UserData	Long	User's private data.

TargetServers

Methods

Name	Returns	Description
Item	TargetServer	Retrieves a TargetServer object from the collection.
ItemByID	TargetServer	Retrieves a TargetServer object from the collection by ID.
Refresh		Refreshes data in the collection.
Remove		Removes a TargetServer object from the collection.

Properties

Name	Returns	Description
Application	Application	The top-level application object for SQL-DMO.
Count	Long	The number of items.
Parent	IVSQLDMO StdObject	The hierarchical parent object.
TypeOf	SQLDMO_ OBJECT_TYPE	The type of SQL-DMO object.
UserData	Long	User's private data.

TransactionLog

Methods

Name	Returns	Description
Truncate		Removes all records from transaction log.

Properties

Name	Returns	Description
Application	Application	The top-level application object for SQL-DMO.
CreateDate	String	The creation date of the database.
LastBackup	String	Date and time of last database transaction backup.
LogFiles	LogFiles	A collection of log files.
Parent	IVSQLDMO StdObject	The hierarchical parent object.
Properties	Properties	A list of properties for the object.
Size	Long	The log size in MB.
SpaceAllocated OnFiles	Long	Log space allocated on specified database.
SpaceAvailable	Long	Log space available in KB.
SpaceAvailable InMB	Single	Log space available in MB.
TypeOf	SQLDMO_ OBJECT_TYPE	The type of SQL-DMO object.
UserData	Long	User's private data.

TransArticle

Methods

Name	Returns	Description
AddReplicated Columns		Adds columns to the replication list.
BeginAlter		Begins multi-property object alter.
CancelAlter		Cancels multi-property object alter.
DoAlter		Executes an object alter.
ListReplicated Columns	SQLObjectList	List names of columns replicated by this TRANSARTICLE.
Remove		Drop this object and remove from parent collection.
Remove Replicated Columns		Remove columns from the replication list.
Script Destination Object	String	Generate SQL script to create the schema for this object.

Properties

Name	Returns	Description
Application	Application	The top-level application object for SQL-DMO.
ArticleType	SQLDMO_ ARTICLE_TYPE	The type of article.
CommandOptions	SQLDMO_ COMMANDOPTION_TYPE	The command options.
Creation ScriptOptions	SQLDMO_ CREATIONSCRIPT_TYPE	The creation script options.
Creation ScriptPath	String	The path to snapshot creation script.

Table Continued on Following Page

Name	Returns	Description
DeleteCommand	String	The command to replace DELETE with while distributing transactions.
Description	String	A descriptive text about the object.
Destination ObjectName	String	The name of destination table or stored procedure.
Destination OwnerName	String	The owner name of destination table or stored procedure.
FilterClause	String	The filter clause to auto-generate sync object and filter procedure.
ID	Long	The ID value for the object.
InsertCommand	String	Command to replace INSERT with while distributing transactions.
Name	String	The name of the object.
Parent	IVSQLDMO StdObject	The hierarchical parent object.
PreCreation Method	SQLDMO_ PREARTICLE_TYPE	Article pre-creation methods on destination table.
Properties	Properties	A list of properties for the object.
Replicate AllColumns	Boolean	Replicate all columns for this article
Replication FilterProcName	String	None qualified name of procedure to use as data replication filter, or name for auto-generated procedure if filter clause supplied.
Replication Filter ProcOwner	String	Owner name of procedure to use as data replication filter, or owner name for auto-generated procedure if filter clause supplied.
Snapshot ObjectName	String	None-qualified name of table or view to use as template for initial sync, or name for auto-generated view if filter clause supplied.
Snapshot ObjectOwner	String	Owner name of table or view to use as template for initial sync, or owner name for auto-generated view if filter clause supplied.

Name	Returns	Description
SourceObject Name	String	None-qualified name of object being published.
SourceObject Owner	String	Owner name of object being published.
Trans Subscriptions	Trans Subscriptions	Collection of subscriptions for this article.
TypeOf	SQLDMO_ OBJECT_TYPE	The type of SQL-DMO object.
UpdateCommand	String	Command to replace UPDATE with while distributing transactions.
UserData	Long	User's private data.

TransArticles

Methods

Name	Returns	Description
Add		Adds a TransArticle object to the collection.
Item	TransArticle	Retrieves a TransArticle object from the collection.
ItemByID	TransArticle	Retrieves a TransArticle object from the collection by ID.
Refresh		Refreshes data in the collection.
Remove		Removes a TransArticle object from the collection.

Properties

Name	Returns	Description
Application	Application	The top-level application object for SQL-DMO.
Count	Long	The number of items.
Parent	IVSQLDMO StdObject	The hierarchical parent object.
TypeOf	SQLDMO_ OBJECT_TYPE	The type of SQL-DMO object.
UserData	Long	User's private data.

Transfer

Events

Name	Returns	Description
PercentComplete AtStep		Percent completed in the current stage of transfer.
ScriptTransfer PercentComplete		Percent completed in scripting files.
StatusMessage		Status message during Transfer process.
TransferPercent Complete		Percent completed in transferring schema and data to destination.

Methods

Name	Returns	Description
Abort		Aborts a transfer in process.
AddObject		Adds an object to the list of objects to be copied.
AddObjectByName		Adds an object to the list of objects to be copied by name reference.
ListObjectNames	NameList	Lists objects added explicitly.
RetrieveErrors	String	Retrieves the error messages when the non-stop scripting option is on.
RetrieveWrite FileErrors	String	Retrieve the error messages for the non-scripting related errors.

Properties

Name	Returns	Description
Application	Application	The top-level application object for SQL-DMO.
CopyAllDefaults	Boolean	Copy all source defaults?
CopyAllObjects	Boolean	Copy all source objects?

Name	Returns	Description
CopyAllRules	Boolean	Copy all source rules?
CopyAll StoredProcedures	Boolean	Copy all source stored procedures?
CopyAllTables	Boolean	Copy all source tables?
CopyAllTriggers	Boolean	Copy all source triggers?
CopyAllUser DefinedDatatypes	Boolean	Copy all source user-defined data types?
CopyAllViews	Boolean	Copy all source views?
CopyData	SQLDMO_ COPYDATA_TYPE	Copies all source data.
CopySchema	Boolean	Copy the source schema?
DestDatabase	String	The destination database name.
DestLogin	String	The destination database login.
DestPassword	String	The destination database login password.
DestServer	String	The destination server name.
DestUseTrusted Connection	Boolean	Use integrated security for destination login?
DropDestObjects First	Boolean	Drop specified objects from destination database before transfer?
Include Dependencies	Boolean	Include objects depended on by specified objects?
IncludeGroups	Boolean	Copy source database groups to destination database?
IncludeLogins	Boolean	Copy source database user logins?
IncludeUsers	Boolean	Copy source database users?
Parent	IVSQLDMO StdObject	The hierarchical parent object.
Properties	Properties	A list of properties for the object.
Script2Type	SQLDMO_ SCRIPT2_TYPE	Sets the output file type.
ScriptType	SQLDMO_ SCRIPT_TYPE	What's included in the script and transfer.
TypeOf	SQLDMO_ OBJECT_TYPE	The type of SQL-DMO object.
UserData	Long	User's private data.

TransPublication

Methods

Name	Returns	Description
Activate Subscriptions		Activate all the subscriptions to this publication.
BeginAlter		Begins a multi-property object alter.
CancelAlter		Cancels a multi-property object alter.
DoAlter		Executes a single job alter.
EnumPublication Accesses	QueryResults	Enumerate the logins in the access list of this publication.
Enum Subscriptions	QueryResults	Enumerate the subscriptions.
GrantPublication Access		Adds a login to the access list of this publication.
RefreshChildren		Refresh the object and its child collections.
ReInitialize AllSubscriptions		Re-synchronize subscriptions on all subscribers.
Remove		Drop this object and remove from parent collection.
Revoke PublicationAccess		Removes a login to the access list of this publication.
Script	String	Generate SQL script to setup this publication.

Properties

Name	Returns	Description
AllowSynchronous Transactions	Boolean	Does the publication allow synchronous transactions?
Application	Application	The top-level application object for SQL-DMO.
AutogenerateSync Procedures	Boolean	Does the sync procedure get auto-generated?

Name	Returns	Description
Description	String	A descriptive text about the object.
Enabled	Boolean	Is the publication available?
HasSubscription	Boolean	Whether the publication has any subscription except unsynchronized anonymous subscriptions.
ID	Long	The ID value of the object.
Name	String	The name of the object.
Parent	IVSQLDMO StdObject	The hierarchical parent object.
Properties	Properties	A list of properties for the object.
Publication Attributes	SQLDMO_ PUBATTRIB_TYPE	The attributes the publication supports.
Replication Frequency	SQLDMO_ REPFREQ_TYPE	The frequency of replication.
RetentionPeriod	Long	The retention period.
SnapshotAvailable	Boolean	Is the publication's snapshot available for use?
SnapshotJobID	String	The job ID of the snapshot.
SnapshotMethod	SQLDMO_ INITIALSYNC_TYPE	The snapshot method.
SnapshotSchedule	Schedule	The schedule for the snapshot agent with the publication.
TransArticles	TransArticles	A collection of articles for this publication.
Trans Subscriptions	Trans Subscriptions	A collection of subscriptions for this publication.
TypeOf	SQLDMO_ OBJECT_TYPE	The type of SQL-DMO object.
UserData	Long	User's private data.

TransPublications

Methods

Name	Returns	Description
Add		Adds an object to the collection.
Item	TransPublication	Retrieves a TransPublication object.
ItemByID	TransPublication	Retrieves a TransPublication object by ID.
Refresh		Refreshes the collection data.
Remove		Drops the object and removes it from the collection.
Script	String	Generates a SQL script for the object.

Properties

Name	Returns	Description
Application	Application	The top-level application object for SQL-DMO.
Count	Long	The number of items.
Parent	IVSQLDMOStdObject	The hierarchical parent object.
TypeOf	SQLDMO_OBJECT_TYPE	The type of SQL-DMO object.
UserData	Long	User's private data.

TransPullSubscription

Methods

Name	Returns	Description
BeginAlter		Begins a multi-property TransPullSubscription alter.
CancelAlter		Cancels a multi-property TransPullSubscription alter.

Name	Returns	Description
DoAlter		Executes a `TransPullSubscription` alter.
EnumJobInfo	QueryResults	Enumerate the job info for this subscription.
ReInitialize		Re-initialize this subscription.
Remove		Drops the object and removes it from the collection.
Script	String	Generates a SQL script for the object.

Properties

Name	Returns	Description
Application	Application	The top-level application object for SQL-DMO.
Description	String	A descriptive text about the object.
Distribution JobID	String	Returns the distribution job ID.
Distribution Schedule	Schedule	The schedule for the distribution agent associated with this subscription.
Distributor	String	Name of the distribution server.
Distributor Security	Replication Security	The replication security attributes for the distributor.
EnabledFor SyncMgr	Boolean	Register this subscription with SyncMgr?
FTPAddress	String	The address of the FTP server.
FTPLogin	String	The login ID for access to the FTP server.
FTPPassword	String	The password for the Login ID on the FTP server.
FTPPort	Variant Long	The IP port of the FTP server.
LastDistribution Date	String	Last date time that the distribution agent ran.
Name	String	The name of the object.
Parent	IVSQLDMO StdObject	The hierarchical parent object.
Properties	Properties	A list of properties for the object.

Table Continued on Following Page

Name	Returns	Description
Publication	String	The name of the publication.
Publication Attributes	SQLDMO_ PUBATTRIB_TYPE	The attributes the publication supports.
PublicationDB	String	The name of the publication database.
Publisher	String	The name of the publisher server.
Publisher Security	Replication Security	The replication security attributes for the publisher.
SubscriberLogin	String	The login used by the distribution agent to logon to the subscribing server.
Subscriber Password	String	The password used by the distribution agent to logon to the subscribing server.
Subscriber SecurityMode	SQLDMO_ SECURITY_TYPE	The security mode used by the distribution agent to logon to the subscribing server.
SubscriberType	SQLDMO_ TRANSUBSCRIBER_ TYPE	The type of subscriber.
SubscriptionType	SQLDMO_ SUBSCRIPTION_ TYPE	The type of subscription.
TypeOf	SQLDMO_ OBJECT_TYPE	The type of SQL-DMO object.
UserData	Long	User's private data.

TransPullSubscriptions

Methods

Name	Returns	Description
Add		Adds a TransPullSubscription object to the collection.
Item	TransPull Subscription	Retrieves a TransPullSubscription object from the collection.

Name	Returns	Description
Refresh		Refreshes data in the collection.
Remove		Removes a `TransPullSubscription` object from the collection.
Script	String	Generates a SQL Script for the object.

Properties

Name	Returns	Description
Application	Application	The top-level application object for SQL-DMO.
Count	Long	The number of items.
Parent	IVSQLDMO StdObject	The hierarchical parent object.
TypeOf	SQLDMO_ OBJECT_TYPE	The type of SQL-DMO object.
UserData	Long	User's private data.

TransSubscription

Methods

Name	Returns	Description
BeginAlter		Begin a multi-property object alter.
CancelAlter		Cancel a multi-property object alter.
DoAlter		Executes the object alter.
ReInitialize		Resets the subscription.
Remove		Drops the object and removes it from the collection.
Script	String	Generates a SQL script for the object.

Properties

Name	Returns	Description
Application	Application	The top-level application object for SQL-DMO.
Distribution JobID	String	Retrieves the distribution job ID value.
Distribution Schedule	Schedule	The schedule for the distribution agent associated with this subscription.
EnabledFor SyncMgr	Boolean	Is the subscription registered with SyncMgr?
Full Subscription	Boolean	Is this a full or partial subscription?
Name	String	The name of the object.
Parent	IVSQLDMO StdObject	The hierarchical parent object.
Properties	Properties	A list of properties for the object.
Status	SQLDMO_ SUBSTATUS_TYPE	The status of the subscription.
Subscriber	String	The name of the subscriber server.
Subscriber Type	SQLDMO_ TRANSUBSCRIBER_ TYPE	The type of the subscriber.
Subscription DB	String	The name of subscription database.
Subscription Type	SQLDMO_ SUBSCRIPTION_ TYPE	The type of subscription.
SyncType	SQLDMO_ SUBSYNC_TYPE	The synchronization type for this subscriber.
TypeOf	SQLDMO_ OBJECT_TYPE	The type of SQL-DMO object.
UserData	Long	User's private data.

TransSubscriptions

Methods

Name	Returns	Description
Add		Adds a `TransSubscription` object to the collection.
Item	TransSubscription	Retrieves a `TransSubscription` object from the collection.
Refresh		Refreshes data in the collection.
Remove		Removes a `TransSubscription` object from the collection.
Script	String	Generates a SQL script for the object.

Properties

Name	Returns	Description
Application	Application	The top-level application object for SQL-DMO.
Count	Long	The number of items.
Parent	IVSQLDMO StdObject	The hierarchical parent object.
TypeOf	SQLDMO_ OBJECT_TYPE	The type of SQL-DMO object.
UserData	Long	User's private data.

Trigger

Methods

Name	Returns	Description
Alter		Alters the text for this existing trigger.
Enum Dependencies	QueryResults	Lists objects that have a dependency on this object.
Remove		Drops the object and removes it from the collection.
Script	String	Generates a SQL script for the object.

Properties

Name	Returns	Description
AnsiNullsStatus	Boolean	Check if ANSI NULLS was on when the object was created.
Application	Application	The top-level application object for SQL-DMO.
CreateDate	String	The date the object was created.
Enabled	Boolean	Enables or disables the object for use.
ID	Long	The ID value for the object.
Name	String	The name of the object.
Owner	String	The owner of the object.
Parent	IVSQLDMO StdObject	The hierarchical parent object.
Properties	Properties	A list of properties for the object.
Quoted IdentifierStatus	Boolean	Check if Quoted Identifiers was on when the object was created.
SystemObject	Boolean	Is the object a system object?
Text	String	The text object definition.
Type	SQLDMO_ TRIGGER_TYPE	The type of trigger.
TypeOf	SQLDMO_ OBJECT_TYPE	The type of SQL-DMO object.
UserData	Long	User's private data.

Triggers

Methods

Name	Returns	Description
Add		Adds a Trigger object to the collection.
Item	Trigger	Retrieves a Trigger object from the collection.
ItemByID	Trigger	Retrieves a Trigger object from the collection by ID.
Refresh		Refreshes data in the collection.
Remove		Removes a Trigger object from the collection.

Properties

Name	Returns	Description
Application	Application	The top-level application object for SQL-DMO.
Count	Long	The number of items.
Parent	IVSQLDMOStdObject	The hierarchical parent object.
TypeOf	SQLDMO_OBJECT_TYPE	The type of SQL-DMO object.
UserData	Long	User's private data.

User

Methods

Name	Returns	Description
AddAlias		Adds one or more login names to be aliased to this user.
GrantNTUser DBAccess		Grants NT user the explicit database access.
IsMember	Boolean	Checks if the current user is a member of the specified database role.
ListAliases	SQLObjectList	A collection of all logins aliased to this user.
ListDatabase Permissions	SQLObjectList	Lists database-level permissions.
ListMembers	NameList	Lists the roles the user is a member of.
ListObject Permissions	SQLObjectList	List object-level permissions for this user.
ListOwnedObjects	SQLObjectList	Lists objects owned by this user.
Remove		Drops the object and removes it from the collection.
RemoveAlias		Remove one or more login name's aliases to this user.
Script	String	Generates a SQL script for the object.

Properties

Name	Returns	Description
Application	Application	The top-level application object for SQL-DMO.
HasDBAccess	Boolean	Checks to see if the user has explicit access to the database.
ID	Long	The ID value for the object.
Login	String	Gets/Sets the user's login name.
Name	String	The name of the object.
Parent	IVSQLDMOStdObject	The hierarchical parent object.
Properties	Properties	A list of properties for the object.
Role	String	The user's role name.
SystemObject	Boolean	Is the object a system object?
TypeOf	SQLDMO_OBJECT_TYPE	The type of SQL-DMO object.
UserData	Long	User's private data.

UserDefinedDatatype

Methods

Name	Returns	Description
BindDefault		Bind/Unbind the default to UDT.
BindRule		Bind/Unbind the rule to UDT.
GenerateSQL	String	Generates a series of T-SQL statements that can be used to create the UDT in this database.
ListBound Columns	SQLObjectList	Return a list of all bound columns.
Remove		Drops the object and removes it from the collection.
Script	String	Generates a SQL script for the object.

Properties

Name	Returns	Description
AllowIdentity	Boolean	Checks if the columns of this type allow identity fields.
AllowNulls	Boolean	Checks if the columns of this type allow Nulls.
Application	Application	The top-level application object for SQL-DMO.
BaseType	String	Name of UDT's physical base datatype.
Default	String	Name of UDT's default.
DefaultOwner	String	The owner of the UDT's default.
ID	Long	The ID value for the object.
IsVariable Length	Boolean	Checks if this datatype is a variable length datatype.
Length	Long	The length of the datatype if it is not a fixed length datatype.
MaxSize	Long	The maximum length size of the data type.
Name	String	The name of the object.
Numeric Precision	Long	The precision of the data type if it is numeric or decimal.
NumericScale	Long	The scale of the data type if it is numeric or decimal.
Owner	String	The database owner of the object.
Parent	IVSQLDMO StdObject	The hierarchical parent object.
Properties	Properties	A list of properties for the object.
Rule	String	The name of the UDT's rule.
RuleOwner	String	The name of the rule's owner.
TypeOf	SQLDMO_ OBJECT_TYPE	The type of SQL-DMO object.
UserData	Long	User's private data.

UserDefinedDatatypes

Methods

Name	Returns	Description
Add		Adds a UserDefinedDatatype object to the collection.
Item	UserDefined Datatype	Retrieves a UserDefinedDatatype object from the collection.
ItemByID	UserDefined Datatype	Retrieves a UserDefinedDatatype object from the collection by ID.
Refresh		Refreshes data in the collection.
Remove		Removes a UserDefinedDatatype object from the collection.

Properties

Name	Returns	Description
Application	Application	The top-level application object for SQL-DMO.
Count	Long	The number of items.
Parent	IVSQLDMO StdObject	The hierarchical parent object.
TypeOf	SQLDMO_ OBJECT_TYPE	The type of SQL-DMO object.
UserData	Long	User's private data.

Users

Methods

Name	Returns	Description
Add		Adds a User object to the collection.
Item	User	Retrieves a User object from the collection.
ItemByID	User	Retrieves a User object from the collection by ID.
Refresh		Refreshes data in the collection.
Remove		Removes a User object from the collection.

Properties

Name	Returns	Description
Application	Application	The top-level application object for SQL-DMO.
Count	Long	The number of items.
Parent	IVSQLDMOStdObject	The hierarchical parent object.
TypeOf	SQLDMO_OBJECT_TYPE	The type of SQL-DMO object.
UserData	Long	User's private data.

View

Methods

Name	Returns	Description
Alter		Alters the text definition for the existing view.
Deny		Denies access to the view.
EnumDependencies	QueryResults	Enumerates the dependencies of the view.
ExportData	Long	Exports the views data to a bulk copy routine.
Grant		Grants privileges on the object.
ListColumns	SQLObjectList	Lists the view's columns.
ListPermissions	SQLObjectList	Lists users with permissions on the object.
ListUser Permissions	SQLObjectList	Lists specified user's permissions on the object.
Remove		Drops the object and removes it from the collection.
Revoke		Removes a user's privileges for the object.
Script	String	Generates a SQL script for the object.

Properties

Name	Returns	Description
NullsStatus	Boolean	Checks if ANSI NULLS option was on when the object was created.
Application	Application	The top-level application object for SQL-DMO.
CreateDate	String	The date the object was created.
ID	Long	The database ID of the object.
Name	String	The name of the object.
Owner	String	The database owner of the object.
Parent	IVSQLDMOStdObject	The hierarchical parent object.
Properties	Properties	A list of properties for the object.
Quoted Identifier Status	Boolean	Checks if quoted_identifiers option was on when the object was created.
SystemObject	Boolean	Checks to see if the object is a system object.
Text	String	The object definition.
TypeOf	SQLDMO_OBJECT_TYPE	The type of SQL-DMO object.
UserData	Long	User's private data.

Views

Methods

Name	Returns	Description
Add		Adds a View object to the collection.
Item	View	Retrieves a View object from the collection.
ItemByID	View	Retrieves a View object from the collection by ID.
Refresh		Refreshes data in the collection.
Remove		Removes a View object from the collection.

Properties

Name	Returns	Description
Application	Application	The top-level application object for SQL-DMO.
Count	Long	The number of items.
Parent	IVSQLDMO StdObject	The hierarchical parent object.
TypeOf	SQLDMO_ OBJECT_TYPE	The type of SQL-DMO object.
UserData	Long	User's private data.

Global Object Constants

Name	Description
SQLDMO_ALERT_TYPE	The defined alert types.
SQLDMO_ARTICLE_TYPE	The defined article types.
SQLDMO_ARTSTATUS_TYPE	The defined article status types.
SQLDMO_AUDIT_TYPE	The defined audit types.
SQLDMO_BACKUP_LOG_TYPE	The defined backup log types.
SQLDMO_BACKUP_TYPE	The defined backup types.
SQLDMO_BCP_CODEPAGE_TYPE	The defined bcp codepage types.
SQLDMO_CATEGORYTYPE_TYPE	The defined category type types.
SQLDMO_COMMANDOPTION_TYPE	The defined command option types.
SQLDMO_COMP_LEVEL_TYPE	The defined completion level types.
SQLDMO_COMPLETION_TYPE	The defined completion types.
SQLDMO_CONFIGVALUE_TYPE	The defined configuration value types.
SQLDMO_CONSTANTS_TYPE	The defined constants types.
SQLDMO_COPYDATA_TYPE	The defined copy data types.
SQLDMO_CREATIONSCRIPT_TYPE	The defined creation script types.
SQLDMO_DATAFILE_TYPE	The defined data file types.
SQLDMO_DBCC_REPAIR_TYPE	The defined DBCC repair types.

Table Continued on Following Page

Name	Description
SQLDMO_DBSTATUS_TYPE	The defined database status types.
SQLDMO_DBUSERPROFILE_TYPE	The defined database user profile types.
SQLDMO_DBUSERROLE_TYPE	The defined database user role types.
SQLDMO_DEPENDENCY_TYPE	The defined dependency types.
SQLDMO_DEVICE_TYPE	The defined backup device types.
SQLDMO_ENUMNOTIFY_TYPE	The defined enumerated notification types.
SQLDMO_ERROR_TYPE	The defined error types.
SQLDMO_EVENT_TYPE	The defined event types.
SQLDMO_EXEC_TYPE	The defined execution types.
SQLDMO_FIND_OPERAND	Find operands.
SQLDMO_FREQRELATIVE_TYPE	The defined frequency relative types.
SQLDMO_FREQSUB_TYPE	The defined frequency subscription types.
SQLDMO_FREQUENCY_TYPE	The defined frequency types.
SQLDMO_FULLTEXT_START_TYPE	The defined full-text start types.
SQLDMO_FULLTEXTSTATUS_TYPE	The defined full-text status types.
SQLDMO_GRANTED_TYPE	The defined grant types.
SQLDMO_GROWTH_TYPE	The defined file growth types.
SQLDMO_INDEX_TYPE	The defined index types.
SQLDMO_INITALSYNC_TYPE	The defined initial synchronization types.
SQLDMO_INTSECLOGIN_TYPE	The defined internal security login types.
SQLDMO_JOB_TYPE	The defined job types.
SQLDMO_JOBEXECUTION_STATUS	The defined job execution types.
SQLDMO_JOBOUTCOME_TYPE	The defined job outcome types.
SQLDMO_JOBSERVER_TYPE	The defined job server types.
SQLDMO_JOBSTEPACTION_TYPE	The defined job step action types.
SQLDMO_KEY_TYPE	The defined key types.
SQLDMO_LINKEDTABLE_TYPE	The defined linked table types.
SQLDMO_LOGIN_TYPE	The defined login types.

Name	Description
SQLDMO_MEDIA_TYPE	The defined media types.
SQLDMO_MERGESUBSCRIBER_TYPE	The defined merge subscriber types.
SQLDMO_MONTHDAY_TYPE	The defined month day types.
SQLDMO_NOTIFY_TYPE	The defined notification types.
SQLDMO_NTACCESS_TYPE	The defined Windows NT Access types.
SQLDMO_OBJECT_TYPE	The defined object types.
SQLDMO_OBJSORT_TYPE	The defined object sort types.
SQLDMO_OS_TYPE	The defined operating system types.
SQLDMO_PACKAGE_TYPE	The defined package types.
SQLDMO_PERFMON_TYPE	The defined performance monitor types.
SQLDMO_PREARTICLE_TYPE	The defined prearticle types.
SQLDMO_PRIVLEGE_TYPE	The defined privilege types.
SQLDMO_PROCEDURE_TYPE	The defined stored procedure types.
SQLDMO_PUBATTRIB_TYPE	The defined published attribute types.
SQLDMO_PUBLICATION_TYPE	The defined publication types.
SQLDMO_PUBSTATUS_TYPE	The defined publication status types.
SQLDMO_QUERY_DATATYPE	The defined query datatypes.
SQLDMO_REPFREQ_TYPE	The defined replication frequency types.
SQLDMO_REPLAGENT_TYPE	The defined replication agent types.
SQLDMO_REPCONSTANTS_TYPE	The defined replication constants types.
SQLDMO_REPLICATION_TYPE	The defined replication types.
SQLDMO_REPLSECURITY_TYPE	The defined replication security types.
SQLDMO_REPLSCRIPT_TYPE	The defined replication script types.
SQLDMO_RESOLVECONFLICT_TYPE	The defined resolve conflict types.
SQLDMO_RESTORE_TYPE	The defined restore types.
SQLDMO_ROLE_TYPE	The defined role types.
SQLDMO_RUNPRIORITY_TYPE	The defined run priority types.
SQLDMO_SCRIPT_TYPE	The defined script types.
SQLDMO_SCRIPT2_TYPE	The defined enhanced script types.

Name	Description
SQLDMO_SECURITY_TYPE	The defined security types.
SQLDMO_SERVERBCP_DATAFILE_TYPE	The defined server side bcp data file types.
SQLDMO_SESSION_TYPE	The defined session types.
SQLDMO_SHRINK_TYPE	The defined database shrink types.
SQLDMO_SQL_VER	SQL Server version.
SQLDMO_SRVOPTION_TYPE	The defined server option types.
SQLDMO_SRVUSERPROFILE_TYPE	The defined server user profile types.
SQLDMO_STAT_AFFECT_TYPE	The defined statistics affect types.
SQLDMO_STAT_SCAN_TYPE	The defined statistics scan types.
SQLDMO_STATUSINFO_TYPE	The defined statistics information types.
SQLDMO_SUBSCRIBER_TYPE	The defined subscriber types.
SQLDMO_SUBSCRIPTION_TYPE	The defined subscription types.
SQLDMO_SUBSTATUS_TYPE	The defined subscription status types.
SQLDMO_SUBSYNC_TYPE	The defined subscription synchronization types.
SQLDMO_SVCSTATUS_TYPE	The defined service status types.
SQLDMO_TABLEATT_TYPE	The defined table attribute types.
SQLDMO_TARGETSERVERSTATUS_TYPE	The defined target server status types.
SQLDMO_TASKSTATUS_TYPE	The defined task status types.
SQLDMO_TRANSUBSCRIBER_TYPE	The defined transfer subscriber types.
SQLDMO_TRIGGER_TYPE	The defined trigger types.
SQLDMO_VERIFYCONN_TYPE	The defined verify connection types.
SQLDMO_WEEKDAY_TYPE	The defined weekday types.
SQLDMO_XFRSCRIPTMODE_TYPE	The defined transfer script mode types.

Microsoft SQL Server Namespace Reference

The object model is shown diagrammatically below. The gray boxes represent collection objects and the white boxes represent objects.

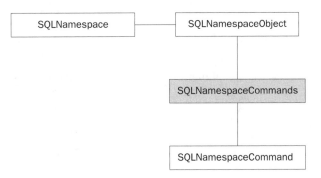

Library File Location

The source file that contains the SQL Namespace Object library is located at `<DRIVE>:\MSSQL7\Binn\Resources\1033\sqlns.rll`.

Objects and Collections

Name	Description
SQLNamespace	The main object for accessing the SQL-NS objects.
SQLNamespaceCommand	The object in charge of executing SQL Server user interface objects.
SQLNamespaceCommands	A collection of SQLNamespaceCommand objects.
SQLNamespaceInternal	A Microsoft internal object; no methods or properties are available.
SQLNamespaceObject	The object interface to the SQL Server Enterprise Manager user interface objects.

SQLNamespace

Methods

Name	Returns	Description
GetChildrenCount	Long	Returns the number of child items an item has.
GetFirstChildItem	Long	Returns the first child item in the SQL Namespace object hierarchy.
GetName	String	Returns the name of the selected member.
GetNextSiblingItem	Long	Returns next child/sibling item in the SQL Namespace object hierarchy.
GetParentItem	Long	Retrieves parent item in hierarchy.
GetPreviousSiblingItem	Long	Returns previous child/sibling item in SQL Namespace object hierarchy.
GetRootItem	Long	Returns handle to the root/parent item.
GetSQLDMOObject	Object	Retrieves the SQL-DMO object associated with SQLNamespace.

Name	Returns	Description
GetSQLNamespaceObject	SQLNamespace Object	Retrieves the SQL Namespace interface object.
GetType	SQLNSObject Type	Retrieves the object type of the item.
Initialize		Initializes the namespace, providing name of client application. Optionally, you can provide the default parent window for the UI, and also the non-default root of the namespace.
Refresh		Refreshes the console tree for the selected node.
SetLCID		Sets the locale identifier for SQL Namespace.

SQLNamespaceCommand

Methods

Name	Returns	Description
Execute		Executes the command selected in the CommandID property.

Properties

Name	Returns	Description
CommandGroup	Long	Returns the ID of the command group to which this command belongs. (For internal Microsoft use only.)
CommandID	SQLNSCommandID	Returns the SQLNSCommandID value of the SQLNamespaceCommand object.
HelpString	String	Returns a help string for the SQLNamespaceCommand object.
Name	String	Returns the name of the SQLNamespaceCommand object.

SQLNamespaceCommands

Methods

Name	Returns	Description
Item	SQLNamespaceCommand	Retrieves a SQLNamespaceCommand object from the collection.

Properties

Name	Returns	Description
Count	Long	Returns the number of SQLNamespaceCommand objects in the collection.

SQLNamespaceInternal

The SQLNamespaceInternal object was developed for use by the Microsoft SQL Server group for internal development only. No methods, properties, or events are defined for this object.

SQLNamespaceObject

Methods

Name	Returns	Description
ExecuteCommandByID		Executes the command on the SQLNamespaceObject object based on the CommandID.
ExecuteCommandByName		Executes the command on the SQLNamespaceObject object based on the command's Name.

Properties

Name	Returns	Description
Commands	SQLNamespaceCommands	Returns the SQLNamespaceCommands collection.
Handle	Long	Retrieves the handle of the SQLNamespaceObject object.
Name	String	Returns the descriptive name of the SQLNamespaceObject object.
Type	SQLNSObjectType	Returns the SQLNameSpaceObject object type.

Global Object Constants

For each constant enumeration described in the table below, there is a corresponding enumeration with a prefix of LP that should be used by C++ programmers (e.g. there is a constant enumeration called LPSQLNSCommandID that corresponds to SQLNSCommandID).

Name	Description
SQLNSCommandID	SQL-NS command Ids.
SQLNSErrors	Error ranges for the SQLNamespace object.
SQLNSModality	The modality of the user interface objects when displayed.
SQLNSObjectType	Available object types for the SQLNamespace object.
SQLNSRootType	The type of object set at the root level.

Microsoft Data Transformation Services Package Object Library Reference

The object model is shown diagrammatically below. The gray boxes represent collection objects and the white boxes represent objects.

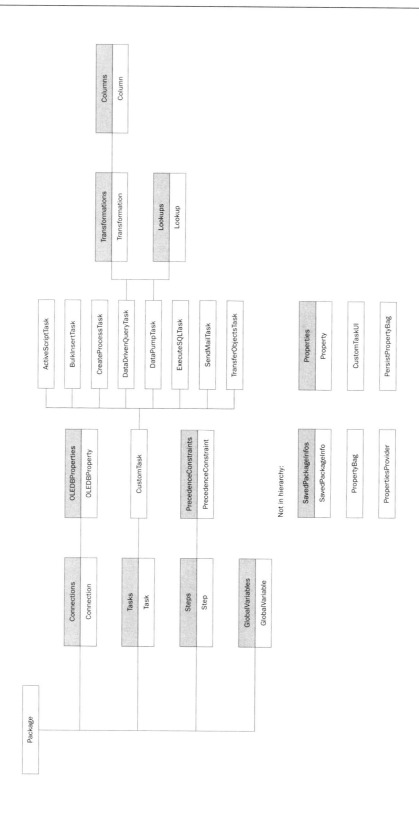

> The source file that contains the Data Transformation Service Object library is located at `<Drive>:\MSSQL7\Binn\Resources\1033\dts.rll`.

Objects and Collections

Name	Description
`ActiveScriptTask`	Defines an ActiveX script task.
`BulkInsertTask`	Provides an interface for rapid copying of lots of data from a text file.
`Column`	Contains information about a source or destination column of information.
`Columns`	A collection of DTS `Column` objects.
`Connection`	Contains information about the connection to the OLE DB service provider.
`Connections`	A collection of DTS `Connection` objects.
`CreateProcessTask`	An object that contains information about running a separate program as a task.
`CustomTask`	A wrapper object that encapsulates a custom DTS package task.
`CustomTaskUI`	Allows for the specification of specialized dialog boxes to support DTS tasks.
`DataDrivenQueryTask`	Contains information regarding the use of individual queries rather than executing an `INSERT` operation at the destination.
`DataPumpTask`	Creates and executes an instance of the DTS data pump as a custom task.
`ExecuteSQLTask`	Allows the execution of a SQL statement on an open connection.
`GlobalVariable`	Allows the definition of global variables for sharing across scripts or tasks.
`GlobalVariables`	A collection of `GlobalVariable` objects.

Name	Description
IDTSStdObject	The top-level hierarchy object for the DTS Package class.
Lookup	Allows the specification of one or more query strings for custom transformation.
Lookups	A collection of Lookup objects.
OleDBProperties	A collection of OleDBProperty objects.
OleDBProperty	Used to set OLE DB session properties for the OLE DB service provider.
Package	Main object that defines DTS transformations.
PackageLog	Internal Microsoft use only.
PersistPropertyBag	For objects carrying out DTS custom tasks this defines an interface for persistent property storage.
PrecedenceConstraint	Contains information about the order that steps are executed.
PrecedenceConstraints	A collection of PrecedenceConstraint objects.
Properties	A collection of DTS Property objects.
PropertiesProvider	Defines an object supplying a DTS Properties collection.
Property	Defines the attributes of a DTS object.
PropertyBag	Defines an index/name container for DTS custom task implementations.
SavedPackageInfo	Contains information about a saved DTS package.
SavedPackageInfos	A collection of SavedPackageInfo objects.
SendMailTask	Contains information that allows users to send an e-mail as a custom task.
Step	Controls the flow and execution of tasks in a DTS package.
Steps	A collection of Step objects.
Task	Sets a unit of work within a DTS package.
Tasks	A collection of Task objects.
TransferObjectsTask	Allows the transfer of objects between a destination and source SQL Server.
Transformation	Contains information about the source, destination, and transformation of columns of data in a DTS Package.
Transformations	A collection of Transformation objects.

ActiveScriptTask

Methods

Name	Returns	Description
CheckSyntax		Parses the active script for syntax errors.
Execute		Executes an ActiveScriptTask.

Properties

Name	Returns	Description
ActiveXScript	String	Specifies an ActiveX script.
AddGlobalVariables	Boolean	Specifies whether global variables may be used within an ActiveX script.
Description	String	A descriptive string for the ActiveScriptTask.
FunctionName	String	Identifies the function name to call within the ActiveX script.
Name	String	The name of the ActiveScriptTask.
Properties	Properties	Returns the Properties collection for the ActiveScriptTask object.
ScriptLanguage	String	Identifies the scripting language (VBScript, JScript, or PerlScript).

BulkInsertTask

Methods

Name	Returns	Description
Execute		Executes a BulkInsertTask.

Properties

Name	Returns	Description
BatchSize	Long	Sets the number of rows to load in a batch.
CheckConstraints	Boolean	Set this value to indicate whether any constraints should be checked while data is loaded.
Codepage	String	Sets code page to use while loading data.
ConnectionID	Long	Sets the ID of the Connection object.
DataFile	String	Sets the UNC path of the file to be loaded.
DataFileType	DTSBulkInsert _DataFileType	Sets the file type of the data to be inserted.
Description	String	The descriptive string for the BulkInsertTask.
DestinationTableName	String	Specifies the name of the table that data will be inserted into.
FieldTerminator	String	Sets the column terminator value for batch inserted files.
FirstRow	Long	Sets the first source row to copy.
FormatFile	String	Specifies a bcp format file to use for load operations.
KeepIdentity	Boolean	Shows whether the data in the file should be used as values of an identity column(s).
KeepNulls	Boolean	Sets whether NULL columns should keep NULL values.
LastRow	Long	Identifies the last row to be loaded from a source file.
MaximumErrors	Long	Sets the maximum number of errors that may occur before a load operation is terminated.
Name	String	The name of the BulkInsertTask.

Table Continued on Following Page

Name	Returns	Description
Properties	Properties	A list of properties for this object.
RowTerminator	String	Sets the row termination file for the source file.
SortedData	String	Sets the order of the loaded data.
TableLock	Boolean	Sets whether to perform a table lock on the destination table.

Column

Properties

Name	Returns	Description
ColumnID	Variant	Sets/Gets the ID of a source/destination column.
DataType	Long	Sets/Gets the data type of a column object.
Flags	Long	Sets/Gets the DBCOLUMNFLAGS value that describes the column
Name	String	The name of the column object.
Nullable	Boolean	Specifies whether the column is or is not nullable.
NumericScale	Long	Sets/Gets the numeric scale of the column if it is a numeric or decimal value.
Ordinal	Long	Gets the ordinal position of the column within the table.
Parent	IDTSStdObject	The parent object of the Column object.
Precision	Long	Set/Gets the column precision if the column is decimal or numeric data type.
Properties	Properties	A list of properties for the object.
Size	Long	Specifies the maximum size of the column.

Columns

Methods

Name	Returns	Description
Add		Adds a DTS Column object to the collection.
AddColumn		Adds a DTS Column object to the collection by name and ordinal position.
Insert		Inserts a DTS Column object by ordinal position.
Item	Column	Retrieves a DTS Column object from the collection.
New	Column	Creates a new DTS Column object.
Remove		Removes a DTS Column object from the object.

Properties

Name	Returns	Description
Count	Long	Specifies the number of DTS Column objects in the collection.
Parent	IDTSStdObject	The parent object of the Columns object.

Connection

Methods

Name	Returns	Description
AcquireConnection		Allows the acquisition of exclusive use of the OLE DB service provider.
ReleaseConnection		Releases ownership of the OLE DB service provider.

Properties

Name	Returns	Description
Catalog	String	Sets the name of the catalog that the Connection object will be initially established in.
Connected	Boolean	Gets the connection status of the Connection object.
ConnectImmediate	Boolean	Identifies whether a package should attempt an immediate connection to the service provider upon starting.
ConnectionProperties	OleDB Properties	Gets the OleDBProperties object for the established connection.
ConnectionTimeout	Long	The number of seconds to wait while establishing a connection before generating an error.
DataSource	String	Sets the server name when an application requests an OLE DB provider for SQL Server.
Description	String	A text description of the Connection object.
ID	Long	Unique identifier for the established connection.
InTransaction	Boolean	Identifies whether the connection is involved in a distributed transaction.
InUse	Boolean	Identifies whether the connection is currently in use.
LastOwnerTaskName	String	Displays the name of the last Task to utilize the connection.
Name	String	The name of the Connection object.
Parent	IDTSStd Object	Specifies the parent object of the Connection object.
Password	String	The password used while making the connection.
Properties	Properties	A list of properties for this object.
ProviderID	String	The ProgID of the OLE DB provider.

Name	Returns	Description
Reusable	Boolean	Identifies whether a connection is reusable by multiple steps within a given task.
UDLPath	String	Path of UDL (data link) file to create connection from, rather than using Connection properties.
UserID	String	The user ID utilized when making a connection.
UseTrustedConnection	Boolean	Specifies whether to use Windows NT Authentication security to establish a connection.

Connections

Methods

Name	Returns	Description
Add		Adds a Connection object to the collection.
BeginAcquire MultipleConnections		Allows the acquisition of multiple connections.
EndAcquire MultipleConnections		Stops the acquisition of multiple connections.
Insert		Inserts a Connection object into the collection.
Item	Connection	Retrieves a Connection object from the collection.
New	Connection	Creates a new Connection object.
NewDataLink	Connection	Gets a new Connection object to populate prior to adding to this collection, using Microsoft Data Links.
Remove		Removes a Connection object from the collection.

Properties

Name	Returns	Description
Count	Long	Specifies the number of DTS Connection objects in the collection.
Parent	Object	Specifies the parent object of the Connections collection.

CreateProcessTask

Methods

Name	Returns	Description
Execute		Executes a CreateProcessTask.

Properties

Name	Returns	Description
Description	String	A text description of the CreateProcessTask.
FailPackage OnTimeout	Boolean	Identifies whether the DTS package fails within the timeout period.
Name	String	The name of the CreateProcessTask object.
Process CommandLine	String	The UNC file name of the file to execute.
Properties	Properties	A list of properties for this object.
Success ReturnCode	Long	The return code that is returned upon successful completion a task.
Terminate ProcessAfter Timeout	Boolean	Sets whether to terminate a process after a timeout period has expired.
Timeout	Long	The number of seconds in the timeout period.

CustomTask

Methods

Name	Returns	Description
Execute		Executes a CustomTask.

Properties

Name	Returns	Description
Description	String	A text description of the CustomTask.
Name	String	The name for the CustomTask.
Properties	Properties	A list of properties for this object.

CustomTaskUI

Methods

Name	Returns	Description
CreateCustomToolTip		Creates a tooltip window for a custom tooltip.
Delete		Deletes a CustomTask object in the user interface.
Edit		Edits a CustomTask object in the user interface.
GetUIInfo		Returns user information about the CustomTask.
Help		Used to invoke help about the CustomTask object.
Initialize		Initializes the CustomTaskUI object.
New		Creates a new custom task.

DataDrivenQueryTask

Methods

Name	Returns	Description
Execute		Executes a `DataDrivenQueryTask`.

Properties

Name	Returns	Description
DeleteQuery	String	Specifies a Transact-SQL statement to delete data from a data source..
DeleteQuery Columns	Columns	Specifies columns to be placed in a parameterized `DeleteQuery`.
Description	String	A text description of the `DataDrivenQueryTask` object.
Destination ColumnDefinitions	Columns	Destination column definitions for a `DTSRowQueue` destination.
Destination CommandProperties	OleDBProperties	The OLE DB command properties for the destination data connection.
Destination ConectionID	Long	Connection object to use for destination.
DestinationObject Name	String	Sets the name of the data destination.
Destination SQLStatement	String	Specifies a SQL statement to execute at the destination.
ExceptionFile ColumnDelimiter	String	The column delimiter for the exception file.
ExceptionFileName	String	The filename where exception rows are written.
ExceptionFileRow Delimiter	String	The row delimiter for the data in the exception file.
FetchBufferSize	Long	Sets the number of rows to fetch during a single operation.
FirstRow	Variant	Gets the first source row.

Name	Returns	Description
InsertQuery	String	Sets a parameterized SQL statement to insert data at a destination.
InsertQuery Columns	Columns	Sets the column parameters for the InsertQuery parameters.
LastRow	Variant	Gets the last row from the source to copy.
Lookups	Lookups	A collection of lookup values.
MaximumErrorCount	Long	The maximum number of error rows before the data pump terminates operation.
Name	String	The name of the DataDrivenQueryTask object.
ProgressRowCount	Long	Sets the number of rows returned between notifications to the connection point during a data pump execution.
Properties	Properties	A list of properties for this object.
SourceCommand Properties	OleDBProperties	The OLE DB command properties for the data source connection.
SourceConnectionID	Long	The ID for the source OLE DB connection.
SourceObjectName	String	Specifies the source object name if no SQL statement is supplied.
SourceSQLStatement	String	Sets the SQL statement to be executed on the source rowset.
Transformations	Transformations	A collection of Transformation objects.
UpdateQuery	String	Sets a parameterized SQL query to update data.
UpdateQueryColumns	Columns	Specifies the column parameters for the UpdateQuery property.
UserQuery	String	Sets a parameterized user-defined SQL query.
UserQueryColumns	Columns	Specifies the column parameters for the UserQuery property.

DataPumpTask

Methods

Name	Returns	Description
Execute		Executes a `DataPumpTask`.

Properties

Name	Returns	Description
AllowIdentity Inserts	Boolean	Specifies whether the SET IDENTITY_INSERT option is ON or OFF.
Description	String	A text description of the `DataPumpTask` object.
DestinationColumn Definitions	Columns	Destination column definitions for a `DTSRowQueue` destination.
DestinationCommand Properties	OleDBProperties	OLE DB command properties for the destination.
Destination ConnectionID	Long	Connection object to use for destination.
DestinationObject Name	String	Sets the name of the data destination.
Destination SQLStatement	String	Specifies a SQL Statement to execute at the destination.
ExceptionFile ColumnDelimter	String	The column delimiter for the exception file.
ExceptionFileName	String	The file name where exception rows are written.
ExceptionFileRow Delimiter	String	The row delimiter for the data in the exception file.
FastLoadOptions	DTSFastLoad Options	Used for the `UseFastLoad` property to set SQL OLE DB destination connection options.
FetchBufferSize	Long	Sets the number of rows to fetch during a single operation.

Name	Returns	Description
FirstRow	Variant	Gets the first source row from the source.
InsertCommitSize	Long	Number of successful InsertRows between Commits.
LastRow	Variant	Gets the last row from the source to copy.
Lookups	Lookups	A collection of lookup values.
MaximumErrorCount	Long	The maximum number of error rows before the data pump terminates operation.
Name	String	The name of the DataPumpTask object.
ProgressRowCount	Long	The number of rows returned between notifications to the connection point during a data pump execution.
Properties	Properties	A list of properties for this object.
SourceCommand Properties	OleDBProperties	OLE DB command properties for the source.
SourceConnectionID	Long	The ID for the source OLE DB connection.
SourceObjectName	String	Specifies the source object name if not SQL statement is supplied.
SourceSQLStatement	String	Sets the SQL statement to be executed on the source rowset.
Transformations	Transformations	A collection of Transformation objects.
UseFastLoad	Boolean	Specifies whether to use the IRowsetFastLoad interface to insert rows at the data destination.

ExecuteSQLTask

Methods

Name	Returns	Description
Execute		Executes an ExecuteSQLTask.

Properties

Name	Returns	Description
CommandProperties	OleDBProperties	Sets the OleDBProperties object for the connection.
CommandTimeout	Long	The number of seconds before the command is presumed to have failed.
ConnectionID	Long	The ID for the OLE DB connection.
Description	String	A text description of the ExecuteSQLTask object.
Name	String	The name of the ExecuteSQLTask object.
Properties	Properties	A list of properties for the object.
SQLStatement	String	The SQL statement to execute on the source rowset.

GlobalVariable

Properties

Name	Returns	Description
Name	String	The name of the GlobalVariable object.
Parent	IDTSStdObject	The parent object of the GlobalVariable object.
Properties	Properties	A list of properties for the object.
Value	Variant	The value of the GlobalVariable object.

GlobalVariables

Methods

Name	Returns	Description
Add		Adds a GlobalVariable object to the collection.
AddGlobalVariable		Adds a GlobalVariable object to the collection by name.
Insert		Insert an object at an ordinal position or prior to a named object.
Item	GlobalVariable	Retrieves a GlobalVariable object by index.
New	GlobalVariable	Creates a new GlobalVariable object.
Remove		Removes a GlobalVariable object from the collection.

Properties

Name	Returns	Description
Count	Long	The number of GlobalVariable objects in the collection.
Parent	IDTSStdObject	The parent object of the GlobalVariable object.

IDTSStdObject

There are no methods, events, or properties designed for this object.

Lookup

Properties

Name	Returns	Description
ConnectionId	Long	The ID for the established OLE DB connection.
MaxCacheRows	Long	The maximum number of rows to cache.
Name	String	The name of the Lookup object.
Parent	IDTSStdObject	The parent object of the Lookup object.
Properties	Properties	A list of properties for the object.
Query	String	A parameterized query to execute.

Lookups

Methods

Name	Returns	Description
Add		Adds a Lookup object to the collection.
AddLookup		Adds a Lookup object to the collection by name.
Insert		Inserts a Lookup object into the collection by index.
Item	Lookup	Retrieves a Lookup object by index.
New	Lookup	Creates a new Lookup object.
Remove		Removes a Lookup object from the collection.

Properties

Name	Returns	Description
Count	Long	The number of Lookup objects in the collection.
Parent	IDTSStdObject	The parent object of the Lookup object.

687

OleDBProperties

Methods

Name	Returns	Description
Item	OleDBProperty	Retrieves a OleDBProperty object by index.

Properties

Name	Returns	Description
Count	Long	The number of OleDBProperty objects in the collection.
Parent	IDTSStdObject	The parent object of the OleDBProperties object.

OleDBProperty

Properties

Name	Returns	Description
Name	String	The name of the OleDBProperty.
Parent	IDTSStdObject	The parent object of the OleDBProperty.
Properties	Properties	A list of properties for the object.
PropertyID	Long	The ID of the OleDBProperty.
PropertySet	String	The GUID of the property.
Value	Variant	The value of the OleDBProperty.

Package

Methods

Name	Returns	Description
EndPreparation ForSteps Executing OnMainThread		Internal Microsoft use only.
Execute		Executes a `Package` object.
GetDTSVersion Info		Returns the DTS object version information.
GetLast ExecutionLineage	String	Returns information about the lineage of a package stored in the Microsoft Repository.
GetSaved PackageInfos	Saved PackageInfos	Returns a list of versions in the specified storage location.
LoadFromRepository		Loads the DTS package from the specified Repository.
LoadFromSQLServer		Loads the DTS package from the specified SQL Server.
LoadFromStorage File		Loads the DTS package from the specified storage file.
RemoveFrom Repository		Removes the selected DTS package from the selected Repository.
RemoveFrom SQLServer		Removes the selected DTS package from the selected SQL Server.
SaveAs		Creates a new package ID and assigns a new name to create a new package.
SaveToRepository		Saves a package to a selected Repository.
SaveToSQLServer		Saves a package to a selected SQL Server.
SaveToStorageFile		Saves a package to a selected file.
Start Preparationfor StepsExecutingOn MainThread		Internal Microsoft use only.
UnInitialize		Clears all state information and releases all objects.

Properties

Name	Returns	Description
AutoCommit Transaction	Boolean	Sets whether a specified transaction should be committed or terminated upon completion.
Connections	Connections	A collection of Connection objects.
CreationDate	Date	The package creation date.
CreatorComputer Name	String	The name of the computer that created the package.
CreatorName	String	The username of the package creator.
Description	String	A descriptive text about the object.
FailOnError	Boolean	Sets whether to stop execution upon package error.
GlobalVariables	GlobalVariables	A global variable collection.
LineageOptions	DTSLineageOptions	Specifies how the execution lineage should be shown.
LogFileName	String	The name of the log file.
MaxConcurrent Steps	Long	The maximum concurrent steps for the package.
Name	String	The name of the Package object.
PackageID	String	The ID value for the package (GUID).
PackagePriority Class	DTSPackage PriorityClass	The Win32 thread priority for the class.
Parent	IDTSStdObject	The parent object (IDTSStdObject) for the Package object.
PrecedenceBasis	DTSStepPrecedence Basis	Indicates whether to use step status or result in PrecedenceConstraint.
Properties	Properties	Lists the properties of the object.
Repository MetadataOptions	DTSRepository MetadataOptions	Specifies metadata scanning and resolution options when storing the DTS Package to a Repository.
Steps	Steps	A collection of Step objects to be executed for the package.

Table Continued on Following Page

Name	Returns	Description
Tasks	Tasks	A collection of Task objects to be performed during the package execution.
Transaction IsolationLevel	DTSIsolationLevel	The isolation level for the transaction for the package.
UseOLEDBService Components	Boolean	Sets whether to use OLE DB components to initialize data sources.
UseTransaction	Boolean	Sets whether the Package object should create a transaction for supporting tasks.
VersionID	String	The GUID of this version of the package.
WriteCompletion StatusTo NTEventLog	Boolean	Whether to write completion status to the Windows NT Event Log.

Events

Name	Returns	Description
OnError		Executes when error condition occurs.
OnFinish		Executes when finish condition occurs.
OnProgress		Executes during progress intervals.
OnQueryCancel		Executes on query cancel status.
OnStart		Executes on start of package.

PackageLog

No methods, events or properties are defined for this object.

PersistPropertyBag

Methods

Name	Returns	Description
Load		Loads a custom tasks property storage.
Save		Gets a custom task to carry out property storage.

PrecedenceConstraint

Properties

Name	Returns	Description
Parent	IDTSStdObject	The parent object of the PrecedenceConstraint object.
Precedence Basis	DTSStep PrecedenceBasis	Indicates whether to use step status or result in PrecedenceConstraint.
Properties	Properties	The properties of the object.
StepName	String	The name of the Step object that will be evaluated.
Value	Variant	The value of the constraint.

PrecedenceConstraints

Methods

Name	Returns	Description
Add		Adds a PrecedenceConstraint object to the collection.
AddConstraint		Adds a PrecedenceConstraint object to the collection by name.
Insert		Inserts a PrecedenceConstraint object into the collection by index.
Item	Precedence Constraint	Retrieves a PrecedenceConstraint object by index.
New	Precedence Constraint	Creates a new PrecedenceConstraint object.
Remove		Removes a PrecedenceConstraint object from the collection.

Properties

Name	Returns	Description
Count	Long	The number of `PrecedenceConstraint` objects in the collection.
Parent	IDTSStdObject	The parent object of `PrecedenceConstraints` collection.

Properties

Methods

Name	Returns	Description
Item	Property	Returns a `Property` object by index value.

Properties

Name	Returns	Description
Count	Long	The number of `Property` objects in the collection.
Parent	IDTSStdobject	The parent object of the `Properties` collection.

PropertiesProvider

Methods

Name	Returns	Description
GetProperties ForObject	Properties	Gets a `Properties` collection for the specified automation object.

Property

Properties

Name	Returns	Description
Get	Boolean	Retrieves a property value.
Name	String	The name of the property.
Parent	IDTSStdObject	The parent object of the Property object.
Properties	Properties	The properties of the object.
Set	Boolean	Returns TRUE when a property's value may be changed.
Type	Long	The type property specifies the value type of the Property object.
Value	Variant	The value for the Property object.

PropertyBag

Methods

Name	Returns	Description
Read		Reads a property value.
Write		Writes a property value.

SavedPackageInfo

Properties

Name	Returns	Description
Description	String	A text description of the SavedPackageInfo object.

Table Continued on Following Page

Name	Returns	Description
IsVersionEncrypted	Boolean	Specifies whether this version of the package is encrypted.
PackageCreationDate	Date	The package creation date.
PackageID	String	The GUID ID value of the package.
PackageName	String	The name of the package.
VersionID	String	The GUID version ID of the package.
VersionSaveDate	Date	The date and time the package was last saved.

SavedPackageInfos

Methods

Name	Returns	Description
Item	SavedPackageInfo	Retrieves a SavedPackageInfo object by index.

Properties

Name	Returns	Description
Count	Long	The number of SavedPackageInfo objects in the collection.

SendMailTask

Methods

Name	Returns	Description
Execute		Executes a SendMailTask.
GetDefaultProfileName		Returns the default profile name.
InitializeMAPI		Initializes the MAPI provider.
Logoff		Ends a MAPI session.

Name	Returns	Description
Logon	String	Creates a MAPI session.
ResolveName	String	Resolves an e-mail address.
ShowAddressBook	String	Displays the address book user interface.
UnInitializeMAPI		Uninitializes the MAPI provider.

Properties

Name	Returns	Description
CCLine	String	The e-mail addresses for the CC: line.
Description	String	A text description of the SendMailTask object.
FileAttachments	String	Set the file attachments.
IsNTService	Boolean	Sets whether the caller is a Microsoft Windows NT Service.
MessageText	String	The message body of the e-mail.
Name	String	The name of the SendMailTask object.
Password	String	Specifies the password for making the MAPI connection.
Profile	String	The profile to use to send the e-mail.
Properties	Properties	The properties of the object.
SaveMailInSent ItemsFolder	Boolean	Specifies whether to move the sent e-mail to the Sent Items folder.
Subject	String	The subject line for the e-mail.
ToLine	String	The TO: line for the e-mail.

Step

Methods

Name	Returns	Description
Execute		Executes the Step object.
GetExecutionErrorInfo		Returns the details about the execution if it fails.

Properties

Name	Returns	Description
ActiveXScript	String	The ActiveX script.
AddGlobalVariables	Boolean	Sets whether global variables may be referenced from other ActiveX scripts.
CloseConnection	Boolean	Sets whether to close a connection on step completion.
CommitSuccess	Boolean	Sets whether to commit a step if it completes successfully.
Description	String	A text description of the step.
DisableStep	Boolean	Specifies whether a step should be executed.
ExecuteInMainThread	Boolean	Whether the step should be executed in the main thread of the package object.
ExecutionResult	DTSStepExec Result	Returns step execution results.
ExecutionStatus	DTSStepExec Status	Returns the status of the step.
ExecutionTime	Double	Specifies the total execution time in seconds.
FinishTime	Date	The date/time when the step was completed.
FunctionName	String	The name of the function from the ActiveX script.
IsPackageDSORowset	Boolean	When the package is a rowset provider, this property sets when the current step executes and returns a rowset.
JoinTransaction IfPresent	Boolean	Whether a step executes within a Package object's transaction.
Name	String	The name of the Step object.
Parent	IDTSStdObject	The parent object of the Step object.
Precedence Constraints	Precedence Constraints	The execution constraints for the step.

Name	Returns	Description
Properties	Properties	The properties of the object.
RelativePriority	DTSStep Relative Priority	The Win32 thread execution priority.
RollbackFailure	Boolean	Sets whether to rollback a step if there is a failure.
ScriptLanguage	String	The scripting language for the step (VBScript, JScript, or PerlScript).
StartTime	Date	The date/time the step began.
TaskName	String	The name of task to execute in the step.

Steps

Methods

Name	Returns	Description
Add		Adds a Step object to the collection.
Insert		Adds a Step object to the collection by index.
Item	Step	Retrieves a Step object from the collection.
New	Step	Creates a new Step object.
Remove		Removes a Step object from the collection.

Properties

Name	Returns	Description
Count	Long	The Step objects in the collection.
Parent	IDTSStdObject	The parent of the Steps collection.

Task

Methods

Name	Returns	Description
Execute		Executes a Task.

Properties

Name	Returns	Description
CustomTask	CustomTask	Returns the CustomTask object.
CustomTaskID	String	The ProgID or CLSID of the CustomTask object.
Description	String	A descriptive text about the Task object.
Name	String	The name of the Task object.
Parent	IDTSStdObject	The parent object of the Task object.
Properties	Properties	The properties of the object.

Tasks

Methods

Name	Returns	Description
Add		Adds a Task object to the collection.
Insert		Adds a Task object to the collection by index.
Item	Task	Retrieves a Task object from the collection.
New	Task	Creates a new Task object.
Remove		Removes a Task object from the collection.

Properties

Name	Returns	Description
Count	Long	The number of Task objects in the collection.
Parent	IDTSStdobject	The parent of the Tasks collection.

TransferObjectsTask

Methods

Name	Returns	Description
AddObjectForTransfer		Adds an object to the list of objects to be transferred.
CancelExecution		Cancels task execution.
Execute		Executes the TransferObjectsTask.
GetObjectForTransfer		Iterates through objects on the list.
ResetObjectsList		Clears the list of objects.

Properties

Name	Returns	Description
CopyAllObjects	Boolean	Sets whether to transfer all objects from the source database.
CopyData	DTSTransfer _CopyData Option	Specifies whether data should be copied, and whether existing data should be replaced or appended to.
CopySchema	Boolean	Specifies, based on the CopyData property, whether or not data will be copied.
Description	String	A text description of the TransferObjectTask.
Destination Database	String	The name of the destination database.
DestinationLogin	String	The login ID on a destination server.

Table Continued on Following Page

Name	Returns	Description
Destination Password	String	The password for the user ID on the a destination server.
DestinationServer	String	The destination server name.
DestinationUse TrustedConnection	Boolean	Sets whether to use a trusted connection to a destination server.
DropDestination ObjectsFirst	Boolean	Specifies whether to drop objects, if they already exist on the destination.
Include Dependencies	Boolean	Specifies whether dependent objects will be scripted and transferred during an object transfer operation.
IncludeLogins	Boolean	Specifies whether logins will be scripted and transferred during an object transfer operation.
IncludeUsers	Boolean	Specifies whether users will be scripted and transferred during an object transfer operation.
Name	String	The name of the TransferObjectTask.
Properties	Properties	The properties of the object.
ScriptFile Directory	String	The directory where the script file and log files are written.
ScriptOption	DTSTransfer _Script Option	Sets the scripting option for the object.
ScriptOptionEx	DTSTransfer _Script OptionEx	Sets the extended scripting option for the object.
SourceDatabase	String	The name of the source database.
SourceLogin	String	The login ID on a source server.
SourcePassword	String	The password for the login ID on a source server.
SourceServer	String	The source server name.
SourceUseTrusted Connection	Boolean	Sets whether to use a trusted connection to a source server.

Transformation

Properties

Name	Returns	Description
DestinationColumns	Columns	The collection of columns for a destination transformation.
ForceBlobsInMemory	Boolean	Specifies whether to always store each source BLOB column in a transformation as a single memory allocation.
ForceSourceBlobs Buffered	DTSForce Mode	Specifies whether to always buffer each source BLOB column in a transformation.
InMemoryBlobSize	Long	Specifies the size in bytes of per-column allocation for in-memory BLOBs in a transformation.
Name	String	The name of the Transformation object.
Parent	IDTSStd Object	The parent object of the Transformation object.
Properties	Properties	The properties of the object.
SourceColumns	Columns	The collection of columns for a source transformation.
TransformFlags	Long	Sets the transformation flags that indicate characteristics of a transformation.
TransformServer	Object	Contains specification of the dispatch interface of the custom COM server object for a transformation.
TransformServerID	String	Returns the programmatic identifier (ProgID) or class identifier (CLSID) of the Transformation.
TransformServer Parameter	Variant	Specifies a transform server's initialization parameter.
TransformServer Properties	Properties	Specifies the collection of Automation objects available on the TransformServer IDispatch interface.

Transformations

Methods

Name	Returns	Description
Add		Adds a Transformation object to the collection.
Insert		Adds a Transformation object to the collection by index.
Item	Transformation	Retrieves a Transformation object from the collection.
New	Transformation	Creates a new Transformation object.
Remove		Removes a Transformation object from the collection.

Properties

Name	Returns	Description
Count	Long	The number of Transformation objects in the collection.
Parent	IDTSStdObject	The parent of the Transformations collection.

Global Constants

For each constant enumeration described in the table below, there is a corresponding enumeration with a prefix of LP that should be used by C++ programmers (e.g. there is a constant enumeration called LPDTSErrorMode that corresponds to DTSErrorMode).

Name	Description
DTSBulkInsert_DataFileType	Specifies the type of data file used for bulk insert operations.
DTSCustomTaskUIFlags	Indicates the type of user interface supported by a custom task.
DTSErrorMode	Error conditions during step execution of a DTS package.
DTSFastLoadOptions	Specifies fast load options for the DataPumpTask.UseFastLoad method.

Name	Description
DTSForceMode	Overrides the default handling of associated properties.
DTSIsolationLevel	The isolation level of a package's transaction.
DTSLineageOptions	Specifies how package execution lineage should be presented and recorded.
DTSPackageError	Error conditions for DTS package creation and execution.
DTSPackagePriorityClass	Win32 process priority class for a DTS package.
DTSRepositoryMetadataOptions	Specifies metadata scanning and resolution options when storing the DTS package to a Repository.
DTSRepositoryStorageFlags	The Repository options when saving or loading the DTS Package.
DTSSQLObjectType	Indicates types of objects available on Microsoft SQL Server.
DTSSQLServerStorageFlags	Specifies Repository options when saving or loading the DTS package.
DTSStepExecResult	The execution result of a DTS Step object.
DTSStepExecStatus	The execution status of a DTS Step object.
DTSStepPrecendenceBasis	The values for a step's precedence value.
DTSStepRelativePriority	The Step object's Win32 thread relative priority.
DTSStepScriptResult	The return code from an ActiveX script step execution.
DTSTaskExecResult	The execution results of a DTS task.
DTSTransfer_CopyDataOption	Specifies flags indicating whether data should be copied, and whether existing data should be replaced or appended to.
DTSTransfer_ScriptOption	Sets the scripting option for a DTS transfer.
DTSTransfer_ScriptOptionEx	Sets the extended scripting options for a DTS transfer.

Microsoft Data Transformation Services DataPump Scripting Object Library Reference

Objects and Collections

Name	Description
DataPumpTransformScript	Provides access to script level functions.
DTSDataPumpColumn	Provides access to column level data from an ActiveX DTS script.

Table Continued on Following Page

Name	Description
DTSDataPumpColumns	A collection of DTSDataPumpColumn objects.
DTSDataPumpLookup	Provides data about columns in a lookup to an ActiveX DTS script.
DTSDataPumpLookups	A collection of DTSDataPumpLookup objects.
DTSErrorRecords	Allows capture or removal of Script errors that are encountered.

DataPumpTransformScript

Note: This is incorrectly listed as DataPumpTransformationScript *in MSDN.*

Properties

Name	Returns	Description
FunctionEntry	String	Get/Set function to call in the script file.
Language	String	Script language (VBScript, JScript, or PerlScript).
Text	String	Script text entry.

DTSDataPumpColumn

Methods

Name	Returns	Description
AppendChunk		Sets the current value of the column.
GetChunk		Retrieves the current value of the column.

Properties

Name	Returns	Description
ActualSize	Long	Returns the size of the column.
Attributes	Long	Returns one or more characteristics of a column.
DefinedSize	Long	Returns the maximum size of the column.

Name	Returns	Description
Name	String	Retrieves the name of the column.
NumericScale	Byte	Sets the scale for numeric values in a column.
OriginalValue	Variant	Specifies the value of the column before it was modified.
Precision	Byte	Sets the precision of numeric values for a column.
Type	Long	Sets the type of data for a column.
UnderlyingValue	Variant	Same as OriginalValue property.
Value	Variant	Current value of a selected column.

DTSDataPumpColumns

Methods

Name	Returns	Description
Item	DTSDataPumpColumn	Retrieves a DTSDataPumpColumn object based on an ordinal index value.

Properties

Name	Returns	Description
Count	Long	Returns number of DTSDataPumpColumn objects in the collection.

DTSDataPumpLookup

Methods

Name	Returns	Description
AddToCache		Add a key to the Lookup object cache.
Execute		Retrieves a key based on key values.
RemoveFromCache		Removes a key from the Lookup object cache.

Properties

Name	Returns	Description
LastRowCount	Long	Returns the number of rows executed during the last lookup.
Name	String	Returns the name of the column.

DTSDataPumpLookups

Methods

Name	Returns	Description
Item	DTSDataPumpLookup	Retrieves a DTSDataPumpLookup object based on an ordinal index value.

Properties

Name	Returns	Description
Count	Long	Returns the number of DTSDataPumpLookup objects in the collection.

DTSDataErrorRecords

Methods

Name	Returns	Description
Add		Adds an error to the error stack.
Clear		Clears all errors from the error stack.

DTS Global Constants

For each constant enumeration described in the table below, there is a corresponding enumeration with a prefix of LP that should be used by C++ programmers (e.g. DTSDataPumpError has a corresponding constant enumeration called LPDTSDataPumpError).

Name	Description
DTSDataPumpError	Available values for data pump errors.
DTSExecuteStatus	Available values for various execution statuses.
DTSTransformFlags	Available values for controlling transformations.
DTSTransformStatus	Available values for return status from transformations.

Index

Q

R

741

wrox
PROGRAMMER TO PROGRAMMER™

Wrox writes books for you. Any suggestions, or ideas about how you want information given in your ideal book will be studied by our team. Your comments are always valued at Wrox.

Free phone in USA 800-USE-WROX
Fax (312) 893 8001

UK Tel. (0121) 687 4100   Fax (0121) 687 4101

Professional SQL Server 7.0 Development with SQL-DMO, SQL-NS, and DTS - Registration Card

Name _____

Address _____

_____

_____

_____

City _____ State/Region _____

Country _____ Postcode/Zip _____

E-mail _____

Occupation _____

How did you hear about this book? _____

☐ Book review (name) _____

☐ Advertisement (name) _____

☐ Recommendation _____

☐ Catalog _____

☐ Other _____

Where did you buy this book? _____

☐ Bookstore (name) _____ City _____

☐ Computer Store (name) _____

☐ Mail Order _____

☐ Other _____

What influenced you in the purchase of this book?

☐ Cover Design

☐ Contents

☐ Other (please specify) _____

How did you rate the overall contents of this book?

☐ Excellent   ☐ Good

☐ Average   ☐ Poor

What did you find most useful about this book? _____

_____

What did you find least useful about this book? _____

_____

Please add any additional comments. _____

_____

What other subjects will you buy a computer book on soon? _____

What is the best computer book you have used this year?

_____

Note: This information will only be used to keep you updated about new Wrox Press titles and will not be used for any other purpose or passed to any other third party.

wrox
PROGRAMMER TO PROGRAMMER™

NB. If you post the bounce back card below in the UK, please send it to:

Wrox Press Ltd., Arden House, 1102 Warwick Road,
Acocks Green, Birmingham B27 6BH. UK.

——— *Computer Book Publishers* ———

BUSINESS REPLY MAIL
FIRST CLASS MAIL   PERMIT#64   CHICAGO, IL

POSTAGE WILL BE PAID BY ADDRESSEE

**WROX PRESS INC.,
29 S. LA SALLE ST.,
SUITE 520
CHICAGO IL 60603-USA**